THE KINGFISHER
CHILDREN'S
ENCYCLOPEDIA

Published 2012 by Kingfisher
an imprint of Macmillan Children's Books
a division of Macmillan Publishers Ltd
20 New Wharf Road, London N1 9RR
Basingstoke and Oxford
Associated companies throughout the world
www.panmacmillan.com

First published 1998 by Kingfisher
This revised and updated edition published in 2012

ISBN: 978-0-7534-3268-6
032
Copyright © Macmillan Children's Books 2012

9 8 7 6 5 4 3 2 1
1TR/0312/UTD/TWP/128GEMA

A CIP catalogue record for this book is available from
the British Library

Printed in Singapore

The websites listed in this book are correct at the time of publishing. However,
due to the ever-changing nature of the internet, website addresses and content
can change. Websites can contain links that are unsuitable for children. The publisher
cannot be held responsible for changes in website addresses or content, or for
information obtained through third-party websites. We strongly advise that
internet searches should be supervised by an adult.

THE KINGFISHER
CHILDREN'S
ENCYCLOPEDIA

KINGFISHER

Editorial Director
Jennifer Justice

Managing Editor
Sarah Allen

Editorial team
Trevor Anderson, Max Benato, Jane Birch, Harry Boteler, Anne Davies, Rebecca Fry, Aimee Johnson, Tracey Kelly,
Sarah Kovandzich, Elizabeth Longley, Miren Lopategui, Rupert Matthews, Jayne Miller, Vicky Weber, Brian Williams

Creative Director
Val Pidgeon

Art Director
Mike Davis

Art Editor
David Noon

Design team
Liz Black, Pete Byrne, John Jamieson, Ruth Levy, Emma Skidmore, Nina Tara

Picture Research
Veneta Bullen, Davina Bullen, Sophie Mortimer, Yannick Yago

Maps
Hardlines

Contributors & Consultants
Sue Aldridge, Sarah Angliss, Max Benato, Martyn Bramwell, Enid Broderick, Tim Brown, David Burnie,
Catherine Halcrow, Jack Challoner, Michael Chinery, Maria Constantino, Chris Cooper, Sophie Cooper,
Alan Cowsill, Jeff Daniel, David Darling, Dougal Dixon, John Farndon, Sue Gordon, John Graham, Ian Graham,
Catherine Headlam, Lesley Hill, Caroline Juler, Anne Kay, Robin Kerrod, J.C. Levy, Keith Lye, Tim Madge,
David Marshall, Bob McCabe, Iain Nicolson, Steve Parker, Jane Parker, John Paton, Malcolm Porter, Sue Reid,
Meg Sanders, Bill Shapiro, Philip Steele, Richard Tames, John Tipler, Ian Westwell, Brian Williams
2012 Edition Contributors & Consultants David Burnie, Clive Carpenter, Clare Hibbert

Illustrators
David Ashby, Julian Baker Illustration, Julian Baum, Michelle Brand, Andy Burton, Tom Connell, Maggie Downer,
Richard Draper, Andrew Farmer, Chris Forsey, Mick Gillah, Trevor Hill, Karen Hiscock, Christian Hook,
Kevin Jones Associates, Ruth Lindsay, Ceri Llewellyn, Kevin Maddison, Nicki Palin, Peter Ross, Peter Sarson,
Mike Saunders, Ron Tiner, Martin Woodward, Black Hat: Kevin Lyles, Blue Chip: Keith Harmer,
David Lewis Agency: Mark Stacey, J.M. & A: Steinar Lund, Linda Rogers Associates: Peter Dennis,
Linden Artists: Lindsay Graham, Richard Hook, Sebastian Quigley, Clive Spong, Specs Art: Richard Berridge,
Virgil Pomfret: Luigi Galanti, W.L.A: Cy Baker, Derick Bown, Robin Budden, Robin Carter, Barry Croucher,
Sandra Doyle, Brin Edwards, David Hardy, Dan Harvey, Philip Hood, Ian Jackson, Bridgette Jones, Rachel Lockwood,
Pond/Giles, Jonathan Potter, Steve Roberts, Andrew Robinson, Mike Rowe, Chris Shields, Paul Staveley,
Mark Stewart, Mike Taylor, Richard Tibbitts, Chris Turnbull, Simon Turvey, David Woods

INTRODUCTION

The word *encyclopedia* comes from the Greek for 'all-round education', and *The Kingfisher Children's Encyclopedia* provides just that, in a way that is both accessible and stimulating.

This brilliant encyclopedia covers everything from ancient history to up-to-the-minute developments in technology; from animal and plant life on Earth to the latest plans for exploring outer space. Geography, natural history, religion, the human body – all the topics that children explore at home and at school are included here.

Detailed, in-depth coverage of an impressive range of topics makes this encyclopedia perfect for project work and homework assignments. At the same time, the text is broken up into manageable paragraphs, suitable for both confident readers and younger browsers. Colourful photographs and superb illustrations and maps not only enhance the text, but also encourage readers to find out more for themselves.

Easy access is the key to this encyclopedia. Major subject areas such as ELECTRICITY have been arranged alphabetically, but the encyclopedia also has a comprehensive index so that readers can refer quickly to related topics, such as CIRCUITS and SWITCHES.

The encyclopedia has been written and checked by a team of specialist authors and consultants, and produced by a team of editors and designers with years of experience in children's reference. We are confident that it is a book in which children, and parents, can put their trust.

The Editors

How to use this Encyclopedia

This book is fun and easy to use. All the entries are arranged alphabetically and provide information on two levels – quick reference and in-depth knowledge. The features explained in the guide below will help you to get the most from your encyclopedia.

Eye-catching colour photographs bring subjects to life

Main headings always appear in the top left corner of the page for quick reference

All entries begin with a concise definition of the subject

Headings divide the text into self-contained sections

Authoritative text is approachable and packed with facts

Typeface is clear and easy to read

Colourful identification panels amplify the main topic by highlighting specific subjects

Architecture

Architecture is the art of designing buildings and other structures that are soundly built, pleasing to look at and suitable for their purpose.

The classical style uses flat beams, columns and sculpture.

The style of architecture used for a building depends on the materials available, the architect's ideas and what the building is going to be used for.

ARCHITECTS AT WORK
As well as needing to know a building's purpose, an architect must know the space allocated and how much money can be spent. Detailed models and drawings are produced for the builders, showing every part of the building and how it is to be constructed. These plans include practical features, such as heating and lighting systems, pipe work and plumbing.

The Romans built aqueducts with rounded arches and thick walls.

WESTERN STYLES
Western architecture began in Greece around 500BC with the classical style. Pillars were built to precise mathematical patterns, such as those in the Parthenon, Athens, built 447–438BC. From about 200BC, the Romans used curved arches and domes to make bridges and aqueducts.

Japanese castles have upturned roof edges and contrasting colours.

MEDIEVAL IDEAS
During the Middle Ages, the pointed arches and colourful stained glass of the Gothic style began to appear, especially in

▲ Today's architects use modern materials to create startling new designs. Disney World's EPCOT Center in Florida is a geodesic dome. These are strong, lightweight domes with no internal supports or straight walls. They are constructed from ready-made sections.

churches. Like the classical styles of the Romans and Greeks, the Gothic style has been used by many architects since then.

MODERN MATERIALS
Since the 19th century, inventions such as heating and lighting, and new building materials such as steel, plastic and reinforced concrete have revolutionized architecture. Steel-framed skyscrapers were first developed in the USA after the invention of the elevator in 1854. Modern architecture is often characterized by a combination of borrowed ideas with the newest materials and techniques.

India's Taj Mahal features domes and minarets typical of Islamic architecture.

HI-TECH BUILDINGS
The Sydney Opera House in Australia uses hi-tech materials such as glass, concrete and ceramics in its structure. Complex mathematics were needed to work out if the materials would take the weight of its unusual component parts. Modern architects begin with a series of drawings, and use computers to calculate weights and forces. Then building begins.

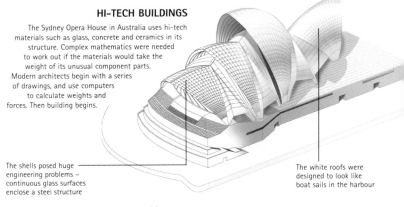

The shells posed huge engineering problems – continuous glass surfaces enclose a steel structure

The white roofs were designed to look like boat sails in the harbour

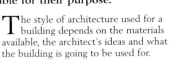
Glass walls and tall office blocks dominate modern architecture.

18

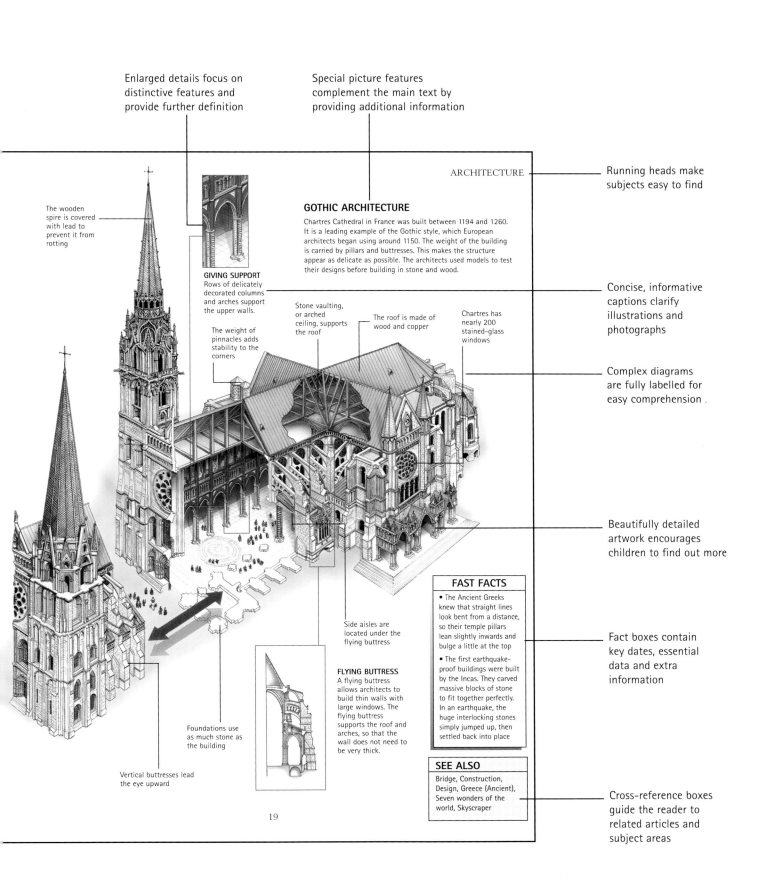

Enlarged details focus on
distinctive features and
provide further definition

Special picture features
complement the main text by
providing additional information

Running heads make
subjects easy to find

The wooden
spire is covered
with lead to
prevent it from
rotting

GOTHIC ARCHITECTURE

Chartres Cathedral in France was built between 1194 and 1260.
It is a leading example of the Gothic style, which European
architects began using around 1150. The weight of the building
is carried by pillars and buttresses. This makes the structure
appear as delicate as possible. The architects used models to test
their designs before building in stone and wood.

GIVING SUPPORT
Rows of delicately
decorated columns
and arches support
the upper walls.

Concise, informative
captions clarify
illustrations and
photographs

The weight of
pinnacles adds
stability to the
corners

Stone vaulting,
or arched
ceiling, supports
the roof

The roof is made of
wood and copper

Chartres has
nearly 200
stained-glass
windows

Complex diagrams
are fully labelled for
easy comprehension

Beautifully detailed
artwork encourages
children to find out more

Side aisles are
located under the
flying buttress

FAST FACTS

• The Ancient Greeks
knew that straight lines
look bent from a distance,
so their temple pillars
lean slightly inwards and
bulge a little at the top

• The first earthquake-
proof buildings were built
by the Incas. They carved
massive blocks of stone
to fit together perfectly.
In an earthquake, the
huge interlocking stones
simply jumped up, then
settled back into place

Fact boxes contain
key dates, essential
data and extra
information

FLYING BUTTRESS
A flying buttress
allows architects to
build thin walls with
large windows. The
flying buttress
supports the roof and
arches, so that the
wall does not need to
be very thick.

Foundations use
as much stone as
the building

Vertical buttresses lead
the eye upward

SEE ALSO

Bridge, Construction,
Design, Greece (Ancient),
Seven wonders of the
world, Skyscraper

Cross-reference boxes
guide the reader to
related articles and
subject areas

ABORIGINAL PEOPLE

The term 'aboriginal' is used to describe the native inhabitants of any country. The Aboriginal people are the first inhabitants of Australia.

The Aboriginal people arrived in Australia from Southeast Asia. They lived in nomadic groups, travelling around their territories, hunting with spears and boomerangs, fishing from canoes and gathering fruits and vegetables. They had no written language, but passed on valuable knowledge by word of mouth and in song.

▶ A songman, accompanied by a didgeridoo player, tells stories through songs and poetry.

▲ These pieces of bark are painted with clan signs of the Napaljarri people of the Northern Territory. Originally, there were about 500 Aboriginal clans, each with its own territory and complex language.

EUROPEAN SETTLERS

When the British settled in Australia in the late 18th century, there were more than 300,000 Aboriginal people. Many were killed by the settlers or driven off their land. By the mid-1900s, their population had dropped to around 45,000. Today, it has risen to more than 515,000. In 2008, the government formally apologized to the Aboriginal people for past mistreatment.

THE ABORIGINAL WAY OF LIFE

The Aboriginal people traditionally lived out in the open or in shelters made from branches and bark.

They wore little apart from body paint, ornaments and waistbands or fur coats made from kangaroo skin. Today, a small number live in the Outback (interior) in the same way as their ancestors, but most have moved to towns and cities.

ART AND MUSIC

Aboriginal art mainly portrays religious beliefs in paintings on cave walls and on bark, or in poetry and songs. Today, some Aboriginal artists live by selling paintings made with earth pigments and charcoal. Aboriginal music is played on a didgeridoo (a long, wooden pipe) and two clapping sticks, which are traditionally boomerangs.

▶ Witchetty grubs are the large, white larvae of the goat moth. The grubs are high in protein and are traditionally regarded as a great delicacy by Aboriginal people.

DREAMTIME

Rituals play an important role in Aboriginal beliefs, and body painting is a part of many rituals. Their beliefs are centred on the land and include an idea of eternity called Dreamtime – a world with no beginning and no end. Through Dreamtime, the ancestors – spirits that shaped mountains, rivers, plants, animals and people – can be contacted.

SEE ALSO

Australia

AFRICA

Africa is the second largest continent and covers about one fifth of the Earth's land area. It includes 54 countries, six of which are islands.

▲ The Tuareg are a nomadic people who inhabit a large area of the Sahara Desert. Some still travel the desert with camel trains laden with goods such as dates and salt.

KEY FACTS

- **Area:** 30,306,000 sq km
- **Population:** 1,046,000,000
- **Number of countries:** 54
- **Largest country:** Algeria (2,381,741 sq km)
- **Smallest country:** Seychelles (455 sq km)
- **Highest point:** Mount Kilimanjaro (5,895m)
- **Largest lake:** Lake Victoria (69,484 sq km)
- **Longest river:** Nile

▼ Chobe National Park in Botswana is home to herds of elephants and impala. Many African countries have set aside large stretches of land as wildlife reserves.

The world's hottest continent, Africa has rainforests and tree-scattered grasslands (known as savanna), which are inhabited by a huge variety of wild animals. A third of Africa is covered by the Sahara, the largest desert on Earth.

HIGHS AND LOWS
Much of Africa is made up of plateaux, flat areas of land high above sea level. The plateau in East Africa is broken up by two extinct volcanoes – Mount Kenya and Tanzania's Mount Kilimanjaro – and the Great Rift Valley. The Rift is a long crack in the Earth's crust that runs from Mozambique, through East Africa, the Red Sea and into southwestern Asia. Elongated lakes have formed in the valley. Africa's spectacular natural features include the Nile, the longest river in the world, and Lake Tanganyika, the world's longest lake, which stretches for 620km.

HOT AND DRY
Because Africa lies across the Equator, most of the continent gets extremely hot. The world's highest temperature in the shade was recorded in Libya in 1922 at 58°C. The land around the tropics, each side of the Equator, is starved of rain and more than half of Africa's land has less than 500mm of rain per year.

RAINFORESTS AND SAVANNA
In some regions, particularly around the Equator in West and Central Africa, rainfall is high and large rainforests grow. Monrovia, the capital of Liberia, has an average of 5,140mm of rain per year. Between the rainforests and the deserts are immense areas of tropical savanna. Savanna is prone to drought, with a mixture of rainy and dry seasons.

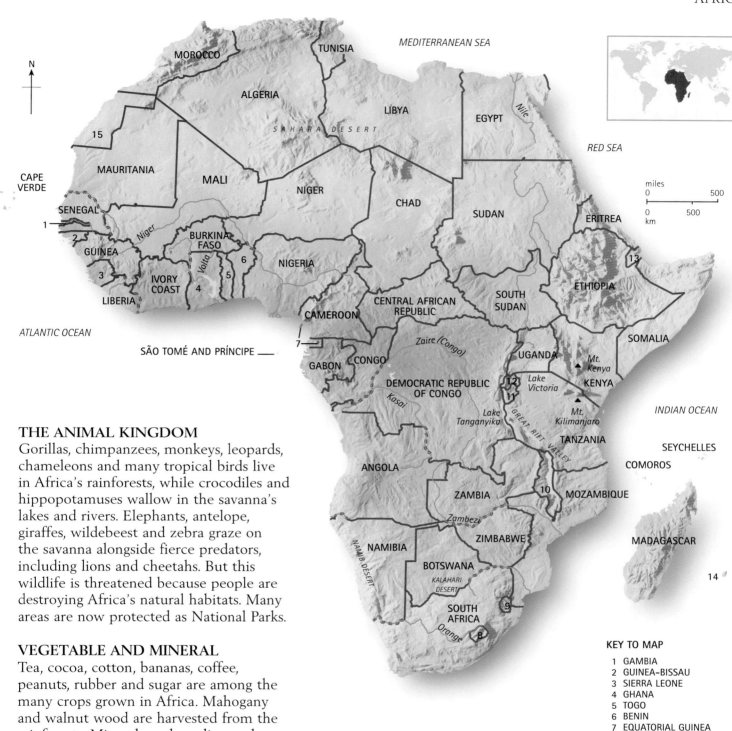

MEDITERRANEAN SEA

RED SEA

ATLANTIC OCEAN

INDIAN OCEAN

N

miles
0 — 500
km
0 — 500

MOROCCO
TUNISIA
ALGERIA
LIBYA
EGYPT
SAHARA DESERT
Nile
15
MAURITANIA
MALI
NIGER
CHAD
SUDAN
ERITREA
CAPE VERDE
SENEGAL
1
2
GUINEA
3
BURKINA FASO
Niger
Volta
6
5
4
NIGERIA
CENTRAL AFRICAN REPUBLIC
SOUTH SUDAN
ETHIOPIA
13
IVORY COAST
LIBERIA
CAMEROON
SÃO TOMÉ AND PRÍNCIPE
7
SOMALIA
GABON
CONGO
Zaire (Congo)
UGANDA
Mt. Kenya
KENYA
DEMOCRATIC REPUBLIC OF CONGO
Kasai
12
11
Lake Victoria
Mt. Kilimanjaro
Lake Tanganyika
GREAT RIFT VALLEY
TANZANIA
SEYCHELLES
COMOROS
ANGOLA
ZAMBIA
10
MOZAMBIQUE
Zambezi
MADAGASCAR
14
NAMIBIA
NAMIB DESERT
ZIMBABWE
BOTSWANA
KALAHARI DESERT
SOUTH AFRICA
Orange
9
8

THE ANIMAL KINGDOM

Gorillas, chimpanzees, monkeys, leopards, chameleons and many tropical birds live in Africa's rainforests, while crocodiles and hippopotamuses wallow in the savanna's lakes and rivers. Elephants, antelope, giraffes, wildebeest and zebra graze on the savanna alongside fierce predators, including lions and cheetahs. But this wildlife is threatened because people are destroying Africa's natural habitats. Many areas are now protected as National Parks.

VEGETABLE AND MINERAL

Tea, cocoa, cotton, bananas, coffee, peanuts, rubber and sugar are among the many crops grown in Africa. Mahogany and walnut wood are harvested from the rainforests. Minerals such as diamonds, gold, bauxite (aluminium ore), iron ore and copper are mined for export. Oil is exported from Gabon, Libya and Nigeria.

PEOPLE AND LANGUAGES

Many Africans live in tribal villages with their own cultures. Over 1,000 languages are spoken south of the Sahara alone. Country borders take little account of tribal differences, and in one country there may be many tribal groupings. ▶

KEY TO MAP

1 GAMBIA
2 GUINEA-BISSAU
3 SIERRA LEONE
4 GHANA
5 TOGO
6 BENIN
7 EQUATORIAL GUINEA
8 LESOTHO
9 SWAZILAND
10 MALAWI
11 BURUNDI
12 RWANDA
13 DJIBOUTI
14 MAURITIUS
15 WESTERN SAHARA
(occupied by Morocco)

◀ The Korup National Park in Cameroon is one of Africa's densest rainforest areas.

▲ The people of Tahoua in Niger build reed huts from locally available materials. Huts like these are typical of the Sahel region, an area of dry grassland on the edge of the Sahara.

RELIGIOUS BELIEFS

The people who live in northern Africa are mostly Arabs and Berbers who speak Arabic and follow Islam. The countries in southern Africa are largely populated by black Africans. Although most are Muslims or Christians, ancient local traditions still flourish and more than a quarter of Africa's people follow local beliefs.

THE EARLY DAYS

Many scientists believe Africa is the continent where human beings first evolved, about seven million years ago, but little is known about this very early history. Around 10,000 years ago, the Sahara had a moist climate and many people lived there, hunting animals, gathering plants for food, and later raising crops and herding cattle.

ANCIENT EGYPT AND ISLAM

In about 3100BCE, Ancient Egypt – one of the world's greatest early civilizations – was formed out of Upper and Lower Egypt in northern Africa. It thrived on the fertile banks of the Nile until, in 30BCE, it became part of the Roman Empire. In the 7th century CE, the Arabs conquered northern Africa and converted the people of Egypt and its neighbours to Islam.

GREAT KINGDOMS

For centuries, people outside Africa knew little about the continent south of the Sahara. Between 1100 and 1500, Arabs trading

◀ The Masai people of East Africa are one of many tribal groups that live in Africa. A nomadic people, they raise cattle and hunt wild animals.

▲ The snakes coming out of the nostrils of this 18th-century Benin bronze head represent the belief that those with magic powers could release snakes to destroy their enemies.

for gold, ivory and slaves brought back news of great empires in West Africa such as Ghana, Mali, Benin, Songhai and Kanem. Kingdoms such as Benin, which was founded in about 900CE, produced beautiful bronze sculptures which are highly prized today. Many of the sculptures symbolize the magical aspects of the *obas* (kings) of Benin. Kingdoms arose in the south, such as the huge stone city of Great Zimbabwe. News of Africa's wealth attracted great curiosity among Europeans.

CONQUERING A CONTINENT

Portuguese explorers were the first Europeans to map the coasts of Africa. In 1498, the navigator Vasco da Gama rounded the tip of southern Africa, the Cape of Good Hope, on a journey that led him to discover a new route to India. Others later sailed on to East Africa. The Portuguese were also the first Europeans to export slaves from West Africa, a trade which continued until the 19th century.

EUROPEAN INFLUENCE

The Dutch took over many Portuguese trading posts in the 17th century and in

◄ About three fifths of Africa's people live in villages. In some areas, the markets are full of fresh produce, but in others, drought, poverty and civil war have led to food shortages and widespread famine.

1652 they founded a settlement at Cape Town, which became part of South Africa. By the late 19th century, almost all of Africa was ruled by European powers.

INDEPENDENCE

Colonial rule continued until the 1950s, when colonies began to gain independence. By the early 1970s, most countries were independent, but economic problems have led to instability in many areas. The African Union, which took over from the Organization of African Unity in 2001, aims to promote economic, political and cultural co-operation in Africa.

▲ Harare, named after the African chief Neharawe, is the capital of Zimbabwe in southern Africa. It is a modern city, with tall skyscrapers and tree-lined streets.

A HARD WAY OF LIFE

Two thirds of the world's poorest nations are in Africa. Most Africans live in villages and farm the land. Poverty, disease and war in many parts mean that people often do not reach old age. In Angola, Nigeria, Chad, Swaziland, Guinea-Bissau, South Africa and Zimbabwe, the average life expectancy is less than 50 years.

BUSY CITIES

Although most Africans live in villages, the continent has some large, bustling cities. Cairo, the capital of Egypt, is the largest, with a population of 15,500,000. It is followed by Lagos in Nigeria, which has 12,400,000 inhabitants, and Kinshasa in the Democratic Republic of Congo, with a population of 9,400,000.

TIME OF EQUALITY

One of the most important events in Africa's history took place in 1994, when South Africa became a democracy under the leadership of Nelson Mandela. This finally ended apartheid, the official policy that separated people of different races from the whites. Since 1948, this policy had given whites power, while denying people of other colours basic rights in education, at work and in everyday life.

▲ Africa has produced some world-class soccer players. They include Senegal's El Hadji Diouf (above) and Samuel Eto'o of Cameroon, who is the highest-paid African player.

SEE ALSO

Civil war, Continent, Egypt, Egypt (Ancient), Empire, Explorer, Grassland, Kenya, Nigeria, Roman Empire, Slavery, South Africa, Sudan

AIRCRAFT

An aircraft is a vehicle that can fly through the air. Aeroplanes, helicopters, gliders, airships and balloons are all different types of aircraft.

KEY DATES

1903 Orville and Wilbur Wright make first powered, controlled flight in their aircraft *Flyer 1*

1937 British engineer Frank Whittle designs jet engine. In 1939 the Heinkel He 178 is first jet plane

1939 American engineer Igor Sikorsky designs first modern helicopter

1947 In the USA, the rocket-powered Bell X-1 is first aircraft to fly at supersonic speed

1950s The first jet airliners, the DeHavilland Comet and Boeing 707, enter service

1970 The Boeing 747 'jumbo jet' enters service

1976–2003 Concorde ran its supersonic service

The Wright brothers' *Flyer 1* made the first controlled, powered flight in 1903. It covered 36m.

A gas burner heats the air inside a hot-air balloon to make it rise. It can only go where the wind takes it.

Like all gliders, the Delphin SF-34 uses air currents to stay airborne. Long, thin wings give maximum lift.

The first aircraft were balloons and airships, which relied on lighter-than-air gases to keep them up. Sir George Cayley in Britain and Otto Lilienthal in Germany flew the first gliders in the 19th century. But it was the invention of the petrol engine in the 1880s that led to powered flight in heavier-than-air craft, such as helicopters and aeroplanes.

EARLY AEROPLANES
Aeroplanes are aircraft with fixed wings that provide the upward force known as lift, engines to provide thrust, and hinged control surfaces for steering. Aeroplanes were developed at the start of the 20th century and were originally built of wood and canvas to make them light.

WHAT KEEPS A PLANE UP?
An aeroplane's wings hold it up as it flies. They have a curved upper surface and a flat lower surface. Air travels more slowly across the bottom of the wing than the top, creating an upward push.

PROPELLER VERSUS JET
All early aeroplanes had small piston engines that drove propellers. As the propeller turned, it pulled the aircraft forward. Most modern large aeroplanes are powered by jet engines. These burn fuel and air to produce a stream of exhaust gases that thrusts the aeroplane forward. Jets provide more power but are costly to maintain.

THE FUSELAGE
The main body of a plane is called the fuselage. It contains the crew, passengers, cargo and equipment. The front of the fuselage houses the cockpit where the pilot sits, and at the rear is the tailplane, made up of a vertical fin and two small wings.

Short wings

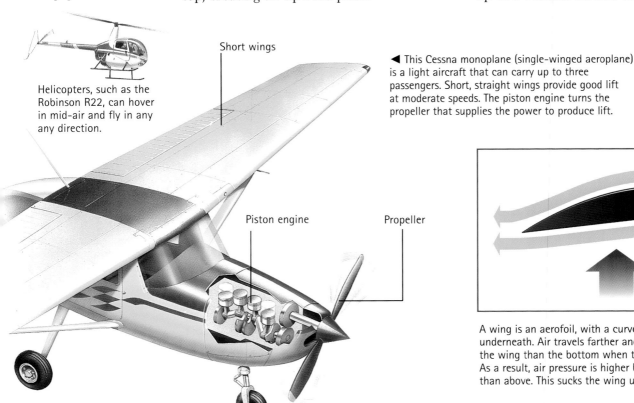

Helicopters, such as the Robinson R22, can hover in mid-air and fly in any any direction.

Piston engine   Propeller

◀ This Cessna monoplane (single-winged aeroplane) is a light aircraft that can carry up to three passengers. Short, straight wings provide good lift at moderate speeds. The piston engine turns the propeller that supplies the power to produce lift.

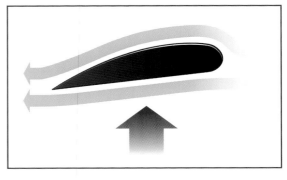

A wing is an aerofoil, with a curved top and a flat underneath. Air travels farther and faster over the top of the wing than the bottom when the plane is in the air. As a result, air pressure is higher beneath the aerofoil than above. This sucks the wing up, creating lift.

THE JET AIRLINER

Long-distance travel has been made cheap and reliable by jet airliners. The first wide-bodied jet was the Boeing 747, or jumbo jet. It can carry up to 524 passengers as far as 13,450km. More than 1,400 Boeing 747s have been produced in over ten different versions. Swept-back wings cut down air resistance, or drag, at high speeds. This reduces lift, however, so airliners need long runways and high speeds to take off and land. All new aeroplanes now have to meet strict environmental and safety rules.

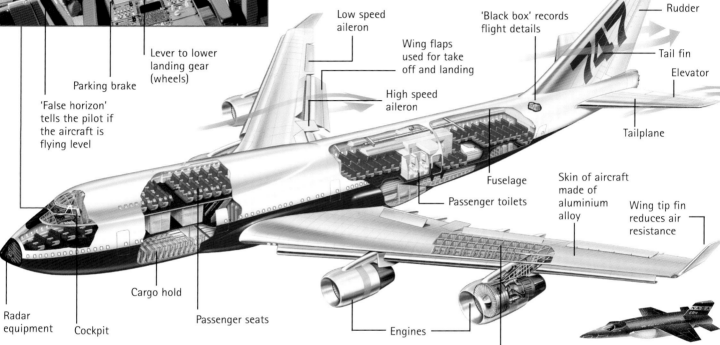

Low speed aileron
Wing flaps used for take off and landing
High speed aileron
'Black box' records flight details
Rudder
Tail fin
Elevator
Tailplane
Fuselage
Passenger toilets
Skin of aircraft made of aluminium alloy
Wing tip fin reduces air resistance
Lever to lower landing gear (wheels)
Parking brake
'False horizon' tells the pilot if the aircraft is flying level
Radar equipment
Cockpit
Cargo hold
Passenger seats
Engines
Fuel tanks located inside wings

FLY-BY-WIRE

Large flaps on the back edge of the wings increase lift and reduce speed for landing, while ailerons, elevators and the rudder change direction. These are usually controlled by the pilot, but some modern aircraft use a system called 'fly-by-wire', whereby the flaps and ailerons are adjusted with the help of computers.

FLYING AND FLOATING

Aeroplanes come in many forms. Jet airliners fly all around the world, while small aeroplanes, called light aircraft, ferry people, mail and supplies over short distances. Some planes have floats instead of wheels to land on water. Military planes hold radar, cameras and bombs. Biplanes (aeroplanes with double wings) are used by display teams and as crop-sprayers because they can fly slowly and make sharp turns.

Propelled by rocket engines, the supersonic X-15 holds the world air speed record at 7,274km/h set in 1967.

Concorde ran the world's only supersonic passenger service, with a cruising speed of about 2,175km/h.

The Harrier Jump Jet uses the downward thrust of its engines to rise straight up without needing a runway.

▶ The B-2 Stealth Bomber has flat, slab-like panels made of special materials. These scatter beams from enemy radar, making the craft almost undetectable. Special paint also absorbs radar waves.

SEE ALSO
Airport, Balloon and airship, Engine, Helicopter, Transport, Warfare

AIRPORT

Airports are places that airline passengers pass through and where freight is handled. They are also where aircraft are refuelled, repaired and maintained.

The biggest airports are like small cities with tens of thousands of people working in them 24 hours a day. Domestic airports handle passengers flying within the same country. People flying to or from another country go through international airports. Specialist services here include passport control, immigration and customs.

◀ Air traffic controllers are positioned high above the airport in the control tower. They use radar to track each plane on their screens and computers to plan flight paths. They radio their instructions to the pilots.

FAST FACTS

• Atlanta Hartsfield is the world's busiest airport, handling over 89 million passengers a year

• Of the ten busiest airports in the world, five are in the USA

• London Heathrow airport handles more international passengers (over 60 million per year) than any other airport

• People in the USA fly more than any other nation – together they fly 1,650 billion km/year

ON ARRIVAL
All passengers arriving on international flights must pass through customs to check they are not bringing anything illegal, such as drugs, into the country. Customs officers are entitled to stop and search anyone they believe to be carrying illegal goods. They also check for goods on which travellers should pay tax.

KEEPING SAFE
Security at airports has become a high priority since the 1960s, as the number of terrorist attacks on planes has increased.

All passengers boarding a flight must go through a metal detector while their hand luggage is put through an X-ray machine. This is to check that they are not carrying any weapons or explosives onto the aircraft. International travellers also use passports to prove their identity.

CONTROLLING AIR TRAFFIC
Aircraft landing and taking off have to comply with air traffic control to make sure they do not collide, either on the ground or in the air. At very large airports, the area under air traffic control extends for hundreds of kilometres horizontally and thousands of metres vertically in all directions. Aircraft circle the sky above the airport waiting for permission to land.

ON LANDING
Aeroplanes land on runways and then taxi (move slowly) to a gate. Here the doors of the aircraft can be safely opened. Passengers leave the aircraft with their hand luggage and either walk or are driven by bus to the main terminal buildings.

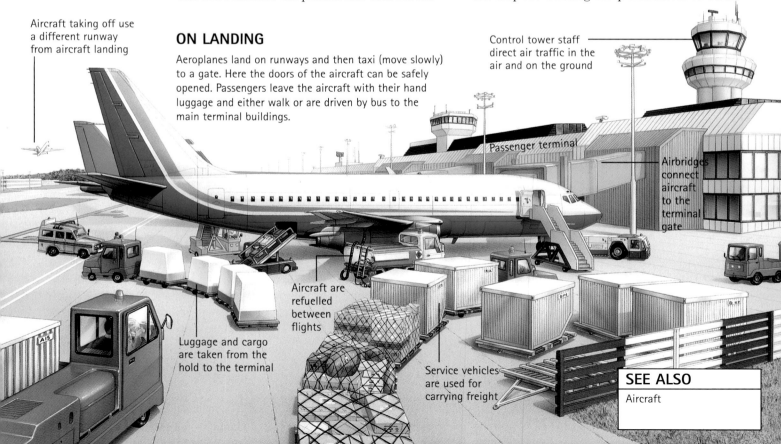

Aircraft taking off use a different runway from aircraft landing

Control tower staff direct air traffic in the air and on the ground

Passenger terminal

Airbridges connect aircraft to the terminal gate

Aircraft are refuelled between flights

Luggage and cargo are taken from the hold to the terminal

Service vehicles are used for carrying freight

SEE ALSO
Aircraft

ALLIGATOR AND CROCODILE

Alligators and crocodiles are large, scaly reptiles with powerful jaws. They live on the banks of rivers and in swamps, feeding on fish, mammals, turtles and birds.

An alligator's lower teeth are not visible when its jaws are shut.

The fourth tooth on the lower jaw of a crocodile sticks out.

Closely related to alligators, caimans feed on fish and other prey.

The gharial has a long, thin, tooth-lined snout and feeds mainly on fish.

Alligators and crocodiles are some of the largest living reptiles on the planet – the biggest crocodiles can grow to around 7m and weigh over 1,120kg. Alligators are usually smaller. Together with caimans and gharials, alligators and crocodiles belong to a group called crocodilians. An alligator's snout is broader and flatter than the snout of a crocodile, and its teeth are hidden when its jaws are closed.

STRONG JAWS

Like crocodiles, alligators float with only the tip of their snout and their eyes protruding, waiting to pounce on prey. Although crocodiles have been known to attack humans, alligators rarely do so, even though their jaws are strong enough to crack the bones of an animal such as a pig. Alligators eat a wide variety of animals. Young ones feed on insects, crayfish, frogs and minnows, while the diet of an adult may include water birds, turtles and small mammals, including the occasional dog.

◄ A crocodile pounces on a wildebeest, seizing it in its strong jaws and spinning it around in the water.

ALLIGATOR HOLES

During the winter, alligators stay in the water to keep warm, burying themselves in mud or in holes they have made with their bodies. In times of drought, these holes are often the only places where water can still be found, and they are used as a refuge by alligators and other aquatic animals until the rain returns.

ENDANGERED CREATURES

There are 13 species of crocodile, but only two species of alligator: the American alligator of southeast USA and the Chinese alligator of the Chang Jiang (Yangtze). All crocodilians are hunted for their skin and meat. Their habitats are also threatened. The American alligator became so rare that it was protected by law from 1969 to 1987.

DEVOTED PARENTS

Alligators lay between 30 and 80 eggs in a concealed nest. After incubating for 60 days in the heat of the Sun, the young make high-pitched yelps from inside the eggs. The mother then scratches away the earth and waits until the young hatch out to carry them to the water in her mouth. She watches over them in their first year.

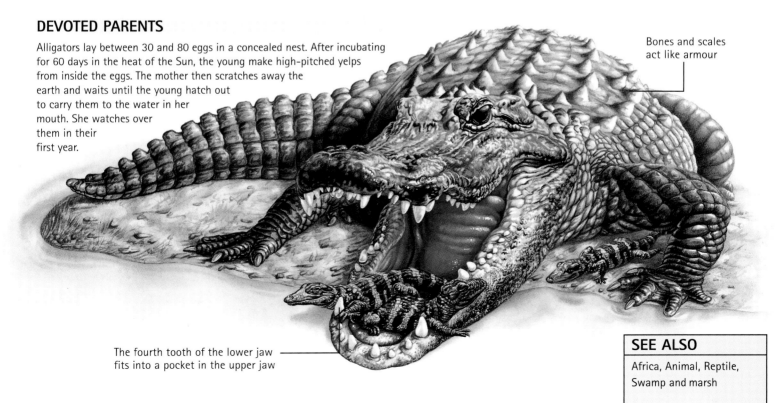

Bones and scales act like armour

The fourth tooth of the lower jaw fits into a pocket in the upper jaw

SEE ALSO

Africa, Animal, Reptile, Swamp and marsh

AMPHIBIAN

Amphibians are cold-blooded animals that are able to live both in water and on land. Most start life with gills, but later develop lungs for breathing.

Like many frogs, the European common frog has smooth, moist skin and long legs for jumping.

Like many toads, the European common toad has dry, lumpy skin and walks rather than leaps.

The long-tailed salamander's bright colour helps it warn off predators.

Newts, such as this smooth newt, are salamanders that spend long periods in water.

Caecilians have no legs and live undergound. They are found only in tropical areas and many are blind.

Frogs, toads, salamanders, newts and caecilians are all types of amphibian. They are cold-blooded creatures that rely on their surroundings for warmth, and are found in most parts of the world. Adult amphibians usually have soft, thin, moist skin that absorbs oxygen from the air, helping them to breathe. But some frogs and toads have thick, warty skin to help them survive in drier conditions. There are around 6,260 amphibian species, but one third of them are endangered.

JELLIED EGGS
The way amphibians breed and develop is unique in the animal kingdom. Females lay their jelly-covered eggs, called spawn, in water. These hatch into tadpoles, which develop limbs and lungs so that they can live on dry land. Some amphibians need only a small amount of water in which to lay their eggs. The tree frog lays its eggs on moist leaves and the male midwife toad carries the female's eggs on its back legs, dipping them in pools of water.

▲ The extraordinary Mexican axolotl salamander usually spends its life as a tadpole, breathing through gills.

BIG EATERS
All amphibians are hunters. Many use their bulging eyes to track fast-moving prey, swallowing it whole. Small frogs and salamanders eat insects and tiny fish. Large toads gulp down mice and birds. They usually sit and wait, or crawl towards their prey, before lunging with mouth open. Some frogs and salamanders have a long, sticky-tipped tongue attached to the front of their mouth, which they can flick out to grab insects.

LEAPING FROGS AND TOADS
Over 80 per cent of all amphibians are frogs and toads, known as anurans. They have long, five-toed back legs for leaping and shorter, four-toed front legs used to cushion the landing. There is no scientific difference between frogs and toads, but anurans with smooth, moist skin that usually jump are called frogs, and those that waddle and have drier, lumpy skin are called toads.

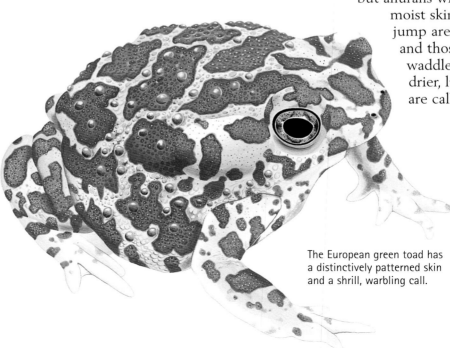

The European green toad has a distinctively patterned skin and a shrill, warbling call.

THE GLANDS
Pores that hold the salamander's poison can be found across its back and on the sides of its head.

THE POISON
When the fire salamander is attacked by a predator, poison oozes out of the pores in its skin.

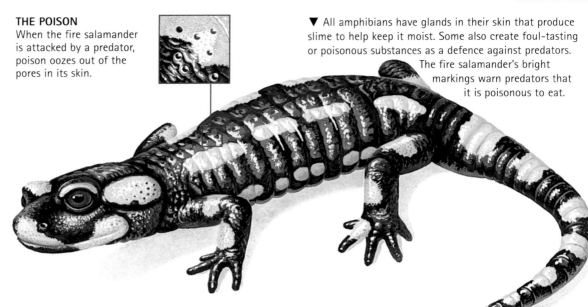

▼ All amphibians have glands in their skin that produce slime to help keep it moist. Some also create foul-tasting or poisonous substances as a defence against predators. The fire salamander's bright markings warn predators that it is poisonous to eat.

SALAMANDERS AND CAECILIANS

Newts and salamanders (urodelans) have short limbs and long tails. Salamanders in Europe and North America that spend long periods in water are called newts. Most salamanders breathe with lungs and through their skin, although some have no lungs. Caecilians (apodans) are the third and smallest group of amphibians. They are worm-like, with blunt snouts for tunnelling, tiny eyes and wide mouths. They hunt mainly at night.

▼ The spectacled salamander has a bright red tail that it curls along its back when alarmed.

THE AMPHIBIAN LIFE-CYCLE

When frogs mate, the male usually sits on the female's back for up to three days. As soon as the female lays her eggs in the water, the male releases sperm to fertilize them. The eggs hatch into tadpoles, which eventually metamorphose (change) into froglets (young frogs) and leave the water for life on land.

1 The female frog lays her eggs, or spawn, in large masses in a pond or stream. The eggs are protected by a special jelly.

2 The larvae, or tadpoles, develop inside the eggs. About a week later, the tadpoles hatch out and attach themselves to plants.

3 The tadpoles breathe through feathery gills and start to swim at about three days old. They feed on waterweeds and algae in the water.

4 The tadpoles slowly turn into frogs, developing limbs and lungs so that they can live on land. Their tails are absorbed into their bodies.

5 Fully-grown, the young frogs leave the water. They feed on small insects and will not reproduce themselves until they are a year old.

SEE ALSO

Animal, Frog and toad, Hibernation

ANIMAL

Animals are multi-cellular living creatures that can move, eat food, sense their surroundings and reproduce, usually by mating with a partner.

The rotifer is one of the smallest animals – seen only through a microscope.

The octopus is a type of mollusc, a group that also includes snails and squid.

The angel fish is just one of 32,000 different species of fish.

The shield bug is part of the largest group – insects, with a million known species.

The peacock is one of 10,000 species of bird, most of which can fly.

The rabbit is a mammal. Its young are fed on milk produced by the mother.

More than 1.8 million kinds of animal live on Earth, and many more are discovered each year. Every animal is unique, but there are common features that set creatures in the animal kingdom apart from other living beings such as plants, fungi and single-celled organisms.

THE MATING GAME

Like all living creatures, animals must reproduce. Most do this by mating with a partner. It is usually the female that chooses a mate, so many males are brightly coloured or use elaborate courtship rituals to lure a suitable partner to them.

BILLIONS OF TINY CELLS

All adult animals are multi-cellular, which means they are made up of more than one cell. Some animals, such as rotifers and hydras (aquatic animals), have just a few dozen cells, but large animals, such as humans, are much more complex and can have up to 50 billion cells.

▲ The bushbaby is a nocturnal animal, so it comes out at night to feed. Huge, round eyes, a good sense of smell and an excellent sense of hearing are essential for hunting prey at night.

FOOD FOR LIVING

Unlike plants, animals cannot make their own food – they must eat ready-made plant or animal food. Most have some sort of mouth, but the way in which the food is broken down inside their body varies. Birds have no teeth, so the food is ground up by stones in their stomach. Snakes swallow prey alive and whole, digesting it slowly with strong juices. The tapeworm has no mouth, but lives in another animal's intestines, soaking up digested food through its skin.

MOTHERLY LOVE

Many animals go to great lengths to keep their babies alive. For example, the female scorpion, best known for her sting, is a very caring mother. She carries her newborn young on her back for up to 12 days, until they can fend for themselves.

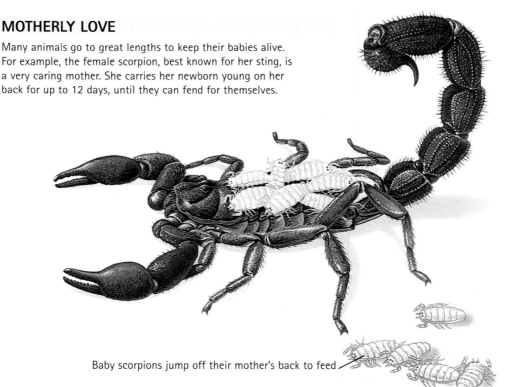

Baby scorpions jump off their mother's back to feed

NERVES AND SENSES

All animals sense their surroundings with a set of nerves and sense organs that are adapted to suit the way they live. For example, many night hunters have whiskers to find their way in the dark, and some snakes have infra-red sensors to 'see' the body heat of their prey. Sharks can smell blood in the water many kilometres away and home in on it accurately, while migrating animals, such as grey whales, have an extra sense that allows them to travel great distances without getting lost.

ON THE MOVE

All animals, from the slowest snail to the fastest gazelle, move, usually by using an efficient set of muscles. The way they move varies: some crawl or walk, some slither, while others hop or run – in the case of crabs, sideways. Even a drifting jellyfish pulsates to move itself up or down in the water. This ability to move has allowed some species to spread all over the world. Some animals, such as sponges and corals, can only move when young, but remain in one place as adults. ▶

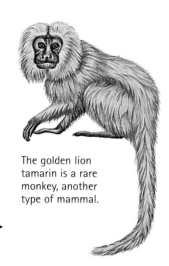

The golden lion tamarin is a rare monkey, another type of mammal.

THE FASTEST ANIMAL

Predatory animals use many methods to catch their food. Some use stealth, others use camouflage, but the cheetah's strategy is speed. It is the fastest animal on four legs, reaching speeds of 110km/h in mid-chase. Its favourite food is the young antelope that graze on the African savanna. But a cheetah's stamina is poor – if it does not catch the antelope in the first few hundred metres, the prey usually gets away.

1 The cheetah creeps forward slowly, getting as close as possible to its victim before breaking into a high-speed sprint.

2 The cheetah bounds forward, covering several metres in each leap. Its claws do not retract, giving it extra grip on the ground.

3 The antelope suddenly changes direction to confuse the cheetah, but the cat's flexible back allows it to turn sharply.

4 The gap closes. The cheetah swipes with strong paws at the antelope's legs to knock it off balance and bring it down, before killing it with a bite.

A QUESTION OF CLASS

Zoologists divide the animal kingdom into about 30 major groups, or phyla (the largest of which are shown in this chart). Each group, or phylum, can be further divided into sub-phyla, classes (shown), then orders, families, genuses and species (not shown). Animals from different species cannot breed together, except in rare circumstances.

INVERTEBRATES
(animals without backbones)

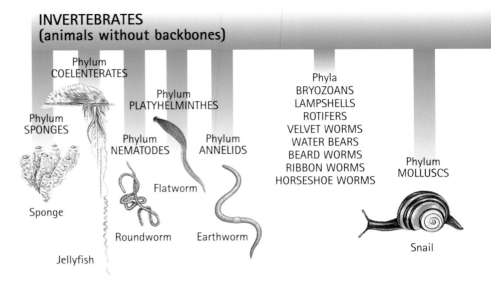

Phylum
COELENTERATES

Phylum
PLATYHELMINTHES

Phylum
SPONGES

Phylum
NEMATODES

Phylum
ANNELIDS

Phyla
BRYOZOANS
LAMPSHELLS
ROTIFERS
VELVET WORMS
WATER BEARS
BEARD WORMS
RIBBON WORMS
HORSESHOE WORMS

Phylum
MOLLUSCS

Sponge

Flatworm

Roundworm

Earthworm

Jellyfish

Snail

▲ The marbled polecat belongs to a family of carnivores (meat-eating mammals) that includes weasels, badgers, otters and skunks. All of these animals have short legs and long, sinuous bodies.

FAMILY GATHERINGS

Zoologists classify, or group, animals by their common features. For example, all insects have six legs, all birds have feathers, and all mammal mothers feed their young on milk from their own bodies. The grouping of animals in this way is known as taxonomy. It helps zoologists to work out when animals first appeared on Earth, how they have changed over time, and which creatures are closely related.

WITH BACKBONES

All animals can be divided into two main groups: those with backbones, called vertebrates, and those without backbones, called

invertebrates. Vertebrates include fish, amphibians, reptiles, birds and mammals. All other animals are invertebrates.

THE MYSTERIOUS BARNACLE

It can be difficult for zoologists to tell if some creatures are animals at all. For example, an acorn barnacle attached to a rock on the seashore does not even look alive, let alone animal-like. By studying its life-cycle, zoologists discovered that before the barnacle attaches itself to a rock, it looks like a young prawn. This proved that barnacles are crustaceans, along with crabs and lobsters.

▲ Acorn barnacles

WHO IS RELATED TO WHOM?

Scientists study the genetic make-up of animals compared to other animals to reveal who is related to whom. For many years zoologists argued over whether red pandas were related to bears, raccoons or

► The anteater is an edentate. This is an order of mammal with few or no teeth. Other members of the group include sloths, which are herbivores (plant-eaters) and armadillos. The anteater is an insectivore (insect-eater), living solely on ants and termites, which it sniffs out with its snout and licks up with its long, sticky tongue. Its powerful front claws are used for digging.

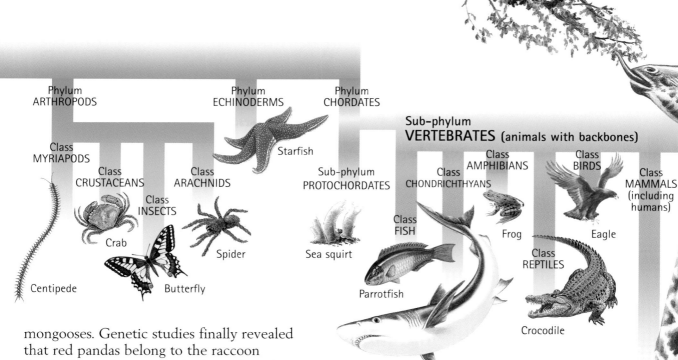

Phylum
ARTHROPODS

Phylum
ECHINODERMS

Phylum
CHORDATES

Class
MYRIAPODS

Class
CRUSTACEANS

Class
ARACHNIDS

Class
INSECTS

Crab

Spider

Centipede

Butterfly

Starfish

Sub-phylum
VERTEBRATES (animals with backbones)

Sub-phylum
PROTOCHORDATES

Class
CHONDRICHTHYANS

Class
AMPHIBIANS

Class
BIRDS

Class
MAMMALS
(including
humans)

Class
FISH

Frog

Eagle

Class
REPTILES

Sea squirt

Parrotfish

Crocodile

Great white shark

mongooses. Genetic studies finally revealed that red pandas belong to the raccoon family. In another study, the kiwi, thought to be one species of bird, was shown to have two species – they look very similar, but cannot breed together.

DEEP-SEA TREASURES
In the 1970s, when scientists sent deep-sea equipment down to new depths, over 200 new animal types were discovered living around deep-sea hydrothermal vents (jets of hot, mineral-rich water spurting out from the ocean floor). Transparent fish, 2m-long tube worms, plate-sized clams and blind white crabs were among the amazing finds.

SPECIES UNDER THREAT
Many animals in the world are now rare or nearly extinct. Once an animal species has

died out, it is lost forever, which is why zoos have breeding programmes for threatened species. Estimates vary, but scientists agree that there are millions of animal species still waiting to be discovered. These too are under threat as many of the natural areas of the world, including coral reefs and tropical rainforests, are being destroyed or polluted by people.

▶ The giraffe is the tallest animal. It is a mammal and can grow up to 5.5m tall. It lives in Africa and eats thorny acacia leaves, which it strips from the branches with its 50cm-long tongue.

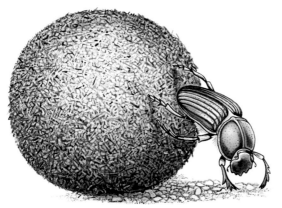

▲ Some animals, called detritivores, help to recycle other animals' waste products. The dung beetle eats animal dung. Some species eat the dung where they find it, while others dig a hole and bury it to eat later.

AMAZING ANIMAL FACTS

• Insects are the most numerous animals on Earth. It is estimated that for every human there are 200 million insects

• The largest animal to have lived on Earth is the blue whale. Belonging to the order of mammals called cetaceans, blue whales can grow to over 30m in length

• The fastest-moving animal is the peregrine falcon, which can swoop at speeds of up to 350km/h

• Unlike most animals, the sponge can regrow its entire body from a tiny fragment of itself

• The giant squid has the largest eye of any animal ever to have lived. It is about 40cm in diameter, or ten times the size of a human eye

SEE ALSO
Amphibian, Conservation, Evolution, Fish, Insect, Mammal, Micro-organism, Prehistoric animal, Reptile, Zoology

ANTARCTICA

Antarctica is the fifth largest continent. It surrounds the South Pole and 98 per cent of it lies buried beneath a thick sheet of ice.

▲ Norwegian explorer Roald Amundsen was first to reach the South Pole on December 14, 1911.

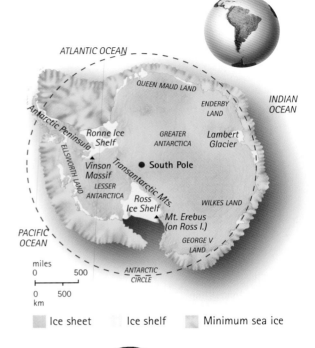

miles 0 — 500

0 — 500 km

Ice sheet   Ice shelf   Minimum sea ice

KEY FACTS

• **Area:** 14,000,000 sq km

• **Population:** no permanent population

• **Number of countries:** none, although some countries claim sections of the continent

• **Highest point:** Vinson Massif (4,897m)

• **Largest ice shelf:** Ross ice shelf (192,000–208,000 sq km)

• **Position of South Pole:** 1,235km from the nearest coastline

Only a few mountains and barren, rocky areas show above the ice that hides Antarctica. The thickness of the polar ice sheet makes Antarctica the highest continent. It is also the windiest continent and largely a frozen desert, with snowfall near the Pole equivalent to less than 150mm of water per year. The world's coldest air temperature, –89.2°C, was recorded there, at Vostok scientific station.

FIRE AND ICE

A string of mountains cuts across the icy mass. On their eastern side, near the coast, the ice sheet reaches depths of 4,800m. Ross Island, to the west, holds the active volcano, Mount Erebus. Ice flows down to the coast as glaciers and spreads out over the sea, creating huge ice shelves. When the ice becomes too heavy, parts of it break away to form enormous, flat-topped icebergs up to 60m high and many kilometres long.

FUR AND FEATHERS

Antarctica has few land animals because, even in summer, most of the continent is covered with ice. The animals live mainly in the air or sea and have thick fur,

◄ Two emperor penguins with their chick. To withstand the winter cold, emperors have very dense feathers and large fat reserves. They also huddle together in groups of up to 5,000 birds to keep warm.

feathers or blubber (fat) to keep them warm. The ocean is home to many types of krill (tiny shrimp-like creatures), squid, fish, seals, whales and eight types of penguin. Antarctic birds include the predatory skua and large-winged albatross.

STUDIES ON ICE

Antarctica has a temporary population of up to 4,000 scientists from 18 countries. Their interests vary from space research to microbiology, and all must abide by the Antarctic Treaty. This agreement bans the mining of valuable mineral resources buried beneath the ice, and prevents any military or industrial activities on the continent. More than 20,000 tourists also visit Antarctica each summer.

◄ Icebergs break away from the ice shelves that surround Antarctica. The ice builds up in layers over thousands of years.

SEE ALSO

Animal, Bird, Climate, Conservation, Explorer, Glacier, Magnetism

ARCHAEOLOGY

Archaeology is the study of the remains of the past that people have left behind them, such as objects and buildings. Often remains are buried or sunken.

CHINA'S BURIED ARMY

In 1974, thousands of life-sized clay soldiers were found near the tomb of Shi Huangdi, the first emperor of the Qin dynasty in China who died in 210BCE. They were part of a massive burial complex built to protect the emperor in the afterlife.

2 The site is divided into a grid with string. Squares are excavated one by one. Top soil is removed with diggers and trowels.

1 Archaeologists use computerized equipment to find buried objects.

3 Finds are carefully cleaned by brushing away soil. Each find is recorded and numbered before it is removed.

4 The position of an object can reveal important information.

5 Objects are carefully examined before being restored and preserved. They can then be put on display.

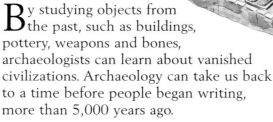

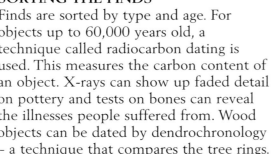

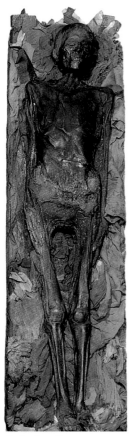

▲ An Egyptian mummy, or preserved body, from c. 600BCE. Remains like this reveal a lot about the lives of ancient people.

By studying objects from the past, such as buildings, pottery, weapons and bones, archaeologists can learn about vanished civilizations. Archaeology can take us back to a time before people began writing, more than 5,000 years ago.

CLUES TO THE PAST

To know where to dig, archaeologists often start from a small clue such as a coin or a fragment of pottery. Many archaeologists now work on rescue digs – recording a site before it is destroyed, usually by building work. Aerial photography and scanners are used to reveal what is under the ground.

SORTING THE FINDS

Finds are sorted by type and age. For objects up to 60,000 years old, a technique called radiocarbon dating is used. This measures the carbon content of an object. X-rays can show up faded detail on pottery and tests on bones can reveal the illnesses people suffered from. Wood objects can be dated by dendrochronology – a technique that compares the tree rings.

LOST CITIES

Sites may be as small as a grave or as large as an entire city. The ancient city of Troy, for example, was uncovered in Turkey by German archaeologist Heinrich Schliemann in 1870, after years of searching. Many sites, however, are discovered by accident. The Indus Valley civilization in Asia, which was destroyed in about 1700BCE, was found by chance in the 1920s by railway workers.

◀ A Minoan vase from about 1500BCE, found on the island of Crete. Distinctive styles in art and pottery allow archaeologists to identify different groups of people.

SEE ALSO

Aztecs, Babylon, China, Egypt (Ancient), Greece (Ancient), Roman Empire

ARCHITECTURE

Architecture is the art of designing buildings and other structures that are soundly built, pleasing to look at and suitable for their purpose.

The classical style uses flat beams, columns and sculpture.

The Romans built aqueducts with rounded arches and thick walls.

Japanese castles have upturned roof edges and contrasting colours.

India's Taj Mahal features domes and minarets typical of Islamic architecture.

Glass walls and tall office blocks dominate modern architecture.

The style of architecture used for a building depends on the materials available, the architect's ideas and what the building is going to be used for.

ARCHITECTS AT WORK
As well as needing to know a building's purpose, an architect must know the space allocated and how much money can be spent. Detailed models and drawings are produced for the builders, showing every part of the building and how it is to be constructed. These plans include practical features, such as heating and lighting systems, pipe work and plumbing.

WESTERN STYLES
Western architecture began in Greece around 500BCE with the classical style. Pillars were built to precise mathematical patterns, such as those in the Parthenon, Athens, built 447–438BCE. From about 200BCE, the Romans used curved arches and domes to make bridges and aqueducts.

MEDIEVAL IDEAS
During the Middle Ages, the pointed arches and colourful stained glass of the Gothic style began to appear, especially

▲ Today's architects use modern materials to create startling new designs. Disney World's EPCOT Center in Florida is a geodesic dome. These are strong, lightweight domes with no internal supports or straight walls. They are constructed from ready-made sections.

in churches. Like the classical styles of the Romans and Greeks, the Gothic style has been used by many architects since then.

MODERN MATERIALS
Since the 19th century, inventions such as heating and lighting, and new building materials such as steel, plastic and reinforced concrete have revolutionized architecture. Steel-framed skyscrapers were first developed in the USA after the invention of the elevator in 1854. Modern architecture is often characterized by a combination of borrowed ideas with the newest materials and techniques.

HI-TECH BUILDINGS
The Sydney Opera House in Australia uses hi-tech materials such as glass, concrete and ceramics in its structure. Complex mathematics were needed to work out if the materials would take the weight of its unusual component parts. Modern architects begin with a series of drawings, and use computers to calculate weights and forces. Then building begins.

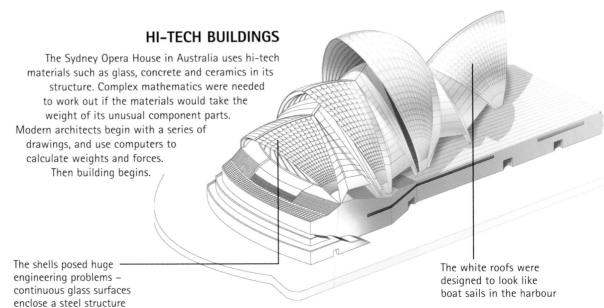

The shells posed huge engineering problems – continuous glass surfaces enclose a steel structure

The white roofs were designed to look like boat sails in the harbour

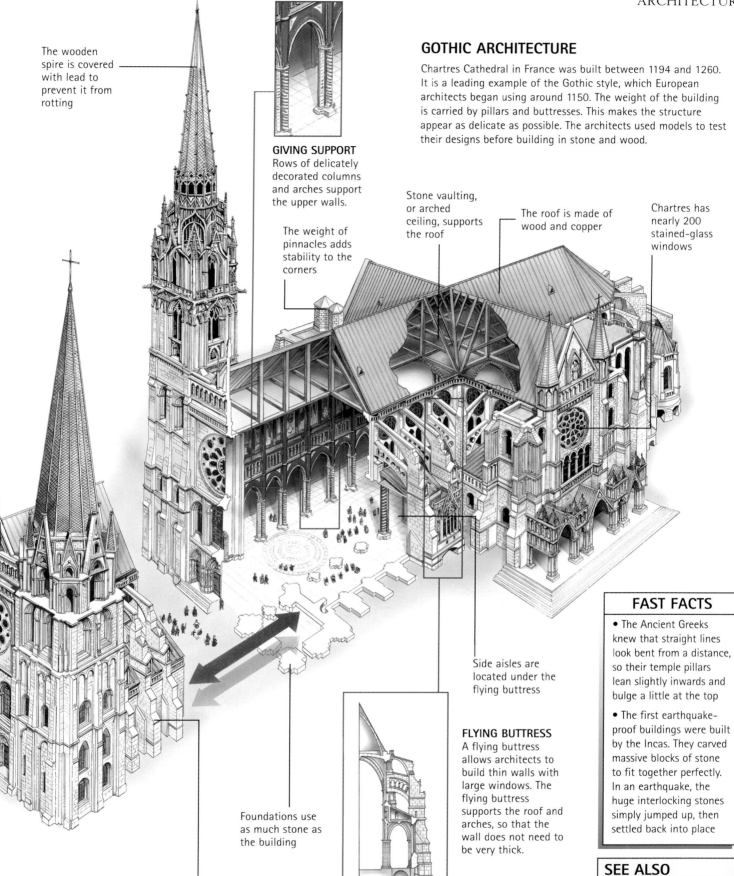

The wooden spire is covered with lead to prevent it from rotting

GIVING SUPPORT
Rows of delicately decorated columns and arches support the upper walls.

The weight of pinnacles adds stability to the corners

GOTHIC ARCHITECTURE

Chartres Cathedral in France was built between 1194 and 1260. It is a leading example of the Gothic style, which European architects began using around 1150. The weight of the building is carried by pillars and buttresses. This makes the structure appear as delicate as possible. The architects used models to test their designs before building in stone and wood.

Stone vaulting, or arched ceiling, supports the roof

The roof is made of wood and copper

Chartres has nearly 200 stained-glass windows

Side aisles are located under the flying buttress

FLYING BUTTRESS
A flying buttress allows architects to build thin walls with large windows. The flying buttress supports the roof and arches, so that the wall does not need to be very thick.

Foundations use as much stone as the building

Vertical buttresses lead the eye upward

FAST FACTS
• The Ancient Greeks knew that straight lines look bent from a distance, so their temple pillars lean slightly inwards and bulge a little at the top

• The first earthquake-proof buildings were built by the Incas. They carved massive blocks of stone to fit together perfectly. In an earthquake, the huge interlocking stones simply jumped up, then settled back into place

SEE ALSO
Bridge, Construction, Design, Greece (Ancient), Seven wonders of the world, Skyscraper

ARCTIC

The Arctic is the area within the Arctic Circle – an imaginary line around the northern part of the globe with the North Pole at its centre.

The Arctic is made up of the frozen Arctic Ocean, the surrounding seas and small islands, and the northern parts of Canada, Alaska, Russia, Finland, Sweden, Norway and Greenland.

LAND OF THE MIDNIGHT SUN

Temperatures creep above freezing point for only about four months of the year. There are some days during the summer when areas near the North Pole are in constant daylight because the Sun never sets. This is why the Arctic is sometimes known as the Land of the Midnight Sun.

TUNDRA LIFE

Treeless plains, or tundra, cover the land. In the summer, these plains are home to animals such as reindeer, lemmings, musk ox and Arctic hares, which graze on scrubby plants and shrubs. Migratory birds, such as the Arctic tern, return from winter homes to breed in the short warm season.

▲ Arctic hares live on the tundra. In summer, their fur is brown. They grow a new white coat in winter.

THE DARK OF WINTER

Wintertime in the Arctic is cold, dark and long. For a short time the Sun does not come above the horizon at all. The ocean is frozen and the tundra snow-covered, with only a few mosses and lichens growing. Most animals and birds migrate south until summer returns. Polar bears thrive in these harsh conditions, hunting seals and catching fish in the icy water.

▼ An aeroplane arrives with supplies for the store at Savissivik, Greenland. Aircraft are a vital link for scattered settlements around the Arctic.

PEOPLE IN THE ARCTIC

A number of different peoples live in the Arctic, including the Inuit of Greenland, Canada and northeast Asia, and the Sami (Lapps) of Scandinavia. Those on the coast live by hunting and fishing. Those living inland hunt wild caribou or, like the Nenet tribe from Siberia in northern Russia (below), herd reindeer for a living.

SEE ALSO

Asia, Canada, Climate, Magnetism, Migration, Native Americans, North America, Ocean and sea, Russia and the Baltic States, Scandinavia, USA

20

ARGENTINA

Bordered by the Andes Mountains to the west, Argentina is the second largest country in South America and the eighth largest in the world.

Area: 2,766,890 sq km
Population: 40,117,000
Capital: Buenos Aires
Language: Spanish
Currency: Argentinian peso

Argentina has two warm and rainy regions in the north: the Gran Chaco and Mesopotamia. The central areas are made up of a fertile, grassy plain called the Pampas, while Patagonia in the south is largely desert. In the far south is the cold and windswept land of Tierra del Fuego.

UNIQUE WILDLIFE
Jaguars, monkeys and tapirs are found in rainforests in the north. Patagonia is home to unique animals, such as the pudu, a tiny deer, and rhea, a flightless ostrich-like bird.

TOWN DWELLERS
Ninety-seven per cent of Argentinians are of European descent, with *mestizos* (people of mixed European and Indian descent) and others making up just 3 per cent. Skilled cowboys, known as *gauchos*, herd cattle across the plains. Around 92 per cent of the population live in cities and towns. Many people work in meat-packing industries and in factories using farm products, including wool and hides.

SPANISH TREASURE-SEEKERS
Spanish explorers reached Argentina in 1516. They were looking for treasure and they named the country after *argentum*, the Latin word for 'silver'. European

▲ Cacti flourish in the warm, dry air of the plateaux (flat areas of land high above sea level) in the Andes Mountains. Many species of cactus grow all across Argentina.

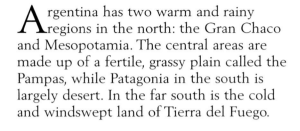

▲ Argentina's capital, Buenos Aires, whose name means 'favourable winds', is one of the world's great ports.

settlers arriving soon afterwards became rich by farming the fertile land.

MODERN TIMES
In 1816, Argentina declared independence after almost 300 years of Spanish rule. Since the 1930s, the country has faced many problems, including harsh military rule and high unemployment. In 1982, Argentina invaded the Falkland Islands, a British dependency, but was defeated. Elections in 1983 ended military rule.

◄ Gauchos work on the huge cattle ranches of the Pampas. They are regarded as folklore heroes.

SEE ALSO
Grassland, South America

21

ART

Art can be any creative work used to portray images and to express feelings – from drawing, painting and sculpture to architecture and computer graphics.

▲ René Magritte's *The False Mirror* (1928) is typical of his work, which often put together two ordinary images to produce something dream-like and surreal.

The first examples of art were cave paintings and images carved out of stone, the oldest of which were made about 40,000 years ago. Most early art was dedicated to gods, as religion and worship were important influences, but over the centuries new styles of art have evolved.

Japanese silk screen prints, like this one from the 1800s, greatly influenced 20th-century Western art.

CLASSICAL STYLE
It was during the Renaissance in the 14th, 15th and 16th centuries that the word 'artist' was first used. Before that, painters were thought of as skilled craftworkers. Renaissance means rebirth, and artists such as Michelangelo and Leonardo da Vinci took their ideas from the classical lines of the Ancient Greeks and Romans.

Native American art, such as this mask carved around 1850, combine geometric styles with strong colours.

PAINTING FROM LIFE
The Renaissance artists were the first to use live models. By using light and shade, these artists gave their images depth, resulting in a three-dimensional appearance on the canvas. They also began to use perspective to indicate whether objects were near or far away.

This pot by Clarice Cliff is typical of the 1930s' Art Deco style, with its bold lines, colours and shape.

STRONG FEELINGS
In the late 16th century, art started to become more personal. Scientific advances made people question their religious beliefs and this was reflected in the art of the baroque movement.

Caravaggio's *The Death of a Virgin* was rejected by the priest who commissioned it, because it showed the Virgin Mary as an old woman. As the style evolved, artists like Rubens showed this passion of feeling in paintings full of drama.

EVERYDAY LIFE
In the 17th century, artists began to paint everyday life and ordinary people. Until then, only important people and grand themes were thought to be worth painting. Artists such as Rembrandt seemed to reveal the sitter's character, while Hogarth's work commented on social conditions.

► Jeweller Carl Fabergé (1846–1920) was famous for the jewel-encrusted eggs he made for the tsars of Russia.

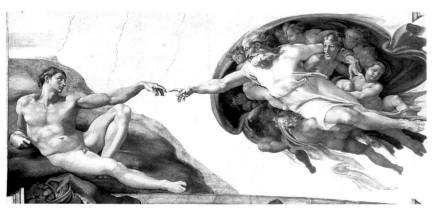

▲ This scene, *The Creation of Adam*, is on the ceiling of the Sistine Chapel, Rome. It is one of nine scenes from the Old Testament, painted by Michelangelo between 1508 and 1512.

▲ The vibrant, rapid strokes of Edgar Degas' *Dancer Fastening her Pump* (1880s) capture a sense of movement.

◀ *As I Opened Fire* (1964) by Roy Lichtenstein, who was a leading exponent of pop art. This used mass-produced imagery to create a powerful impact.

Pablo Picasso tried to see subjects from many different angles as in his *Little Girl with Hoop* (1919).

CAPTURING SUNLIGHT

By the 1700s and 1800s, many artists were beginning to feel the need to try out new methods and ideas. In the late 1800s, the French Impressionists, such as Claude Monet, Auguste Renoir and Edgar Degas, became more spontaneous, daubing their canvases with bold strokes of colour to try to capture the fleeting effects of light.

THE SHOCK OF THE NEW

During the 1900s, artists experimented in other new ways. Cubists such as Picasso and Georges Braque began to show images as though they were seeing them from several sides at once, opening the door for different forms of abstract art. Surrealists like René Magritte and Salvador Dali used dreams to explore hidden feelings, painting unlikely objects together in surprising situations. Photography gained a new status as an art form, with haunting images of landscapes or witty and innovative surrealist images. Artists today continue to discover new styles and materials, including video and multimedia techniques, as well as taking inspiration from traditional folk art.

EASTERN ART

In some cultures, artistic styles have changed little over thousands of years. Chinese art has been very influential with its accurately observed landscapes executed with simple brush strokes on silk and paper.

DECORATIVE ARTS

Distinctive styles can also be seen in the decorative arts – in ceramics, textiles and metalwork. Art deco of the 1930s, for example,took art into every aspect of life.

Man Ray started a trend for surreal photography as in this image entitled *The Violin* (1925).

▲ *Marriage à la Mode* (1743) by William Hogarth was a series of scenes criticizing manners.

◀ Duane Hanson's life-size fibreglass work *Old Couple on a Bench* (1994) is an example of realism in the 1990s.

SEE ALSO

Aboriginal people, Architecture, Colour, Design, Paint and dye, Photography, Renaissance, Sculpture

ASIA

Asia is the world's largest continent. It covers 30 per cent of the Earth's land area and has a bigger population than all the other continents put together.

▲ A dragon boat festival in Taiwan. At the end of the race, the winning team raises its oars. Boats are an important means of transport along Asia's wide rivers.

KEY FACTS

- **Area:** 31,773,000 sq km
- **Population:** 4,228,000,000
- **Number of countries:** 48
- **Largest country:** Russia, 75% of which is in Asia
- **Smallest country:** Maldives (298 sq km)
- **Highest point:** Mount Everest (8,848m)
- **Largest lake:** Caspian Sea (371,800 sq km)
- **Longest river:** Chang Jiang (Yangtze) (6,300km)

The immense size of Asia means it has a huge variety of environments and weather conditions. Its natural habitats include dense tropical forests, fertile plains, Arctic regions and deserts – both hot and cold. The world's ten highest mountains are found in Asia, as well as the lowest point on land: the shores of the Dead Sea, at 393m below sea level.

NATURAL BORDERS

Asia is separated from Europe by the Ural Mountains in the northwest and from North America by the Bering Strait, a strip of water only 88km wide, in the northeast. The Red Sea and the Suez Canal divide Asia from Africa in the southwest.

EXTREMES OF TEMPERATURE

Northern Asia is cold and often desolate, with few plants to support people or animals. Noril'sk in northern Russia is the coldest city in the world with average temperatures of –10.9°C. By contrast, Tirunelveli in India, southern Asia, has average temperatures of 29°C.

WET AND DRY

Devastating floods occur in Asia, notably in China, Bangladesh, India and Pakistan. The monsoon winds from the Indian Ocean bring heavy rain to much of southern and eastern Asia. Vast areas of central Asia, on the other hand, have very little rain, and deserts such as the Gobi dominate the landscape.

DANGER ZONE

Because Asia lies on faults in the Earth's crust, many Asian countries, especially Japan, have experienced devastating earthquakes. The coasts of eastern and Southeast Asia are also prone to typhoons – violent storms that come from the China Sea.

▲ The snow leopard is found in some of the most remote areas of central Asia. Its pale, spotted coat allows it to blend in with its surroundings.

▶ The yak is used in the mountainous regions of Tibet (a region of China since 1950) as a source of food, milk and clothing, and for carrying goods.

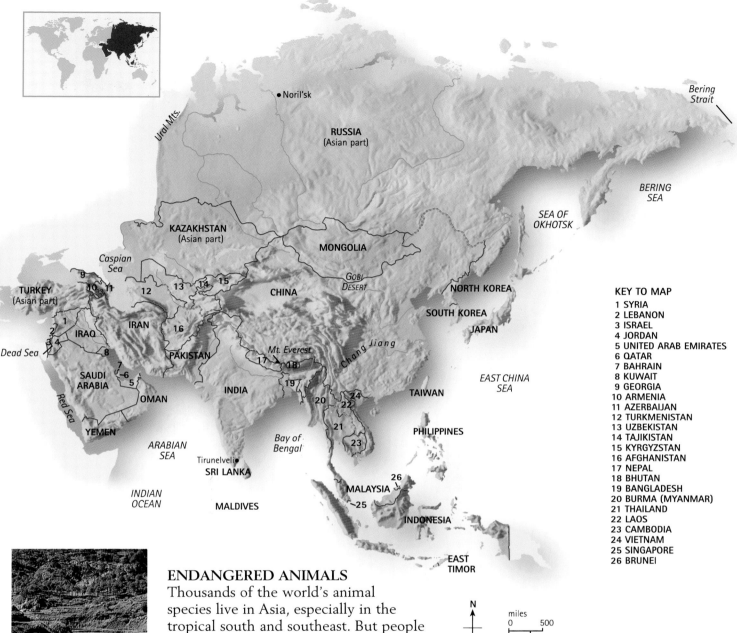

- Noril'sk
- Bering Strait
- **RUSSIA** (Asian part)
- *BERING SEA*
- *SEA OF OKHOTSK*
- **KAZAKHSTAN** (Asian part)
- *Caspian Sea*
- **MONGOLIA**
- *GOBI DESERT*
- **NORTH KOREA**
- *Ural Mts.*
- **TURKEY** (Asian part)
- 9
- 10 11
- 12
- 13 14 15
- **CHINA**
- **SOUTH KOREA**
- **JAPAN**
- *Dead Sea*
- 1
- 2
- 3 4
- **IRAQ**
- **IRAN**
- 16
- *Mt. Everest*
- 17 18
- *Chang Jiang*
- *EAST CHINA SEA*
- 8
- **PAKISTAN**
- 7
- 6
- 5
- **SAUDI ARABIA**
- **OMAN**
- **INDIA**
- 19
- 20 24
- 22
- **TAIWAN**
- *Red Sea*
- **YEMEN**
- 21
- 23
- **PHILIPPINES**
- *ARABIAN SEA*
- Tirunelveli
- **SRI LANKA**
- *INDIAN OCEAN*
- **MALDIVES**
- *Bay of Bengal*
- 26
- **MALAYSIA**
- 25
- **INDONESIA**
- **EAST TIMOR**

KEY TO MAP
1 SYRIA
2 LEBANON
3 ISRAEL
4 JORDAN
5 UNITED ARAB EMIRATES
6 QATAR
7 BAHRAIN
8 KUWAIT
9 GEORGIA
10 ARMENIA
11 AZERBAIJAN
12 TURKMENISTAN
13 UZBEKISTAN
14 TAJIKISTAN
15 KYRGYZSTAN
16 AFGHANISTAN
17 NEPAL
18 BHUTAN
19 BANGLADESH
20 BURMA (MYANMAR)
21 THAILAND
22 LAOS
23 CAMBODIA
24 VIETNAM
25 SINGAPORE
26 BRUNEI

N

miles
0   500
0   500
km

▲ Terraces are cut in the hillsides in the Philippines to provide land for growing rice and other crops.

ENDANGERED ANIMALS

Thousands of the world's animal species live in Asia, especially in the tropical south and southeast. But people clearing the land for farming and hunting animals for their skins have put several species in danger of extinction, including the giant panda, the orang-utan, the tiger and the snow leopard.

THE LAND PROVIDES

Rice is the main crop of warm, wet southern Asia, while wheat, barley and millet grow in the colder, drier north. Spices such as pepper and cloves have been a source of wealth for India, Sri Lanka and Indonesia for centuries. Other major crops include tea, tobacco, cotton, sugar, coffee, cocoa, jute and fruits. Forests cover nearly a third of Russia, and nearly 20 per cent of the rest of the continent.

NATURAL RESOURCES

Raw materials are among Asia's most important exports. Asia provides more than half of the world's tin. Coal, gas, aluminium and other metals needed for manufacturing are exported worldwide. Seven of the ten countries with the largest oil reserves are in Asia: Saudi Arabia, Iran, Iraq, Kuwait, the United Arab Emirates, Russia and Kazakhstan.

WAY OF LIFE

In the desert areas of Saudi Arabia and Iran, and the steppes (dry, grassy, treeless plains) of Mongolia and neighbouring ▶

countries, there are many nomadic (wandering) tribes. These nomads live by herding camels, goats, sheep and horses. Farming is the most common occupation for the people of many Asian countries, including China, India and Indonesia.

▲ Mongolians have traditionally survived off the infertile land of central Asia by herding cattle. Bactrian (two-humped) camels are used as beasts of burden.

▼ Sana, the capital of Yemen, is one of the most beautiful Islamic cities. Handmade goods, such as cloth, leatherware, glassware and pottery, are sold in its bazaars.

CROWDED CITIES
In Asia, 46 per cent of people live in a city, compared to 76 per cent in Europe and 82 per cent in the USA. Seven of the ten cities with the largest populations are in Asia: Tokyo, Seoul, Jakarta, Mumbai, Karachi, Osaka and Delhi.

BIG BUSINESS
Industry is a major employer in countries such as Japan, South Korea and Taiwan, and it is becoming increasingly important in Thailand and Malaysia. Other areas such as Singapore and Hong Kong have become important financial centres, while fishing and forestry, as well as manufacturing, are important industries in many Asian countries. Japan is the

▲ Chinese workers produce many goods, including salt (above). China is also the world's largest rice producer.

world's largest manufacturer of cars, while South Korea makes more televisions than any other country. China has one of the world's fastest-growing economies.

CRADLE OF CIVILIZATION
Asia was the birthplace of some of the world's most ancient civilizations, including Mesopotamia (in modern-day Iraq), China, and the Indus Valley (in modern-day Pakistan). These areas had large cities and were ruled by a small governing class of priests, officials and warriors. Their rich culture attracted both trade and conquering armies.

▲ Followers of Buddhism worship outside a temple in Yangon (Rangoon), the former capital of Burma (Myanmar). Nearly 90 per cent of Burma's population are Buddhist.

GAINING INDEPENDENCE

Colonial rule continued until the 20th century, when many of the colonies won their freedom, and created independent nations such as India and Jordan. In other countries, such as the former Soviet Union and China, communism took a firm hold. Since the break-up of the Soviet Union in 1991, republics such as Kazakhstan and Tajikistan have become independent nations. In 2002, after years of violent clashes, East Timor, formerly part of Indonesia, became Asia's newest country. The Arab Spring of 2011 saw uprisings in many nations of the Middle East, including Syria, Bahrain and Yemen.

MULTI-RELIGIOUS SOCIETY

Asia was where the world's major religions had their roots. Buddhism and Hinduism were spread from India by merchants and missionaries. Islam was carried from Asia to Europe and Africa by conquering armies such as the Mongols in the 12th century. Judaism and Christianity were exported from Asia as well as silk and spices during the Roman period. Today, these five religions still thrive in Asia, although Islam has the most followers.

GLITTERING EMPIRES

By the 16th century, the Ottoman Empire in the Middle East, the Safavid Empire in Iran, the Mogul Empire in India and the Ming Empire in China were the richest and most powerful states in the world. They had grown rich on exports such as silk, spices, ceramics and jewels. But these riches attracted European explorers.

COLONIAL RULE

From the beginning of the 19th century, much of Asia was colonized by European powers, whose steamships and modern weapons gave them superior mobility and firepower. The colonists transformed large areas of Asia into plantations for growing tea, coffee, cotton and rubber which they then exported for sale in Europe.

▲ Trade routes, known as the Silk Road, were used to carry goods between Asia and Europe from 1000BCE until the 1400s. Luxury items, such as the Ming vase shown here, as well as silks and spices, were carried through Pakistan, Tajikistan, Uzbekistan and Kazakhstan to the Middle East, from where they were taken by boat to Europe.

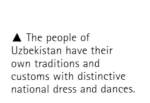

▲ The people of Uzbekistan have their own traditions and customs with distinctive national dress and dances.

SEE ALSO

China, Communism, Crop, Earthquake, Empire, Indian subcontinent, Indonesia, Japan, Mesopotamia, Middle East, Religion, Russia and the Baltic States, Southeast Asia

ASTRONAUT

Astronauts are people who are specially trained to work in space. They often spend weeks or months carrying out research in a space station or spacecraft.

On April 12, 1961, Yuri Gagarin of the USSR became the first man in space on board *Vostok 1*.

Valentina Tereshkova from the USSR became the first woman in space on June 16, 1963 on board *Vostok 6*.

Apollo 11 astronaut Neil Armstrong of the USA was the first to walk on the Moon, on July 21, 1969.

Experiments carried out by astronauts help us to discover what exists in space and how conditions in space affect life on Earth. Since the first human space journey was made in 1961, astronauts have walked on the Moon and lived in orbit.

JOBS IN SPACE
Work on board a spacecraft includes maintaining the equipment, conducting scientific experiments and launching and repairing satellites. To fly a spacecraft, an astronaut must be trained as a military pilot, while mission specialists must be highly qualified engineers or scientists.

CRUSHING FORCES
Astronauts must be prepared for the unusual conditions found in space. First, they are trained to survive the G-forces (crushing forces of take-off) which make the body seem up to six times heavier than usual. To get used to the lack of gravity in space, astronauts train in giant

▲ Astronauts train for long periods in a giant water tank, known as the Neutral Buoyancy Simulator, in order to prepare for the work they will do on space walks. These astronauts are training for repair work on a satellite.

water tanks and high-altitude aircraft, which provide a sense of weightlessness.

SPACE SICKNESS
Over 40 per cent of astronauts suffer from space sickness for the first few days, because weightlessness affects their sense of balance. Gradually, a lack of gravity also reduces the number of red cells carrying oxygen in the astronauts' blood, causing tiredness.

ASTRO-GYMS
Astronauts can 'grow' about 5cm in space due to the lack of gravity, and their heart, muscles and bones weaken. These changes

FAST FACTS

• Russian astronauts are called cosmonauts

• In 1957, the USSR sent the first animal into space – a dog called Laika

• The longest period anyone has spent in space is 437 days

• Over 520 people have now travelled in space

• In 2001, Dennis Tito became the first 'space tourist' when he paid for a return flight to space

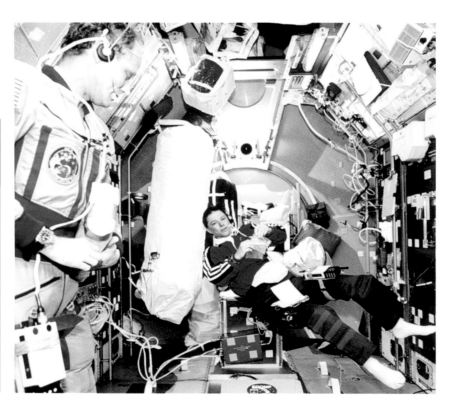

▲ Scientific experiments are carried out in space to observe the effects of the lack of gravity on such things as fungi and plants.

◄ Everything in the spacecraft, including the astronauts, floats around the cabin unless it is tied down.

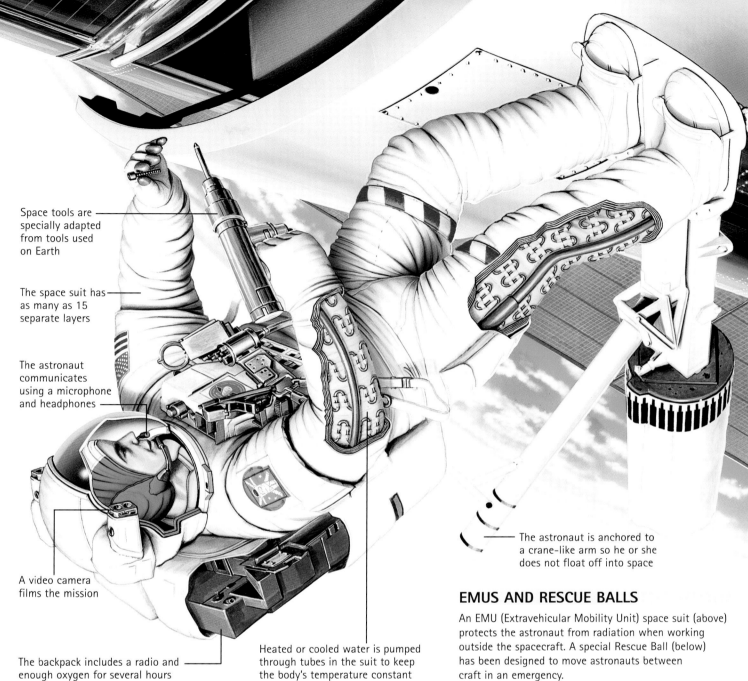

Space tools are specially adapted from tools used on Earth

The space suit has as many as 15 separate layers

The astronaut communicates using a microphone and headphones

A video camera films the mission

The backpack includes a radio and enough oxygen for several hours

Heated or cooled water is pumped through tubes in the suit to keep the body's temperature constant

The astronaut is anchored to a crane-like arm so he or she does not float off into space

EMUS AND RESCUE BALLS

An EMU (Extravehicular Mobility Unit) space suit (above) protects the astronaut from radiation when working outside the spacecraft. A special Rescue Ball (below) has been designed to move astronauts between craft in an emergency.

can be controlled with a special diet and by carrying out a regular exercise routine in a gym on board the spacecraft.

THE OUTER LIMITS

Spacecraft are constantly bombarded with radiation particles that would normally be blocked by the Earth's atmosphere. Each astronaut carries an instrument to measure his or her exposure to radiation. The recommended limit in a lifetime is 100 rads (units of radiation). This restricts the amount of time an astronaut can spend in space and could jeopardize plans for long-distance missions to Mars or

more remote planets, which would take two or more years to reach.

NO DAYS AND NIGHTS

Temperature in space can change from extremes of −200°C to more than 100°C when the craft is in the full glare of the Sun. It is important to maintain a steady temperature in the spacecraft, and this is done in the same way as in an air-conditioned office on Earth. There is no day or night in space, but astronauts keep to a routine that imitates the cycle on Earth so that they know when to sleep and when to work.

SEE ALSO
Gravity, Planet, Rocket, Satellite, Spacecraft, Space exploration

ASTRONOMY

Astronomy is the scientific study of objects in space, such as planets, stars, comets and black holes, using equipment such as telescopes and space probes.

Nicolaus Copernicus discovered that the planets orbit the Sun.

Johannes Kepler claimed that the planets move in elliptical (oval) orbits.

Galileo Galilei was the first astronomer to use a telescope.

E arly civilizations watched the stars and planets to predict the coming of the seasons. But it was the Ancient Greeks who first studied them as a science. The word astronomy comes from two Greek words meaning 'star laws'.

COPERNICUS TO EINSTEIN

Modern astronomy began with Nicolaus Copernicus, who realized that the Sun, not the Earth, was at the centre of our solar system. His ideas were published in 1543, the year he died. When Galileo Galilei used his newly invented telescope in 1610, he helped prove those ideas. In 1667, Isaac Newton put forward his laws of gravity, which explained how objects move in

▲ Our galaxy seen through a telescope.

▶ An X-ray picture of our galaxy. The central red and yellow area may be a black hole.

space, and Albert Einstein published a new theory of gravity in 1915, which led to ideas such as black holes and the Big Bang.

SIGNALS TO THE PLANETS

Today's astronomers can calculate Earth's distance from other planets in our solar system by bouncing radar signals off the planets' surfaces and timing how long they take to return to Earth. The distance to faraway stars can be worked out from their brightness and by using a method called parallax (see diagram far right).

Isaac Newton described how gravity affects cosmic objects.

THE KECK OBSERVATORY

Observatories are special buildings used to study the skies. The Keck in Hawaii, USA is one of the highest in the world. At the top of an extinct volcano, it is 4,200m above sea level and has two telescopes in twinned domes that track the stars like binoculars.

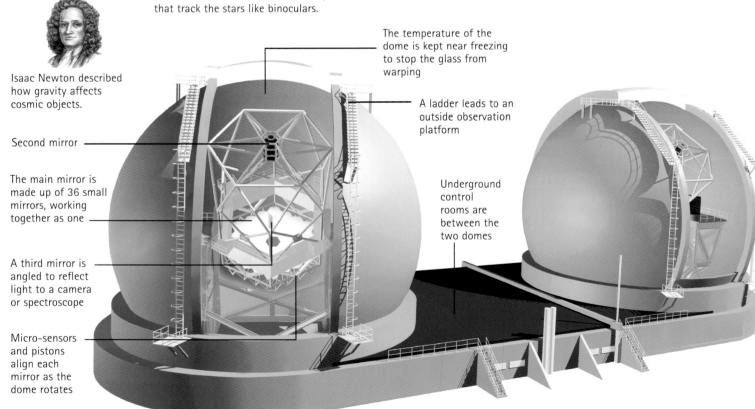

The temperature of the dome is kept near freezing to stop the glass from warping

A ladder leads to an outside observation platform

Second mirror

The main mirror is made up of 36 small mirrors, working together as one

A third mirror is angled to reflect light to a camera or spectroscope

Underground control rooms are between the two domes

Micro-sensors and pistons align each mirror as the dome rotates

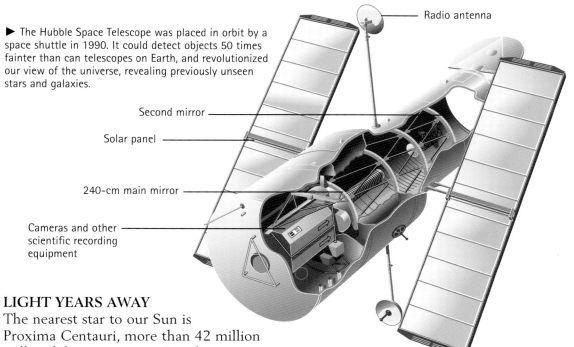

Radio antenna

▶ The Hubble Space Telescope was placed in orbit by a space shuttle in 1990. It could detect objects 50 times fainter than can telescopes on Earth, and revolutionized our view of the universe, revealing previously unseen stars and galaxies.

Second mirror

Solar panel

240-cm main mirror

Cameras and other scientific recording equipment

Edmond Halley predicted that the comet of 1682 would return in 1758.

Albert Einstein created important theories about space and time.

LIGHT YEARS AWAY

The nearest star to our Sun is Proxima Centauri, more than 42 million million kilometres away. Star distances are measured in light years (light travels 9.46 million million kilometres in one year). Proxima Centauri is 4.26 light years away, which means its light takes four years and three months to reach Earth.

SECRETS OF STARLIGHT

The temperature and chemical make-up of objects in space are revealed by the radiation that they give off. This radiation includes light, radio waves, microwaves, infrared, ultraviolet, X-rays and gamma rays. Astronomers use optical and radio telescopes as well as spectroscopes (radiation detectors), set up in observatories, to study cosmic radiation.

PLANETARY PROBES

Sending unmanned spacecraft to planets is very technically challenging. Spacecraft are launched aboard rockets and either land on the planet or send down a probe that transmits information back to Earth.

In 1997, a probe entered Jupiter's clouds, and the first remote-controlled, robotic probe roamed around on Mars. In 2004, two more rovers carried out research on Mars. In the same year, a spacecraft visited Saturn and its moons, and released a probe that landed on the surface of Titan, Saturn's largest moon. In 2006, *New Horizons* was launched. It flew by Jupiter, Saturn and Uranus on its way to the dwarf planet Pluto and the Kuiper Belt.

◀ In 1997, a probe from the *Galileo* spacecraft plunged into Jupiter's gas clouds. It sent back photographs and chemical data to Earth for over an hour before being destroyed.

KEY DATES

3000BC First known records of astronomy made by the Babylonians

125BC Hipparchus groups stars according to brightness

1543 Copernicus proposes that Earth orbits the Sun

1600 Kepler discovers that the planets orbit the Sun in elliptical (oval-shaped) paths

1781 Herschel discovers Uranus

1846 Neptune discovered

1908 Giant and dwarf stars first noted

1930 Clyde Tombaugh discovers Pluto

1955 76-m radio telescope built at Jodrell Bank, UK

1997 Probe enters Jupiter's atmosphere to collect data; first rover, *Sojourner*, lands on Mars

2004 *Spirit* and *Opportunity* rovers land on Mars; the *Cassini* spacecraft arrives at Saturn

2006 *Venus Express* orbits Venus

2011 *Messenger* enters orbit around Mercury

PARALLAX

The distances of nearby stars can be calculated by plotting their positions at different times of the year, and then applying a simple geometric equation. The bigger the parallax angle, the closer the star.

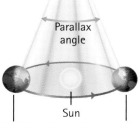

Where the star seems to be on January 1

Where the star seems to be on July 1

Real position of star

Parallax angle

Sun

Position of Earth on July 1

Position of Earth on January 1

SEE ALSO

Big Bang theory, Black hole, Galaxy, Gravity, Solar system, Space exploration, Star, Telescope

ATMOSPHERE

The atmosphere is an envelope of gases surrounding the Earth. It shields us from the Sun and contains the air we breathe. Without it life would not exist.

The gases that form the atmosphere are held in place around the Earth by gravity. They can be divided into four layers: the troposphere, stratosphere, ionosphere and exosphere. Each contains a mixture of gases, which gets thinner the farther away the layer is from the Earth.

THE WEATHER ZONE
The lowest and densest layer is the troposphere, which extends about 13km above the Earth's surface. It contains 78 per cent nitrogen, 20 per cent oxygen and small amounts of other gases, and is where life exists, clouds form and where most of Earth's weather occurs.

OZONE LAYER
Above the troposphere, up to about 50km, is the stratosphere. This is where jet planes usually fly, and near its top is the ozone layer, which absorbs most of the Sun's harmful ultraviolet radiation.

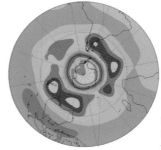
◄ Scientists produce ozone maps using data gathered by satellites. This map shows a North America-sized hole over Antarctica in September 2008. The hole forms each spring, then mixes in with the rest of the stratosphere.

The holes developing in the ozone layer have been linked to industrial chemicals such as the CFCs that were used in aerosol spray cans, fire extinguishers and fridges.

HIGH-ENERGY RAYS
Above the stratosphere is the ionosphere. In this layer, the Sun's rays break up some gas atoms into charged particles, or ions. Temperatures in the upper ionosphere (which is called the thermosphere) can reach 2,000°C.

MERGING INTO SPACE
Above 500km the ionosphere merges into the exosphere, which stretches away into space to a height of several thousand kilometres. Any gas molecules found here are on their way out towards space.

▲ In the atmosphere above the Arctic and Antarctic, colliding particles from the Sun create flickering bands of light known as auroras.

EVOLVING ATMOSPHERE

The atmosphere is constantly evolving. At first it was made up of high levels of carbon dioxide. Oxygen appeared about 1,800 million years ago, but advanced life was possible only after the ozone layer formed.

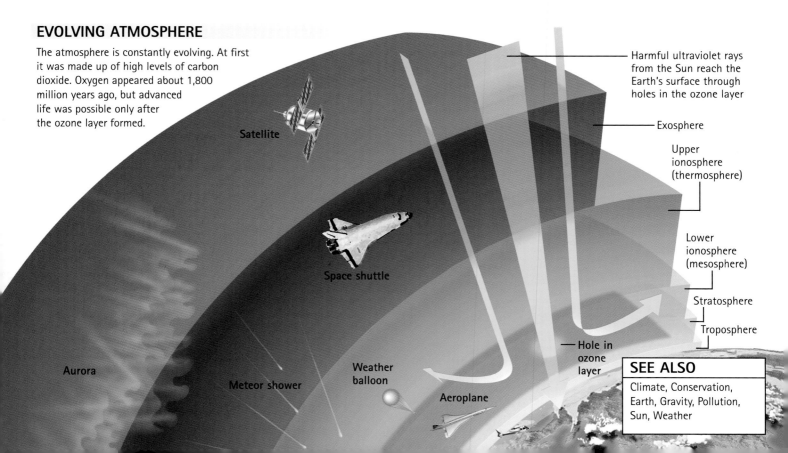

Satellite

Space shuttle

Aurora

Meteor shower

Weather balloon

Aeroplane

Hole in ozone layer

Harmful ultraviolet rays from the Sun reach the Earth's surface through holes in the ozone layer

Exosphere

Upper ionosphere (thermosphere)

Lower ionosphere (mesosphere)

Stratosphere

Troposphere

SEE ALSO
Climate, Conservation, Earth, Gravity, Pollution, Sun, Weather

ATOM AND MOLECULE

Atoms are the basic building blocks of everything around us, from plants and animals to planets and stars. A molecule is two or more atoms joined together.

Crystals form regular shapes as their atoms are arranged in fixed patterns.

Pencil 'lead' is soft because its atoms slide easily over each other.

Diamonds are very hard because their atoms are in a rigid framework.

DNA, the basis of life, consists of two coiled strands of molecules.

Every substance in the universe is made of atoms. An atom is the smallest part of any substance that can exist on its own – it is less than ten billionths of a metre in diameter. The full-stop at the end of this sentence contains billions of atoms.

EMPTY SPACE

Most of an atom is made up of empty space, but at its centre is a tiny nucleus. If an atom were scaled up to the size of a football pitch, the nucleus would be no bigger than a peppercorn.

THE NUCLEUS

The nucleus is the densest part of the atom and usually contains an equal amount of smaller, 'sub-atomic' particles called protons and neutrons. Electrons are even lighter sub-atomic particles that whiz round the nucleus in all different directions at the speed of light.

INSIDE AN ATOM

The nucleus of every atom consists of particles called protons and neutrons (except for the hydrogen atom, which has no neutrons). Other particles, called electrons, flit around the nucleus in a random motion, making billions of trips in a millionth of a second.

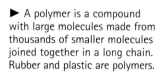

▶ A polymer is a compound with large molecules made from thousands of smaller molecules joined together in a long chain. Rubber and plastic are polymers.

FORMING BONDS

Some substances consist of molecules that are formed from only one type of atom, and these are called elements. But when different types of atoms join to make molecules, they form compounds. A water molecule is a compound of one oxygen atom and two hydrogen atoms.

SOLID, LIQUID OR GAS

Water is a liquid, which means its molecules can move around (flow), whereas the molecules in a solid such as wood are fixed together in a definite pattern. Gas molecules buzz around randomly, filling all the available space.

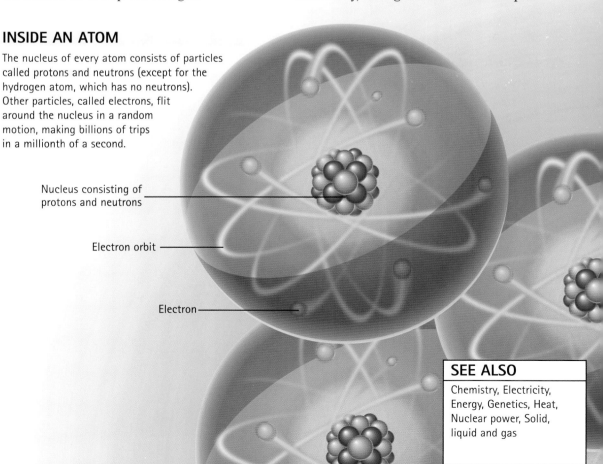

Nucleus consisting of protons and neutrons

Electron orbit

Electron

FAST FACTS

• The word 'atom' comes the Greek word *atomos*, meaning 'uncut'

• A tiny speck of dust, just visible to the naked eye, contains a million billion atoms

• The lightest atom is hydrogen. The heaviest naturally occurring atom is uranium, which is 238 times the mass (weight) of hydrogen

SEE ALSO

Chemistry, Electricity, Energy, Genetics, Heat, Nuclear power, Solid, liquid and gas

AUSTRALIA

Australia is the sixth largest country in the world, covering about four per cent of the Earth's surface. It is also the smallest, flattest continent.

Area: 7,702,315 sq km
Population: 22,329,000
Capital: Canberra
Language: English
Currency: Australian dollar

KEY FACTS

• **Number of states: six** (Western Australia, South Australia, Queensland, New South Wales, Victoria and Tasmania)

• **Number of territories: three** (Northern Territory, the Australian Capital Territory and Jervis Bay)

• **Highest point:** Mount Kosciuszko (2,230m)

• **Longest river:** Murray–Darling (3,750km)

• **Largest Lake:** Eyre (9,583 sq km)

▲ Rainforests on the northeast coast of Queensland, where the climate is wettest, are now National Parks.

Australia is often referred to as Down Under because it lies below the Equator, in the Earth's Southern Hemisphere. It is both a country and a continent.

THE GREAT DIVIDING RANGE

With the exception of a few mountain ranges, Australia is low and flat. The mountains of the Great Dividing Range run down the coast of Queensland and New South Wales. Fertile plateaux (flat areas of land high above sea level) lie along the top, where dense forests once grew. Today, many of the forests have been cleared for cities and farms.

SUNSHINE AND MONSOONS

The weather is cool and wet in the southernmost parts of the country, but most of Australia is hot or warm all year round. There are just two seasons in the far north: wet and dry. The wet season, from November to April, is hot and humid, with monsoon rains that turn huge areas of land into lakes.

THE OUTBACK

The country's vast central region, which the Australians call the Outback, is hot and dry and mostly a desert – the second largest in the world. The temperature at Alice Springs, in central Australia, is often over 38°C. The rest of the interior is made up of land covered in coarse grass, low shrubs and trees, and provides grazing for cattle and sheep.

LIFE-BRINGING WATER

The many billabongs (waterholes) and rivers in the Outback are dry most of the year, and the parched plants sometimes catch fire. There are occasional heavy rains, however, when the buried seeds of flowering plants come to life and the rivers fill with water. The Australian lung

▼ Uluru (Ayers Rock) is a huge outcrop of sandstone right in the middle of Australia. It is sacred to the Aboriginal people.

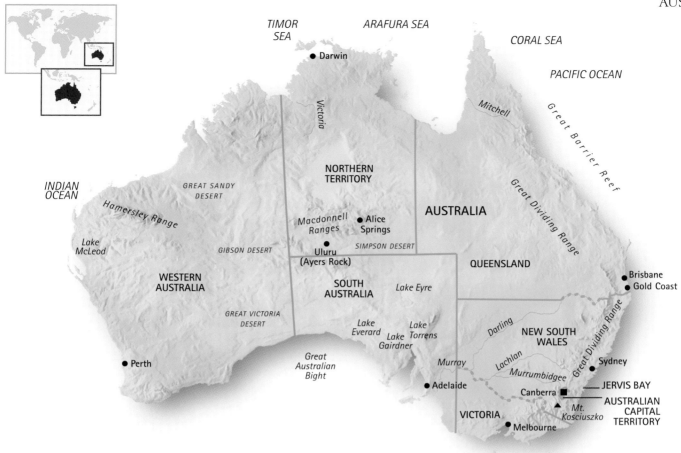

TIMOR SEA
ARAFURA SEA
CORAL SEA
PACIFIC OCEAN

● Darwin

Victoria

Mitchell

NORTHERN TERRITORY

Great Barrier Reef

INDIAN OCEAN

GREAT SANDY DESERT

AUSTRALIA

Hamersley Range

Macdonnell Ranges
● Alice Springs

Great Dividing Range

Lake McLeod

GIBSON DESERT

● Uluru (Ayers Rock)

SIMPSON DESERT

QUEENSLAND

WESTERN AUSTRALIA

SOUTH AUSTRALIA

Lake Eyre

● Brisbane
● Gold Coast

GREAT VICTORIA DESERT

Lake Everard
Lake Gairdner
Lake Torrens

Darling

NEW SOUTH WALES

Great Dividing Range

● Perth

Great Australian Bight

Murray
Lachlan
Murrumbidgee

● Sydney

● Adelaide

JERVIS BAY

Canberra ■

AUSTRALIAN CAPITAL TERRITORY

VICTORIA

▲ Mt. Kosciuszko

● Melbourne

N

miles
0   500
0   500
km

TASMANIA

TASMAN SEA

● Hobart

fish has adapted to this changing climate by developing both gills and lungs.

A LAND ON ITS OWN

Australia has been isolated from any other land mass since about 65 million years ago, when it split from Antarctica. About 130 million years ago, Australia and Antarctica were both part of a great southern continent. Many species of animal that are unique to Australia evolved during this time. These include marsupials (pouched mammals), such as kangaroos, koalas and wombats, as well as two unusual egg-laying mammals, the duckbilled platypus and the echidna (also known as the spiny anteater).

AUSTRALIA'S EXPORTS

Australia's farms produce wheat, beef, mutton and wool, as well as wine made from grapes grown in the south. Australia is rich in minerals, such as coal, gold, iron ore, bauxite (aluminium ore), uranium, diamonds and opals. Minerals and farm products are the country's main exports, with manufactured goods representing about 15 per cent. Australia's factories ▶

▲ The kookaburra is often seen in parks and gardens. Its strange call, like a chuckling laugh, led to the name 'laughing jackass'.

◀ The Great Barrier Reef is a chain of more than 2,500 small reefs and coral islands that stretch for 2,010km along the northeast coast.

▲ New South Wales and Western Australia produce more than half of Australia's wool.

▼ Sydney is Australia's oldest and largest city, with a population of more than 4.5 million. The city is built around a huge natural bay, jutting out into which is the world-famous Sydney Opera House.

England. The cattle live and breed freely until it is time for market, when the farmer rounds them up, often with a helicopter.

SCHOOL ON THE AIRWAVES

People living on sheep stations and cattle runs are often hundreds of kilometres from the nearest town. They must rely on flying doctors, who arrive by light aircraft, for medical help. Children in the Outback send and receive schoolwork by mail and listen to lessons broadcast on the radio. They can communicate with their teachers via two-way radios.

produce goods such as motor vehicles, textiles, chemicals and household goods. Australia also has a film industry, which is rapidly expanding.

SHEEP STATIONS

Most of the Outback is too dry to grow crops, but vast sheep farms, called sheep stations, cover thousands of hectares. Huge beef cattle ranches are known as cattle runs, a few of which are the size of

IN THE BIG CITIES

Nearly 90 per cent of people in Australia live in cities, where most of the jobs are to be found. The largest cities – Sydney, Melbourne and Brisbane – lie on the south and east coasts. In Sydney, the population of more than 4.5 million enjoys the attractions of city life, including the world-famous Sydney Opera House, as well as the beach. Bondi Beach lies about 8km south of the centre and attracts many swimmers and surfers.

▲ A favourite pastime in coastal cities is surfboat racing. Lifeguards give demonstrations of their skills at festivals.

THE GOLD RUSH

In 1851, many more people dashed to Australia with news that gold had been found in New South Wales and Victoria. This became known as the Gold Rush. Melbourne, the capital of Victoria, soon became a wealthy city and Australia's population more than doubled. In 1854, gold miners at the Eureka Stockade rebelled against their colonial rulers, hastening reform and self-government.

FIRST INHABITANTS

Australia's first inhabitants were the Aboriginal people who arrived 50,000 years ago from Southeast Asia. They lived off the land, hunting animals, gathering plants and fishing for thousands of years, until European settlers destroyed their way of life in the 18th century.

CAPTAIN COOK LANDS

The Dutch were the first Europeans to explore the coast in the 1600s, but they never established any settlements. The first Europeans to settle in Australia were the British. In 1770, Captain James Cook reached the east coast of Australia and immediately claimed it for Britain, calling it New South Wales.

CONVICTS ARRIVE

The first British fleet landed at Botany Bay in January 1788, with soldiers, convicts and the colony's first governor, Arthur Phillip. The first settlement, named Sydney, was set up nearby, and as more free settlers arrived, other farming settlements grew up around the coast.

AUSTRALIA – THE NATION

In 1901, Australia became a nation. The colonies became states and united as the Commonwealth of Australia. During World War I, Australian troops helped the British and in World War II they defended their country from Japanese invasion. People from many countries migrated to Australia after both wars and the population rose from five million in 1918 to more than 22 million today. English is not the first language for 15 per cent of Australians. Increasingly Australia now looks to Asia and the Pacific countries for trade links, especially to Japan.

▲ Cattle ranches, or runs, can be thousands of kilometres in size. Farmers use helicopters to round up huge herds of livestock.

◄ Tasmania has a cooler, wetter climate than the Australian mainland. Much of the island is unpopulated and covered in thick forest.

◄ Britain sent many thousands of convicts to Australia between 1788 and 1853 under the system of transportation. The early years in prison settlements were harsh.

SEE ALSO

Aboriginal people, Architecture, Continent, Explorer, Gold, Kangaroo, Platypus

AZTECS

The Aztecs were members of one of the last great native civilizations of the Americas. They created a large empire in Mexico during the 15th century.

Quetzalcóatl (meaning plumed serpent) was one of the main Aztec gods.

This ceremonial mask was made from precious stones on a human skull.

The Aztecs' rise to power began in the 14th century, when they built the city of Tenochtitlán on an island where Mexico City now stands. They began to create their great empire by conquering nearby cities, largely to the south and east.

THE PEOPLE

The Aztec ruler was an emperor who relied on a warrior class to defend and expand the empire. Next in importance were the priests. Ordinary people were farmers, merchants, craftworkers and slaves. Food was farmed on floating gardens (called *chinampas*) on Lake Texcoco, which surrounded Tenochtitlán. Maize, vegetables and cotton were grown and turkeys and dogs were kept for meat. The Aztecs were among the first to use cocoa beans to

▶ The Aztecs used two calendars: this solar one, divided into 18 months, and a sacred one.

make a chocolate drink, and the words 'tomato' and 'avocado' come from the Aztec language.

TEMPLES OF DOOM

The main religious building was the Great Temple at Tenochtitlán, a stone pyramid with sacrificial altars at the top. Each Aztec ruler built a bigger, more impressive temple on the same site. It was rebuilt six times.

CONQUERED BY A LEGEND

The Aztec Empire was at its height when Montezuma II became emperor in 1502 and built a vast palace. Under his rule the empire stretched across Mexico from the east to the west. In 1519, a small force of Spanish soldiers and bounty hunters, led by Hernán Cortés, arrived in Mexico. Many Aztecs, including Montezuma, believed Cortés was the legendary god Quetzalcóatl, and at first welcomed the Spaniards. By 1521, Cortés' army had completely destroyed Tenochtitlán and Cortés was made governor of Mexico.

HUMAN SACRIFICE

Religion was very important to the Aztecs. They worshipped many gods – of war, rain, Sun and wind – and carried out human sacrifices to win the favour of their gods. Captives taken in battle were killed by the priests. They cut out the still-living hearts using ceremonial knives made of very sharp stone. The blood was used to bathe statues of the gods.

Stone knives were used to cut out the heart

Feathers from the quetzal bird were used for headdresses

SEE ALSO

Mexico, Native Americans

BABYLON

Babylon was a large and wealthy city beside the river Euphrates in modern Iraq. It was founded around 2300BCE and flourished for 2,000 years.

▼ These standard Babylonian weights were used in ancient markets.

The city of Babylon was famous for its power, beauty and architecture. The name Babylon means 'gate of god', and the city was a great religious centre.

PYRAMID TOWERS
The city was dominated by its pyramid-shaped temple-towers called *ziggurats*, made from sun-dried bricks. Around the city was a great wall and canals fed water from the river to fields outside the city for growing grain, vegetables and fruits.

MATHS EXPERTS
The Babylonians were skilled in science, mathematics and astronomy. They divided the circle into 360 degrees and the hour into 60 minutes, and grouped numbers into tens. They studied the Sun and stars in order to predict the future, and they used a form of writing, called cuneiform, scratched with pointed reeds in soft clay.

▲ Hammurabi's army conquered neighbouring cities to form a large, strong empire.

RIGHTS FOR CHILDREN
Babylon's rulers had military, religious and legal powers. One of their greatest leaders was Hammurabi, who ruled from 1792BCE to 1750BCE. He drew up a set of laws, the oldest surviving in the world, that protected women, children and slaves. The Code of Hammurabi was carved on a black pillar, which is now in the Louvre museum in Paris, France.

RISE AND FALL OF BABYLON
After Hammurabi, the Babylonians were ruled by Assyrians until a new Babylonian empire arose under Nebuchadnezzar II in 605BCE. He fortified Babylon and built fine buildings. After he died in 562BCE, Babylon collapsed into civil war. It fell to the Persians in 539BCE, and was conquered in 331BCE by the Greeks, led by Alexander the Great.

GRAND ENTRANCE
Babylon's narrow streets were crowded with traders, who entered through one of eight gates in the double city walls. The grand Ishtar Gate, named after a fertility goddess, was the main entrance. It was covered with blue tiles and decorated with figures of bulls and dragons.

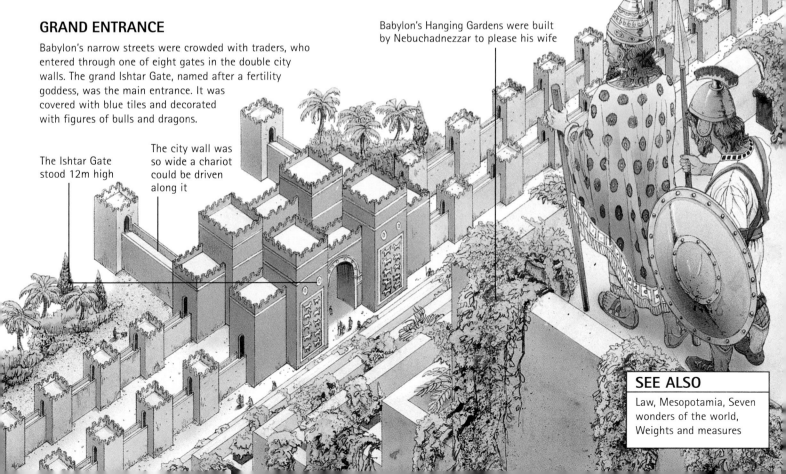

Babylon's Hanging Gardens were built by Nebuchadnezzar to please his wife

The Ishtar Gate stood 12m high

The city wall was so wide a chariot could be driven along it

SEE ALSO
Law, Mesopotamia, Seven wonders of the world, Weights and measures

BALLOON AND AIRSHIP

Balloons and airships are aircraft that use gas, which is lighter than air, to fly. They consist of a gas-filled bag, or envelope, with a basket or cabin underneath.

In 1783, the Montgolfier brothers built the first ever passenger hot-air balloon from paper and linen.

Count Ferdinand von Zeppelin set up the first airship service in 1910. They could fly at 95km/h.

Richard Branson's 1997 round-the-world balloon had a pressurized cabin to protect the passengers.

Like aeroplanes, modern airships are steered with joysticks, which move fins on the tail.

The gas in a balloon or airship is lighter than the surrounding air, and so it lifts the aircraft off the ground, like a bubble floating upwards in water. Airships have engines and equipment for steering, while hot-air balloons drift with the winds.

LIGHT GAS

The weight that a balloon or an airship can carry depends on the gas used. Hydrogen provides the most lift, but it catches fire very easily. Today, airships usually use helium because it is safer. Balloons are usually filled with nothing more than hot

CHANGING COURSE

Hot-air ballooning is a popular sport. A burner heats the air inside the balloon. This takes the balloon up, because hot air is lighter than cold air. To come down, the pilot pulls a rip line which opens a vent in the bag to let hot air escape.

▶ Modern hot-air balloons are twice as tall as a house. They are made of nylon and carry up to five people.

air. They have a burner that reheats the air whenever the balloon starts falling. Hot air expands, making it lighter, or less dense, than cold air, so the balloon rises.

FLYING AN AIRSHIP

The first airships were rigid with a huge hull, or body, made out of a frame covered with a skin. These were no longer built after 35 people died on the *Hindenburg* in 1937 when the hydrogen gas caught alight. Today's airships are non-rigid and are made from a gas bag stretched into shape by the gas inside pressing against it. They are powered by engines and are used for advertising, pleasure trips and as television camera platforms at big sporting events.

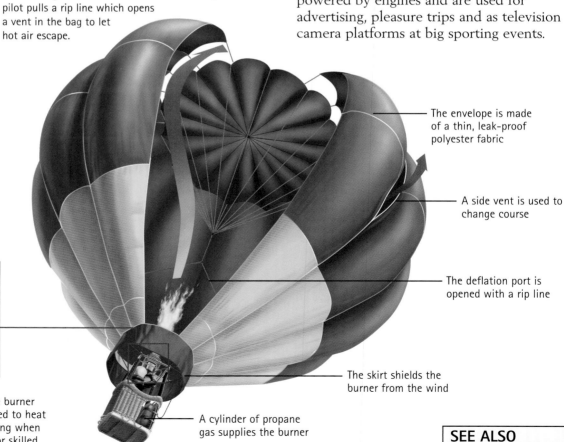

The envelope is made of a thin, leak-proof polyester fabric

A side vent is used to change course

The deflation port is opened with a rip line

The skirt shields the burner from the wind

A cylinder of propane gas supplies the burner

THE BURNER
Propane gas is fed to the burner through tubes. It is ignited to heat the air in the bag. Deciding when to use the burner calls for skilled judgement, especially when the balloon is coming down to land.

SEE ALSO
Aircraft, Atmosphere, Solid, liquid and gas, Transport

BAT

Bats are the only mammals that are capable of true flight. Most are nocturnal (active at night). They live all over the world, except at sea and in polar regions.

Large ears enable the bat to hear the returning echoes

A clawed thumb is used for scrambling up rocks inside caves

The big brown bat of North America gives birth to twins, unlike other bats, which have only one young.

Bats use their tails to brake or change direction in flight

Kitti's hog-nosed bat from Thailand is the world's smallest mammal. It was first recorded in 1974.

Sound waves bounce off the moth and back to the bat

Free-tailed bats have a tail that extends beyond the wing membrane. These bats can fly high and fast.

Horseshoe bats have circular flaps of skin around the nose to direct sound while hunting.

ECHOLOCATION

Most bats can see in the dark but the micro-bat also uses echolocation to find its way around. It makes very high-pitched (ultrasonic) squeaks – as many as 500 per second. The sound waves from these squeaks 'hit' objects or prey in front of the bat, making an echo return. The bat can tell from these echoes exactly where the prey is.

The Rodrigues fruit bat lives on an island in the Indian Ocean. Its forest home has now almost gone.

With their large wings of leathery, lightweight skin held stretched out by very long finger bones, bats are the only mammals that can truly fly. There are so many different species of bat that, added together, they make up almost a quarter of the whole mammal group.

A MAMMAL WITH WINGS
Apart from its wings, the bat has the typical features of a mammal. It has a furry body, warm blood, and its young are fed on their mother's milk. When resting, the bat wraps its wings around its body and hangs upside down by its claws in a roost, such as a cave, a hollow tree, high up in a roof, or down in a cellar.

GROUPS OF BATS
Bats are divided into two main groups according to their size. Fruit bats are large bats, often called flying foxes because they have a face that looks like a fox. Most live in tropical forests and eat leaves and fruits. Other bats, called micro-bats, are much smaller and eat mainly insects, which they hunt in flight. Micro-bats look like winged mice.

Some bats are specialist feeders. The fishing bat of South America grabs fish in its long claws. Vampire bats, from South and Central America, feed on the blood of cattle and horses, but rarely of humans.

KEEPING WARM
Bats living in colder climates hibernate in winter by clustering in cool, dry places. Others, such as the Mexican free-tailed bat, migrate. Most bats give birth to one offspring a year, early in the warm season. The young cluster together in nursery roosts while the parents go off to feed.

PROTECTED BY LAW
Many bat species are threatened because their habitats have been destroyed by people building roads and houses. Bats are also often treated as pests. Fruit bats especially are accused of destroying crops and damaging trees. In many countries, bats are now protected by wildlife laws.

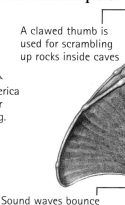

> ### SEE ALSO
> Conservation, Hibernation, Mammal, Migration, Radar and sonar, Seed and pollination

BEAR

Bears are large, strong mammals with stocky bodies, thick fur and big claws. There are seven species, living mainly in Europe, Asia and North America.

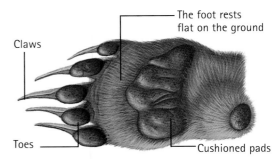

The foot rests flat on the ground

Claws

Toes

Cushioned pads

▲ Bears use their front feet for digging, hunting and climbing. Their claws may grow up to 12cm long.

Sloth bears love honey so much they are also known as honey bears.

The spectacled bear is the only bear that lives in South America.

The American black bear lives in remote areas and feeds on almost anything.

There are several types of brown bears. The Kodiak is the world's largest bear.

Meat is the main source of food for most bears. They are classified as carnivores (meat-eaters), but bears will eat just about anything and are particularly fond of fruits, nuts, fish and honey. They use their strong sense of smell to track down food, because their small eyes provide only poor vision.

LIVING IN A DEN
Bears spend most of the year alone, but come together to mate or to scavenge on the bodies of dead animals. In regions with cold winters, most bears spend long periods asleep in dens, which can be caves, tree stumps or holes under rocks. This is not true hibernation as they often wake up. It is during this time that the cubs are born – usually two every second year. The female polar bear gives birth to her cubs in a snow den.

COLOUR AND MARKINGS
The seven species of bear include the polar bear, white-coated for camouflage in the snow, and two black bears, the American and the Asian. The sloth bear hangs from forest trees in India and Sri Lanka. South America's spectacled bear gets its name from white markings around its eyes, while the Malayan or sun bear has a sun-like patch on its chest. Brown bears include the grizzly and Kodiak.

IN DANGER
Bears have almost no predators – except for humans, who hunt and kill them for their fur, teeth or claws. Largely peaceful, bears will defend themselves and their cubs fiercely only if under attack. Wildlife conservation groups are fighting to protect the remaining bear population from human cruelty and destruction.

AS WHITE AS SNOW
The polar bear lives among the treeless tundra and cold seas of northern polar regions. It is white-coated for snow camouflage and can grow to over 1,000kg in weight. Thick, water-repellent fur allows the bear to swim in icy seas, where it hunts seals, fish, walruses and small whales. Polar bears are known to ambush seals by lying in wait at breathing holes in the pack-ice.

SEE ALSO
Animal, Arctic, Forest, Hibernation, Mammal

42

BICYCLE AND MOTORBIKE

Bicycles, which rely on pedal-power, are the most energy-efficient form of transport. Motorbikes are based on the bicycle design, but are powered by an engine.

▶ Off-road motorbikes are strong for rough terrain and jumping obstacles.

The dandyhorse, built in 1817 by Karl von Drais, had no pedals and was pushed along by foot.

The penny farthing, produced in 1870, had solid tyres and a step to help the rider climb on.

Bicycle design has changed little since the 1880s, when the chain-driven rear wheel and air-filled tyres arrived.

Early motorcycles, such as this one built by Gottlieb Daimler in 1885, were slow and uncomfortable to ride.

The first bicycle with pedals appeared in the 1860s, when Frenchman Pierre Lallement introduced the velocipede. Twenty years later, the German Gottlieb Daimler fitted a petrol engine to a bicycle frame and made the first motorcycle.

MODERN BICYCLES

All modern bicycles have the same basic design. The front wheel, connected to the handle bars, steers the bike, while the back wheel drives it. Types include BMXs and touring, road, mountain and racing bikes. Modern bikes are built for speed and strength from tough, yet lightweight materials, including aluminium and carbon fibre. The number of gears on a bicycle ranges from three to 21, and tyres can be very thin to reduce friction or extra wide to absorb shocks from rough, uneven ground as on cross-country bikes.

ENGINE POWER

Motorbikes have either a four-stroke engine like a car, or a simpler two-stroke engine. The smallest are just 50cc (cubic centimetres) in size, while the most powerful can be over 1,100cc. Scooters and mopeds are the smallest motorbikes. Most have electronic ignition and up to five gear speeds.

RACING MOTORBIKES

Motorbike racing is an international sport and includes motocross (dirt-track racing), enduros (endurance racing) and speed racing. The fastest superbikes can have 18 gear ratios and reach speeds of 280km/h.

BICYCLE GEARS

Gears make it easier to cycle. If the cyclist selects a low gear, a device called a derailleur moves the chain onto the largest sprocket on the rear wheel. This allows the back wheel to turn with less pedalling, making it easier (but slower) to go uphill. Selecting a high gear to go downhill has the opposite effect.

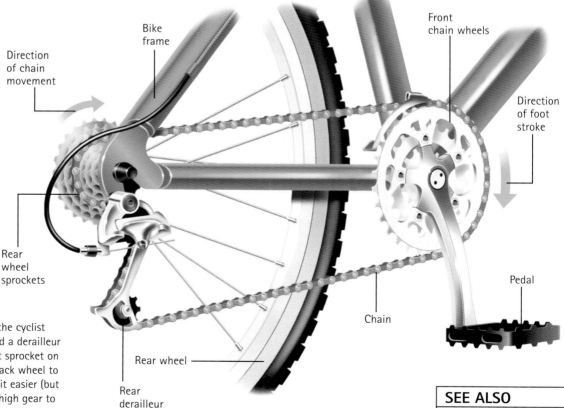

Direction of chain movement

Bike frame

Front chain wheels

Direction of foot stroke

Rear wheel sprockets

Rear derailleur

Rear wheel

Chain

Pedal

SEE ALSO

Engine, Sport, Transport

BIG BANG THEORY

The Big Bang is the term used to describe a huge explosion that scientists believe happened about 13.7 billion years ago, creating our universe.

Matter, energy, space and time are all thought to have been created in a fraction of a second 13.7 billion years ago, when there was a colossal explosion called the Big Bang that created tremendous heat.

PEA-SIZED UNIVERSE
Nobody knows what caused the Big Bang, as we cannot look back to a time before it. But just after the event, the universe is believed to have been a knot of tightly packed particles only about the size of a pea. Its temperature was ten thousand trillion, trillion degrees Celsius.

COSMIC COOLING
From that moment on, the universe began to expand and cool. First, hydrogen and helium (the two most common atoms in the universe) were created. Over the next billion years, the first stars and galaxies formed, gathered together by the force of gravity. Finally planets began to form.

MICROWAVES IN SPACE
A discovery made in 1965 seems to support the Big Bang theory. A steady glow of microwave radiation comes from every direction in space. Scientists believe that this is the cooled remains of the fireball in which the universe was formed.

SPEEDING GALAXIES
Scientists have also found that, apart from a few nearby galaxies, everything in space is racing away from us. This suggests that all matter and energy in the universe was once concentrated at a single point, just before the Big Bang. The universe may expand forever, or it may eventually stop expanding and collapse inwards.

▲ A microwave map of our galaxy, showing radiation ripples thought to be left over like an afterglow of the Big Bang.

FAST FACTS
- Most of the helium nuclei in the universe today were made in the first 15 minutes after the Big Bang
- The Oscillating Universe theory says that the universe will eventually contract. When all the matter collides, a new Big Bang will be triggered

THE UNIVERSE IS BORN
In the first split second after the Big Bang, matter was created in the heat of the newborn universe. As it cooled down, a dense fog of atoms, made up of protons, neutrons and electrons, appeared.

5 One billion years later: gravity pulls matter together to form galaxies.

6 13.7 billion years later: the ever-expanding universe that we see today.

4 300,000 years later: electrons begin to orbit the nuclei to form atoms. The universe fills with light.

3 Three minutes later: protons and neutrons combine to form hydrogen and helium nuclei.

2 A fraction of a second later: the temperature begins to drop. Protons and neutrons form.

1 The Big Bang takes place.

SEE ALSO
Atom and molecule, Energy, Galaxy, Planet, Solar system, Star, Universe, Wavelength

BIRD

Birds are warm-blooded, egg-laying vertebrates (animals with backbones). They have wings, and are the only animals with feathers.

The large beak of the toucan is useful for plucking fruit from trees.

An avocet's long, slender bill probes for shellfish in soft mud.

The eagle uses its hooked beak to tear meat into chunks.

A swift gathers insects in its wide beak while flying.

There are about 10,000 different kinds of bird. They are found all over the world, even on polar ice-caps. Only a few birds cannot fly at all. These include the long-legged, fast-running ostrich of Africa, the rhea of South America, the emu of Australia and penguins in the Southern Hemisphere, which use their flipper-like wings to 'fly' through water.

HOLLOW BONES
A bird is designed for lightness. Its bones are thin and hollow and its beak is toothless. In the front limb, the upper-arm and forearm bones are long. The wrist, hand and three finger bones are joined together to support the feathers.

BIRD SENSE
Birds have excellent eyesight and good hearing, but their sense of smell is less developed. A bird's feeding habits vary with habitat and species. Some, such as the parrot, are nut-eaters; others, such as

▶ A humming-bird can flap its wings 100 times per second, creating a humming sound as it hovers to drink nectar.

the snipe, feast on worms. Some birds like to scavenge dead bodies. The raven has a reputation as an evil bird because it used to peck at the dead bodies of executed criminals in medieval times.

CHEWING STONE
As they have no teeth to chew with, seed-eating birds grind their food in the gizzard, a muscular stomach part. Digestion is aided by pieces of stone and grit that they have swallowed for this purpose. ▶

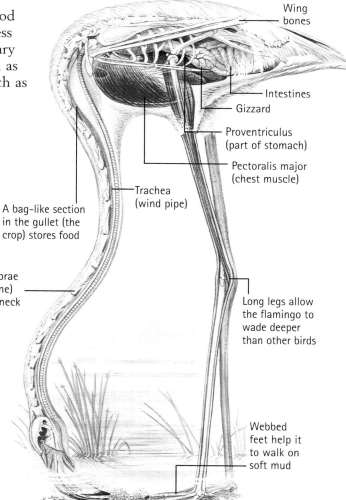

Wing bones

Intestines

Gizzard

Proventriculus (part of stomach)

Pectoralis major (chest muscle)

Trachea (wind pipe)

A bag-like section in the gullet (the crop) stores food

Sections of short vertebrae (as in a human backbone) allow flexibility of the neck

Long legs allow the flamingo to wade deeper than other birds

Webbed feet help it to walk on soft mud

THE FLAMINGO'S BEAK AND DIET
The shape of a bird's beak depends on what it eats. The flamingo sieves its food from water, so its long beak contains a filter of little hooks to trap tiny plants and crustaceans (shellfish). It is the algae that the shellfish eat that give the flamingo its bright pink colour. If the flamingo doesn't eat them, its feathers turn greyish white.

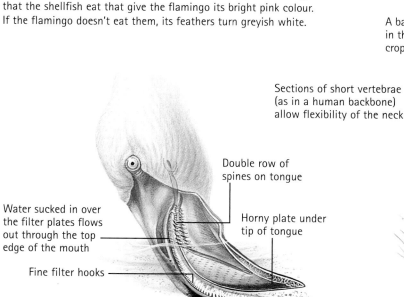

Water sucked in over the filter plates flows out through the top edge of the mouth

Fine filter hooks

Double row of spines on tongue

Horny plate under tip of tongue

NESTS

Birds' nests vary widely, from the bare cliff-ledge of the guillemot, to the stick-and-twig pile of an eagle's eyrie.

Swallows build nests of mud high up on cliffs or on the sides of buildings.

The Indian tailor bird uses spider silk to sew leaves together.

A plover lays its eggs on shingle – their only protection is camouflage.

Some ducks, grebes and other water birds build floating nests.

The ovenbird builds an oven-shaped nest of mud on a branch or fence post.

Down feather

Contour feather

Flight feather

FEATHERS

Birds have three types of feather. Fluffy down feathers near the body keep the bird warm. Contour feathers give the body a streamlined shape. Flight feathers on the wings have barbs that form smooth, flat surfaces.

COLOURS AND BREEDING

The colours of a bird's feathers usually help to conceal, or camouflage, it in its natural habitat. Most birds moult (shed) their old feathers and grow new ones each year. This moulting may be linked to breeding, as some male birds, such as the bird-of-paradise and peacock, grow colourful feathers to attract mates. The females, however, tend to be drab in colour so that they are hidden from predators while sitting on the nest.

COURTING COUPLES

As the spring or mating season arrives, a male and female pair up to mate. Most birds court with a variety of calls and displays. Some males give gifts of food such as insects to the females. Usually the males show off their colours and skills in flight and on perches, or try to out-sing and out-dance rivals. Grebes perform a very elaborate dance that involves crouching, headwagging and swaying.

LAYING EGGS

Most bird pairs breed alone, but some, such as rooks or puffins, breed in large groups called colonies. The female lays hard-shelled eggs and sits on them to keep them warm until they are ready to hatch. This process is called incubation. The number of eggs laid in one clutch varies – a kiwi lays a single egg, while a North American bobwhite can lay up to 25. Eggs can take at least ten days to hatch; albatross eggs take the longest, up to 70 days.

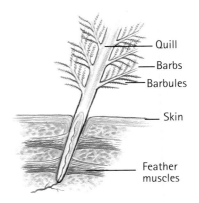

Quill

Barbs

Barbules

Skin

Feather muscles

MICROSCOPIC HOOKS

Each feather is made of keratin (found in the hair and nails of humans) and has a long, stiff shaft, or quill, with side parts called barbs, linked by tiny hook-like barbules.

MATCH-MAKING

Larger, long-lived birds, such as gannets, storks, cranes and albatrosses, often return to the same nest site and the same partner each year. The male ostrich, however, courts several females which all lay eggs in one nest. He then guards all the eggs (there may be as many as 30) and – when they hatch out – the chicks.

▲ Male birds-of-paradise have beautiful feathers. They show off their plumes in a dance to attract a mate.

HOW A BIRD FLIES

The goose, like other birds in flight, lowers its wings using its strong pectoral (chest) muscles. The wings push the air down and back, thrusting the bird up and forwards in the air. The wing and tail feathers can be twisted and fanned to help the goose manoeuvre as it flies.

1 The powerful downstroke lifts the bird upwards.

2 Legs and tail are in line with body to keep the bird streamlined as it flies.

3 The upstroke is less powerful. Feathers are twisted, letting air through.

4 The tail is used for steering and for braking.

MOVING HOUSE

Birds are warm-blooded. Their average body temperature is 41°C – slightly hotter than that of humans. This means they can stay active in cold weather but they need food, so many species leave colder climates and migrate to warmer places somewhere else in the world.

BETWEEN CONTINENTS

Birds such as geese and waders fly from the Arctic to Europe, Asia and North America. Birds from Europe, such as swifts and bee-eaters, fly south to Africa and India. The Arctic tern is the greatest migrator of all birds, flying an amazing 15,000km all the way to the Antarctic.

FAST FACTS

- A large bird such as a swan has about 25,000 feathers, whereas a tiny humming-bird has 1,000

- The world's largest bird, the ostrich, is too heavy to fly. The largest flying bird is the Kori bustard, which weighs 18kg

- The pitohui of New Guinea is the only bird that is poisonous

FEEDING THE CHICKS

The crow belongs to the group known as perching birds, which is the largest of the 26 bird groups. Its toes are designed for gripping, as crows build their nests in trees or on the side of cliffs. The chicks are often born blind and helpless and the parents feed them until they are ready to leave the nest.

The bones are thin and hollow so that birds are very light

The inside of the chick's mouth is bright red to attract the parent's attention

Like all birds, the crow has thousands of feathers

These two-week-old chicks have soft, downy feathers, and their eyes are now open

SEE ALSO

Animal, Eagle, Migration, Prehistoric animal, Zoology

BLACK DEATH

The Black Death was a disease that struck Asia, Europe and North Africa in the 14th century. It killed over one third of the people living there.

Fleas passed on the bubonic plague when they bit people.

The fleas lived on black rats, which thrived in the close-packed town houses.

Medieval artists often portrayed the Black Death as a murderous skeleton.

More people were killed by the Black Death in the late 1340s than by any other disease in history. Milder outbreaks of the disease, also called the bubonic plague, continued for about 300 years.

DEADLY SYMPTOMS

The name Black Death came from the blood spots that turned black under the skin. Some victims died within hours. Only about five per cent of people who caught the disease survived. Fleas from diseased rats spread the plague by biting humans. It was also possible to catch the plague from another person.

THE PLAGUE SPREADS

The Black Death began in central Asia in about 1339, and in 1347 Italian soldiers brought it back from the Crimea, on the Black Sea. It spread rapidly through North Africa and Europe, where rats and fleas thrived in conditions of poor hygiene. As people fled the disease-infested cities, the Black Death was spread farther afield.

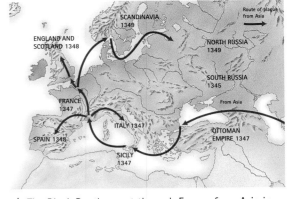

▲ The Black Death swept through Europe from Asia in 1347, reaching its peak in 1349. Only a few areas, such as Belgium and eastern Germany, were unaffected.

A TERRIBLE PUNISHMENT

The appearance of the Black Death was a terrible mystery in the Middle Ages. Many people regarded it as a punishment from God, and some people whipped themselves in public and prayed to be saved. Doctors had little idea how to treat the disease, because they did not know what caused it. Many people believed dogs and cats spread the disease so they killed them. As a result, the true carriers, black rats, only increased.

DEVASTATED POPULATIONS

Many doctors and priests died looking after the sick, leaving few educated people alive. Because so few workmen survived, after the worst of the plague was over, those who remained could demand wages instead of simply working to pay rent for land. The economy became based on money, as it is today.

'BRING OUT YOUR DEAD!'

During an outbreak of the plague, people tried to control the disease. Infected houses were marked with a cross to warn visitors. Prisoners or volunteers patrolled the streets with barrows, calling for people to bring out the bodies of the dead. The bodies were then taken to large plague pits outside the town and buried quickly.

SEE ALSO
Asia, Disease, Medicine, Middle Ages

BLACK HOLE

A black hole is a region of space where the pull of gravity is so strong that nothing can escape from it, not even light.

Nearby star

INVISIBLE FORCE

When a black hole lies close to another star, its immense gravity sucks particles or gas away from the star. These are pulled into a gassy spiral, called an accretion disc. The gas inside the disc is heated to millions of degrees Celsius and gives off X-rays. It is these powerful, flickering X-rays that reveal the presence of a black hole.

Black hole

Particles, gas and matter spiral downwards

Scientists believe that a black hole forms after a massive, heavy star has exploded at the end of its life. The outer parts are hurled into space but the core of the dead star, with no light and heat left to support it, shrinks very quickly.

DEAD STARS
The gravity of a dead star is thought to pull all the material left behind inwards, squeezing it tighter to make it smaller and extremely compact. A tiny black hole, the size of a full-stop, could hold enough matter to make a mountain. Vast black holes, thought to exist at the centre of galaxies, may contain as much matter as tens of millions of stars.

COSMIC VACUUM
Black holes are invisible – they can only be tracked down by their effect on a nearby object. They tug matter away from

the surface of a star, like a vacuum cleaner. This debris enters a whirlpool, which spins around the black hole at speed before disappearing inside, like water going down a giant plug hole.

THROUGH A WORMHOLE
Some black holes may be the entrances to strange tunnels through space and time known as wormholes. It has been suggested that a spacecraft could travel along a wormhole and reappear in a different part of the universe.

▲ A black hole is shaped like a funnel. Objects are pulled into the funnel and, once inside, never escape.

◄ This ultraviolet image shows galaxy M77. Its centre is thought to be a black hole with the mass of several million suns.

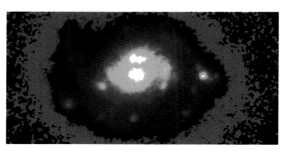

SEE ALSO
Astronomy, Big Bang theory, Constellation, Galaxy, Gravity, Star

BLOOD

Blood is a vital liquid that is pumped through arteries and veins around the body by the heart. Blood carries oxygen, nutrients, hormones and waste products.

KARL LANDSTEINER
This Austrian-born pathologist (1868–1943) discovered blood groups, making blood transfusions safe for the first time.

FAST FACTS
• An average human has about 5 litres of blood
• A blood spot the size of a pin-head contains about 5 million red cells, 10,000 white cells and 250,000 platelets
• Anaemia is a lack of oxygen in the blood

Most animals have a blood-like fluid. It is red in most vertebrates (animals with backbones), but can be different colours in other animals. Lobsters have blue blood, snails have grey blood, some insects have green blood, and a worms' blood is colourless.

BLOOD PLASMA
Just over half (55 per cent) of human blood is a pale yellow liquid called plasma. This contains hundreds of substances, including nutrients, sugars, salts, minerals, hormones and chemicals.

OXYGEN CARRIERS
About 45 per cent of blood is made up of blood cells and platelets. The vast majority of blood cells are small, red and doughnut-shaped. They are made inside the bones and released into the blood, where they carry oxygen around the body. When red cells have plenty of oxygen, as in most arteries, they are bright red. When low in oxygen, as in most veins, they are dark red.

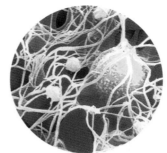

◀ Chemicals in the blood form a net over a wound. The net traps red blood cells, platelets and white blood cells (shown in yellow) to form a clot.

DEFENDING THE BODY
Less than one per cent of blood is made up of white blood cells and platelets. There are several types of white blood cell, all of which defend the body. Some fight invading bacteria and viruses by bombarding them with chemicals. Others surround invaders and eat them.

CLOTTING AND HEALING
Platelets are cell fragments that help wounds to heal. They gather around a cut and release chemicals to slow blood loss and form a clot. This stops the blood flow and seals the wound, stopping germs from getting in while new skin grows.

BLOOD GROUPS
There are several different types of human blood, including A, B, AB and O. The blood group depends on the chemicals that the white blood cells produce. If a person needs blood in an operation, the right blood group must be given as some chemicals do not mix. The wrong chemicals may clot with the existing blood and make the illness worse or even cause death.

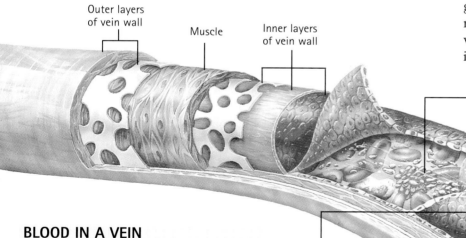

Outer layers of vein wall

Muscle

Inner layers of vein wall

White blood cell that makes chemicals to fight disease

White blood cell that eats dying and dead germs

Red blood cell

Valve to stop blood flowing the wrong way

Platelets help blood to clot

White blood cell that attacks invaders

BLOOD IN A VEIN

Blood is carried toward the heart by veins and away from the heart by arteries. Red blood cells returning to the lungs from the heart are dark red in colour because they are no longer carrying oxygen. All blood contains plasma, platelets, red blood cells and several types of white blood cells.

SEE ALSO
Cell, Disease, Heart, Immune system, Medicine

BOAT

Boats are watercraft powered by an engine, sails or oars. They are smaller than ships – usually no more than about 20m long.

Boats in Ancient Egypt were made by tying reed bundles together.

A coracle is a round boat made of animal skin stretched over a frame.

A junk is a traditional Chinese boat that is still in use today.

A catamaran is a sailing boat with two hulls arranged side by side.

A paddle steamer's engine turns a huge paddle wheel to drive the boat forward.

Small, powerful tug boats are used to tow much larger vessels into port.

▶ A sailing boat can travel in almost any direction, but at different rates. Sailing with the wind behind the boat (running) is not the fastest. Sailing across the wind (reaching) is faster. To sail into the wind a boat must tack, or zigzag, at an angle of 45° to the wind direction with the sails drawn in as close as possible.

Close hauled
Reach
Broad reach
Wind direction
Run
With the wind
Into the wind
Across the wind

Working boats are used for fishing, transporting goods and people, and moving ships in harbours. Yachts, powerboats, sailing dinghies and canoes are all used for racing and for fun.

HOLLOWED-OUT TRUNKS
The first boats were built in prehistoric times, when people hollowed out tree trunks to make dug-out canoes. Boats such as Inuit kayaks were made from animal skins, and the Ancient Egyptians made their boats from bundles of reeds.

DESIGNED FOR THE JOB
A boat's design depends on its use. A lifeboat must be built to travel long distances quickly and to cope with rough seas. A small motorboat must be tough enough to withstand the pounding of the waves as well as its engine vibrations.

PARTS OF A BOAT
The keel runs along the base of a boat. It keeps it stable and provides a framework from which to build up the boat. The hull, or outer shell, can be made of wood, but plastic and fibre glass are tougher and cheaper. The bow, or front of the boat, cuts through the water and pushes it aside so that the hull can glide through smoothly.

POWERED BY THE WIND
The skill in sailing lies in positioning the sail so that it catches the wind most efficiently. Sails are adjusted by a sheet (rope). Sideways movement is reduced by the centreboard (keel) reaching far down into the water. The boat is steered using the tiller to adjust the position of the rudder (a board attached to the back of the boat).

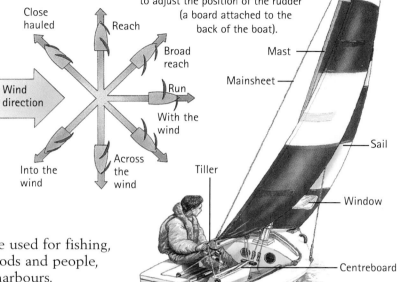

Mast
Mainsheet
Sail
Window
Tiller
Centreboard
Rudder

ON THE MOVE
Rowing boats are moved by muscle-power, using oars which have a broad blade at one end. The paddles of some canoes have blades at each end, this makes them easier to steer in fast-moving rapids. Sailing boats, or yachts, use sails to catch the wind and drive them through water. Most working boats and some sports boats are powered by an engine. This makes a propeller spin in the water, moving the boat forward.

▲ Small, light speedboats lift out of the water when they travel at speed.

SEE ALSO
Egypt, Engine, Fishing industry, Ship, Transport, Wind power

BRAIN AND NERVOUS SYSTEM

The brain is the body's control centre, responsible for action, thought, memory, behaviour and emotion. It is linked to the body by the nervous system.

Fish have simple brains, with areas that process smell extending forward to the tip of the nose.

Snakes have brains with large sight areas, showing the importance of sight for hunting.

Birds have brains with large movement centres which control the complex movements used in flight.

Cats, like other mammals, have brains with large cerebrums for complex and adaptable behaviour.

The average adult human brain weighs 1.4kg, looks like a giant, grey walnut and has the texture of blancmange. It is made up of tiny cells that send electrical messages to the body along a network of nerves known as the nervous system.

IN THREE PARTS

All vertebrates (animals with backbones) have a brain that can be divided into three main areas: brain stem, cerebellum and cerebrum. The brain stem and cerebellum keep the body functioning. The cerebrum deals with thought, memory and sensation.

BRAIN STEM

The brain stem lies at the bottom of the brain, where it joins the spinal cord (the bundle of nerves linking the brain to the body). The stem controls the body's automatic processes, such as heartbeat, breathing, body temperature, blood pressure, digestion and getting rid of waste.

THE CEREBELLUM

The cerebellum lies at the back of the brain. When movement instructions come from the cerebrum, the cerebellum sorts them, fills in the details and sends out signals to the muscles to make movements smooth and co-ordinated. The cerebellum also controls posture and balance.

THE CEREBRUM

About 90 per cent of the human brain is taken up by the cerebrum – the centre of all thought. It is split into two halves, called cerebral hemispheres, which contain grey matter and white matter. Grey matter lies on the surface and is made of nerve cell bodies, which create messages. The inner white matter is packed with nerve fibres carrying the messages to the body.

CEREBRAL CENTRES

The human cerebrum looks the same all over, but different areas carry out special functions. One area receives and processes nerve signals from the eyes. Another is for touch, processing nerve signals from the skin. Just in front of this is the motor

FAST FACTS

• About 0.85 litres of blood pass through the brain every minute

• Brain activity uses up one fifth of the body's energy supply

• The longest nerve, the sciatic, runs from the base of the spine to the knee. Some nerve signals travel at up to 400km/h

• Meningitis is the inflammation of the meninges. Encephalitis is inflammation of the brain

HOW NERVE CELLS PASS ON MESSAGES

The brain and nervous system are made of microscopic nerve cells called neurons. Each nerve cell has two parts: a spider–like cell body and a long nerve fibre. The cell body receives signals from other nerve cells and passes these along its fibre, like a tiny telephone wire, to yet more nerve cells, until the message reaches its final destination.

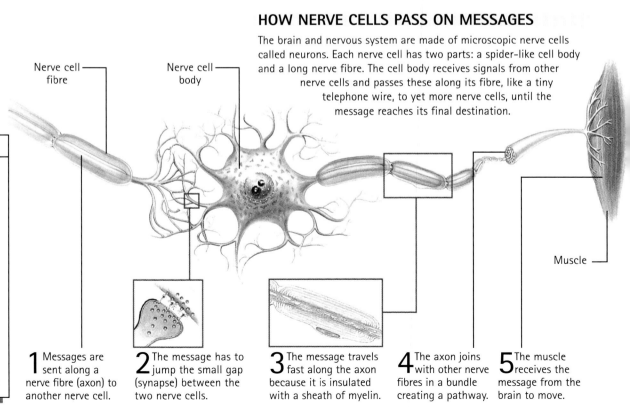

Nerve cell fibre

Nerve cell body

Muscle

1 Messages are sent along a nerve fibre (axon) to another nerve cell.

2 The message has to jump the small gap (synapse) between the two nerve cells.

3 The message travels fast along the axon because it is insulated with a sheath of myelin.

4 The axon joins with other nerve fibres in a bundle creating a pathway.

5 The muscle receives the message from the brain to move.

THE BRAIN AND SKULL

The brain is protected by a bony skull, three thin layers of membrane, called meninges, and a pool of fluid. The two sides of the cerebrum (the cerebral hemispheres) are joined by the corpus callosum. The left side of the brain usually controls logic while the right side is more active in creative pursuits.

Bony skull

Fluid

Meninges

Cerebrum

Corpus callosum

Cerebellum

The hypothalamus is the site of emotion and instinct

The pituitary gland controls the hormones

Planning

Skilled movement

Touch

Spatial awareness

Thought and consciousness

Speech

Hearing

Sight

Memory

Brain stem

Cerebellum

Spinal cord

centre, which sends nerve signals to the muscles. There are also areas for hearing, taste, speech and other body processes. Consciousness and thought are believed to originate at the front of the cerebrum.

CROSSING THE DIVIDE

Nerve signals arriving or leaving one side of the brain cross over to affect the opposite side of the body, so signals from the body's right side go to the brain's left hemisphere and vice versa. The two sides are joined by a strip of nerve fibres, the corpus callosum.

INSTINCTS AND EMOTIONS

Basic instincts, such as hunger, thirst and sleep, as well as strong emotions, such as

fear, anger and joy, come from the hypothalamus, which lies at the top of the brain stem. Dangling beneath it is the pituitary, a pea-sized gland that controls the body's hormones (chemical messages).

THOUGHTS AND MEMORIES

The human brain contains 100 billion nerve cells and is far more complex than the most advanced supercomputer. One thought or memory involves millions of nerve signals, flashing around billions of brain cells, along trillions of pathways. An electroencephalogram (EEG) machine is used to record these electrical nerve signals.

A NETWORK OF NERVES

The brain is linked to a branching network of nerves by the spinal cord. Sensory nerves bring information from the senses to the brain. Motor nerves carry signals from the brain to the muscles. The brain and spinal column make up the central nervous system. The nerves in the rest of the body make up the peripheral nervous system.

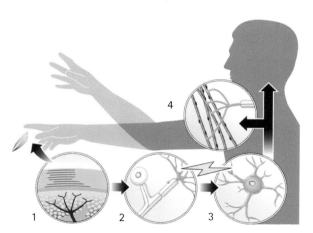

▲ A reflex is an automatic response. The flame's heat stimulates pain sensors in the finger (1) that send a signal to the spinal cord (2). The signal passes to a motor nerve (3), which makes muscles contract (4), pulling away the hand. Signals also pass to the brain, which registers pain.

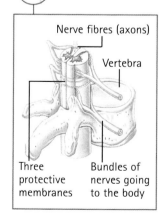

Nerve fibres (axons)

Vertebra

Three protective membranes

Bundles of nerves going to the body

▲ The spinal cord runs through a tunnel formed by vertebrae in the spine. Its nerves are surrounded by protective membranes.

SEE ALSO

Cell, Gland, Hearing, Human body, Sight, Taste and smell, Touch

BRAZIL

Brazil is the largest country in South America, covering almost half the continent. It is also South America's richest and most heavily populated country.

Area: 8,511,965 sq km
Population: 185,713,000
Capital: Brasília
Language: Portuguese
Currency: Real

Two thirds of Brazil is covered by the vast Amazon river basin, which contains the world's largest rainforest. The 6,437km-long Amazon flows across the northwest of the country and carries about a fifth of the world's river water.

ON THE EQUATOR

Brazil is warm all year round, with temperatures rarely dropping below 20°C, because the Equator lies across the north of the country. Rainfall is highest inland, with more than 280mm of rain falling in January, the wettest month.

LIFE IN THE RAINFOREST

The Amazon rainforest is a dense and steamy region, with at least 40,000 kinds of plants and thousands of different insects, exotic birds and wild animals including macaws, monkeys, jaguars, sloths, armadillos, piranha fish and anaconda snakes. But the wildlife and the way of life of the small groups of Indians that inhabit the rainforest are under threat because of the number of trees being cut down. Efforts to protect the rainforest – an area of global environmental importance – are now being made. Farming, timber and logging all threaten the region.

◄ Many families living in the heart of the Amazon rainforest still build houses of thatched palm leaves.

FARMING THE LAND

Most of Brazil's wealth comes from the crops grown in the highlands. Coffee is the country's largest export – Brazil produces about a third of the world's supply. Other exports include orange juice, soya beans, rice, sugar cane and cotton. Valuable timber, such as mahogany, as well as nuts, rubber and medicines are harvested in the forests.

INDUSTRY AND MINING

Factories around the major cities make cars, aircraft, cement and chemicals. Brazil's vast mineral wealth includes iron, lead, copper, magnesium, uranium, gold and diamonds. Most of Brazil's power is hydroelectric, from projects such as the Itaipu Dam on the Paraná river at the Paraguay border.

▲ São Paulo, Brazil's largest city, is ringed by shanty towns called *favelas*. Poverty is a serious problem for Brazil's rapidly growing population.

► Sugar Loaf Mountain overlooks the beautiful natural harbour of Rio de Janeiro, once the capital of Brazil. The mountain gets its name from the days when sugar was sold in pyramid-like, solid blocks.

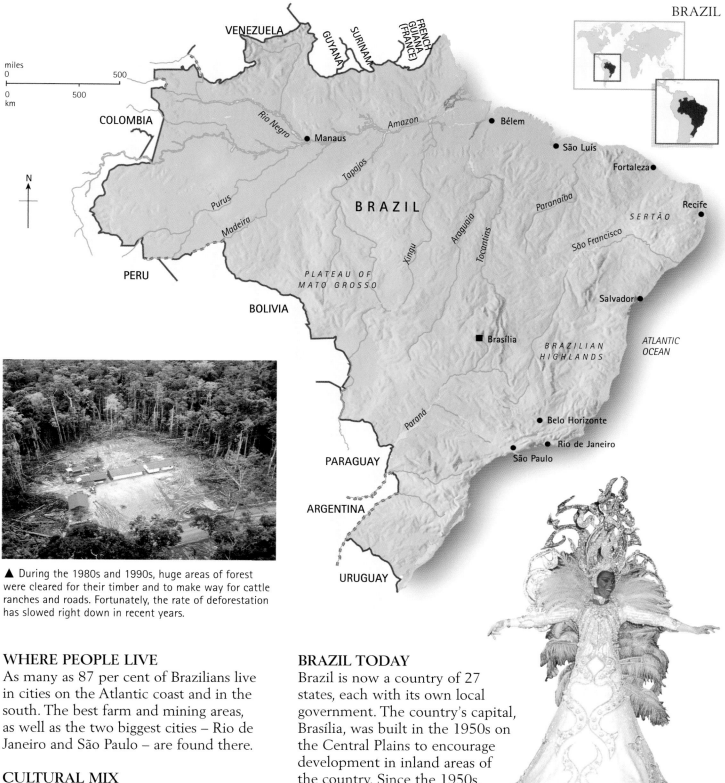

miles
0   500
0   500
km

VENEZUELA
GUYANA
SURINAME
FRENCH GUIANA (FRANCE)

COLOMBIA

Rio Negro

Amazon

● Bélem

● São Luís

Manaus ●

Tapajos

Fortaleza ●

Purus

B R A Z I L

Paranaíba

Recife

SERTÃO

Madeira

Araguaia

São Francisco

PERU

Xingu

Tocantins

BOLIVIA

PLATEAU OF
MATO GROSSO

Salvador ●

■ Brasília

BRAZILIAN
HIGHLANDS

ATLANTIC
OCEAN

Paraná

● Belo Horizonte

PARAGUAY

● Rio de Janeiro

São Paulo ●

ARGENTINA

URUGUAY

▲ During the 1980s and 1990s, huge areas of forest were cleared for their timber and to make way for cattle ranches and roads. Fortunately, the rate of deforestation has slowed right down in recent years.

WHERE PEOPLE LIVE

As many as 87 per cent of Brazilians live in cities on the Atlantic coast and in the south. The best farm and mining areas, as well as the two biggest cities – Rio de Janeiro and São Paulo – are found there.

CULTURAL MIX

Just under half of Brazilians are of European origin, many with Portuguese ancestry. The rest are of mixed Indian, European and African descent. The Indian tribes have lived in Brazil for thousands of years, while the Portuguese arrived in the 1500s, bringing African slaves with them. Brazil declared its independence from Portugal in 1822.

BRAZIL TODAY

Brazil is now a country of 27 states, each with its own local government. The country's capital, Brasília, was built in the 1950s on the Central Plains to encourage development in inland areas of the country. Since the 1950s, Brazil's economic status in the world has grown, but at the expense of many of its natural resources. More than a quarter of Brazilians are under 15 years of age. The population is set to reach 207 million by 2050. It is important that the country continues its economic growth if its population is to be housed, educated and employed.

▲ The Brazilian carnival lasts for five days just before Lent. It is especially spectacular in Rio de Janeiro.

SEE ALSO

Conservation, Native Americans, Rainforest, South America

BRIDGE

Bridges are structures that are built to allow people, animals or vehicles to cross rivers, canals, canyons, railways or roads.

Most bridges are fixed, but some are movable – all must be carefully designed to withstand the effects of traffic, floods, high winds, earthquakes and changes of temperature. The main types of fixed bridge in use today are beam, arch, suspension and cantilever.

STRAIGHT ACROSS
The earliest bridges were made by laying logs or large, flat stones laid across a river. Beam or girder bridges take this simple idea a step further. They have a flat deck, sometimes supported by piers (pillars), and can span gaps of up to 300m. A cantilever bridge is a type of beam bridge with two halves balanced on piers and joined by a short span in the middle.

ARCH BRIDGES
Because of its curved shape, the arch bridge can reach farther than the beam bridge. Its supports at either end are called abutments. They take the strain of the outward thrust created by the weight of the arch. The Romans were the first to build arch bridges, using bricks or stone.

BRIDGES IN SUSPENSION
Suspension bridges can cover very long distances where piers cannot be used, perhaps because the river is too deep. The traffic deck is suspended

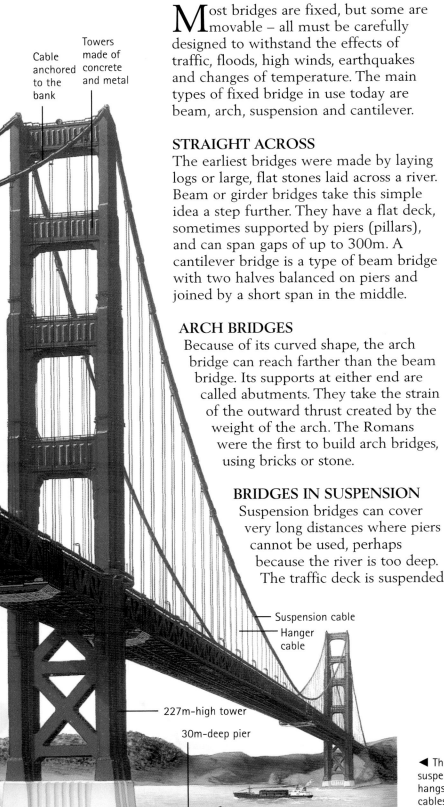

Cable anchored to the bank

Towers made of concrete and metal

Suspension cable

Hanger cable

227m-high tower

30m-deep pier

HOW BRIDGES WORK
Bridges are designed to withstand huge forces (shown by the arrows in the diagrams below). They must be strong enough to carry their own weight, as well as that of the people and vehicles that use them. Bridges must also withstand the strong vibrations set up by high winds.

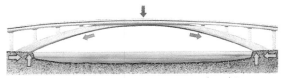

In an arch bridge, the downward pressure (load) is pushed out towards the foundations on each bank.

In a cantilever bridge, the load on the central span is balanced equally over each supporting pier.

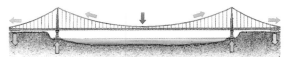

In a suspension bridge, curving cables transfer the bulk of the load to anchored points on each bank.

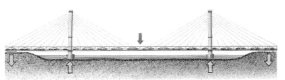

In a cable-stayed bridge, the load is balanced equally over one or more central supports.

→ Load   → Support   → Tension   → Compression

from towers by steel cables. A modern version of this is the cable-stayed bridge, which does not need the heavy anchorages required to stabilize a suspension bridge.

MOVABLE BRIDGES
Some bridges are built to move so that large ships can pass through. Drawbridges lift up by splitting in the middle or at one end, swing bridges turn sideways, and lift bridges have a central section that can be raised. Deck sections can also be floated on pontoons to create temporary bridges.

◄ The 1,280m-long Golden Gate suspension bridge in San Francisco hangs from two 1m-thick suspension cables, each made of 27,450 wires.

SEE ALSO
Architecture, Construction, Industrial Revolution, Iron and steel

BUDDHISM

Buddhism is a religion that was first practised in Asia about 2,500 years ago. Today, it is estimated that there are around 376 million Buddhists across the globe.

▲ The Wheel of Life symbolizes the process of change and rebirth. When we reach Nirvana, the process stops and we come off the wheel.

▲ A Buddhist monastery in Tibet. Buddhism was introduced into Tibet in 749CE. Tibetan monks are called lamas. The chief lamas are the Dalai Lama and the Panchen Lama.

Buddhism was founded in northeast India by a prince called Siddhartha Gautama. Born around 563BCE, he left his home at the age of 29 to lead a life of meditation and preaching. He became a great religious teacher before his death in about 483BCE.

THE ENLIGHTENED ONE
While sitting under a fig tree, Gautama entered a peaceful state of mind, called enlightenment, or Nirvana ('absence of sorrow'). He then taught others how to find this peace and gained the title Buddha, which means 'Enlightened One'. The Buddhist religion spread from India to China, Japan and other parts of Asia.

REBIRTH
Buddhists believe in reincarnation – being reborn until Nirvana is reached. The form of each new life depends on how the being behaved during previous lives. A human might have been an animal in the last life; a male might have been female. This is known as their karma.

FOUR NOBLE TRUTHS
Buddha's teachings are based on the Four Noble Truths. These state that all suffering is caused by attachment to the material world. Buddhists believe that

▲ A young Thai Buddhist, in traditional orange robes, sits contemplating under a tree. Buddhists believe that meditation plays a vital role in the path to enlightenment.

they will be free of these attachments, and therefore of suffering, if they follow the Eightfold Path. This consists of eight steps involving wisdom, understanding, morality and meditation.

TYPES OF BUDDHISM
There are two main types of Buddhism: Theravada is common in Southeast Asia and teaches that Buddha was an ordinary human being who achieved enlightenment; Mahayana is popular in northern Asia and claims that Buddha was the divine spirit in human form. A branch of Mahayana, called Zen Buddhism, was established in Japan in the 1100s.

◀ Many images of Buddha show him sitting serenely with crossed legs in the lotus position. The image reminds followers of Buddha's goodness and helps them to meditate and pray.

EIGHTFOLD PATH TO ENLIGHTENMENT
- Right views
- Right thought and intention
- Right speech, plain and truthful
- Right action, including never taking a life
- Right occupation, harming no one
- Right effort, always persevering
- Right awareness of the past, present and future
- Right contemplation or meditation

SEE ALSO
Asia, Japan, Religion

BUTTERFLY AND MOTH

Butterflies and moths are flying insects with two pairs of wings, which are often brightly coloured. They hatch as caterpillars and change into moths or butterflies as adults.

The turquoise blue has been hunted almost to extinction by collectors for its beautiful wings.

A peacock butterfly's eye spots may help it scare off small birds when it suddenly opens its wings.

The white admiral is a woodland butterfly. Its caterpillar is covered with protective spines.

Swallowtails are large and colourful butterflies, found in North Africa, Europe and across Asia.

The large white is a very common butterfly. Its caterpillars feed in groups, often on cabbage plants.

There are more than 170,000 kinds of butterflies and moths in the world. They form the group of insects known as Lepidoptera, which means 'scale-wing'. Their wings are covered with thousands of tiny scales that give the wings their colourful appearance.

COLOURFUL BUTTERFLIES
Most butterflies fly by day and have brightly coloured wings, which close together over their backs when they are resting. They have a slim body and thin antennae (feelers) with clubbed tips, which are used to detect smells. The monarch, cabbage white, tortoiseshell and peacock are all types of butterfly.

DULL MOTHS
Most moths are dull in colour, fly at night, have feathery or hairy antennae and a stout and hairy body. At rest, a moth holds its wings open. A moth's forewing is often linked to its hind-wing on each side by tiny hairs that act like hooks. The hawk moth, ermine, eggar and tussock are all

◄ The back part of the hawk moth caterpillar looks exactly like a viper in order to deceive any predators into leaving it alone.

▲ Tropical birdwing butterflies, such as the Rajah Brooke, can have a wingspan of up to 28cm.

types of moth. The scarlet tiger and burnet are examples of moths that are brightly coloured and fly by day.

SENSING THE WORLD
An adult butterfly or moth sees well with its large eyes. Its sensitive antennae pick up the scents of flowers and fruits and can detect the smell of a mate. Most species of butterfly or moth feed on flower nectar, which is sucked up by a long, straw-like mouth, called a proboscis.

EGG TO CATERPILLAR
After mating, female butterflies and moths lay their eggs on or near the plant that their caterpillars like to eat. The brimstone butterfly likes buckthorn, while the green oak tortrix moth chooses oak leaves. Some species will feed only on one type of plant.

LIVING TO EAT
Butterfly and moth eggs hatch into soft-skinned, wingless larvae called caterpillars. Their job is to eat – a large group of caterpillars can destroy crops within a few weeks. A caterpillar sheds its skin (moults) four or five times as it feeds and grows. To protect themselves against predators, some caterpillars are covered in hairs that release a chemical when broken. Others are brightly coloured as a warning.

◄ This peppered moth is a pale, speckled grey in colour to camouflage it against lichen on tree bark.

LIFE SPAN

Most butterflies and nearly all moths live for just one breeding season or year. A few butterflies, such as peacock and monarch, survive the winter as adults. Their main predators are birds by day and bats at night. The breeding season is usually in the spring or summer, although tropical species can breed at any time of the year.

ALL CHANGE

When they are ready to become adults, caterpillars enter a pupal stage (chrysalis). Many moth caterpillars spin cocoons of silk. Butterfly caterpillars grow a hard skin. Inside these cases, they gradually change. After a few weeks, or the following spring, the chrysalis splits and the adult winged insect (imago) emerges.

Like all hawk moths, the privet hawk moth is a fast flyer. Its caterpillars have a curved horn at the end.

CATERPILLAR TO BUTTERFLY

The monarch butterfly lays its eggs on a milkweed plant. A week later a single caterpillar emerges from each egg. First it eats its egg case, then it feeds on the plant. Once fully grown, the caterpillar becomes a chrysalis (pupa). Inside, it metamorphoses (changes form), before emerging as a butterfly. The whole cycle from egg to adult takes about five weeks.

1 The female monarch lays a cluster of eggs on the leaves of a milkweed plant.

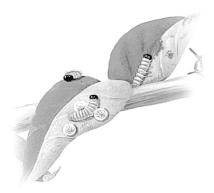

2 Each tiny caterpillar (larva) hatches and starts to eat. It grows very quickly.

3 When fully grown, the caterpillar spins a silken thread and firmly attaches itself to a twig.

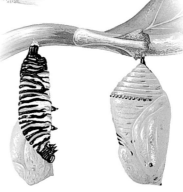

4 The caterpillar sheds its stripey skin, revealing a chrysalis (pupa). It now looks still and lifeless.

5 Inside the chrysalis a new body slowly begins to form. Finally, the skin splits and an adult butterfly emerges.

6 The butterfly clings to the twig of the milkweed plant, letting its new wings hang down to help force blood into them.

7 When the wings have dried and hardened, metamorphosis is complete and the adult monarch butterfly can fly away.

SEE ALSO

Animal, Flower, Insect

CANADA

Canada is the second largest country in the world. It is the north part of the continent of North America and a large percentage of its area lies within the Arctic Circle.

Area: 9,970,610 sq km
Population: 34,019,000
Capital: Ottawa
Languages: English, French
Currency: Canadian dollar

▲ Forestry is one of Canada's most important industries. Trees are cut down to make paper as well as to build homes.

FAST FACTS

• The Yukon Territory is rich in metal ore. During the 1890s, it was the site of the Klondike gold rush

• Alberta has some of the world's best dinosaur remains. *Albertosaurus* is just one example

• The border between Canada and the USA is the longest undefended border in the world

▶ The 553m-high Canadian National (CN) Tower dominates Toronto's skyline. The city is Canada's financial, manufacturing and communication centre.

The Rocky Mountains run down the west of Canada, and four of the five Great Lakes lie on its border with the United States. These, together with other Canadian lakes, contain more than 17 per cent of the world's fresh water.

CANADIAN FORESTS
Forests cover 53 per cent of the land. British Columbia is the leading province in timber production, with 75m-high trees, such as Douglas fir, growing in its moist, coniferous forests. Maple syrup is collected in the maple trees in Ontario and Quebec, and in the southwest there are orchards and vineyards.

THE GREAT PLAINS
Canada has vast grassland areas called prairies, stretching across its centre. Only about seven per cent of these Great Plains is used for growing crops, but this land produces enough to make Canada the world's second largest exporter of wheat. Cattle ranches on the drier grasslands supply beef and dairy produce.

▲ Moose are just one of the animals living in Canada's forests, which are also home to bears, beavers, bobcats, caribou, foxes, wolves, mountain lions and goats.

INDUSTRY AND MINING
Canada's manufacturing industries lie mostly in Ontario and Quebec. They make vehicles, aircraft, machinery, steel, chemicals and paper, as well as processing food and minerals. Canada is rich in resources such as gold, iron ore, copper, petroleum and natural gas, many of which are exported. Fishing has long been an important industry in Canada, but overfishing has reduced stocks.

SPORT AND LEISURE
Most Canadians live in cities around the Great Lakes and St Lawrence River, or on the west coast. They share a love of the outdoors, enjoying ice hockey, baseball, soccer and football. Rodeo enthusiasts

◀ In wintertime, temperatures can fall as low as −30°C. Lakes and rivers freeze over, and people play games on the ice.

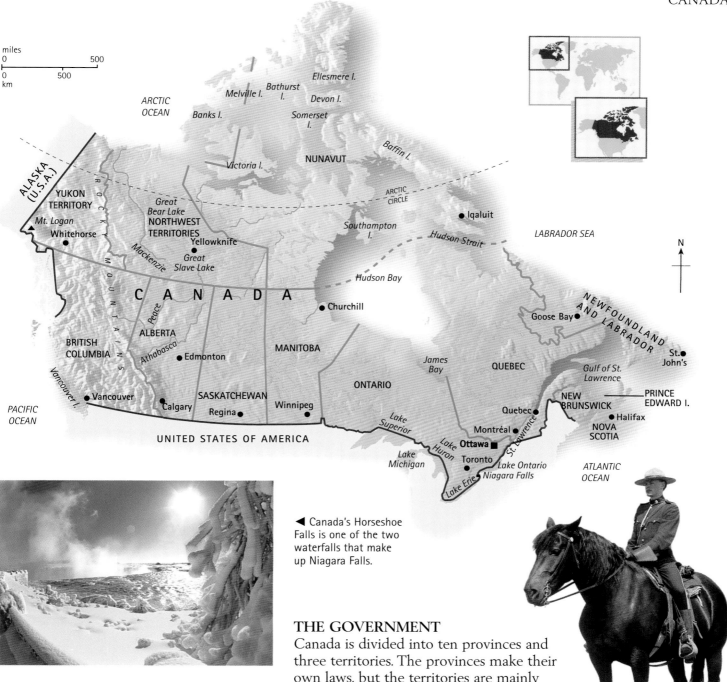

miles
0   500
0   500
km

◀ Canada's Horseshoe Falls is one of the two waterfalls that make up Niagara Falls.

flock to the annual Calgary Stampede, and there are 36 National Parks.

CANADIAN PEOPLES

Canada's native peoples are the Inuit and Native Americans, whose ancestors came from Asia, probably around 13,000 years ago. Europeans arrived in Canada in the 1500s, and in the 1700s Britain and France fought for control of the country. Since 1867, Canada has been self-governing, with Newfoundland becoming a part of the country in 1947.

THE GOVERNMENT

Canada is divided into ten provinces and three territories. The provinces make their own laws, but the territories are mainly under government control. National laws are made by the parliament in Ottawa. There is an elected House of Commons and an upper house called the Senate, whose job it is to advise parliament.

TRANSPORT

Canada has a good system of roads, including the Trans-Canada Highway, which is more than 7,000km long. The St Lawrence Seaway, a waterway linking stretches of river and canals, allows ships to carry cargoes inland from the Atlantic Ocean as far as the Great Lakes.

▲ The Royal Canadian Mounted Police, nicknamed the Mounties, are Canada's national police force.

SEE ALSO

Arctic, Native Americans, North America

CAR

Cars are motorized vehicles with an engine, wheels and steering mechanism. They are designed to carry passengers or to race in competition.

There are over 600 million cars on the road today. They have had a huge impact on society and are one of the world's most important inventions.

Cugnot's steam gun carriage of 1769 was the first motorized vehicle.

Daimler's first car, built in 1886, was a coach fitted with an engine.

The Rolls Royce Silver Ghost of 1906 used automatic engine controls.

The 1914 Model T Ford was the first car made on a moving assembly line.

Volkswagen produced more than 20 million Beetles between 1938 and 2003.

The 1984 Ferrari Testarossa can reach a speed of 290km/h.

The GM Sunraycer of 1987 used solar energy from sunlight to power it.

THE FIRST CARS
The first successful petrol-powered vehicles were developed by the German engineers Karl Benz and Gottfried Daimler in the 1880s. Benz designed a complete vehicle. Daimler simply added his engine to a horseless carriage.

HOW A CAR MOVES
Most cars today are powered by petrol or diesel engines, or by electric motors. The engine turns a drive shaft, which is linked to the wheels by gears.

STREAMLINING
A car's shape is now designed using computers. It must look good, be safe and comfortable, and work well. The sleeker or more streamlined the car, the faster and more economical it will be to drive.

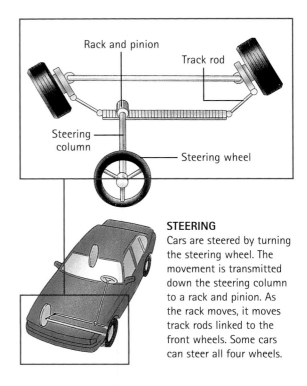
Rack and pinion
Track rod
Steering column
Steering wheel

STEERING
Cars are steered by turning the steering wheel. The movement is transmitted down the steering column to a rack and pinion. As the rack moves, it moves track rods linked to the front wheels. Some cars can steer all four wheels.

Objects that stick out, such as windscreen wipers, can be tucked away under panels to reduce wind resistance and wind noise. In some modern designs, front and rear panels on the car can be adjusted electronically to change the air-flow around the car's body.

Racing cars are designed to have minimum air resistance. They have a sleek shape and pointed nose.

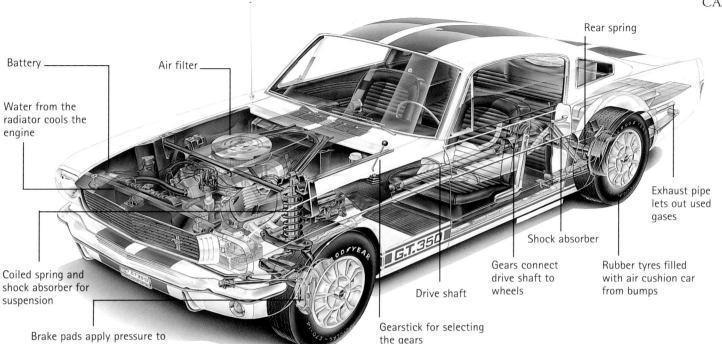

Rear spring

Battery

Air filter

Water from the radiator cools the engine

Coiled spring and shock absorber for suspension

Brake pads apply pressure to discs to slow the car down

Exhaust pipe lets out used gases

Shock absorber

Gears connect drive shaft to wheels

Rubber tyres filled with air cushion car from bumps

Drive shaft

Gearstick for selecting the gears

CONTROL SYSTEMS

Gearboxes have up to five forward gears to vary the speed and power of the car, and one gear for reversing. Gears are selected by a shift lever, although many gearboxes are automatic. An electrical system controls the engine, lights and other instruments. The electric circuits are powered by a battery, which is charged from the engine. Computerized engine management systems in modern cars mean that problems can be diagnosed more easily.

ROAD SAFETY

Road safety is very important in the design of modern cars. Experiments using life-size dummies are carried out by safety experts to establish how a car collapses on impact and how this affects the passengers inside. These experiments have led manufacturers to introduce improvements in the design of the steering wheel, seats and seat belts, and to the invention and use of new safety devices such as inflatable air bags.

IMPROVING COMFORT

Passenger comfort is improved by smooth braking and suspension. Brakes are linked to all four wheels to slow the car down. Modern cars use anti-locking brakes to prevent skidding when roads are wet or slippery. The suspension system cushions the car from bumps in the road and usually consists of a coiled spring and shock absorber (to reduce the spring's vibrations) attached to each of the four wheels.

THE ENVIRONMENT

Cars have caused huge environmental and social changes, bringing mobility to millions of people. Thousands of kilometres of motorways have been built, while the ability to travel long distances to work has helped towns to spread. In some cities, however, poisonous gases from car exhausts and traffic congestion do cause serious problems. It is hoped that the use of new fuels, such as ethanol, as well as electric motors, will reduce this pollution.

▼ Crash test dummies are used to test cars for road safety. Here an air bag is shown exploding after a crash. The dummy mimics how a person would be affected in the accident.

KEY DATES

1891 René Panhard and Emile Levasor build first 'horseless' carriage powered by a Daimler engine

1896 Karl Benz patents first motor car

1901 First mass-produced car, the Oldsmobile

1906 First Grand Prix held at Le Mans, France

1908 Henry Ford introduces the Model T

1934 André Citroën introduces front-wheel drive

1979 Catalytic converter is introduced

1997 Toyota launches its hybrid electric Prius

SEE ALSO

Invention, Transport, Truck and bus

CARIBBEAN

The Caribbean islands lie between North and South America, forming a curving chain about 3,200km long. They include Cuba, Jamaica and Haiti.

ANTIGUA & BARBUDA
Area: 442 sq km
Population: 86,000
Capital: St John's
Language: English
Currency: East Caribbean dollar

BAHAMAS
Area: 13,939 sq km
Population: 354,000
Capital: Nassau
Language: English
Currency: Bahamian dollar

BARBADOS
Area: 430 sq km
Population: 274,000
Capital: Bridgetown
Language: English
Currency: Barbados dollar

CUBA
Area: 110,861 sq km
Population: 11,241,000
Capital: Havana
Language: Spanish
Currency: Peso

DOMINICA
Area: 739 sq km
Population: 70,000
Capital: Roseau
Language: English
Currency: East Caribbean dollar

The region known as the Caribbean includes three island groups: the Greater Antilles and the Lesser Antilles, which lie in the Caribbean Sea, and the Bahamas, in the Atlantic Ocean. These islands are also known as the West Indies because, when the explorer Christopher Columbus first saw them in 1492, he did not know he was off the coast of North America, but believed he was near India.

TROPICAL ISLANDS
The tropical climate in the Caribbean means that temperatures rarely drop below 25°C, although the hot days are often relieved by coolingy sea breezes. Violent hurricanes sometimes strike the islands, causing great damage to property.

FOREST ANIMALS
Vegetation on the islands includes palm trees and exotic flowers such as orchids. Some islands also have very dense rainforests – home to parrots and macaws, as well as bats, snakes and insects. In many places, these forests have been cleared to make way for crop plantations.

▲ Bananas are one of the chief crops. They are picked while still green and exported in refrigerated cargo ships.

HOME-GROWN PRODUCE
Sugar cane is the main crop grown on the islands. The stalks are crushed to produce raw juice or refined to make crystallized sugar. Other important crops are bananas and other fruit, coffee, cocoa and cotton.

ISLAND INDUSTRY
As well as farming, there is some mining. Jamaica has bauxite (aluminium ore), Trinidad has offshore oil and gas, and there is some manufacturing. Tourism is by far the largest employer – on some islands, more than one fifth of the working population is employed, directly or indirectly, by the tourist industry.

THE ORIGINAL ISLANDERS
The first settlers in the Caribbean were the Caribs and Arawaks from South America. Most were killed by Europeans who arrived

▼ Large markets, where people sell home-grown goods, are a familiar aspect of island life.

DOMINICAN REPUBLIC
Area: 48,433 sq km
Population: 9,379,000
Capital: Santo Domingo
Language: Spanish
Currency: Peso

GRENADA
Area: 344 sq km
Population: 104,000
Capital: St George's
Language: English
Currency: East
Caribbean dollar

HAITI
Area: 27,750 sq km
Population: 9,923,000
Capital: Port-au-Prince
Languages: French, Creole
Currency: Gourde

JAMAICA
Area: 10,991 sq km
Population: 2,699,000
Capital: Kingston
Language: English
Currency: Jamaican dollar

ATLANTIC OCEAN

BAHAMAS

GREATER

CUBA

CAYMAN IS. (UK)

TURKS AND
CAICOS IS. (UK)

JAMAICA

ANTILLES

HAITI DOMINICAN
REPUBLIC

HISPANIOLA

CARIBBEAN SEA

PUERTO
RICO (USA)

1 2   3 4

ST KITTS & NEVIS

MONTSERRAT (UK)

ANTIGUA &
BARBUDA

GUADELOUPE (FRANCE)

DOMINICA

MARTINIQUE (FRANCE)

ST LUCIA

ST VINCENT &
THE GRENADINES

BARBADOS

GRENADA

TRINIDAD
& TOBAGO

LESSER

ANTILLES

◄ This square in Cuba
has architecture typical
of that built by the
European colonials.

KEY TO MAP
1 VIRGIN IS. (USA)
2 VIRGIN IS. (UK)
3 ANGUILLA (UK)
4 ST MARTIN (FRANCE/NETHERLANDS)
*Countries in parentheses are countries of which that island or group
is a dependency. Aruba and Curaçao (both Netherlands) are not shown.*

miles
0   100

0   100
km

soon after Columbus sighted the islands.
The Europeans brought slaves from Africa
to work on sugar and cotton plantations.
After the abolition of slavery in the 19th
century, people from India and China came
to work in the Caribbean.

A CULTURAL MIX
The people of the Caribbean reflect its mix
of cultures. They speak Spanish, French or
English, often with a local dialect. Religion
is an important part of life. As well as
Christians, Hindus and Muslims, there are
Rastafarians, who worship Haile Selassie
(emperor of Ethiopia until 1974) as a god.
On Haiti, many people practise voodoo, a
blend of African and Christian beliefs.

SELF-GOVERNING
Most larger islands are independent. Others
are dependent on the USA, France, UK or
the Netherlands. They include Puerto Rico
(USA), Guadeloupe and Martinique
(France) and Curaçao (Dutch). Caribbean
governments are working to develop the
islands, many of which are poor. In the last
50 years, many islanders have migrated to
Britain, Canada or the USA to find work.

ST KITTS & NEVIS
Area: 269 sq km
Population: 52,000
Capital: Basseterre
Language: English
Currency: East
Caribbean dollar

ST LUCIA
Area: 617 sq km
Population: 166,000
Capital: Castries
Language: English
Currency: East
Caribbean dollar

**ST VINCENT & THE
GRENADINES**
Area: 389 sq km
Population: 109,000
Capital: Kingstown
Language: English
Currency: East
Caribbean dollar

TRINIDAD & TOBAGO
Area: 5,128 sq km
Population: 1,318,000
Capital: Port of Spain
Language: English
Currency: Trinidad dollar

▲ The beautiful sandy beaches and warm waters of the
Caribbean islands lure tourists from all over the world.

SEE ALSO
Empire, Explorer, North
America, Slavery

CARTOON AND ANIMATION

A cartoon can be an animated film, a comic strip or a single picture. The first printed cartoons, in the 1840s, ridiculed prominent people or political events.

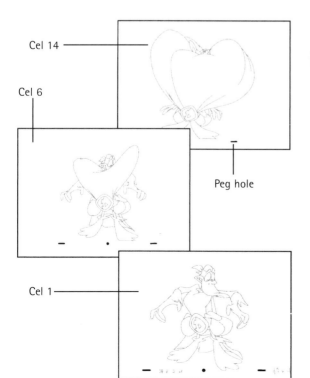

©Marvel Comics

▲ Spiderman, created in 1962, has crossed over from comic book to animated film.

The word 'cartoon' was originally used by artists to describe the picture that they produced as part of their preparation for a painting or tapestry. Today, cartoons are seen on screen and in print.

CEL ANIMATION

The traditional way of making cartoons for TV and film involves creating a moving sequence from a collection of individual images. This process is known as cel animation. Each action or change of expression of a character is made by using a number of slightly different hand-drawn pictures. When these are shown one after another on film, they give the viewer the illusion of movement by the character.

A CAST OF THOUSANDS

Between 15,000 and 20,000 images are used for a 20-minute animated film, so a whole studio of artists is often needed for

longer films. Painters create a background picture for each scene, while illustrators draw the characters. Then other artists touch up the images. Disney's *Beauty and the Beast* had 90 artists whose only job was to touch up the lines! Once the image has been coloured in, it is placed on a clear plastic sheet of celluloid, called an acetate, by a paint and trace artist. Then, finally, the animation is shot onto film.

COMPUTER ANIMATION

Many artists still draw by hand and use computers to add colour. Computers also speed up the rendering (the planning of the movements and the creation of the frames). Disney's *Toy Story*, made in 1995, was the first full-length film to be made entirely by computer animation.

COMIC STRIPS

Comic strips use a smaller creative team than animated films. A strip tells a story in a series of pictures. Speech balloons are used to put words into the mouths of characters.

Cel 14

Cel 6

Peg hole

Cel 1

COMPUTER EFFECTS

In *The Duck* by Uli Meyer Animation, the figures were hand-drawn on transparent plastic, then scanned into a computer to be coloured in and made three-dimensional. About 750 drawings were used in a five-second scene where Duck foils two robbers. The drawings (cels) are pegged one over the other to check the order of movement.

SEE ALSO

Computer, Film, Newspaper and magazine

CASTLE

Castles are fortified homes that were owned by rich and powerful families during the Middle Ages. Some are still in use, but many are now in ruins.

Early castles, known as motte and baileys, were made of wood and soil.

Massive stone keeps began to be erected around 1070.

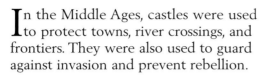

Concentric castles had two or more walls and strongly guarded gatehouses.

In the Middle Ages, castles were used to protect towns, river crossings, and frontiers. They were also used to guard against invasion and prevent rebellion.

MOTTE AND BAILEY
Castles were first built around 950CE by knights or lords. The castles included a hill or mound surrounded by a ditch and topped by a wooden tower called a motte. A bailey, or courtyard, contained living quarters, stables, granaries, and barns. These early castles were protected by a high wooden fence, called a palisade.

STONE CASTLES
From about 1070, larger castles had a stone tower called a keep. The Tower of London, the first keep in England, was begun in 1078. Food and weapons were stored inside the tower, and the knight and his staff lived there. Prisoners were kept in dungeons.

TOWERS AND WALLS
From the 1100s onward, stone curtain walls were built to surround the keeps. Towers were added to the outside of the walls so that attackers could be shot at from different directions. After about 1270, a second outer wall was added to some castles to make them harder to attack. These castles, often built by Crusaders in the Middle East, were called concentric because of their double walls.

UNDER ATTACK
A castle was attacked with catapults, rams, and siege towers. Boulders and flaming missiles were hurled at it, and its walls undermined. If a castle was not captured quickly it was besieged. Most castles fell because of bribery, disease, or famine.

CANNON FIRE
By the 1450s, cannons and gunpowder became powerful enough to destroy walls. Castles were no longer safe from attack. Most fell into ruin, but some continued to be used as palaces or luxurious homes.

UNDER SIEGE
Armies attacked castles by smashing walls with catapults or rams and by digging out foundations so that the walls collapsed. The moat was drained and filled in so that siege machines could be wheeled right up to the walls. Attackers were shielded by frames covered with wet hides.

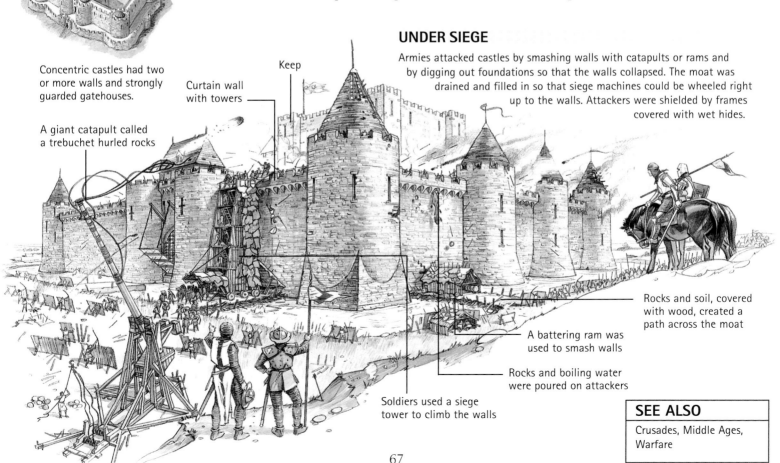

Keep

Curtain wall with towers

A giant catapult called a trebuchet hurled rocks

Rocks and soil, covered with wood, created a path across the moat

A battering ram was used to smash walls

Rocks and boiling water were poured on attackers

Soldiers used a siege tower to climb the walls

SEE ALSO
Crusades, Middle Ages, Warfare

CAT

Cats are agile, hunting mammals with keen senses and sharp teeth and claws. Domestic cats make some of the most popular pets.

The long-haired Persian needs regular grooming to keep its coat sleek.

The hairless sphynx was bred in the 1960s from a kitten born without fur.

The Manx cat from the Isle of Man, in the UK, is famous for its lack of a tail.

The blue shorthair has copper eyes and a quiet, affectionate nature.

The Cornish rex has a curly coat of short, thin hair and large, open ears.

The Siamese has long been one of the most popular pedigree (purebred) cats.

HUNTER IN THE HOME

Even a domestic cat, like this tabby, has the hunting instincts of its wild relations. Cats often toy with their prey, rather than killing it immediately. They hunt mostly at night, catching mice, small birds and insects.

Whiskers are modified hairs with nerves at their base and are ultra-sensitive to touch

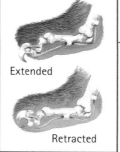

Extended

Retracted

THE CLAWS
Cats retract (pull back) their claws to keep them sharp when not in use. Each claw is attached to a toe bone. It is retracted by ligaments, which are worked by muscles.

Large, sensitive ears pick up sounds too faint for human ears to hear

Pupils open wide to let in a maximum amount of light. A mirror-like layer at the back of the eye intensifies the light

The cat family is divided into two main groups, based largely on size. The first group is made up of big cats such as tigers, lions and leopards. The second includes cougars, bobcats and lynxes, as well as the many small wild cats and the domestic cat. In all there are 37 species of cat.

PET CATS
It is thought that the domestic cat was originally a small wild cat living in Africa. By 2000BCE it had been tamed by the Ancient Egyptians, who used it to protect their food stores from mice and rats. Today, there are many breeds of domestic cat, including longhaired Persians and Angoras and the shorthaired Manx and Siamese.

CAT CHARACTERISTICS
Domestic cats resemble their wild relatives in many ways. They are excellent hunters, strong and agile, with a keen sense of hearing and very good eyesight. They have curved claws, strong jaws, sharp teeth and whiskers that are sensitive to touch. Cats are naturally inquisitive and are expert climbers and jumpers. Their flexible backbones allow them to swivel their bodies into a wide range of positions.

CAT BEHAVIOUR
Cats spend at least an hour a day grooming their fur by licking it with their rough tongues. This helps to keep their fur in good condition and keeps them cool in hot weather. Cats sleep, on average, twice as long as other mammals, spending up to three quarters of the day asleep, usually in short intervals called cat naps.

HUNTING TACTICS
Although most domestic cats do not have to catch their own food, their instinct (inborn behaviour) is to hunt. A cat's sensitive nose quickly picks up the scent of its prey. With its soft, padded paws, a cat can stalk its prey without being noticed until it is close enough to pounce. Then it grabs the prey with its claws and kills it with a powerful bite – usually at the back of the head, breaking the victim's neck.

SEE ALSO
Animal, Mammal, Sight, Tiger

CAVE

Caves are hollows that are formed in rock and ice by erosion (wearing away), usually by water. The largest, most impressive caves are found in limestone rock.

Some caves consist of just one hole barely large enough for a person to enter; others are intricate mazes of passageways and chambers. The Mammoth Cave network in Kentucky, USA, is the world's longest. Its labyrinth of caves stretches for 560km.

ROCK, ICE AND LAVA

Caves sometimes form in sea cliffs, where waves attack weak spots in the rock. The pressure of the water and the salty spray gradually erode (eat away at) the cliff. Long, tunnel-like caves can also develop in glaciers where streams of melted water run beneath the ice. Similar caves can be found in volcanoes, where a crust forms over a liquid stream of molten lava.

LIMESTONE CAVES

The largest and most impressive caves are found in limestone rock, where rainwater (which is slightly acidic) trickles through cracks in the rock. The rock slowly dissolves and the thin cracks get wider and wider. The trickle of rainwater swells into a stream, which carves hollows in the stone to form caves and pot-holes.

THE INSIDE STORY

Where streams meet, they carve out very large caves, or caverns. The floor of the cavern may be filled by underground lakes, so that it can only be explored by diving. Water dripping from the ceilings of limestone caves is rich in minerals, such as calcium carbonate, from the dissolved rock. As the water drips, these minerals are often deposited in dramatic columns – long, slender stalactites hang down from the ceiling, while shorter, stumpier stalagmites grow up from the floor. Where they join together, a pillar is formed.

MAKING CAVES

It takes thousands of years for a limestone cave to form. The process begins when rainwater starts to wear away the stone and seep through cracks. Horizontal caverns are made where the water forms underground lakes. These are left dry when the level of ground water falls.

1 Rain falls on the ground and seeps through cracks in the rock.

2 The cracks get wider and form a pot-hole.

3 Passages appear as the water continues to dissolve the rock.

4 The water becomes an underground stream, gradually eroding more rock to form a cave.

5 Stalactites and stalagmites are formed from minerals deposited by the dripping water.

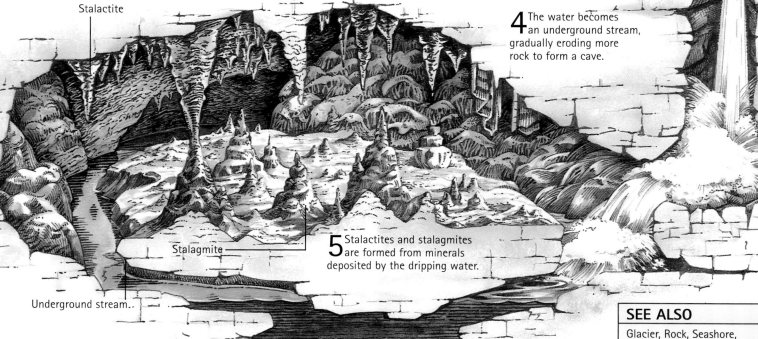

Stalactite

Stalagmite

Underground stream

SEE ALSO

Glacier, Rock, Seashore, Volcano, Water

CELL

Cells are the smallest units capable of all the functions of life. Some living things are single cells, while others (such as ourselves) are made up of billions of cells.

Bacteria have only one cell, and can multiply fast.

Onions, like most plants, have box-shaped cells.

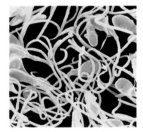

Sperm cells are used in reproduction.

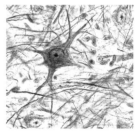

Nerve cells take messages to and from the brain.

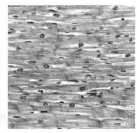

Muscle cells are long and thin and lie in bundles.

Every living thing is made up of tiny chambers, called cells – the basic building blocks of all organisms. Every cell has its job, but works with the others to keep the plant or animal alive. Some living things, such as bacteria, are just one cell; this contains all they need to survive.

THROUGH THE WALLS
A cell is surrounded by a thin film, or membrane. This gives it shape and allows chemicals and waste to pass in and out. Inside the membrane, tiny structures float in a jelly-like fluid called cytoplasm.

INSIDE THE CHAMBER
Each tiny structure, or organelle, in a cell has a job. The nucleus, for example, contains genes (instructions that decide the cell's shape and function). Sausage-shaped structures called mitochondria release the energy in food. Other organelles store energy, make proteins, keep the cell clear of debris or defend it against bacteria.

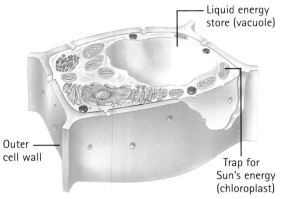

▲ Plant cells have a thick wall of cellulose, which gives them a rigid shape. Up to 90 per cent of their space is taken up by the vacuole – a sack full of sugary water.

PLANT CELLS
Unlike animal cells, plant cells have a thick cell wall and extra structures called chloroplasts. These structures are filled with a green pigment called chlorophyll. This traps the Sun's energy and uses it to make food in a process called photosynthesis.

SPLITTING IN TWO
Cells multiply by splitting in two. Under a microscope, you can see some bacteria split as fast as once every 15 minutes. Most animal and plant cells multiply much more slowly than this for growth, to repair damage and for reproduction.

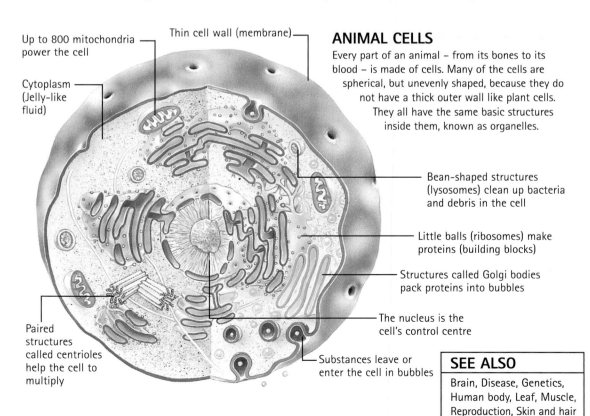

ANIMAL CELLS
Every part of an animal – from its bones to its blood – is made of cells. Many of the cells are spherical, but unevenly shaped, because they do not have a thick outer wall like plant cells. They all have the same basic structures inside them, known as organelles.

SEE ALSO
Brain, Disease, Genetics, Human body, Leaf, Muscle, Reproduction, Skin and hair

CELTS

The Celts are a group of people who lived in Europe from about 2,500 years ago. They were fierce warriors who fought frequently.

This Celtic silver and gold drinking cup was made in Ireland in the 8th century.

A Celtic noble or priest would have worn this gold torc around his neck.

A 6th-century brooch used to fasten a heavy woollen cloak around the shoulders.

The first Celts lived in Central Europe from about 500BCE and came to live in countries such as Germany, France, Britain and Spain. Most of what we know about Celtic life and culture has been passed down in accounts written by the Romans.

FARMING AND METALWORK
The Celts lived by farming the land, growing grain, root crops and fruit, and breeding cattle, sheep and pigs. They were skilled metalworkers, famous for gold jewellery. During the Iron Age, they made high-quality weapons and armour.

TRIBAL WARS
Celtic tribes fought fierce battles with their rivals. Warriors wore little armour, often fighting naked to prove their bravery. Many tribes built fortifications on hills for protection. In Britain, Queen Boudicca (or Boadicea) led her tribe, the Iceni, in a failed attack on the Romans in 61CE.

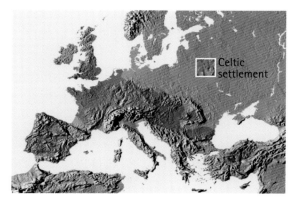

▲ This map shows the major areas of Celtic settlement in about 200BCE. Celtic peoples living in Turkey were called Galatians, while in France they were called Gauls.

Celtic settlement

GODS AND DRUIDS
The Celts had no written language, but passed on stories of their gods and history in songs and poems. They worshipped many different gods and goddesses, offering sacrifices in their honour. Ceremonies and rituals were performed by Druidic priests.

TODAY'S CELTS
Most Celtic tribes were conquered by about 150CE, during the spread of the Roman Empire. Today, descendants of Celtic people can be found in the British Isles and in Brittany, in France.

WARRIOR QUEEN
Queen Maeve ruled Celtic Connaught in Ireland in about 100CE. According to a later legendary story, 'The Cattle Raid of Cooley', she attacked Ulster in order to capture a brown bull to complete her collection of prized items. She captured the animal, but was later defeated by another Celt, Cuchulainn.

SEE ALSO
France, Ireland, Roman Empire

CENTRAL AMERICA

Central America is a strip of land between North and South America. It consists of Belize, Guatemala, Costa Rica, El Salvador, Honduras, Nicaragua and Panama.

BELIZE
Area: 22,965 sq km
Population: 333,000
Capital: Belmopan
Languages: English and Spanish
Currency: Belize dollar

COSTA RICA
Area: 51,100 sq km
Population: 4,439,000
Capital: San José
Language: Spanish
Currency: Costa Rican colon

EL SALVADOR
Area: 21,041 sq km
Population: 6,095,000
Capital: San Salvador
Language: Spanish
Currency: Colón

GUATEMALA
Area: 108,889 sq km
Population: 14,362,000
Capital: Guatemala City
Language: Spanish and Mayan languages
Currency: Quetzal

Poverty, political instability and civil war have troubled Central America for the last 100 years. All seven countries in this region are rich in natural resources, but wealth is unevenly spread. A growing number of people earn money from tourism. About 25 per cent work on the land – far fewer than previously.

LAND AND CLIMATE
Lowland forests, plains and swamps lie along the Central American coasts and rivers and mountains criss-cross the region. Its many volcanoes include Guatemala's Tajumulco, the highest peak in Central America. The region's climate is hot and moist, with temperatures seldom dropping below 24°C. Land along the coast has the highest temperatures, with cooler areas inland on the mountains and plateaux (flat areas of land high above sea level). More than 300mm of rain per month falls in some areas from July to September.

FORESTS IN DANGER
Central America has some of the richest forests in the world, containing valuable hardwood trees, such as mahogany. But in

▲ The Mayan temple of Altun Ha lies deep in the rainforest of Belize. Hundreds of palaces and pyramids were built by the Maya in Central America between 300CE and 900CE.

some places, including Costa Rica, the trees are being cut down so fast for timber, or to make space for farming, that national parks have been set up to protect the remaining trees. Jaguars, monkeys, snakes, caymans (like small alligators), iguanas, many species of birds, as well as colourful butterflies and other insects are all at risk from deforestation.

AGRICULTURAL LIFE
A quarter of people in Central America are farmers. Cattle and sheep are raised in the highlands, while export crops, such as bananas, sugar cane, cotton and coffee, are grown on plantations. Chicle is collected from sapodilla trees to make chewing gum and cacao beans are farmed for chocolate. Maize, beans and rice are grown for food.

▼ Most Central Americans are Roman Catholic, but their religious festivals often have a local flavour. For example, All Saints' Day (November 1) is celebrated in Guatemala with riotous horse races.

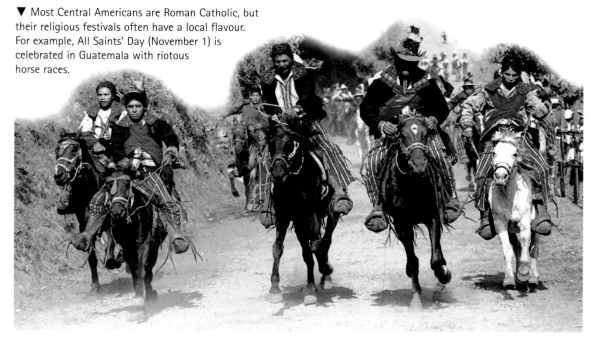

▲ The Panama Canal, opened in 1914, is an important shipping link between Atlantic and Pacific ports.

◀ There are many Indian communities in Guatemala, each with its own distinct style of dress.

HONDURAS
Area: 112,088 sq km
Population: 8,046,000
Capital: Tegucigalpa
Language: Spanish
Currency: Lempira

INDEPENDENT NATIONS

Honduras, Guatemala, El Salvador, Costa Rica and Nicaragua gained independence from Spain in the 1800s. Panama separated from Colombia in 1903, and Belize was a British colony until 1981. In the 1990s, the Central American Common Market, which had been set up in the 1960s, was replaced by the Central American Integration System. Since the 1990s, dictatorships and military rule in Guatemala, Nicaragua, Honduras, El Salvador and Panama have been replaced by democratic governments.

NICARAGUA
Area: 130,670 sq km
Population: 5,142,000
Capital: Managua
Language: Spanish
Currency: Córdoba

INDUSTRIAL GROWTH

Low labour costs have attracted industry to Central America, particularly clothing and textile manufacture, with Far Eastern companies setting up factories. Panama has a higher living standard than its neighbours, with insurance, banking and other service industries.

PEOPLE AND LANGUAGE

Most Central Americans are of mixed European and Indian descent. In the 1500s, Spanish soldiers and gold seekers conquered the region. Before then, it was home to various Indian tribes, including the Maya, who ruled between 300CE and 900CE. Many of the first European settlers brought African slaves, whose descendants still live in Nicaragua, Belize and Panama. Spanish is spoken all over the region, although English is the official language in Belize. Many people also speak local Indian languages.

PANAMA
Area: 75,990 sq km
Population: 3,406,000
Capital: Panama City
Language: Spanish
Currency: Balboa

◀ Many Guatemalan village women weave traditional textiles to sell to tourists.

SEE ALSO

Aztecs, Civil war, Conservation, Maya

73

CHEMISTRY

Chemistry is the study of chemicals. These are substances that are used in, or created by, a reaction involving changes to atoms or molecules.

ANTOINE LAVOISIER
(1743–94). Lavoisier was a French chemist. He explained how chemical reactions worked. He was the first to understand the role of oxygen in combustion (burning).

Oxygen is an element. The two atoms that make up its molecules are of the same kind. The chemical formula for oxygen is O_2.

Carbon dioxide gas is a compound of two oxygen atoms with one carbon atom. Its chemical formula is written CO_2.

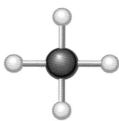

A molecule of methane gas has a carbon atom in the middle bonded to four hydrogen atoms. Its formula is written CH_4.

Water has one oxygen atom and two hydrogen atoms, giving it probably the best-known chemical formula, H_2O.

CHEMICAL ANALYSIS

Chemists use flame tests as a way of identifying chemical elements – by seeing which colour they give off when held in the flame of a Bunsen burner. A compound of an element is burned on the end of a piece of platinum wire or asbestos. The flame burns a distinctive colour, so the element can be identified. This type of chemical analysis is called qualitative and shows what elements a substance contains. To show how much of an element is present, chemists use quantitative analysis.

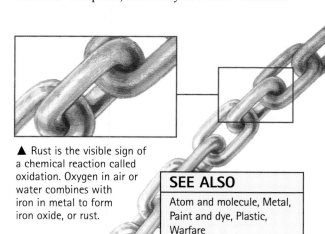

Barium
Potassium
Lithium
Sodium
Copper
Calcium

The compound is put into the flame on a platinum wire

Bunsen burner

Flame colours of elements

Chemistry explains the way substances behave and how they combine with each other. Chemists use chemical reactions to create many substances that are used in everyday life, including plastics, dyes, glues, detergents and medicines.

ELEMENTS AND COMPOUNDS

An element is a substance in which all the atoms are of the same kind. A compound is a combination of two or more elements. The compound sodium chloride (common salt), for example, is a combination of the elements sodium and chlorine. Many compounds, including salt and water, occur naturally. Others, such as nylon and plastic, were first made artificially in laboratories.

CHEMICAL REACTIONS

When different substances combine to form new materials, a chemical reaction has taken place. A substance's atoms are bonded together into molecules. During a reaction, the bonds between atoms break, allowing new molecules to form. A rusting car is an example of a chemical reaction, as iron in the car and oxygen in the air form iron oxide, or rust. Chemists use symbols (such as Fe for iron and O for oxygen) to record what happens in a reaction.

ALCHEMISTS TO SCIENTISTS

Medieval alchemists studied reactions, but it was not until the 1770s that Antoine Lavoisier showed how reactions work. In 1869, Russian chemist Dmitri Mendeleyev worked out the periodic table, grouping elements by how they react with each other.

WEAPONS AND DRUGS

Today, chemical substances of all kinds are mined or manufactured. Chemists search for new reactions to create fertilizers or drugs, which may contain long chains of molecules. Industry mass-produces useful chemicals through large-scale reactions. Poison gas and other chemicals have been used as weapons, but they are now banned.

▲ Rust is the visible sign of a chemical reaction called oxidation. Oxygen in air or water combines with iron in metal to form iron oxide, or rust.

SEE ALSO

Atom and molecule, Metal, Paint and dye, Plastic, Warfare

CHINA

China is the third largest country in the world and the nation with the largest population. Almost a fifth of the Earth's people live in China.

Area: 9,560,790 sq km
Population: 1,328,886,000 (including Hong Kong and Macau)
Capital: Beijing
Language: Guoyo (Mandarin Chinese)
Currency: Yuan

China is one of the world's oldest civilizations. Its name comes from an ancient Chinese ruling family called Qin (pronounced Ch'in). The Chinese call their country Zhongguo, which means 'middle land'. China's 1.3 billion citizens are ruled by one of the world's few remaining communist governments.

NATURAL BARRIERS

China lies in the eastern half of Asia, and deserts and mountains form natural barriers with its neighbours. The Gobi Desert, which covers 1,300,000 sq km, straddles China's border with Mongolia. The Himalayas – the highest mountains on Earth, rising to over 8,000m – stretch along the border with India, Bhutan and Nepal. The Chang Jiang (Yangtze) river is the longest in Asia and flows from the Tibetan highlands to the East China Sea, dividing the warm, moist southern regions from the drier and cooler north.

▲ The bicycle is the main method of transport for people in China. As many as 80 million bicycles are made there each year.

▲ The giant panda lives in the bamboo forests of central and western China. So few now survive in the wild that it has become a worldwide symbol for conservation.

CHINA'S WILDLIFE

Plant life ranges from bamboos and other subtropical plants in the south to coniferous forests in the north. Many garden plants now common around the world, such as the climbing plant wisteria, first came from China. With much of the country covered by mountains and desert, forests have been cleared to make way for villages and farms. This has reduced the habitats of animals such as the tiger (which is also prey to hunters) and the giant panda, making them rare in the wild. ▶

THE GREAT WALL OF CHINA

One of China's greatest early empires was ruled by the Qin dynasty. The first Qin emperor, Shi Huangdi, came to the throne in 221BCE. He ordered the construction of the Great Wall to keep out invaders from the north. Stretching for 6,400km, the wall was built by joining together shorter walls that had been built earlier. The wall has been rebuilt many times. Most of the present wall was constructed during the Ming Dynasty (1368–1644).

RUSSIA

KAZAKHSTAN

RUSSIA

• Yining

KYRGYZSTAN

Tian Shan

Harbin •

MONGOLIAN UPLANDS

TAJIKISTAN

TAKLIMAKAN DESERT

MONGOLIA

Shenyang •

NORTH KOREA

PAKISTAN

GOBI DESERT

Beijing ■

Tianjin •

Karakorum Mts.

• Hotan

INDIA

Kunlun Mts.

Huang He

SOUTH KOREA

N

Xining •

Lanzhou •

YELLOW SEA

C H I N A

PLATEAU OF TIBET

Xi'an •

miles

0   500

0   500

km

Himalaya Mts.

CENTRAL UPLANDS

Nanjing •

Shanghai •

NEPAL

Wuhan •

Mt. Everest

BHUTAN

Chongqing •

Chang

EAST CHINA SEA

INDIA

TAIWAN

Nanning •

Guangzhou •

Shenzhen •

HONG KONG

BURMA (MYANMAR)

LAOS

VIETNAM

MACAO

SOUTH CHINA SEA

Hainan Island

FARMING

About 42 per cent of people in China still farm the land. They face the threat of floods, drought, erosion and other environmental problems. Important crops include rice, which is the main food of the south, and wheat, which is used to make bread and noodles in the north.

▼ Traditional ways of life are still strong in many parts of China. Here, fishermen use birds called cormorants to bring up fish from the water. They tie a thong around the bird's throat to stop it swallowing the catch.

Millet, tea, vegetables, soya beans and cotton are also grown; and many farmers breed pigs, ducks and chickens.

INDUSTRIAL GROWTH

Industry within China has grown rapidly in the last 40 years. Chinese factories produce machinery, transport equipment, clothing and electrical goods. Shanghai is the leading industrial city. In 1997, Hong Kong – then a British colony and wealthy financial and industrial centre – was returned to China.

WRITING IN CHARACTERS

Over 90 per cent of the people are Han Chinese, originally from the north of China. Mandarin is the main dialect, but many others are also spoken. Chinese writing does not use an alphabet. Instead, it uses symbols called characters that stand for words or ideas, not letters.

PHILOSOPHY AND FAMILY

For more than 2,000 years, Confucianism has been China's main religion. It teaches respect for parents and ancestors and has strongly influenced family life in China. At one time, several generations of the same family lived in the same house. Today, in an effort to curb China's population growth, the government rewards one-child families with priority housing and medical care. This has led to much smaller families.

RULED BY DYNASTIES

For thousands of years, China was an empire ruled by emperors from successive royal families called dynasties. Many great inventions were made by the Chinese, including paper, ink, silk, printing and gunpowder. China remained isolated from most of the rest of the world until the 19th century, when foreign powers forced China to open its borders to trade. In 1911, dynastic rule was ended and the country became a republic.

COMMUNIST RULE

In 1949, China adopted a communist government and was re-named the People's Republic of China, under the leadership of Mao Zedong. His strict policies meant that there were many changes as all aspects of life came under state control, and people found their freedom restricted.

▲ Preparing food on a street stall. Rice, noodles and vegetables are the main ingredients used in Chinese cooking.

◀ China's largest city, Shanghai, has a population of around 14,231,000. It is also China's leading industrial centre.

CHINA TODAY

Since Mao's death in 1976, China's government has encouraged economic reform and foreign trade. By 2008, its economy was the second largest in the world. However, China's rapid growth has led to problems such as air pollution, huge energy consumption and water shortages. Political change is limited and the state maintains tight controls on its people.

► This man is performing a traditional form of exercise that develops both mind and body. Called wushu, it is an ancient Chinese martial art.

◀ Farmers bring their produce to sell at a market in southern China. Here, farmers harvest three crops a year – two of rice and one of vegetables.

SEE ALSO

Asia, Communism, Mongols, Paper

CHRISTIANITY

Christianity is a religion based on the teachings of Jesus Christ, who lived in Palestine about 2,000 years ago. Today, it is practised throughout the world.

The most well-known symbol of Christianity is the cross. It represents the cross on which Jesus was crucified.

Greek Christians used the fish as a code. The Greek word for fish spelled out the first letters of 'Jesus Christ, God's Son, Saviour'.

The Christian Bible consists of the Hebrew Bible (Old Testament) and Christ's life and teachings (New Testament).

More people follow the Christian religion than any other. About 2.2 billion people believe that there is only one God and that he sent his son, Jesus Christ, to Earth to proclaim his law and to save people from sin.

THE LIFE OF CHRIST

The life and teachings of Jesus Christ are contained in the New Testament of the Bible, the Christians' holy book. (The Old Testament of the Bible contains the sacred writings of the Jews.) Jesus is said to have performed miracles and healed the sick. The Roman rulers of Jerusalem crucified him by nailing him to a cross. Christians believe that three days later Jesus was resurrected, or came back to life, and that some 40 days later he rose into Heaven.

CHRISTIANITY SPREADS

Jesus' teachings were spread by his disciples, or followers, who formed the early church. Despite persecution, Christianity became the religion of the Roman Empire in 324CE and later spread across the world. Today, there are three main divisions in the Christian Church: Roman Catholic,

▲ Upon entering the Christian faith, followers are baptized with water. This symbolizes cleansing and reflects the way Jesus was baptized by John the Baptist.

Protestant and Eastern Orthodox. More than half of Christians are Catholics.

THREE-IN-ONE GOD

Christians believe God has three forms: the Father (God), the Son (Jesus) and the Holy Spirit (God's influence on Earth). Together they form the Holy Trinity.

THE HOLY MEAL

Before his Crucifixion, Jesus ate the Last Supper with his disciples. Christians re-enact this meal with bread and wine in a special church ceremony called Holy Communion, or Mass, when Christ 'becomes present' again. They celebrate Christ's birth at Christmas, his Resurrection at Easter and the coming of the Holy Spirit at Pentecost.

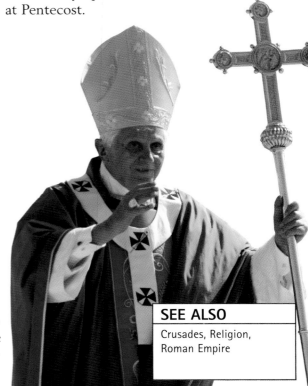

▲ On Palm Sunday (the Sunday before Easter) many Christians carry palms in church. This commemorates Jesus' entry into Jerusalem, when he was greeted with branches of palm.

▶ Pope Benedict XVI became the leader of the Roman Catholic Church in 2005. Before him, Pope John Paul II reigned for 26 years.

SEE ALSO

Crusades, Religion, Roman Empire

CITY

A city is a large community where thousands of people live and work. About half of the world's population lives in cities.

Most cities are commercial or administrative centres. They are usually larger and more important than other towns in their region. Not all cities are huge. In Europe, a city is a town with a cathedral. In the USA, the name 'city' is applied to an urban area with definite boundaries. The world's largest city is Tokyo in Japan, with more than 34 million people, including those living in suburbs.

CITY LOCATIONS

The earliest cities grew in areas where the climate was suitable for growing crops. Easy access was also important so that trade could develop. Venice in Italy, London in England and Kolkata (Calcutta) in India all grew because of their closeness to water, which provided transport routes.

PLANNING AHEAD

Most of today's cities were not planned; they spread out as they grew. But in 1692, William Penn, the founder of the US state of Pennsylvania, drew a plan for the city of Philadelphia that resembled a grid. This became the pattern for most US cities. In the mid-1800s, a French administrator called Baron Georges-Eugene Haussmann redesigned Paris with wide boulevards and open squares rather than the chaotic jumble of narrow streets that the city had been before.

CAPITAL CITIES

Every country has a capital city where the national government is located. A few capital cities have been built from new, including the 20th-century cities of Canberra in Australia, Brasília in Brazil and Islamabad in Pakistan. But more often, capitals have grown over time and have a mixture of old and new buildings alongside each other. The oldest parts of a city often form the centre. Many people live outside the city centre in areas known as suburbs.

HOW CITIES WORK

With city centres becoming busier and more densely packed, high-rise buildings make the most of limited space. People working in the city often move farther out, where land is cheaper. This means that good road and rail systems are necessary to bring them into the centre.

▲ Large, elegant department stores attract tourists and shoppers to cities.

▲ The opera and other forms of entertainment bring people to the city centre. They are often performed in grand and ornate buildings.

▲ Placing mass transit systems underground reduces traffic congestion and creates more space.

▲ A good road network and public transport are important to link the city centre with the suburbs.

SEE ALSO

Housing, Road, Skyscraper, Train, Transport

CIVIL RIGHTS

Civil rights are the laws and customs that entitle everyone to fair and equal treatment. They give people the freedom to speak and act within the law.

▲ Amnesty International works for the freeing of political prisoners and prisoners of conscience. It campaigns against torture and the death penalty.

▲ The flag of the United Nations, which was set up in 1946, after the end of World War II. The UN's aim is to maintain international peace and co-operation.

The idea of civil rights in the West dates back to the writings of Ancient Greek and Roman philosophers, and to the ideas of Judaism and Christianity. In some countries, civil rights are protected by a written constitution, as in the USA, and in others, such as the United Kingdom, they consist of laws and customs built up over hundreds of years.

FAIR AND EQUAL

Civil rights mean people must be treated fairly and equally, no matter what their sex, religion or ethnic origin. They are allowed freedom to express what they believe in speech or in the media. They also have the right to organize a political party, to have a fair trial if accused of a crime and to vote in elections.

THE FIGHT FOR THE RIGHT

Many rights have been won only after a long and painful struggle. During the 1950s and 1960s, Dr Martin Luther King led the civil rights campaign to win equality for

▲ A demonstration held in 1997 against the military government in Burma (Myanmar). The government had refused to recognize the results of multi-party elections.

black Americans. In South Africa, Nelson Mandela was imprisoned in 1962 for opposing apartheid (the separation of whites and non-whites). He was finally released in 1991, when apartheid was abolished. In 1994, Mandela was elected South Africa's first black president. He led the country until he retired, in 1999.

CIVIL RIGHTS ABUSES

International bodies, such as the United Nations and the European Court of Human Rights, protect civil rights; other organizations, like Amnesty International, campaign on behalf of people who are persecuted. However, some governments continue to ban civil rights. Dictators and single-party states deny rights to their people because they do not want their power threatened. Communist countries, such as China, traditionally stress the importance of social rights – for example, the right to work – often at the expense of human rights like freedom of speech.

'I HAVE A DREAM'

In 1963, Martin Luther King led 200,000 people on a civil rights march in Washington, DC. In his speech he declared, 'I have a dream', demanding equal rights for Black Americans. The Civil Rights Act of 1964 followed. King was awarded the Nobel Peace Prize. In 1968, he was shot dead.

SEE ALSO
Communism, Democracy, Fascism, South Africa

CIVIL WAR

Civil war is an armed struggle between people who live in the same country or nations. Civil war is usually triggered by political, religious or ethnic differences.

Families, communities and whole countries have been divided by civil war. Because fighting takes place wholly within a country, no one escapes its effects. Prisoners are often murdered, homes destroyed and civilians terrorized.

FIGHTING FOR RIGHTS
Civil wars erupt because of a difference in people's beliefs. They are often begun by minorities fighting for greater political or religious rights, for union with a similar group in a nearby state, or for the right to keep their way of life. These minorities are often headed by strong leaders.

OUTSIDE INFLUENCE
In some civil wars, outside countries give their support to one side, often for political gain or to protect human rights. During the 1980s, for example, a desperate civil war raged in Nicaragua between the socialist government and the right-wing Contras. The USA supported the Contras in order to combat the spread of left-wing socialist and communist regimes in Central America. Such foreign interference was typical of the Cold War, a period of rivalry and deep distrust between the Soviet Union, the USA and their supporters.

▲ An Angolan UNITA rebel soldier pictured in 1986. Angola suffered years of civil war, backed, until 1990, by countries such as Cuba, the Soviet Union, South Africa and the USA.

▲ A United Nations soldier helps an old woman cross the main street in Sarajevo, in the former Yugoslavia. An armoured vehicle shields them from sniper fire.

KEY DATES

1918—21 Russian Civil War. Fought after the Russian Revolution between Bolsheviks and anti-communists. Bolsheviks win

1967—70 Nigerian Civil War. Fought between Biafra and the Federal government. Biafra is defeated

1991—95 and **1998—99** In Yugoslavia, Slovenia, Croatia, Bosnia and Kosovo fight for independence

1998—2002/3 The Dem. Rep. of Congo, supported by troops from Angola, Namibia and Zimbabwe, fights rebels aided by Rwanda and Uganda

ETHNIC CLASHES
Civil wars started by ethnic (racial) hatred have produced some of the worst cruelties of recent times. In the early 1990s, fighting broke out in Yugoslavia, as three provinces – Bosnia, Croatia and Slovenia – fought for independence from the Serbian-dominated state. During the long-running war, thousands of civilians became the innocent victims of ethnic cleansing – the murder or forced eviction of one racial group by another through the use of violence and terror.

AFRICAN UNREST
When colonial rule ended in many African nations in the 1960s and 1970s, civil war followed. Within countries like Nigeria and Angola, different peoples had been forced together by colonial boundaries and these differences caused conflict. Some of the bloodiest civil wars caused by political and ethnic differences have broken out in Somalia, Congo and Chad.
▶

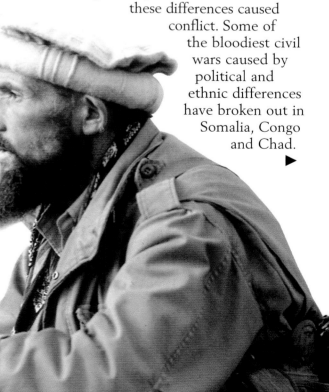

▶ A guerrilla fighter in Afghanistan. During the 1980s, Afghans fought to free their country from Soviet control. Guerrillas carried out surprise attacks on depots and patrols.

▼ Spanish army soldiers forcing Republicans to surrender at Sanosierra on August 6, 1936.

▲ Posters are often used to rally support. This poster declares 'Peasants, the land is yours.' It was designed by Republicans in the Spanish Civil War.

CHARLES I
English ruler (1600–49), came to the throne in 1625. He was executed during the English Civil War.

OLIVER CROMWELL
(1599–1658) ruled England, Scotland and Ireland as Lord Protector after the king's execution.

▶ The Roundheads' crushing defeat of Royalist forces at Naseby in 1645 was the decisive victory of the English Civil War.

ROMAN CIVIL WAR
Civil wars are not a new phenomenon. Many of the earliest civil wars were fought between influential individuals and their backers in the search for power. In 49BCE, civil war was started in Ancient Rome when Julius Caesar ordered his armies to cross the River Rubicon and march on Rome. He drove out his opponents and succeeded in making himself dictator.

ENGLISH CIVIL WAR
The English Civil War, which lasted from 1642 to 1649, was a struggle between the English king, Charles I, and parliament over who should govern the country. Charles believed that kings were appointed by God and should rule alone. Parliament believed it should have greater power. Parliament refused to co-operate with the king and this caused civil war.

ROYALISTS AND ROUNDHEADS
England divided into two factions: the Royalists, or Cavaliers, supported the king, and the Roundheads supported parliament. Two great generals, Lord Fairfax and Oliver Cromwell, led the Roundheads and, after initial royal victories, the king's forces were defeated. In 1649, Charles was executed and England was declared a republic.

THE SPANISH CIVIL WAR
In 1936, a left-wing Republican government was elected in Spain. Most of the right-wing army rebelled and tried to overthrow the government. The right, led by General Franco, received support from Germany and Italy. Thousands of Spaniards died in the war. In 1939, the Republican army collapsed and Franco became dictator of Spain.

Royalist

Roundheads

SEE ALSO
Africa, Civil War (American), Greece and the Balkans, Refugee, Spain, Warfare

CIVIL WAR, AMERICAN

More Americans died in the American Civil War than in any other US conflict. It was caused by the deep divisions between northern and southern states.

The Union flag (above) and the Confederate flag (left)

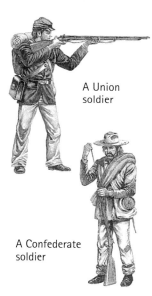

A Union soldier

A Confederate soldier

The American Civil War (1861-65) was caused by deep political differences. The southern states believed in the right of states, not Congress, to make their own laws, including the right to hold slaves. The South felt that this right was threatened by the election of Abraham Lincoln in 1860.

NORTH AND SOUTH
The North was a land of industry and manufacturing – and home to a strong movement against slavery. The South was a land of farms and plantations and depended on slaves for labour.

DECLARATION OF WAR
After Lincoln's election, 11 southern states seceded (separated) from the Union, to create the Confederate States of America. Southern forces attacked Fort Sumter (a US military post in South Carolina) on April 12, 1861. Lincoln, determined to keep the nation intact, formed the Union army against the slave-holding states.

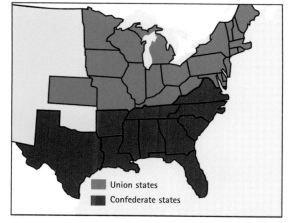

Union states
Confederate states

▲ The American Civil War was fought mainly in the east and southeast of the country, between the 11 Southern, or Confederate, states and the 23 Northern, or Union, states, including Oregon and California on the west coast.

FOUR YEARS OF FIGHTING
The American Civil War was a fight the South could not win. More people lived in the North, it had a stronger industrial base, better communications and a navy capable of stopping food and supplies reaching the South. In 1865, the South surrendered. More than 600,000 had died in the long and bloody struggle, and most southern cities had been destroyed by the war. That same year, the 13th Amendment was added to the Constitution, abolishing slavery. Five days after the South's surrender, Lincoln was assassinated.

THE BATTLE OF GETTYSBURG

The Battle of Gettysburg in July 1863 was a major turning point in the American Civil War. About 85,000 Union troops, led by General George Meade, defeated some 75,000 Confederate soldiers led by General Robert E. Lee. The Confederates never truly recovered from the crushing defeat.

SEE ALSO

Slavery, USA, Warfare

CLIMATE

The climate of a region is its weather pattern over a long period of time. The weather may change from day to day, but the climate stays the same.

▼ The world can be divided into different climate zones. These vary from tropical regions, characterized by hot and humid weather, to freezing polar areas.

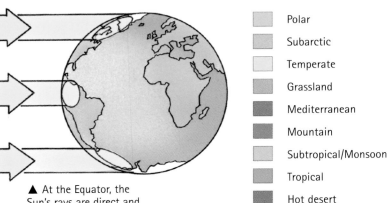

▲ At the Equator, the Sun's rays are direct and strong. Away from the Equator, the Sun's rays are weaker because they strike the Earth at an angle and must travel farther through the cool air of the atmosphere.

- Polar
- Subarctic
- Temperate
- Grassland
- Mediterranean
- Mountain
- Subtropical/Monsoon
- Tropical
- Hot desert

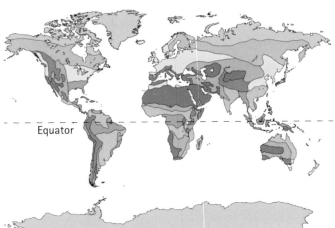

Equator

The climate of a region depends on how close the region is to the sea, how high up it is (its altitude) and, most importantly, how far it is from the Equator (its latitude). Climate is usually measured as a combination of the average rainfall in an area and the temperature.

THE POWER OF THE SUN
The two extremes of climate on Earth are found at the Equator and at the Poles. The climate is hottest in the zones each side of the Equator, known as the tropics, because the Sun is almost directly overhead. The Poles are the coldest areas on Earth: temperatures drop below –50°C.

THE TROPICS
The tropics are not only the hottest areas but also the wettest. The Sun is so hot here that it evaporates water from the rivers and oceans, forming rain clouds that drench the region. Some of the world's largest deserts, such as the Sahara in Africa, lie either side of the tropics because the air moving out from the tropics has lost most of its moisture by the time it reaches them.

COLDER HIGHER UP
Mountainous regions have a colder climate than nearby low areas. This is because air is cooler the higher up you go in the atmosphere. On a mountain, air cools by 6°C for each 1,000m climbed.

CHANGING CLIMATE
Climates can change over time. Volcanic eruptions may have a sudden, local effect, but deforestation and destruction of the ozone layer by pollutant gases may have long-term effects all over the world.

WIND CIRCULATION
At the Poles, cold air sinks and disperses and is replaced by warmer air flowing in from above. The cold air moving away from the Poles meets warm winds from the subtropics and pushes the warm air back to the Equator.

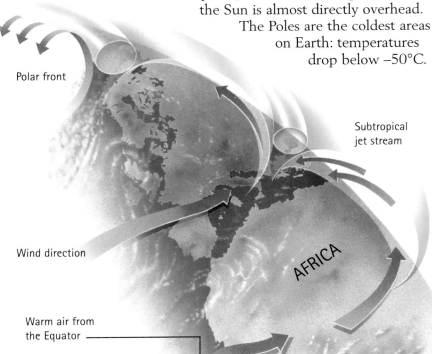

Polar front

Subtropical jet stream

Wind direction

AFRICA

Warm air from the Equator

SEE ALSO
Desert, Forest, Habitat, Mountain and valley Pollution, Water, Weather

CLOCK

Clocks are instruments used to measure time in hours, minutes and seconds down to the smallest fraction. They include mechanical, quartz and atomic clocks.

Chinese candle clocks 'chime' when the candle burns the string to release a weight onto the cymbal.

Sundials show the time by plotting the changing position of the Sun's shadow during the day.

Chronometers, invented in the 1700s for use on ships, have a slowly unwinding spring, not a pendulum.

A quartz watch tells the time by recording the vibrations of a quartz crystal inside.

Atomic clocks count the vibrations of light given off by atoms, and are used in satellites and aircraft.

People first learned to tell the time using sundials, sandglasses, marked candles and water clocks. But during the 13th century, the first mechanical clocks were made.

MECHANICAL CLOCKS
Mechanical clocks are set in motion in one of two ways – by winding up a spring or by raising a weight. Gear wheels with teeth, or cogs, move the hour, minute and second hands – this is called the clock's movement. Some clocks need to be wound every day, but others can run for about a week.

THE PENDULUM
In 1582, the Italian scientist Galileo Galilei discovered that every swing of a pendulum, or hanging weight, takes the same length of time. The time the swing takes depends on the length of the pendulum arm. A Dutch astronomer called Christiaan Huygens used this knowledge to make the first pendulum clock 74 years later. In a pendulum clock, the swinging weight moves from side to side to regulate the movements of the clock's hands around the clock face.

QUARTZ CRYSTAL
Most of today's clocks and watches are battery operated and have a tiny quartz crystal inside. The crystal vibrates when it receives a charge of electricity from the battery. It gives out regular, fast pulses of current, which are slowed down by a microchip to one per second.

ATOMIC CLOCKS
The most accurate clocks are caesium-beam atomic clocks, which were first made in 1955. These measure the frequency of an atom's vibrations. They lose only a fraction of a second every million years.

TURNING TIME
When a grandfather clock is wound up, a weight is pulled up to the top of its case. As the weight falls, tiny toothed gearwheels turn and move the hands around the clock face. The swing of the pendulum makes the weight fall evenly as the cogs catch against the pallet at every swing, turning one notch of the escape wheel. This makes the 'tick-tock' sound.

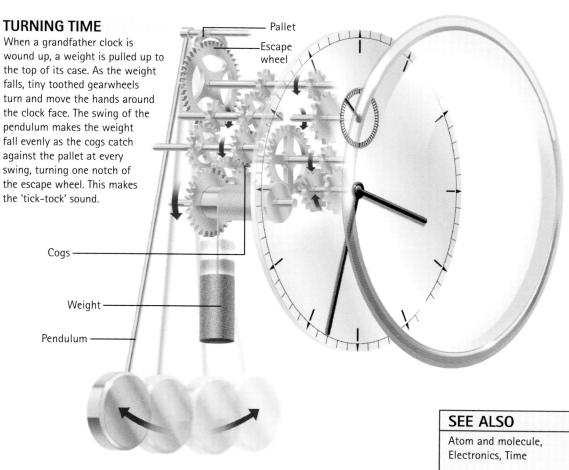

Pallet

Escape wheel

Cogs

Weight

Pendulum

SEE ALSO

Atom and molecule, Electronics, Time

CLOTHING

Clothing is worn to protect the body and to make it look attractive. The kind of clothes people wear reflects where they live, their lifestyle and their personality.

People started wearing clothes more than 100,000 years ago in colder parts of the world. Ice Age hunters 25,000 years ago stayed warm by sewing together animal furs. About 10,000 years ago, early farming communities learned how to spin plant and animal fibres to make thread that could be woven into cloth. Wool, cotton, silk and flax for linen were used. Woollen cloth was used in cold northern areas, while linen was preferred in hot countries such as Egypt.

THE FIRST TROUSERS

Among the first people to cut clothes into the kinds of shapes used today were the ancient tribes of Persia (Iran). Men wore coats with sleeves and an early form of trousers designed for life on horseback.

READY TO WEAR

In 1785, the steam-powered loom marked the birth of the modern clothing industry; and in the 1850s, sewing machines

▲ Fire-fighters' protective suits were developed from space suit technology. The suits have many layers, which were originally intended to protect astronauts from the Sun's lethal radiation while they worked in space.

arrived. Clothing factories soon started making large amounts of inexpensive, ready-to-wear clothes so that people could afford to buy garments instead of making their own or having expensive designs made up by dress-makers and tailors.

CHANGING SHAPES

Advances in technology have continued to shape fashion in the 20th and 21st centuries. Synthetic nylon was first used to make stockings in the 1940s, polyester appeared in the 1960s, Lycra in the 1980s and smart fabrics in the 2000s.

▲ In the 1960s, designers responded to a new teenage market and the mini-skirt arrived. Twiggy, shown here, was a British fashion model who became the symbol of the new look.

▲ Simple lengths of linen draped in loose styles kept both women and men cool in Ancient Egypt. Children often went naked.

▲ Richly embroidered fabrics were used to make clothes for wealthy people in the 1400s. Men's shoes had long, pointed toes.

▲ Knee breeches in pale colours were worn by gentlemen in the 1700s. Trousers did not become fashionable until the 1800s.

▲ In the mid-1800s, ladies wore tight corsets and hoops made of wicker or steel, called crinolines, to make their skirts stick out.

FASHION VICTIMS

Wearing the latest styles to be fashionable began as a way for rich people to show their wealth. But sometimes, staying in fashion was painful. During the 1800s, women in search of the 'hour-glass' figure wore laced corsets with whalebone inside. This compressed the waist, making it as tiny as possible. People still follow design trends, but since World War II, when many women started working in factories, clothes have become more practical.

WORKWEAR TO CLASSICS

Trends do not always come from designers. Tough denim jeans, originally made as workwear for Californian gold miners in the 1850s, have become fashion classics. Many people today choose clothes to express their personality.

NATIONAL DRESS

In many parts of the world, traditional dress is worn every day. The *sari*, worn by Hindu women, is a long wrap of light fabric worn over a tight-fitting top called a *choli*. In some countries, national dress is kept for festivals and family celebrations.

MIX AND MATCH

National dress has had a strong influence on Western fashion. American cowboys learned to make leather trousers (chaps) by watching Native Americans stretch and soak buffalo hides. Today, designers continue to borrow from different eras and cultures in a constant search for new ideas.

▲ This wet suit is made of neoprene (a synthetic rubber). It gives the diver protection and warmth under water. Clothes like these allow people to explore previously inaccessible places.

▲ Designer creations are shown on the catwalk, then toned down and reproduced for a ready-to-wear market.

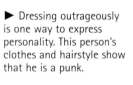

◄ Clothes for sports must be light, protective and easy to move in. Sports clothes often promote a sense of team spirit and are popular as everyday wear for both men and women.

▶ Dressing outrageously is one way to express personality. This person's clothes and hairstyle show that he is a punk.

▲ In the 1800s, young boys and girls from wealthy families dressed alike. Both wore dresses over ankle-length pantaloons.

KEY DATES

1300s Clothes for wealthy people are tailored to fit

1500s Whalebone is first used to stiffen corsets

1850s Tightly laced corsets and crinolines are used to create the 'hour-glass' figure

1870s The bustle is used to create the 'S'-bend shape

1920s Coco Chanel revolutionizes women's fashion by creating short, simple shift dresses

1947 Christian Dior's 'New Look' with very full skirts ends the austerity of the war years

1960s André Courréges (France) introduces the mini-skirt, which is popularized in the UK by Mary Quant

1980s Lycra is used to create body-hugging designs

SEE ALSO

Design, France, Material, Paint and dye, Textile

COAL

Coal is a rock formed under the ground from the remains of decayed prehistoric plants. It burns easily and is widely used as a fuel.

Anthracite is the highest quality coal. It gives the most heat but little smoke.

Most coal mined today is used in power stations to produce light and heat.

Some perfumes are made from coal tar – a black liquid produced from coal.

Coal, like petroleum and gas, is a fossil fuel. It was formed under the ground from the remains of rotting plants over millions of years. It is used to make fires and to make electricity, chemicals and steel.

CARBON CONTENT
Coal is made up of carbon, tar, oils and minerals. There are three different types of coal, depending on the amount of carbon each contains. Lignite, or brown coal, contains less than 50 per cent carbon, bituminous coal around 70 per cent, and anthracite, the most valuable, has about 95 per cent carbon. Over 3.4 billion tonnes of coal are mined each year and 826 billion tonnes remain underground.

INDUSTRIAL COAL
In about 1750, the Industrial Revolution led to a huge demand for coal as a fuel for steam engines. Today, many power stations burn coal to produce electricity. The iron industry uses coke – coal which has been heated to make the tar and oils evaporate – to produce iron and steel. The tar and oils are then used to produce dyes, fertilizers and fibres such as nylon.

POLLUTION
When coal is burned, it releases smoke containing soot and poisonous gases, such as carbon monoxide. These can harm the environment, so power stations usually have filters to clean the smoke.

▲ A great deal of mechanized equipment is used to mine coal. Cutting machines dig out coal at the coal face while a conveyor belt transports it back up the shaft.

HOW COAL IS FORMED
About 300 million years ago, in an age known as the Carboniferous period, the climate was warm and wet, ideal for swampy forests. Dead plants rotted and formed peat, which was buried under layers of sand and mud as sea levels rose, flooding the swamps. These layers slowly turned to rock. Their weight squeezed the peat, turning it into coal.

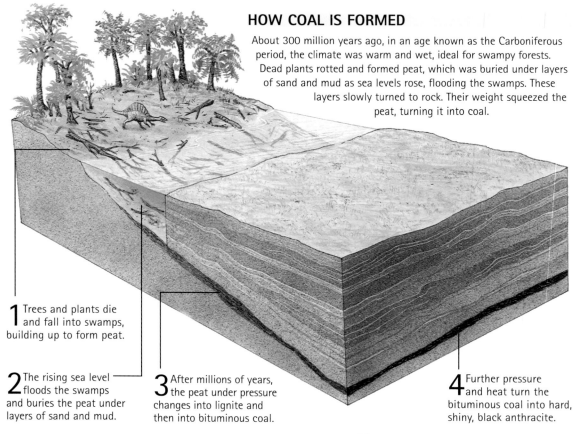

1 Trees and plants die and fall into swamps, building up to form peat.

2 The rising sea level floods the swamps and buries the peat under layers of sand and mud.

3 After millions of years, the peat under pressure changes into lignite and then into bituminous coal.

4 Further pressure and heat turn the bituminous coal into hard, shiny, black anthracite.

▲ A shaft is dug down to a seam several hundred metres down. A few mines are open-cast – coal is mined at the surface.

SEE ALSO
Electricity, Fossil, Gas, Industrial Revolution, Iron and steel, Mining, Oil, Pollution

COLD WAR

The Cold War was a period of hostility between the capitalist and communist countries of the world. It began after the end of World War II.

▲ The USSR's Nikita Khrushchev (left) and US President John F. Kennedy, fingers poised over their nuclear buttons, confront each other in this 1962 cartoon.

FAST FACTS

• In 1955, a Soviet-led alliance of Eastern European states, the Warsaw Pact, was set up to oppose NATO

• In 1945, there were only three nuclear weapons in the world; by 1962, there were over 2,000

• In 1956, an anti-Soviet uprising in Hungary was brutally crushed

▼ US soldiers in a burning village during the Vietnam War. The USA backed South Vietnam in its fight against Viet Cong guerrillas and Soviet-backed North Vietnam.

For more than 45 years, between 1945 and 1991, two superpowers, the USA and the Soviet Union (USSR), fought each other using spies, alliances, trading bans and local wars as their weapons.

IRON CURTAIN
After World War II, the USSR and the USA distrusted each other. As communist governments took control of Eastern Europe, the Western nations reacted by forming a military alliance called the North Atlantic Treaty Organization (NATO). The frontier between West and East became known as the Iron Curtain.

CONFRONTATION
The Cold War was marked by a series of crises. The first was the Berlin Airlift in 1948, when the West flew in supplies to a Soviet-blockaded Berlin, the former capital of Germany. The superpowers began

stockpiling nuclear weapons. They took opposing sides in other conflicts, such as the Korean War (1950–53) and Vietnam War (1954–75). In 1962, people feared that nuclear war would break out when the USA demanded that the USSR withdraw nuclear missiles from Cuba. Eventually, the Soviets backed down and the crisis ended.

THE COLD WAR THAWS
After 1970, tension between the superpowers began to ease. The Cold War finally ended in 1991 with the fall of communism in many European countries, and the break-up of the USSR, as states such as Lithuania, Kazakhstan, Belarus and Georgia gained independence.

THE BERLIN AIRLIFT

After World War II, Germany was divided up. The UK, France and USA controlled the West and the USSR controlled the East. The capital, Berlin, was also divided. In 1948, the West, including West Berlin, was united into one country, West Germany, with one currency, the German mark. In protest, the USSR cut off West Berlin's road, rail and water links with the West. For 11 months US and British flew food, fuel and other vital supplies into the city until the Soviets lifted their blockade.

SEE ALSO
Civil war, Communism, Democracy, Germany, Russia and the Baltic States, USA, World War II

COLOUR

Colour is what we see when light from an object reaches our eyes. White light seems colourless, but it is actually made up of a mixture of colours.

When you see a rainbow, you are seeing sunlight split apart by raindrops. The rainbow has seven colours – red, orange, yellow, green, blue, indigo and violet. This range is called the spectrum.

The primary colours of light are red, blue and green. Mixed together they make up white light.

The primary colours of paint are yellow, blue and red. Mixed together they produce black.

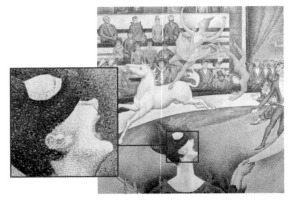

▲ Georges Seurat's *The Circus* (1891) is painted using a technique called pointillism. Pure colour is applied as dots, which merge at a distance to create the subtler shades.

REFLECTING LIGHT
An object only appears to be a particular colour because of the light it reflects. For example, a leaf looks green because it reflects green light and absorbs all the other colours in the spectrum.

PRIMARY COLOURS
In the 19th century, scientists were amazed to discover that almost any colour of light can be created by combining different amounts of a basic set of three colours – red, blue and green. These are known as the primary colours of light.

MIXING IT UP
If equal amounts of red, blue and green light are mixed together, they make white light. Mixing just red and green light together makes yellow; blue and green makes cyan (a green-blue); and blue and red makes magenta. In photography, printing, film and television, light is mixed to produce millions of different colours.

PAINTING A DIFFERENT PICTURE
Pigments (used in paints) have a different set of primary colours. The primary colours are yellow, blue and red, and when they are mixed together they make black.

SEEING IN COLOUR
We see colour when light falls on the retina at the back of the eye. The retina is full of cells, called cones and rods, that are sensitive to light. Cones are sensitive to particular colours, and rods, which are not colour-sensitive, help us to see in dim light.

REFLECTION AND ABSORPTION

When light hits an object, the object absorbs (soaks up) some of the colours of the spectrum and reflects (throws off) others. A tomato, for example, looks red because it reflects red light back into our eyes, but absorbs the other colours of the rainbow: orange, yellow, green, blue, indigo and violet light.

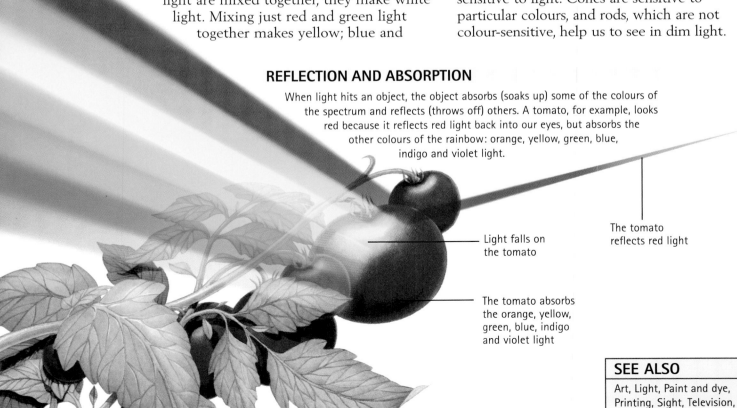

Light falls on the tomato

The tomato reflects red light

The tomato absorbs the orange, yellow, green, blue, indigo and violet light

SEE ALSO

Art, Light, Paint and dye, Printing, Sight, Television, Wavelength

COMET, METEOR AND ASTEROID

Comets, meteors and asteroids are chunks of ice, rock or metal that circle the Sun. As they travel closer to the Earth, some can be seen lighting up the night sky.

Shooting stars are meteors burning up as they enter Earth's atmosphere.

The 19km-long asteroid Gaspra was photographed by the *Galileo* space probe.

Arizona's Barringer Crater was made by a meteorite over 20,000 years ago.

The space between the planets is littered with debris left over from when the solar system formed. Balls of ice and rock with tails are called comets, small particles that blaze through Earth's atmosphere are meteors, and larger chunks of rock and metal are asteroids.

ICE-COLD COMETS
A comet has a fuzzy head and one or more tails. Its head is a lump of ice, dust and rock measuring from 10km to 30km across. Surrounding it is a cloud of gas and dust called a coma. The Sun's heat and the solar wind (a stream of particles given off by the Sun) drive dust and gas out from the coma to form the comet's tails.

SHOOTING STARS AND SHOWERS
Many meteors have been around since our solar system formed, but others are chips off comets and asteroids, or even the Moon and Mars. These can be as small as grains of sand and most

burn up as they hurtle into the Earth's atmosphere, travelling at speeds of up to 40km/second. These are called shooting stars. Some travel in swarms and create a meteor shower in the night sky. Such showers can appear at the same time each year, when Earth crosses the swarm's path. Every year, a few meteors hit the Earth's surface and are called meteorites.

THE ASTEROID BELT
Asteroids (sometimes called minor planets) are chunks of rock and metal smaller than planets that circle the Sun. There are billions of asteroids in the solar system, and more than 90 per cent of them are in the asteroid belt between Mars and Jupiter.

A COMET IN FLIGHT

Comets are surrounded by clouds of dust, called comas, which can be up to a million kilometres across. Comets travel in long loops around the Sun. Each time they approach the Sun, more gas and dust evaporate from their centres, making the comas grow larger and the comets form tails. Comets' tails always point away from the Sun.

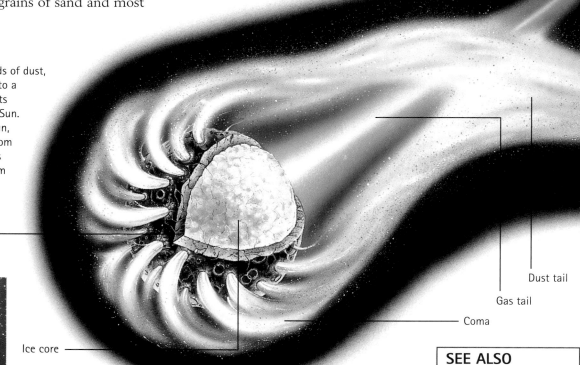

Rocky crust

Ice core

Dust tail

Gas tail

Coma

▲ Halley's Comet is visible from Earth every 76 years. It was closely studied on its last return in 1986.

SEE ALSO

Astronomy, Moon, Planet, Solar system, Spacecraft, Space exploration, Sun, Universe

COMMUNICATION

Communication is the process of sending and receiving messages. This can be done by using spoken and written language or recognized signs and signals.

◀ Sign language for the deaf uses hand signals and is based on ideas, not words.

People usually communicate with each other individually or in small groups. However, they sometimes need to relay messages to a much larger audience. This is known as mass communication.

SIGNS AND SIGNALS

Humans have developed ingenious ways of conveying messages to each other, using signs and signals when language cannot be used. Some Native Americans sent smoke signals and African tribes-people used drumbeats. Signals are still in use today – navies send messages using flags (known as semaphore) and road users rely on roadside signs and traffic lights.

POSTAL COMMUNICATIONS

One of the earliest, cheapest and most reliable forms of communication is the postal service. The first stamps were used in Britain in 1840. Most letters today are sorted by machine, and then transported by road, rail or air to their destination.

TELEGRAPH MESSAGES

For a long time, the fastest way to communicate over long distances was to deliver messages on foot, on horseback or by boat. Then in 1840, the American inventor Samuel Morse introduced the first simple telegraph, which used electricity to send messages down wire cables. The messages were coded using a system of dots and dashes. This became known as Morse code.

FASTER THAN EVER

Since the 1800s, many inventions, such as the telephone, radio and television, have made communication across the world faster and easier. Today, a message can be sent to the other side of the world in seconds by using satellite and computer links. The Internet enables all types of computers to communicate and share services. Video conference centres allow people thousands of kilometres apart to see and talk to each other directly.

The Sumerians developed the first known writing system in about 3500BCE.

From the 1400s, printing became a means of mass communication in Europe.

The telephone, invented in 1876, allowed long-distance communication.

A satellite dish receives images and sounds sent from around the world.

THE PONY EXPRESS

In 1860, the Pony Express was the fastest delivery system in the USA, delivering letters along a 3,164km trail in less than ten days, where previously it had taken over three weeks by boat or stagecoach. The riders rode in all weather, changing to fresh horses at each pony express station – spaced 16-20km apart. The service was closed in October 1861, once the telegraph and Morse code came into use.

SEE ALSO

Computer, Internet, Language, Media, Printing, Radio, Satellite, Technology, Telecommunication, Telephone, Television

COMMUNISM

Communism is a political theory based on the idea that everybody should share all wealth, property and industry equally.

The German journalist Karl Marx developed the idea of communism in the 1800s.

Mao Zedong led the Communists to victory in China in the 1940s.

Guerilla warfare brought Fidel Castro to power. He led Cuba from 1959 to 2008.

Ho Chi Minh led North Vietnam for most of the Vietnam War.

▶ Vladimir Lenin, leader of the Bolshevik Party, led a revolution that overthrew tsarist rule in Russia. He set up the world's first communist regime in 1917.

In 1848, Karl Marx and Friedrich Engels published the *Communist Manifesto*, which stated that private ownership should be replaced by common ownership. Marx wanted to see an end to the way of life in which most people worked for a low wage while a few wealthy people owned the factories and land. He believed that the only way to achieve this was by revolution.

THE FIRST REVOLUTION

The first successful communist revolution took place in Russia in 1917, after which the Union of Soviet Socialist Republics (USSR) was set up under the leadership of Vladimir Lenin. The state took control of farms, factories and railways in the name of the people. Lenin and his successor, Joseph Stalin, ruled as dictators. Most people were better fed and housed, but personal freedoms were severely restricted.

SPREAD OF COMMUNISM

After World War II, communism spread to Eastern Europe, China and countries in Africa, Asia and Central America. During the Cold War, there was hostile rivalry between the communist countries and the US-led Western democracies.

◀ Since North Korea became communist in 1948, many statues to heroic workers have been erected.

THE COLLAPSE

From 1989 to 1992, communism in countries such as Poland, Hungary and East Germany collapsed. With the break-up of the USSR in the 1990s, China remains the only major nation with a communist government.

KEY DATES

1848 Journalist Karl Marx and philosopher Friedrich Engels publish the *Communist Manifesto*

1917 Lenin leads Russia's Bolshevik Revolution

1949 China becomes a communist state under Mao Zedong

1989 Communism collapses in Eastern Europe

1991 The break-up of the USSR leaves only China, Cuba, Vietnam and N. Korea as communist states

SEE ALSO

China, Cold War, Democracy, Eastern Europe, Fascism, Revolution, Russia and the Baltic States

COMPUTER

Computers are machines that handle information according to sets of instructions. They then give the results in a form that people can understand.

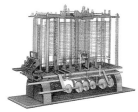

In 1834, Charles Babbage (1792-1871) designed the first mechanical computer, but he never saw it built.

In the 1960s, computers used transistors and stored data on tape. They could fill a whole room.

The 1981 Sinclair ZX81 was one of the first home computers to be launched on the world market.

Portable laptop computers, small enough to fit inside a briefcase have been available since the 1980s.

Smartphones have powerful operating systems. They run small programs called apps.

The computer is an electronic device that can do calculations millions of times faster than the human brain. First, the computer receives data, or information, put in by the user, then it processes the data as simple electrical signals according to its program, and produces a result.

BINARY NUMBERS
All computers use a language called the binary system. Binary numbers are entirely made up of the digits 0 and 1. When a letter is typed on the keyboard or when the mouse or joystick is moved, tiny electric currents are sent to the computer. These currents are stored by the computer as binary numbers.

MINIATURIZATION
The first computers took up a whole room, but by the 1960s, electronic components had become much smaller and computers began to shrink in size. The home computer became possible through the invention of the microchip, which contains tens of thousands of electronic components within a space no larger than a fingernail.

HIGHLY VERSATILE
A PC (personal computer) can tackle jobs from word-processing to 3-D design and animation. Music can be recorded, edited and played back on the PC. Desktop publishing means books and magazines can be designed on the PC.

HOW IT WORKS
Data (information) in a PC is usually stored in random-access memory (RAM). The central processing unit (CPU) calls it up when it is needed, according to a list of instructions (the program), which is also stored in memory. Data flows to and from the CPU along an electronic pathway called the bus. After processing, data is stored in RAM again.

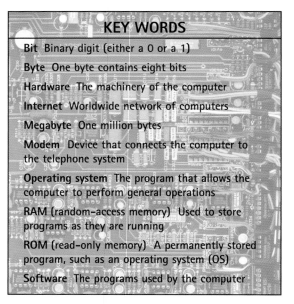

KEY WORDS
Bit Binary digit (either a 0 or a 1)

Byte One byte contains eight bits

Hardware The machinery of the computer

Internet Worldwide network of computers

Megabyte One million bytes

Modem Device that connects the computer to the telephone system

Operating system The program that allows the computer to perform general operations

RAM (random-access memory) Used to store programs as they are running

ROM (read-only memory) A permanently stored program, such as an operating system (OS)

Software The programs used by the computer

SCIENCE FRONTIERS
Computers have revolutionized science and technology. Space probes, satellite TV and weapon detection systems all rely on computers. Computers make it possible to test chemical and nuclear reactions without real-life experiments.

AUTOMATION
In the car industry, computers are used to design a vehicle and then build it with the aid of robots. Inside the car itself, a computer can check the engine, the brakes and the steering. Computers can even be used in the home to control temperature, lighting and security.

GLOBAL LINKS
Computers are increasingly changing the way we live by connecting people and places all over the world. The Internet links up computers all over the world, allowing messages and information to be sent across the globe in a matter of seconds.

BILL GATES (born 1955) In 1975, American Bill Gates founded Microsoft, now the largest software company in the world.

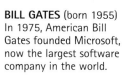

HOW THE COMPUTER WORKS

A computer system has four basic parts. An input device such as the keyboard, mouse or dual controller enters information into the computer. Then the central processing unit (CPU) performs the tasks. The information is sent to an output device, such as the screen or printer, to display the results. And finally a memory unit stores programs and data.

A plasma screen is a light and quiet computer screen which provides sharp, vivid, high-quality images

The CD-ROM drive uses compact discs to read and store data

The CPU is the brains of the computer

Speakers are used to output sound from the computer

The keys on the keyboard act as switches, sending tiny electric currents to the computer when pressed

The hard disk inside the CPU is made up of magnetic layers that store information when the computer is turned off

A mouse is used to point to different areas of the screen

COMPUTER ADD-ONS

Game Pad
A game pad is a powerful, dual-control input device used to play computer games.

Digital Camera
Photographs can be viewed on the screen of the camera and then imported to a computer for storage.

MP3 Player
This is a digital music player which can store and play songs downloaded from the computer.

SEE ALSO

Electronics, Internet, Robot, Satellite, Space exploration, Technology, Telecommunication

CONSERVATION

Conservation is the protection and careful use of the Earth's natural resources, such as animals, plants and fossil fuels. It also includes care of historical treasures.

◀ The care and preservation of paintings is a painstaking process. An art conservator must understand a painting's history and content in the same way that an animal conservationist must know the habits of an endangered animal.

Conservationists try to find a balance between the needs of human beings and care of the environment. There are around seven billion people alive today and they all need land to live on, food to eat and fuel for power. Without care, habitats can be destroyed, resources used up and the Earth damaged.

▲ Recycling plastics, paper, tin and glass conserves the Earth's resources. In many US states, laws have been passed by which households can be fined for failing to separate rubbish for recycling.

GLOBAL AWARENESS
Some conservation issues are local, as when an ancient oak tree is threatened with felling to make way for a new road. Others, such as recycling, saving energy and stopping animals from becoming extinct, are shared worldwide. In 1992, world leaders got together at the Earth Summit in Brazil to draw up the very first global action plan to save the planet. One scheme that was introduced to encourage

people to stop destroying their habitats – by logging trees or draining marshes – is the 'debt-for-nature' idea. This means that a poor country has some of its international debt cancelled in exchange for setting aside areas for conservation.

FACING EXTINCTION
Around 150 rare plant and animal species become extinct each day – far more than when the dinosaurs died out, 65 million years ago. The tiger, rhinoceros, Asian snow leopard and even some species of insect are all in danger of disappearing forever. The last 700 to 800 mountain gorillas live on the borders of Rwanda, Uganda and the Democratic Republic of Congo, in Africa. Their rainforest home has been destroyed by farmers and timber firms, and they are also killed for food.

NATURE RESERVES
One of the best ways of protecting wildlife is to preserve an entire habitat in a national park. Zoos also help by breeding rare animals, such as the giant panda.

SAVING THE HELPLESS GIANT

Many species of large whale, such as the humpback whale (below), are threatened with extinction because they have been over-hunted for their blubber, meat, oil and bones. A global conservation body known as the International Whaling Commission (IWC) outlawed the killing of such rare whales in 1985, but not all countries have agreed to stop hunting.

SEE ALSO

Animal, Asia, Dinosaur, Ecology, Energy, Habitat, Pollution, Rainforest, Whale and dolphin, Zoology

CONSTELLATION

Constellations are groups of stars that form recognizable patterns in the night sky. Astronomers have named a total of 88 constellations.

▲ The Northern and Southern Hemispheres are domes of sky seen above and below the Equator.

Thousands of years ago, people in Asia, Europe and the Middle East realized that the stars formed patterns in the sky, and named them after characters and creatures in their lives and legends. By 300CE, the Greek astronomer Ptolemy had named 48 constellations. Many of the names he gave them are still in use, including Taurus (the Bull), Ursa Major (the Great Bear) and Andromeda (a mythical Ancient Greek heroine). Today, astronomers use the position of the constellations to map the stars.

THE ZODIAC
If we could see the stars during the day, the Sun would pass in front of 13 constellations over the course of the year. The ancient astronomers counted only 12 constellations and called them the signs of the zodiac – claiming that babies born under each sign would have certain traits.

NEAR AND FAR
Stars in a constellation seem close to each other, but are usually far apart. Orion contains the stars Betelgeuse (300 light years away from Earth), Rigel (900 light years away) and Mintaka (2,300 light years away). One light year equals 9.46 million million kilometres.

MAPS OF THE STARS

Two maps of the constellations are needed because people who live north of the Equator (in the Northern Hemisphere) see different stars from those who live south of the Equator (in the Southern Hemisphere). The constellations in the centre of both maps can usually be seen all year round, while those near the edge can be seen only during particular seasons or at certain times of the night.

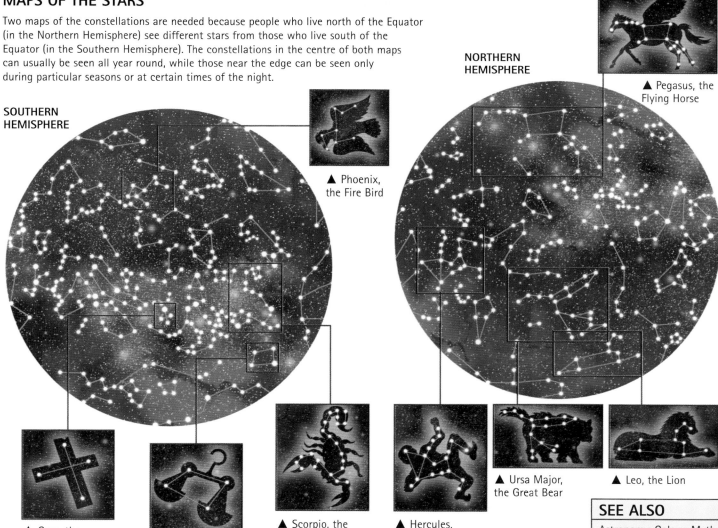

SOUTHERN HEMISPHERE

NORTHERN HEMISPHERE

▲ Pegasus, the Flying Horse

▲ Phoenix, the Fire Bird

▲ Crux, the Southern Cross

▲ Libra, the Scales

▲ Scorpio, the Scorpion

▲ Hercules, the Giant

▲ Ursa Major, the Great Bear

▲ Leo, the Lion

SEE ALSO
Astronomy, Galaxy, Myth and legend, Solar system, Star

CONSTRUCTION

Construction is the process of putting something together. It includes erecting houses, skyscrapers, bridges, dams and roads, as well as building ships.

Bricks are still the most popular construction material in house building.

Carpentry is used to make the main frame, doors and windows in many houses.

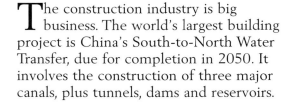

The frames of tall buildings and ships used to be fixed with hot nails, or rivets.

The construction industry is big business. The world's largest building project is China's South-to-North Water Transfer, due for completion in 2050. It involves the construction of three major canals, plus tunnels, dams and reservoirs.

TRADITIONAL TECHNIQUES
In the past, most construction was domestic – each family built a house, pens for animals and dams to irrigate their crops. The materials were usually natural and found locally, and included wood, clay, stone, bone, skin or grass. Work was done by hand.

THE DAWN OF CIVILIZATION
As more complex civilizations developed, so did building skills. The first bricks were made in Palestine in 6000BCE, and the construction of the pyramids in Egypt required thousands of workers, as well as skilled mathematicians. Ancient cranes were used on Roman building sites.

▲ Hong Kong Harbour Bridge under construction in 1996. The last road section is being lifted from a barge below.

MODERN CONSTRUCTION
The size and height of constructions used to be limited by the skill of the stonemason or carpenter. But from the late 1800s, new techniques using steel frames and moulded concrete allowed skyscrapers to be built.

A BUILDING GOES UP
There are two main stages in constructing a building. First, the foundations must be laid below ground to support the structure. Tough materials are used, such as concrete (poured in trenches) or steel columns (driven into the ground). The second stage is the construction of the building above ground. Either the walls or a steel frame are constructed first to support floors and other features. Finally, the roof is added.

STEEL-FRAMED CONSTRUCTION
Modern high-rise buildings usually have a steel frame onto which floors and wall panels are bolted. The frame supports the weight of the building so walls can be thin with large windows.

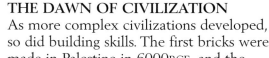

▲ H-shaped, reinforced steel joists are bolted together to form the building's frame.

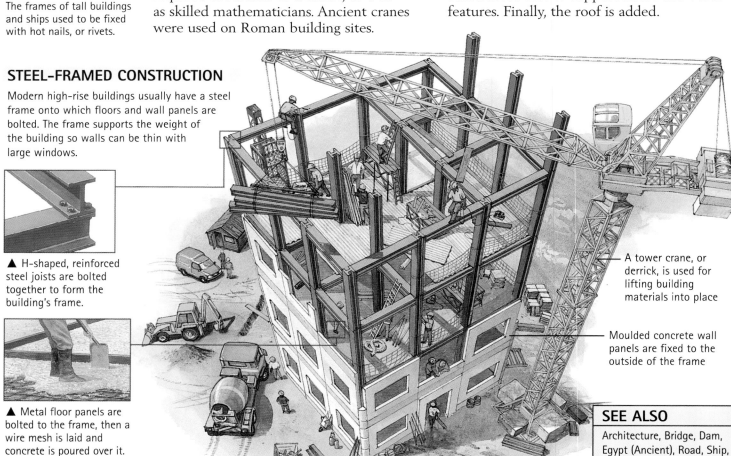

▲ Metal floor panels are bolted to the frame, then a wire mesh is laid and concrete is poured over it.

A tower crane, or derrick, is used for lifting building materials into place

Moulded concrete wall panels are fixed to the outside of the frame

SEE ALSO
Architecture, Bridge, Dam, Egypt (Ancient), Road, Ship, Skyscraper, Tunnel

CONTINENT

Continents are large stretches of land unbroken by sea. There are seven continents on Earth.

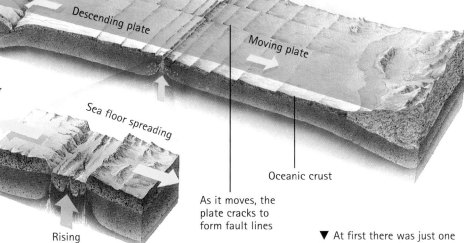

HOW CONTINENTS DRIFT

All the land on Earth is fixed to giant plates which float on a sea of magma (melted rock). As the magma moves slowly, so do the continents, but some towards each other and others apart. Where two giant plates rub together, a crack sometimes appears in the Earth's surface, allowing magma to escape. Two such cracks, known as mid-ocean ridges, run through the Atlantic and Indian oceans.

Plate edge — — — Fault line ————

▲ The continents are attached to tectonic plates, the pieces which form the Earth's surface.

Continental crust

Volcano

Trench

Mid-ocean ridge

Descending plate

Moving plate

Sea floor spreading

Rising magma

As it moves, the plate cracks to form fault lines

Oceanic crust

The Earth's crust is like a giant jigsaw puzzle made up of eight large pieces and several small pieces, called tectonic plates. On top of these plates sit seven land masses, or continents: Africa, Antarctica, Asia, Australia, Europe, North America and South America. Together they make up 95 per cent of Earth's land surface, with islands forming the rest. The largest continent is Asia, with an area of just over 44 million sq km, and the smallest is Australia, covering about 7.7 million sq km.

CONTINENTAL CRUST

The continents are the thickest parts of the Earth's outer layer, or crust – in some places reaching down 60km to 70km. At the centre, the continents contain the oldest rocks on the planet, with some dating back three billion years. As newer rocks were added around the fringes of these ancient cores, the continents grew.

FLOATING WORLD

The tectonic plates on which the continents sit are floating on a hot, molten layer called magma. Heat from deep inside the Earth keeps the magma moving slowly, and as it moves, so do the plates and continents. The slow movement of the continents is called continental drift.

VANISHED LANDS

More than 300 million years ago, all the land on Earth formed just one continent, called Pangaea. Then, about 180 million years ago, it split into two continents, called Gondwanaland and Laurasia. Slowly, North and South America broke away, India joined Asia, and Australia split from Antarctica and moved northwards, until today's seven continents were created.

TOMORROW'S CONTINENTS

The movement is still continuing, and the continents we know today will look very different in 50 million years' time. Africa and the Americas, for example, will be even farther away from each other. North and South America will no longer be joined and Australia will have moved farther northwards.

▼ At first there was just one large continent, then two, and finally today's seven continents were formed.

Laurasia

Gondwanaland

180 million years ago

North America · Europe & Asia · South America · Africa · India · Antarctica & Australia

65 million years ago

SEE ALSO

Africa, Antarctica, Asia, Australia, Earth, Europe, North America, Ocean and sea, Rock, South America

CRAB AND OTHER CRUSTACEANS

Crabs belong to a group of animals called crustaceans. These creatures have no bones and are covered with a hard shell called an exoskeleton.

The male fiddler crab has a very large claw, which it waves as part of a display to attract the female.

The hermit crab lives in an empty seashell, which it drags around with its two pairs of walking legs.

The lobster has one narrow claw for slicing dead fish, and a heavier claw for crushing clams.

The crayfish grows up to 40cm long, lives in fresh water and has ten legs, like lobsters and crabs.

The water flea is one of the smallest crustaceans, growing to between 0.2mm and 18mm long.

The woodlouse is the only crustacean that lives entirely on land. It can roll itself up for defence.

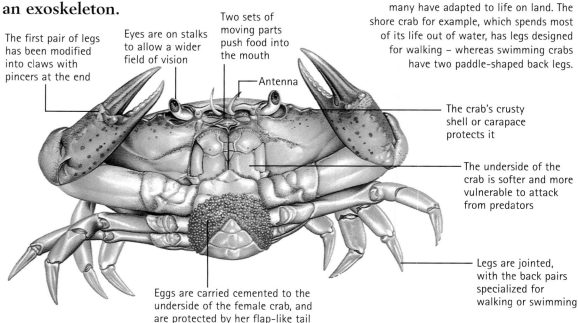

The first pair of legs has been modified into claws with pincers at the end

Eyes are on stalks to allow a wider field of vision

Two sets of moving parts push food into the mouth

Antenna

The crab's crusty shell or carapace protects it

The underside of the crab is softer and more vulnerable to attack from predators

Legs are jointed, with the back pairs specialized for walking or swimming

Eggs are carried cemented to the underside of the female crab, and are protected by her flap-like tail

LIVING ON THE SHORELINE

Most crabs live in or near the sea, but many have adapted to life on land. The shore crab for example, which spends most of its life out of water, has legs designed for walking – whereas swimming crabs have two paddle-shaped back legs.

Crustaceans include shrimps, lobsters, woodlice, water fleas and barnacles. Altogether, there are about 45,000 species of crustacean. Beneath its hard body shell, a crustacean's body is divided into sections, with jointed legs attached. Crabs, lobsters and barnacles have especially thick shells, which contain a lot of chalk-like material. This makes their shells feel like crusts.

EYES ON STALKS

There are about 10,000 species of crab. The smallest are the tiny pea crabs, which are less than 1cm across. The biggest are spider crabs, which live on the sea bed and measure up to 4m across from the tip of one leg to another. Crabs have ten legs, two of which are claws, and their eyes can move up and down on the end of stalks.

CRAB HABITS

Crabs usually live in water or close to the shore. Large crabs feed mainly on dead animals, which they tear up with their claws, while small crabs pick tiny scraps of food from the sea bed. Many crabs move sideways on land. The robber crab climbs palm trees to pick young coconuts, which it bores into with its powerful claws.

WITHOUT A SHELL

A crab's body is armoured by a shell which moults as the crab grows. The hermit crab, however, does not have a shell and must inhabit empty mollusc shells to protect its soft abdomen. As it grows, it searches for a bigger shell to make its home.

HATCHED FROM EGGS

Crabs and other crustaceans reproduce by laying eggs. On hatching, the tiny larvae drift about in water, passing through several body changes before they become adults. In a few species, such as the woodlouse, the young hatch out looking like mini adults.

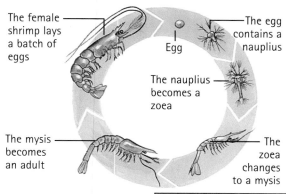

The female shrimp lays a batch of eggs

Egg

The egg contains a nauplius

The nauplius becomes a zoea

The zoea changes to a mysis

The mysis becomes an adult

▲ A shrimp larva must pass through several stages before becoming an adult.

SEE ALSO
Animal, Seashore

CROP

Crops are plants that people grow in fields, to provide food such as wheat and potatoes or other useful materials such as cotton and linen.

Wheat grows worldwide, in areas with moist mild winters and dry summers.

Rice grows best in warm, wet areas such as China, where it is a staple food.

Potatoes, originally from Peru, have long been an important crop in Europe.

Sugar beet is grown for its sugar-rich root. Its leaves are used as animal fodder.

Coffee is the major cash crop in tropical regions. It is grown on plantations.

Grapes are grown in vineyards and harvested for wine, raisins and fresh fruit.

The type of crop grown by farmers depends on the climate of the country, the quality of the soil and its demand in the market. In developing countries, especially in tropical parts of the world, people grow just enough of a crop for their own needs. These are called subsistence crops. Other people, usually farmers, grow large amounts of crops, so that they can be sold. These are called cash crops.

ESSENTIAL CEREALS

The most important food crops are cereals – large grasses grown for their seeds or grains. Cereals include wheat, rice, maize, oats, sorghum and millet, which cover about three quarters of the world's farmland. Wheat is the most popular cereal, with about 690 million tonnes grown every year, mainly for humans to eat, but also as animal feed. Rice is the main ingredient in the diet of over half the world's people, particularly in Asia.

◄ Cotton is a cash crop. It is grown for its fibres, which are spun to make fabric or cotton wool. Its seeds are also crushed to produce oil and fodder.

ROOTS TO FRUITS

Another vital food source are the root crops – plants with edible fleshy roots. The potato is an important root crop in Europe, and yams and cassavas are staples in many parts of Africa. Cotton and flax are grown for their fibrous flowers which are used to make cotton and linen. Other major crops include tea and tobacco, which are grown for their leaves, and fruit such as bananas and apples.

WILD ANCESTORS

All crops have come from wild plants, but they have been bred over time to provide bigger and better yields in soils or climates that are not their natural home. Some crops have changed so much that it is hard to say which wild plants were their ancestors. As field and crop sizes have grown, the use of fertilizers, insecticides and fungicides has also risen.

HARVESTING THE CROP

Combine harvesters automatically cut, thresh and clean cereals such as wheat ready for transportation to market. Special attachments can be added to harvest different crops such as soya beans and maize.

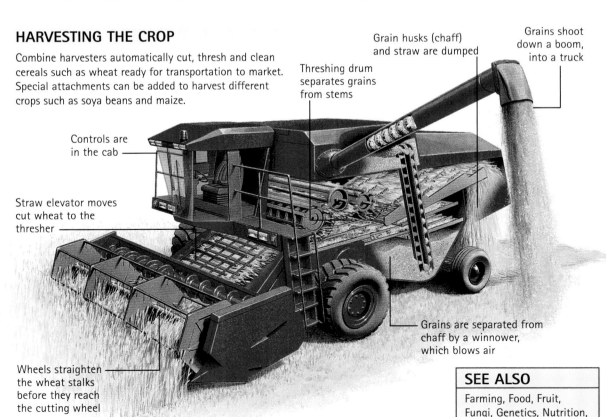

Grain husks (chaff) and straw are dumped

Grains shoot down a boom, into a truck

Threshing drum separates grains from stems

Controls are in the cab

Straw elevator moves cut wheat to the thresher

Grains are separated from chaff by a winnower, which blows air

Wheels straighten the wheat stalks before they reach the cutting wheel

SEE ALSO

Farming, Food, Fruit, Fungi, Genetics, Nutrition, Vegetable

CRUSADES

The Crusades were a series of religious wars that took place in the Holy Land in the Middle Ages. They were fought between Christians and Muslims.

Nuredin was the Muslim leader who united the Islamic forces that Saladin took into battle at Hattin.

Sultan Saladin led the united Muslim armies and took Christian strongholds after the Second Crusade.

For nearly 200 years, starting in 1096, Christians from Europe marched to Palestine to fight the Muslims for control of the Holy Land, especially Jerusalem. They carried the Pope's blessing, but many fought for power and wealth.

THE BEGINNING

From the 7th century, Muslim Arabs ruled the Holy Land, but Christian pilgrims were allowed to visit Jerusalem. Then, in 1071, the Muslim Turks captured Jerusalem and threatened the Christian Byzantine Empire. Pope Urban II called for Christian soldiers to unite and march to the Holy Land to recapture Jerusalem and protect pilgrims.

PILGRIM PEASANTS

The response to the Pope's call was vast. With cries of *Deus Vult!* (meaning 'God wills it' in Latin), thousands of people began the long march eastwards. The first to set out for the Byzantine capital of Constantinople were bands of poorly armed pilgrim peasants under the leadership of Peter the Hermit and Walter the Penniless. Many died on the way, and the

▲ The Crusaders travelled to the Holy Land by land and sea from all the Christian kingdoms of Europe. They built more than 100 castles and fortresses in the area. One of the best preserved is Krak des Chevaliers in Syria, which withstood 12 sieges before falling to the Muslims in 1271.

——— First Crusade (1096–99)
——— Second Crusade (1147–49)
——— Third Crusade (1188–92)
——— Fourth Crusade (1202–4)

rest were killed by the Muslims as soon as they reached Anatolia.

AN ARMY OF KNIGHTS

The First Crusade began in November 1096, when a large army, mostly consisting of French and Norman knights under the leadership of noblemen such as Godfrey de Bouillon, gathered at Constantinople. The army defeated the Muslims, capturing the cities of Antioch and Jerusalem, and establishing a Christian kingdom along the Palestinian and Syrian coast.

THE BATTLE OF ARSUF

In 1191, King Richard I secured victory over the Muslim leader Saladin at Arsuf, with a charge of armoured knights. The charge was led by the Knights Templars and Knights Hospitallers – two military orders of skilled knights who were fanatical enemies of Islam and, like monks, took religious vows.

JERUSALEM IS LOST

Muslim counterattacks started the Second Crusade (1147–49), in which King Louis VII of France and King Conrad II of Germany led separate attacks on Anatolia. These ended in failure for the Christians and weakened their hold on the Holy Land. In 1187, a new Muslim leader, Saladin, led Islamic opposition and wiped out the Crusaders at the Battle of the Horns of Hattin. He then captured Jerusalem and most of the Holy Land.

RICHARD THE LIONHEART

The Third Crusade (1189–92) was led by Richard I (Richard the Lionheart of England), Frederick I of Germany, and Philip II of France. Unfortunately, Frederick drowned on the way, but the Crusaders defeated Saladin and retook much of the Holy Land, except Jerusalem.

LATER CRUSADES

The Fourth Crusade (1202–4) ended in chaos. Its leaders wanted power and riches, and concentrated on Constantinople instead of fighting for the Holy Land. The Christians had little success in the Fifth Crusade (1217–21), but gained Jerusalem by treaty during the Sixth (1222–29). The Seventh Crusade (1248–54) ended with the capture of Louis IX of France, who was freed only after a ransom was paid.

FINAL BATTLE

During the Eighth Crusade (1270–72), the Muslims continued to advance. In 1291, they secured the last of the vital ports of Acre. No more Crusades took place and many of the knights settled on the island of Cyprus.

In 1212, thousands of children went on a children's crusade to the Holy Land. They did not reach their destination and many of them died or were sold as slaves.

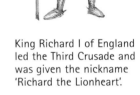

King Richard I of England led the Third Crusade and was given the nickname 'Richard the Lionheart'.

Louis IX ruled the coast around Acre, Syria, for four years between the Seventh and Eighth Crusades.

The Knights Hospitallers built many castles to defend land they had captured. The largest of these was Krak des Chevaliers which was built in the desert of what is now Syria. It held a garrison of 2,000 men and only fell to the Saracens in 1271 when its defenders surrendered after a year-long siege.

SEE ALSO

Castle, Christianity, Empire, Islam, Middle Ages, Middle East, Warfare

CUSTOM

Customs are the traditions, rituals and ways of behaving in a society which are passed on from generation to generation and are sometimes turned into laws.

Some Portuguese fishermen paint eyes on their boats to watch over them at sea and bring them back safely.

The *haka*, performed by New Zealand rugby teams before a match, is based on a Maori war dance.

The custom of carving pumpkin faces comes from the Celtic Day of the Dead, celebrated on October 31st.

The *chanoyu*, a Japanese tea ceremony which can last for four hours, came originally from China.

The painting of eggs is a symbol of new life which has been adopted by Christians at Easter time.

DANCING DRAGON

During the Chinese New Year festival, dancers inside a dragon costume move through the streets while fire crackers are set off. The dragon is believed to bring rain for a successful crop and so has become a symbol of good fortune for the coming year. The fire crackers are to frighten away evil spirits.

Every society has its own set of customs, whether it is waiting in a queue, or wearing a particular costume during a celebration. Learning about different customs helps us to understand people from other countries or cultures.

RITES OF PASSAGE
Across the world, customs are different, but there are times of life, known as rites of passage, when a person's status changes. Such times include birth, coming of age, marriage and death – occasions that are marked by elaborate customs in every society. The custom of keeping mother and baby secluded from society for a month after birth is a common custom in many countries, probably based on fear of infection. There are also many customs marking a young person's move from childhood to adulthood, ranging from throwing a party to a religious ritual.

LINKS WITH THE PAST
Customs may be adapted over time, often due to industrialization or contact with other cultures. A custom's original meaning may be forgotten, or it may continue as a way of keeping a link with the past. In the USA, for example, families hold special meals at Thanksgiving to celebrate the first harvest of the Pilgrim Fathers, even though few people today are farmers.

CUSTOMARY GREETINGS
Everyday customs help people to bond with other members of their society. For instance, every culture has a customary way of greeting – Europeans kiss or shake hands, the Inuit rub noses and the Chinese bow. By taking part in customs, people demonstrate their membership of a group or society.

GOING AGAINST THE GRAIN
Refusing to follow a custom can offend, and may lead to the exclusion of an individual from a group of society. Customs are not laws, but because they are designed to help us understand what is acceptable behaviour in a society, they are often included in laws or religious codes.

▲ In Hindu weddings, everything is brightly coloured, and the bride usually wears a red sari with lots of gold jewellery.

SEE ALSO
Clothing, Dance, Judaism

DAM

A dam is a barrier built across a river or stream to hold back water. The stored water may be used for irrigation, as drinking water, or to provide power.

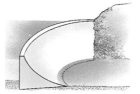

Arch dams, used in tall, narrow canyons or gorges, are often surprisingly thin.

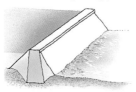

Concrete gravity dams are built to hold back water in broad, shallow valleys.

Embankment dams have a reinforced inner wall to hold back shallow lakes.

The earliest dams were built in the Middle East about 5,000 years ago. These dams were used to direct water to fields of crops, through canals called irrigation channels. A dam built on the Orontes River in Syria about 1300BCE still irrigates fields near the city of Homs.

CONTROLLING THE FLOW

Today, dams are still built for irrigation, as well as to stop flooding and to provide water power for electricity. In low-lying areas of China, Bangladesh and the USA, dams have been built to stop flood disasters. Other dams are built so that water can be stored in artificial lakes called reservoirs. The water is then supplied to homes and industry.

HYDROELECTRIC DAM

Hydroelectric dams use water power to produce electricity. They require large quantities of water and a very long drop from the top to the bottom of the dam. About 6.6 per cent of the world's electricity is generated by hydroelectric dams.

EMBANKMENT DAMS

The simplest dams are embankment dams. They are made from earth and rock and have a waterproof core to stop water seeping through. The Aswan High Dam in Egypt controls the annual flooding of the River Nile as well as providing hydroelectric power for the whole country.

GRAVITY AND ARCH

Gravity dams are made of stone or concrete. They rely on their weight and strength to hold back the water. Arch dams are curved so that the weight of the water is pushed out from the dam to the canyon or gorge. This means they can be very thin – for example, the Vaiont Dam in the Italian Alps is 265m high but only 23m thick at its base.

ENVIRONMENTAL IMPACT

Dam-building affects the surrounding environment, and wildlife can be destroyed. Some dams have fish ladders, which enable fish such as salmon to make their journey upstream to breed.

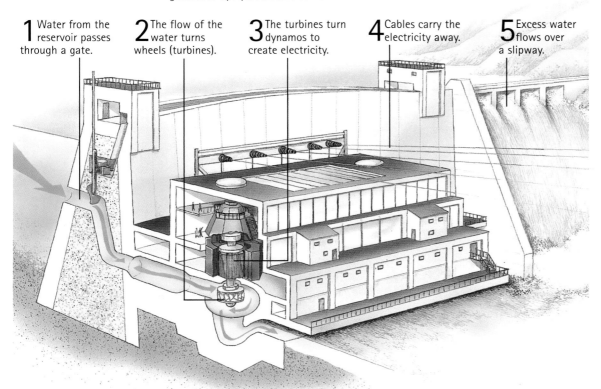

1 Water from the reservoir passes through a gate.

2 The flow of the water turns wheels (turbines).

3 The turbines turn dynamos to create electricity.

4 Cables carry the electricity away.

5 Excess water flows over a slipway.

SEE ALSO

Construction, Egypt, Water power

DANCE

Dance is one of the oldest art forms. It is the rhythmic movement of all or part of the body, and includes ballet, the waltz, flamenco, tap, rumba and disco.

Dancing can express emotion, tell a story, create a specific atmosphere or show off physical strength. There are two main types of dance: social dancing for enjoyment, and dance created to entertain an audience.

DANCING THROUGH HISTORY

People have been dancing for thousands of years – dancing figures appear in cave paintings in Europe and Africa dating back to prehistoric times. Many of the earliest dances that are still popular today were connected with religious ceremonies or superstitious beliefs. English morris dancing is based on ancient war rituals and voodoo dancers in Haiti go into a trance in which they attempt to summon the spirits. The expressive dance drama of the Ancient Greeks has had a long-lasting influence in the West.

▶ Ice-skating competitions feature ice dancing in their freestyle section. Couples are not allowed to lift one another, but often imitate traditional ballroom dance routines using daring athletic poses.

GETTING TOGETHER

Formal social dances, where set steps are followed, go back many centuries. Bugaku dancing in Japan originated in the 7th century. In medieval Europe, grand social dances were popular at court. Most were adapted from the simple country dances of ordinary people. As early as the 15th century, there were dance teachers who taught the steps to the latest dances.

CLASSIC BEAUTY

Ballet originated in the royal courts of Italy during the 1400s, but was developed in France. King Louis XIV was an enthusiastic dancer, and opened the first European dance academy in Paris in 1661. Until then, most dancers had been amateur, but professional dancers soon began to appear. The academy's director, Charles-Louis Beauchamp, helped to standardize the classic movements. He is thought to have set out the five basic ballet positions of the feet and arms. By the mid-1800s, romantic ballets such as *La Sylphide* were popular in Europe.

▲ Contemporary dance is less structured than ballet and does not always tell a story. It often uses choreography of the dancers' bodies to form striking poses.

▼ Ballet tells a story, whether it is a classical tale such as *Swan Lake*, or a favourite children's story like *Alice in Wonderland*. Here, Alice (far right) meets the fearsome Queen of Hearts during her journey through Wonderland.

◀ Music and dance are important in the cultures of many tribal countries, such as Zimbabwe, Africa. Here a Shangaan dancer, in an elaborate costume with wings, mask and grass skirt, performs a tribal dance.

▲ Dancing to repetitive music with a powerful underlying beat, often in strobe lighting, swept clubs in the 1990s.

BREAKING AWAY

The second half of the 1800s was the era of classical Russian ballet, with great masterpieces such as Tchaikovsky's *Swan Lake*. But by the early 1900s, some dancers were beginning to create a freer style, breaking away from the rigid patterns and training of classical ballet. The American dancer Isadora Duncan was a big influence on contemporary dance. She performed barefoot, basing her moves on ideas inspired by Ancient Greece.

TAKE YOUR PARTNERS

As time went by, trends in social dances changed along with styles of music. In the 1800s, the waltz caused a scandal because the man and woman dancing held each other so closely. Exciting new dances in the 20th century were based partly on African-American and Irish traditions, like jazz and tap. In the 1920s, while dramatic Russian ballets toured Europe, ordinary people in the USA were dancing the popular and high-kicking Charleston.

YOUTH MOVEMENTS

Jitterbugging, made popular by American GI soldiers, became the fashion in the 1930s and 1940s, and developed into the sensational rock'n'roll jive of the 1940s and 1950s. The twist was a popular dance in the 1960s, and the latter part of the last century was marked by disco, breakdancing and free expression.

▶ In the popular Japanese theatre of Kabuki, an all-male cast performs comic dance, drama and singing shows, often in female dress. To give a visual climax, each scene ends with a pose called the *mie*.

SEE ALSO

Africa, Custom, Music, Theatre

DEMOCRACY

Democracy is a form of government in which the people take part in ruling the state. The people may rule directly or through elected officials.

◄ Two metal voting discs were given to each man in ancient Athens. They were used in criminal trials to vote guilty or not guilty.

People who live in a democracy either vote for officials who make laws for them, or they vote directly on laws in a meeting known as an assembly. Democracy allows people freedom of speech and the right to choose between competing political parties in regularly held elections.

◄ In some elections today, a person votes by making a mark against the candidate's name on a ballot paper. The papers (votes) are posted in a sealed ballot box, to be counted later.

POWER TO THE PEOPLE
The first democracy appeared in Ancient Greece in the 6th century BCE, when men in cities could vote in assemblies. The word democracy is Greek for 'people-power'.

ELECTION VICTORY

India is the world's largest democracy and election time plays an important part in the life of the people. Candidates make speeches, distribute leaflets, advertise and design posters to persuade people to vote for them. Most candidates belong to a political party whose members share the same ideas about how the country should be run.

ELECTED ASSEMBLIES
The reign of Alexander the Great and a succession of Roman emperors gradually put an end to democracy, and the Middle Ages saw the rise of feudalism and monarchy. Democracy reappeared in the 17th century, when elected assemblies, known as parliaments, began to take power in some countries. At first only wealthy men could vote but today nearly every adult in a democracy is allowed to vote.

MAJORITY RULE
Voters choose people to represent them in legislatures (law-making bodies), such as the British House of Commons or the US Congress. For a new law to be passed, a majority in the legislature must vote for it. On important issues, there may be a vote of all the people, known as a referendum.

CHOOSING REPRESENTATIVES
Some elections are decided by a 'first past the post' system: the candidate with the most votes wins. Others are decided by proportional representation: each party gets candidates in parliament in relation to the number of votes it receives.

GOVERNMENTS AND THE LAW
There are many kinds of democracy. In Britain, there is a monarchy, but an elected parliament makes laws. France is a republic with a president and prime minister, as well as a legislature. Russia is becoming more democratic after the fall of its communist government.

SEE ALSO

Civil rights, Government, Greece (Ancient), Law, Politics

DESERT

Deserts are dry areas of land with relatively few plants or animals. Most deserts are hot, get very little rain, and are sandy or rocky.

▲ Deserts are not always hot. Some places in Antarctica and Greenland are known as polar deserts because the ground there is so dry. For example, on the western side of Antarctica, there are areas that receive less than 13cm of snow each year.

More than a fifth of the world's land surface is so dry that it is known as desert. Most deserts receive less than 250mm of rain each year. Others receive more rain than this but it evaporates quickly in the strong heat and winds, or sinks into the parched ground. The driest place in the world is the Atacama Desert in Chile, parts of which have less than 0.1mm of rain each year.

WHERE DESERTS FORM
Most deserts, such as the Kalahari and Sahara in Africa, lie between the tropics of Cancer and Capricorn (25° to the north and south of the Equator). The air in the tropics is often too hot and dry for rain clouds to form. The cold Gobi Desert in central Asia exists, however, because it is far from the sea's moist winds. Other deserts occur because the winds that sweep across them lost all their moisture passing over neighbouring mountainous regions.

SURVIVAL TACTICS
Desert plants and animals have developed ways of coping with the lack of water. Plants usually have long, spreading roots to reach any available moisture. Most have spines or small leaves that are rolled or waxy to cut down on water loss through evaporation. Other plants spend most of their lives as seeds – only growing when rain falls. Desert animals often hide during the heat of the day and come out at night. Camels can go for many days without water.

POCKETS OF WATER
Oases are pockets of fertile land in a desert. These occur where an aquifer, or underground stream, comes to the surface. Plants such as palm trees thrive, and animals and people gather there.

CREEPING DESERTS
Deserts can spread. This may happen because the climate becomes drier or nearby land is overgrazed by farm animals.

IN THE SHADOW OF THE SIERRA NEVADA
The deserts of North America are shielded from rain by the towering mountain wall of the Sierra Nevada. In some areas, less than 100mm of rain falls, making the gravelly ground inhospitable except to a few plants and animals. Temperatures during the day can reach 100°C, but at night it is often near freezing because there is no cloud cover.

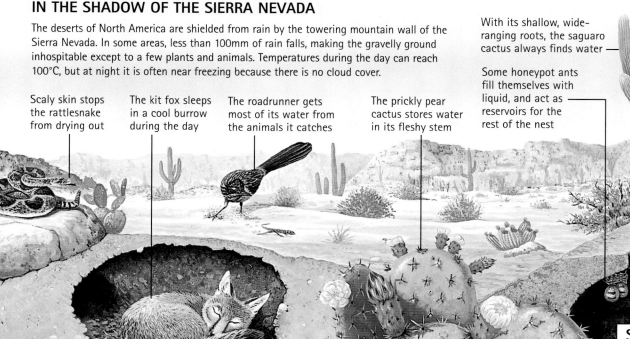

With its shallow, wide-ranging roots, the saguaro cactus always finds water

Scaly skin stops the rattlesnake from drying out

The kit fox sleeps in a cool burrow during the day

The roadrunner gets most of its water from the animals it catches

The prickly pear cactus stores water in its fleshy stem

Some honeypot ants fill themselves with liquid, and act as reservoirs for the rest of the nest

SEE ALSO

Africa, Antarctica, Climate, Habitat, Plant, South America

DESIGN

Everything we use today, from a toothbrush to a car, has been designed according to its function, to trends in fashion and art and the latest available materials.

▲ Fashion designers sketch their ideas first. They show the outfits from different angles and in a variety of colours, adding swatches of fabric.

Spanish painter Salvador Dali designed this 'Eye of Time' watch.

Even household appliances, such as the kettle, are always being re-designed.

Scottish designer and architect Charles Rennie Mackintosh designed all his chairs with unusually high backs.

Professional designers must create an object that does the job it is supposed to do as efficiently as possible. But they must also think carefully about the aesthetic value, or appearance, of the object, how and where it will be used, who will be using it, and changing trends in technology and materials.

AGE OF DESIGN
The word design comes from the Italian word *disegno*. Between the 14th and 16th centuries, during the great Italian artistic era called the Renaissance, the word was used to describe the basic idea behind a work of art, as well as rough sketches of it. Today, the term covers a huge area from detailed drawings and engineering plans for buildings to the graphic design of books, magazines and product wrappers.

SKETCHING IT OUT
The first step for many designers, whether painters, architects, film set designers or fashion designers, is to sketch out their ideas, or create storyboards on paper. If it is a building or product, they may then make up a small model to scale. Fashion designers often make up a sample garment, using inexpensive cloth.

DESIGNING ON COMPUTERS
Computers are now used extensively in design, especially for industry. They allow people to experiment with three-dimensional, often animated, models on the screen. Using CAD (Computer Aided Design), a designer can quickly change a detail and the computer will calculate and apply the changes to the rest of the design. Specialist programs help experts create cars, shoes and electrical goods.

THE CREATIVE PROCESS
Computers can be used to highlight stress points, illustrate aerodynamics and show other crucial design features of a prototype car. Newspapers and magazines are designed on computer and sent to the printer on a disk, as was this book.

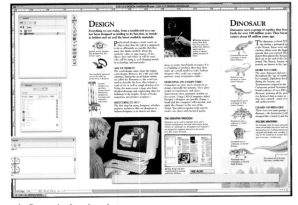

▲ Page design has been revolutionized by desktop publishing software, which allows changes to be made in seconds.

SEE ALSO
Architecture, Art, Clothing, Computer

DINOSAUR

Dinosaurs were a group of reptiles that lived on Earth for over 160 million years. They became extinct about 65 million years ago.

Tyrannosaurus rex was a theropod, or 'beast-footed' dinosaur.

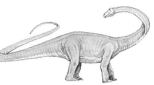

Diplodocus was a sauropod, or 'lizard-footed' dinosaur.

Camptosaurus was an ornithopod, or 'bird-footed' dinosaur.

Stegosaurus was a stegosaur, or 'roofed' dinosaur.

Sauropelta was an ankylosaur, or 'jointed' dinosaur.

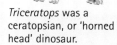

Triceratops was a ceratopsian, or 'horned head' dinosaur.

The dinosaurs evolved 225 million years ago during a geological period known as the Triassic. Some were only the size of a chicken, others were the biggest land animals that ever existed. They roamed the planet throughout the Jurassic period and died out at the end of the Cretaceous period. The Triassic, Jurassic and Cretaceous periods are known as the 'age of reptiles'.

MORE TO COME

The same dinosaurs did not exist throughout the 'age of reptiles'. For example, *Diplodocus* lived during the Jurassic, and *Tyrannosaurus* reigned in the Cretaceous period. Scientists have found evidence of over 500 types of dinosaur, spanning all the periods, but it is believed that as many as 1,300 types may have existed – most of which are still undiscovered.

LIZARD OR BIRD-LIKE

There were two main groups, or orders, of dinosaur – the Saurischia (with hip bones arranged like a lizard's) and the Ornithischia (with hip bones arranged like

a bird's). The Saurischia can be divided into two smaller groups known as the theropods and the sauropods. The Ornithischia include four groups: the ornithopods, the stegosaurs, the ankylosaurs and the ceratopsians.

MEAT-EATERS

The theropods were meat-eaters, all built to the same design. They had long mouths full of meat-tearing teeth, they walked on their hind legs, and had small bodies which they balanced with long, heavy tails. Some, such as *Compsognathus*, were chicken-sized, while the biggest were 12m-long killers, such as *Tyrannosaurus*. ▶

KILLING MACHINE

The theropods were the meat-eating dinosaurs, which all had large jaws full of teeth for tearing flesh. *Deinonychus* was a terrifying killing machine equipped with deadly tools, including a slashing claw on the second toe of its back foot which gave it its name – 'terrible claw'.

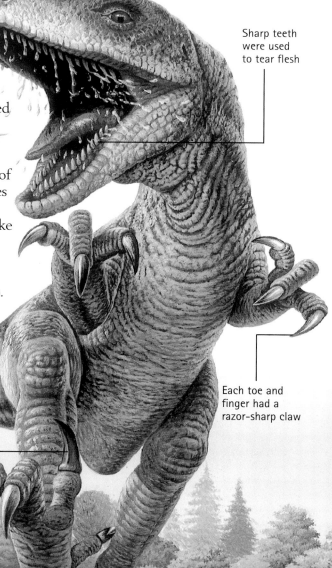

Sharp teeth were used to tear flesh

Each toe and finger had a razor-sharp claw

The second toe of its back foot had a 'terrible claw'

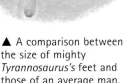

▲ A comparison between the size of mighty *Tyrannosaurus*'s feet and those of an average man.

▼ This fossil skeleton of *Tuojiangosaurus* was discovered in China in the 1970s. *Tuojiangosaurus* was a stegosaur that lived in the late Jurassic period, about 150 million years ago.

DINOSAUR GIANTS

Sauropods were plant-eaters. They had big, heavy bodies and moved around on all fours, using their long necks to reach leaves on trees. They were the biggest land animals that ever lived and included *Diplodocus* and *Brachiosaurus*.

CHEEKY PLANT-EATERS

The Ornithischia dinosaurs were also all plant-eaters. The only ones that could walk on their hind legs were the ornithopods. They had a more sophisticated chewing system than the long-necked sauropods, with cheeks for holding the food while they chewed it. *Iguanodon* is probably the most famous of the ornithopods.

▲ In 1978, a fossilized nest of 15 young *Maiasaura* was found in Montana, USA. Evidence showed that the young were very small and would have had to be cared for by the mother to survive. *Maiasaura* means 'good mother lizard'.

BONY ARMOUR

Three ornithischian groups evolved from the ornithopods (bird-footed dinosaurs). They all had armour of some kind, which made them heavy and so they walked on four legs. The first were the stegosaurs – the 'roofed' dinosaurs. They had big bodies and either a double row of bony plates down the back like *Stegosaurus*, or an arrangement of spines like *Kentrosaurus*.

A SCENE FROM THE LATE JURASSIC

The late Jurassic is the period from 157–145 million years ago. It is known for its many plant-eating dinosaur species, such as spiny *Stegosaurus* and long-necked sauropods, including *Apatosaurus*. The main dinosaur predator was the meat-eating *Allosaurus* – although the reptile *Diplosaurus*, an ancestor of today's crocodile, was pretty fearsome.

Archaeopteryx – one of the first birds

A SCENE FROM THE LATE CRETACEOUS

The Late Cretaceous was a period from 95–65 million years ago. It was dominated by herds of duckbilled *Edmontosaurus*es, which had replaced the sauropods as the main plant-eaters. Meat-eating *Tyrannosaurus* probably hunted these animals, because other plant-eaters like *Triceratops* and *Ankylosaurus* had developed spectacular defensive armour. Large flying reptiles may have scavenged like vultures on the bodies of dead dinosaurs .

JOINTED DINOSAURS

The second ornithischian group was the ankylosaurs, or 'jointed' dinosaurs. They had bony armour that lay flat over their broad backs, and were also armed with spikes along the sides, as in *Edmontonia*, or a tail with a club, as in *Euoplocephalus*.

HORNED HEADS

The last ornithischian group was the ceratopsians. They had armour on their faces and heads, where it formed big bony frills around the neck. These 'horned head' dinosaurs included *Triceratops*, which had a small horn on the nose and two long horns over the eyes, and *Styracosaurus*, which had an enormous horn on the nose and a series of smaller horns around the frill.

REPTILE NEIGHBOURS

Dinosaurs were not the only reptiles that lived at the time. Many groups of swimming reptiles, such as the fish-shaped ichthyosaurs and the long-necked plesiosaurs, lived in the sea, while pterosaurs flew in the air.

DINOSAUR FACTS

- The smaller meat-eating dinosaurs hunted in packs like wolves, preying on young or weak plant-eaters
- Large plant-eating dinosaurs like Diplodocus must have had to eat continuously to avoid starvation
- Dinosaurs may have been warm-blooded like mammals and birds
- Many different types of insect and mammal also lived during the time of the dinosaurs
- The dinosaurs' legs were not at the side like reptiles, but under their bodies like mammals

DEATH OF THE REPTILES

All these unusual reptiles became extinct along with the dinosaurs at the end of the Cretaceous period. Nobody knows for sure how this happened, or why other reptiles, such as crocodiles and turtles, survived. It may have been a gradual process, due to a slow climatic change, or there may have been a sudden catastrophe, such as the Earth being hit by a gigantic meteorite. The dinosaurs did leave some relatives, however. During the Jurassic period, birds evolved from the small meat-eating theropods, which means today's birds are the direct descendants of the dinosaurs.

Male

Female

▲ *Parasaurolophus* had a hollow crest extending upwards from its nose, through which it may have hooted a warning or called its mate.

SEE ALSO

Evolution, Fossil, Mammal, Prehistoric animal, Reptile

DISEASE

A disease is an illness which disturbs the normal healthy functioning of a plant, animal or person. Each disease produces symptoms (physical changes).

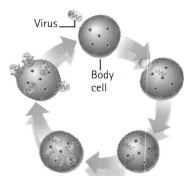

VIRUS ATTACK
A virus spreads in the body by using the body's cells to make copies of itself. As the replicas break out, they destroy the body's cell, and each virus starts the process again.

The human body may be attacked by thousands of diseases. These range from relatively harmless ones, such as the common cold and athlete's foot, to life-threatening diseases, such as typhoid and some cancers. Plants and animals also suffer from diseases – potatoes suffer from blight and cats can get the flu (influenza).

▲ Many diseases have almost been wiped out by the widespread use of inoculation (also called immunization and vaccination). This is when a milder form of the disease is introduced into the body, by injection or via the mouth, so that the person develops long-term resistance to the disease.

VIRUSES AND BACTERIA
Flu, AIDS and tetanus are all types of infectious disease. They are caused by harmful microscopic organisms called germs, which invade the body and multiply. Tetanus is caused by bacteria (living creatures), while flu and AIDS are caused by viruses (bundles of DNA wrapped in protein). Infectious diseases are spread from person to person by, for example, breathing in germs. A sudden outbreak of an infectious disease which affects many people is called an epidemic.

Some infectious diseases can be prevented with vaccinations, and others can be treated with medicines such as antibiotics.

NON-INFECTIOUS DISEASES
Many diseases are not caused by germs, but are the result of poor diet. An example of this is scurvy, which is the result of not eating enough vitamin C. Others may be caused by an unhealthy lifestyle. For example, smoking and stress can lead to heart disease. Some diseases, such as haemophilia, run in families as a result of faulty genes.

LOOKING FOR CLUES
Symptoms such as pain or fever tell the person suffering from a disease that something is wrong and give clues to doctors as to the cause. A doctor can also detect signs of disease by taking X-rays or blood tests.

AFRICAN SLEEPING SICKNESS

The tsetse fly spreads a disease called sleeping sickness in some areas of Africa. When it feeds on human blood, this tiny fly injects some of its saliva into the person's bloodstream. If its saliva contains micro-organisms called *Trypanosoma brucei*, these also enter the bloodstream, and multiply inside the body, causing fever, headaches and sleepiness. The person may die if not treated quickly.

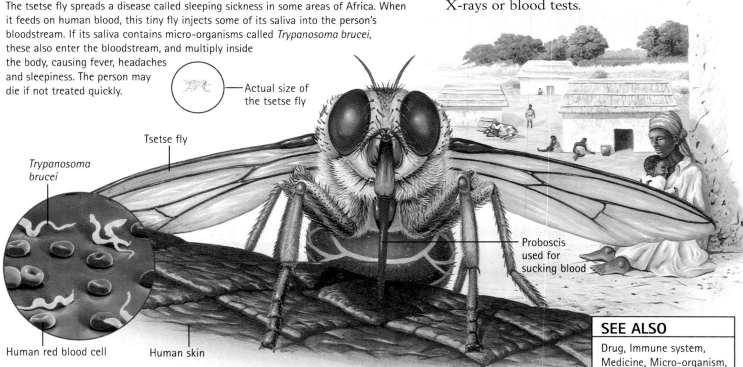

Actual size of the tsetse fly

Trypanosoma brucei

Tsetse fly

Proboscis used for sucking blood

Human red blood cell

Human skin

SEE ALSO
Drug, Immune system, Medicine, Micro-organism, Surgery

Dog

The domestic dog (*Canis familiaris*) belongs to the dog family, known as Canidae, and is believed to be descended from the grey wolf.

The chihuahua is the smallest dog in the world: only 15cm to the shoulder.

The poodle is an intelligent dog, used for finding truffles (fungi) in France.

The greyhound, bred for speed, can easily reach 57km per hour.

The bulldog was originally bred for the 'sport' of bull-baiting in the Middle Ages.

The husky is a powerful sledge dog, able to pull twice its own weight.

The Airedale is the largest breed of terrier, probably bred for hunting otters.

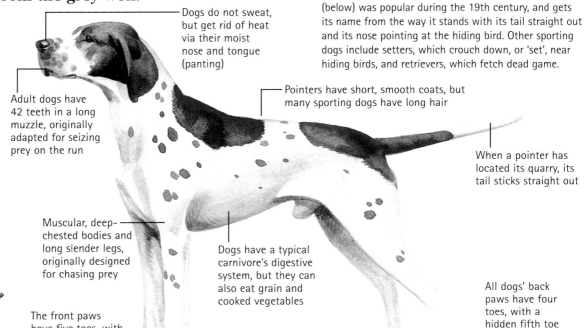

Dogs do not sweat, but get rid of heat via their moist nose and tongue (panting)

Adult dogs have 42 teeth in a long muzzle, originally adapted for seizing prey on the run

Muscular, deep-chested bodies and long slender legs, originally designed for chasing prey

The front paws have five toes, with strong, blunt, non-retractable claws

Dogs have a typical carnivore's digestive system, but they can also eat grain and cooked vegetables

Pointers have short, smooth coats, but many sporting dogs have long hair

When a pointer has located its quarry, its tail sticks straight out

All dogs' back paws have four toes, with a hidden fifth toe

Dogs were the first animals to be tamed. Fossil remains of a domestic dog dating back to 10,500 years ago have been found in Idaho, USA. The relationship between human and dog probably began because dogs are natural scavengers, and hung around camps looking for food scraps.

BREEDS AND GROUPS

Since then, humans have selectively bred dogs – the American Kennel Club (AKC) recognizes 161 breeds of dog, and the British Kennel Club includes 210. These breeds are divided into seven groups by appearance, use and size: Hounds, Working dogs, Gundogs, Terriers, Utility dogs, Pastoral dogs and Toy dogs. The dog's most acute senses – smell and hearing – were selectively bred early on for guarding and hunting. Other physical features were bred for specific uses. For example, the dachshund's short legs were selected for going down badger sets, and the bulldog's set-back nose was selected to help it breathe while biting. Nowadays, a gentle, non-aggressive nature is selected for pets.

SPORTING DOGS

Sporting dogs are bred for their acute sense of smell, which they use to track down game birds. The pointer (below) was popular during the 19th century, and gets its name from the way it stands with its tail straight out and its nose pointing at the hiding bird. Other sporting dogs include setters, which crouch down, or 'set', near hiding birds, and retrievers, which fetch dead game.

A DOG'S LIFE

Most domestic dogs are fully grown by the age of two, are old by the age of 12, and rarely live past 20. Bitches (females) can become pregnant from about seven months, and give birth to an average of three to six puppies, although some breeds may have up to ten puppies. The puppies open their eyes on the tenth day and are ready to leave their mother at six weeks. Dogs are pack animals and follow a leader. This loyalty can be transferred to a human master, especially if the dog is trained while young.

▲ The border collie uses the hunting instincts of its wild ancestors to round up sheep.

SEE ALSO
Hearing, Mammal, Wolf

DRUG

Drugs are substances that affect the way in which the body or mind works. Most drugs are used medicinally, to cure or prevent an illness.

Medicinal liquids called syrups make swallowing drugs easy for children.

Tablets and capsules are the most common form of drugs.

A drug is injected into the blood when a quick response is needed.

Eye drops and inhalers act fast by sending the drug to the exact spot.

Creams and gels often contain drugs which disinfect a cut or graze.

Skin patches release drugs slowly through the skin into the blood.

Cigarettes are made from tobacco leaves, which contain the drug nicotine.

▶ The foxglove is listed in the oldest surviving book on drugs and their uses, written between 20CE and 70CE by the Ancient Greek doctor Dioscorides.

Over 4,000 years ago, Emperor Chi'en Nung of China put together a book of more than 300 medicinal plants, many of which are still used in medicine today. But it was not until the 18th century, when the English doctor William Withering studied the heart drug digitalis (extracted from foxgloves), that drugs were looked at scientifically. The modern drug industry began in 1899, when the German company Bayer manufactured the painkiller aspirin.

TYPES OF DRUG

Doctors use many types of drug to treat patients. For example, antibiotics such as penicillin kill the bacteria that cause infections. Analgesics (painkillers), such as aspirin and codeine, stop pain messages from reaching the brain. Sedatives have a calming effect and can help a person to sleep. Anaesthetics deaden the body's nerves and are used in operations. Vaccines help the immune system to fight diseases, and insulin is given when the body fails to make enough naturally.

DANGERS AND ADDICTION

Some drugs, such as heroin or cocaine, are addictive, which means people cannot stop taking them. They are illegal because they are so dangerous. Even medicinal drugs or everyday drugs, such as alcohol, caffeine in tea and coffee or nicotine in cigarettes, can be harmful if taken in large amounts.

SLOW-RELEASE CAPSULES

Drugs sometimes need to be released into the bloodstream slowly over a few hours, especially if they are painkillers. Slow-release capsules contain hundreds of tiny pellets with coatings of different thicknesses. Some of the pellets release the drug in the stomach, while others release it later in the intestines.

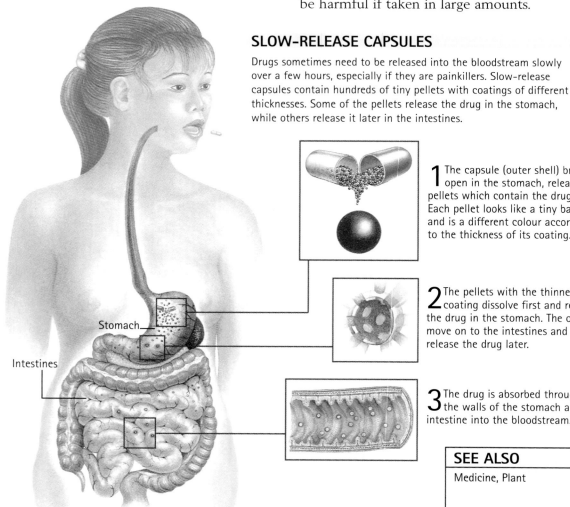

Stomach

Intestines

1 The capsule (outer shell) breaks open in the stomach, releasing pellets which contain the drug. Each pellet looks like a tiny ball and is a different colour according to the thickness of its coating.

2 The pellets with the thinnest coating dissolve first and release the drug in the stomach. The others move on to the intestines and release the drug later.

3 The drug is absorbed through the walls of the stomach and intestine into the bloodstream.

SEE ALSO

Medicine, Plant

EAGLE AND OTHER BIRDS OF PREY

Eagles and other birds of prey survive by hunting other animals. They swoop on their prey from the air, grabbing them with their sharp talons.

► Unlike hawks and eagles, owls, such as this little owl, hunt their prey at night.

The Andean condor is the largest bird of prey. It can weigh up to 12kg.

When peregrine falcons dive, they can reach speeds of over 250km/h.

Northern goshawks can strike in mid-air, often attacking from below.

Vultures, such as this black vulture, feed on the bodies of dead animals.

The golden eagle is the most widespread eagle in the Northern Hemisphere.

Birds of prey are born hunters. They have sharp eyesight to spot far-off prey, sharp, curved talons to catch their food and strong, hooked beaks to tear at flesh. Most have large, broad wings with flight feathers that spread out when they soar in updrafts. As well as eagles, birds of prey include buzzards, falcons, hawks, kites, ospreys and vultures. Owls are also often included, but belong to a different bird group.

HUNTING SKILLS
Most birds of prey soar high into the air and then swoop down on their prey on the ground at high speed. Some, such as the peregrine falcon, can also attack birds in mid-air. The kestrel is unusual because it hovers just a few metres above the ground before swooping. Vultures usually scavenge dead meat.

DIFFERENT TASTES
There are more than 60 species of eagle scattered throughout the world, although many are endangered. Most live in wild, remote places where humans cannot disturb them. Eagles eat a wide range of animals. The golden eagle attacks hares, small rodents and other birds, while the bateleur eagle gorges on snakes. Some are experts at snaring fish, and the harpy eagle catches monkeys.

FISH FOR DINNER
The bald eagle, the national bird of the USA, is one of the most endangered birds of prey. It feeds on birds and small animals, but particularly likes fish. It scoops them from the surface of the water and flies off, gripping them in its sharp talons.

NEST RECYCLING
Many eagles use the same nest, or eyrie, again and again, adding more material each time they breed. Their nests can become enormous – a bald eagle's can measure 3m across and weigh over a tonne. Most eagles lay just two eggs. Once the young have hatched, they do not leave the nest for up to two months.

SEE ALSO
Bird

EARTH

Our planet, Earth, is one of the nine planets that move around the Sun. It is made up of rock and metal, and is the only planet known to support life.

Planet Earth is an almost perfect ball of rock with a metal core, which travels around the Sun. It is surrounded by a blanket of gases called the atmosphere, has one moon, and as far as we know, is the only planet that supports life.

NIGHT AND DAY
Approximately every 24 hours, the Earth does a full circle on its axis – an imaginary line joining the North and South Poles. As it spins, one side turns to face the Sun and is in daylight, while the other side turns away, experiencing night. The Earth spins eastward, which is why the Sun seems to rise in the east and set in the west.

Magnetic fields
Magnetic North Pole
Magnetic South Pole

▲ As the Earth spins, electrical currents beneath the surface turn the planet into a huge magnet, with a north and south pole just like any ordinary magnet.

AROUND THE SUN
As well as spinning on its own axis, the Earth is constantly moving around the Sun. One complete path around the Sun is an orbit. The length of a year is determined by the time it takes a planet to make one orbit. This means that the Earth travels 958 million kilometres at an average speed of 30km per second.

CHANGING SEASONS
The Earth is tilted towards the Sun at an angle of 23.5°. As the Earth orbits, those places that are tilted towards the Sun receive more warmth and light for the part of the year that is known as summer. As these places move further round, they tilt away from the Sun, experiencing winter.

THE EARTH'S MAKE-UP
Beneath its thin shell, or crust, the interior of the Earth is very hot. Below about 70km, there is a mantle of rock that is semi-molten (partly melted). The outer layer of the Earth's core is molten too, but enormous pressure keeps the inner core (the centre) solid, even though temperatures here reach over 6,000°C. The upper layer of the mantle is made of plates, like pieces of a jigsaw, with the continents on top. Sometimes, the plates rub together, causing pressure. Earthquakes occur when the plates move.

FROM CORE TO CRUST

If we could cut a piece out of the Earth like a giant apple, we would see a planet made in four layers. At its centre is a solid inner core of almost pure iron, surrounded by an outer core of liquid iron and nickel. Enveloping this is a mantle of silicon compounds, crystals and lighter metals, topped with a hard rock crust.

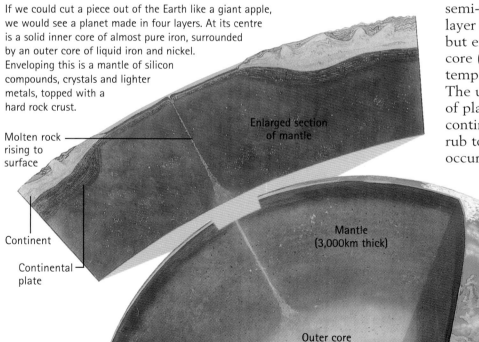

Enlarged section of mantle

Molten rock rising to surface

Continent

Continental plate

Mantle
(3,000km thick)

Outer core
(2,200km thick)

Inner core
(2,500km across)

The Earth is wrapped in a blanket of gases known as the atmosphere, which stretches up more than 500km into space. It is held in place by the gravitational pull of the planet

THE EVOLVING EARTH

Astronomers believe that the Earth began to form about 4.6 billion years ago, when the solar nebula (a vast cloud of hot debris circling the newly formed Sun) began to cluster together into lumps that eventually became the planets of our solar system. The process took millions of years to complete and Earth, like the other planets, developed a unique chemistry and atmosphere.

1 Hot clouds of dust and gases spin around the newly formed Sun. As the specks of dust collide, they stick together in lumps.

2 The forces of gravity pull more passing lumps into the spinning ball. Heavy elements such as iron sink to the centre.

3 Lighter metals and rocks come to the surface and the red-hot Earth cools enough for a hard shell to form.

4 Gases escaping from the Earth form clouds and rain falls, creating oceans containing small oxygen-producing plants.

5 Originally one large mass of land, the Earth's land surface is now split into seven chunks, known as continents.

LIFE ON EARTH

Why exactly there is life on Earth is still a mystery to scientists. The theories are numerous, but the answer is probably a combination of reasons. Firstly, Earth's distance from the Sun is ideal – not too hot like Venus, nor too cold like Mars. Secondly, Earth has water, which covers more than 70 per cent of its surface. Scientists believe that electrical storms on the newly formed planet caused chemical reactions between gases in the atmosphere. these created the first building blocks of life, which fell into the oceans, where they combined to form simple plant-like creatures. All plants make oxygen, and so an ideal atmosphere was soon created for the evolution of oxygen-breathing life forms.

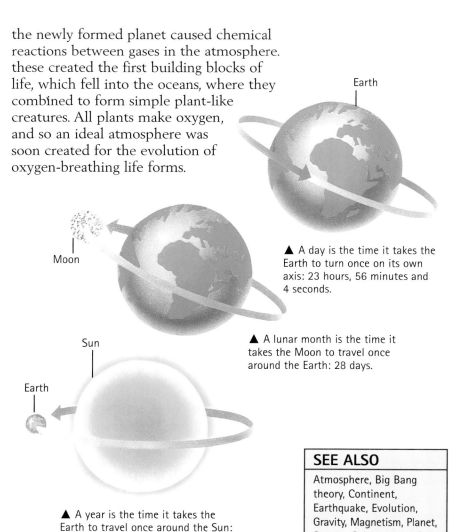

▲ A day is the time it takes the Earth to turn once on its own axis: 23 hours, 56 minutes and 4 seconds.

▲ A lunar month is the time it takes the Moon to travel once around the Earth: 28 days.

Earth

Moon

Sun

Earth

▲ A year is the time it takes the Earth to travel once around the Sun: 365 days, 6 hours and 9 minutes.

EARTH FACTS AND FIGURES

• The Earth's diameter (the distance from Pole to Pole through the centre) is 12,714km

• The Earth's circumference (the distance around its middle at the Equator) is 40,075km

• As the Earth spins, places near the Equator move much faster than places at the Poles, causing the planet to bulge slightly in the middle and be flattened at the top and bottom

• The temperature of the Earth's inner core may be as hot as 6,200°C

• Of the eight planets in our solar system, Earth is the third closest to the Sun

• The Sun and the Earth are about 150 million kilometres apart

• The Earth's path around the Sun is not a circle but an ellipse (an oval), which means it is closer to the Sun on January 1 than on June 1

SEE ALSO

Atmosphere, Big Bang theory, Continent, Earthquake, Evolution, Gravity, Magnetism, Planet, Season, Solar system, Sun, Time, Volcano

EARTHQUAKE

An earthquake is a shaking of the Earth's surface. It is caused by the sudden release of pressure through weak parts of the Earth's crust.

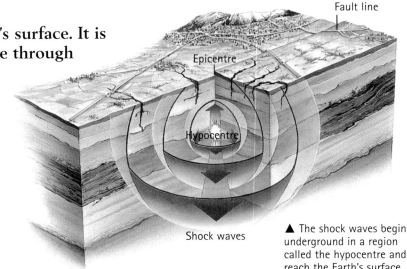

The vast majority of earthquakes do not cause any serious damage. Small tremors can happen with an erupting volcano, an avalanche or a landslide. However, the largest earthquakes occur as a result of pressure or tension deep under the ground being released through weak areas (fault lines) in the Earth's crust.

TECTONIC PLATES

The Earth's crust is broken into giant slabs called tectonic plates. Sometimes, pressure builds up underground as a result of the plates moving against each other. The pressure is suddenly released, sending out shock waves in all directions and causing the Earth's crust to shake and even crack.

EARTHQUAKE ZONES

Two great earthquake zones exist. Both are where two tectonic plates meet. One stretches across southern Asia, through the Mediterranean and into East Africa. The other is the 'ring of fire' around the Pacific Ocean, which includes the USA. In 1906, a large part of San Francisco was destroyed by an earthquake in this zone.

▲ The shock waves begin underground in a region called the hypocentre and reach the Earth's surface directly above, at the epicentre. From here, they radiate out in all directions.

SHOCK WAVES

Earthquake shock waves are known as seismic waves. They are detected using a measuring instrument called a seismometer. A severe earthquake can be felt as much as 400km away. Geologists measure the size of an earthquake using the Moment Magnitude Scale (MMS), which indicates how much energy it has released.

DISASTER IN JAPAN

In 2011, Japan was devastated by the effects of a Magnitude 9.0 offshore earthquake. It triggered powerful tsunamis up to 40m high. The worst-hit region was Tohoku, in the northeast. More than 19,500 people died, 125,000 buildings were destroyed or damaged and reactors at the Fukushima nuclear plant blew up, leaking radiation into the countryside.

SEE ALSO
Continent, Earth, Mountain and valley, Ocean and sea, Volcano

EASTERN EUROPE

Eastern Europe is a geographical region of countries that were once part of the communist bloc controlled by the Soviet Union.

BELARUS
Area: 207,546 sq km
Population: 9,481,000
Capital: Minsk
Languages: Belarusian and Russian
Currency: Belarusian rouble

CZECH REPUBLIC
Area: 78,864 sq km
Population: 10,507,000
Capital: Prague
Language: Czech
Currency: Czech koruna

HUNGARY
Area: 93,030 sq km
Population: 9,986,000
Capital: Budapest
Language: Hungarian
Currency: Forint

MOLDOVA
Area: 33,873 sq km
Population: 4,090,000
Capital: Chisinau
Language: Moldovan
Currency: Moldovan leu

POLAND
Area: 312,685 sq km
Population: 38,187,000
Capital: Warsaw
Language: Polish
Currency: Zloty

Eastern Europe lies between the Baltic Sea, the Balkan peninsula, the Black Sea and Russia. It makes up more than one sixth of Europe's land area, and is a region of plains, low hills and mountains.

PEAKS AND PLAINS
To the south lie the rugged Carpathian Mountains and Transylvanian Alps. The highest point is Gerlachovsky Stit, a peak of 2,656m in the Carpathians. To the west is the Hungarian Plain and to the east are the vast rolling steppes (grasslands) of Ukraine.

A REGION OF RIVERS
The area is watered by some of Europe's major rivers. The Danube, Europe's second longest river (2,858km), forms much of Romania's southwestern border, while the Dnieper and the Dniester both flow through Ukraine. Europe's largest swamp, the Pripet Marshes, straddles the border between Belarus and Ukraine.

▼ The medieval city of Prague, capital of the Czech Republic, has some of Europe's most beautiful and well-preserved architecture.

▲ Huge expanses of steppe once covered Ukraine but this land, covered with rich soil, is now heavily farmed.

CONTINENTAL CLIMATE
Away from the mountains, Eastern Europe has warm summers with average temperatures reaching 20°C or more in July. Winters get colder as you travel from west to east. Most of the region has moderate rainfall, with 500mm to 1,000mm per year, but the southeast is drier, with less than 500mm of rain a year.

BREAD BASKET OF EUROPE
In the lowlands, many of the region's forests have been cleared for farming. The fertile steppes, once an area of natural grassland, are also farmed. Ukraine is sometimes called 'the bread basket of Europe' because of its high production of grains and other crops. ▶

N

BALTIC SEA

LATVIA

LITHUANIA

RUSSIA

■Minsk

BELARUS

RUSSIA

miles
0   100
0   100
km

GERMANY

Vistula

Warsaw ■

POLAND

Pripet
Marshes

■Prague

CZECH REPUBLIC

Kiev ■

UKRAINE

Dnieper

SLOVAKIA

Gerlachovsky Stit

Dniester

AUSTRIA

■Bratislava

Carpathian Mountains

MOLDOVA

HUNGARY

■Budapest

Hungarian Plain

Chisinau ■

SLOVENIA

Danube

CASPIAN SEA

CROATIA

ROMANIA

BLACK SEA

Transylvanian Alps

SERBIA

Bucharest ■

Danube

BULGARIA

BALKAN PENINSULA

ROMANIA
Area: 237,500 sq km
Population: 21,462,000
Capital: Bucharest
Language: Romanian
Currency: Leu

SLOVAKIA
Area: 49,036 sq km
Population: 5,425,000
Capital: Bratislava
Language: Slovak
Currency: Euro

UKRAINE
Area: 603,700 sq km
Population: 45,779,000
Capital: Kiev
Language: Ukrainian
Currency: Hryvnia

▶ Old-fashioned factories, such as this one in Romania, cause air, water and soil pollution in many parts of Eastern Europe.

DISAPPEARING WILDLIFE

As in the rest of Europe, the wildlife in Eastern Europe has been reduced by the destruction of forests and grasslands. A number of large mammals that once grazed on the steppes, such as the saiga antelope, have now disappeared. The rare wisent (European bison) is found in western Belarus and central Poland, while the Danube delta on the Black Sea is a major wetland and home to many birds.

HEAVY AND LIGHT INDUSTRY

Coal, oil and natural gas, iron ore and other minerals are found in this region. Heavy industry produces machinery,

▲ The practice of Eastern Orthodox Christianity is widespread in Belarus, Moldova, Romania and Ukraine. Here, Holy Communion is celebrated in Kiev, Ukraine.

transport equipment and steel, and the manufacture of electronic goods, clothes and processed food is increasing.

CITY DWELLERS

Many people live in rural areas, and a few people still follow a nomadic lifestyle. But more than two thirds of the people live and work in towns and cities. Kiev, in Ukraine, is the largest city in Eastern Europe, with a population of 3,250,000.

RELIGIOUS WORSHIP

Religion is an important part of life for many people in Eastern Europe. The two dominant faiths in the region are Roman Catholic and Eastern Orthodox Christianity. There is a Muslim minority in Romania, which was once part of the Muslim Ottoman Empire.

FOREIGN POWERS

All of the countries of Eastern Europe have at times in their history been under the influence of a foreign power. In 1793, Poland disappeared after being divided up among Prussia, Austria and Russia. Hungary and Czechoslovakia formed part of the Habsburg Empire until 1918. Romania gained its independence from Turkey in 1878. More recently, Ukraine, Belarus and Moldova were part of the Russian-dominated Soviet Union.

COMMUNIST RULE

After World War II, all the countries of Eastern Europe came under communist rule, either as part of the Soviet Union or as members of the Soviet bloc. Romania remained outside Soviet control, but under the communist dictator Nicolae Ceausescu.

THE NEW MAP

Belarus, Moldova and Ukraine gained their independence in 1991, following the break-up of the Soviet Union. In 1993, Czechoslovakia split peacefully into two countries: the Czech Republic and Slovakia. All but Belarus, Ukraine and Moldova are now part of the European Union. All these countries have experienced considerable migration of people to western Europe in search of work since 1990.

▲ Holiday-makers in Budapest play chess in one of Hungary's many natural hot springs.

DEMOCRACY IN HUNGARY

From the end of World War II, Hungary, like the rest of Eastern Europe, came under Soviet communist rule. However, demonstrations in favour of democracy, such as this one in Budapest in 1988, indicated people's unhappiness with the government. In 1989, Hungary was the first Eastern European country to shake off communism. In March 1990, it elected its first democratic government in 42 years.

EUROPA!

CAVE
CANEM

SEE ALSO

Cold War, Communism, Democracy, Europe, Russia and the Baltic States

ECOLOGY

Ecology is the study of how plants, animals and humans live together in their natural surroundings, and the ways in which they affect one another.

THE FOOD CHAIN

Each organism in a food chain feeds on and gets energy from the level above. Ecologists divide plants and animals in a chain into groups, depending on how they get their energy. Plants are energy producers, using the Sun's energy to produce new growth. Animals are consumers, obtaining energy by eating plants or other animals.

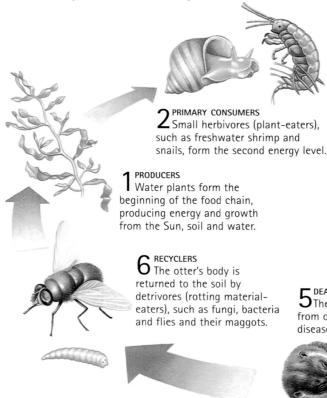

2 PRIMARY CONSUMERS
Small herbivores (plant-eaters), such as freshwater shrimp and snails, form the second energy level.

1 PRODUCERS
Water plants form the beginning of the food chain, producing energy and growth from the Sun, soil and water.

3 SECONDARY CONSUMERS
The third level of energy usage is by larger carnivores (meat-eaters) such as trout, which feed on the shrimp and snails.

4 TOP PREDATOR
In the fourth level of energy transfer, a bigger carnivore such as an otter preys on the trout.

6 RECYCLERS
The otter's body is returned to the soil by detrivores (rotting material-eaters), such as fungi, bacteria and flies and their maggots.

5 DEATH
The otter dies from old age or disease.

Every plant and animal depends on a cycle of food, energy and waste disposal that links it to other plants and animals. Ecologists study how plants and animals are linked to each other in food chains and webs.

CHAINED TOGETHER

All living things need energy. Plants use light energy from the Sun to turn substances in the soil, air and water into food. Insects eat the plants, and fish, birds and other animals eat the insects. In this way, energy is passed along a food chain. When living things die, their bodies break down and release nutrients back into the ground to start the process again.

ECOSYSTEMS

An ecosystem is made up of the plants and animals in a certain area, together with the air, soil, climate and other non-living things. A forest is one type of ecosystem, but there are many others. An ecosystem can be as small as a pond or as large as an ocean.

HUMANS INTERVENE

Humans are part of the biggest ecosystem of all – the Earth itself. Some human actions can affect the entire planet. Logging a rainforest, for example, affects the forest by destroying its plants and animals. Since trees produce the oxygen needed by humans and other life forms, the world's oxygen supply is also affected.

GREY SQUIRREL INVASION

The introduction of animals or plants from foreign lands can have harmful effects on the ecology of an area. When grey squirrels from North America were introduced to Britain, the native red squirrels were pushed out of the food chain in most areas.

▲ Many timber companies manage their forests ecologically using a process known as artificial reforestation. This means that a constant supply of seeds is sown in a nursery and transplanted to the forest to replace felled trees.

SEE ALSO

Animal, Brazil, Conservation, Forest, Habitat, Plant, Pollution

EDUCATION

Education is the development of skills and knowledge. It can be formal, as provided by schools, or informal – via playing, watching and learning in everyday life.

Learning to play a musical instrument is free as part of the curriculum in some countries. In other places, pupils must pay for lessons.

School trips are a fun and exciting way of relating subjects learnt in the classroom to real-life objects and situations.

Many people feel that the main reason for educating children is to benefit society, by teaching skills needed to keep the community going. Others feel that it is more important to develop an individual's talents and interests. The Ancient Greek philosopher Socrates believed that education could make people happier.

SCHOOL FOR ALL

The Ancient Greeks were the first to set up a formal education system, but only for boys of rich families. Lessons included the art of public speaking for budding politicians. In many countries, the church or charities governed schooling. It wasn't until the 1800s that governments began to take control, and the 1900s before education became free for most girls and boys. However, millions of people worldwide still do not possess the basic skills of reading and writing.

BEST YEARS OF YOUR LIFE

In most countries, it is compulsory for children to go to primary school at the age of five or six, then on to a secondary (high) school at about 11 years of age. Some start earlier. Friedrich Froebel opened the first kindergarten (nursery) in Germany in 1837. In many parts of the world, attendance drops after the age of 11, but education can continue into adulthood at colleges or universities. Courses offer vocational (career) training or specialist qualifications.

THE CURRICULUM

The curriculum (subjects taught) varies in each country. It may emphasize religion, local crafts or history. Many 19th-century schools concentrated on reading, writing and arithmetic. Subjects and teaching methods have changed over the years, as have educational theories. The 17th-century Czech educationalist, Comenius, thought pictures were a vital teaching tool. Italian reformer Maria Montessori (1870–1952) devised wooden apparatus to help children learn through exploration.

SCHOOLS OF THOUGHT

Styles of teaching, subjects taught and classroom settings have changed over the years. Once children had to sit in rows in silence while the teacher lectured them. Now, there is more emphasis on interaction and small group tuition. Educators argue about which is best – formal instruction (presenting facts to learn) or learning through activity and experience.

▲ A government health advisor visits a classroom in the USA in 1925 to instruct children on healthy eating.

SEE ALSO

Greece (Ancient)

125

EGYPT

Egypt lies in the northeast of Africa. More people live there than in any other African nation except Nigeria and Ethiopia, yet just four per cent of its land is inhabited.

Area: 997,739 sq km
Population: 77,775,000
Capital: Cairo
Language: Arabic
Currency: Egyptian pound

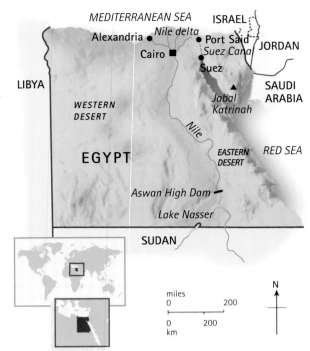

Most Egyptians live around the Nile delta and valley, and along the Suez Canal, a vital shipping link for world trade. The River Nile, controlled by the Aswan High Dam, provides fertile land stretching from Egypt's border with Sudan in the south right up to the Mediterranean Sea in the north. Egypt's main cities are its capital, Cairo, and the port of Alexandria – two of the largest cities in Africa.

DESERT AREAS
On either side of the Nile lie two deserts that together cover more than 90 per cent of the country – the vast, low-lying Western Desert and the hilly Eastern Desert, which borders the Red Sea.

AGRICULTURAL LIFE
Agriculture is the country's most important industry, employing about a third of all Egyptians. These farmers, known as *fellahin*, grow cotton and food crops such as maize and rice in the fertile Nile delta. The manufacturing industry is growing, and tourists attracted by the ancient ruins also generate income for many Egyptians. Oil, cotton and cloth are major exports.

Traders, such as this man selling herbs and tea, set up their stalls in open street markets, or bazaars.

A MUSLIM POPULATION
Most Egyptians are descended from the people of Ancient Egypt or from Arabs who invaded in the 7th century CE. Ninety per cent of the people are Muslims.

EGYPT TODAY
Egypt was part of the Ottoman Empire from 1517 until 1922. Britain controlled the Suez Canal and had administrative power in the country from the 1880s until the 1950s. President Hosni Mubarak ruled as dictator from 1981 until 2011, when massive protests forced him to step down.

Egypt's main port of Alexandria was the world's greatest trading city 2,000 years ago.

▶ Triangular-sailed wooden boats called feluccas carry goods and passengers along the Nile.

> **SEE ALSO**
> Africa, Egypt (Ancient), Islam, Middle East

EGYPT, ANCIENT

Ancient Egypt developed along the River Nile around 5,000 years ago. Over the next 2,500 years, it grew into one of the greatest civilizations of all time.

The funeral mask of Tutankhamen, boy-king of Egypt (1361-52BCE), was discovered in1922.

The tombs of important officials contained models of items that they might need in the next world.

The Ancient Egyptians chose to settle by the Nile in Africa because each year the river flooded, spreading mud over the banks. This provided them with fertile land to farm.

PYRAMID BUILDERS
The Ancient Egyptians were the first real engineers and built impressive temples, cities and pyramids. The largest of the pyramids needed over two million blocks of stone, each weighing as much as 2.5 tonnes. Some were cut from distant quarries and floated down the Nile by raft.

IMPORTANT INVENTORS
The Egyptians used papyrus reeds to make shoes, boats, ropes and writing paper. Papyrus scrolls preserve Ancient Egyptian hieroglyphic writing. The Egyptians also invented a 365-day calendar.

▲ Pyramids were burial monuments for kings. A Sphinx (half man, half lion) stands beside the pyramids at Giza.

LIFE AFTER DEATH
Many gods were worshipped, including the sun-god Ra, and Osiris, god of the dead. The Egyptian kings, or pharaohs, were also believed to be gods. When they died, the kings and queens were buried in tombs full of things they might need in the next world – food, jewels, even small statues of servants (*shabtis*). Most royal tombs were later robbed, but in 1922, the tomb of the boy pharaoh Tutankhamen was found with most of its treasures untouched.

THREE GREAT ERAS
Ancient Egypt included three great ages: the Old Kingdom, Middle Kingdom and New Kingdom. In 31BCE, Cleopatra died and Egypt fell to the Roman Empire.

MUMMIFIED BODIES

The Ancient Egyptians believed in life after death. Their bodies were mummified (preserved) before burial to prevent decay. It took 70 days to mummify a body.

The body was preserved in salt for 40 days to dry. Before being bandaged, the dried body was rubbed with oils and spices and the heart placed inside

Most of the internal organs were put into canopic jars. This human-headed one held the liver

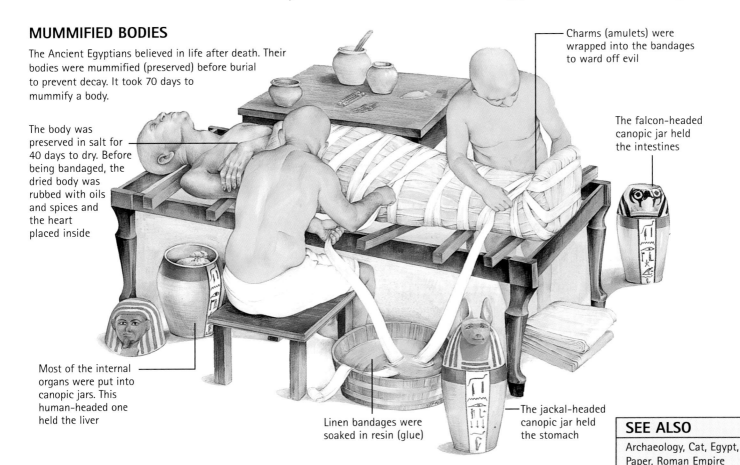

Charms (amulets) were wrapped into the bandages to ward off evil

The falcon-headed canopic jar held the intestines

Linen bandages were soaked in resin (glue)

The jackal-headed canopic jar held the stomach

SEE ALSO
Archaeology, Cat, Egypt, Paper, Roman Empire

ELECTRICITY

Electricity is a form of energy. It can be stored in batteries or sent along wires to make electric trains, computers, light bulbs and other devices work.

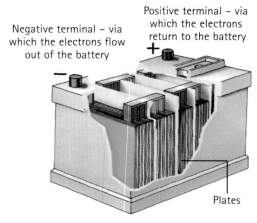

Negative terminal – via which the electrons flow out of the battery

Positive terminal – via which the electrons return to the battery

Plates

▲ Wet batteries, like those in cars, store electricity and can be recharged. Six cells contain lead and lead dioxide plates in a solution of dilute sulphuric acid. The battery is first charged by an outside electrical source, but after that a generator, run by the car's engine, keeps it charged.

Electricity is an invisible form of energy created by the movement of charged particles. It flows into our homes along wires and can be easily converted into other energy forms, such as heat and light.

▲ Each light bulb in a circuit creates resistance to the flow of electric current, and so light bulbs wired in series do not glow brightly.

PASSING ON ELECTRONS

Everything in the world, including humans and the air they breathe, is made of atoms. Each of these tiny particles has a positively charged centre (nucleus), with smaller, negatively charged electrons whizzing around it. Electricity is created when one of the electrons jumps to another atom. This can be caused by the magnetic field in a generator, by chemicals in a battery, or by friction (rubbing materials together).

THALES THE PHILOSOPHER

The discovery that an electric charge could be created by rubbing two materials together was first made by the Greek philosopher Thales over 2,600 years ago. He found that if he rubbed the fossilized tree sap, amber, with silk, it attracted feathers and dust. We now know that this happened because electrons had been passed between the silk and the amber,

▲ Light bulbs wired in parallel all glow brightly, because each light bulb is connected directly to the battery.

making them electrically charged. In recognition of his discovery, our word electron comes from the Greek word *elecktron*, meaning amber.

CONDUCTORS AND INSULATORS

The electricity of substances such as amber is called static electricity because the charge stays put once the electrons have moved between the atoms. In other substances, the electrons carry on flowing. These substances are called conductors. Most electrical wires are made of copper because it is a good electrical conductor, as are all metals. Water also conducts electricity, which is why it is dangerous to

HOW A GENERATOR WORKS

An electric generator works by using the principle of electro-magnetic induction discovered in 1831 by the British chemist and physicist Michael Faraday (1791–1867). He discovered that if a coil of wire is spun between two magnets, electrons begin to flow inside the wire coil. An alternating current (AC) and a direct current (DC) can be created in this way.

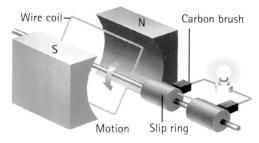

Wire coil · Carbon brush · S · N · Motion · Slip ring

▲ The two magnets naturally produce an alternating current (AC). As the coil spins, the magnetic field inside the coil points first one way and then the other. This makes the electric current change direction, or alternate.

Wire coil · S · N · Carbon brush · Commutator · Motion

▲ To create a direct current (DC), which flows in only one direction, the coil must be attached to a device called a commutator which is able to reverse the current.

▶ Practical DC generators are used to power large industrial motors. Unlike Faraday's simple model, a generator has many coils of wire wound on a rotor.

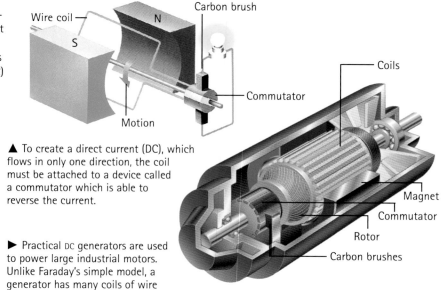

Coils · Magnet · Commutator · Rotor · Carbon brushes

ELECTRICAL TERMS

Conductor Any substance through which an electric current can flow

Coulomb (C) The measurement of electric charge

Current How fast electrons flow along a conductor – it is measured in amperes (A)

Insulator Any substance through which an electric current cannot flow

Resistance How hard it is for current to flow through a conductor – it is measured in ohms (Ω)

Static electricity Electric charge created by two objects rubbing together and exchanging electrons

Voltage (V) A unit of measurement describing how powerfully a battery sends electric current

Watt A unit of measurement that describes how much electrical energy can be converted into heat and light energy per second

operate electrical appliances with wet hands. Other materials are made of atoms between which it is almost impossible for electrons to flow. These materials are known as insulators, and include plastic, wood and amber. A flow of electrons is known as a current, and the term 'resistance' is a measure of how difficult it is for current to flow through a conductor.

COMPLETING THE CIRCUIT

For an electrical appliance such as a torch to work, its electricity source (the battery) must be connected to the bulb by wires in an unbroken loop. This is known as a circuit. The job of the torch's ON/OFF switch is to open or close a gap in the circuit. When the switch is on, electricity is allowed to flow around the circuit, lighting the bulb. When the switch is off, the circuit is broken and the current cannot flow.

MAINS SUPPLY

Batteries have a limited amount of chemicals and can only provide a certain amount of electricity. That is why most electrical devices are powered by a mains supply. Wires connect millions of wall sockets to a power station. An electric current flows from the power station along the wires, out of the sockets and into the equipment being used. To complete the circuit, the current returns to the power station through yet more wires.

PRODUCING ELECTRICITY

All power stations have a generator which produces electricity. In nuclear power stations, the nuclear reactor creates the heat needed to turn water into steam. The steam turns giant wheels, called turbines, which power the generator. The electricity it produces then flows along wires to homes, shops and offices.

THE POWER STATION

The nuclear reactor splits atoms to create the heat needed to produce steam to spin the turbines.

Water heats up and turns to steam

Nuclear reactor

Condenser

Cooling tower

Generator

Transformer

Steam spins the turbine which powers the generator

THE ELECTRICITY GRID

Electricity from the power station travels via step-up and step-down transformers which convert it to the voltage needed for distribution.

Nuclear power station

Step-up transformer

Substation

Step-down transformer

Large factory

Underground transformer

Substation

Homes

Transformer

ALTERNATING CURRENT

The electricity that comes out of a power station is in the form of alternating current (AC). Unlike a battery, which produces a steady one-way current called a direct current (DC), the mains supply flows first in one direction and then the other. The current changes direction very rapidly (about 50 times a second).

SEE ALSO

Atom and molecule, Electronics, Energy, Heat, Magnetism, Nuclear power

ELECTRONICS

Electronics is a branch of engineering which studies the components and circuits that make up modern electrical devices, such as radios and toasters.

Modern electrical devices contain tiny electronic parts called components, which are joined together by lines of metallic paint on circuit boards. Electronic engineers know how to put together the right components to make circuits that can perform specific jobs.

WORKING PARTS
Components affect the way electrons (tiny charged particles) flow through a circuit. The simplest component, the switch, breaks the flow of electrons, or current. Resistors make it harder for the current to flow, while capacitors store current as electrical charge. Diodes let current flow in only one direction.

TRANSISTOR TECHNOLOGY
The first circuits used bulky glass valves, or vacuum tubes, which could magnify a current or switch it on or off. This ability to turn a current on or off electronically is the principle behind all computers. In the

1950s, the valve was replaced by a device called the transistor, which was much smaller, cheaper and more durable, paving the way for the huge electronic advances that were to follow.

BIRTH OF THE MICROCHIP
In the 1970s, the invention of the microchip, which contained thousands of tiny transistors on a piece of material smaller than a stamp, enabled complex circuits to be squeezed into a tiny space. This made the home computer possible. More recently, Very Large Scale Integration (VLSI) has allowed hundreds of millions of transistors to be put on a single chip, meaning that even smaller computers can be made.

ELECTRONICS TODAY
Electronics is now part of virtually all electrical devices. The microprocessor, a complex circuit fitted onto a single chip, is used in devices ranging from space rockets and robots to DVD players, laptops and smartphones.

Until the 1950s, radios used glass valves, which were bulky and fragile.

In the 1950s, the small, robust transistor began to replace the valve.

In the 1970s, microchips made hand-sized radio-cassette players possible.

Today's radios are often tiny, and digital radios are replacing analogue radios in many cases.

HOW A DIGITAL WATCH WORKS
A digital watch is powered by a battery. Its timing is controlled by a quartz crystal, which vibrates thousands of times a second. The microchip uses these vibrations to keep time, which it displays in numbers.

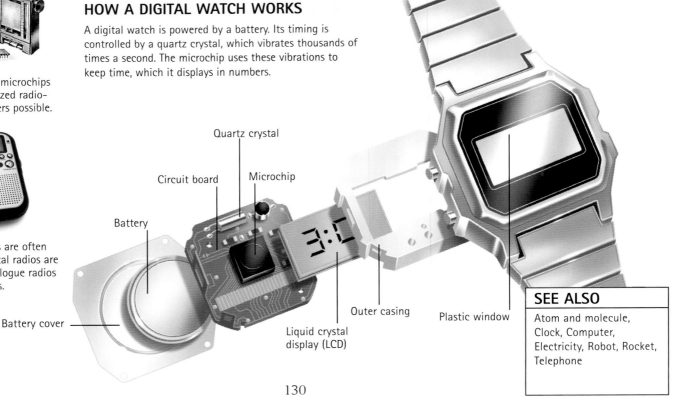

Quartz crystal

Circuit board

Microchip

Battery

Battery cover

Outer casing

Plastic window

Liquid crystal display (LCD)

SEE ALSO

Atom and molecule, Clock, Computer, Electricity, Robot, Rocket, Telephone

ELEPHANT

Elephants are the largest animals on land. They have very thick skin, a trunk and ivory tusks. There are three species: two live in Africa and one in Asia.

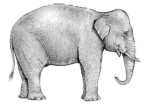

The Asian or Indian elephant grows to around 3m at the shoulder and weighs up to 5 tonnes.

The African savanna elephant is the largest land animal. It stands 4m and weighs up to 6 tonnes.

The African savanna elephant lives in open grassland. The African forest elephant, only recognized as a separate species in 2000, lives in rainforests. The Asian elephant also lives in forests. It has smaller ears than a savanna elephant, and its trunk ends in one tip, not two.

EATING MACHINES
Elephants live on a diet of leaves and bark, eating up to 200kg of food a day. They use their strong trunks, which are giant, flexible nostrils, to pull up plants and to bring food and water to their mouths. They have 12 back teeth (molars), but only four are fully developed and in use at any one time. All elephants have tusks, or extra long curved teeth, which they use to strip bark off trees and to dig for water.

PROTECTIVE INSTINCTS
Female elephants start to breed when they are about ten years old. They are pregnant for 20 months, before giving birth to a single calf. When a calf is about to be born, other females gather around the mother and the herd stays in one place until the young calf, which stands nearly a metre tall, is on its feet and ready to move on.

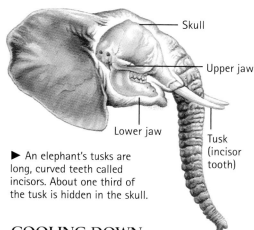

▶ An elephant's tusks are long, curved teeth called incisors. About one third of the tusk is hidden in the skull.

Skull — Upper jaw — Lower jaw — Tusk (incisor tooth)

COOLING DOWN
Because elephants have no sweat glands, they lose very little body heat. They cool down by hiding in the shade and flapping their ears, or by bathing in water and using their trunks to shower themselves.

OLD AGE
All elephants, except the old bull males, are sociable animals and live in herds led by the oldest females. They can live for over 60 years, but many are killed for their ivory tusks. In many places the bull elephants, which have the biggest tusks, have become rare. The spread of human settlements has also led to both Asian and African elephants becoming endangered.

SEE ALSO
Africa, Animal, India, Mammal

EMPIRE

An empire is a group of nations or states under the control of a single power. Most empires are built up when one country conquers others.

Octavian, later called, Augustus, became the first Emperor of Rome in 27BCE.

From 527 to 565, Justinian ruled the Byzantine Empire with his wife Theodora.

In 1525, Babar founded the Mughal Empire by conquering northern India.

Suleiman strengthened and enlarged the 16th-century Ottoman Empire.

Maria Theresa and Francis I unified the Habsburg Empire in the 1740s.

Haile Selassie, emperor of Ethiopia, was overthrown by the army in 1974.

BRITISH INDIA
Over 600 small states, ruled by leaders including rajahs and maharajahs, came under the British Empire in India. They had their own laws, armies and finances, but British troops were stationed in some states to ensure loyalty.

Some of the greatest empires in history were the Roman, Byzantine, Japanese, Ottoman, Russian and British empires. Each was ruled by an emperor or empress, but there have been other types of rule.

POWER GROWTH
Empires are usually built up when a country becomes richer or has larger armed forces than its neighbours, allowing it to spread its power and influence. The Greek king Alexander the Great trained his army with new weapons and tactics before conquering a vast empire from 334 to 323BCE. The European Habsburg dynasty used royal marriages and treaties to expand its Holy Roman Empire for more than 300 years from the 15th century. In the 1800s, the British Empire was won by economic strength, backed up by military superiority when needed.

IMPERIAL RULE
Many empires are ruled by a single state or nation, often with great brutality. The Assyrians in the Ancient Middle East used their army to enforce the king's rule and to collect taxes. Those who disobeyed were cruelly punished. The Mongol Empire was run as a dictatorship in which the khan's wishes were enforced by the army. Other empires allowed some freedoms to their subjects. The states in the Athenian Empire of the 5th century BCE met each year to discuss events. Many of the cities and states in the Holy Roman Empire were free to run their own affairs, make their own laws and even go to war.

KEY DATES

1500–1100BCE Egyptian New Kingdom rules an empire in southwest Asia

850–609BCE Assyrian Empire rules the Middle East.

559–326BCE Persian Empire flourishes

264BCE–410CE Rome expands to rule vast areas before falling to barbarian invasion

228BCE China united under the Qin Dynasty

800CE Holy Roman Empire begins with the coronation of Charlemagne

1206 Genghis Khan founds the Mongol Empire

1492–1828 Spain conquers an empire in the Americas before colonies win independence

1880–1950s European powers build empires in Africa and Asia, then grant colonies independence

COLONIAL ADVENTURES

The Industrial Revolution made European states richer and better armed than other peoples. By 1850, several European nations owned colonies in Africa and Asia, which produced wealth and trade. In 1882, the British took over Egypt, prompting other European nations to conquer vast areas of Africa, Asia and the Pacific and turn them into colonies. Within 40 years, it became clear these new colonies produced little wealth, but were costly to maintain.

COLLAPSE OF EMPIRES

Empires may collapse as the result of foreign attack, member states breaking away or internal dispute. The Ancient Persian Empire was defeated in war by the Greeks under Alexander the Great. The Roman Empire was weakened by internal power struggles, and then fell to barbarian attacks in the 5th century. In 1917, the German and Habsburg Empires were divided up into smaller states by the victorious Allies at the end of World War I and the new states were racked by revolution, bringing an end to the Empires.

A POST-IMPERIAL WORLD

Since 1945, very few empires have continued to exist. The colonial empires of the British, French and other European

▲ The great palace of Persepolis was the centre of the Persian Empire, founded by Darius the Great in 559BCE. Nations subject to the Persian 'King of Kings' brought tributes to Persepolis each spring as part of a great festival.

nations broke up when, weakened by World War II, they could not afford to keep the colonies in the face of nationalist independence movements. In 1990, the Soviet Union broke up as the states of the old Russian Empire declared themselves independent. There are few multi-national empires in the world today, because most nations are able to survive economically and do not need to be part of an empire to be protected from invaders.

▲ The Forbidden City, Beijing, was the Palace of the Chinese emperors from 1421 to 1911. It now houses museums and galleries.

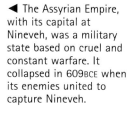

◄ The Assyrian Empire, with its capital at Nineveh, was a military state based on cruel and constant warfare. It collapsed in 609BCE when its enemies united to capture Nineveh.

SEE ALSO

Aztecs, Babylon, Incas, Mongols, Napoleonic Wars, Roman Empire

ENERGY

Energy is the ability to do work. An object or substance has energy if it can move or if it can generate such things as heat, sound, or electricity.

The Sun provides most of the heat and light energy that we use on Earth.

When anything moves, such as a car, it is using kinetic energy.

Dynamite's explosive power comes from stored chemical energy.

A radio produces sound energy by making the atoms in the air vibrate.

A hammer coming down to strike a nail uses the potential energy of gravity.

Nuclear energy takes its most dramatic form in a nuclear explosion.

Energy is everywhere – in sunlight as heat and light energy, in a CD player as sound energy, even in a lump of coal as stored chemical energy. Energy can be converted from one form into another, but it can never be destroyed.

MOVING OBJECTS

One of the most basic forms of energy is the energy of movement, or kinetic energy. Heavy, fast-moving objects have more kinetic energy than light, slow-moving ones. The kinetic energy of a car is less than that of a lorry travelling at the same speed. A parked car has no kinetic energy at all.

HEAT ENERGY

Kinetic energy is also closely related to heat energy. An object is hot because its atoms (the tiny particles that it is made of) are constantly in motion. So an object's heat energy can be thought of as the kinetic energy of its atoms. The faster its atoms move, the hotter the object becomes.

SAVING IT FOR LATER

Energy can be stored to be used later. This energy in storage is called potential energy.

▲ A runner waiting on the blocks to start a race is like a coiled spring ready to expand. When the starter's gun goes, the potential (stored) energy in the runner's muscles is converted into the kinetic (motion) energy of running.

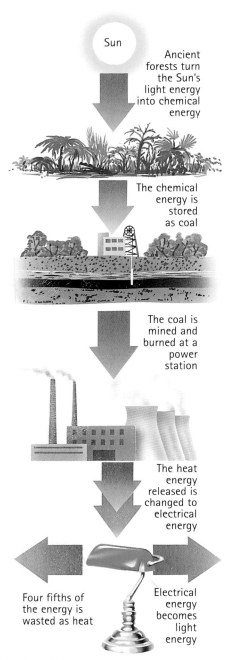

Sun

Ancient forests turn the Sun's light energy into chemical energy

The chemical energy is stored as coal

The coal is mined and burned at a power station

The heat energy released is changed to electrical energy

Four fifths of the energy is wasted as heat

Electrical energy becomes light energy

ENERGY CYCLE

The Sun is our main source of energy on Earth. Every time it is used, the energy changes form. Other natural sources include oil, gas and coal, but we use them wastefully.

A spring stores energy as it is squeezed. When it is released and expands back to its original shape, the potential energy becomes motion (kinetic energy).

CHANGING FORM

The law of conservation of energy says that energy can never be destroyed or lost, but will change its form. For example, if a boy gliding on a pair of roller-skates slowly comes to a halt, his kinetic energy will gradually decrease to zero. But the energy does not vanish, it is transformed into two other energy forms: heat and sound. The heat, created by the friction of the roller-skate wheels rubbing on the ground, warms up both the wheels and the ground. The sound energy can be heard as a swish or squeak of the wheels.

ENERGY AND POWER

Scientists measure energy using units called joules (J). Power – the rate at which energy is used – is measured in watts (W). The idea of power involves time. If two kettles heat a litre of water from 10°C to 100°C, they both give the water the same amount of heat energy. But if one kettle does the job in half the time, it has twice the amount of power as the other. Nuclear power works by releasing the energy locked up inside the nucleus of an atom and using it to do work.

MAKING IT WORK

Energy is never lost, but can be wasted if it is not put to work. Heat is the main cause of energy wastage. For example, an ordinary light bulb converts only one fifth of its electrical energy into light – the rest is wasted as heat. Inefficiency of car engines also means that the Earth's natural energy resources, such as oil, are constantly being wasted.

AN ENERGETIC GAME OF PINBALL

Energy is constantly changing its state. In a game of pinball, potential energy is converted into kinetic energy. The moving ball will tend to slow down through friction as it comes into contact with parts of the machine. Energy is used up in overcoming friction, but it is not lost – it is changed into heat. When the player adds energy to the ball, by pushing it with a flipper, the ball speeds up.

1 Pulling back the plunger coils a spring just behind the ball. In energy terms, the potential energy in the player's hand is transferred to the spring.

2 Letting go of the plunger shoots the ball into play. The spring's potential energy is changed into the kinetic energy of the moving ball.

3 As the ball moves inside the machine, it starts to slow down – its kinetic energy is being changed, mainly into heat. Flippers and obstacles have springs to speed the ball up.

SEE ALSO

Ecology, Electricity, Force and motion, Heat, Light, Magnetism, Nuclear power, Solar power, Sound

ENGINE

Engines are machines which convert energy into mechanical work to power vehicles, to drive other machines or to generate electricity.

▲ A microlite is a hang-glider with an engine. It uses a two-stroke engine, which is lighter, cheaper and more powerful for its size than a four-stroke engine.

FRANK WHITTLE
(1907–87) An officer in the British Royal Air Force, he built the first successful jet engine, known as a gas turbine.

WERNHER VON BRAUN
(1912–77) He was head of the team of German scientists that created the V2 – the first rocket-powered guided missile, and the inspiration for later moon rockets.

The main types of engine are steam, petrol, diesel, jet and rocket. Each one is supplied with energy by burning, or combusting, fuels such as coal, petrol and diesel oil. Nearly all engines are internal combustion engines, which means the fuel is burnt inside the engine. The exception to this is the steam engine, which uses external combustion.

EARLY STEAM ENGINES
In the 18th century, much of the power for the Industrial Revolution was provided by the steam engine. In 1712, Englishman Thomas Newcomen developed the first practical steam engine for pumping water from mines. In 1765, a Scottish engineer, James Watt, began to improve the Newcomen steam engine and developed a much more efficient machine. Soon steam engines were powering factory machinery, as well as railway vehicles such as the *Rocket* locomotive, built by English engineer George Stephenson in 1829.

THE POWER OF STEAM
In a steam engine, a fire is used to boil water to produce high-pressure steam. As the steam expands, it pushes a piston to and fro in a cylinder, or turns the blades of a fan-like wheel called a turbine. These then drive the machine. Most steam engines have been replaced by internal combustion engines. However, many power station generators today are still worked by steam turbines.

PETROL ENGINES
Nowadays, cars, trucks, buses and many trains and aircraft use internal combustion

STEAM LOCOMOTIVE
Steam locomotives powered the railways of the world for over 130 years. Hot gases from the burning coal surround the water tubes, turning the water to steam. The steam passes to the cylinder, driving the piston backwards and forwards. The piston in turn pushes the connecting rod backwards and forwards, which rotates a crank and drives the wheels. Water and coal are carried in the tender.

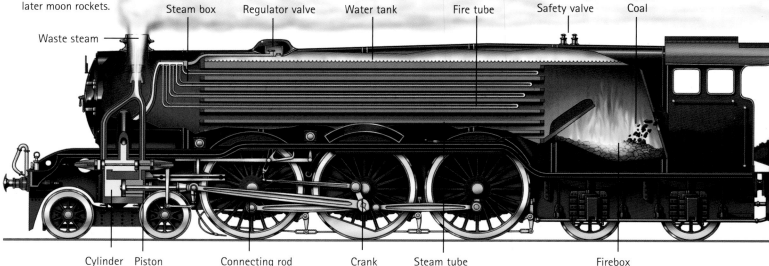

Waste steam — Steam box — Regulator valve — Water tank — Fire tube — Safety valve — Coal

Cylinder Piston Connecting rod Crank Steam tube Firebox

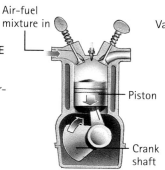
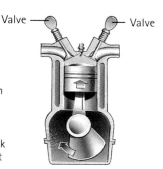

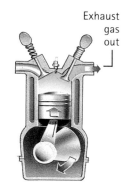

A FOUR-STROKE ENGINE
Cars have internal combustion engines with pistons that work in a four-stroke cycle (the piston makes two movements up and two down). Air and fuel are let into the piston cylinder by valves at the top. The explosion of ignited fuel moves the piston, which turns a crankshaft. This spins the drive shaft.

Air-fuel mixture in

Piston

Crank shaft

1 **Induction.** As the piston goes down, it draws a mixture of air and petrol into the cylinder.

Valve — Valve

2 **Compression.** The piston rises, squashing the fuel and air mixture ready for ignition.

Spark plug

3 **Power.** A spark lights the fuel, forcing the piston down and turning the crankshaft.

Exhaust gas out

4 **Exhaust.** On the final stroke of the engine, the piston rises to expel exhaust (waste) gases.

engines fuelled by diesel oil, petrol or biofuels. In a petrol engine, the fuel mixes with air inside a cylinder, and a spark sets the mixture alight, pushing the piston up and down (see above).

DIESEL ENGINES
Like petrol engines, diesel engines have cylinders, pistons, valves and a fuel supply, but there are no spark plugs or ignition system. The fuel explodes because of the immense heat created when the piston compresses the fuel and air inside a cylinder. The explosion of fuel pushes the piston up and down, powering the vehicle.

THE GAS TURBINE
A jet, or gas-turbine, engine does not have pistons. Instead, air is sucked in at the front of the engine and compressed, or squashed, by the rotating blades of the compressor. The air is blown into the combustion chamber and ignited with aviation fuel. The hot gases are expelled from the back of the engine, pushing the plane forward.

TO THE STARS
Like jet engines, rocket engines also use their exhaust gases to push the vehicle forward. Unlike jets, however, rockets cannot burn fuel by taking in oxygen from the air, as there is no air in space. Instead, they carry their oxygen supply with them, usually as liquid oxygen. The fuel either ignites spontaneously when mixed with the oxygen, or is lit by a spark.

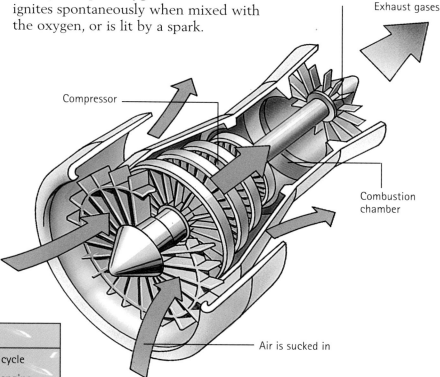

Turbine

Exhaust gases

Compressor

Combustion chamber

Air is sucked in

A JET ENGINE
In a jet aeroplane engine, air is sucked in at the front of the engine by giant rotating blades. The air is then compressed and passed into a combustion (burning) chamber, where it is ignited. The plane is thrust forward by the exhaust gases. These gases also turn a turbine, which drives the compressor.

KEY DATES
1862 Alphonse Beau de Rochas invents the four-stroke cycle

1876 Nikolaus Otto develops the prototype automobile engine

1878 Sir Dougald Clerk invents the two-stroke cycle

1892 Rudolph Diesel patents the diesel engine

1930s C. P. Steinmetz's *Future of Electricity* predicts air pollution from use of coal as fuel

1939 The first jet-engined aircraft, the Heinkel, flies in Germany

1944 The first V2 missile is fired on enemy targets

SEE ALSO
Aircraft, Car, Electricity, Energy, Rocket, Train, Transport

EUROPE

Europe is the second smallest of the world's seven continents. It has 48 countries, including parts of Russia, Turkey and Kazakhstan.

KEY FACTS

- **Area:** 22,887,000 sq km
- **Population:** 713,800,000
- **Number of countries:** 48
- **Largest country:** Russia, 25 per cent (4,309,400 sq km) of which is in Europe
- **Smallest country:** Vatican City (0.44 sq km)
- **Highest point:** Mount Elbrus (5,642m)
- **Largest lake:** Lake Ladoga (17,700 sq km)
- **Longest river:** Volga (3,688km)

▼ Wine is produced throughout Europe, particularly in France (shown here), Germany, Spain, Italy and Bulgaria.

Only the continent of Australia is smaller than Europe, but Europe's moderate climate, rich resources and fertile land support a large population. Between them, the people speak about 50 languages and many more dialects. With its 48 countries, Europe is a continent of diverse cultures.

NEVER FAR FROM WATER

The northwest and west of Europe are bordered by the Arctic and Atlantic Oceans, while the Mediterranean Sea surrounds the south. The coastline is broken up by thousands of fjords and other inlets. However, 16 European countries have no access to the sea.

NORTH EUROPEAN PLAIN

Many of Europe's most populated areas lie on the North European Plain, which stretches from the southern part of the United Kingdom through northern France, Germany and Poland to the Ural Mountains in Russia. To the north are

▲ Iceland in the North Atlantic Ocean is known as the Land of Ice and Fire because of its volcanoes and hot springs set against a landscape of ice fields and glaciers.

forests of coniferous trees such as fir, larch and pine. Deciduous forests of ash, elm and oak grow in central and southern Europe. In the southeast are large areas of dry grassland called steppes.

SCANDINAVIA

In the far north of Europe lies the cold and mountainous region of Scandinavia, which includes the countries of Norway, Sweden, Denmark and Finland. The climate around the Arctic Ocean is cold and snowy, with temperatures in January averaging below –16°C. Few trees grow in the extreme north, but the forests farther south contain large animals such as brown bears, reindeer and wolves.

ARCTIC OCEAN

ICELAND

NORWEGIAN SEA

FINLAND

Lake Ladoga

RUSSIA (European part)

NORWAY

SWEDEN

BALTIC SEA

ESTONIA

LATVIA

NORTH SEA

DENMARK

RUSSIA

LITHUANIA

EUROPEAN PLAIN

BELARUS

KAZAKHSTAN (European part)

UNITED KINGDOM

IRELAND

1 NORTH

GERMANY

POLAND

2

3

ATLANTIC OCEAN

CZECH REPUBLIC

SLOVAKIA

UKRAINE

Carpathian Mts

Volga

5

FRANCE

4

AUSTRIA

HUNGARY

18

10 11

ROMANIA

Caspian Sea

Mt. Elbrus

Pyrenees

7

6

9

12

13

BLACK SEA

PORTUGAL

SPAIN

8

ITALY

14 15

16

BULGARIA

Bosporus

TURKEY (European part)

MEDITERRANEAN SEA

17

GREECE

CYPRUS

MALTA

miles
0   500
0   500
km

N

KEY TO MAP
1 THE NETHERLANDS
2 BELGIUM
3 LUXEMBOURG
4 SWITZERLAND
5 LIECHTENSTEIN
6 MONACO
7 ANDORRA
8 VATICAN CITY
9 SAN MARINO
10 SLOVENIA
11 CROATIA
12 BOSNIA–HERZEGOVINA
13 SERBIA
14 MONTENEGRO
15 KOSOVO
16 MACEDONIA
17 ALBANIA
18 MOLDOVA

THE MEDITERRANEAN

The southern part of Europe is divided from the north by three mountain ranges: the Pyrenees, the Alps and the Carpathian Mountains. The Mediterranean countries of southern Europe, including Italy, Spain and Greece, have mild, rainy winters and hot, dry summers.

A FERTILE CONTINENT

Europe is a fertile continent with farms covering more than half the land. Crops include barley, oats, potatoes and wheat, and citrus fruits and olives in the south. Vast areas of steppes in southern Russia and Ukraine and are farmed for grain.

OIL, GAS AND COAL

Oil and natural gas are produced in the North Sea, and coal is found in large quantities in Europe. These fuels help power the continent's many factories – Europe produces more manufactured goods than any other continent, including cars, electronic goods, ships and steel.

A MIXED POPULATION

Most Europeans are the descendants of people who lived on the continent in prehistoric times, but there is a long history of immigration from Africa, Asia and the Caribbean region. About 77 per cent of the population lives in cities and towns, working in factories or service industries, such as finance and tourism. ▶

▲ The number of red squirrels decreased in Europe in the 20th century, following the introduction of the grey squirrel from North America and loss of large areas of woodland.

BRANCHES OF CHRISTIANITY

Christianity is Europe's leading religion. Many follow the Roman Catholic Church, which has its headquarters in Vatican City. The Vatican covers just 0.44 sq km in Rome, Italy, and is the world's smallest independent country. Protestantism is a branch of Christianity popular in northern Europe, while the Orthodox Church flourishes in the east and southeast.

HISTORICAL CITIES

Many of Europe's large cities are steeped in history, but are also characterized by modern architecture and a modern way of life. Paris in France contains magnificent buildings dating from the Middle Ages. Moscow in Russia and London in the UK are important international cities, as well as historic sites. Athens and Rome, the capitals of Greece and Italy, have impressive ruins surviving from the days of Ancient Greece and the Roman Empire.

DEMOCRACY AND LAW

Throughout history, Europe has had an important influence on world politics. The system of democracy – where the government is chosen by the people – was first tried in Ancient Greece about 2,500 years ago. Similarly, many of the laws developed during the Roman

▲ Istanbul in Turkey lies on the shores of the Bosporus, which divides Europe from Asia. Its buildings reflect a mixture of Eastern and Western styles.

▲ The ruins of Delphi, a sacred site from as early as 1100BCE, stand on Mount Parnassus in the southern part of mainland Greece.

civilization (from 590BCE to 476CE) still influence legal systems today.

THE RENAISSANCE

From the 1300s, Europe became an increasingly important centre of art and learning, with people interested in new ideas about art, science and literature. This period is known as the Renaissance. At the same time, a desire for trade led European seafarers to set out to explore unknown lands and later to start colonies abroad. In the late 18th century, the continent was the birthplace of the Industrial Revolution, which brought great power and prosperity to the West.

END OF EMPIRES

The map of Europe has often changed throughout history, largely because of wars between rival countries. In the 20th century, two great world wars were fought between European powers. In the years following World War II (1939–45), the empires created in African and Asia by European countries such as Belgium, Britain, France, the Netherlands and

◀ Many European countries, such as Germany, the Netherlands, Romania and Italy, have strong national football teams and attract keen supporters such as these from Switzerland.

Portugal came to an end. Former colonies became independent countries, but many people living there continued to follow European customs and speak European languages. A large number of them have since made their homes in Europe.

EAST AND WEST

By the 1950s, Europe was divided between the non-communist countries of the west and the Soviet-backed communist countries of the east. Until the 1980s, the two sides remained armed and hostile throughout the period known as the Cold War. But from the late 1980s,

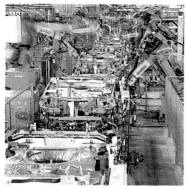

◀ German car-making factories are among the most highly automated in the world, and the cars they produce are exported worldwide.

the Eastern European countries threw off their communist governments. A new map of Europe was shaped, with new countries and partnerships. Yugoslavia split up into five countries at this time; a sixth nation was added in 2006, when Montenegro broke away from Serbia. In 2008, Kosovo declared its independence from Serbia and became Europe's newest country.

▲ After World War II, about a seventh of Berlin was in ruins. The city was divided between East and West until 1990, when Germany was reunited.

THE EUROPEAN UNION

In the 1950s, a group of countries in western Europe set up the European Community, or Common Market, to encourage greater economic unity in Europe. Over the years, the Community grew into the European Union, which aims for both economic and political unity. There are 27 member states.

SEE ALSO

Eastern Europe, France, Germany, Greece and the Balkans, Italy, Netherlands, Belgium and Luxembourg, Scandinavia, Spain and Portugal, Switzerland and Austria, UK

EVOLUTION

Evolution is the way in which an organism changes over many generations, resulting in a species that is very different from its early ancestors.

JEAN BAPTISTE LAMARCK
(1744–1829) was a French biologist who believed, mistakenly, that animals evolved during their own lifetimes. For example, each giraffe, by stretching, elongated its neck.

CHARLES DARWIN
(1809–1882) shook the world, and especially the Church, with his theory of natural selection, which he published in *On the Origin of Species* in 1859.

Most scientists believe that the first simple organisms appeared on Earth over 3,000 million years ago and that all today's plants and animals have arisen from these by a process of gradual change. This process, which is constantly happening from one generation to the next, is known as evolution.

DARWIN'S THEORY
The idea of evolution has been around since the time of the Ancient Greeks. However, the first convincing theory of how evolution works was only provided in the middle of the 19th century by the English naturalist Charles Darwin. He recognized that plants and animals produce lots of offspring but that only a small number of these offspring survive. Darwin concluded that only the individual with the most useful characteristics is able to survive in a process that he called the struggle for existence.

SURVIVAL OF THE FITTEST
Darwin noticed that individuals that are not well suited to their surroundings die out. This leaves only the fittest individuals

EVOLUTION FACTS AND FIGURES

• Scientists estimate that 99.9 per cent of all the species that have ever lived are now extinct

• The idea of evolution was first suggested by the Ancient Greeks more than 2,500 years ago

• Another naturalist called Alfred Wallace came up with the same theory of evolution as Darwin (and at the same time), but Darwin published his ideas first

• By looking at fossilized animals in different layers of rock, scientists can see how the animals evolved

• When Darwin visited the Galapagos Islands he saw that all the finches had different beaks to suit their food, such as a long, hooked beak for catching insects or a nutcracker-shaped beak for eating seeds

to breed and pass the useful characteristics that have allowed them to survive on to their offspring. In popular terms, this process is known as 'the survival of the fittest'. It explains the enormous variety of plant and animal life that is found throughout the world – because the conditions vary from place to place, animals and plants adapt to fit their environment.

LITTLE BY LITTLE
With each new generation of plant and animal life, the struggle for existence continues. The result is that, over a long period of time, plants and animals gradually change and become better

THE EVOLUTION OF MAN

The earliest humans evolved from ape-like ancestors around seven million years ago. Australopithecines, such as *Australopithecus afarensis* (3.9-2.9 mya), walked upright on their back legs. *Homo habilis* (2.4-1.5 mya) made basic tools from stone and bone, while *Homo erectus* (1.8 mya - 70,000 ya) was probably the first human to use fire. The Neanderthals (*Homo neanderthalensis*, 230,000-28,000 ya) lived alongside and even interbred with modern humans (*Homo sapiens*), who first appeared 195,000 ya.

AUSTRALOPITHECUS   HOMO HABILIS   HOMO ERECTUS   NEANDERTHAL MAN   HOMO SAPIENS

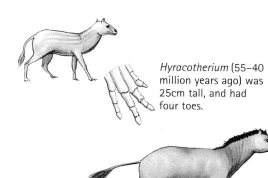

Hyracotherium (55–40 million years ago) was 25cm tall, and had four toes.

THE EVOLUTION OF THE HORSE

All life forms probably developed from single-celled sea organisms. From there on, evolution branched out in different directions. One group of fishes, for instance, evolved into amphibians and one group of amphibians then gave rise to the reptiles. Birds and mammals evolved from different groups of reptiles. Today's hoofed horse evolved over millions of years form an animal the size of a dog.

Mesohippus (40–25 mya) was much larger and had three toes.

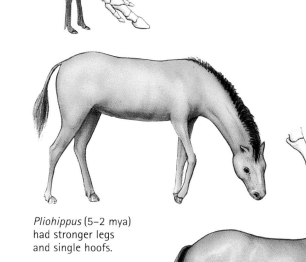

Merychippus (25–5 mya) was better suited to firm, grassy plains.

▲ Hungry explorers arriving on the island of Mauritius in the 1500s were new predators for the flightless dodo, which was extinct by 1680.

adapted to the place they live in and the dangers that surround them. To an observer, each change may be almost invisible, but over millions of years they can make a big difference.

NATURAL SELECTION

Conditions of habitat and climate are not the same everywhere, so a variation in the evolution of a plant or animal that is useful in one area of the world might be less useful in another. A species that spreads out may therefore evolve, or change, over a long period of time into several different species. Because this process of weeding out the inefficient individuals and favouring the fittest ones is an entirely natural one, Darwin gave it the name natural selection.

Pliohippus (5–2 mya) had stronger legs and single hoofs.

EVIDENCE FROM THE ROCKS

Some of the strongest support for the idea of evolution comes from the fossilized remains of plants and animals that are found in rocks formed from layers of sand and mud on ancient sea beds. In each layer of rock, the organisms look slightly different from the ones below. This provides the evidence for a process of change over hundreds, thousands or even millions of years.

A COMMON ANCESTOR

The bone structure of living animals also gives clues to evolution. A human arm, a

Equus caballus (1.5 mya) was similar to today's horses.

bird's wing and a whale's flipper all look very different and have different uses in everyday life. However, their bones are actually very similar. This suggests that these animals have all evolved from a common ancestor, which spread out over a wide geographical area. The arms were then adapted for different jobs according to the demands of the different environments.

SEE ALSO

Dinosaur, Fossil, Genetics, Horse, Prehistoric animal, Prehistoric people

EXPLORER

People explore to discover the unknown. Through exploration we have learnt much about the Earth. We are still exploring the oceans and the vastness of space.

Christopher Columbus opened up America to European trade in 1492.

Captain Robert Scott died on the way back from the South Pole in 1912.

Jacques Cousteau helped invent the aqualung so he could explore underwater.

The Phoenicians were among the first explorers, sailing the Mediterranean around 3,000 years ago. Pytheas, a Greek sailor, ventured into the Atlantic Ocean in 300BCE and, in 1000CE, Norway's Leif Ericsson reached North America.

THE SILK ROAD

Chinese and Arab travellers made long journeys overland. In 138BCE, Zhang Qian became the first Chinese man to explore Central Asia. Later, European merchants took the Silk Road to China, visited by the Italian Marco Polo in 1275 and described in his book, *Description of the World*.

AGE OF DISCOVERY

In the 15th century, stronger ships and the invention of navigational aids such as the backstaff (used to plot the ship's position by the Sun and stars) prompted European explorers to head to sea. They went in search of lands to conquer and for trade, riches and slaves. Seeking a sea route to India, Portuguese sailors headed south along the African coast. In 1488, Bartholomeu Días reached the southern tip of Africa, and in 1498, Vasco da Gama crossed the Indian Ocean. Columbus arrived in America from Spain in 1492.

MAP-MAKERS

In 1522, Ferdinand Magellan's ship from Spain completed the first voyage around the world. He died on the way, but the trip proved that the Earth was round. In the 1770s, James Cook, of the British navy, sailed the Pacific, mapping the coast of New Zealand and landing in Australia.

LAST FRONTIERS

Later explorers moved inland. The Scot David Livingstone travelled into Africa. Others ventured into uninhabited areas. The American Robert Peary conquered the North Pole in 1909, and Norway's Roald Amundsen reached the South Pole in 1911. In 1960, the bathyscaphe *Trieste* dived 10,910m under the sea, and in 1969, man walked on the Moon.

INTO THE UNKNOWN

Early sea voyages advanced navigational knowledge and helped map-makers to produce more accurate maps. In the 1400s, Henry the Navigator, a Portuguese prince skilled in mathematics and astronomy, helped organize 50 expeditions to West Africa. These trips pushed back the frontiers of navigation and paved the way for future trade and exploration.

SEE ALSO

Antarctica, Asia, Australia, Map, Ocean and sea, Space exploration, Submarine, Vikings

EXPLOSIVE

An explosive is a substance such as gunpowder or dynamite that creates a huge burst of energy and a shock wave when it is triggered.

GUY FAWKES
(1570–1606) A member of the Gunpowder Plot to blow up King James I of England and parliament on November 5, 1605. He was caught returning to light the fuse and was hanged.

Demolition gangs use explosives to bring down old buildings. Mining companies use them to blast apart rocks, tunnellers to blow holes in mountains and scientists to send rockets into space. Fireworks are pyrotechnic explosions that create a display of sound, light and smoke.

CREATING SHOCK WAVES

When explosives release energy, they heat up the surrounding air. Fuels such as petrol and coal release heat slowly, but an explosive heats the air rapidly. As the air around an explosive heats, it expands, creating a fast-moving shock wave that breaks apart any objects in its path. We hear the shock wave as a bang.

GUNPOWDER AND DYNAMITE

Gunpowder is the oldest explosive – it was discovered by the Chinese over 1,400 years ago. Its main ingredients are charcoal (burnt wood), sulphur and saltpetre, which are ground up and set alight in air. Gunpowder is still used in fireworks today.

DETONATING SAFELY

The destructive power of an explosive is great and it is therefore essential that people are able to control the explosive. When nitroglycerine (a combination of carbon, hydrogen, nitrogen and oxygen) was invented in 1846, it was too dangerous to use, as it could be detonated (ignited) by shaking it. The Swedish scientist Alfred Nobel solved the problem in 1867 by adding a porous earth called kieselguhr, which created a new, safe explosive – dynamite. Dynamite does not need air to work and is today widely used for demolition.

1 Sticks of dynamite are removed from their waxed wrappers and a detonating cap inserted.

2 Holes are bored in the bricks and the dynamite is inserted. Fuse wire links each detonator cap.

3 The structure of the chimney is weakened by carefully knocking out rows of bricks near the ground, leaving a zigzag of concrete struts.

4 The demolition team has now finished its job, so everyone stands well clear and the electronic switch is flicked.

UP THE CHIMNEY AND DOWN AGAIN

Demolishing a tall structure, such as a gas chimney, using explosives is an act needing precision and patience. The preparation work can take days, using many kilograms of dynamite and metres of fuse wire. The skill lies in ensuring that the construction falls safely, in the right direction, away from obstacles such as old gas pipes.

5 The dynamite has been placed so that the chimney falls without damaging the nearby gas pipes.

SEE ALSO
Chemistry, Energy, Mining

FARMING

Farming is the business of growing crops and raising livestock on the land to produce food, drink, textiles and other products.

Items such as food, leather, cotton and rubber come from farms. Farming is the world's biggest employer, taking up 35 per cent of the working population.

ORIGINS OF FARMING
Archaeological evidence shows that farming began around 11,000BCE, when Stone Age peoples began to herd wild animals. By around 8000BCE, people had learnt that scattered seeds would grow and multiply, providing food for themselves and their animals. The first crops were probably wheat and barley.

AGRICULTURAL REVOLUTIONS
Dramatic developments in farming have occurred since then. Irrigation of crops in Mesopotamia in 4000BCE and the ox-drawn plough, invented in about 3000BCE, made it possible to work difficult soils. From the

▲ Rows of green crops growing in the middle of a barren, sandy desert are evidence of the enormous achievements in farming and irrigation techniques.

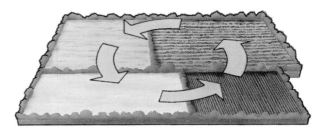

▲ In the early 1700s, English politician Charles Townshend created a four-field crop rotation system, which meant that a field did not have to be left fallow (empty) each year.

14th century, the potato, tomato, turkey, chilli and maize were brought from America to Europe and Asia. New machinery, such as Jethro Tull's seed drill (1700), Eli Whitney's cotton gin (1793) and steam-powered tractors (mid-1800s) made farming less labour-intensive.

GREATER PRODUCTIVITY
Since the 1970s, a 'Green Revolution' based on artificially-improved crops and fertilizers has increased food production in poorer nations. In developed countries, new machines and the rearing of livestock on mechanized farms has increased production.

DAIRY FARMING

Milk is produced on dairy farms from cattle, although goats, buffalo and sheep may also be kept for their milk. On modern dairy farms, cattle are milked by machine. The milk is cooled and stored in a large tank before being transported to a plant for bottling or processing into butter, cheese and other products.

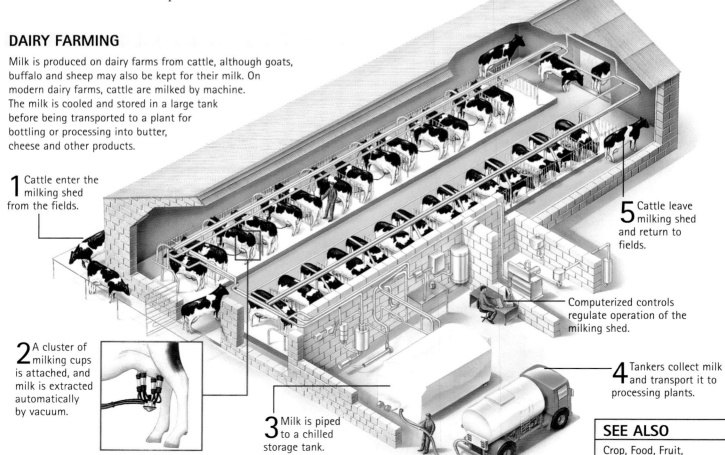

1 Cattle enter the milking shed from the fields.

2 A cluster of milking cups is attached, and milk is extracted automatically by vacuum.

3 Milk is piped to a chilled storage tank.

4 Tankers collect milk and transport it to processing plants.

5 Cattle leave milking shed and return to fields.

Computerized controls regulate operation of the milking shed.

SEE ALSO
Crop, Food, Fruit, Mesopotamia, Vegetable

FASCISM

Fascism is a political belief which states that the government of a country is all-powerful and that the citizens must obey it for the good of the nation.

Juan Perón, with his wife Eva, ruled Argentina in the 1940s and 1950s.

General Francisco Franco won a civil war before ruling Spain (1939–75).

Antonio Salazar was dictator of Portugal from 1932 until 1968.

Oswald Mosley was the leader of the British Union of Fascists in the 1930s.

Fascist ideas gained support after World War I (1914–18), with the first fascist government appearing in Italy in the 1920s. The term 'fascism' comes from *fasces*, bundles of rods with an axe which were symbols of power in Ancient Rome.

SUCCESS THROUGH STRENGTH

Fascism is based on the idea that a nation will only succeed through disciplined, ruthless action and a determined will. Fascists believe that achieving a worthwhile aim makes all actions acceptable. Schools, religion, newspapers, the arts and sciences are expected to serve the nation. Military power and a secret police back up a fascist government. Fascists often believe that their race or nation is superior to all others.

SEIZING POWER

In 1922, the Italian fascist leader Benito Mussolini took advantage of chaos caused by a general strike to seize power. He called himself *Il Duce* (The Leader) and, with backing from big business, brought prosperity to Italy. But he led Italy to defeat in World War II and in 1945 was murdered by his own people. Fascist-style governments held power in Japan and Hungary in the 1930s and 1940s.

NAZI GERMANY

In Germany, the Nazi leader Adolf Hitler was voted into power in 1933, promising to end unemployment and poverty. As *Führer* (Leader), he crushed opposition, and ordered the murder of millions of Jews, gypsies and others. In 1939, he started World War II, but killed himself in 1945, when Germany faced defeat.

MODERN EXTREMISTS

Some governments still follow fascist ideas, but none admit to fascism because of its association with the regimes of Hitler and Mussolini. Small, extremist political parties in many countries openly support racism and fascism, but gain few votes at election.

PACT OF STEEL

In May 1939, the two fascist dictators, Adolf Hitler in Germany and Benito Mussolini in Italy, agreed a military treaty called The Pact of Steel. In 1940, Mussolini entered World War II on Hitler's side. They were later joined by other fascist states in Eastern Europe when Hitler invaded the Soviet Union in 1941. All shared in Hitler's downfall four years later at the end of World War II.

SEE ALSO
Government, Politics,
World War I, World War II

FILM

A film is made up of a number of photos, or frames, projected in rapid sequence onto a screen to create moving images. It is a popular form of entertainment.

In 1877, a British-American photographer, Eadweard Muybridge, took a series of photographs of a horse running, using 24 cameras. By putting the photos together in sequence, Muybridge created the concept of moving pictures on film. This led to the movies – the most popular art and entertainment form of the 20th century.

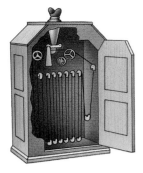

The kinetoscope, invented by Thomas Edison, was the first machine to produce moving pictures. Fifty metres of film revolved on spools and the viewer looked through an eyehole to see the pictures move.

THROUGH THE PEEPHOLE

Thomas Edison picked up Muybridge's idea and made a machine called a kinetoscope, which showed up to 90 seconds of moving pictures, viewed through a peephole. The French brothers Louis and Auguste Lumière took things one step further by inventing a machine that took these images, stored on rolls of celluloid, and projected them onto a wall for an astonished audience to see.

ADVENT OF AN INDUSTRY

Film screenings became popular right around the world, but especially in the United States. The film that broke new ground in cinema history was Edwin Porter's 11-minute dramatic epic *The Great Train Robbery* of 1903, in which a group of gunmen robs a train and are tracked down and brought to justice.

MAKING MOVIES

Making films can involve literally hundreds of technicians, actors and cameramen, but it is the director of the film who controls what is seen on screen. He or she decides how a film should be shot, where the cameras should be set, and what kind of lighting to use. Today, many directors use computer-generated special effects in their films, and some of the footage shot in the conventional way with the camera is changed completely by computer enhancement.

Second camera takes shot from different angle

Cameraman

Director

Microphone

Console controls sound

HISTORICAL SCREENPLAY

The principles of Porter's film still define film-making today. A written script details the scenes to be shot; these scenes are filmed in any order, and then edited together in the order of the original script. This is known as post-production. It is at this stage that the soundtrack and computer effects are added.

SUN AND STARS

The sunny weather and open landscape of a small suburb of Los Angeles, California, called Hollywood, made it the centre of film-making in America, and later the world, from 1907. Once sound was added to films in 1927, other countries formed film industries too.

SMALL-SCREEN COMPETITION

The popularity of television in the 1950s left cinema in a slump. Film-makers tried gimmicks such as 3-D (viewers wore green and red tinted glasses) or 'smell-o-vision' to attract audiences. This slump continued until the 1970s when the modern film blockbuster was born. *Jaws*, Steven Spielberg's tale of a deadly killer shark, started the trend in 1975, but was eclipsed two years later by George Lucas's *Star Wars*. The 2000s saw 3-D films return to popularity (viewers now wore dark-tinted, polarized glasses): the beginning of this new wave came with the release of *Avatar*.

EARLY MOVIES
Early movies were in black and white. Props and scenery provided the special effects, as in *Modern Times* (1936), one of Charlie Chaplin's first films with sound.

MUSICALS
Colour was introduced in the 1930s, when films such as *The Wizard of Oz* (1939), shot in Technicolor, were made possible. However, many films were still made in black and white right up to the 1950s.

ANIMATED FILMS
In the past, cartoons were hand-drawn. Today, most animations are produced on computer, using CGI (Computer Generated Imagery). Many, like *Kung Fu Panda 2* (2011), are released in 2-D and 3-D simultaneously.

FILM FRANCHISES
Franchises are movie series, where the same characters star in multiple films. Successful series have included the *Pirates of the Caribbean* (above), *X Men*, *Star Wars* and *James Bond* films.

SEE ALSO
Cartoon and animation

FISH

Fish are vertebrates (backboned animals) which breathe oxygen dissolved in water through their gills. They are found in salty and fresh water around the world.

FOUR TYPES OF FISH

Fish can be divided into groups by body structure. Examples are jawless fish, sharks and rays, and bony fish – primitive and modern.

Lampreys (above) and hagfish are ancient fish. They have no jaws and, like sharks, their skeletons are made of soft cartilage.

Sharks usually have a torpedo-shaped body with a skeleton of cartilage. All have strong jaws, many with several rows of teeth.

Primitive bony fish, such as the coelacanth (above) and lungfish, are related to fish that lived over 400 million years ago.

Perch (above) are modern bony fish. Unlike primitive bony fish they do not have a fleshy lobe at the base of each fin.

KEY TO TEMPERATE SEA

1 PLAICE
2 SAND EEL
3 BASS
4 COD
5 CONGER EEL
6 HERRINGS
7 MACKEREL

Most fish are streamlined for easy movement through water. The tail pushes the fish forward, and the fins are used for steering and balance. Most fish have two pairs of fins on their sides. There is one dorsal fin, running down the middle of the back, and another fin at the base of the tail. The tail is usually forked.

COLD-BLOODED CREATURES

As cold-blooded creatures, fish stay at the same temperature as the water they live in. If the water is very cold, fish slow down and may stop moving altogether. Apart from using sight and smell, fish also have a row of sensors on their sides known as the lateral line, that picks up vibrations in the water even if the fish cannot see clearly.

BONE OR GRISTLE

There are over 32,000 known species of fish – more than all other vertebrates put together. Fish can be divided into cartilaginous fish and bony fish. Cartilaginous fish, whose skeletons are made of soft cartilage, or gristle, include sharks, skates and rays. There are only

Mudskippers survive low tides in the swamps of Africa and Southeast Asia by breathing air. They use their strong pectoral fins as 'arms' to climb trees in search of food.

about 900 species, all of which live in the sea. Bony fish include some of the most colourful animals on earth, and the fastest – sailfish – can reach speeds of 100 km/h.

BROWN AND GRISTLY

Most cartilaginous fish are brown or grey and have five or more gill slits on each side. Their fins are solid and their bodies are covered with rough, tooth-like scales. Sailors once used shark skins to scrub the decks of wooden ships. The whale shark is the largest fish, measuring 12m long and weighing up to 20 tonnes.

FISH BONES

Bony fish have smooth, overlapping scales. Their fins are delicate membranes stretched over slender spines. The gills are covered by a flap called an operculum, so there is only one gill opening on each side of the body.

TEMPERATE SEAS

Fish are adapted to suit their environment. Sea fish constantly lose water and must drink a lot, whereas freshwater fish take in water through their skin. Temperate waters, which get colder in winter, are home to dull-coloured fish, commonly caught for food. These fish often swim deeper or migrate in cold weather.

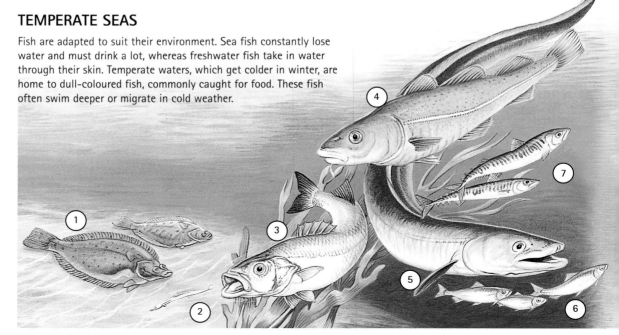

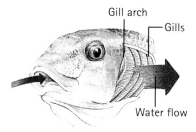

Gill arch
Gills
Water flow

▲ Oxygen from the water passes through the thin walls of the gills (tiny blood-filled threads arranged in pockets on each side of the throat) and into the blood. The water then passes out through the gill slits.

INSIDE A TYPICAL FISH

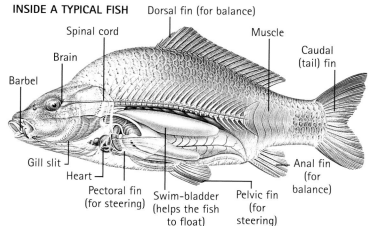

Dorsal fin (for balance)
Spinal cord
Brain
Barbel
Muscle
Caudal (tail) fin
Gill slit
Heart
Pectoral fin (for steering)
Swim-bladder (helps the fish to float)
Pelvic fin (for steering)
Anal fin (for balance)

Most bony fish have an air-filled swim-bladder, allowing them to float motionless in the water. Sharks have no swim-bladder and would sink if they stopped swimming.

JAWLESS FISH

There are 70 species of lamprey and 43 species of hagfish. These eel-shaped creatures make up the jawless fish. Lampreys have round, sucker-like mouths and toothed tongues, used to rasp flesh from other fish. Hagfish have slit-shaped mouths and sharp teeth. They eat dead fish.

MILLIONS OF EGGS

Some fish give birth to live young, but most species lay eggs. These are usually released into the water by the female, where they are fertilized by the male. Fish lay many eggs, as most of them get eaten. The ocean sunfish may lay 300 million eggs in its lifetime. Fish that protect their eggs do not lay many, and it is often the male that looks after them. The female sea horse lays eggs in a pouch on the male's abdomen, where they can be protected.

FRESHWATER FISH

About two fifths of all fish live in freshwater streams, lakes, rivers, ponds, marshes and swamps.

Guppies, native to the Caribbean islands, are attractive and popular aquarium fish.

Piranha live in South American rivers, feeding on fish or other animals with their razor-like teeth.

This African catfish is typical of its group, which has long barbels (whiskers) and fins that lock upright.

Rainbow trout are native to North America, but because of trout farming, now live in European rivers.

The climbing perch can be seen taking short 'walks' across land, as it has a gill chamber for breathing air.

TROPICAL SEAS

The most brightly coloured fish live in the tropics, blending in with the vivid coral reefs, their camouflaged colours hiding them from predators.

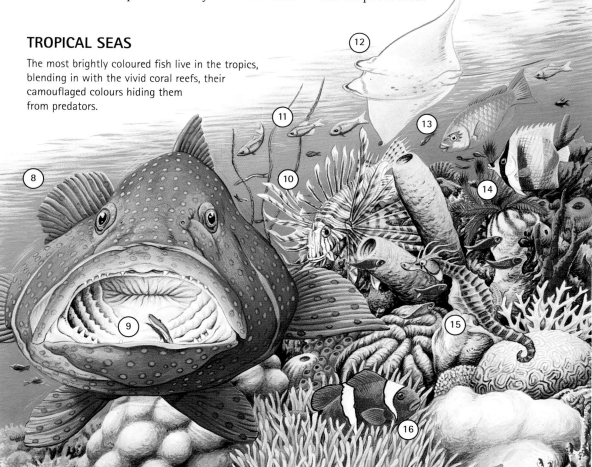

KEY TO TROPICAL SEA
8 GROUPER
9 CLEANER WRASSE
10 LION FISH
11 FAIRY BASSLET
12 MANTA RAY
13 PARROT FISH
14 BUTTERFLY FISH
15 SEA HORSE
16 TOMATO CLOWNFISH

SEE ALSO

Animal, Fishing industry, Fossil, Jellyfish, Ocean and sea, Prehistoric animal, Shark

FISHING INDUSTRY

The fishing industry is the organized business of catching or breeding fish and shellfish for food, from seas, rivers or lakes.

Gill nets hang like curtains beneath the surface with weights to hold them down.

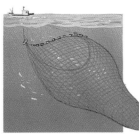

Trawl nets are dragged along the bottom to catch demersal (sea bed) fish.

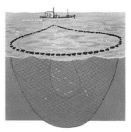

Purse seines are nets pulled in a circle around pelagic (surface) fish.

Fishing is one of the world's most important industries. About 101 million tonnes of fish are caught each year. China, Peru, the USA, Indonesia, Chile, Japan, India and Russia catch the most. People have caught fish since prehistoric times, but commercial fishing did not begin until the 1600s.

FISHING GROUNDS

The oceans are vast, but most fish are caught in well-known fishing grounds within 100km of land, in the shallower waters of the continental shelf. There are rich fishing grounds off Canada's east coast, near Iceland and around Japan. Fish are attracted to these places by plentiful supplies of plankton to eat.

FISH TYPES

Two types of fish are caught at sea: pelagic and demersal. Pelagic fish, including herring, salmon, tuna and anchovies, live

HARVESTING THE SEA

Many large fishing boats are equipped as floating fish factories. The net is winched in, and the haul is sorted into types of fish. Often they are cleaned and gutted before being placed in ice boxes and stored in freezer compartments below deck to keep them fresh on the way to market. Long-range fishing craft may be at sea for several months at a time.

near the sea's surface. Demersal fish, including cod, sole and haddock, live near the sea bed. Fishermen use different fishing methods and nets to catch the two types of fish. Nowadays, the size of fishing catches is limited by international agreements. This is because some species of fish have been overfished and are in danger of extinction.

FISH FARMING

Keeping fish for food in tanks, ponds or underwater cages is called fish farming. Fish and shellfish, including salmon, trout, oysters, mussels and scallops, are farmed. Fish farms produce nearly half of the fish people eat. In China, fish farms yield more than 32 million tonnes of fish a year. By comparison, Chinese fishing boats bring in 17 tonnes of fish a year.

▲ On board large trawlers, sonar equipment detects large groups of fish.

SEE ALSO

Fish, Ocean and sea

FLAG

There almost 200 independent countries in the world, each of which has a national flag that is flown at home and outside the country's embassies abroad.

Flags were originally used in warfare to lead the troops and identify friend or foe. The colour and design of national flags reflect the nations' history or religion. For example, the United Kingdom flag is based on the Christian cross, first flown during the Crusades. In European heraldry, white and yellow represented metal, and were not placed next to each other on emblems. European flags still reflect this – only the Vatican City flag breaks the rule. ▶

Afghanistan

Albania

Algeria

Andorra

Angola

Antigua and Barbuda

Argentina

Armenia

Australia

Austria

Azerbaijan

The Bahamas

Bahrain

Bangladesh

Barbados

Belarus

Belgium

Belize

Benin

Bhutan

Bolivia

Bosnia-Herzegovina

Botswana

Brazil

Brunei

Bulgaria

Burkina Faso

Burma (Myanmar)

Burundi

Cambodia

Cameroon

Canada

Cape Verde

Central African Republic

Chad

Chile

China

Colombia

Comoros

Congo Republic

Costa Rica

Côte d'Ivoire

Croatia

Cuba

Cyprus

Czech Republic

Democratic Rep. of Congo

Denmark

Djibouti

Dominica

Dominican Republic

East Timor

Ecuador

Egypt

El Salvador

Equatorial Guinea

Eritrea

Estonia

Ethiopia

Fiji

Finland

153

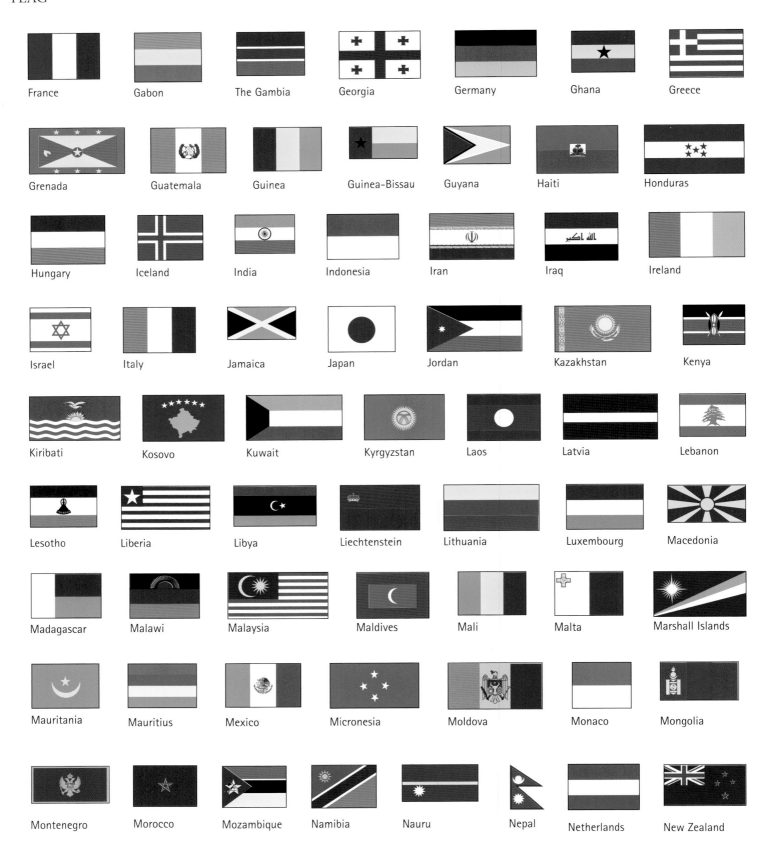

France

Gabon

The Gambia

Georgia

Germany

Ghana

Greece

Grenada

Guatemala

Guinea

Guinea-Bissau

Guyana

Haiti

Honduras

Hungary

Iceland

India

Indonesia

Iran

Iraq

Ireland

Israel

Italy

Jamaica

Japan

Jordan

Kazakhstan

Kenya

Kiribati

Kosovo

Kuwait

Kyrgyzstan

Laos

Latvia

Lebanon

Lesotho

Liberia

Libya

Liechtenstein

Lithuania

Luxembourg

Macedonia

Madagascar

Malawi

Malaysia

Maldives

Mali

Malta

Marshall Islands

Mauritania

Mauritius

Mexico

Micronesia

Moldova

Monaco

Mongolia

Montenegro

Morocco

Mozambique

Namibia

Nauru

Nepal

Netherlands

New Zealand

Nicaragua

Niger

Nigeria

North Korea

Norway

Oman

Pakistan

Palau

 Panama

 Papua New Guinea

 Paraguay

 Peru

 Philippines

 Poland

 Portugal

 Qatar

 Romania

 Russia

 Rwanda

 St Kitts-Nevis

 St Lucia

 St Vincent and the Grenadines

 Samoa

 San Marino

 São Tomé and Príncipe

 Saudi Arabia

 Senegal

 Serbia

 Seychelles

 Sierra Leone

 Singapore

 Slovakia

 Slovenia

 Solomon Islands

 Somalia

 South Africa

 South Korea

 South Sudan

 Spain

 Sri Lanka

 Sudan

 Surinam

 Swaziland

 Sweden

 Switzerland

 Syria

 Taiwan

 Tajikistan

 Tanzania

 Thailand

 Togo

 Tonga

 Trinidad and Tobago

 Tunisia

 Turkey

 Turkmenistan

 Tuvalu

 Uganda

 Ukraine

 United Arab Emirates

 United Kingdom

 United States of America

 Uruguay

 Uzbekistan

 Vanuatu

 Vatican City

 Venezuela

 Vietnam

Yemen

Zambia

Zimbabwe

FLOWER

Flowers are the reproductive parts of some kinds of plants. They make seeds that will form a new generation of the same type of plant.

Bats are attracted to the nighttime scent and infra-red colours of some tropical flowers.

Many alpine flowers are tough and lie low on the ground, to help them withstand the cold.

Desert plants, such as cacti, have bright flowers to attract insects for the few weeks they are in bloom.

Water flowers, such as white water-lilies, float above the surface to attract insect pollinators.

Flowers are really specialized leaves that have evolved over millions of years to help plants reproduce efficiently. There are more than 300,000 species of flowering plants, called angiosperms, which range from huge, long-lived trees to tiny annuals. Flowers may vary greatly in appearance, but they are all made up of the same basic parts.

MALE AND FEMALE PARTS

The main reproductive parts of a flower are the female carpel and the male stamens. Each stamen is made up of the anther, which produces tiny powdery grains of pollen, and the filament, or stalk. The carpel has a stigma, which is often sticky and coloured. The stigma is found at the end of a style – a kind of stalk that leads down to the ovary. Inside the ovary are egg cells that develop into the seeds which will later become new plants.

POLLINATION

For seeds to form, pollen grains from the anther must come into contact with the

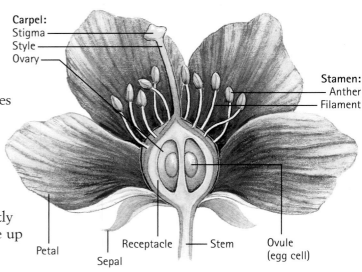

Carpel:
Stigma
Style
Ovary

Stamen:
Anther
Filament

Petal
Sepal
Receptacle — Stem
Ovule (egg cell)

▲ Flowers have four main parts: sepals and petals (the outer parts), and carpels and stamens (the reproductive parts). The stamens are male and the carpels are female.

stigma. This process is called pollination. Most flowering plants are pollinated by insects. As an insect such as a bee pushes inside the flower looking for nectar, its body gets dusted with pollen from the anthers of the flower. The insect will then transfer the pollen dust to the stigma of the next flower it visits.

FLOWER APPEAL

The varying colours, scents and shapes of individual flowers have developed to appeal to pollinators – usually insects, but also birds and small mammals, such as bats. Many flowers have glands called nectaries, which produce nectar – a sugary liquid on which the pollinators feed. The pollinators must push past the male and female parts of the flower to reach the nectar.

▲ One of the petals of the bee orchid looks like a real bee. This signals to other pollinators that the flower is a good source of nectar, and they land on it to find food. Other flowers attract bees with ultraviolet markings on their petals that only bees can see.

FLOWER FACTS

• The first flowering plant – thought to have been a magnolia – appeared about 160 million years ago

• The world's largest flower, *Rafflesia arnoldii*, grows in Indonesia and can measure up to 1m in diameter. Its smell of rotting meat is irresistible to the flies that pollinate it

• Opium, which comes from the opium poppy, is used to make pain-killing drugs such as codeine

• The Madagascan periwinkle, once thought of as a weed, is now farmed to produce anti-cancer drugs

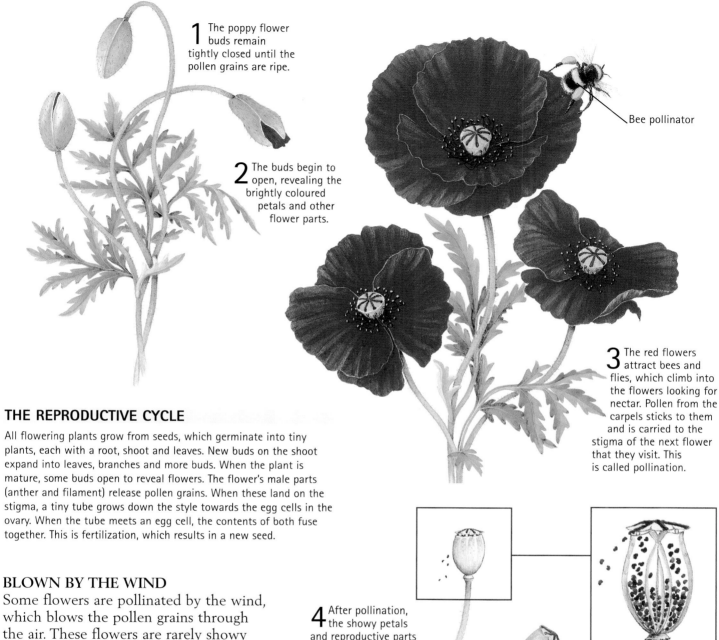

1 The poppy flower buds remain tightly closed until the pollen grains are ripe.

2 The buds begin to open, revealing the brightly coloured petals and other flower parts.

Bee pollinator

3 The red flowers attract bees and flies, which climb into the flowers looking for nectar. Pollen from the carpels sticks to them and is carried to the stigma of the next flower that they visit. This is called pollination.

THE REPRODUCTIVE CYCLE

All flowering plants grow from seeds, which germinate into tiny plants, each with a root, shoot and leaves. New buds on the shoot expand into leaves, branches and more buds. When the plant is mature, some buds open to reveal flowers. The flower's male parts (anther and filament) release pollen grains. When these land on the stigma, a tiny tube grows down the style towards the egg cells in the ovary. When the tube meets an egg cell, the contents of both fuse together. This is fertilization, which results in a new seed.

BLOWN BY THE WIND

Some flowers are pollinated by the wind, which blows the pollen grains through the air. These flowers are rarely showy or scented. They often have feathery stigmas to catch the clouds of pollen as they fly through the air.

A GARDEN IN BLOOM

Particular flowering plants are selected for a garden because of when, and how often, they produce their flowers. This can depend on how long the flowering plants live. Annuals are plants that sprout, mature, flower, produce seeds and die all in the same year. Biennials live for two years, and perennials live for three years or longer. Most garden plants are perennials, because once they have flowered, they flower every year for as long as they live.

4 After pollination, the showy petals and reproductive parts are discarded, leaving just the seed capsule.

Petals fall off to leave seed head

5 As it sways in the wind, the seed capsule shakes out the ripened seeds through holes, like pepper from a pepperpot.

6 Most poppies are annuals (plants that live for one year). This means that the plant puts all its energy into flowering and producing seeds, and then dies.

SEE ALSO

Desert, Fruit, Grassland, Leaf, Plant, Rainforest, Seed and pollination

FOOD

Food is any substance that is a source of nutrition to a living organism. Without it, nothing can live. The food we eat is supplied by plants and animals.

Modern diets contain a wide range of foods. Some, such as fruits and vegetables, are still in the original state in which they were grown. Others, such as bread and hamburgers, are processed foods, which means they arrive at our tables looking very different from the ingredients that were used to make them.

THE FIRST FARMERS

Until 15,000 to 10,000 years ago, humans were hunter-gatherers, spending much of their time hunting animals and gathering fruits and vegetables for food. By about 8000BCE, people in fertile parts of the world were managing the land for agriculture. They started to grow food crops and to domesticate animals such as cattle, sheep and poultry for milk, meat and eggs.

DIFFERENT DIETS

Meat and dairy products are a major part of the diet in the West, but in many places people do not eat dairy at all – fewer than 30 per cent of people in the world can digest lactose (the sugar in milk). In tropical countries, people eat mainly rice, cassava and potatoes, with few vegetables, while in Mediterranean countries, it is usual to have a high intake of all kinds of different fruits and vegetables.

FOOD INTAKE WORLDWIDE

Although there is more than enough food to support the world's population, it does not always reach those in need. One in seven people goes hungry – and 65 per cent of the world's hungry live in only seven countries. Around 20 million people die of hunger each year. In the USA, people eat 60 per cent more food than they need, which can cause its own set of health problems.

STAPLE FOODS

Our food comes from many different sources, either plant or animal. The main foods obtained from plants are grains, fruits and vegetables. Products made from grains, or cereals, such as rice or bread, have been the basis of the human diet for thousands of years. Food from animals includes meat, eggs and dairy products. They cost more to produce than plant foods.

► Cereals such as wheat (right), rice and maize make up more than 60 per cent of the world's food intake.

Breakfast cereal

Bread

Flat bread

Noodles

Biscuits

Pasta

FOOD PROCESSING

Humans have been processing food – by cooking it – ever since the discovery of fire. Today, there are many other ways of processing food, such as milling, freezing, canning and ultra-heat treatment. Processing makes some foods, such as potatoes and wheat, easier to digest. It also stops food from rotting, which encourages germs to grow. Heat treatment kills germs, while chilling and freezing slows down their growth to a safe level.

ADDITIVES

Substances known as additives are usually added to foods during processing. Some, such as the vitamins and minerals added to bread and cereals, improve the nutritional value of food. Other additives include preservatives, which are added to foods to stop them going rotten, and colourings, such as the natural pigment of beetroot.

FRUIT AND VEGETABLES

We eat fruits, such as oranges, and vegetables, such as cauliflowers, in their natural state. However, oranges can also be processed to make juice or preserved by canning. Vegetables such as peas can be frozen or dried to last longer.

Picking in an orange grove

Cauliflower

Fresh oranges

Orange juice

FOOD SAFETY

A small percentage of the population suffers from food poisoning each year, usually caused by food contaminated with harmful bacteria such as *E coli* or *Salmonella*. Preparing food hygienically lowers the risk of food poisoning. Foods such as meat, fish, milk and eggs should be heated and cooked thoroughly before eating to kill any dangerous bacteria.

RELIGION AND CULTURE

The food people eat often depends on their culture or religion. For example, some Jews eat a kosher diet, governed by religious laws such as cooking and eating meat and dairy produce separately. In the Hindu religion, every living creature is believed to have a soul, so eating animals is often avoided. Many vegetarians believe animals should not be killed for humans to eat.

▲ Paella is a Spanish dish made with rice, shellfish, vegetables and chicken, named after the shallow frying pan in which it is cooked. Each country has unique local ways of preparing food that have often been passed down through the generations, and are usually made from local produce.

DAIRY PRODUCTS

Dairy cattle produce milk, from which other products such as butter, cheese and yoghurt are made. Beef comes from cattle that have been specially reared for their meat. Beef is cut up into joints or steaks, or minced for foods such as burgers.

Milk

Cheese

Butter

Beefburger

Yoghurt

SEE ALSO

Crop, Custom, Farming, Nutrition, Prehistoric people

FORCE AND MOTION

A force changes the way an object moves. If the object is stationary, a force will set it in motion. If it is moving, a force will change its speed or direction.

Force is a word we use in everyday speech. For instance, we may talk about forcing a door open or forcing a suitcase shut. In both, a force – either a push or pull – is being applied by a person to move the door or suitcase lid.

▲ An object's weight affects how fast it moves and how long it takes to stop. This is called its momentum, and it can be transferred from one object to another, as between two pool balls.

FAST FACTS

• A bus is harder to push than a car because an object with greater mass (more material) has more inertia, which means it needs a greater force to accelerate

• Two forces that balance each other exactly, producing no movement, are known as static forces. A bridge stays up in this way

CHANGING VELOCITY

A force is anything that changes an object's velocity (speed in a given direction). A ball rolling along the ground has a certain velocity, but if it is kicked, the ball increases velocity. An increase in velocity is known as acceleration, and a decrease in speed is called deceleration.

STATE OF INERTIA

An object that stays at the same velocity – neither speeding up, nor slowing down or changing direction – is said to be in a state of inertia. This rarely happens, however, because moving objects usually slow down because they bump into something, come into contact with the ground or are blown by the wind. The force created by wind, or when two items rub together, is known as friction. It works against motion, slowing things down.

▲ The people on this fairground ride are kept spinning in a circle by two competing forces: centrifugal force, which pulls outwards, and centripetal force, which pulls inwards.

MIGHTY FORCES

Pulling a door open or pushing it shut requires direct force and human strength. But sometimes we are not strong enough (do not have enough force) to move an object. People have invented machines such as levers and pulleys to increase the effect of our force. Powerful natural forces such as electricity and magnetism have also been harnessed to work for us. Another natural force, gravity, literally keeps our feet on the ground.

NEWTON'S LAWS

Most of the principles of force and motion were first discovered in the 1660s by the English scientist Isaac Newton. Today, in honour of his work, we measure force in newtons (N). One newton is roughly the force that you feel when you hold a large orange in the palm of your hand.

ACTION AND REACTION

Whenever force is applied to an object, it always creates another force, called a reactionary force, that works in the opposite direction. A canoeist paddling through water moves forward by such action and reaction. The canoeist's paddle pushing the water backwards is the action, while the reaction is the force exerted by the water on the paddle, which pushes the canoe forward through the water.

Action: the paddle pushes against the water

Reaction: the canoe moves forward in the water

SEE ALSO

Bridge, Electricity, Gravity, Heat, Invention, Machine, Magnetism

FORENSICS

Forensics is the scientific investigation of a crime, such as theft or murder, by scientists such as doctors, dentists, chemists and biologists.

▲ Surfaces are dusted for fingerprints. Victims have their fingerprints taken, so that only unknown prints are included in a search.

▲ Dried blood is scraped off the murder weapon, diluted and analyzed for blood type and DNA code.

No matter how careful a criminal may be, he or she will leave clues behind. It is the job of the forensic team to examine the scene of the crime for fingerprints and footprints, bloodstains and other evidence.

AT THE SCENE OF THE CRIME
Equipment such as cameras, lasers and plaster casts are used to make a record of the position of everything at the scene. Samples of hair, paint, glass and other substances are also taken away for analysis. These samples have to be handled very carefully. The investigating team wears paper bodysuits, overshoes, and gloves so that they do not contaminate the samples. They will also wrap the samples in plastic before sending them for analysis.

ANALYZING CLUES
Fingerprints can reveal the identity of a criminal if they can be matched to samples kept on computer. Analysis of DNA (genetic code) from blood and other samples taken from the scene of the crime has been used since 1986 for more serious crimes. Each person has a unique DNA 'fingerprint' or profile, which can be checked against samples taken at the scene. Laboratory analysis of a single fleck of paint is enough to identify a car used in a crime, for example. Similarly, bite marks in food found at the scene can lead to an arrest, if they can be matched with dental records.

CAUSE OF DEATH
Suspicious deaths involving murder, suicide or accident are usually investigated by a coroner (an official who specializes in forensics). The coroner orders an autopsy (an examination of the body to determine the cause of death). The forensic pathologist (a doctor who specializes in autopsies) examines the external appearance of the body and then dissects it, looking at each organ in turn. He or she also analyzes blood and flesh samples.

WHO DUNNIT?
Every item at the scene of the crime tells a story. Criminals often wear gloves, so fingerprints are rare, but clothing fibres caught on the corner of a photocopier in a scuffle may lead police to the murderer.

FIBRES
Fibres from clothing worn by the criminal and the victim are taken away and studied under a microscope.

FINGERPRINTS
Finding just one print can solve the crime – even identical twins have different fingerprints.

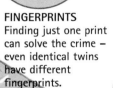

BLOOD
Originally only the blood group could be established, but now a unique DNA code can be found.

FOOTPRINTS
Footprints may reveal the criminal's shoe size and the shop where the shoes were bought.

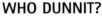

SEE ALSO

Chemistry, Genetics

FOREST

Forests are large areas of land covered mainly by trees and other plants. Today, they occupy almost 30 per cent of the world's land area.

There are three basic types of forest: coniferous (boreal), broad-leaved deciduous, and dense, tropical rainforests. Many forests include a combination of coniferous and deciduous trees.

CONIFEROUS FORESTS
Coniferous forests are found in the cold northern areas of Canada, Europe and Asia and include spruce, fir or pine. These trees are evergreens (do not shed their leaves in winter) and carry their seeds in cones.

DECIDUOUS FORESTS
The temperate regions of the USA and Europe have warm summers, mild winters and rain all year round. Here, the forest trees, such as oak, ash and beech, are all deciduous, which means they drop their leaves in the autumn.

▲ In deciduous forests, the fallen leaves form a carpet on the floor, which nourishes new growth.

FAST FACTS

• Before forests were cleared to make way for farms and cities, forests covered about 60% of the world's land area

• 29% of the forests are boreal, 21% temperate and 50% tropical

• Some rainforests have up to 300 different trees in 100 sq metres

• In the United States, under 10% of the original forests remain

THE LIFE OF THE FOREST
A forest's highest layer is formed by the tree tops and is called the canopy. Below this are shorter trees, then a layer of bushes and shrubs. Lower still, there are ferns, grasses and wild flowers, and then the mosses and fungi that grow on the forest floor. In addition to the larger animals, such as deer and squirrels, there are thousands of smaller creatures living under the leaves, and in the bark and forest soil.

THE TROPICS
In the hot, permanently wet regions of the tropics, there are dense rainforests full of teak, ebony, rosewood, mahogany and other evergreen trees. Often the trees grow so closely together that sunlight cannot reach the ground. Other regions in the tropics with both wet and dry seasons have deciduous woodlands and savanna – grasslands with scattered clumps of trees.

WHY WE NEED FORESTS
Forests provide food and shelter for animals and refresh the atmosphere by turning carbon dioxide into oxygen. More than 3,000 million people use firewood for cooking and heating. There is also a huge trade in forest products: softwood (conifers) for building and making paper, and hardwoods (deciduous) for furniture. Other products include fruits, nuts and spices, gums and resins, rubber and many vital medicines.

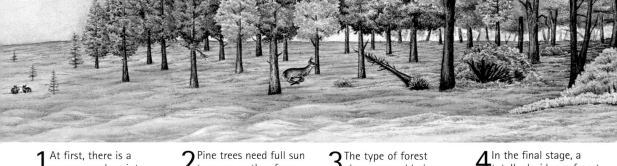

1 At first, there is a grassy meadow, into which pine seeds fall and grow to become seedlings.

2 Pine trees need full sun to grow, so they form the top layer of forest, with deciduous trees beneath.

3 The type of forest changes as old pines die and deciduous trees fill in gaps in the canopy.

4 In the final stage, a totally deciduous forest develops. It is the climax of this ecological succession.

SEE ALSO
Brazil, Habitat, Plant, Rainforest, Tree

FOSSIL

Fossils are the remains of once-living things found in rocks. They are preserved in different ways and show us what conditions were like in the past.

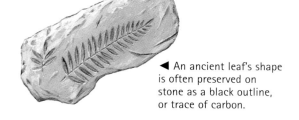

◀ An ancient leaf's shape is often preserved on stone as a black outline, or trace of carbon.

Dead insects can be preserved whole in tree resin (sap) that has turned into amber over time.

Ammonites (fossilized shells of extinct molluscs) are often found as moulds or casts in rock.

A dinosaur footprint, made over 65 million years ago, may be preserved in rock as a trace fossil.

Fossils can include shells, bones, teeth, leaves, skeletons, or even whole animals. Most fossils are found in areas that were once in, or near, water, such as the sea or a river. Layers of mud in the water settle over the animal, creating the perfect conditions for its remains to be preserved.

TYPES OF FOSSIL

A living substance can be preserved whole, but more often it is changed in some way over time. It can be replaced by another material, such as stone, or may rot away leaving an empty mould of the organism.

PRESERVED WHOLE

An insect stuck in resin (sap) oozing from a tree will be preserved whole when that resin turns to the semi-precious stone amber. When larger animals die, usually only the hard parts like bones and teeth, are preserved. Sometimes, pools of natural tar can preserve mammoth bones unaltered since the Ice Age (over 10,000 years ago).

PETRIFIED WOOD

Fossilized wood is petrified. This means that the wood has been replaced, molecule by molecule, by a stony material. The carbon in a leaf can survive as a black outline on a stone surface. Millions of leaves preserved in this way produce coal.

A STONE REPLICA

Stone copies of plants or animals are created when water seeps through the rock in which they lie, removing all of the remains. This leaves an empty mould in the shape of the living creature, which is filled by minerals seeping into the rock – creating an exact copy of the creature, known as a cast. Seashells are often fossilized as casts in limestone. Trace fossils are marks in the rock that show where an animal once existed, as in the case of worm burrows.

USEFUL FOSSILS

We can tell how old a rock is from its fossils. Many animals existed for only a short time in history and, when we find their fossils in rock, we can tell the age of that rock. Other fossils tell us about the climate or habitat of an area in the past. For example, finding a fossil palm leaf in a cool region indicates it once had a tropical climate, and fossil seashells found far inland reveal that the area was once under the sea.

HOW FOSSILS ARE FORMED

When a dinosaur dies, its flesh rots away, leaving only the bones behind. Scavengers may also remove parts of the body, so complete fossilized remains are rare. Over time, the bones are covered by layers of soil, which harden into rock. Millions of years later, the fossil is exposed by wind and rain or movements in the Earth's crust.

1 The dinosaur's body falls into a sea, river, lake or swamp. Under water the remains are more likely to be buried fast by soil and sand deposited by the water.

2 The dinosaur's flesh rots away or is eaten by water animals. Its bones and teeth are covered by many layers of sand and soil, which change to rock over time.

3 Thousands of years later, the strata of rock shift, bringing the bones to the surface.

SEE ALSO

Coal, Dinosaur, Evolution, Oil, Prehistoric animal, Rock

FRANCE

France is Europe's third largest country. Only Russia and Ukraine are bigger. France has a rich cultural tradition and a turbulent history.

Area: 547,030 sq km
Population: 62,134,000
Capital: Paris
Language: French
Currency: Euro

Much of the French landscape is either plains or low hills. Three of its borders are high mountain ranges: the Vosges in the northeast; the Pyrenees in the southwest; and the Alps, including France's highest point, Mont Blanc (4,807m), in the southeast. The Massif Central rises in central France. Paris, the capital, lies in flat country on the River Seine. Other big rivers include the Loire, Rhône and Gironde.

A NATION OF FARMERS

France is the European Union's leading farming nation. Its soil and climate are good for crops. The north is cool and moist, averaging about 35mm of rainfall per month. The south is drier and hotter, with summer temperatures above 25°C. French farmers grow wheat, barley, oats, flax, sugar beet, fruits and vegetables, and raise cattle and sheep. France is famous for its wines and cheeses, and French cooking is admired and copied all over the world.

PARIS THE CAPITAL

Paris is the centre of government, arts and fashion. It is France's biggest city – home to about a sixth of the nation's people. Its 2,000-year-long history means the buildings are a mixture of old and new. Visitors come to see the Louvre Museum, the tomb of Napoleon, Notre Dame Cathedral, the Eiffel Tower and other famous sights.

▲ Peaceful rural communities across the country are farm-based. Typical crops include wheat, apples and grapes.

FRENCH LIFE

Although France is a land of forests and green countryside, 85 per cent of the French people live in towns and cities. People meet in pavement cafés and restaurants, or enjoy a game of boules (bowls). Favourite sports in France include cycle racing, soccer, rugby football and tennis. There are parades and speeches on Bastille Day (July 14), France's national day, which celebrates the start of the French Revolution in 1789.

AN INDUSTRIAL GIANT

After Paris, the largest French cities are Marseille (the main seaport), Lyon, Lille, Nice and Toulouse. France has a highly developed industrial economy. French factories produce many goods, including cars, aircraft, chemicals, machinery and textiles. Fishing and mining are important. France also has a world reputation for luxury goods, such as perfume and elegant clothes. Europe's fastest trains speed between French cities, and there is a fine road system.

▲ Many French people, and other Europeans, go on winter skiing holidays in the Alps on the border between France and Italy.

► This spectacular glass pyramid, finished in 1989, is the entrance to the Louvre Museum in Paris. The Louvre, originally built as a fortress in about 1200, was expanded during the mid-1500s by King Francis I, who wanted to transform it into a palace. It now houses one of the world's largest art collections.

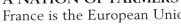

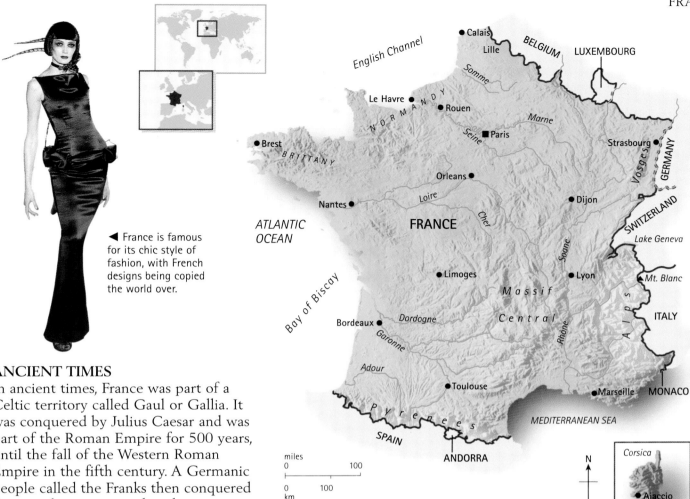

◀ France is famous for its chic style of fashion, with French designs being copied the world over.

ANCIENT TIMES

In ancient times, France was part of a Celtic territory called Gaul or Gallia. It was conquered by Julius Caesar and was part of the Roman Empire for 500 years, until the fall of the Western Roman Empire in the fifth century. A Germanic people called the Franks then conquered the area, bringing it within their empire. France gets its name from the Latin *Francia*, meaning 'country of the Franks'.

▲ Each summer, the world's top cyclists take part in the Tour de France, a race across the country. The final stage is through Paris, from Disneyland to the Champs Elysées.

A TURBULENT HISTORY

France became an independent country in the 9th century, but there was no common language until the founding of the French Academy in the 1630s. France has had a turbulent history, including wars with Spain and England and rule by greedy or inept kings. The revolution of 1789 removed the king and many of the old ways, and during the rule of Napoleon Bonaparte (1799 to 1815), France dominated Europe. France suffered great damage and loss of life in two world wars, but recovered to become a founder member of the European Union and a strong voice in world affairs.

ACROSS THE WORLD

France also ruled colonies overseas, which is why today French language and culture are found in places as far apart as Quebec (Canada) and North Africa. There are still many French dependencies, mainly in the Caribbean and the Pacific. The island of Corsica, which lies 170km off the southeast coast, is also a region of France.

▲ The 300-m high Eiffel Tower in Paris was the winning entry in a design competition for the World's Fair in 1889.

SEE ALSO

Celts, Europe, Napoleonic Wars, Revolution, World War I, World War II

FROG AND TOAD

Frogs and toads belong to the group of animals known as amphibians. Most spend their early life as tadpoles in water, but the adults live mainly on land.

◄ The male edible frog has large vocal sacs to call females in the mating season.

Gliding frogs have rounded sucker pads to help them climb.

Bullfrogs can grow up to 20cm, and may even eat newly-hatched alligators.

Arrow-poison frogs are among the most colourful and poisonous animals.

Frogs are related to toads, but frogs generally have slimmer bodies with a smooth skin, while toads have a drier, warty skin. All amphibians have thin skin, as their lungs are inefficient and they use their skin to breathe through. Oxygen from the air passes through the skin into tiny blood vessels just under the surface. This can happen only if the skin is moist, so frogs and toads are usually found in damp places.

STICKY TONGUES
Most frogs feed on slugs, insects and worms, which they catch with a long, sticky tongue. Larger frogs, such as the American bullfrog, also feed on prey such as mice, and even small ducklings.

MUSCULAR LEGS
Frogs are great jumpers. Their long, muscle-packed hind legs can send them shooting over 12 times their own length through the air. Webbed feet help frogs swim, while tree frogs make huge leaps from branch to branch, aided by sticky pads on their toes. Toads have less powerful back legs than most frogs and waddle.

BRIGHT COLOURS
Green or brown is the typical colour of most frogs, but some tropical frogs are brilliantly coloured. Some species change their skin colour with changes in light or temperature and all frogs shed the outer layer of their skin several times a year, pulling it over their head with their legs.

NOISY COURTSHIP
Frogs and toads can be very noisy at breeding time, when males croak to attract females. The European marsh frog is one of the noisiest – a colony sounds like a crowd of people laughing.

INSIDE A FROG

A frog's internal organs are similar to those of higher animals such as dogs. Externally, their bulging eyes help them look around in many directions, while the disc above the eye is the eardrum (called a tympanum). Some frogs have sticky-tipped tongues fixed to the front of their mouths which they flick out to capture prey.

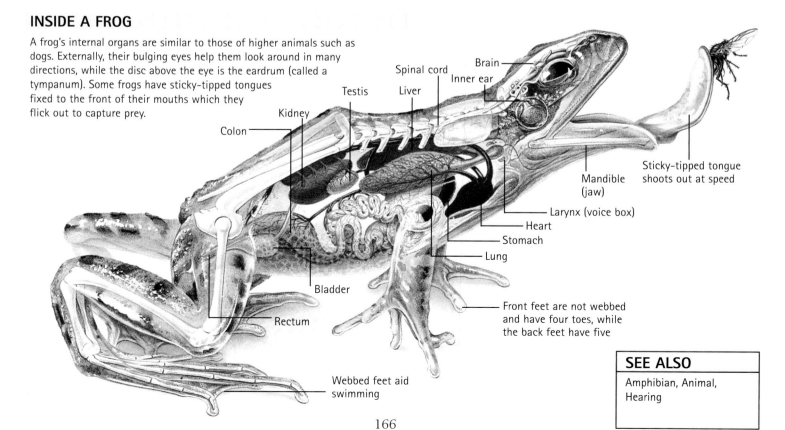

Colon
Kidney
Testis
Liver
Spinal cord
Brain
Inner ear
Sticky-tipped tongue shoots out at speed
Mandible (jaw)
Larynx (voice box)
Heart
Stomach
Lung
Bladder
Rectum
Front feet are not webbed and have four toes, while the back feet have five
Webbed feet aid swimming

SEE ALSO
Amphibian, Animal, Hearing

FRUIT

Fruits contain the seeds of flowering plants. They protect the developing seeds and help them to reach a suitable place to grow into new plants.

Pomes are fleshy fruits like pears, which have their seeds in a core formed from the flower stem.

Berries, such as tomatoes, cucumbers and oranges, hold many seeds inside a single fruit with soft pulp.

Drupes have a single stone which contains the seed. Blackberries are a cluster of many small drupes.

Dry fruits range from chestnuts to corncobs, but all are seed-bearing.

For a new generation of plants to grow successfully, the seed must be spread away from the parent plant so that the new plants are not all grouped together. Fruits are the means by which flowering plants ensure that their ripe seeds get to new, fertile locations.

FLESHY FRUITS

Fruits can be divided into two basic groups: fleshy and dry. Fleshy fruits are juicy and taste good to mammals and birds, which eat the seeds along with the fruit. The seeds pass through the animals bodies undigested and drop to the ground, where they grow into new plants. Strawberries are false fruits. They develop from a swollen stem. The pips on the surface are the real fruits.

DRY FRUITS

Fruits such as poppy seedheads or walnuts become dry as the seed ripens. Some, such as pea pods, split open so the seed is scattered in all directions. Others, such as the sycamore key, are light and can be blown by the wind. Nuts are also fruits. They have a hard outer casing that rots when the seed inside is ripe and ready to germinate (start growing).

SEED CONTAINERS

Fruits develop from the ovary of the flower after it has been pollinated. The seeds inside the fruit develop from the fertilized egg cells within the ovary. Some fruits, including peaches, cherries and plums, contain a single seed. However, most fruits, such as apples, raspberries, tomatoes and marrows, contain more than one seed. Occasionally, the sepals (leaves outside the flower petals) remain after the petals of the flower have fallen, and enclose the fruits, as in acorns.

FRUIT TO EAT

Some fruits are poisonous to humans, but there are many that are delicious and nutritious. Fleshy fruits often contain fruit sugars, which are a useful source of energy, and the fibre provided by the skin, flesh, and sometimes the seeds, ensures healthy digestion. Fruits contain vitamins, minerals and other nutrients that help the body fight off illness. Nuts are also an excellent source of protein.

EATING THE FRUIT

The bright colour and pleasant smell of fruits such as blackberries attracts birds and animals to eat them. After digesting the soft outer part, they pass the seeds out of their body with the rest of their waste. By this time, they will often be at some distance from the original plant.

1 The dispersed seed falls on fertile soil and the first shoots appear.

2 Flowers on the mature plant are pollinated and produce seeds.

3 The petals drop off and the fruit forms. It is hard and unappealing to birds.

4 The fruit becomes succulent and sweet when it is ready to be eaten.

SEE ALSO

Flower, Food, Leaf, Nutrition, Plant, Seed and pollination

FUNGI

Fungi are neither plants nor animals, but have their own kingdom, which has over 80,000 species and includes mushrooms, toadstools, moulds and yeasts.

◄ The mould on these nectarines comes from airborne spores that have started to breed.

The earth star lifts its fruit body clear of the ground on star-like rays.

The giant puffball is as big as a man's head and makes billions of spores.

Truffles are considered the tastiest of fungi. They grow close to tree roots.

Unlike plants, fungi need a supply of organic food in order to grow and reproduce. Plants have a green pigment, called chlorophyll, which allows them to make their own food using the Sun's energy. Fungi have no chlorophyll, so they take food from plants and animals.

WHERE THEY LIVE

There are more than 80,000 different types of fungi. Some, like yeast, are only a single cell. Most form masses of threads, called mycelium, which spread inside whatever they feed on. Many live inside plants, or in the soil, where they help to break down dead plant and animal matter.

HOW THEY BREED

To reproduce, fungi must release minute spores into the air. Some fungi, such as mushrooms and toadstools, grow large fruit bodies to help the spores to travel farther. Others grow tall, thread-like stalks with spore capsules at the end. If they land in a suitable place, the spores will grow to form new fungi of the same type. There are fungus spores around us all the time.

USEFUL FUNGI

Some fungi are useful as they help to break down the remains of dead plants and animals or make medicines. An example is the antibiotic penicillin. Certain yeast fungi are used to make bread and alcohol. Some mushrooms are good to eat, but others contain deadly poison, and it is difficult to tell them apart.

NO-FUN FUNGI

Fungi can grow on and spoil food, paper, wood in buildings, and damp clothes. Fungus diseases can damage and even kill plants, including crops such as potatoes and strawberries. Some affect animals and people: athlete's foot is a common fungal disease that causes itchy, flaky skin between the toes.

HOW FUNGI BREED

Like nearly all fungi, the fly agaric grows a web of thread-like mycelium through which it feeds on decaying matter. In order to reproduce, it releases spores from the surface of its gills into the air. When the spores land, they develop their own mycelium. But they can only grow fruit bodies by joining up with mycelium from the same species of fungi.

Cap

Developing gills

Developing cap

Mycelium

Upturned cap allows spores to disperse farther.

Gills, where spores are produced

Spores

Stipe (stem)

SEE ALSO

Medicine,
Micro-organism, Plant

GALAXY

A galaxy is a huge collection of stars held together by gravity. The Sun is just one of about 200 billion stars contained within our home galaxy, the Milky Way.

There are probably over a thousand million galaxies in the universe. They come in three basic shapes: spiral, elliptical and irregular.

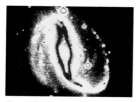
Barred-spiral galaxies have a well-defined bar with arms attached to it.

Elliptical galaxies can be round or oval, and have very little gas or dust.

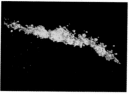
Irregular galaxies are small and shapeless, and contain a lot of gas.

THE NUCLEUS
The central part of a galaxy is called the nucleus. Here, stars are crowded much closer together than on the galactic outskirts. Astronomers now believe that massive black holes may lie deep within the nucleus of many large galaxies. There is probably a black hole at the centre of our own galaxy.

LIGHT YEARS AWAY
Enormous distances separate galaxies. The closest large galaxy to the Milky Way is the Andromeda Galaxy, located about two million light years away. It is the farthest object visible to the naked eye.

CLUSTERS AND SUPERCLUSTERS
Galaxies are arranged in clusters, which are themselves part of superclusters. The Milky Way and the Andromeda Galaxy are the two largest members of a small cluster of about 30 galaxies known as the Local Group. This, in turn, forms a tiny part of the Local Supercluster.

ACTIVE GALAXIES
Galaxies vary greatly in the amount of energy they give off. Some galaxies, known as active galaxies, are so called because they give out more energy than is available from all the stars they contain. The extra energy is believed to be supplied by matter falling into a black hole at their centre.

ELLIPTICAL GIANTS
Elliptical galaxies are round or oval in appearance and usually have very little gas or dust. They vary greatly in size, from giants to dwarfs. Giant ellipticals may contain up to ten trillion stars and are the largest type of galaxy.

THE MILKY WAY
The Milky Way is a large spiral galaxy measuring about 100,000 light years across (a light year equals 9.46 million million kilometres). It is about 13.6 billion years old and takes 225 million years to rotate once. Like all spirals, it contains plenty of gas and dust, from which new stars are formed. The dense nucleus is the oldest part and has no gas left for new stars.

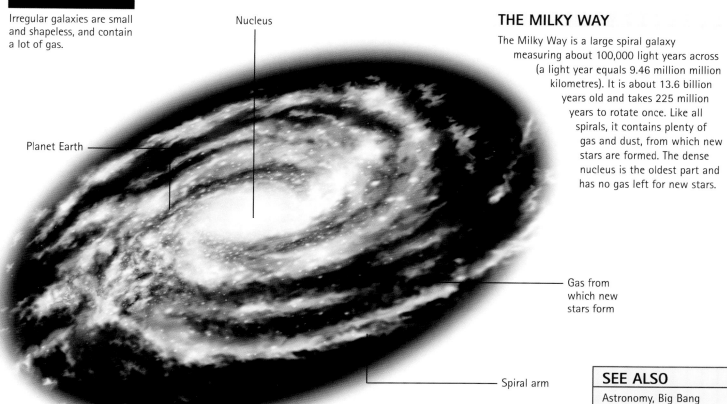

Nucleus

Planet Earth

Gas from which new stars form

Spiral arm

SEE ALSO
Astronomy, Big Bang theory, Black hole, Constellation, Solar system, Star, Universe

GAS

Gas that is burned for cooking and heating is a fossil fuel consisting mainly of methane. It is usually brought into homes and industries via pipelines.

Gas is useful because it releases heat when it burns. It is used for heating and cooking in homes and many industries burn gas for welding or smelting.

FOSSIL FUEL
Most domestic gas is natural gas, found underground, often with oil or coal but sometimes on its own. Like oil, gas was formed over millions of years from the remains of plants and animals. These organisms are made up largely of hydrogen and carbon, which change to a hydrocarbon called methane when they decay. The natural gas is then mined. Bottled gas, used by campers, is not natural gas. It is propane or butane, two by-products of oil refining.

PROCESSING GAS
Most natural gas is found under the sea. It flows under pressure through

92% Methane

3.5% Ethane

2.5% Nitrogen

1% Propane

1% Other

◄ The composition of natural gas varies, although its main ingredient is always methane. These are the percentages for North Sea gas.

a pipe connected to a gas terminal on land, although some is made into a liquid and shipped across the sea. There are a few unwanted substances in natural gas, which are removed at the terminal. The resulting gas does not smell, which means that a leak could go unnoticed. For this reason, a smelly chemical called a thiol is added.

GAS – THE BURNING ISSUE
The Ancient Chinese first used natural gas thousands of years ago to evaporate sea water to obtain salt. In the early 1800s, oil prospectors in the USA set light to wells which produced only gas. Then, in the 1870s, experiments were carried out into piping natural gas into US homes. The UK first began prospecting for gas in the 1930s.

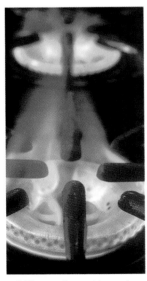

1 Exploration teams search for gas by drilling from rigs in areas with the right rock formation. Gas is often found with oil.

2 The gas reaches terminals in seamless steel pipes.

3 Smaller pipes then supply homes and industries.

4 The gas is used in cookers and heating systems.

DRILLING FOR GAS
Gas is usually found thousands of metres below the Earth's surface in a rock such as sandstone. A layer of hard impermeable rock above it prevents the gas from reaching the surface unless it is drilled by a gas or oil company.

SEE ALSO
Mining, Oil, Rock

GENETICS

Genetics is the science that studies how animals and plants pass their features to their offspring, generation after generation.

Gregor Mendel (1822–84) bred pea plants and studied how they passed features onto offspring.

Nobel Prize-winning scientists James Watson, from the USA and Francis Crick from the UK discovered the structure of DNA in 1953.

Babies look like their parents. This tendency for offspring to resemble their parents was known in ancient times. People selected particular plants or animals with features they wanted, such as cows that gave most milk, and bred them. Over many generations, this selective breeding led to cows which gave even more milk.

PATTERNS OF INHERITANCE
In the 1850s, an Austrian monk called Gregor Mendel discovered the basics of inheritance by breeding pea plants. He found that some features of pea plants, such as height and colour, were not passed on to the next generation as a blend of both parents' features. Instead, a feature from one parent was dominant.

IT IS IN THE GENES
We now know that the features inherited by the peas were decided by their genes.

▶ Dolly, the first artificially cloned sheep, was created from a cell taken from another adult sheep. This meant that both sheep had exactly the same genes.

Genes are the instructions which decide the appearance and function of each living cell or organism. They are arranged on corkscrew-shaped chemicals called DNA (deoxyribonucleic acid), visible only under an electron microscope.

PASSING ON GENES
When a human or other living thing reproduces, it passes on a copy of half of its genes to its offspring. Each reproductive cell (sperm or egg) contains a different combination of genes, guaranteeing that each offspring will be unique.

GENETIC ENGINEERING
Scientists can now change animals and plants by genetic engineering. The required gene is extracted from the DNA using chemicals called enzymes and inserted into a host organism to obtain the desired characteristic.

PASSING ON THE MESSAGE

DNA is made of thousands of chemical sub-units (known as bases), strung in a line like beads on a necklace. There are four different bases, called A, T, G and C, which are arranged along the DNA. Their sequence determines the cell's genetic code, in the same way that letters of the alphabet arranged in a certain order become a sentence.

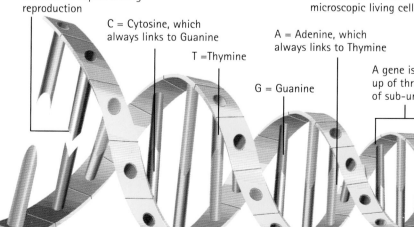

The DNA is unzipped while the code is copied during reproduction

C = Cytosine, which always links to Guanine

T =Thymine

G = Guanine

A = Adenine, which always links to Thymine

A gene is made up of three pairs of sub-units

Genes are contained inside the nucleus of each microscopic living cell

Nucleus

The DNA strand looks like a twisted ladder – a shape known as a double helix

The DNA strands are coiled up into chromosomes – human cells contain 23 pairs

The DNA is wrapped around a core of proteins

SEE ALSO
Atom and molecule, Cell, Crop, Farming, Forensics

GERMANY

Germany is a large country which lies in the middle of Europe and borders nine other countries. East and West Germany were reunited in 1990.

Area: 357,021 sq km
Population: 81,752,000
Capital: Berlin
Language: German
Currency: Euro

Germany has a varied landscape, with a broad, flat plain in the north and highlands in the central region. The south is mountainous and includes the South German Hills, Black Forest and Bavarian Alps. The country is crossed by several major rivers, including the Danube, Rhine, Oder, Weser, Ems and Elbe. The climate is rarely severe, with warm summers and mild winters, and most places receive from 500mm to 1,000mm of rainfall a year.

FARMING AND INDUSTRY
Less than three per cent of Germans are farmers, growing crops such as wheat, barley, rye and potatoes, as well as grapes to make wine. Many more people work in manufacturing or service industries. There are factories almost everywhere, especially in the Ruhr region – the heart of the iron, steel and chemical industries. German goods include cars, cameras, computers and textiles. Factories in the east are being modernized to match those in the west, the most prosperous part of the country.

GETTING AROUND
Germany has a high standard of living and many people own cars. Motorways, called *autobahns*, were built from the 1930s, and

▲ The Rhine is one of Europe's most important rivers. Its slopes are lined with vineyards and picturesque towns.

the country also has an efficient modern rail system. Barges are used to carry heavy goods along the Rhine and the country's other waterways.

FESTIVALS, FOOD AND RECREATION
Germans are fond of food and drink. A famous annual get-together is the Munich Beer Festival, held in October. Popular German foods include sausages, such as frankfurters, sauerkraut (a dish made with pickled cabbage), pastries and cheese. For recreation, many people enjoy sports such as soccer, tennis and athletics, and other outdoor activities, including walking, climbing and boating.

ARTS AND ARCHITECTURE
Many of the world's great philosophers, such as Immanuel Kant, writers, including Goethe, and composers, such as Beethoven and Wagner, have been German. Engineers Daimler and Benz invented the motor car, and German scientists pioneered the jet engine and space rocket. The country is also famous for Meissen china, and for its architecture, which includes many magnificent churches and palaces.

WARS AND RECOVERY
For hundreds of years, Germany was a patchwork of independent states, each with its own rulers. By the 1700s, Prussia

▲ Many locals wear Bavarian national costume during the famous Munich Beer Festival, held every October. It attracts thousands of people from all over the world.

▶ Germany is the world's fourth largest producer of cars after China, Japan and the USA. Car manufacturers from all over the world exhibit their latest models at the Frankfurt Motor Show each year.

emerged as the strongest, uniting most of the other states to form a German empire in 1871. Germany suffered defeat in World War I (1914–18) and was then ruled by the Nazi dictator, Adolf Hitler, who led the country into World War II (1939–45). Defeat in this war left Germany divided. East Germany was under communist rule, while West Germany became the richest capitalist democracy in Europe. In 1990, the two parts – an economically prosperous west and an impoverished east – were reunited, bringing many economic and social problems. However, Germany is still a powerful economic and political force within the European Union.

DENMARK

BALTIC SEA

NORTH SEA

Rostock

Hamburg

Bremen

Elbe

POLAND

Oder

NETHERLANDS

Ems

Weser

Hannover

Berlin

Rhine

Harz Mts.

Dortmund

GERMANY

Leipzig

Essen

Dresden

Düsseldorf

Cologne

RUHR

ORE MTS.

Bonn

BELGIUM

Frankfurt

Mosel

Main

CZECH REPUBLIC

Mannheim

Nürnberg

LUXEMBOURG

Stuttgart

Danube

N

Munich

AUSTRIA

FRANCE

BLACK FOREST

Bavarian Alps

SWITZERLAND

miles
0   100

0   100
km

▲ An East Berlin guard hands a flower to West Berliners sitting on top of the Berlin Wall in 1990 – the year the Wall came down, after dividing the city for over 25 years.

▼ Sigmaringen Castle, built on top of a mountain in the Black Forest region, is typical of many castles that dot the German landscape.

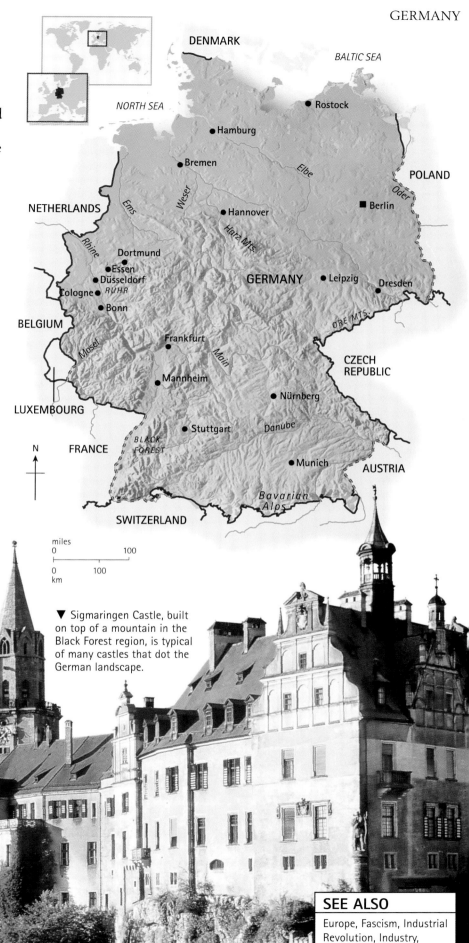

SEE ALSO

Europe, Fascism, Industrial Revolution, Industry, World War I, World War II

GLACIER

A glacier is a mass of ice that flows slowly, under the influence of gravity, either from high in the mountains or in polar regions where it is very cold.

Take a handful of snow and squeeze it hard. It turns to ice in your hand. This is what happens when snow falls, year after year, in the valleys of high mountains. The snow at the bottom of the valley is compressed by the weight of the snow above, until it turns to ice.

ICE RIVERS

As the ice comes under greater pressure from the snow above, it begins to soften and flow like putty. At this point, a glacier has formed. The movement of the glacier is very slow – only a few metres per year.

DESTRUCTIVE POWER

A heavy glacier is a powerful force of erosion. As it moves downwards, it grinds the valley into a distinct U-shape. A valley that once held a glacier is obvious from its flat bottom and vertical sides.

GATHERING RUBBLE

The debris that is worn away by the glacier is carried along, either embedded in the ice or lying on the top. This rubble is called moraine. When it is dropped at the glacier's snout as the ice melts, moraine forms a landscape of irregular heaps of clay, sand and rocks.

POLAR ICE CAPS

Glaciers that form near the North and South Poles can cover whole countries or continents, and are usually known as ice caps or ice sheets. Snow falls at the centre of the continent and spreads out towards the sea. Antarctica and Greenland are both covered by such ice sheets.

THE ICE AGE

Between 1,600,000 and 10,000 years ago, the Earth went through periods of intense cold, known as Ice Ages. For thousands of years in each Ice Age, vast glaciers covered much of North America, Asia and Europe as far south as London, England. Many of the lakes, valleys and hills that we see today were carved by these ice sheets. The first people to settle the Americas crossed from Asia to what is now Alaska on 1,000-m high ice bridges.

1 The top of the valley is eroded by the glacier into an armchair shape called a cirque.

2 As the glacier travels, its surface cracks to form crevasses.

3 The glacier picks up rubble (moraine), which piles into ridges.

4 Melting ice forms a lake at the bottom of the glacier.

SEE ALSO

Antarctica, Arctic, Lake, Mountain and valley, Prehistoric animal, Prehistoric people

GLAND

Glands are organs that make and release chemicals that the body needs. One group of glands makes hormones, which control growth, life and development.

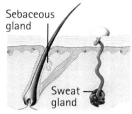

▲ The skin has two exocrine glands beneath its surface: sebaceous glands, which make oil to keep skin and hair soft; and sweat glands, which keep the body cool.

FAST FACTS

- Tear glands are exocrine glands that release tears to clean the front of the eye
- Human endocrine glands produce over 50 hormones between them
- Women's breasts are mammary glands, which produce milk

Some glands in the body have little tubes known as ducts, through which they release chemicals directly to an area where they are needed. These are the exocrine glands. They include sweat glands in the skin and salivary glands in the mouth. Other glands have no ducts and release chemicals called hormones into the blood. These are the endocrine glands.

THE MASTER GLAND
The pituitary gland is the smallest but most important gland in the body. It is attached to part of the lower brain called the hypothalamus. Together these two areas of the brain control all the body's nerves and endocrine glands.

SUGAR IN THE BLOOD
The body stores and uses energy as glucose (blood sugar). A gland in the neck, called the thyroid gland, makes a hormone called thyroxin which controls metabolic rate (how fast the cells use up glucose). The amount of glucose in the blood is regulated by two more hormones, called insulin and glucagon, which are made in the pancreas.

HEALTHY BONES AND TEETH
On the thyroid gland are four tiny, pea-sized glands called parathyroids. Together, the thyroid and parathyroids make hormones which affect levels of calcium for healthy bones and teeth.

PUMPING UP THE ADRENALINE
There is an adrenal gland on top of each kidney. The outside of each gland makes steroid hormones that control the body's water balance, and bodily reactions to stress and illness. The inside of each gland makes a hormone called adrenaline, which gets the body ready for emergency action. A fast heartbeat, more sweat and the need to go to the toilet frequently are all effects of adrenaline. Today we may feel these effects in a stressful situation, such as an exam, but their original purpose was to prepare the body to run from danger, such as a wild animal.

ENDOCRINE GLANDS

Hormones circulate around the body in the bloodstream. Their levels are often regulated by a system known as feedback. This means that sensor cells check how much of each hormone is present in the blood, and tell the glands to release more or less, as it is needed.

The pituitary gland makes over 12 hormones

The thyroid gland makes thyroxine which controls the body's use of energy

Four parathyroids are embedded in the thyroid gland

The thymus gland helps the immune system to develop in childhood, then gradually shrinks

As well as being an endocrine gland, the pancreas is also an exocrine gland which makes digestive juices

An adrenal gland sits on the top of each kidney

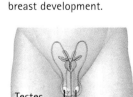

▲ Ovaries make female hormones which control the menstrual cycle and breast development.

Ovaries

Testes

▲ Testes make male hormones which control sperm production and growth of facial hair.

SEE ALSO

Brain, Hearing, Human body, Mammal, Reproduction, Sight, Skin, Stomach

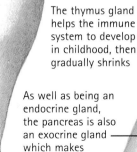

GLASS

Glass is a transparent material made by melting together sand, salt and other substances at high temperatures, then leaving them to cool gradually.

People first made glass over 6,000 years ago, to use as a coloured glaze on stone or clay beads. The earliest surviving glass containers, dating from about 1500BCE, came from Egypt and Mesopotamia. They were moulded around stones as they cooled, or carved once they had set. There are many more ways to make glass today. It can be moulded, blown into shape or rolled into flat sheets like pastry.

USES FOR GLASS

Glass is used to make countless objects around us – from window panes and lenses in spectacles to cookware and ornaments. It can also be pulled into long strands, like spaghetti, to make glass fibre. Glass fibre can be spun into thicker strands, called fibre-optic cables, that carry information as pulses of light over vast distances. It can also be matted to make glass wool, a material that traps heat like a blanket. Glass wool is often used to insulate attics.

SODA-LIME GLASS

Modern, manufactured glass is about 75 per cent silica (the main ingredient of sand), but also contains other substances to make it easier to produce. Ninety per cent of all glass is a type called soda-lime glass, which contains soda (sodium carbonate), to reduce its melting temperature from 1,300°C to 700°C, and lime to stop it dissolving in water.

TOUGHENING IT UP

Tiny amounts of other chemicals can be added to glass to change its properties. Boron, for example, can make it ovenproof, copper can make it a red colour and lead can make it more transparent. Because glass shatters easily it can be laminated (toughened by sandwiching Perspex or wire mesh between layers of glass.) Such glass can be made to withstand bullets.

1 A powder containing about 72% silica (the quartz-like part of sand), 15% soda, 6% lime, 4% magnesia, 2% alumina and 1% boric oxide is poured into the furnace.

2 The glass is heated until it is soft and workable – the soda in the glass gives it a melting point of about 700°C.

3 The glass passes between rollers and onto a bath of hot metal, usually tin, where it floats until its surface is smooth and hard.

FLOAT GLASS FOR WINDOWS

Traditionally, window glass was made by hand, either by spinning or blowing a gob of melted glass flat and cutting it. Then, at the beginning of the 20th century, sheet glass began to be made by drawing melted glass straight from the furnace through rollers. The surface was rough, though, and needed costly polishing, so in the 1950s English glass manufacturer Alistair Pilkington invented the float process shown here.

4 The glass passes over cooling rollers until its surface is hard enough not to be scratched by handling.

5 The glass is cut for use in windows and mirrors.

▲ Stained-glass windows are made from small pieces of coloured glass, joined together with lead strips. The colours come from metal oxides which are added to the glass during smelting. For example, red is from copper and yellow is from manganese and ferrous oxide. Features are painted on later.

SEE ALSO

Materials,
Telecommunication

GOLD

Gold is a shiny, yellow precious metal. It is a stable chemical element that is not affected by air or water, which means that it never rusts or tarnishes.

Unlike most metals, gold occurs in its pure state. Some of it is found as grains in sand or gravel, but most of it is found as veins in rock. It has been valued by people for thousands of years because of its qualities as an attractive metal that never tarnishes and is easy to shape.

GOLD MINING
Most gold – over 2,300 tonnes a year – is extracted by mining. After crushing the rock in which it is found, gold is collected using one of several chemical methods, the most common of which is the cyanide process. Sodium cyanide is added to a pulp of powdered rock and water. This dissolves the gold, which is filtered before zinc is added. The gold settles as a fine mud and the zinc is dissolved.

ORNAMENTAL AND PRACTICAL
Gold has been used for making jewellery and ornaments for thousands of years. Today, it is used for many other things, including wiring electronic circuits, making teeth fillings and forming part of satellite reflector shields.

▲ Most gold is found in lodes, or veins, in rock. This must be crushed before the gold can be collected.

STRENGTHENING GOLD
Pure gold is very soft and needs to be hardened by mixing it with other elements, such as copper or silver. The amount of gold in an object is measured in carats. Eighteen-carat gold contains 18 parts of gold and six parts of silver and copper. The purest gold is 24-carat gold.

THE GOLD RUSHES
Nearly half of all the gold in the world today is held by governments as ingots (gold bars). Gold has always been prized. Between 1840 and 1900, thousands of people tried to seek their fortune in the USA, Canada, South Africa and Australia, during what are known as 'gold rushes'.

▶ Ornate gold knife belonging to the Ashanti king Kofi Karikari in the 19th century. Kings of this West African empire were also enthroned on the Golden Stool, a carved gold throne used as a symbol of power.

PROSPECTING FOR GOLD
Rocks containing tiny nuggets, veins or flakes of gold may become eroded (worn away) by rain or ice. When this happens, the gold can be carried into streams. During a 'gold rush', prospectors would be seen standing in streams panning for gold. After dipping the pan into the stream they would swirl and tip it gently to throw off water, leaving gravel and perhaps gold.

▶ If the prospector was lucky, he would find small grains of gold mixed in with the gravel at the bottom of the pan.

SEE ALSO

Australia, Chemistry, Metal, Mineral and gem

GOVERNMENT

The government of a country is the system by which laws are made, social services provided and the country organized.

The structure of governments varies, but most governments are responsible for the same tasks and have a constitution, a set of rules which they must obey.

BRANCHES OF GOVERNMENT

Most governments today have three branches: the executive (a prime minister or president), the legislative (an assembly, parliament or congress) and the judiciary (the highest courts of law). The legislature is composed of elected representatives and it makes the laws by which the country is governed. New laws are debated by the legislature, then a vote is taken. Once a law is passed it is enforced by the judiciary.

LOCAL GOVERNMENT

National affairs, such as defence and foreign policy, are usually supervised by national government. At local level, services such as education, town planning, refuse collection, parks, fire services, police and road-building are handled by regional and town governments. Depending on the economic state of a country and the political beliefs of the party in government, social services may be provided, such as help for the sick, unemployed or those on low income.

DICTATORS AND OLIGARCHS

In Ancient Rome an oligarchy (men from a small number of noble families) met in the Senate to run the government. In 82BCE, Lucius Sulla was made dictator with supreme power to solve disputes. Against strong opposition he reformed the constitution and the legal system and cut government power. In 79BCE, Sulla retired to his country estate.

RAISING TAXES

Running a country is expensive. Governments raise money by placing taxes on how much people earn or inherit and how much they spend. Income tax rates vary wildly – in some countries, people pay nothing on their earnings, while in others top rates can be as high as 67 per cent. To pay for local services, local governments may collect additional taxes.

▲ The House of Commons, inside the Houses of Parliament at Westminster, London, is where elected members of the British parliament sit and vote on new laws.

TYPES OF GOVERNMENT

Communism A system based on the 19th-century political theories of Karl Marx and Friedrich Engels. They advocated class war and a society in which all the property is owned by the people. Communist states are usually dictatorial.

Dictatorship Rule by one person, a group or a committee whose word is law. Often accompanied by censorship and restricted rights. The idea of dictatorship comes from Ancient Rome when the Roman Senate could appoint individuals as 'dictators' in times of national emergency.

Federalism A union of two or more states which can pass individual state laws, but which accept the national government's rule in matters such as the country's defence. Countries with federal governments include the US, Australia and Switzerland.

Monarchy Rule by a king, queen, emperor or empress. Traditionally, a monarch would have supreme power, but nowadays most monarchs have only constitutional power. This means their power is limited by the country's constitution or government to ceremonial duties. The UK has this system.

Oligarchy Government by a small ruling group. A republic would be an oligarchy if only a few people were entitled to vote for the leader. Most Ancient Greek city-states were oligarchies because only the free men (not slaves or women) could vote. Ancient Rome was an oligarchy ruled by a few nobles.

Republic A state or country where power is held by elected representatives acting on behalf of those who elected them. An elected president is head of state and sometimes of the government. The most common form of government in the world today.

SEE ALSO

Civil rights, Democracy, Empire, Revolution, Women's rights

GRASSLAND

Grasslands are large areas of flat or gently rolling land covered by grasses, often with trees and bushes scattered across them or clustered along streams.

▲ Damp long-grass prairies are rich in bluestem, switch grass and needlegrass.

Between dry, rainless deserts and dense, wet forests there are usually areas known as grasslands. These regions have definite wet and dry seasons. The grasses grow quickly, flower, and produce seeds in the wet season, then die back or do not grow in the dry season. Most of a grass plant is below ground. This means that it can survive droughts and fires better than other plants.

GRASSLAND TYPES
Different types of grass grow all over the world, and grasslands are given different names wherever they exist. In North America, they are called prairies or plains; in Africa they are known as savannas. The cooler grasslands of Argentina are Pampas, and in Russia they are steppes.

AFRICAN SAVANNA
Temperatures on the savanna are hot all year, but rain falls only during the summer. The long red oat, bluestems and dropseed grasses plus scattered trees produce up to 45 tonnes of vegetation per hectare each year, providing food for animals that include zebra, antelope and ostriches. Frequent fires encourage fresh growth of grasses and trees.

ANIMALS AND PLANTS
Herds of antelope in Africa, kangaroos in Australia and buffalo in the USA graze the grasslands. Marmots, rabbits, and ground squirrels burrow for roots and shelter. These plant-eaters are hunted by lions, wolves and hyenas, and birds of prey, such as hawks and eagles. Invertebrates (animals without backbones), such as insects, are the largest group of grassland animals. These provide food for rodents and small birds.

HARVESTING THE LAND
Wild grasslands once covered almost a third of the world's land, but most have been changed by humans. Sheep farmers in Australia, cattle ranchers in the USA, dairy farmers in Europe and nomadic goat herders in North Africa, all depend on natural or cultivated grasslands to feed their animals. Grasslands have also been ploughed to produce cereal crops such as wheat, maize, and oats.

Scattered trees grow where roots can reach deep, permanent water

Waterholes fill during the wet season, storing water for the dry season

Grazing animals wander across the grasslands in herds, usually settling near a source of water

SEE ALSO
Africa, Animal, Argentina, Canada, Crop, Farming, Food, Habitat

GRAVITY

Gravity is a force that exists between any two objects, pulling them together. On Earth, the force of gravity pulls you towards the ground and gives you weight.

◀ The speed at which a rocket is launched determines whether it escapes Earth's gravity and flies off into space or plummets back to Earth.

When you jump up in the air, you come back down again. This is because the Earth's gravity pulls you down towards the planet. If there were no gravity, we would drift off the Earth and into space. Gravity explains why the stars and planets move in the way that they do and how the Moon affects the tides each day. It is also the force that gives us our weight.

MASS AND WEIGHT

The less gravity there is, the less you weigh. If you were in outer space, far away from any other objects, you would not feel any gravity. This means you would be completely weightless, even though your mass (quantity of matter) would not have changed. On Earth, the weight of something depends on its mass. A walrus has more mass than a mouse, for example, so it feels a greater force of gravity. That is why a walrus weighs more than a mouse.

FREE–FALL

Skydivers experience a feeling of weightlessness in a free-fall from a high aeroplane. In fact, they are still being pulled by the Earth's gravity, but the air resistance is pushing against them. Only outside the Earth's atmosphere, in space, are we truly weightless.

▲ Astronauts and fighter pilots feel the effects of gravity, or G-force, during take-off. Not only does gravity distort their faces, but it can also send all the blood to their legs, often

FAST FACTS

- Sir Isaac Newton (1643-1727) discovered the Law of Gravity, supposedly when he saw an apple fall from a tree
- Gravity keeps the rings of Saturn in orbit around the planet
- To escape the Earth's gravity, a spacecraft must reach a speed of 11.2km/sec. This is known as the 'escape velocity'

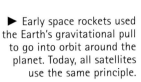

▶ Early space rockets used the Earth's gravitational pull to go into orbit around the planet. Today, all satellites use the same principle.

PULLING TOGETHER

We normally think about gravity only as it applies to the Earth, but gravity exists between any two objects. The greater their mass and the closer they are together, the larger the force of gravity between them. Two ships at sea, for example, will attract each other, but their gravitational pull is so small compared to other forces on Earth, that it is not noticeable. However, two nearby spaceships, far away from other objects in space, will create a noticeable gravitational attraction, called microgravity.

DROPPED FROM ON HIGH

Like all forces, gravity alters the velocity (speed) of objects. Near the Earth's surface, gravity makes all objects accelerate at the same rate (9.81m/sec.^2), no matter how heavy they are. If you dropped a full and an empty box from the top of a tall building, they would reach the ground together.

SEE ALSO

Earth, Force and motion, Moon, Solar system, Spacecraft

GREAT DEPRESSION

The Great Depression was a worldwide slump in trade and the economy which began with the Wall Street stock market crash in 1929 and lasted into the 1930s.

► In the USA, President Roosevelt, launched the New Deal: a government programme to aid the poor through community projects. Preparations for World War II aided recovery in Europe.

In the 1930s, trade between nations collapsed, businesses closed and millions of people lost their savings and their jobs. This worldwide slump was known as the Great Depression.

THE CAUSES
Trouble began after World War I (1914–18). The loser, Germany, was ruined by having to pay huge compensation to the victorious Allies. Many Germans lost all their savings as the value of their money collapsed. There were fears of a revolution like that in Communist Russia (1917).

HOME FROM WAR
In Britain, France and the United States, factories struggled to adjust to peacetime trade. Millions of soldiers came home and looked for jobs. Trade unions called workers to strike against employers who demanded wage cuts. The first-ever General Strike in

Britain happened in 1926. Food prices fell so low that many farmers were ruined and gave up their land.

THE CRASH
In 1929, the United States' financial market crashed after a period of frantic buying. Share prices fell sharply, ruining many investors. Banks and businesses shut down. The Wall Street Crash (named after New York's financial district) affected money markets around the world. World trade plunged. The Great Depression had begun.

EFFECTS OF THE SLUMP
The Great Depression cast a shadow across the 1930s. Jobless people lined up for food and clothing handouts. Some lost their homes and wandered the streets, begging or looking for work. Droughts and dust storms brought more misery to farming communities in the United States.

▲ Few were immune to the effects of the Great Depression. Many well-qualified people were out of work and forced to walk the streets.

FLEEING THE DUST BOWL
In 1930, a drought hit large areas around Oklahoma, where grassland had been ploughed to produce wheat. By 1933 the soil had turned to dust, leaving farms useless. Thousands of poverty-stricken families, called Okies, fled the Dust Bowl looking for work in California and elsewhere. By the 1940s the grassland had regrown.

SEE ALSO

Communism, Money, Revolution, World War I, World War II

Greece and the Balkans

Southeast Europe is a mountainous region that includes Greece and the Balkan countries, named after the mountain range that runs through the Balkan Peninsula.

ALBANIA
Area: 28,748 sq km
Population: 3,195,000
Capital: Tirana
Languages: Albanian, Greek
Currency: Lek

BOSNIA–HERZEGOVINA
Area: 51,129 sq km
Population: 3,840,000
Capital: Sarajevo
Languages: Croatian, Serbian, Bosnian
Currency: Marka

BULGARIA
Area: 110,993 sq km
Population: 7,365,000
Capital: Sofia
Languages: Bulgarian, Turkish
Currency: Lev

CROATIA
Area: 56,542 sq km
Population: 4,291,000
Capital: Zagreb
Language: Croatian
Currency: Kuna

GREECE
Area: 131,957 sq km
Population: 10,788,000
Capital: Athens
Language: Greek
Currency: Euro

► Remains of the Parthenon, a temple built in the 5th century BCE to honour the goddess Athena, stand in Athens city centre.

The Balkan peninsula has seas on three sides: the Adriatic and Ionian to the west, the Mediterranean to the south, and the Aegean and Black Sea to the east.

MOUNTAIN COUNTRY

Apart from the Balkan mountains, there are several other mountain ranges in the region. One of the most famous peaks is Mount Olympus in Greece, which is 2,911m high. The Danube river is the most important waterway, forming the border between Romania and Bulgaria. The Balkans has a mild climate, with summer temperatures reaching 30°C, but winters can be cold and snowy in the mountains.

LAND OF THE SLAVS

There is a rich cultural and religious diversity as a result of the many invaders to the region. Ancient Greece ruled an empire until the Roman invasion in 146BCE. Then, in the 4th century, the Roman Empire became split into east and west, and the Balkans fell into the eastern part, known as the Byzantine Empire. During the 5th and 7th centuries, Slavs came down from the north, scattering into distinct tribes, which are reflected in the languages present today: Bulgarian, Serbian, Croatian, Slovenian and Macedonian. The Ottoman Turks ruled the region from the 1400s, but most Balkan people stayed Christian under Islamic rule.

▲ Fish is important in the diet of many Greek people, especially on the islands. Here, a fisherman rows out from the harbour of Symi, a Greek island near the Turkish coast.

THE BALKANS TODAY

In 1929, King Alexander I became dictator of Yugoslavia, a nation made up of Bosnia-Herzegovina, Croatia, Montenegro, Serbia and Slovenia, and introduced a common language, Serbo-Croatian. After World War II (1939–45), Yugoslavia, Bulgaria and Albania became communist countries. Josip Tito was leader of the communist Federal People's Republic of Yugoslavia until he died in 1980. Savage civil wars began in 1991, and the former Republic of Yugoslavia broke up. It is now divided into seven independent countries. All the Balkan

KOSOVO
Area: 10,887 sq km
Population: 2,009,000
Capital: Pristina
Languages: Albian, Serbian
Currency: Euro

MACEDONIA
Area: 25,713 sq km
Population: 2,057,000
Capital: Skopje
Languages: Macedonian, Albanian
Currency: Dinar

MONTENEGRO
Area: 13,812 sq km
Population: 620,000
Capital: Podgorica
Languages: Montenegrin, Serbian
Currency: Euro

SERBIA
Area: 77,468 sq km
Population: 7,121,000
Capital: Belgrade
Language: Serbian
Currency: Dinar

SLOVENIA
Area: 20,273 sq km
Population: 2,047,000
Capital: Ljubljana
Language: Slovenian
Currency: Euro

TURKEY
Area: 779,452 sq km
Population: 73,723,000
Capital: Ankara
Languages: Turkish, Kurdish
Currency: Turkish lira

▲ The Festival of Roses is held each year in Kazanluk, Bulgaria, one day before rose picking begins. The petals are crushed for their oil, called attar of roses, used in perfume.

countries are striving to modernize their economies. Greece, Slovenia and Bulgaria are members of the European Union.

HOW PEOPLE LIVE
Many of the Balkan people are farmers, living in small towns and villages as their ancestors did before them. They grow maize, barley, fruits and vegetables, and raise sheep, goats, cattle and pigs. Donkeys and horse-drawn wagons can still be seen carrying produce to market. There are few big cities, apart from national capitals such as Athens (Greece) and Belgrade (Serbia), where skyscrapers tower over older buildings. Factories make vehicles, textiles, chemicals and electronic goods, and mines produce coal, iron and lead.

WHERE EAST MEETS WEST
Along the sunny Balkan coasts, with their beaches and medieval towns, tourism is an important industry. New hotels and roads cater for the growing tide of visitors. Eastern and Western building styles can be seen side by side: here a Christian church in Byzantine style, there an Islamic mosque. Bulgaria is famous for growing roses to make perfume. Visitors from all over the world visit Greece to see the wonders of its ancient civilization.

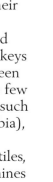

▼ Albanian children stand in front of an air raid bunker.

SEE ALSO
Civil war, Empire, Europe, Greece (Ancient), Refugee

GREECE, ANCIENT

The Ancient Greeks created one of the world's greatest civilizations. They gave us lasting styles of architecture, art, literature and government.

Not many paintings are left from Ancient Greece, but there are many decorated pots – usually showing myths or festivals.

This silver four-drachma piece, made in Athens, was used all over Ancient Greece. The owl symbolized Athena, goddess of wisdom.

Corrupt politicians were ostracized (sent into exile) if enough voters scratched their name onto an *ostraka* (a piece of broken pottery).

The Greeks moved south into what is now Greece some 4,000 years ago. The Minoans were the first to develop a great civilization around 2000BCE, on the island of Crete, but most achievements in the arts, sciences and government were made during the Golden Age. This was a period between 477 and 431BCE, when Athens was the ruling city state.

A RUGGED COUNTRY

The nature of the Greek countryside helped to shape the country's history. Its mountain ranges made travel by land difficult. Fiercely independent and patriotic communities grew up in the fertile pockets between the mountains, and Ancient Greece became a country divided into many city states.

THE OLYMPIANS

The people were deeply religious. They believed in many gods – all of whom had human form, but possessed superhuman powers and were, of course, immortal. The chief gods were known as the Olympians because they were believed to live at the top of Mount Olympus in northern Greece. Zeus ruled the gods with his wife Hera. Other gods and goddesses included: Aphrodite, goddess of love; Apollo, god of the Sun, music and light; Ares, god of war, and Athena, goddess of wisdom. The Ancient Greeks built temples to their gods, in which they made offerings of food, wine and sometimes live animals. Rich families had shrines in their homes to smaller house gods.

▲ Women were usually married at the age of 13 or 14 to men more than twice their age. They were in charge of the house and wove all the material for the loose-fitting garments, known as chitons, worn by men and women.

DECORATIVE ARTS AND FESTIVALS

The Greeks decorated their temples and palaces in a new, natural style of marble statues and reliefs. Music, drama, dance and sport were celebrated at festivals, such as the Olympic Games, held every four years from 776BCE in honour of the gods.

LITERATURE AND LEARNING

The poet Homer, who created the epic poems the *Odyssey* and *Iliad*, was just one of many great writers. Dramatists such as Aeschylus, Euripedes and Sophocles wrote plays for open-air theatres. Socrates, Plato and Aristotle discussed philosophy in *agoras* (market places) and academies, while scientific discoveries were made by Pythagoras, Archimedes and others.

◄ The ruggedness of the Greek countryside meant that most trade and warfare was carried out at sea. Greek warships known as triremes had up to 170 oarsmen, arranged on three decks (above), which gave them great speed.

ATHENS VERSUS SPARTA

The two most powerful city states were Athens and Sparta, which were constantly at war with each other. They had different approaches to education, the arts and warfare. Athens and other city states had a democratic government where all male citizens could vote, and their children were educated in the arts and sciences. Sparta was a military kingdom with a tough, warlike people. Boys were sent away to military camps at the age of seven, and girls were also trained in gymnastics and warfare – a fact which shocked the Athenians.

EMPIRE AND LEGACY

Early in the 5th century BCE, Athens and Sparta united against a new common enemy, Persia. The Ancient Greeks won, but fighting resumed and the city states began to crumble. Then, in 335BCE, Alexander the Great united Ancient Greece once more, and went on to conquer almost the entire Middle East, from Egypt to northern India. In 146BCE, the Romans conquered Greece, but adopted much of its culture and ways.

▲ The actors in the amphitheatres wore clay masks so that even people in the top rows could tell the characters apart.

▲ Lyres were stringed instruments made from turtle shells. Athenian boys learned to sing and play the lyre and aulos (flute) at music schools.

▲ Amphitheatres, like this one at Delphi, were carved into the sides of hills. Their clever design meant that a whisper on stage could be heard by the whole audience.

KEY DATES

2000BCE Minoan civilization in Crete flourishes

1600-1200BCE Mycenean civilization on the mainland rules Greece

900-800BCE Homer writes the *Iliad* and the *Odyssey*

490BCE Persian army invades Greece – the Greeks win at the battle of Marathon

480BCE Battles of Thermopylae and Salamis

431-404BCE Peloponnesian war between Athens and Sparta. Plague kills a third of Athenians. Sparta wins

356-323BCE Reign of Alexander the Great

146BCE Roman Empire conquers Greece

BATTLE OF THERMOPYLAE

The Greek cities fought frequent wars with each other, but in 480BCE they united against an invasion by the Persian Emperor Xerxes. A force of 300 hoplites (armoured infantry) from Sparta held thousands of Persians at the mountain pass of Thermopylae for three days before being wiped out. This gave the Greek fleet of ships time to gather at the Strait of Salamis and defeat the invasion.

SEE ALSO

Architecture, Astronomy, Democracy, Europe, Greece and the Balkans, Medicine, Mesopotamia, Myth and legend, Olympic Games, Sculpture, Seven wonders of the world, Theatre

HABITAT

A habitat is the home of particular species of animal or plant. It provides them with the food, shelter and conditions that allow them to survive.

◄ Oystercatchers living on the Dutch coast depend on clean seas for the survival of their diet: mussels (left), oysters and limpets.

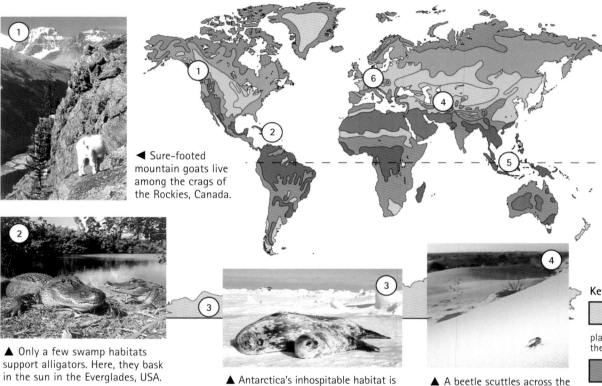

◄ Sure-footed mountain goats live among the crags of the Rockies, Canada.

▲ Only a few swamp habitats support alligators. Here, they bask in the sun in the Everglades, USA.

▲ Antarctica's inhospitable habitat is home to animals with a thick layer of fat, such as this Weddell seal and pup.

▲ A beetle scuttles across the cold desert of Turkmenistan. Its small size helps it keep warm.

▲ An orang-utan sits in a rainforest canopy in Borneo – a threatened habitat.

Key

Cold desert: cold region with little rain. Animals and plants must be able to survive the lack of water and cold.

Tundra: treeless plains near Arctic. Snow-covered in winter. Migratory animals, moss and lichens in summer.

Temperate woodland: tree-covered areas in climate that changes between winter and summer. Trees usually shed their leaves.

Coniferous forest: areas (usually northern) with trees bearing pine cones. Wildlife includes deer, bears, wolves.

Savanna grassland: grassland areas with scattered trees, lying between desert and rainforest. Large predators and herbivores.

Tropical rainforest: dense forest around Equator in Asia, Africa and South America. Habitat with the most wildlife.

Steppe and dry grassland: hot summers and cold winters. Short grasses, with many snakes and rodents.

Hot desert: hot with little rain. Can be sandy or rocky. Many animals hide during the day.

Climate, soil, plants and animals – from the tiniest insect to the tallest tree – all create a habitat. Scientists classify them into types, such as grassland, forest, desert, mountain-top, river, marsh or ocean. All these groups show great variation.

HABITATS AND BIOMES
When scientists talk about a habitat in general, they use the word biome. For example, a grassland is a biome, but a specific grassland such as the Argentinian Pampas is known as a habitat. Within each habitat there are also thousands of small, specialized living spaces, such as the dark, damp world under a rock on a river bank, or a pool of water in the fork of a forest tree. These are known as micro-habitats.

OCEAN WORLDS
The biggest biome of all is the oceans, which cover 71 per cent of the Earth's surface. This biome is divided into layers according to how warm or salty the water is and how far down the Sun's light reaches. It also varies from place to place – from the warm blue seas of the Caribbean to the cold, windswept Antarctic Ocean. Around the edges of the seas are other special habitats, such as coral reefs, rocky and sandy shores and river mouths.

UPSETTING THE BALANCE
Each habitat is a complex system, with all the plants and animals perfectly suited to, and yet dependent on, their environment, as well as on one another. When something upsets the balance, a habitat can be badly damaged. Parts of Africa's savannas have been turned into desert because too many people, goats and cattle have stripped off the vegetation. Lakes and rivers in many countries have been poisoned by industrial chemicals. Forests may be damaged by acid rain, and some seashores are being scarred by oil spillages.

SEE ALSO
Desert, Forest, Grassland, Ocean and sea, Pollution, Rainforest, Seashore

186

HEARING

Hearing is one of the five senses. It depends on the detection of sound waves in the air which are changed into nerve signals and sent to the brain for processing.

Bats use their high-pitched (100,000Hz) squeaks to locate flying insects to eat.

Frogs can hear only low frequency sounds of 5,000Hz and below.

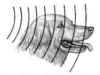

Dogs hear both high and low-pitched sounds. Dog whistles are 35,000Hz.

Human ears hear frequencies from about 30 to 18,000Hz.

For most people, hearing is the second most important sense, after sight. It allows communication, warns us of danger and gives pleasure, from music to bird song.

THE OUTER EAR

We hear with our ears. The outer ear is just a skin-covered flap of gristle, or cartilage, that catches sound waves in the air. Most of the delicate working parts are behind it, protected inside the skull.

INSIDE THE EAR

Sound waves funnel into the ear canal. At its end, they hit a small patch of flexible skin, the eardrum. The sound waves bounce off it and make the eardrum vibrate (shake to and fro). Vibrations pass from the eardrum, along a chain of three tiny bones, called the hammer (malleus), anvil (incus) and stirrup (stapes). These bones pass the vibration to the oval window.

THE COCHLEA

The oval window is a membrane in the wall of a fluid-filled chamber, the cochlea, which is coiled like a snail, small enough to sit on your fingernail. Vibrations of the oval window push ripples into the fluid inside the cochlea. As the ripples go around the coil, they shake almost two million tiny hairs sticking out from 25,000 hair cells.

SOUND TO ELECTRICITY

The hair cells send nerve signals, millions every second, along the cochlear nerve to the brain. Here they are analyzed for volume and frequency, and compared with 'soundprints' in the memory. Sound waves travel at about 340m/sec. If the sound comes from the side, the waves reach the nearer ear a fraction of a second before the farther ear. The brain detects this tiny difference and works out the direction of the sound source. This is only possible with two (or more) ears, and is called stereophonic hearing. Frequency of a sound is measured in vibrations per second, Hertz (Hz), and our ears can hear only certain frequencies.

CAPTURING SOUNDS ON THE AIRWAVES

The outer ear works in the same way as a satellite dish, collecting sound waves in the air and sending them towards the eardrum. They travel through the middle ear, via the hammer, anvil and stirrup to the cochlea, where they become electrical messages that are sent to the brain.

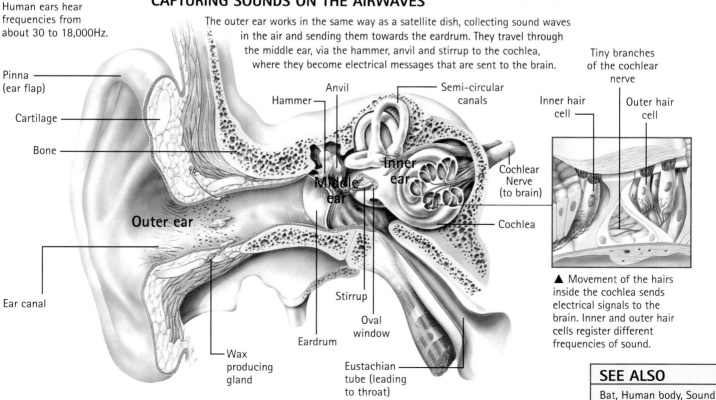

Pinna (ear flap)
Cartilage
Bone
Outer ear
Ear canal
Wax producing gland
Hammer
Anvil
Middle ear
Stirrup
Eardrum
Oval window
Eustachian tube (leading to throat)
Semi-circular canals
Inner ear
Cochlear Nerve (to brain)
Cochlea
Tiny branches of the cochlear nerve
Inner hair cell
Outer hair cell

▲ Movement of the hairs inside the cochlea sends electrical signals to the brain. Inner and outer hair cells register different frequencies of sound.

SEE ALSO

Bat, Human body, Sound

HEART AND CIRCULATORY SYSTEM

The heart is a hollow, muscle-walled pump in the chest. It squeezes at least once every second to pump blood around the body. If it stops, so will life.

WILLIAM HARVEY
(1578–1657) The English doctor who showed that blood circulates (moves around the body) in only one direction, along arteries and veins.

The heart is a muscular pump with four chambers (pockets) which drives the blood around the body via a network of arteries, veins and capillaries known as the circulatory system.

IN AND OUT
As the muscles in the heart contract, blood is squeezed from the heart into arteries, which carry the blood around the body. As the heart muscles relax, blood flows into the heart from the body, via veins. Each squeeze-relax cycle is a heartbeat.

A TIRELESS MUSCLE
Cardiac (heart) muscle never tires. In an average lifetime, a human heart beats more than 2,500 million times. On

average, the heart beats 70 times per minute, although heartbeat rate varies with age or health. Each heartbeat pumps about 70ml of blood. As the body has only about 5,000ml (five litres) of blood, all the blood passes through the heart in one minute. An active body uses more energy and oxygen, so the heart beats faster and pumps more blood with each beat.

CHECKING THE HEART
Each heartbeat starts in a small patch of the wall in the right atrium. This is the heart's natural pacemaker. It sends tiny electrical signals through the heart's walls, telling them to contract. The action is controlled by nerve signals from the brain and chemicals in the blood called hormones. Electronic sensors placed on the skin can detect the electrical signals of the heart. The signals are displayed as a graph on an ECG (electrocardiograph) machine.

TWO PUMPS IN ONE
The heart is not one pump but two, separated by a muscular dividing wall. The right pump receives low-oxygen blood from the body, along the main veins. It sends this blood out through the pulmonary arteries to the lungs, where it receives oxygen, and returns to the heart's left pump. This sends it out around the body again.

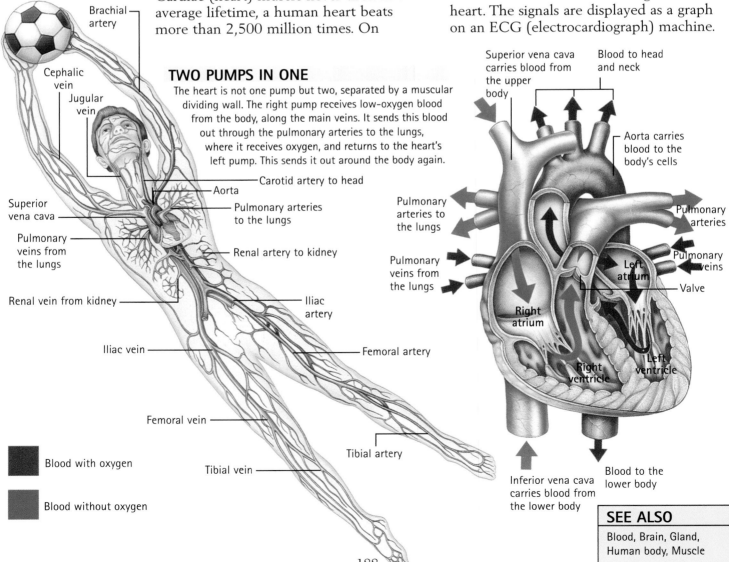

Brachial artery
Cephalic vein
Jugular vein
Superior vena cava
Pulmonary veins from the lungs
Renal vein from kidney
Iliac vein
Femoral vein
Tibial vein

Carotid artery to head
Aorta
Pulmonary arteries to the lungs
Renal artery to kidney
Iliac artery
Femoral artery
Tibial artery

Blood with oxygen

Blood without oxygen

Superior vena cava carries blood from the upper body
Blood to head and neck
Aorta carries blood to the body's cells
Pulmonary arteries to the lungs
Pulmonary arteries
Pulmonary veins from the lungs
Pulmonary veins
Left atrium
Valve
Right atrium
Right ventricle
Left ventricle
Inferior vena cava carries blood from the lower body
Blood to the lower body

SEE ALSO
Blood, Brain, Gland, Human body, Muscle

HEAT

Heat is a form of energy that is created by the vibration of atoms within a substance. Heat always moves from warm places to cooler ones.

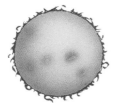
Only a fraction of the Sun's rays reaches us, yet it is our most important heat source.

Everything is made up of atoms and molecules which are always moving, even when an object is perfectly still. Their motion gives the object internal energy, or heat. The faster the atoms and molecules move, the hotter an object is. We usually measure heat with a thermometer in degrees Celsius.

▲ The Earth's inner heat escapes through cracks in the crust, creating hot springs in Iceland. People bathe in them, and geothermal plants use the heat to make electricity.

CONDUCTION

If two objects of different temperatures touch each other, the hotter object will always transfer some of its heat to the cooler object. For example, when you stir a hot coffee with a cold teaspoon, the heat from the coffee flows into the teaspoon. This happens because atoms in the coffee bump into atoms in the spoon, making them vibrate more. This is called conduction. Metal is a good conductor of heat but some materials, such as polystyrene, transfer heat poorly. They are called insulators.

By striking a match, we start a chemical reaction which produces heat.

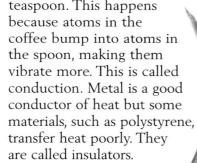
Pressure deep inside the Earth produces heat which escapes via volcanoes.

CONVECTION AND RADIATION

Heat also travels by radiation and convection. The Earth is warmed by heat which radiates (spreads out) through space from the Sun to the Earth. Heat radiates very fast – it takes just over 8 minutes for heat to radiate from the Sun to the Earth. Convection occurs only in liquids or gases that are unevenly heated. Warm parts of a liquid or gas flow into cooler ones, spreading heat with them.

HEAT IN OUR LIVES

When we eat food, our bodies break it down, releasing energy that heats us inside. We burn fuels, such as wood and coal, to help us stay warm, or to make heat to drive machines. Power stations make electricity, which we convert into heat in our homes.

FEELING THE HEAT

Boiling water in a kettle over an open fire requires heat to travel in each of its three ways: radiation, conduction and convection. Air molecules are set in motion by heat radiating from the fire. The hot air molecules hit the kettle bottom, making its molecules vibrate. The heat travels through the metal via conduction and through the water by convection.

The flow of electricity through wires creates heat that we use to toast bread.

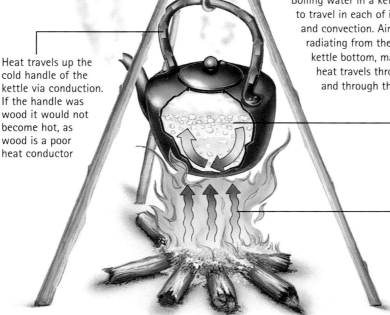
Heat travels up the cold handle of the kettle via conduction. If the handle was wood it would not become hot, as wood is a poor heat conductor

Heat circulates through the water via convection until all of the water is the same temperature

Heat from the fire radiates through the air until it hits the bottom of the kettle

Friction (two objects rubbing together) creates heat used to start a fire.

SEE ALSO

Atom and molecule, Electricity, Energy, Solid, liquid and gas

HELICOPTER

Helicopters are aircraft with spinning rotor blades instead of wings. These enable them to fly in ways that are impossible for most other aircraft.

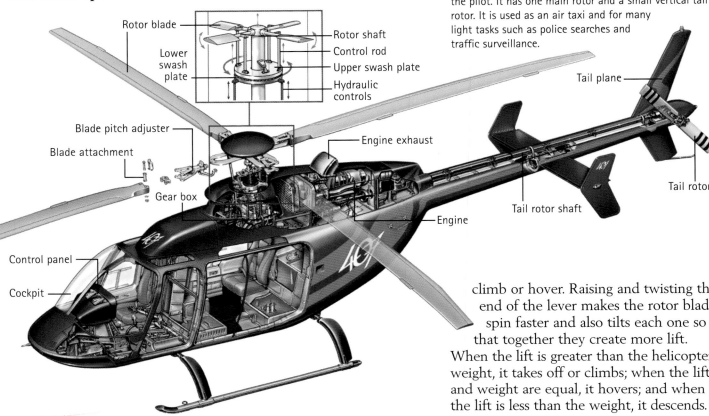

Rotor blade
Lower swash plate
Rotor shaft
Control rod
Upper swash plate
Hydraulic controls

Blade pitch adjuster
Blade attachment
Gear box

Control panel
Cockpit

Engine exhaust
Engine

BELL 407

The Bell 407 helicopter is a popular commercial helicopter, capable of carrying six passengers as well as the pilot. It has one main rotor and a small vertical tail rotor. It is used as an air taxi and for many light tasks such as police searches and traffic surveillance.

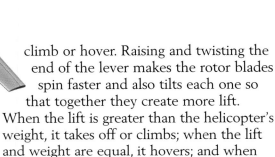

Tail plane
Tail rotor
Tail rotor shaft

The Ka-26 Kamov Hoodlum has two sets of main rotors, rotating in opposite directions.

The Russian Mil-24 gunship has one main rotor on top and a small vertical rotor at the back.

The Boeing CH-47 Chinook military helicopter has two rotors – one at each end.

Helicopters are very manoeuvrable aircraft – they can take off and land vertically in a small space, hover in one place and fly in any direction: forwards, sideways, even backwards!

ONE ROTOR OR TWO
Most helicopters have one set of long, thin rotor blades (the main rotor) on top and a smaller tail rotor. The main rotor provides lift to keep the helicopter in the air. The tail rotor is used for changing direction. It also stops the helicopter from being spun around by the main rotor. Some helicopters have two main rotors which rotate in opposite directions to prevent the vehicle from spinning around.

TAKING OFF
The angle of the rotor blades is called the pitch. By changing the pitch of the blades, with a control lever in the cockpit, the pilot can make the helicopter take off, land, climb or hover. Raising and twisting the end of the lever makes the rotor blades spin faster and also tilts each one so that together they create more lift. When the lift is greater than the helicopter's weight, it takes off or climbs; when the lift and weight are equal, it hovers; and when the lift is less than the weight, it descends.

MOVING AND STEERING
A helicopter moves forward when the whole of the main rotor is tipped forward. To slow down, the rotor is tipped back. Tipping the blades to the side makes the helicopter fly sideways. To turn, the angle of the tail rotor is altered with foot pedals.

SPINNING INTO ACTION
The first helicopters flew in the early 1900s, but they were clumsy and could barely take off. The first successful modern helicopter was the Vought-Sikorsky VS-300, built by Igor Sikorsky in 1940.

HELICOPTERS AT WORK
The helicopter's versatility in flight means it can be used for search and rescue at sea, police observation, or as an air ambulance. Military helicopters can fly lower than planes, and take off from small clearings or the decks of ships.

SEE ALSO
Aircraft

HIBERNATION

In the cooler parts of the world, many mammals pass the winter months in a very deep sleep. This is known as hibernation.

Many types of bat are active during the night and go into a type of hibernation each daytime.

Some butterflies, such as the monarch, hibernate in large groups in hollow trees or attics over winter.

The deep winter sleep of some bears is hibernation, but their body temperature only drops slightly.

Snakes, such as adders, hibernate under rocks or in holes under the ground when the weather is cold.

Some animals, such as the lungfish, aestivate (become inactive in summer to survive drought).

Many animals hibernate during the winter when it is cold and there is little food about. While hibernating, their body temperature falls greatly until it is little more than that of the surroundings.

GETTING READY
During the autumn, an animal will eat a lot to increase its body fat, which will give it energy while hibernating. It then looks for a safe spot in which to settle down. Most rodents take food supplies into their sleeping quarters to hibernate.

ONLY JUST ALIVE
While hibernating, an animal's heart and breathing rates drop until it is only just alive. It may stir and stretch itself from time to time, but does not really wake up until the outside temperature rises in the spring. By this time, most animals have used up all their food reserves and are very thin. They have to look for food right away, and will die if they do not find any.

WHO HIBERNATES?
Insect-eating bats in cool climates have to hibernate because there are not enough insects for them to eat in the winter. Dormice, hedgehogs and ground squirrels also hibernate. Among the birds, only the American poorwill and some other nightjars are known to hibernate. Small humming-birds also huddle together each night in a type of nightly hibernation.

COLD BLOODED ANIMALS
Reptiles, amphibians and many fish living in cold climates become inactive in the winter. As the air or water temperature falls, the animals get slower and slower and then come to a complete stop. But there is not such a dramatic change as in the hibernating mammals because they are cold-blooded animals and their temperature is always similar to that of the surroundings.

WARM WINTER SLEEP
Before hibernating, the chipmunk tunnels underground and builds a nesting place. It also collects seeds and nuts, which it stores in the tunnel. After it has pushed the earth out, it often loosely plugs up the entrance with earth. The chipmunk sleeps through most of the winter but may wake up on warm winter days, when it will eat some of its food.

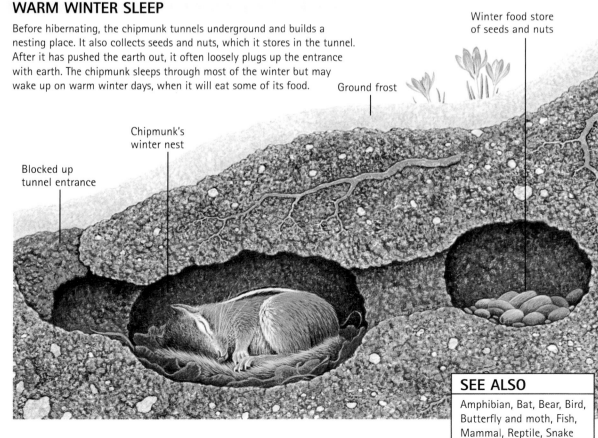

Winter food store of seeds and nuts

Ground frost

Chipmunk's winter nest

Blocked up tunnel entrance

SEE ALSO
Amphibian, Bat, Bear, Bird, Butterfly and moth, Fish, Mammal, Reptile, Snake

HINDUISM

Hinduism is one of the oldest existing religions. It began in north India about 4,000 years ago and is now the most popular religion in southern Asia.

▲ Many small shrines exist by the sides of roads as well as at most Hindu homes. Here food and flowers are offered and incense and candles burned.

Today, about 80 per cent of Indians are Hindu and there are 900 million Hindus worldwide. Much of Hinduism was developed by people called Aryans, who settled in India from about 1500BCE.

▲ Shiva is one of the most important of Hindu gods and represents destruction and rebirth.

EARLIEST WRITINGS
The Aryans produced the earliest Hindu writings, called the *Vedas*, in about 1000BCE. Later there were the famous epic stories, the *Ramayana* and *Mahabharata*. Other important writings led to the creation of the Indian caste system. This is a social and religious system where people are divided into different groups by birth.

MANY GODS
Hindus have three main gods: Brahma (the creator of the universe), Shiva (the destroyer) and Vishnu (the preserver).

But they also worship many other gods and goddesses and believe that all kinds of people and objects can become divine. The cow and the crow, for example, are sacred to Hindus and cannot be killed.

CYCLE OF LIFE
Like Buddhists, all Hindus believe in reincarnation, or being born again after death. They also believe in the importance of living a good life, and in karma, which means that one is punished or rewarded for one's past actions in the next life.

HINDU TEMPLES
Like most Hindu temples, this one in India's capital city, Delhi, is highly ornate. The goddess of good fortune, Lakshmi, is worshipped here in religious rituals, which are usually led by Hindu priests and teachers, who are members of the Brahman caste.

FAST FACTS
- Unlike Buddhism, Hinduism does not have a founder or a rigid system of beliefs
- There are all kinds of religious festivals and pilgrimages. Thousands travel to bathe in the sacred waters of the River Ganges every year
- Hindu wedding celebrations are very colourful and elaborate. When Hindus die, they are cremated

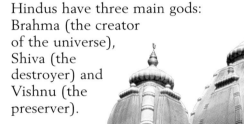

SEE ALSO
Buddhism, Religion

HIPPOPOTAMUS

Hippopotamuses are large, thick-skinned animals with short legs and a massive head and muzzle. They live in the lakes and rivers of tropical Africa.

▲ Hippos normally stay under water for up to six minutes without breathing, and they can actually run under water.

The large, or river, hippo has thick, grey skin and spends much of its time wallowing in shallow water.

The small pygmy hippo has oily, blackish skin and spends less time in the water than the river hippo.

Hippopotamus means 'river-horse' and comes from the Greek words *hippos* (horse) and *potamus* (river). In reality, however, the animal is more like a giant pig.

BARREL ON SHORT LEGS

After the elephant and rhinoceros, the hippopotamus is the world's largest land animal. It is like a barrel with short legs – about 3.5m long, weighing up to 4 tonnes and only about 1.5m high. Hippos generally live in groups of around five to 30 strong. They spend most of the daytime wallowing in mud pools or shallow water, usually with their heads appearing just above the surface. Their eyes, ears and nostrils are all at the top of the head, so they can see, hear and breathe without being seen themselves. They have a good sense of smell, although their eyesight is relatively poor.

FEEDING HABITS

In the evening, hippos leave the water to feed. Grass is their favourite food, but they also eat crops and often damage them by trampling them. Adult hippos have no enemies apart from people. Calves (young hippos) are sometimes eaten by lions on land and by crocodiles in the water, but they are usually well protected by the adults. An adult hippo can easily bite a crocodile in half with its huge jaws.

A SMALL COUSIN

The pygmy hippopotamus is no more than about 1.75m long, has oily, blackish skin and a rounded head. It lives in the swamps and damp forests of west Africa, but spends less time in the water than its larger, grey-skinned cousin.

FEROCIOUS FIGHTERS

The hippopotamus has a huge head and can open its mouth very wide to reveal curved, dagger-like teeth up to 50cm long. With its mouth wide open, the hippo looks as if it is yawning, but this is really a challenge made by one male to another. The males often fight and can cause terrible wounds with their teeth.

▲ Huge tusk-like teeth are used for fighting.

▲ The ears remain closed when under water.

▲ Each hoofed foot has four webbed toes.

▲ The hippo's nostrils close up under water.

SEE ALSO

Africa, Animal, Mammal

HORSE

Horses are four-legged, plant-eating mammals with a single hoof on each foot. Long ago they were wild but today almost all horses are domesticated.

THE HORSE FAMILY
All animals that have a single-toed hoof on the end of each leg belong to the horse family – the group called Equidae.

The common zebra has black and white stripes and lives wild in Africa.

The ass is smaller than the horse, has long ears and is usually coloured grey.

The Shetland pony is a hardy breed of horse with thick coat and long mane.

Przewalski's horse, found in Mongolia in 1870, is the only truly wild horse left.

Most grazing mammals are cloven-hoofed, which means that their feet end in a pair of hoofed toes. Horses' feet, however, end in a large single hoof. This feature, combined with long and powerful legs, makes horses fast and tireless runners. They are therefore perfectly suited to life in open places, where there is nowhere to hide from danger.

WILD HORSES
Horses are sociable animals, and in the wild live in herds about 10 to 20 strong. Mares (female horses) usually breed at the age of about two or three years, and normally have one foal a year. At one time, herds of wild horses roamed across the grassy plains of eastern Europe and central Asia. They were preyed upon by wolves and other predators, and hunted by people for food. But about 6,000 years ago, humans began to tame horses. From that moment, the history of the horse abruptly changed.

PRZEWALSKI'S HORSE
Domesticated horses soon outnumbered wild ones, which became increasingly rare. There were originally two kinds of wild horse: the tarpan and Przewalski's horse. The last tarpan died in a zoo in 1909. Przewalski's horse died out in the wild but has been successfully reintroduced to the grasslands of Mongolia.

PULLING POWER
Horses have been bred for a wide variety of purposes. Some of them were originally bred for their pulling power, and were used by farmers to pull ploughs and farm carts in the days before tractors were invented. Today, there are hundreds of different breeds of horses. They include huge shire horses, which can measure as much as 2m high at the shoulder, child-sized Shetland ponies, and the Falabella horse from Argentina, which is smaller than many dogs.

▲ Many North American rodeo events such as steer wrestling have evolved from working with cattle.

HORSES TODAY
Today, horses are used in every continent except Antarctica. In many countries, they still carry on traditional roles of providing transport and a livelihood for their owners. In North America, they have played a vital role in cattle herding since the mid-1800s, while Australians still use the hardy horses called Walers that were bred by early settlers. Other uses today include policing, ceremonial and sports events, hunting and riding for fun. But one of the most popular events is horse-racing. For this, thoroughbreds descended from 18th-century Arabian stallions are mostly used.

▲ Horses used for show jumping need to have a combination of power, stamina, boldness and agility in order to be able to handle the tough demands of the sport.

PARTS OF THE HORSE

The overall shape and appearance of a horse is called its conformation, while the parts of the horse's body are called the points. A horse's skeleton gives clues about its breed. For example, a cart-horse has large, thick bones which it needs to support its weight whereas a racehorse has long, fine bones that help it to run swiftly.

Crest

Mane

Poll

Quarters

Dock

Flank

Croup

Back

Withers

Forelock

Thigh

Muzzle

Chest

Molar teeth

Incisor teeth

▲ The incisor (front) teeth can be used to tell a horse's age. As the horse grows older, they change in shape, becoming longer and projecting farther forward. The gap between the incisor and molar teeth is where the bit (mouthpiece) is placed when the horse is bridled.

Stifle

Forearm

Shoulder

Knee

Fetlock

Hoof

Hock joint

Cannon bone

Splint bone

Long pastern bone

Short pastern bone

Coffin bone

Heel

Frog

Hoof wall

Sole

Shoe

FAST FACTS

• The Roman emperor Caligula is said to have made his horse, Incitatus, consul – a very high rank in Roman government

• The earliest ancestor of the horse had four toes and was the size of a fox

• Horses are measured in hands from the ground to the top of the withers. A hand is 10cm

• A horse goes through four paces, from slow to fast: walk, trot, canter and gallop

SEE ALSO

Animal, Evolution, Mammal, Mongols, Sport, Transport, World War I

▲ The modern horse stands on only one toe (its hoof), but the two splint bones on either side of the cannon bone are remnants of the early horse's other toes.

▲ Horses have metal shoes nailed to their hooves to protect the hoof wall from wearing down on rough or hard ground. Shoes must be replaced every few weeks. Before they can be fitted, the new growth of hoof has to be trimmed and the hoof reshaped.

HOUSEHOLD APPLIANCE

Household appliances are devices that make day-to-day jobs around the house easier. They have changed our lifestyles and improved public hygiene and diet.

► Percy Spenser (USA) invented the microwave oven in 1945 using technology developed for military defence during World War II.

Most toasters 'pop up' when sensors inside detect that a set temperature has been reached.

Houses in developed countries contain a wide range of appliances. Many are used in the kitchen to keep and prepare food, including cookers, kettles, food processors, refrigerators, freezers and microwave ovens. Others, such as washing machines, tumble dryers, dishwashers and vacuum cleaners, help with cleaning. Since the invention of electricity – a form of energy which can be converted into movement or heat – more sophisticated appliances have been produced.

WASH DAY

Before labour-saving appliances, routine housekeeping was a full-time job. A day was set aside to wash clothes using a washboard and a mangle. Perishable food could not be stored easily, so people shopped most days and preparing meals

Cookers can be designed to burn any fuel. This wipe-clean ceramic hob uses electricity.

The first washing machine (invented by Hamilton Smith, USA, 1858) still relied on muscle power.

Early refrigerators (invented by Ferdinand Carre, France, 1858) were cooled by blocks of ice.

Irons have been used for centuries, first heated on a stove, then by gas, then in 1891, by electricity.

VACUUM CLEANERS

While the suction pulls dirty air in, a spinning brush helps dislodge dirt. Bags are finely perforated and act as a filter, while bagless designs (right) use a whirling vortex of air to spin dirt out – air is pushed out, but dirt is trapped inside.

Air spins at up to 1486 km/h

Air minus dirt and dust

Brush

Dirty air

took longer. Rugs had to be hung up outside and beaten to get the dust out.

MAKING A MEAL OF IT

Most cookers use gas or electricity, as these are easy to control. Methane, butane or propane gas goes through a valve and burns in the air, releasing heat. Electric cookers have elements containing wire which resists the flow of electricity. As the current is forced along this wire, electrical energy is turned into heat energy. Kettles and toasters work in the same way.

MICROWAVE OVENS

Microwave ovens contain a magnetron, which turns electricity into microwaves, or high-frequency radio waves. Microwaves make molecules of water and fat in the surface of the food vibrate very fast, producing heat. This heat spreads from the outside to the middle of the food.

WASHING MACHINES

These have microprocessor control systems. A powerful electric motor turns the drum full of wet clothing back and forth through a series of cycles, which duplicate the stages of washing by hand. The clothes are agitated in hot detergent, then rinsed and spun at high speed which forces out most of the water.

Dust particles

The electric motor turns a fan which creates a partial vacuum and causes air to rush in, pulling dust with it

SEE ALSO

Design, Invention, Machine, Technology, Wavelengths

HOUSING

Housing includes any form of building or structure in which people live. It can provide shelter for a single person, a family or several family groups.

Roma of Europe lived in horse-drawn caravans.

Indonesians build houses on stilts in damp areas.

The Mongolian *yurt* can be folded and moved.

Native American *pueblos* are made of mud brick.

Sudanese huts have small windows to keep out heat.

Suburban houses have garages and gardens.

Since at least 50,000 years ago, people have built tents and shelters from sticks, animal hides or turf. When people settled down to farming, they began to build more permanent houses.

BUILDING MATERIALS
For thousands of years, people used natural materials, such as wood or stone, that they found close by. Clay and chopped straw were mixed, shaped into bricks and dried in the sun. Later, people learned to bake the bricks in ovens to make them tougher and more waterproof. Modern houses may still be made of bricks, or of modern materials such as concrete, steel and glass.

INTO THE CITY
In the 1700s and 1800s, during the Industrial Revolution, people crowded into cities to find work. Builders, or architects, put up rows of houses and flats to meet the rising demand for living space. Today, cities continue to expand. Around them are sprawling suburbs of houses, most with private gardens.

CLIMATE AND DESIGN
In forested areas of North America and Scandinavia, wood is an important building material. Elsewhere, houses are more likely to be built of brick or stone.

▼ Energy-saving fittings, such as these solar panels, make modern houses more efficient.

▲ The ramshackle shanty homes of beggars contrast with blocks of apartments for the wealthy in Mumbai, India.

In hot countries, houses have thick walls to keep the inside cool. Houses in areas with a lot of snow or rain usually have sloping roofs so the water can run off.

COMPUTER CONTROL
Modern houses are equipped with gas, electricity, water and drainage systems. Soon houses may be computer-controlled, with lighting, heating, security, TV and other features running automatically.

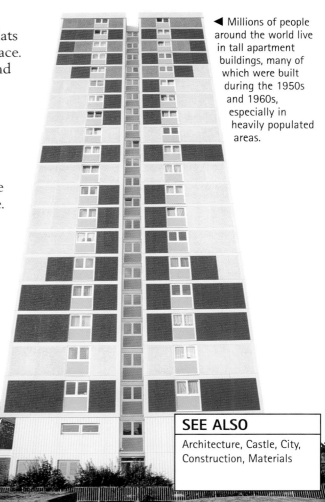
◄ Millions of people around the world live in tall apartment buildings, many of which were built during the 1950s and 1960s, especially in heavily populated areas.

SEE ALSO
Architecture, Castle, City, Construction, Materials

HOVERCRAFT

Hovercraft travel on a cushion of air, which greatly reduces water resistance. They can travel over both water and land – something no other craft can do.

The British SRN6 hovercraft, built in 1965, is still in service over 30 years later.

The ABS hovercraft circumnavigated the Baltic Sea in 1994.

The Russian giant assault hovercraft delivers troops and equipment onto land.

The American Hovermarine was designed to seat up to 150 passengers.

When a boat moves, the surrounding water pushes against it and slows it down. It could go much faster if it could travel above the water instead of through it. The hovercraft and its cousin, the hydrofoil, both provide a solution to this problem.

CUSHIONS AND SKIRTS
The air cushion that holds a hovercraft up is created by one or more powerful lift fans. Air pumped beneath the vehicle by these fans is prevented from escaping too quickly by a flexible rubber skirt all around the edge. A hydrofoil, on the other hand, uses wing-like foils to lift it from the water as it picks up speed.

THE FIRST HOVERCRAFT
People experimented with vehicles supported by air cushions as long ago as 1877, but the technology to build a

▲ Hydrofoils have aerofoil-shaped underwater wings, or foils, which lift the craft's hull out of the water as it speeds up. They are powered by propellers or water jets.

hovercraft was not available until the 20th century. The first successful hovercraft was built by the British engineer Christopher Cockerell in 1959.

SKIMMING WAVES
Hovercraft have a number of uses. The largest hovercraft carry passengers and their cars across short stretches of water. Small, one-person hovercraft often race against each other in competitions. Military hovercraft transport troops and equipment onto beaches.

HOW THE HOVERCRAFT WORKS

Because a hovercraft is raised up on a cushion of air, it can travel over water or land and reach speeds of up to 130km/h, much faster than an ordinary ship. Two large fans on each side of the hovercraft suck in air and push it underneath the craft to lift it up. Another two large fans at the rear, with rudders for steering, propel the craft forward.

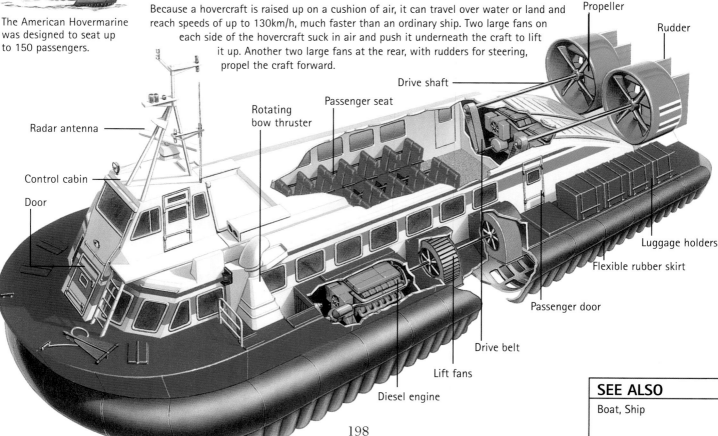

Propeller

Rudder

Drive shaft

Passenger seat

Rotating bow thruster

Radar antenna

Control cabin

Door

Luggage holders

Flexible rubber skirt

Passenger door

Drive belt

Lift fans

Diesel engine

SEE ALSO

Boat, Ship

HUMAN BODY

The human body is made up of a skeleton, organs, outer skin and specialized systems, all of which work together to make it one of the most complex of all life forms.

▼ The human face reveals a person's identity – his or her age, gender and genetic inheritance.

The human body is similar to the bodies of other large mammals, especially apes. But it is also unique in many ways. It can walk upright on its two back legs. Its fingers are capable of precise, delicate movements, and its large brain is far more complex than that of any other creature. These features make humans a separate species in the animal kingdom, called *Homo sapiens*.

BUILDING BLOCKS
The human body is made up of more than 50 million million tiny building blocks, called cells. These are all microscopic in size and vary in shape and structure according to their functions. Every second, the body makes more than five million cells of various kinds, to replace those that wear out and die.

BODY TISSUES
Cells of the same kind are grouped together to form tissues. For example, bone tissue is strong and stiff, to provide the body with an inner supporting framework – the skeleton.

▶ Athletes train hard in order to build up their muscles and reach peak body fitness.

▶ Through regular stretching exercises, the human body can become very supple and capable of bending and twisting in extreme ways.

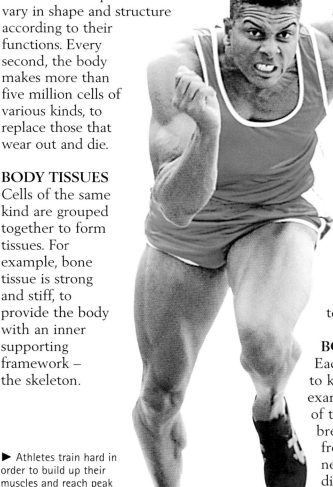

Cartilage tissue is also strong, but softer and smoother. It covers bones where they join, and is found inside bendy parts of the body such as the nose and ears.

BODY ORGANS
Groups of tissue make up the main parts of the body, called organs. Examples are the intestines, which absorb digested food into blood; the kidneys, which filter waste products from blood; and the heart, which pumps blood. Several organs work together as a major body system.

BODY SYSTEMS
Each system has a very important job to keep the body alive and healthy. For example, the respiratory system consists of the nose, windpipe and lungs. It breathes in air and absorbs oxygen from the air into the blood. Oxygen is needed to release the energy from digested food substances in order to power life processes. ▶

DIGESTIVE SYSTEM

The body needs to maintain its cells and tissues, and repair worn-out parts. The raw materials for growth and repair come from food, which is processed by the digestive system: the mouth, teeth, gullet, stomach and intestines. Food is broken down into nutrients and energy-rich chemicals, which pass into the bloodstream. Waste matter passes out of the body as faeces.

URINARY SYSTEM

The life processes inside cells produce waste products, some of which are removed by the urinary, system. This consists of the kidneys, which filter the wastes from the blood to form urine; and the bladder, which stores the urine before it is removed from the body.

CO-ORDINATION AND CONTROL

The body parts and organs do not work on their own. Two main control systems keep them functioning together in a co-ordinated fashion. The hormonal system consists of body parts called endocrine glands that make substances named hormones. These pass into the blood and around the body. Each hormone affects the chemical activity of certain cells and tissues, making them speed up or slow down.

NERVOUS SYSTEM

The second control system, the nervous system, is a network of wire-like nerves throughout the body, with the brain as the control centre. The brain receives information as tiny nerve signals from the sensory system – mainly the eyes, ears,

SKIN AND MUSCLES

The skin protects the inside of the body from dirt, too much dryness or wetness, injury, harmful rays and germs. It also helps to keep the body warm in cold weather and cool in hot conditions. The muscular system consists of more than 640 muscles. In most cases, each end of a muscle is joined to a bone. When the muscle shortens or contracts, it pulls on the bones and moves that part of the body.

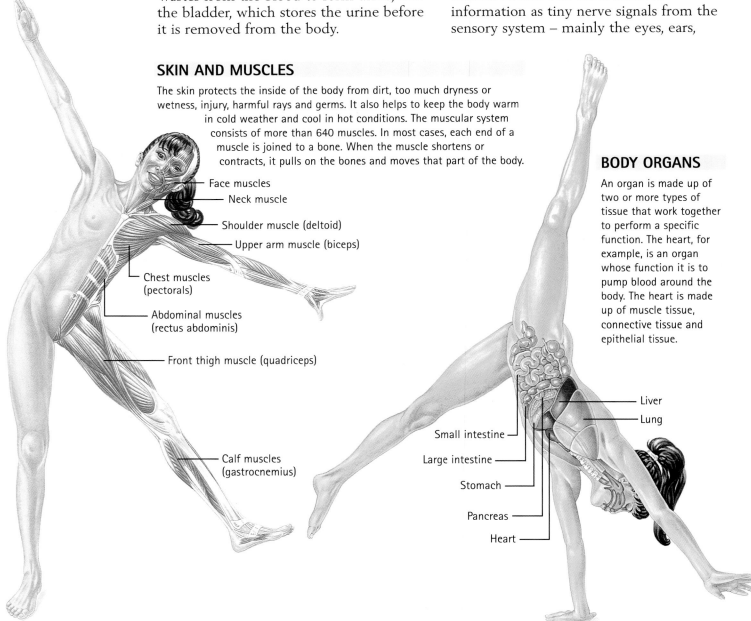

Face muscles

Neck muscle

Shoulder muscle (deltoid)

Upper arm muscle (biceps)

Chest muscles (pectorals)

Abdominal muscles (rectus abdominis)

Front thigh muscle (quadriceps)

Calf muscles (gastrocnemius)

BODY ORGANS

An organ is made up of two or more types of tissue that work together to perform a specific function. The heart, for example, is an organ whose function it is to pump blood around the body. The heart is made up of muscle tissue, connective tissue and epithelial tissue.

Liver

Lung

Small intestine

Large intestine

Stomach

Pancreas

Heart

nose, tongue and skin. These sense organs detect what is happening around the body. The brain also sends signals to muscles, telling them when and how to contract and produce movements. It is also the site of mental processes such as thoughts, feelings, emotions and memories.

REPRODUCTION

The human body reproduces like any other mammal. The reproductive system consists of either female or male sex organs. The male ones make sperm cells. The female ones contain egg cells. When a sperm cell fertilizes an egg cell, the egg begins to multiply rapidly. Over a period of nine months, it grows and develops within the mother's body into an embryo, then a foetus, and is born as a baby.

◄ The average body reaches its peak physical power and maximum size around the age of 18 to 25 years. After this it begins to age. Signs of ageing include wrinkled skin, grey hair, balding in men, shrinking, weaker muscles, slower reactions and less sharp senses.

GROWING UP

Some animals are active and independent within minutes of birth. But a human baby needs food, warmth and care for many months. As it grows into a child, it learns to sit, stand, walk, talk, read, write and acquire many other skills. This takes years because human society is very complex, with many customs, traditions, rules and laws.

CIRCULATORY AND LYMPHATIC SYSTEMS

The circulatory system consists of the heart, blood vessels and blood. It transports oxygen from the lungs, nutrients and energy-rich substances to all parts of the body. The lymphatic and immune systems produce antibodies which are released into the bloodstream to fight off disease.

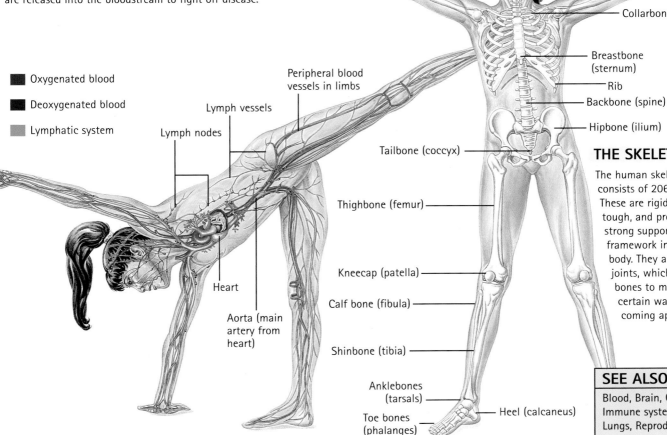

■ Oxygenated blood
■ Deoxygenated blood
■ Lymphatic system

Peripheral blood vessels in limbs
Lymph vessels
Lymph nodes
Heart
Aorta (main artery from heart)

Finger bones (phalanges)
Palm bones (metacarpals)
Skull (cranium)
Upper arm bone (humerus)
Inner forearm bone (ulna)
Outer forearm bone (radius)
Collarbone (clavicle)
Breastbone (sternum)
Rib
Backbone (spine)
Hipbone (ilium)
Tailbone (coccyx)
Thighbone (femur)
Kneecap (patella)
Calf bone (fibula)
Shinbone (tibia)
Anklebones (tarsals)
Toe bones (phalanges)
Heel (calcaneus)

THE SKELETON

The human skeleton consists of 206 bones. These are rigid and tough, and provide a strong supporting framework inside the body. They are linked at joints, which allow the bones to move in certain ways without coming apart.

SEE ALSO

Blood, Brain, Gland, Heart, Immune system, Kidney, Lungs, Reproduction

IMMUNE SYSTEM

The body protects itself from disease and ill-health through its immune system, which constantly cleans the blood and tissues, and attacks invading germs.

EDWARD JENNER
Jenner was a British doctor (1749–1823) who developed the technique of vaccination – a way to provide artificial immunity against disease. In 1796 he injected patients with harmless cowpox to protect them against deadly smallpox.

The immune system is one of the body's most complicated systems. It includes a series of glands – known as lymph glands, or lymph nodes – that are found throughout the body, but especially in the neck, armpits and groin. These glands are connected by a network of tubes called lymph vessels, and both glands and vessels contain a pale, milky fluid called lymph.

MILLIONS OF CELLS
Lymph and lymph glands are home to the main kind of cell in the immune system, called the lymphocyte. These cells are also found in large quantities in the blood, where they form one kind of white blood cell, and in the fluids that bathe all the body parts. There are about two million million lymphocytes in the human body.

RECOGNIZING INVADERS
Germs such as bacteria and viruses are continually entering the body by being breathed in, or swallowed, or through a wound. As soon as they enter, lymphocytes called T- and B-cells identify them as 'non-self', or foreign particles. They do this by detecting unfamiliar substances, or antigens, on the germs' outer surface.

ON THE ATTACK
Some of the B-cells then start to multiply and form plasma cells. These cells produce Y-shaped substances known as antibodies that attach themselves to the antigens and cause the germs to burst, or clump together so they cannot multiply. T-cells produce chemicals that kill infected cells. They also help another type of white blood cell, called a macrophage, to destroy germs by engulfing, or eating, them.

LONG MEMORIES
Different germs carry different antigens. When a germ infects the body, causing an illness, B-cells known as memory cells remember its antigens so that, if the germ enters again, the memory cells can quickly activate the immune system to fight off the illness. This protection against disease is called immunity.

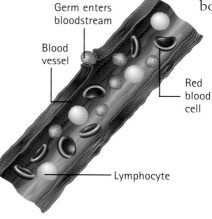

Germ enters bloodstream
Blood vessel
Red blood cell
Lymphocyte

1 When a germ enters the bloodstream – for example, through a cut – white blood cells, known as lymphocytes, are drawn to the site.

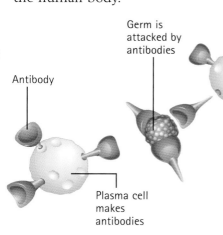

Germ is attacked by antibodies
Antibody
Plasma cell makes antibodies

2 Some lymphocytes multiply and form plasma cells which make antibodies that attack the germ.

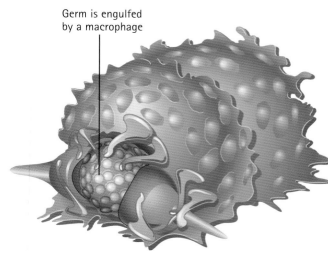

Germ is engulfed by a macrophage

3 Other lymphocytes – certain types of T-cell – help to attract macrophages to the site. These swallow the germ and dissolve it.

IMMUNITY AGAINST DISEASE

Lymphocytes and macrophages work together to destroy germs that cause disease. Often, they do not succeed in killing a new germ before it has multiplied and caused an illness. However, once the memory cells have been primed, the immune system is ready for action. Next time it meets the germ it can quickly make the right antibodies to fight off the infection. Immunity can also be artificially induced. A specially weakened form of the germ is swallowed or injected into the body. It is not strong enough to cause illness but it activates the immune system to remember the real germ in the future.

SEE ALSO
Disease, Gland, Human body, Medicine

INCAS

The Incas were people who lived in the Andes Mountains of South America from about 1200 to the mid-1500s. They ruled a rich and sophisticated empire.

The Inca Empire was centred around Cuzco – a highland valley in the Andes mountains of Peru. The empire stretched into present-day Ecuador, Colombia, Bolivia, Argentina and Chile. Although made up of many tribes, its ruling emperor and nobles were members of the Inca tribe. The empire collapsed after the Spanish invaded in 1532.

The Incas had no writing system. They used knotted, coloured strings, called *quipus*, to keep records.

GOD ON EARTH

The first great Inca emperor was Pachacuti Yupanqui, a warrior who came to power in 1438. His son, Tupac, and grandson, Huayna Capac, extended the empire. The emperor was known as the 'Inca'. He was considered a god, a descendant of the Sun.

RUNNING AN EMPIRE

The empire was strictly governed. The ordinary people worked many days each year for the emperor, planting crops, fighting battles or building bridges and roads. The roads ran throughout the empire, crossing mountain ravines

Gold, silver and precious stones were used to craft beautiful objects used by noble families and in religious rituals.

by rope bridges. In places, roads were carved from rock, elsewhere they were paved. The roads were mostly used by *chasquis*, the royal messengers, and merchants, who used llamas to carry goods. There were no wheeled vehicles.

EVERYDAY LIFE

Most of the 12 million people were farmers. They kept llamas and alpacas for wool and meat, and grew maize, potatoes and other vegetables in terraced fields. Wool and cotton cloth were woven by hand and pots made from clay. Stone fortresses guarded cities and roads, but most families lived in houses made from mud bricks.

GREAT FESTIVAL OF THE SUN

The Capac Raymi, the Great Festival of the Sun, was held in Cuzco on the longest and shortest days of the year. At dawn, the emperor offered a golden cup of sacred beer and sacrificed a white llama to Inti, the Sun god, to gain his help and protection. Other important gods included the supreme deity Viracocha and the goddesses of the earth and the sea.

SEE ALSO

Aztecs, Empire, South America

INDIAN SUBCONTINENT

The Indian subcontinent is a huge land mass which includes the countries of India, Pakistan, Bangladesh, Nepal and Bhutan. It makes up one tenth of Asia.

BANGLADESH
Area: 147,570 sq km
Population: 142,319,000
Capital: Dhaka
Language: Bengali
Currency: Taka

BHUTAN
Area: 46,500 sq km
Population: 696,000
Capital: Thimphu
Language: Dzongkha
Currency: Ngultrum, Indian rupee

INDIA
Area: 3,165,596 sq km
Population: 1,210,000,000
Capital: New Delhi
Languages: Hindi, English, Bengali and 20 other official languages
Currency: Rupee

MALDIVES
Area: 298 sq km
Population: 299,000
Capital: Malé (Malé Island)
Language: Divehi
Currency: Rufiyaa

NEPAL
Area: 147,181 sq km
Population: 26,621,000
Capital: Katmandu
Language: Nepali
Currency: Nepalese rupee

Three quarters of the Indian subcontinent is covered by India itself. As well as Pakistan, Bangladesh, Nepal and Bhutan on the mainland, there are two island nations in the south – Sri Lanka and the Republic of the Maldives.

FROM HIGH TO LOW
High mountain ranges lie in the north of the region, including the Himalayas, which contain the world's highest peak, Mount Everest (8,848m), on the border between Nepal and China. Southern India consists largely of a plateau called the Deccan. Bordering the Deccan are two low mountain ranges, the Eastern and Western Ghats, fringed by narrow coastal plains.

WATER AND WINDS
The longest river in the region, the Indus (2,897km), flows from the Himalayas through Pakistan, where its waters are used by farmers. The Rivers Brahmaputra (2,704km) and Ganges (2,494km) join together in Bangladesh and flow across the world's largest delta, into the Bay of Bengal. Mawsynram, near Shillong, just

▲ Religion and festivals play an important part in Indian life. Many people go on pilgrimages to holy places like the city of Varanasi on the banks of the River Ganges. The waters of the river are considered sacred.

north of Bangladesh, is the rainiest place on Earth – a record of about 26,000mm fell there in 1985. Most rain comes between June and October, when moist monsoon winds blow from the sea. These have little effect on the dry northwest – the Thar Desert along the Pakistan-India border has less than 250mm of rain a year.

TROPICAL TREES
Few plants grow in the northwest, except on the wetter mountain slopes, but most of the Indian subcontinent has plenty of farming and grazing land. Valuable trees in tropical forests include ironwood, rosewood and teak. Bamboo also grows in many areas.

▼ Spices provide a major industry for India and are sold at markets like this one in Udaipur.

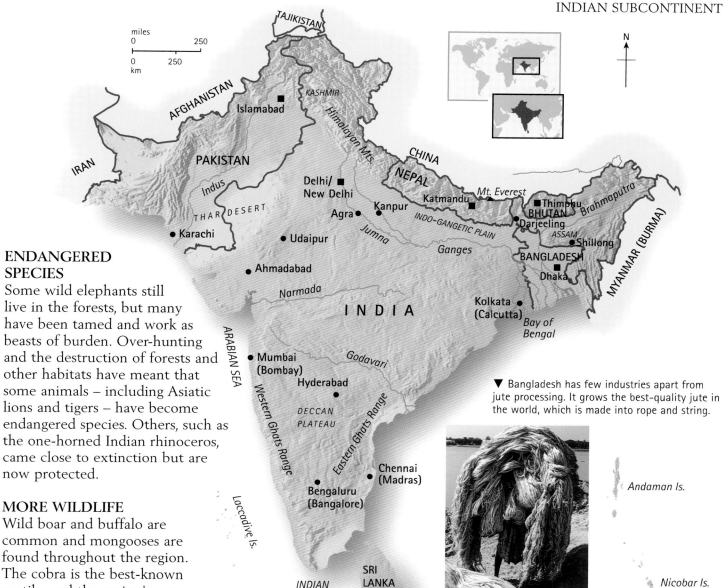

N

ENDANGERED SPECIES

Some wild elephants still live in the forests, but many have been tamed and work as beasts of burden. Over-hunting and the destruction of forests and other habitats have meant that some animals – including Asiatic lions and tigers – have become endangered species. Others, such as the one-horned Indian rhinoceros, came close to extinction but are now protected.

MORE WILDLIFE

Wild boar and buffalo are common and mongooses are found throughout the region. The cobra is the best-known reptile, and the region's many birds include the myna bird, which can imitate human speech. Mountain animals include brown and black bears, deer, the rare snow leopard, the markhor (a kind of wild goat), various kinds of wild sheep and wild yaks.

▲ Ihuhu Island is one of 1,200 coral islands that make up the Maldives. Most are just 2m above sea level.

▼ Bangladesh has few industries apart from jute processing. It grows the best-quality jute in the world, which is made into rope and string.

GROWING POPULATIONS

With a population of over one billion, India has more people than any other country apart from China. Pakistan, with a population of 162 million, ranks sixth in the world, and Bangladesh, with 158 million people, is the world's seventh most populous country.

INDIA'S LANGUAGES

India has 23 major languages and more than 1,650 dialects and minor languages. The two main language groups are the Indo-European, which includes Hindi – the most widely spoken language – and the Dravidian languages, including Tamil, which are spoken mainly in the south. English is also spoken by some Indians. ▶

PAKISTAN
Area: 880,254 sq km
Population: 162,508,000
Capital: Islamabad
Languages: Urdu, English and Punjabi
Currency: Pakistan rupee

SRI LANKA
Area: 65,610 sq km
Population: 20,450,000
Capital: Kotte (Colombo)
Languages: Sinhala and Tamil
Currency: Sri Lankan rupee

▲ Agriculture is Sri Lanka's main economic activity. Important crops, including tea, are grown on large plantations.

URDU AND BENGALI

Pakistan's official language is Urdu, but only eight per cent of the people speak it as their first language. Instead, they speak the language of their community. The largest communities are the Punjabi, Pashtun, Sindhi and Sariaki. In Bangladesh, more than 95 per cent of the people speak the official language, Bengali.

RELIGIONS OF INDIA

Beautiful temples, mosques and other religious buildings are everywhere. In places such as Udaipur, India, there are spectacular palaces built hundreds of years ago for princes. Today, Hindus make up 81 per cent of India's population, with Muslims forming another 13 per cent. India also has large numbers of Christians, Sikhs, Buddhists and Jains. Islam, the Muslim religion, is the chief religion in Pakistan, Bangladesh and the Maldives.

INFLUENCE OF BUDDHA

Hinduism is the official religion of Nepal, but the country was the birthplace of Buddha, so many Nepalese have combined the

▲ The Taj Mahal at Agra was built between 1632 and 1653 at the request of the Mogul emperor Shah Jahan, who wanted it as a tomb for his wife.

beliefs and practices of the two religions. Buddhism is the chief religion in Bhutan and of the Sinhalese in Sri Lanka, although a minority group in Sri Lanka, the Tamils, mainly follows Hinduism. Differences between these groups have led to civil war between government troops and Tamil guerrillas, which ended in 2009.

FARM LIFE

Around three fifths of the people of the Indian subcontinent are farmers who live in villages and farm the land around them. Farming is the leading activity and rice is the main food crop in India, Bangladesh and Sri Lanka. In Pakistan, wheat is the leading food crop. Tea is grown in northeast India, around Darjeeling and in Assam, as well as in Sri Lanka. Most farmers have a

▼ Nepal's Sherpa people live on the southern slopes of the Himalaya mountains where the spectacular landscape, which includes Mount Everest, attracts many tourists. Timber is used for cooking and heating by locals and tourists, and less than a third of the country's forests remain.

▲ In Bhutan, local women make cheese from yaks' milk.

sector and is now the ninth largest economy in the world.

CITY LIFE AND EDUCATION
The region has five cities with more than ten million people. Three are in India: Mumbai (formerly Bombay), Delhi (made up of the walled city of Old Delhi, the capital New Delhi and the surrounding urban sprawl) and Kolkata (formerly Calcutta). Karachi in Pakistan and the Bangladeshi capital Dhaka make up the five. Sri Lanka has a good education system, but in the rest of the Indian subcontinent there are millions of people who cannot read or write. The education system in India is, however, gradually improving.

EARLY TIMES
From the late 18th century, India, Pakistan and Bangladesh formed part of a huge colony called British India. In 1947, British India became independent, splitting into two parts – modern India and Pakistan, which was created for Muslims. In 1971, East Pakistan broke away and became the separate country of Bangladesh. Sri Lanka became independent from Britain in 1948, as did the Maldives in 1968.

GANDHI
Mohandas K. Gandhi was born in India in 1869. From the 1920s he used peaceful protests to lead India to independence. He became known as Mahatma, meaning 'Great Soul'. He was assassinated in 1948.

low standard of living and live in houses made of mud and straw. India has more cattle and buffalo than any other country but these animals are considered sacred by Hindus and cannot be killed for food. Fishing is also a major activity.

DEVELOPING INDUSTRY
The Indian subcontinent has plenty of coal, iron ore and other minerals. There is some oil, and petroleum refining is an important industry. Textiles are leading products, and Mumbai and Delhi are developing large electronics industries. India has a fast growing high-tech

▲ Pakistan's national cricketers are world famous. Children play the game from an early age.

DIFFICULT DIVISION
At the time of the partition of British India, the status of Kashmir in the north was not satisfactorily settled. Part of the territory now falls within northeast Pakistan, but the bulk lies within the Indian states of Jammu and Kashmir. Guerillas and governments are in dispute over whether Kashmir should remain part of India, become part of Pakistan, or become independent.

FAST FACTS
• Indians call their country Bharat after a legendary monarch

• The name India comes from an ancient word *Sindhu* meaning 'river'

• India is the world's seventh largest country

• India's railway system is the largest in Asia

SEE ALSO
Asia, Buddhism, Hinduism, Islam, Mountain and valley

INDONESIA AND EAST TIMOR

Indonesia, in Southeast Asia, is the world's largest island group. There are more than 13,700 islands, but only around 3,000 are inhabited.

INDONESIA
Area: 1,904,413 sq km
Population: 237,641,000
Capital: Jakarta
Language: Bahasa (Indonesian)
Currency: Rupiah

EAST TIMOR
Area: 14,874 sq km
Population: 1,067,000
Capital: Dili
Languages: Tetum, Portuguese
Currency: US dollar

The majority of Indonesia's islands lie close to or just south of the Equator. They are mountainous with many volcanoes, 77 of which have erupted in recent times. The climate is hot and humid, and tropical rainforests cover large parts of the country. The main areas are the islands of Java, Sumatra and Sulawesi and the regions of Kalimantan and West Papua. In 2002, East Timor split from Indonesia and became independent.

VARIED WILDLIFE

The western islands of Indonesia were once linked by land to Asia, and many Asian animals such as elephants and orang-utans can be found there. The eastern islands, once linked to Australia, contain animals such as cockatoos and birds of paradise.

WEALTH OF LANGUAGES

Most of Indonesia's people are Malays. Apart from the national language, about 700 other languages and dialects are spoken. More than 86 per cent of the people are Muslims, making Indonesia the world's largest Islamic country.

▲ Rice, Indonesia's main food, is grown on terraced fields. Volcanic ash makes the soil rich and fertile.

LIFE AND WORK

Many Indonesians live in rural villages, some in houses raised on stilts. Industry is growing rapidly, however, leading to the development of large modern cities such as Jakarta and Surabaya on Java. The forests are rich in timber and the seas provide good fishing. Minerals include tin, nickel, copper and oil. Factories make clothing and electrical goods for export.

PREHISTORIC PEOPLES

People have lived in Indonesia since prehistoric times. There were Hindu and Buddhist kingdoms from the 700s, before the arrival of Islam. Portuguese traders came in the 1500s, then the Dutch colonized the area in the late 1800s, calling it the East Indies. Eventually, in 1949, Indonesia became a republic.

◄ Bali is famous for its music and dance. Dyed batik cloth is used to make traditional clothing.

SEE ALSO
Asia, Islam, Malaysia, Rainforest, Southeast Asia, Volcano

INDUSTRIAL REVOLUTION

The Industrial Revolution is the name given to the great changes that took place when people began to use steam power to make goods in factories.

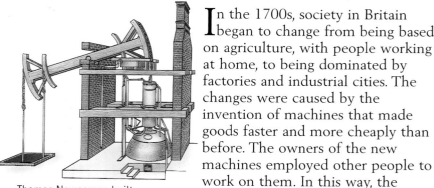

In the 1700s, society in Britain began to change from being based on agriculture, with people working at home, to being dominated by factories and industrial cities. The changes were caused by the invention of machines that made goods faster and more cheaply than before. The owners of the new machines employed other people to work on them. In this way, the factory came into existence, surrounded by houses for the workers. Often several factories were built together, from which a new town developed.

WOMEN'S WORK

Factory jobs often required skill rather than strength. Women were as good as men for such work, and many single women gained independence by earning a wage for themselves. Most women gave up work when they married, to run the household and family.

KING COTTON

The Industrial Revolution began around 1760, when new machines that could spin cotton thread very quickly were invented in Britain. These made thread so fast that hand weavers could not keep up. So weaving machines were invented. At first, water wheels powered the machines, but by 1780, these could not cope. In 1785, the British clergyman Edmund Cartwright (1743-1823) invented a power loom that used steam power to drive it.

THE POWER OF STEAM

Simple steam engines were already being used to pump water out of mines. Between 1764 and 1790, the Scottish engineer James Watt (1736-1819) improved the steam engine so that it used heat more efficiently and could drive machines. By 1800, there were about 500 steam engines at work in Britain. For the first time, people had an artificial source of power, which was cheap and efficient. ▶

Thomas Newcomen built the first steam engine in 1712 to pump water.

The spinning jenny of 1764 could spin several threads at one time.

In 1777, the world's first iron bridge was erected in Shropshire, England.

Eli Whitney's cotton gin of 1794 separated cotton seeds from fibre at speed.

Locomotives, such as the German *Der Adler* of 1835, powered the rail boom.

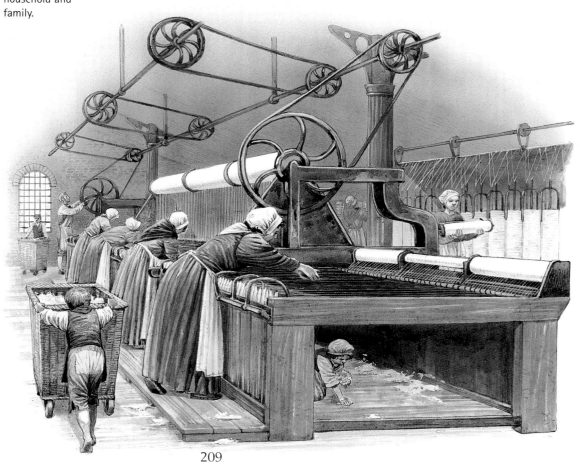

BRUNEL
The British engineer Isambard Kingdom Brunel (1806–59) built railways, bridges and the world's largest ship.

RAW MATERIALS

The Industrial Revolution required iron for machines, coal to burn in steam engines and money to pay for them both. By 1750, Britain had all three and became the first country to industrialize. The iron industry grew quickly after 1709, when Abraham Darby first used coke to smelt iron (melt the iron ore). This was cheaper and more efficient than the old way using charcoal. New coal mines were dug to supply coal for steam engines and coke for ironworks.

CANALS AND RAILWAYS

The new industrial products required a transport system to move them to people. Between 1750 and 1830, canals were dug, linking major cities and rivers. Most roads remained poor, but in 1804, Richard Trevithick built the world's first steam locomotive. By the 1830s, Britain had embarked on a railway craze, and railways were soon built across countries in western Europe and North America. By 1870, most of these nations had linked their cities by rail. Belgium, France, Germany and the USA began industrializing after 1815. By 1900, the USA and Germany had overtaken Britain in steel production.

BUSINESS BOOM

The new machines made goods faster and more cheaply. Factory and mine owners made huge profits, some of which they spent on more machines, so creating new jobs. Investors saved small amounts of money in banks, which then lent large amounts to industrialists. This developing 'capitalist' system raised money to build factories, offices and houses.

A HARD LIFE

For many workers, life in the factories and mines was hard and dangerous. Men, women and children worked 13 or more hours a day, often for low wages. Many workers

DEVELOPING INDUSTRIAL AREAS

New factories were built near canals and railways so that raw materials could be brought in and finished goods taken to markets easily. To begin with, the houses that were built to accommodate the workers in many industrial became slums, with no running water, drains or other basic services.

KEY DATES

1709 Abraham Darby uses coke to smelt iron

1764 The spinning jenny is invented for cotton

1770 The first factories begin producing cotton

1789 The first steam-powered factory opens

1804 Richard Trevithick builds first steam locomotive

1825 The first public railway is opened

1820s Rapid growth of industrialization in USA

In time, reformers won improved working conditions and schooling for all children. Slums were cleared and new laws controlled factory and housing development.

LONG-TERM EFFECTS

During the Industrial Revolution, cities grew rapidly as people began to leave the countryside to find work. Industrialization spread worldwide in the 20th century, and the world economy today is geared to the production of goods, though some countries in Africa and Southeast Asia remain dependent on agriculture or services. People now enjoy higher standards of living than ever before, but at a high cost to the environment. Industrialization has caused pollution and used up resources such as coal, oil and minerals. However, new technology is being developed to solve some of the problems created by industrialization.

CHILD LABOUR
In the 1700s and 1800s, factory owners employed children, many of them under ten years of age, to work in factories and mines. They had to work long hours in dangerous and unhealthy conditions. However, by 1900, most industrialized countries had banned child labour.

were killed or injured by unsafe machinery before new safety laws were enforced. Towns grew rapidly and without proper planning, leaving some areas without drains or clean water. Diseases that were caught from unclean water (such as cholera) or in crowded conditions (tuberculosis) became common and killed thousands of people. These conditions caused social unrest and even riots.

CAMPAIGNERS AND REFORMERS

Gradually, laws to shorten working hours and stop child labour were introduced. Trade unions, at first banned, campaigned for better pay and conditions for workers.

URBAN DEVELOPMENT

Rows of terraced cottages were built around factories to house the workers. Gradually, some factory owners or town councils improved conditions for the workers by building schools and churches.

SEE ALSO

Coal, Engine, Iron and steel, Machine, Train, Transport, Water power

INDUSTRY

Industry covers all the different kinds of work people do, from producing raw materials and manufacturing goods to providing services.

Borer

Grinder

Puncher

Turning machine

▲ Machine tools such as these are widely used to manufacture machinery and motor components.

► Researchers in the chemical industry develop new materials such as drugs and plastics.

Manufacturing industries, such as the aircraft and automobile industries, make goods for people to buy. The electronics industry, for example, produces tiny wafers of silicon that are the brains of our computers, and the chemical industry manufactures a wide range of chemicals, from fertilizers to life-saving antibiotics. The steel industry is one of the most important of all industries because it produces the metal that many other industries rely on. The construction industry uses steel to build towering skyscrapers and massive dams and bridges.

PRIMARY INDUSTRIES
Mining produces the raw materials, such as ores and petroleum, on which the manufacturing industries depend. It marks the beginning of the industrial production process and is therefore called a primary industry. Agriculture, forestry and fishing are also primary industries. Manufacturing is next in the production chain, and is called a secondary industry.

GETTING SERVICE
When the manufacturing industries have produced the goods, they have to be sold to the consumer. This is the job of shops and stores. They do not produce goods themselves, but provide a service by buying goods from the manufacturers and selling them on to customers. Shops are an example of a service industry, often called a tertiary (third) industry. Other examples of service industries include transport and tourism, insurance and banks, restaurants and hotels, hospitals and local government.

MASS PRODUCTION
A key feature of modern industry is mass production – the manufacture of goods in large quantities at a relatively low cost. In a typical mass production operation, goods are built up piece by piece on an assembly line, with people often working side by side with industrial robots.

▲ Some industries, such as this shoe factory in India, involve hundreds of people working together. Others have people working in smaller groups, or alone at home.

AUTOMATION TAKES OVER
Today, many assembly lines are fully automated, with machines now controlled by computers instead of humans. Robots are increasingly being used, particularly in the automobile industry. They are ideal for performing highly repetitive, hazardous or awkward tasks, such as spot welding or paint spraying. Fitted with a gripper, they can also be used to move objects about.

SEE ALSO

Construction, Farming, Fishing industry, Industrial Revolution, Mining, Robot

INSECT

Insects belong to the large group of animals called arthropods, which means 'jointed legs'. An insect's legs are made up of small segments and flexible joints.

Male stag beetles have large jaws that look like the antlers of a stag.

A cricket has long hind legs for hopping and scrapes its wings to 'sing'.

Earwigs are flat with pincers at their tail and wings that fold away.

Aphids have soft brown or green bodies about 2–3mm in length.

A human louse, like all sucking lice, feeds on the blood of mammals.

IDENTIFYING AN INSECT

Adult insects, such as the wasp below, have a body that is divided into three parts: the head, the thorax (where legs and wings are joined) and the abdomen (where the insect digests its food and makes its eggs). They also have three pairs of legs, and a tough body case, or exoskeleton.

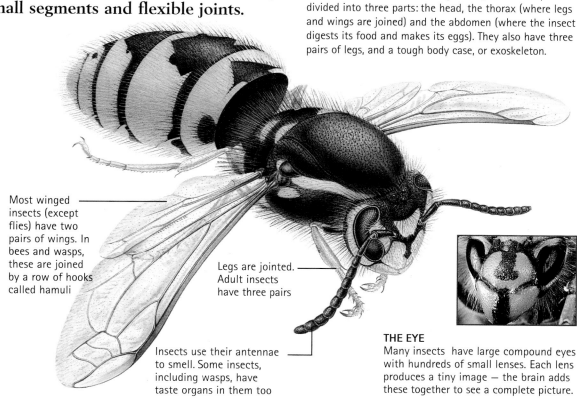

Most winged insects (except flies) have two pairs of wings. In bees and wasps, these are joined by a row of hooks called hamuli

Legs are jointed. Adult insects have three pairs

Insects use their antennae to smell. Some insects, including wasps, have taste organs in them too

THE EYE
Many insects have large compound eyes with hundreds of small lenses. Each lens produces a tiny image – the brain adds these together to see a complete picture.

More than a million kinds of insects have been found on Earth. That's more than all the other types of animals put together. They are split into over 30 groups and include grasshoppers, beetles, butterflies, flies and bees. Insects have no backbone or skeleton inside the body, but the whole insect is covered with a tough, horny material called chitin. This forms an external skeleton rather like a suit of armour. It is made up of segments, some of which are loosely connected by soft membranes so that the insect can move.

WITH OR WITHOUT WINGS
Most insects have two pairs of wings, but some, including fleas and worker ants, never have wings. Flying ants only have wings for a short time, then lose them. Beetles and many bugs look as if they have no wings because their front wings form hard cases and completely cover the delicate hind wings.

BREATHING WITH TUBES
Insects do not have lungs. They breathe by way of a system of fine tubes, called tracheae. These branch through the body and carry air and oxygen. In most insects, air enters the tubes through small holes on the sides of the body – mainly on the abdomen. The openings are called spiracles and they are best seen in large caterpillars, which are the young stages of butterflies and moths.

WATER BUGS
Insects that live in water usually have to come to the surface to renew the air in their breathing tubes, but many young insects can absorb dissolved oxygen straight from the water into their tracheae. ▶

▶ Beetles form the largest insect order, with around 370,000 species.

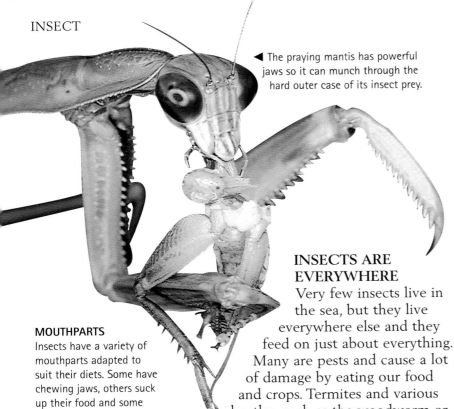

◄ The praying mantis has powerful jaws so it can munch through the hard outer case of its insect prey.

MOUTHPARTS

Insects have a variety of mouthparts adapted to suit their diets. Some have chewing jaws, others suck up their food and some have piercing needles.

Tiger beetles are fierce carnivores (meat-eaters), with prominent biting mandibles (or jaws).

Weevils' mouthparts are extended into a snout. They can be serious pests, infesting flour and grain.

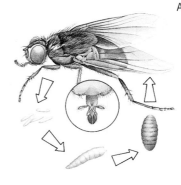

A fly's proboscis is like a straw with a sponge tip. It dribbles on food to dissolve it, then sucks it back up.

INSECTS ARE EVERYWHERE

Very few insects live in the sea, but they live everywhere else and they feed on just about everything. Many are pests and cause a lot of damage by eating our food and crops. Termites and various beetles, such as the woodworm or furniture beetle, can even destroy our houses. Fleas and mosquitoes suck our blood and carry dangerous diseases. But there are also some very useful insects. Honey bees pollinate many of our crops and give us honey, silkmoths give us silk, ladybird beetles eat huge numbers of greenflies (aphids) and other plant pests, and dung beetles and their grubs help to keep the countryside clean by eating up cow-pats and other animal dung.

AN INSECT GROWS UP

Most insects start life as eggs, but the insect that hatches from an egg does not usually look much like its parents. A caterpillar, for example, looks nothing like an adult butterfly or moth: it has no wings and instead of sipping nectar from flowers it munches its way through leaves with its biting jaws. Before it becomes an adult, the caterpillar has to pass through a chrysalis, or pupa, stage, during which its body is broken down and re-built in the adult form. Bees, flies and beetles pass through similar stages as they grow up.

THE EMERGING INSECT

Insects, such as this lacewing, moult several times as they grow up, because their tough outer coats, or exoskeletons, cannot grow. At each moult, the old skin splits open, and the insect crawls out.

INSECT LIFE-CYCLE

Advanced insects, such as flies, have a four-part life-cycle. The eggs hatch into larvae which change their skins twice as they grow. Then comes the pupa stage where they change into the adult form.

Young insects at the worm-like stage are called larvae, and this way of growing up is called a complete metamorphosis, meaning 'a complete change'.

SMALL ADULTS

Grasshoppers, dragonflies and bugs have a slightly different kind of life-cycle. The young insects do not have wings, but they do look fairly like the adults apart from being smaller. They are called nymphs, and they gradually turn into adults without passing through a chrysalis stage. This way of growing up is called an incomplete metamorphosis – 'an incomplete change'.

INSECT HOMES

Ants are the most successful social insects. In the leaf-cutter ant's communal home, the queen lays the eggs, nursery workers look after them, larger workers cut leaves and bring them back to the nest, leaving scent trails by touching the ground with the tips of their abdomens. Soldier ants have a big head with strong jaws and bite to protect the nest; while smaller workers build new tunnels and tend the fungus gardens to feed the others.

Soldier ants use their sting and powerful jaws to defend the colony

Nursery worker

A queen ant can lay one egg every ten seconds.

Ants chew the leaves to pulp and mix it with their droppings. A fungus grows on the mixture and the ants eat the fungus.

Smaller worker protects leaf

A large leaf-cutter can grow up to 2cm and carry a gigantic weight in its mouth.

A worker takes the eggs to the nursery chambers and tends the growing larvae.

The nest has its own air conditioning system – air tunnels keep it at a constant temperature and humidity.

Ants can carry leafs through the network of tunnels.

Rubbish chamber

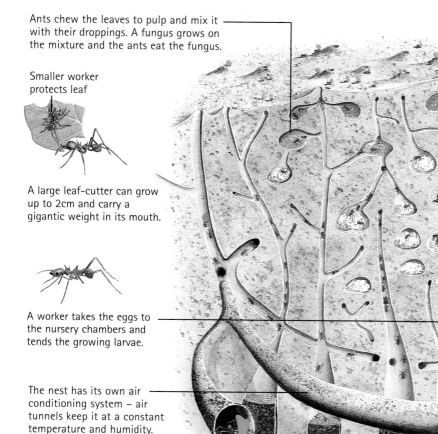

GETTING FATTER

As insects grow they shed their old body cases – but not before growing a soft new one. The insect pumps itself up with air or water for a few hours until the new skin has hardened, and then gets rid of the air or water to leave enough space for the next stage of growth. Most insects moult between four and ten times as they grow up, but some may moult as many as 50 times before they are fully grown adults.

LITTLE AND LARGE

The heaviest insect is the African Goliath beetle, which is about as big as a man's fist and weighs about 100g. Some stick insects are much longer, but their bodies are all quite thin. The tiniest insects are smaller than a full-stop on this page.

HOME ALONE

Most insects are solitary – living alone and finding a safe place to lay their eggs. This may be inside the body of another insect, as in the case of the tarantula hawk wasp which lays an egg on a paralyzed but living spider. Social insects, such as ants, live together in large groups. Each insect has its own job and only the queen lays eggs.

◄ Bumble bees are social insects that have pollen baskets (hairs) on their hind legs to collect pollen.

FAST FACTS

• Ants and bees recognize members of their own colony through smell

• The number of lenses in an insect's eye varies from about six in a worker ant to 30,000 in some dragonflies

• A single swarm of locusts can contain five to ten billion insects!

SEE ALSO

Black Death, Butterfly and moth, Disease, Fossil, Prehistoric animal

INTERNET

The Internet is a globe-spanning computer network, giving people rapid access to information, knowledge, entertainment and opinions from around the world.

▲ Cybercafés allow people who are not on the Internet to make use of it in comfortable surroundings.

The Internet, or 'Net', is often referred to as the Information Superhighway. It allows vast amounts of information to stream around the world from computer to computer, letting the general public have easy and quick access to it.

WHAT THE INTERNET CAN DO

School students can call up pictures and information from galleries in, for example, France, Japan and Britain. They can check unfamiliar words and historical dates in computerized reference libraries based in any country. Alternatively, they can listen to a clip from an album while printing out the guitar chords to go with it. A major use of the Internet is to carry electronic mail, or email. An email message can include pictures and audio clips, as well as words, and can be sent to hundreds of computers as easily and as cheaply as to one.

BIRTH OF THE INTERNET

The Internet began as a military network for communications. In the early 1970s, American engineers designed a system that could keep working even if a nuclear attack knocked out some of the computers. Signals could automatically be re-routed through the surviving computers. This design was later used to set up computer networks linking universities and now it is used in the Internet.

THE WORLD WIDE WEB

The World Wide Web was invented in 1990 so that users could 'surf the Net' quickly. By clicking on links on the screen with the mouse, the user jumps to pages of information consisting of words and pictures located on various computers around the world. Each of these has its own links which lead to further pages.

▼ Search engines greatly speed up the process of finding Web pages and specific pieces of information on the Web.

▼ People can view live video clips of a current US space mission from NASA.

▲ Many goods and services can be ordered and paid for over the Internet.

► Using email, people can send letters and pictures to one another across the world within seconds.

◄ Information on shows, films, zoos, circuses and many other forms of entertainment can be found on the Internet.

SEE ALSO

Communication, Computer, Technology, Telecommunication

INVENTION

An invention is the creation of something new. In the past 200 years, the number of inventions has boomed, changing the world dramatically.

▲ Wheels were used in Mesopotamia about 3200BCE. The cart wheel was developed from the earlier potter's wheel.

Civilization has been driven forward by inventions. Each invention has been based on those that came before it, and has made further progress possible.

GETTING THE BASICS RIGHT

Prehistoric people were the first inventors. They learned how to farm and to make fire, pottery, the wheel and metal tools. One invention often leads to others. Without the wheel, for example, there could be no carts, watermills or machines driven by gears. Key inventions of the 19th century included photography, electric light, plastics and motor vehicles. In 1946, the first electronic computer started up, changing the way we live.

THE INVENTORS

Some people stand out as lone inventors. In the late 1400s, the Italian Leonardo da Vinci designed a flying machine, but could not build it because there was no suitable engine. The American Thomas Alva Edison (1847–1931) is credited with more than 1,000 inventions, among them the light bulb and the phonograph. Other pioneers who worked alone were Alexander Graham Bell (the telephone), Guglielmo Marconi (the radio) and Karl Benz and Gottfried Daimler (the motor car). More recent inventions, such as the television and computers, were developed by large research teams with many specialists.

GOOD OR BAD?

Most people would agree that pain-killing drugs are 'good' inventions and that poison gas is 'bad', but poison gas can be put to good use to kill pests that eat our food. It is how inventions are used that makes them useful or harmful.

The flushing toilet was developed in the 1840s.

Safety matches were invented in 1844.

An early experimental photocopier of 1940.

John Logie Baird invented the television in 1926.

Alexander Graham Bell invented the telephone in 1876.

PHONOGRAPH
Thomas Edison's phonograph of 1877 used a cylinder of tin foil to record sound.

RECORDED SOUND

Sound recording has traditionally been by analogue means. The sound waves in the air are reproduced as peaks and troughs in a groove on a solid object. These were read by passing a needle along the groove. Modern CDs and mp3 players treat sound as digital computer data instead.

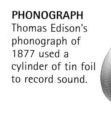

78RPM GRAMOPHONE
In 1921, a flat plastic disc, or record, with sound fed through electric speakers gave better-quality sound.

HI-FI VINYL
In 1958, stereo sound from long-playing records produced high fidelity sound, or hi-fi, for the first time.

COMPACT DISC
The compact disc, or CD, of the early 1980s contained digital music, read by a laser beam for accurate reproduction.

SEE ALSO
Aircraft, Car, Clock, Electronics, Film, Industrial Revolution, Nuclear power, Printing, Warfare

IRELAND, REPUBLIC OF

The Republic of Ireland occupies 80 per cent of the island of Ireland, which lies off the west coast of Britain. It is also called by its Gaelic name, Eire.

Area: 70,285 sq km
Population: 4,581,000
Capital: Dublin
Languages: English and Irish Gaelic
Currency: Euro

Ireland is a land of green fields, rolling hills, lakes, known as loughs, and winding rivers. The centre of the country is flat while low mountain ranges line the coasts. The Shannon (386km) is the longest river in the British Isles and is used to produce hydroelectric power. Ireland has a mild, moist climate and rich green grass grows on the limestone that forms much of the country, giving it the name Emerald Isle.

FARMING AND EUROPE
Ireland is a farming country famous for dairy foods such as butter. Wide bogs in the midlands are full of peat (decayed plants), which is cut and dried for fuel. After joining the European Union (EU), the Republic prospered as EU money helped it to modernize farm machinery and farming methods.

INDUSTRY AND CITIES
Irish factories make electronic equipment, textiles, plastics and other goods. The country also brews alcoholic beverages. Industry is centred mainly around Dublin, Cork and Limerick – three fifths of the people now live in towns or cities, where they are more likely to find work.

▲ Live music, traditional and modern, is a large part of Irish culture. The country has also produced many great writers.

▼ The city of Dublin is popular with tourists. Landmarks include the Ha'penny Bridge over the River Liffey.

IRELAND AND BRITAIN
England gained control of Ireland in the 1500s, after which Protestants from England and Scotland settled there. When Ireland became self-governing in 1921, the six Protestant-dominated counties of Northern Ireland stayed part of the United Kingdom. In the Republic, most people are Roman Catholics. The division of the island causes continuing tensions.

▲ The Irish are famous for breeding horses. Their thoroughbred yearlings are most often used as racehorses.

SEE ALSO
Christianity, Civil war, Europe, UK

IRON AND STEEL

Iron is one of the most common metals in the Earth's crust. It is often used mixed with other ingredients in the form of steel – a cheap, strong building material.

Steel can be shaped in various ways. It can be rolled into tubes...

... or drawn through a hole to make wire.

A series of rollers shapes solid steel into girders.

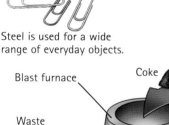

Steel is used for a wide range of everyday objects.

In its natural state, iron is found combined with other elements, such as oxygen, as a rocky material called iron ore. Before it can be used, the iron has to be extracted (removed) from its ore by a process called smelting.

EXTRACTING THE IRON

The iron ore is mixed with coke (a form of carbon) and limestone (a chalky rock). Then it is blasted with hot air until it reaches a temperature of over 1500°C. The iron melts and most of the impurities (unwanted materials) float to its surface. The impurities, known as 'slag', are then removed. The iron remaining is called pig iron. This still contains some impurities, especially carbon, but after further heat treatment, it can be poured into moulds to make cast-iron parts such as engine blocks.

▲ Glowing red-hot, molten iron is poured from a giant ladle into moulds and left to cool as ingots.

MAKING STEEL

Most pig iron goes for refining, or purifying, to make steel. This involves mixing it with scrap steel and blasting it with oxygen so that most of the carbon burns off. Steel is a tough, strong material that is used to make bridges, buildings and many other objects that carry heavy loads. Manufacturers often add other elements to steel to give it special properties. Adding chromium and nickel makes stainless steel – a material that never rusts. This is used to make such things as engine parts and surgical tools.

PROCESSING THE IRON

Iron is extracted from its ore in a blast furnace. The resulting pig iron contains about four per cent carbon, which comes from the coke in the furnace. This carbon makes the iron very brittle, so the iron is processed again before it is used. Steel is made by blasting the pig iron with oxygen inside a furnace called a converter. The oxygen combines with the carbon in the iron to form gases that are easily removed.

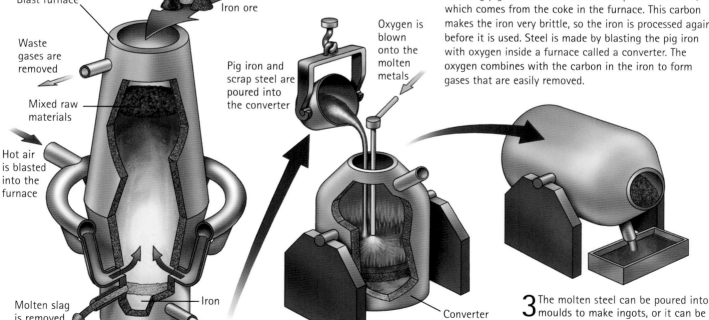

The raw materials are put into the furnace

Limestone

Coke

Iron ore

Blast furnace

Waste gases are removed

Mixed raw materials

Hot air is blasted into the furnace

Molten slag is removed

Iron

Pig iron and scrap steel are poured into the converter

Oxygen is blown onto the molten metals

Converter

Molten pig iron pours into ladle

1 As the coke burns inside the furnace, it removes the oxygen from the iron ore to leave pig iron.

2 Inside the converter, oxygen is used to burn off most of the carbon, leaving steel.

3 The molten steel can be poured into moulds to make ingots, or it can be cast into shape while still fluid.

SEE ALSO

Bridge, Construction, Earth, Metal, Skyscraper

ISLAM

Islam is the second most common religion in the world after Christianity. People who follow Islam are called Muslims.

THE FIVE PILLARS OF ISLAM

There is no god but Allah, and Muhammad is God's messenger

A formal prayer must be said five times every day, while facing the holy city of Mecca

Those who can afford it should give to the poor each year

Followers must fast during the month of Ramadan

Followers must make a pilgrimage to Mecca, if possible, at least once during their lifetime

▲ The crescent and star are the symbols of Islam.

There are 1.5 billion Muslims across the world, many in the Middle East and Africa. They believe in one all-powerful god, who created everything. Their name for God is Allah. Islam means 'submission' in Arabic, and devout Muslims try to live their lives according to Allah's word.

THE STORY OF MUHAMMAD

Islam began with the Prophet Muhammad, an Arab born in about 570CE in the city of Mecca (in what is now Saudi Arabia). When he was 40, Muhammad was called by Allah to preach his words, and he spread Islam throughout much of the Arab world. He died in 632.

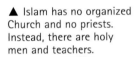

▲ Islam has no organized Church and no priests. Instead, there are holy men and teachers.

PILGRIMAGE TO MECCA

The pilgrimage to Mecca, called the hajj, takes place during the 12th month of the Muslim year. Nearly two million Muslims from across the world converge on Mecca to perform rituals, such as walking round the holy shrine, or Kaaba (the black structure seen below), which contains a black stone dating from ancient times.

LAWS OF ISLAM

Islamic Law, or the Shariah, is very important to Muslims. It was laid down by early Islamic teachers and tells Muslims how they should live their lives. The holy book of Islam is the Koran (or Qur'an), said to be Allah's exact words, as told to Muhammad. A Muslim's main religious duties are the 'Five Pillars of Islam'– faith, prayer, almsgiving, fasting and pilgrimage.

MUSLIMS AT PRAYER

The Muslim place of worship is called a mosque. Five times a day, criers known as *muezzins* call the people to prayer from minarets, or towers, on the mosques. Muslims do not have to go to the mosque to pray, except on Fridays, but can pray in any clean place.

SEE ALSO

Crusades, Middle East, Pilgrim, Religion

ISRAEL, GAZA AND WEST BANK

Israel stands on a narrow strip of land in southwest Asia, on the eastern shore of the Mediterranean Sea. It makes up most of the area once called the Holy Land.

Area: 20,400 sq km
Population: 7,695,000
Capital: Jerusalem
Languages: Hebrew and Arabic
Currency: Shekel

▲ The Dome of the Rock shrine, sacred to Muslims and Jews, stands in East Jerusalem. It is on the site where Muhammad is said to have risen into heaven.

The hills of Galilee lie in northern Israel, while lowlands and fertile plains lie to the west. Most of the south is made up of the Negev Desert.

SALTY SEA
The Jordan river flows along Israel's eastern border from the north, into the Sea of Galilee and then into the Dead Sea. The Dead Sea is actually a lake and contains useful minerals, such as potash, used to make soap. The water is so dense that swimmers can float easily.

WATERING THE LAND
Summers in Israel are dry and hot, while winters are cool. Irrigation schemes have brought water to dry land, making it lush with crops. On collective farms called kibbutzim, families live and work together growing fruit such as oranges – Israel is a major producer of citrus fruits. Other crops include vegetables, cotton and olives. Israel is a highly developed country, however, and about 92 per cent of Israelis live in towns and cities. Many of them work in factories or service industries.

▲ The Dead Sea is the saltiest body of water in the world. The salt crystallizes to form lumps in the water.

THE HOLY LAND
Jews, Christians and Muslims all regard Jerusalem as a holy place. After the Romans conquered the region in 63CE and called it Palestine, most Jewish people were forced to leave. Modern Israel was founded in 1948 as a homeland for the Jews. Several wars followed between Jews and Palestinian Arabs. In 1967, Israel occupied the West Bank and Gaza. Today, nearly six million Palestinians live in Israel, the West Bank and Gaza, and tensions are high.

◄ Since 1993, Palestinians have had limited control over the West Bank and Gaza. Jewish children attend separate schools.

SEE ALSO
Asia, Christianity, Islam, Judaism, Middle East, Pilgrim

ITALY

As the seat of the Roman Empire and cradle of the Renaissance, Italy has been at the centre of European civilization for centuries.

Area: 301,277 sq km
Population: 60,340,000
Capital: Rome
Language: Italian
Currency: Euro

▲ ▼ Venice's annual carnival is a major event, and carnival-goers dress flamboyantly for the occasion. Boats known as gondolas are used for transport in Venice, where the main 'streets' are canals – the Grand Canal at the Rialto Bridge has been the scene of many regattas.

Some of the highest mountains in Europe, the Alps, tower across northern Italy. Another mountain chain, the Apennines, stretches from north to south. The independent state of San Marino stands on the three peaks of Mount Titano in the Apennines – it is the oldest republic in Europe, founded in the 4th century, and covers just 61 sq km.

POWER FROM WATER
Rushing mountain streams are used in hydroelectric schemes to provide much-needed power for a country with little coal or oil of its own. Italy's largest rivers, the Po, Arno and Tiber, are all in northern Italy, as are lakes Garda, Como and Maggiore. Southern Italy, which includes the islands of Sardinia and Sicily, is hotter and drier than the north.

FOOD AND DRINK
Italy is the world's largest wine producer. Italian dishes vary from north to south, and range from veal in subtle, light sauces to seafood in rich, spicy tomato sauces. Italian recipes have inspired cooking around the world, and pizzas and pasta have become international dishes.

▲ Italy has many old and beautiful churches. Even a tiny country church, like this one in Siena, may have a priceless medieval wall painting or carving.

AGRICULTURE
Many Italians are farmers. The major crop is wheat, used to make pasta and bread. Others are olives, grapes, maize and sugar beet. Cattle are reared mainly in the north, and many sheep and goats are kept on rough pasture in Sardinia and Sicily.

INDUSTRIOUS NORTH
In northern Italy, industry is based around the cities of Turin, Milan and Genoa. Factories make a wide range of goods including motor vehicles, clothing, machinery and chemicals. Milan is particularly famous for its fashion houses, where clothes are designed. Many raw materials have to be imported and Italy has a large fleet of merchant ships.

SPEAKING ITALIAN
Almost everyone in Italy speaks Italian, although a few communities speak another language – German is the first language of people

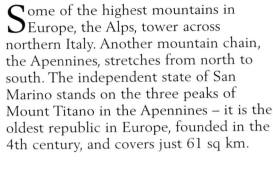

▲ Italy is rich in artistic treasures, spectacular buildings and historic remains such as those of the Colosseum, an ancient amphitheatre in Rome.

living near the Austrian border. Most Italians are Roman Catholics and the head of the Catholic Church, the pope, lives in Vatican City, in Rome.

VATICAN CITY
Vatican City is the smallest independent state in the world, with an area of only 0.44 sq km. St Peter's Basilica stands at its centre. It was built during the fourth century and rebuilt in the 16th century.

VARIETY FOR VISITORS
Tourism is one of Italy's main industries. Every year, millions of people visit the country to enjoy its peaceful countryside, sunny beaches, snow-capped mountains and historic cities such as Venice, Florence, Naples and Rome.

ROME TO RENAISSANCE
Italy was where the Roman Empire was founded. Roman rule ended in 476CE, but Rome remained the headquarters of the Roman Catholic Church. Italy broke up into smaller city states, and in the 15th and 16th centuries, it was the centre of the Renaissance. The country has produced explorers such as Marco Polo, artists such as Leonardo da Vinci and scientists such as Galileo.

UNITING THE STATES
From the 1500s, France and Austria tried to control Italy. In the 19th century, Giuseppe Garibaldi and others led the fight to unite the Italian states. They drove out the Austrians and, in 1861, Italy became an independent and united kingdom.

MODERN ITALY
During the 1920s and 1930s, the fascists, led by Benito Mussolini, held power. After World War II (1939–45), Italy held its first free election for 20 years and a republic replaced the monarchy. Italy had a lively political life from the 1950s to 2000s, with many different governments. Since then, there have been fewer changes. Italy remains a major industrial power, but the country has declined economically.

◄ Motorbikes are a popular form of transport with young Italians, meeting here at the Piazza del Popolo in Rome.

▲ Modern opera began in Italy in the early 1600s, with the composer Claudio Monteverdi. The Italian tenor Luciano Pavarotti helped to popularize opera worldwide.

SEE ALSO
Art, Christianity, Europe, Fascism, Renaissance, Roman Empire, Volcano

JAPAN

Japan is an island country in northeast Asia, off the east coast of China. The Japanese call their country Nippon or Nihon, which means 'source of the Sun'.

Area: 377,819 sq km
Population: 128,057,000
Capital: Tokyo
Language: Japanese
Currency: Yen

▲ Japan is a leading fishing nation. It supplies not only its own people but also many other countries.

▼ Many beautiful temples, like the Kinkaka Ji, with its spectacular gardens, can be found in Japan's former capital, Kyoto.

By area, Japan is Asia's 18th largest country. Its largest island is Honshu, followed by Hokkaido, Kyushu and Shikoku. There are also thousands of small islands, such as the Ryukyu island chain.

ERUPTIONS AND EARTHQUAKES
Most of Japan is hilly or mountainous and the rivers are fast flowing, providing water power for making electricity. Japan's highest peak, Mount Fuji (3,776m), is a volcano which last erupted in 1708. More than 100 of Japan's volcanoes are active and earthquakes are also common.

VARIED CLIMATE
The northernmost island of Hokkaido, just south of Russia's Sakhalin Island, is cool, and snow is common in winter, while Kyushu in the south is much warmer. Most of Japan has plenty of rainfall.

PINK-FACED MONKEYS
Forests cover more than two thirds of the land and many animals, including bears, wild boar, deer and foxes, live in them. Pink-faced monkeys called Japanese macaques live as far north as the northern tip of Honshu. They have long, thick fur and swim in hot springs in the snow to keep warm.

▲ Today, Japan's leading industries include the manufacture of electrical goods such as televisions.

FIRST ARRIVALS
The first people in Japan were probably descendants of a group of people called the Ainu, a few thousand of whom live in Hokkaido today. The ancestors of most modern Japanese people probably reached the islands from mainland Asia around 2,200 years ago. The country ranks tenth in the world by population.

SHARED RELIGIONS
More than two thirds of the people live in crowded cities and towns. The largest city is Tokyo, and other large cities include Osaka and Nagoya, all situated on Honshu, where 80 per cent of the people live. There are two main religions in Japan: Shintoism (the oldest religion) and Buddhism.

MEETING ITS NEEDS

Although it lacks natural resources, Japan is a wealthy country. Because it is so hilly, only about 11 per cent of the land is farmed. Japan produces only 39 per cent of the food it needs. Rice is the leading crop and food. Fruit, sugar beet, tea and vegetables are also important.

MADE IN JAPAN

Manufacturing is the most valuable activity, and Japan ranks third among the world's top industrial countries, after the United States and China. Its products sell around the world and include chemicals, electrical goods and electronic equipment, iron and steel, machinery, ships, textiles, transport equipment and it produces more cars than any country except China.

POWERFUL NATION

Japan became a powerful nation in the late 19th century. It won some important battles against China in 1894 and defeated Russia in 1905. In 1937, it attacked China and, in 1941, it attacked the American naval base in Pearl Harbor, Hawaii. This act drew it and the USA into World War II.

MOVING TO DEMOCRACY

In 1945, after the United States had dropped atomic bombs on Hiroshima and Nagasaki, Japan surrendered. The United States occupied Japan until 1952. During this time, Japan became a democratic country and the once all-powerful emperor became head of state with only ceremonial duties. The country is now ruled by an elected prime minister and government and is one of the world's great economic powers.

SEA OF OKHOTSK

Hokkaido

● Sapporo

● Hakodate

N

JAPAN

Sendai ●

miles
0 — 125
0 — 125
km

SEA OF JAPAN

Honshu

Shinano

Mt. Fuji ▲ ■ Tokyo
● Yokohama

Kyoto ● ● Nagoya
Kobe ●
Hiroshima ● ● Osaka

Shikoku

PACIFIC OCEAN

● Nagasaki

Kyushu

EAST CHINA SEA

Osumi Is.

Ryukyu Is.

Okinawa

Sakishima Is.

▶ Sumo, a Japanese style of wrestling in which opponents try to push each other out of a ring, is a popular national sport.

◀ Japan's bullet train, seen here against Mount Fuji, is one of the fastest in the world. It runs on the island of Honshu.

SEE ALSO

Asia, Buddhism, China, Industry, Southeast Asia, Volcano, World War II

JELLYFISH AND OTHER CNIDARIANS

Jellyfish, sea anemones and corals belong to a group of animals called cnidarians. They all have soft bodies armed with stinging tentacles.

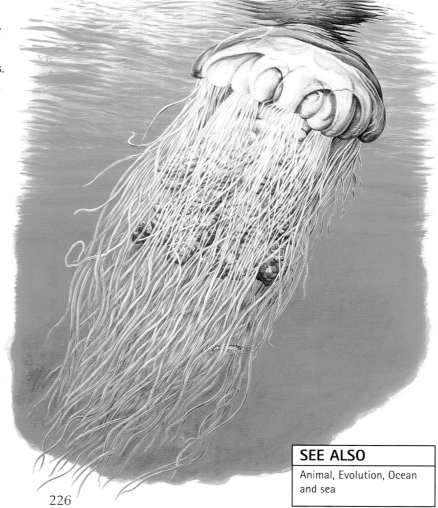

► Jellyfish move by pumping water backwards with their bodies.

A Portuguese man-of-war is not a true jellyfish. Like corals, it is a colony of animals living together.

The hydra is a freshwater cnidarian. It forms new buds that break off and grow into new animals.

Tube-shaped sea anemones attach themselves, with their sucker-like base, to rocks in the sea.

Cnidarians are invertebrates – which means 'no backbone'. In fact they have no trace of a skeleton at all – except for corals, whose soft bodies are surrounded by a hard limestone case. Cnidarians have no brains, but have simple nerves and muscles. The largest individuals are found among the jellyfish, which are nearly all umbrella- or bell-shaped animals with a mouth on the underside. There are about 11,000 different kinds. Most of them are no bigger than a saucer, but there are a few real giants, with bodies up to 2m across and tentacles as long as 70m.

STINGING STRINGS

Most cnidarians use tentacles to catch prey. Even corals are carnivorous, using stinging cells on their tentacles to paralyze microscopic animals in the water. The stings of some jellyfish are very dangerous to swimmers. Those of the Australian sea wasp jellyfish can kill a person within a few minutes.

A STICKY END

Some jellyfish have bodies covered with sticky slime that traps any small animals they bump into. Aurelia, the common jellyfish found washed up on beaches, uses stinging cells and then envelops its paralyzed prey in mucus.

BREAKING UP

Jellyfish scatter eggs or tiny babies into the water, but these do not grow directly into jellyfish. The tiny creatures that hatch from the eggs of common jellyfish settle on a rock or seaweed and grow into cone shapes. They gradually divide until they look like piles of miniature saucers. Each saucer floats away and grows into a new jellyfish.

ENTANGLING PREY

The jellyfish's tentacles are covered with potent stings and are used to catch and kill fish, prawns, and other small animals. The lion's mane jellyfish, here, has a 2-m body and tentacles reaching 40m. The tentacles pull the victim into the mouth, which is hidden under its bell-like body.

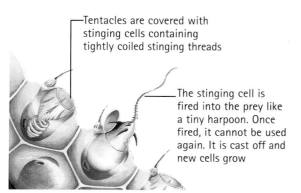

Tentacles are covered with stinging cells containing tightly coiled stinging threads

The stinging cell is fired into the prey like a tiny harpoon. Once fired, it cannot be used again. It is cast off and new cells grow

SEE ALSO

Animal, Evolution, Ocean and sea

JUDAISM

Judaism is the religion of the Jewish people. It teaches that there is one true God, who revealed himself to the Jews and has given the human race rules to live by.

The six-pointed star became a symbol of Judaism during the Middle Ages. It signifies the protection of God given to David, king of Israel, in about 970BCE.

Jews believe that there is one eternal, invisible God who created the universe. There are about 14 million Jews living in Israel and all over the world.

MOSES AND THE HEBREWS

The first followers of Judaism were the Hebrews of the Middle East. According to the Bible (Old Testament), the Jewish holy book, God promised Abraham and his descendants land to live in and protection around 1900BCE. In about 1200BCE, God sent Moses to lead the Hebrews out of slavery in Egypt. God revealed his teachings, about how to live and serve God, to Moses. These teachings are the basis of Judaism and are contained in the Torah, laws based on the first five books of the Bible. Later works, the Talmud, interpret the Torah. They tell people how to lead good lives and how to observe rituals.

Jewish women pray at Jerusalem's Western Wall (Wailing Wall), at the site of the ancient Temple.

THE HOLY SABBATH

The Hebrews worshipped at the Temple in Jerusalem, but this was destroyed in a war with the Roman Empire in 70CE. Modern Jews study their faith in buildings called synagogues. Here, they are guided by teachers known as rabbis. The most religious day of the week is the Sabbath, which lasts from sunset Friday to sunset Saturday. Jews cannot work on this day, because they believe that this was the day when God rested after creating the world.

Jews light a candle a day during the eight days of Hanukkah, to celebrate the rededication of the temple in 165BCE.

▲ A rabbi preparing to sound the *shofar* (ram's horn) at Yom Kippur wears a *tallith* (prayer shawl).

BAR MITZVAH

When a Jewish boy officially becomes a man, at the age of 13, the bar mitzvah ceremony is held. The boy reads from the books of the prophets during the Sabbath service. The service is often followed by prayers and a family celebration.

KOSHER RITUALS

Jews observe various festivals, including Yom Kippur in September or October, when sins are confessed and forgiveness asked. At Passover, in March or April, the departure from Egypt is celebrated. Orthodox Jews have strict rules about what they eat, how their food is prepared and the way ritual objects should be treated. These rules are called kosher.

PERSECUTION

For centuries, Jews have lived among other nations, which have sometimes persecuted them. During World War II, the Nazis murdered millions of Jews in what is called the Holocaust. After this, many Jews created a new homeland, Israel, in the area where the Hebrews lived. But they still face conflict with neighbouring states.

SEE ALSO

Israel, Gaza and West Bank, Religion, World War II

KANGAROO AND OTHER MARSUPIALS

Marsupials are mammals that normally carry their babies in pouches. There are about 320 kinds, most of which live in Australia, New Guinea and the Americas.

Koalas live in and feed off eucalyptus trees.

Common opossums live in Central and North America.

Wombats are nocturnal burrowing animals.

The Tasmanian devil is stocky with sharp teeth.

Kangaroos are the biggest of the marsupials, some of them reaching nearly 2m high. They are Australia's equivalent of the herds of antelope that live on the African plains. Kangaroos are not hoofed animals and they move by leaping instead of running, but they graze and browse like antelope and they have a similar head and jaws. Farmers do not like kangaroos because they eat the grass intended for sheep.

ALL KINDS OF KANGAROO

There are about 50 kinds of kangaroo. The smallest are about the size of a rabbit and are called rat kangaroos. The middle-sized ones are often called wallabies. The red kangaroo and the grey kangaroo are the biggest species. They usually live in small groups called mobs. Although they are about as tall as a man when they stand upright, their young, called joeys, are only about 2.5cm long when they are born.

A WIDE VARIETY

Not all marsupials are grazers. Just like the mammals in other parts of the world, Australia's marsupials have adopted all sorts of habits. Possums and gliders live in the trees like monkeys and squirrels, while the koala is like a small bear. There is even a marsupial mole. There are also many carnivorous, or flesh-eating, marsupials, including the dog-like Tasmanian devil.

EXTINCT SPECIES

The Tasmanian wolf, or thylacine, is another dog-like marsupial, but it has not been seen alive since 1936 and is probably extinct. Farmers hunted it because they thought it killed their sheep. Many other Australian marsupials have died out because they were killed by cats and dogs and other mammals introduced by man.

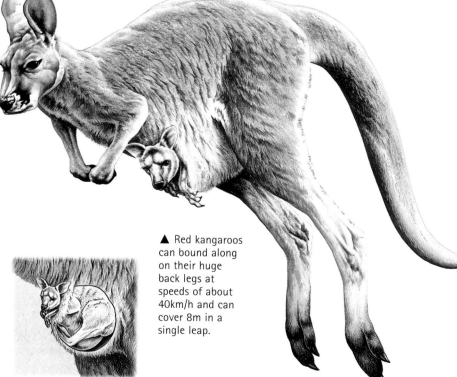

▲ Red kangaroos can bound along on their huge back legs at speeds of about 40km/h and can cover 8m in a single leap.

THE LONG JOURNEY

A kangaroo is born blind and helpless, and looks more like a grub than a kangaroo. As soon as it is born it has to climb up to its mother's pouch, where it starts to feed and grow. It develops long back legs and a long tail, and by six months it is ready to leave the pouch for the first time.

1 The newly born kangaroo crawls over its mother until it reaches the security of the pouch.

2 Inside the pouch, the baby suckles on its mother's milk and starts to grow rapidly.

3 By six months, the joey is old enough to leave its mother's pouch, but it soon jumps back inside if danger threatens.

SEE ALSO
Animal, Australia, Mammal, Zoology

KENYA

Kenya is a country on the east coast of Africa with beautiful scenery and spectacular wild animals. The Equator runs through its centre.

Area: 582,646 sq km
Population: 38,611,000
Capital: Nairobi
Languages: English and Swahili
Currency: Kenyan shilling

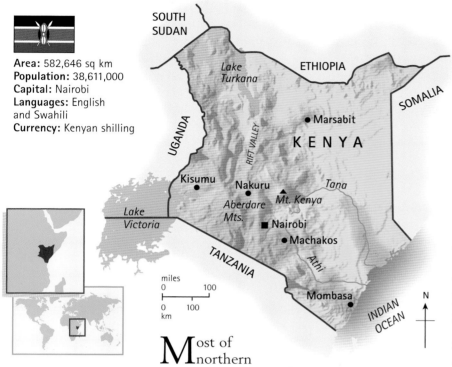

SOUTH SUDAN

ETHIOPIA

SOMALIA

UGANDA

Lake Turkana

• Marsabit

K E N Y A

RIFT VALLEY

Kisumu •

Nakuru •

Aberdare Mts.

▲ Mt. Kenya

Tana

Lake Victoria

■ Nairobi

• Machakos

TANZANIA

Athi

Mombasa •

INDIAN OCEAN

N

miles
0   100

0   100
km

Most of northern Kenya is made up of dry plains. There are also forested highlands in the west and savanna (grassland) to the south. Part of Africa's largest lake, Victoria, is in the west.

MOUNT KENYA

Volcanic mountains lie in the middle of the country close to the Equator. They include Mount Kenya, which is now extinct. At 5,199m, it is the country's highest peak, second only to Tanzania's Mount Kilimanjaro in the whole of Africa.

FARMS AND CITIES

The highlands have fertile soil which is good for farming. On large plantations, Kenyan farmers grow coffee, tea, fruit and vegetables for export. On small plots of land, people raise crops of maize, beans, cassava and potatoes for food. Only 15 per cent of the land is suitable for farming and many Kenyans have left their villages to seek jobs in towns and cities such as Mombasa – the main port – and the capital city, Nairobi.

▲ The Kenyan capital Nairobi has many modern buildings.

▲ Kenya's many national parks and their wildlife are a major tourist attraction.

NATIONAL PARKS

Kenya's wildlife is threatened by poaching. There are 18 national parks, 11 nature reserves and six marine parks where animals are protected. Tourism plays an important part in Kenya's economy.

KENYA'S PEOPLE

Most Kenyans are black Africans, although a small number are of European, Asian and Arab descent. Three fifths of Kenyans are from four ethnic groups: the Kikuyu, the Luhya, the Luo and the Kalenjin. Kenyans are enthusiastic about soccer and athletics. Kenyan runners have won many medals at the Olympic Games.

MODERN KENYA

Some of the earliest-known fossil remains of human beings have been found in parts of Kenya. Kenya was British from 1895. It gained its independence in 1963, and became a republic in 1964. The country's most famous leader of modern times was Jomo Kenyatta, president from 1964 until his death in 1978.

► Peoples such as the Samburu live in Kenya's semi-desert areas.

SEE ALSO

Africa, Animal, Fossil, Mountain and valley

KIDNEY

The kidneys are vital organs that clean the blood by filtering out unwanted substances and excess water. These are then removed from the body as urine.

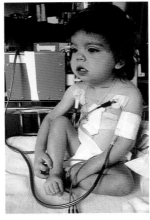

▲ A young girl whose kidneys are not working properly is given regular 'dialysis' treatment. This involves linking her up to a special machine called a hemodialyzer which filters out the waste materials in her blood. Once a suitable donor has been found, she can be given a kidney transplant.

Body processes, such as digesting food or burning energy, produce various waste substances. These are collected from all parts of the body by the blood system and are carried to the kidneys, where they are filtered out. The kidneys are the most important part of the body's excretory system, which is responsible for getting rid of, or excreting, liquid wastes.

A MILLION MICRO-FILTERS

Inside each kidney are two layers. The outer layer – the renal cortex – contains about a million tiny filtering units, called nephrons. Each nephron has a tiny knot of microscopic blood vessels, or capillaries, called a glomerulus, which is surrounded by a double-layered cup – the glomerular, or Bowman's, capsule. As blood flows through the glomerulus, water, minerals, salts and wastes seep out into the glomerular capsule. These substances ooze from the capsule through a long, thin, U-shaped tube, called the nephron loop, or

loop of Henlé, which lies in the kidney's inner layer – the renal medulla.

KEEPING USEFUL SUBSTANCES

Each nephron loop is surrounded by more capillaries, so that useful substances such as minerals and salts can pass from the loop back into the blood. A certain amount of water is also taken back, or reabsorbed. The amount depends on the body's water supplies and is controlled by chemical messengers called hormones.

COLLECTING THE WASTES

The unwanted substances that are left form the urine. This trickles into larger tubes, or collecting ducts, and gathers in the renal pelvis – a space in the middle of the kidney. From here it dribbles into a tube called the ureter and is carried down to the bladder, a stretchy-walled bag in the lower body. The bladder empties by squeezing its muscular wall to force the urine along another tube, the urethra, to the outside.

THE KIDNEYS AT WORK

The kidneys, which are bean-shaped, are positioned centrally in the rear of the body, on either side of the backbone. They receive blood via the renal arteries and, after the blood has been filtered, it is carried away by the renal veins. All the body's blood flows through the kidneys about 350 times a day – that's more than 1,700 litres! It is constantly cleaned and filtered to produce about 1.5 litres of urine each day.

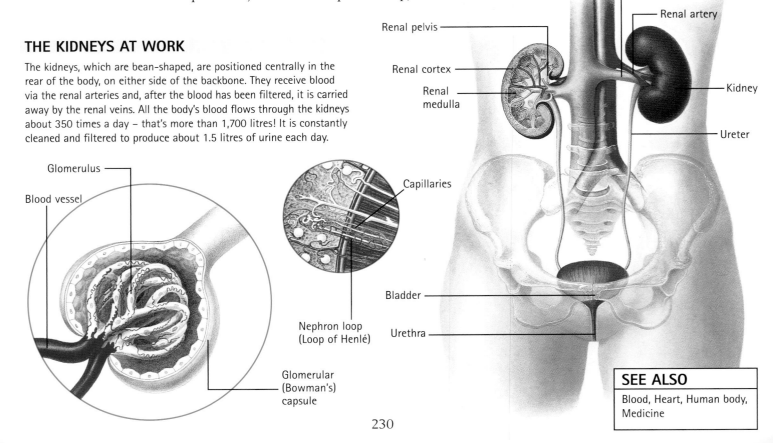

Glomerulus

Blood vessel

Capillaries

Nephron loop (Loop of Henlé)

Glomerular (Bowman's) capsule

Renal pelvis

Renal cortex

Renal medulla

Renal vein

Renal artery

Kidney

Ureter

Bladder

Urethra

SEE ALSO
Blood, Heart, Human body, Medicine

LAKE

A lake is a body of still water that fills a hollow in the Earth's surface. These hollows form in a number of ways, and the water in them can be fresh or salty.

An oxbow lake is a curved section cut off from a meandering river.

Crater lakes form in the tops of old volcanoes or in meteorite craters.

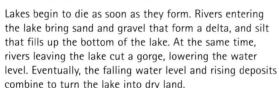
The deepest lakes are fault valley lakes that form where rocks subside.

The water that fills a lake comes from rain, inflowing streams or, sometimes, from springs under the ground. As well as providing an important habitat for many kinds of plant and wildlife, lakes are used by people as a source of water, for fishing, for transport or for fun.

GREAT DEPTHS
The deepest lakes on Earth lie in rift valleys, where parts of the Earth's crust have cracked and sunk. Lake Baikal in Siberia is over 1,600m deep and was formed more than 30 million years ago. It is the world's oldest and deepest lake. Other such lakes include Lake Nyasa in Malawi and Lake Turkana (Rudolf) in Kenya.

THE DEATH OF A LAKE
Lakes begin to die as soon as they form. Rivers entering the lake bring sand and gravel that form a delta, and silt that fills up the bottom of the lake. At the same time, rivers leaving the lake cut a gorge, lowering the water level. Eventually, the falling water level and rising deposits combine to turn the lake into dry land.

GLACIAL WATERS
Most lakes were formed in hollows left behind by the retreating glaciers of the last Ice Age, about 10,000 years ago. Others were formed in depressions between heaps of rocky debris dumped by the glaciers. The Great Lakes of North America and most of the Scottish lochs were formed in this way.

SALT LAKES
Sometimes a lake forms in a hollow with no outlet. Water can then escape only by evaporating, which leaves behind large deposits of salt. The lake between Israel and Jordan known as the Dead Sea is eight times saltier than sea water.

UNIQUE WILDLIFE
Larger lakes support their own wildlife. Lake Baikal is home to 745 animal species and 150 plant species found nowhere else. One example of these is the Baikal seal – one of the few seals found in fresh water. But pollution from industry has become a major problem in many lakes, wiping out numerous species of wildlife.

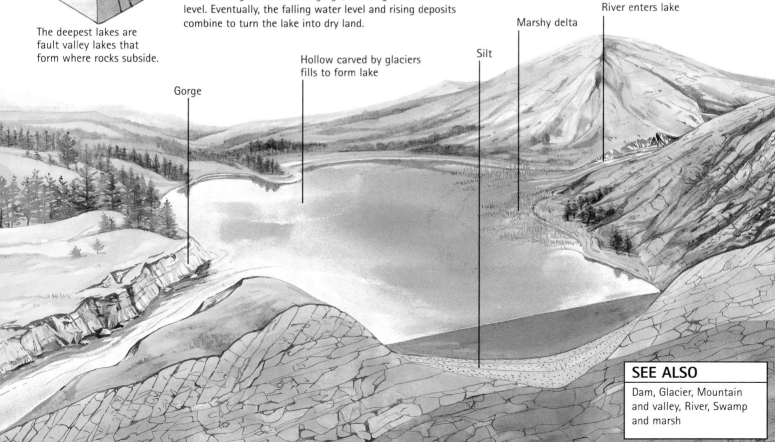
Gorge

Hollow carved by glaciers fills to form lake

Silt

Marshy delta

River enters lake

SEE ALSO
Dam, Glacier, Mountain and valley, River, Swamp and marsh

LANGUAGE

Language is how humans communicate with one another, either through speech, writing or sign language. It comes from the Latin word *lingua*, meaning 'tongue'.

▲ 'Happy New Year' written in a number of different languages.

Language started as a collection of sounds, arranged so that they mean something. Over thousands of years, people developed different languages and then organized the sounds into alphabets. An alphabet is a collection of signs that represent the sounds we use.

▲ The Rosetta Stone, found in Egypt in 1799, helped scholars to read Ancient Egyptian hieroglyphics (left) as the same inscription was written in three languages, including Ancient Greek.

WORLD LANGUAGES

Today, there are around 6,900 languages in the world. Mandarin Chinese is the language spoken by the largest number of people. Next comes English, which is spoken in more countries than any other language. Just over 1,600 languages are spoken in India. People have tried to make up artificial 'universal' languages. The best known and most widely used example is Esperanto, invented in 1887.

HOW LANGUAGES CHANGE

Languages constantly change. New words, such as 'cyberbully', come into use. Old words disappear, for example 'bombard', a cannon. Latin, the language of the Romans, is not spoken but people can read it. Words can also move from one language to another.

English contains many such words, such as 'video' from Latin and 'planet' from Greek.

LANGUAGE FAMILIES

Languages belong to families – groups of related languages which developed from an original parent language. English belongs to the Germanic branch of the large Indo-European language family, while French belongs to the romance branch.

SIGNS AND CODES

Language is not just confined to spoken or written words. Deaf people use sign language, while blind people read Braille, a special alphabet using raised dots. Even codes, such as those used by computers, are called languages.

ABCDE
Roman

ابتثج
Arabic (read right to left)

АБВГД
Cyrillic (Russian)

ΑΒΓΔΕ
Greek

חטיכל
Hebrew (read right to left)

▲ The first five written symbols (letters) of five different alphabets.

香氣治療
Chinese characters

▲ Chinese has no alphabet, but uses up to 40,000 characters, each of which represents an object or idea.

◀ *The Tower of Babel* is the story of how people tried to build a huge tower to reach Heaven. God stopped it from being built by making everyone speak different languages so that they could not understand each other.

SEE ALSO
Communication, Internet, Literature, Media, Newspaper and magazine

232

LASER

A laser is a machine that produces a powerful beam of light. The word 'laser' is short for Light Amplification by Stimulated Emission of Radiation.

Light shows use beams and holograms (3-D images) created by lasers.

Sensors in the nose of a bomb can home in on laser light aimed at a target.

In industry, the high temperature of the laser cuts holes in solid steel.

Lasers give out light in a narrow concentrated beam which is all one wavelength – unlike light from a bulb which goes out in all directions. And while ordinary light spreads out and fades away over long distances, a beam of laser light does not. It can travel for thousands of kilometres as a strong, straight beam.

RUBY OR GAS LASERS
The most common type of laser produces a beam of red light. It is the 'ruby laser', which has a rod-shaped red crystal inside it. Ruby lasers produce flashes or pulses of powerful light. Gas lasers produce a continuous beam. These use coloured liquids or gases instead of crystals. Lasers that use coloured liquids are called 'dye lasers'.

DIRECTING THE BEAM
As laser beams are narrow and intense, they have hundreds of uses. Low-powered laser beams can be reflected (bounced) off objects to find out if they are dark or light, smooth or pitted, still or vibrating. They are used in this way in shops to read price codes on products, to register the pits on CDs or to monitor the vibrations of machines. As laser beams are completely straight, they can also be used as guides on building sites to help in building walls and floors.

THE CUTTING EDGE
High-powered laser beams create enough energy to burn exact holes through solid metal. They are used to cut precise parts for machines

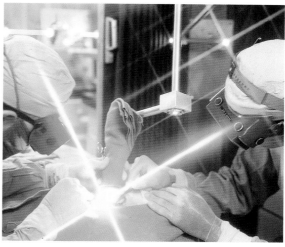

▲ A laser seals as it cuts, so there is less bleeding, making lasers useful for making precision cuts in surgery.

and clothes. Laser beams may also replace the surgeon's knife in delicate operations, such as those on the eye.

3-D IMAGES
One of the most amazing uses of the laser is the hologram. This is a set of ridges that creates a three-dimensional picture (image with depth) when it is seen in the right light. A hologram is produced by scanning a laser beam across the surface of an object. The ridges of the hologram record the way the object reflects light so they can create a 3-D image when light shines on them.

INSIDE A RUBY LASER
A rod of artificial ruby is used as a 'lasing medium'. A powerful lamp directed at the ruby crystal energizes the atoms inside it, so it flashes light. This light is reflected back and forth between two mirrors so that the light waves become 'coherent' (all the same wavelength). It escapes through a tiny hole in one of the mirrors as a narrow 'laser beam' ready to be focused.

Laser beam

Semi-silvered mirror

Totally reflecting mirror

Artificial ruby rod

A coiled fluorescent light provides the energy

SEE ALSO
Astronomy, Light, Surgery, Technology, Telescope

LAW

Laws are the rules people live by. Governments make laws, and law officers and courts see that laws are obeyed and disputes settled.

▲ A traffic policeman in Western Samoa controls the flow of pedestrians across the road. Police act on behalf of the government to enforce the laws of a country and maintain order. They investigate crimes and arrest suspects, patrol the streets, direct traffic, find missing persons and help in times of disaster.

About 4,000 years ago, in Ancient Babylon, King Hammurabi issued a list of laws dealing with such things as stealing and bad workmanship. The ancient Jews based their laws on the Ten Commandments given to Moses by God, as told in the Bible. The early Greeks invented democracy – law-making by all the people – and the Romans gave us most of the kinds of law we still use today, such as family law, property law and criminal law. Emperor Justinian I of the Byzantine Empire drew up his famous Code of Civil Law in 534CE.

TOWARDS MODERN LAW

A big step towards modern law came in 1215, when King John of England signed Magna Carta – an agreement to govern according to the law. Later, parliaments rather than kings began to make laws. In 1804, Emperor Napoleon I of France introduced the Napoleonic Code, which is still the basis for much French law today.

UPHOLDING THE LAW

In a democracy, laws are proposed by governments, passed by legislatures (a congress or parliament) and enforced by the police and courts. People accused of breaking a law may have to go to court, where lawyers (people trained in the law) argue the case, presenting evidence and questioning witnesses. A group of ordinary people, called the jury, decides whether the accused is guilty or not guilty. The judge decides the punishment – this could be a number of years in prison, a fine (payment of money) or community service.

COURT PROCEDURE

A person accused of breaking the criminal law is innocent until proven guilty by a court of law. The lawyers put the case to the jury. The prosecution tries to prove that the defendant is guilty and the defence tries to show that he or she is innocent. Then it is up to the jury to decide.

Jury A body of people (usually 12) who swear under oath to listen to the evidence and make a decision based upon it

Judge The person who oversees court proceedings, rules on law and, where guilt is proven, decides on the form of punishment

Defendant The person accused of breaking the law in the witness box (where he can be questioned by the lawyers)

Prosecution lawyer He or she provides evidence of the defendant's guilt, questioning witnesses and scientific experts, and presenting physical evidence

Stenographer The person who keeps a record of everything that is said during the course of a trial

Defence lawyer The lawyer who acts on behalf of the defendant to show his or her innocence

Physical evidence Items which are put before the jury, presented to prove the defendant's guilt or innocence.

SEE ALSO

Civil rights, Democracy, Mesopotamia, Roman Empire

LEAF

Leaves use energy from sunlight to make food for plants and are themselves a source of food for animals. They also produce the oxygen we need to breathe.

The horse chestnut has a compound leaf made up of separate leaflets.

Maple leaves are hand-shaped, or palmate, with no separate leaflets.

The ash leaf is made up of several pinnate (spindle-shaped) leaflets.

The cherry has a simple pinnate leaf with tiny saw-like serrations at the edges.

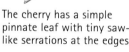

Pine needles are long, thin evergreen leaves that grow in clusters.

Leaves are the food factories of green plants. They come in a variety of shapes and sizes, and help us to identify the different species of plants. The branching pattern of veins on the surface of a leaf is part of a network of tubes that carry water and food to all parts of the plant. The large vein that runs across the centre of the leaf is called the midrib.

MAKING FOOD

The main function of leaves is to make food for the plant. This process, known as photosynthesis, takes place in tiny bodies, called chloroplasts, in the leaf cells. These contain a green-coloured substance called chlorophyll that absorbs light energy. The energy is used to turn water and carbon

LEAF DESIGN

Leaves are designed to catch as much sunlight and lose as little water as possible. Stiff veins hold the leaf out to the light, and cells are transparent so that light can reach the chloroplasts. The outer layer, or cuticle, is waterproof, and most of the stomata are on the underside of the leaf, shielded from drying breezes.

dioxide gas from the air into food molecules, such as starch and sugar. The by-product of this process is oxygen gas, some of which is used by the plant for respiration. The rest passes into the air. Nearly all living things need oxygen to survive.

TRANSPIRATION

Leaves also help the plant to draw water up from the soil, by a process called transpiration. As the water evaporates (dries) from tiny pores, or stomata, in the leaf's surface, more water is sucked up from the roots to replace it. Each pore is bound by two 'guard' cells that can open or close the opening to control water loss. The water moves up the stem through fine tubes called xylem vessels. Another set of tubes, the phloem vessels, carries food around the plant.

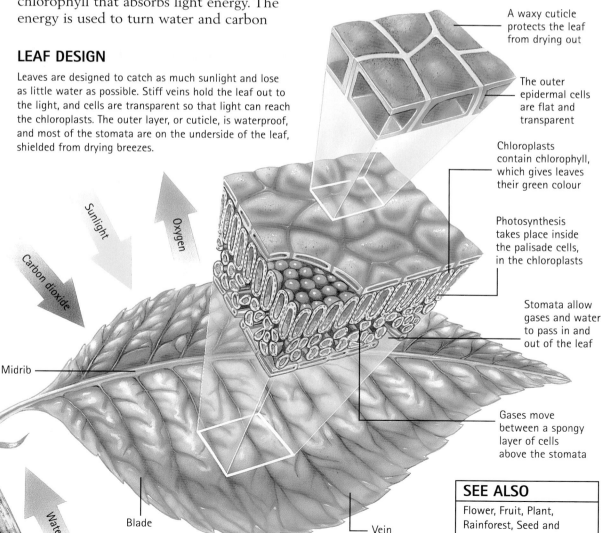

A waxy cuticle protects the leaf from drying out

The outer epidermal cells are flat and transparent

Chloroplasts contain chlorophyll, which gives leaves their green colour

Photosynthesis takes place inside the palisade cells, in the chloroplasts

Stomata allow gases and water to pass in and out of the leaf

Gases move between a spongy layer of cells above the stomata

Sunlight

Oxygen

Carbon dioxide

Water

Midrib

Blade

Vein

SEE ALSO

Flower, Fruit, Plant, Rainforest, Seed and pollination, Tree

LENS

Lenses are transparent objects with at least one curved surface that help us focus on an image by bending rays of light. They are usually made of glass or plastic.

Glasses help us see if our eye lenses don't work properly.

The lens in a camera focuses light onto the film inside.

Optical microscopes use lenses to magnify objects from 100 to 2,000 times.

Lenses in a pair of binoculars help you see things that are far away.

Some periscopes use lenses to enlarge the image reflected from the mirrors at either end.

When light travels through a lens, it slows down. This is because light travels faster through air than through other transparent substances like water, glass and plastic. As it slows down it bends off course. This effect, called 'refraction', is why a straw put in a glass of water at an angle looks bent. The bending distorts the image seen by the eye and can be used to make an object seem bigger or smaller.

DISTORTED IMAGES
If you put a magnifying glass close to the page of a book, you'll see a larger-than-life version of the page below it. This happens

BENDING LIGHT
There are two kinds of simple lens: convex (or converging) lenses which enlarge the image and concave (or diverging) lenses which are thicker at the edges than the middle and reduce the image.

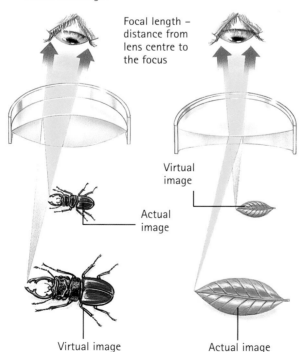

Focal length – distance from lens centre to the focus

Actual image

Virtual image

Virtual image

Actual image

CONVEX LENS
Rays of light passing through the lens are bent inwards. A magnified image is produced behind the object.

CONCAVE LENS
Light rays are bent outwards, so they spread out (diverge) producing a reduced image between the object and the lens.

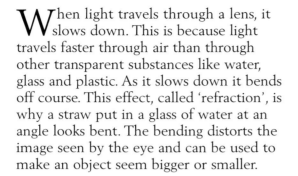

▶ A magnifying glass has a convex lens — a lens that's thicker at the middle than the edges. The image seen depends on how close you hold the glass.

because light rays from the page have been bent away from each other by the lens. Light rays from distant objects are bent towards each other by a magnifying glass. If it's dark enough, you can catch these rays on a sheet of paper. If you put the paper the right distance from the lens, they will form a focused (sharp) image.

GETTING FOCUSED
The distance from the lens to the piece of paper is called the 'focal length' of the lens. In general, a thick lens bends light more than a thin one, so it has a shorter focal length. A camera uses a convex lens to produce sharp images on a sheet of film. Specialist cameras also use concave lenses – that are thicker at the edges than the middle. These are used to reduce large images, like landscapes, onto a photograph.

EYE LENSES
Our eyeballs act like giant convex lenses that focus (bend) light onto the backs of our eyes. The muscles of our eyes pull the lenses flatter when we want to focus on objects in the distance, or make the lenses thicker to help us focus on nearby objects.

SEE ALSO
Astronomy, Laser, Light, Microscope, Photography, Sight, Telescope

LIGHT

Light is a visible form of energy. It moves faster than anything else in the universe, travelling 300,000,000 metres in a single second. Without light we cannot see.

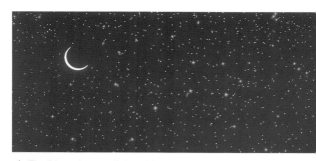
▲ The Moon has no light of its own – it shines only because it reflects the Sun's light. Stars, however, are luminous because they produce their own light.

SIR ISAAC NEWTON
The English scientist and mathematician (1642–1726) demonstrated that light was broken into different colours by shining light through a prism.

The Sun, our nearest star, is our main source of light. Although it is nearly 150 million kilometres away, the light it makes reaches the Earth in only eight minutes and is so strong that it damages our eyes if we look straight at it. At night, when our part of Earth faces away from the Sun, we have to use light bulbs or candles for light. Compared to the Sun, the light energy made by these is tiny. They can only light up objects a few metres away.

CASTING SHADOWS
Light can travel through air, water and other transparent (see-through) materials. Unlike sound, it can also travel through a vacuum, or empty space. Materials that only allow some light through, and are not transparent, are said to be translucent. Many materials, like wood and metal, are opaque – they block light. If you shine a light at an opaque object, you will see a dark patch behind it – the shadow. This has exactly the same outline as the object because light travels in straight lines.

INVISIBLE ENERGY
There are many other types of energy, including radio waves, microwaves and X-rays, that travel just like light. In fact, light is only one tiny part of a huge range of energy forms, called the electromagnetic spectrum. Over the last century or so, people have built a variety of machines, such as scanning equipment, microwave ovens and radios, that can detect or make use of the invisible parts of this spectrum.

▲ When light shines through a prism (a glass triangle), it splits into the colours of the spectrum.
▶ This also happens when light shines through water (rain) causing a rainbow.

▲ There are two basic ways to produce artificial light: through heat (known as incandescence), as in an electric light bulb, or by making a gas glow, as in a fluorescent light.

▲ Glow worms, the glowing larvae of fireflies, have light organs under their abdomen which produce a heatless light known as bioluminescence.
▶ Many deep-sea fish have similar light organs on their sides to help them find food and mates in the dark.

SEE ALSO
Colour, Electricity, Energy, Laser, Lens, Microscope, Moon, Sun, Wavelength

LITERATURE

Literature is the art of writing fine prose or poetry. This often involves story-telling, but may also include history, biography and information books.

People told each other stories and poems long before they learned to write. This is 'oral' (spoken) literature. Most modern literature is written in the form of books or is performed as drama.

GREAT STORY-TELLERS

The Ancient Greeks told stories in poetry and in drama about heroes and gods. The poem by Homer called the *Iliad* tells of

▲ Good literature is written to be enjoyed and it provides hours of entertainment for the cost of a single book.

► Long John Silver, the charming but deadly pirate, appeared in *Treasure Island*, a novel written by the Scottish author Robert Louis Stevenson in 1881.

► Rapunzel used her hair as a climbing rope in a German tale recorded by the Grimm Brothers.

the heroes who fought at the siege of Troy. In China and India, poets told tales of how the world began and the mysteries of life and death.

WRITING IT DOWN

A few oral works were written down, such as the epic English poem *Beowulf* in about 750CE. Books were copied by hand throughout the Middle Ages, when Geoffrey Chaucer (c.1342–1400) wrote a collection of stories called *The Canterbury Tales*. After 1455, the printing press made it possible to copy books cheaply and easily. A 'golden age' of literature began in many countries.

THE NOVEL

The novel is a long story in prose. During the 19th century, ordinary people learned to read and the novel became popular. Some novels were published as serials in magazines. Leading novelists of the time included Britain's Charles Dickens, France's Victor Hugo and Leo Tolstoy in Russia.

POETRY

Poets aim to raise emotions in the reader by putting words together in striking ways. Often poetry has a rhythmical 'beat', and line-endings may rhyme. A poem may be short, like a Japanese three-line *haiku*, or long, like

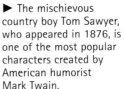
► The mischievous country boy Tom Sawyer, who appeared in 1876, is one of the most popular characters created by American humorist Mark Twain.

◀ Hamlet, the moody Danish prince, was created by the English playwright William Shakespeare, based on an old Danish tale.

John Milton's 12-book *Paradise Lost*. A poem can tell a story, make the reader laugh, or reveal the poet's innermost feelings.

DRAMA

Plays were performed in Ancient Greece, but modern drama dates from the 16th century. Although there may be stage directions, dramatic literature is largely dialogue and relies on acting for its power. Movie scripts use special effects, lighting and camera angles to make the dialogue more effective.

HOW WRITERS WORK

Writers watch and listen, invent plots and characters, and note down interesting

things that happen. Many writers stick to one kind of book, such as humour, horror, crime, romance, religion, art or philosophy. Some writers tell their own life story in an autobiography, others write about famous people in a biography, or about the past as history. Writers

▲ Alice, from the book *Alice in Wonderland* by Lewis Carroll, which appeared in 1865.

▶ The story of Don Quixote and his servant Sancho Panza, by the Spanish author Miguel de Cervantes, has been translated into over 60 languages.

▶ D'Artagnan, hero of the French novel *The Three Musketeers*, was created by Alexandre Dumas in 1844 and has featured in several movies.

work in every field, from aviation to zoology. Writers produce articles for newspapers, magazines and the Internet, and scripts for radio, television and films.

CHILDREN'S WRITERS

There were few books written for children before the 18th century. Today, some of the best writers create stories for children. A few books, such as A.A. Milne's *Winnie the Pooh*, become classics, with their characters known around the world.

PUBLISHING A WORK

There are two main kinds of literature: fiction (stories) and non-fiction (factual books, from cookery recipes to encyclopedias). Every book starts with a writer who either thinks up an idea or is asked to write a book by a publishing company. The publisher pays the writer for the book, and sees to the editing, design, illustration and printing or publishing as an e-book. By selling large quantities of books to readers, the publisher hopes to make a profit.

Charles Dickens (1812–1870) was one of the greatest English novelists.

Dante (1265–1321) began modern Italian literature with his *Divine Comedy*.

The American Edgar Allan Poe (1809–49) wrote poetry and horror stories.

Murasaki Shikibu (c.978–c.1014) wrote the *Tale of Genji* in Japan about 1005.

SEE ALSO

Film, Greece (Ancient), Language, Myth and legend, Printing, Theatre

LUNGS AND RESPIRATORY SYSTEM

The lungs are two pinkish-grey, spongy, cone-shaped organs inside the chest. The respiratory system consists of the nose, throat, windpipe, lower airways and lungs.

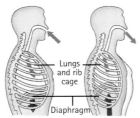

Breathing in   Breathing out

▲ When breathing in, the rib cage expands and the diaphragm is lowered. These actions happen in reverse when breathing out.

Lungs and rib cage

Diaphragm

FAST FACTS

- Adult lungs hold three to five litres of air

- At rest, an average person takes about 12-15 breaths each minute. Each breath consists of about half a litre of air

- After great activity, the breathing rate can rise to 60 breaths per minute with over three litres of air per breath

Oxygen is essential for almost every living thing, including the human body. When we breathe in, our lungs take in fresh air, absorb oxygen from it and pass it to the blood, which carries it to all the parts of the body. Fresh air is taken into the lungs by breathing, or respiration. This process is powered by two sets of muscles – the diaphragm below the lungs and the intercostal muscles between the ribs, in front of the lungs.

IN AND OUT

To breathe in, the diaphragm tenses, shortens and flattens. The intercostals also shorten and pull the ribs upward and forward. These movements stretch the lungs, making them larger, and suck fresh air in through the nose and mouth, down the throat and windpipe, into the lungs. To breathe out, the diaphragm relaxes and the stretched lungs spring back to their normal size, pushing stale air out.

OXYGEN IN

Dark bluish-red, low-oxygen blood flows to each lung along the pulmonary artery. This divides many times to form a vast network of microscopic blood vessels, or capillaries, which enclose tiny balloons called alveoli. Oxygen from the air inside each alveolus seeps easily through its thin lining and the thin capillary wall, into the blood. This makes the blood bright red. The capillaries join to form the pulmonary vein, which carries the high-oxygen blood away.

CARBON DIOXIDE OUT

In addition to taking in oxygen, the respiratory system also removes one of the body's waste products, carbon dioxide. This seeps the opposite way to oxygen – from the blood into the alveolus – and is breathed out as stale air.

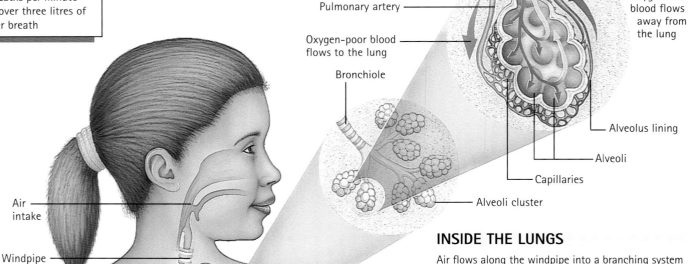

Air intake

Windpipe (trachea)

Pulmonary artery

Oxygen-poor blood flows to the lung

Bronchiole

Pulmonary vein

Oxygen-rich blood flows away from the lung

Alveolus lining

Alveoli

Capillaries

Alveoli cluster

Upper lobe of lung

Bronchus

Lower lobe of lung

INSIDE THE LUNGS

Air flows along the windpipe into a branching system of tubes called bronchi. These divide many times, becoming smaller and thinner. Deep in the lungs they form very fine tubes, or bronchioles, each of which ends in a tiny clump of microscopic air sacs, called alveoli. There are over 350 million alveoli in each lung.

SEE ALSO

Blood, Heart, Human body, Muscle

Machine

A machine is a device that makes work easier by enabling us to use force to complete a task. It can be simple, like a screwdriver, or complicated, like a car.

Simple machines make work easier and can be used as parts of more complex devices. There are six main types of machine: the lever, pulley, and wheel and axle (which are all forms of levers), and the screw, inclined or sloping plane, and wedge (all forms of inclined planes).

BASIC MACHINES

By using a lever, you can increase the effect of the force, or effort, you apply. The machine needs a fulcrum (a fixed point) to support it. By positioning the fulcrum carefully, a small effort applied at one end of the lever, can raise a big load at the other end. Heavy weights can be moved using an inclined plane (pushing goods up a ramp is easier than lifting them), or on rollers, like the logs used by pyramid builders to move slabs, or by a wheel turning on an axle.

MAGNIFIED FORCE

A screw can either pull things together or push them apart (like a jack). A pulley system uses wheels to change the direction of a force produced by pulling on a rope. The wedge (an axe, for example) can be used to split materials.

Corkscrews make use of screw and lever actions. The screw's spiral thread gives a tight grip.

A pair of scissors is a double lever. The screw is the fixed point or fulcrum; the blades pivot around it.

A can opener acts as a wedge, forcing its way into the lid while cogged wheels turn the cutter.

THE EARLIEST MACHINES

The potter's wheel, invented around 3500BCE, was one of the first machines. Others include the spindle, for spinning fibres into yarn; the loom, for weaving yarn into cloth; the plough, for turning heavy soil; and bellows, for blowing air into fires.

WAR AND WORK

Early war inventions include the battering ram (a wedge), and the catapult (a lever). An important development of the wheel was the gear. A gear wheel combines the principles of wheel and lever. As it turns, its teeth, or cogs, mesh with other toothed wheels. In this way it can change the speed and direction of the force applied, depending on the number and spacing of the teeth.

INVENTIVE PAST

The Ancient Greeks used screws, lathes (used for turning wood), construction cranes and watermills – the first machines to use non-animal power. They discovered that steam could be used to drive machines. But neither the Greeks nor the equally inventive Chinese were interested in labour-saving machines, because slaves were cheap and plentiful. ▶

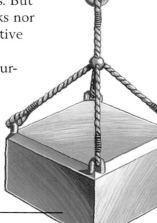

Pulley wheels

Having four wheels allows four times the load to be lifted with the same effort

— Effort

Load —

RAISING THE LOAD

The simplest type of pulley is a wheel with a grooved rim. A rope or chain is passed around the groove. The pulley changes the direction of a force, so by pulling down on the rope, a person can raise a heavy weight. The more pulleys there are with one rope running through them, the greater the load that can be lifted with the same effort.

TAKING THE STRAIN

Lifts can be hydraulic or operated by electric traction, like the one here. Hoisting ropes, made of steel cables, are raised or lowered by a pulley wheel, turned by an electric motor. In the 1850s, engineer Elisha G. Otis invented the first lift featuring an automatic safety device — a safety clamp — which would prevent the lift from falling if the rope broke.

MEDIEVAL MACHINES

Important mechanical inventions of the Middle Ages included the crossbow, windmill, clockwork and the printing press. In the 13th century, the English monk Roger Bacon predicted the use of cars, aeroplanes and submarines long before the technology and materials required for such inventions were even available.

MACHINES REPLACE WORKERS

As labour became more expensive, it made economic sense to make machines do more work. From the 18th century, a new kind of mechanized industry developed. In the United States, the Federal Armory in Springfield, Massachusetts, pioneered the mechanized manufacture of muskets for the army. In Britain, the engineer Marc Brunel designed 43 machines that could make 10,000 pulley-blocks a year, enabling the Royal Navy dockyard to reduce the workforce required for the task from 110 to just ten.

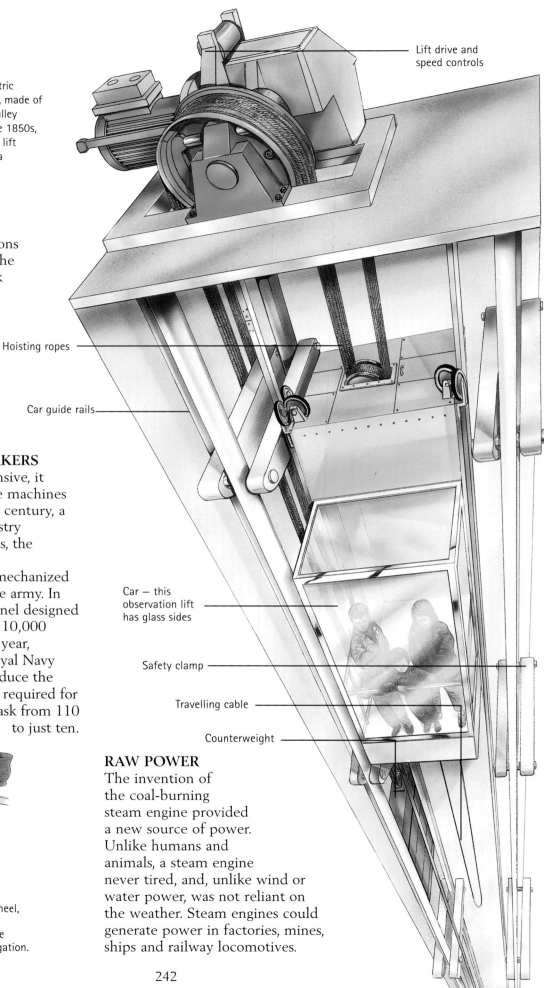

Lift drive and speed controls

Hoisting ropes

Car guide rails

Car — this observation lift has glass sides

Safety clamp

Travelling cable

Counterweight

▲ From the invention of the potter's wheel, someone got the idea for the cartwheel. Fitted with pots, a wheel could also raise water from one level to another, for irrigation.

RAW POWER

The invention of the coal-burning steam engine provided a new source of power. Unlike humans and animals, a steam engine never tired, and, unlike wind or water power, was not reliant on the weather. Steam engines could generate power in factories, mines, ships and railway locomotives.

MACHINES THROUGH HISTORY

100,000 years ago Stone Age people use simple machines like the lever, wedge and inclined plane

5000BCE The plough (a form of wedge) is used

3500BCE The potter's wheel is an early invention

3200BCE Mesopotamians use the cartwheel

2600BCE Ancient Egyptians use the inclined plane and rollers to move stone blocks for pyramids

200BCE The Archimedes screw (like a large corkscrew) is used to raise water from rivers for irrigation

1767 The spinning jenny transforms textile industry

1804 Steam locomotives give power to the wheel

THE FACTORY AGE

To make machines for manufacture, machine tools were needed to stamp out metal plates, cut screws and gears, and shape metals by cutting, drilling, grinding or polishing. Standardization of parts made it easier to keep machines working and repair them quickly. Important new inventions included the dynamo, the electric motor, and the hydraulic press and ram. The clothing and shoe-making industries were transformed by the sewing machine, invented in 1846.

THREAT TO JOBS

The use of machines in industry greatly increased output and made factory goods cheaper. But there was a human cost. Workers, including women and children, toiled for low pay in bad conditions. In the 1880s, social critics like the Englishman William Morris complained that machines were destroying craftsmanship, reducing people to a form of slavery. Some people smashed machines they thought would take away their work.

WORK REVOLUTION

The machine revolution affected farming, where machines took over harvesting, baling and threshing. Transport and trade were revolutionized in the mid–1800s by the locomotive, steamship and conveyor belt. Machines invaded offices and shops, at first in the form of typewriters and cash registers.

THE MODERN WORLD

New machines, such as the car and the aeroplane, began to transform the world at the beginning of the 20th century. The invention of the jet engine and the rocket allowed people to travel at speeds that had been unimaginable before. In the home, ancient devices like the butter churn and the washboard were discarded, and the washing machine, vacuum cleaner and the food processor took pride of place. In industry, robots and increasingly efficient computers took over many basic production processes. New materials, such as plastic, ceramics and carbon fibres, have replaced metals to make machines that are smaller, yet more efficient.

▲ Car jacks can be manual (like the screw car jack above) or hydraulic. They are machines that are designed to raise and support a heavy load, like a car, little by little. By turning a handle many times, the operator applies a small force pushing a long way; this force is converted to pushing a large force (the car) a short way.

▶ A forklift truck is a machine that raises weights using liquid pressure (hydraulics). Simple hydraulic machines have a cylinder with a large and a small piston inside. The cylinder is filled with fluid. A force applied to the small piston is transferred to the larger one, increasing the force.

◀ A snowblower has two engines: one drives the truck, the other turns the drum. As it turns, blades on the drum churn the snow, forcing it upward through the chutes. As the truck moves forward, it takes in more snow.

SEE ALSO

Car, Engine, Household appliance, Industrial Revolution, Industry, Invention, Robot

MAGNETISM

Magnetism is a force that pulls objects made of iron, nickel or cobalt towards magnets. Scientists do not fully understand how this force is created.

The horseshoe magnet has a pole at each end.

So does the simple bar magnet.

A ring magnet has one pole on its outer surface and another pole on its inner one.

If you have ever moved a magnet towards a pin, you have experienced magnetism. Pins are made of steel – a material that consists mainly of iron – and they feel a strong force pulling them towards the magnet, which may even be strong enough to make them stick to it. Any material, like steel, that is attracted towards a magnet in this way is called a magnetic material.

MAGNETIC POLES

When an object is attracted to a magnet, it sticks to its ends – this is where the magnet exerts, or gives out, the greatest force. The two ends of the magnet are called its poles. One of them is north-seeking and the other is south-seeking. They need to be marked in some way so you can tell them apart. If you bring the same poles of two magnets face to face, they will repel each other; if you bring different poles of two magnets face to face, they will attract each other.

► Industrial electro-magnets are powerful enough to lift heavy pieces of scrap iron.

ELECTRO-MAGNETISM

In 1820, a Danish physicist, Hans Christian Oersted, discovered that magnetism was produced by an electric current. This led to the development of the electromagnet – a temporary magnet formed when an electric current passes through a conductor such as wire, which is wrapped around an iron core. Electromagnets are useful because they can be turned on or off and altered in strength. They can produce magnetic fields strong enough to drive generators and electric motors. Smaller ones are used to make doorbells and buzzers work.

MAGNETIC EARTH

The Earth itself acts like a huge magnet with magnetic poles at its north and south ends — known as the magnetic north pole and the magnetic south pole. These poles act like the ends of a magnet and make compass needles point north. They are close to the geographic North and South Poles, which are at the top and bottom of the imaginary line, or axis, around which the earth spins.

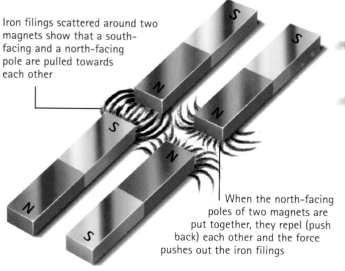

Iron filings scattered around two magnets show that a south-facing and a north-facing pole are pulled towards each other

When the north-facing poles of two magnets are put together, they repel (push back) each other and the force pushes out the iron filings

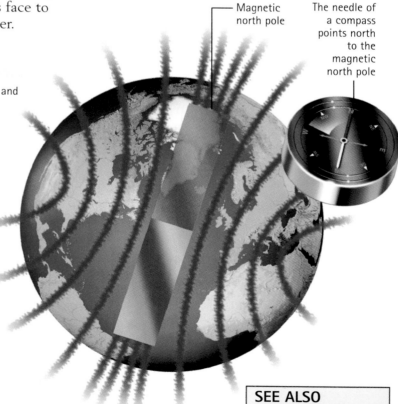

Magnetic north pole

The needle of a compass points north to the magnetic north pole

SEE ALSO

Antarctica, Arctic, Earth, Electricity, Iron and steel, Metal

MALAYSIA

Malaysia is a fast-growing nation in Southeast Asia, consisting of Peninsular Malaysia and the areas of Sabah and Sarawak on the island of Borneo.

Area: 329,847 sq km
Population: 28,334,000
Capitals: Kuala Lumpur and Putrajaya
Language: Bahasa Melayu
Currency: Ringgit (Malaysian dollar)

The two regions that make up Malaysia lie 650km apart, across the South China Sea. The climate is hot, humid and rainy, and there are swamps, rainforests and golden beaches. The many mountains include Mount Kinabalu (4,100m), the highest peak in Southeast Asia.

▲ Sarawak has a swampy coastal plain and many rivers. In some villages, people live in houses raised on stilts.

▲ Workers tap rubber trees for their latex. Rubber is a major export, as well as tin, gas, oil, palm oil, hardwood, tea, cocoa and pineapples.

RURAL AND CITY LIFE
Wildlife includes giant turtles and over a thousand types of orchid. Traditionally, Malays lived in rural areas, in villages called *kampongs*, but 72 per cent of the population now lives in towns and cities. Kuala Lumpur has many modern buildings, including the 452-metre Petronas Twin Towers, and is Malaysia's largest city.

GROWING INDUSTRIES
Malaysia has fertile soil and the most important food crop is rice. It is the second largest palm oil producer after Indonesia and also has large deposits of minerals. The country is growing rapidly as an industrial power and is a major producer of electronic components, textiles, cement, cars and tyres. Tourism is also growing.

MALAYSIA'S PEOPLES
Half the population are Malays and nearly a quarter are Chinese. Other groups include native peoples of Borneo and the Malay peninsula, and Indians (mainly Tamils). Malay is the national language, but Chinese, Tamil and English are also widely spoken. Islam is the official religion, but about 40 per cent of the people practise other religions, including Buddhism, Christianity and Hinduism.

CHINESE ANCESTORS
The ancestors of today's Malays came from China around 2000BCE. The Arabs, Portuguese and Dutch all occupied the area before the British seized control in the early 1800s, eventually granting independence in 1957. Today's Malaysia was formed in 1963.

▲ Traditional crafts include working with textiles. In the north of Peninsular Malaysia, batik work is popular.

SEE ALSO

Indonesia, Rainforest, Southeast Asia

MAMMAL

Mammals are vertebrates (they have backbones). They have adapted to a wider range of habitats and show a greater variety of forms than any other animal group.

◀ The armadillo is covered in bony plates that protect it from predators. When attacked, it curls up into a tight ball.

Orang-utans are one of about 300 primates. This group includes humans.

The bat is the only mammal that can fly. Its forelimbs act as wings.

There are about 320 types of marsupial, mostly found in the Australian region.

Flesh-eating mammals like the hyena have strong teeth called canines.

Marine mammals like the seal have short fur and streamlined bodies.

The duck billed platypus is one of only five species of egg-laying mammal.

All mammals are warm-blooded, which means they can keep their bodies warm and stay active even in the coldest weather. The only other animals that can do this are birds. Most mammals are covered with hair or fur, which helps keep them warm. Unlike other animal babies, young mammals feed on their mother's milk. Mammals also have larger brains than other animals.

A SUCCESSFUL GROUP
The first mammals appeared on Earth about 200 million years ago as small, insect-eating creatures. When dinosaurs died out about 65 million years ago, mammals began to explore different habitats and try different foods. They became larger and took on many different shapes. Thousands of 'experimental' mammals have come and gone during the last 50 million years, but only about 4,660 different species live in the world today.

VARIETY OF HABITAT
Mammals are not as numerous as birds or fish, but they can be found in almost every habitat: some live in seas and rivers; some spend their lives high up in the trees of the forest; antelopes and other grazing mammals form huge herds on grasslands. Some mammals manage to survive in the driest deserts and on the coldest mountain tops. Bats have taken to the air; seals, whales and dolphins to the seas.

THE RIGHT TEETH
Mammals eat a wide range of foods and most have teeth designed to suit their diets. Most plant-eating mammals (herbivores), such as horses and elephants, have large grinding teeth at the back of the mouth. Rodents have sharp, chisel-like front teeth for gnawing nuts and other hard foodstuffs. Flesh-eating mammals (carnivores), such as lions and wolves, have large, sharp canines for stabbing and seizing prey, and sharp-edged cheek teeth for slicing off flesh.

CARE OF THE YOUNG
Young mammals learn many of their survival skills during the period that they are with their mother, feeding on her milk. At birth, lion cubs are blind and helpless, weighing only about 1.5kg. The mother carries them in her mouth, one at a time, from one hiding place to another; the male protects his family from intruders. Only when the cubs are between 18 and 24 months old will the lioness have another litter.

MAMMAL OF THE DESERT

The two-humped Bactrian camel of central Asia is well adapted to life in the desert. It can travel for days or even weeks with no food or water because it carries a large store of fat in its humps, which it converts into food. At the end of a long period without food, the humps lose much of their firmness, and may even flop to one side. With its bushy eyebrows and long lashes, the camel can shield its eyes from the sand. It can even close its nostrils during a sandstorm. A close relative of the Bactrian camel is the Arabian camel, or dromedary, which has only one hump.

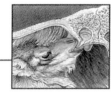

COVERED IN FUR
One of a mammal's main characteristics is its fur. A Bactrian camel's fur can grow to 25cm on its head, neck and humps. Camels grow a new coat once a year.

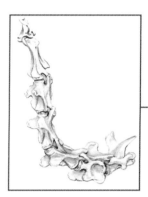

NECK BONES
All mammals, apart from the manatee and sloth, have seven cervical vertebrae (bones that make up the neck).

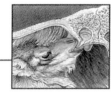

A MOTHER'S MILK
Mammals are the only animals to feed their young with milk – produced in special glands called mammae.

LICKING AND SIFTING

Omnivorous mammals, which include humans, eat plants and animals. Insect-eaters, such as shrews and hedgehogs, have lots of small, sharply pointed teeth, but anteaters have no teeth at all: they lap up ants with their sticky tongue. Some whales have no teeth: they sift tiny creatures from the water through plates of horny material called baleen or whalebone.

EGGS AND POUCHES

A tiny number of mammals, such as the duck billed platypus, are unusual because they lay eggs. Others, called marsupials, are also known as pouched mammals, because the female nurses her babies in a pouch or pocket on her body. About 50 million years ago, marsupials lived all over the world, but they are now found mainly in the Australian region, with a few in North and South America. All other mammals, known as placental mammals, give birth to live young.

THE LARGEST GROUP

Placental mammals are by far the biggest group of mammal. While the baby is inside its mother, it gets food and oxygen from her blood through a structure called the placenta. A placental mammal baby can stay inside its mother's body for much longer than a marsupial baby. A baby elephant, for example, grows inside its mother for about 22 months and is well developed when it is born. Some baby mammals can run about soon after they are born, but many others, including human babies, are quite helpless at birth.

FAST FACTS

• With their relatively large brains, mammals have a greater ability to learn than other animals

• Special mammal senses include the bat's sonar and the mole's ultra-sensitive whiskers

• The largest mammal is the blue whale, which grows up to 30m long

SEE ALSO

Animal, Bat, Bear, Cat, Dog, Hippopotamus, Horse, Kangaroo, Monkey, Platypus, Prehistoric animal, Rat, Rhinoceros, Tiger, Whale and dolphin, Wolf, Zoology

MAP

Maps show the Earth, or a part of it, on paper. They may show travellers a route, or they may display weather patterns, land use and other information.

A pedometer is used to measure distance.

A theodolite gives the direction of distant objects.

Stereo viewers give a 3-D image from aerial photos.

From the earliest times, people have drawn sketch maps to describe a route or place. Only in the past 400 years has science made it possible to draw accurate maps of the entire world.

CHARTS IN CLAY

The first maps were drawn on clay tablets about 2300BC in Mesopotamia. They showed nearby towns and how to reach them, but were not at all accurate. In about AD140 the scientist Claudius Ptolemy produced a book on geography which contained many maps. Soon afterwards, the Roman army produced a map of cities and forts based on accurate measurements of the roads in between.

SEA CHARTS

The European sailors who travelled to other continents from the 1450s onwards needed charts that included information such as depth of the sea, strength of currents and how best to enter a harbour.

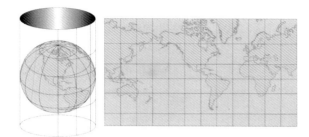

▲ Maps using Mercator's projection, invented in 1569, allow sailors and pilots to plot their course accurately, but distort areas close to the North and South Poles.

▶ Maps using Peter's projection, developed in 1973, give accurate areas but distort shapes.

Modern charts contain similar information, together with locations of lighthouses and radio beacons.

MAPS TO SCALE

Cartographers (map makers) often use computers to draw maps. Most maps are made to a scale, meaning that distances on the map are related to distances on the ground. A map of scale 1:100,000 means that 1cm on the map equals 100,000 cm, or 1km, on the ground. Some maps are deliberately inaccurate. For example, a map of a motorway does not need to show corners or distances, but only which towns can be reached from each exit.

READING THE MEANING

Maps may contain many different types of information. The most familiar maps are those showing road and rail routes for travellers. Scientists may create maps showing how many people live in different areas, what land is used for, or the types of soil to be found. Maps showing temperatures and air conditions are used for weather forecasting. All maps rely on accurate surveying, the collecting of information by people on the ground and the transferring of this to the maps.

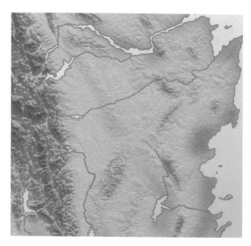

▲ Relief maps show physical features, such as rivers, plains, hills and mountains.

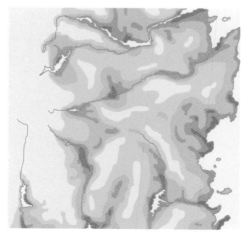

▲ Here, population density is shown by colours. Dark colours are the areas with the most people.

▲ Route maps may show roads, railways and built-up areas to help travellers find their way.

SEE ALSO

Navigation

MATERIALS

People use a huge range of different materials with which to make things. These include wood, clay, metals, plastics, rubber, ceramics and glass.

▲ A lathe spins an object quickly, so that it can be smoothed to a perfect round shape easily.

All the materials people use originally come from the Earth. Materials that are used in their natural state are called raw materials. These may be processed or mixed together to make 'manufactured' or 'synthetic' materials.

Leather is strong but soft and easily cut to shape.

Rubber can be stretched, but bounces back to shape.

Plastic may be soft or hard and can take any shape.

Glass is hard but shatters easily when hit.

Wood is relatively light and strong.

Bricks of clay can bear heavy weights.

RAW AND SYNTHETIC
Wood, which comes from trees, is a raw material. It can be used in its original state or processed to make manufactured materials such as cardboard and paper. Glass is a synthetic material made by mixing together sand, salt and other raw materials at a high temperature.

PROPERTIES
Materials must be carefully chosen. A ladder, for example, must be made of something strong and stiff, like steel. If it is made of something soft and stretchy, like rubber, it will bend when people walk up it, making it dangerous to use. Every material has properties, such as strength and hardness. Other properties

▲ Metal is heated until it becomes liquid, then poured into a mould. When it cools and hardens, the metal takes the shape of the mould.

describe a material as ductile, elastic or plastic. A ductile material is one that can be stretched easily. Metal is ductile when it is hot; it can be pulled into thin wires. Materials like rubber that go back to their original shape after stretching are elastic. Wet clay and other materials that can be pushed into any shape, and then stay like that, are plastic. Most plastics have this property when they are hot, which is how they got their name.

COMPOSITES
Sometimes people need to combine materials that have two properties which a single material does not have. For example, a basement roof window needs to be transparent like glass, but as strong as steel. Manufacturers often mix materials or sandwich them together to make new ones called 'composites'. Laminated glass is a composite material. The strongest type has a thin steel mesh sandwiched between panes of glass. It is almost completely transparent, but is strong enough to stand or walk on.

◄ Clay is an example of a material that changes easily. As clay, it is soft and weak. But when heated, or fired, the clay changes to pottery, which is very hard and strong. Adding different substances, such as bone ash or white clay, gives pottery different properties.

SEE ALSO
Bridge, Construction, Design, Housing, Solid, liquid and gas, Textile

MAYA

The Maya Indians dominated Central America from about 250CE to 850CE, building cities deep in the rainforest. Their descendants still live in the region.

The Maya were great astronomers and carved dates of religious ceremonies on stones.

Maya people wrote using glyphs (picture symbols) to show sounds of words or to convey ideas.

The Maya were among the most highly developed civilizations in Central America. Their achievements in art, architecture and mathematics were outstanding. That is why it is a mystery that their civilization collapsed so suddenly.

MIGHTY MAYA
The first Maya lived in city states, probably led by priest kings. Evidence of these states dates back to around 250CE with stone pillars erected by the rulers to record their achievements. Within a few generations, the Maya were building vast cities, such as Tikal (now in Guatemala) with populations of up to 50,000 people. These spread across the Yucatán Peninsula south to the Pacific Ocean. This was known as the Classic era.

WEALTH FROM THE EARTH
The wealth of the Maya was based on trade and farming. As early as 1500BCE, people in the area were growing maize, the basic

▲ Modern Maya selling their wares at a market on the steps of a church in Guatemala.

food of the Maya. The seeds were often boiled, but were also ground into a powder to make a porridge. Maya farmers grew tomatoes, runner beans, avocados and sweet potatoes. They had no farm animals, but hunted wild game and fish. Most people lived in forest huts, only coming into the city for markets or religious ceremonies.

SCIENCE OF THE STARS
Mayan priests learned how to calculate the solar year, lunar months and even the movements of the planet Venus. For these calculations, the Maya developed complex mathematical skills and used writing more skilfully than any other American peoples.

DEATH OF A CULTURE
In about 800CE, some of the southern cities began to be abandoned; historians are not sure why. By 950CE, most of the great cities had collapsed. People continued to live in their homeland, but in villages. There was a revival around 1200, then, in the 1500s, the Maya were conquered by Spanish invaders.

MAYAN MONUMENTS

With only stone hand tools, the Maya managed to build great pyramids and palaces. The Castillo pyramid in Chichén Itzá reached 30m above the ground. Chichén Itzá survived longer than most Mayan cities — it was inhabited until about 1440.

The Castillo is 55m square at the base

Four staircases each had 91 steps. These, plus the step at the temple entrance, added up to 365 — the number of days in the Mayan year.

SEE ALSO

Central America, Explorer, Mexico

MEDIA

The media are the channels through which news and views are publicized. They include radio, television, newspapers, magazines, teletext and the Internet.

▲ Paparazzi photographers spy on celebrities and take photographs for international papers and magazines.

The media offer a window on the world, bringing events from other countries close to home. Media can be printed (newspapers, magazines or books), broadcast (on radio, television or cinema) or electronic, such as the Internet. It can be aimed at informing and entertaining, or advertising something or someone.

CENSORSHIP

News put out through media can affect public opinion. Some governments try to censor the media, others use them for propaganda. The freedom of the press to print or broadcast what it likes, so long as it is true, is an important civil right. In democratic countries such as the USA, there are laws to protect the press from pressure to print a particular thing. A free press can question the actions of a government and make it difficult for dictators. Most dictators or one-party states allow only news favourable to themselves to be broadcast.

CONTROLLING THE MEDIA

Usually the media are owned by private businesses. Reporters or programme-makers may do as they please, as long as their work fits in with the style and tone of the programme or publication, which may support a particular political party.

MEDIA INFLUENCE

Companies and personalities may try to influence what appears in the media by offering gifts, trips or parties. Journalists may also be threatened with being sued for libel or having access to events withdrawn if unpleasant stories are broadcast.

COVERING AN EVENT

A news event will be covered in different ways by the various media: newspapers send a reporter and photographer; radio shows may have just one broadcaster with an outside broadcast unit; television needs visual images and sound.

Game, set and match to Rusedski

British tennis ace Greg Rusedski wowed spectators with his powerful style on court yesterday to win through to the finals.

CANADIAN-BORN Rusedski beat his opponent 6-0, 6-4 in straight sets, then faced a gruelling fifth set when he eventually took match point on 14-12.

GIRLFRIEND IN CROWD
Rusedski's girlfriend Lucy Connors was among the crowd cheering ecstatically on centre court. He now heads Britain's hopes to take the Grand Slam.

By JANE SMITH

NEWSPAPER
A reporter and photographer will go along to a match to record results and comments from players.

TELEVISION
Television coverage of a news event demands camera operators, sound technicians and a commentator on site.

RADIO
Results are given during a radio news bulletin, while sports programmes are recorded live from events.

THE EVENT
Major sports attractions, such as the Wimbledon or the US Open tennis tournaments, give press passes to TV and radio stations and accredited journalists.

SEE ALSO
Internet, Newspaper and magazine, Photography, Radio, Television

MEDICINE

Medicine is the scientific study of human disease. It covers the causes, prevention, diagnosis and treatment of all types of different illnesses.

The name of the Ancient Greek Hippocrates (c.460–377BCE) lives on in the Hippocratic Oath, a code of principles for doctors.

French chemist Louis Pasteur (1822–95) invented pasteurization – a process of killing germs in liquids such as milk.

English surgeon Joseph Lister (1827–1912) introduced antiseptics into surgery, reducing the risk of bacterial infection.

Alexander Fleming (1881–1955) was a British bacteriologist who discovered the antibiotic drug penicillin.

The Greek physician Hippocrates is often called the 'founding father of medicine'. He examined patients and recorded their symptoms. He also prescribed many remedies, including willow bark tea – later shown to be the source of aspirin. But medicine could not progress in a scientific way until doctors understood how the body works.

UNDERSTANDING THE BODY

The 16th-century Belgian anatomist Andreas Vesalius was the first to show where bones, muscles, blood vessels and organs were situated in the body. Then William Harvey (1578–1657), a British doctor, discovered that the blood was pumped around the body by the heart. When 19th-century scientists showed that microbes (microscopic organisms such as bacteria) could cause disease, medicine began to progress as a modern science.

MAKING A DIAGNOSIS

The identification, or diagnosis, of a disease begins with the doctor taking a history of the illness. This includes asking about symptoms, previous illnesses and details of the patient's lifestyle. Then the doctor carries out a physical examination. This may include listening to the sounds of the patient's chest and abdomen with a stethoscope, feeling organs such as the liver, and looking into the eyes, ears and throat with special instruments. Most illnesses can be diagnosed from the history and physical examination alone. The doctor may also send blood, urine and other samples to a hospital laboratory for testing. Sometimes the patient will need to have an X-ray or a scan. These create pictures of the inside of the body which can give a better idea of what is wrong.

MEDICAL TREATMENT

Most illnesses are treated by drugs or surgery. There are around 6,000 drugs available today, including painkillers, antibiotics, anti-cancer drugs and drugs

MILESTONES IN MODERN MEDICINE

1905 First blood transfusion

1922 First use of insulin to treat diabetes

1928 Discovery of penicillin by Alexander Fleming

1938 First artificial hip replacement

1943 First renal dialysis or artificial kidney machine

1955 Polio vaccine introduced by Jonas Salk

1967 First heart transplant

1979 Vaccination eliminates smallpox worldwide

1981 First cases of AIDS diagnosed

2001 First telesurgery

2008 First full face transplant

◀ Computer technology is widely used in the development of new drugs. Here, a 'virtual reality' system is being used to create a 3-D image of a drug, which can then be manipulated by the researcher.

for mental illness. Surgery is often used in the treatment of heart disease and cancer to remove or repair diseased tissue. It is possible to replace major organs such as the heart, lungs, kidneys and liver by transplant surgery.

PREVENTATIVE MEDICINE

Prevention is always better than cure. Doctors and nurses use what they know about the causes of disease to help stop patients getting ill in the first place. Smoking is known to cause both heart disease and lung cancer, so the medical profession tries to discourage patients from smoking. Smokers can attend anti-smoking clinics, for example, and there are health warnings on cigarette packets. People can also look after themselves by eating a healthy diet, exercising, getting enough rest and having regular check-ups. Vaccination protects people from diseases such as polio.

ALTERNATIVE TREATMENT

There are also complementary or alternative medicines, which take a different approach to healing. Acupuncture comes from the Chinese medical tradition. It depends upon balancing the body's life-force, or *chi*, which flows along invisible channels in the body called meridians. During treatment, an acupuncturist uses needles to help the chi flow more freely. This and other alternative medicines, such as reflexology, homeopathy and aromatherapy, are popular with patients, although their effects may not be scientifically proven.

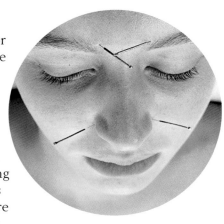

▲ Acupuncture involves thin metal needles being inserted into selected points in a patient's body. In China, where the technique originated, it is used as an anaesthetic during surgical operations.

VIEWING THE BODY IN CROSS-SECTIONS

One of today's fastest and most accurate forms of imaging (to help diagnosis) is the computerized tomography (CT) scanner, which creates a 'virtual reality' image of the patient's body. The patient is moved slowly through the scanner, inside which an X-ray source rotates around the body. A ring of detectors relay the information to a powerful computer for processing. The information is then displayed on screens on the main console as a series of cross-sections, or slices, through the patient's body.

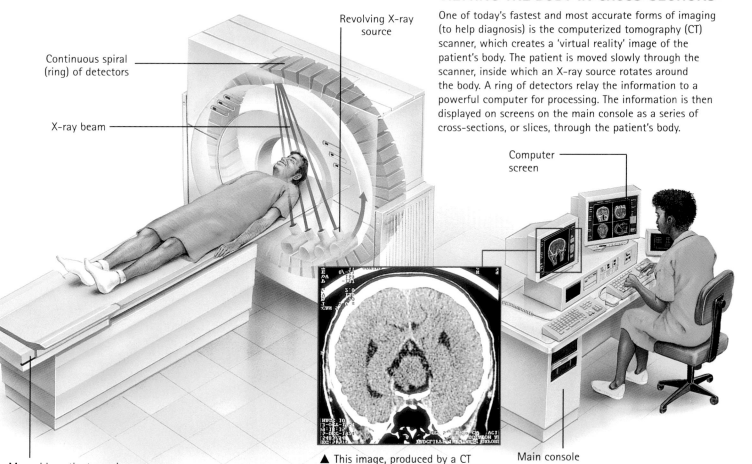

Revolving X-ray source

Continuous spiral (ring) of detectors

X-ray beam

Computer screen

Moveable patient couch

▲ This image, produced by a CT scanner, provides details of a slice through the patient's brain.

Main console

SEE ALSO

Disease, Drug, Human body, Immune system, Nutrition, Surgery, X-ray

MESOPOTAMIA

Mesopotamia lies along the valleys of the Tigris and Euphrates rivers in the Middle East. The world's earliest cities and organized civilizations grew up here.

Cast copper work, a bust of King Sargon of Agade.

A wooden lyre shows the importance of music at Ur.

Elaborate gold jewellery was worn by the nobles.

Cylinder seals were used by merchants and priests.

After 2000BCE, chariots dominated warfare.

Watered by the mighty Tigris and Euphrates rivers, Mesopotamia (a Greek word meaning 'between the rivers') was a fertile and wealthy land. It was here that early farmers developed writing, founded cities and built a series of empires which dominated surrounding lands.

FIRST FARMERS

Farming spread into Mesopotamia from the hills to the north and west. By about 6000BCE, people living along the rivers had learnt how to irrigate fields to grow barley, wheat, dates and beans. Sheep and goats were kept for meat and wool. In the fertile valley more food could be grown and the population boomed. By about 3500BCE, villages along the twin rivers had grown into cities of over 10,000 people.

CITY STATES

The buildings in the cities were made of mud brick, with only a few being built of fired brick. The people learned how to weave wool and flax into clothing, how to make copper tools and produce high-quality pottery for the first time. Each city was independent, but traded with other towns and peoples, even importing ivory and gemstones from India.

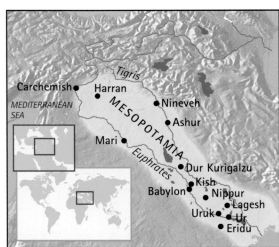

▲ A number of powerful cities ruled the area that surrounded them until the growth of empires.

KEY DATES

15,000–10,000BCE The first farming settlements develop in Mesopotamia

3500BCE Larger villages grow into walled cities ruled by kings, priests or nobles

c. 2370BCE Sargon of Akkad founds the first empire in Mesopotamia

2100–1700BCE The cities of Ur and Babylon dominate Mesopotamia

c. 1792–c. 1750BCE Reign of Hammurabi, king of Babylon, who united the cities of Mesopotamia and is famous for his law code

1250BCE The Assyrian Empire begins to expand

727BCE All of Mesopotamia is brought into the Assyrian Empire by Tiglath Pileser III

627BCE The Assyrian Empire collapses into chaos

626BCE The rise of the Chaldean Empire

539BCE Mesopotamia is captured by the Persians

► A ceremonial helmet made of an alloy of gold and silver, which belonged to King Meskalamdug of Kish in about 2200BCE.

THE WORLD OF GILGAMESH

The vital need to organize irrigation schemes led to the growth of a strong central system of government by kings or priests. Gradually, a few powerful cities, such as Eridu, Kish and Uruk, came to dominate the surrounding area, known as Sumer. Writing was invented and was used to keep track of government and temple records, but it was also soon being used to record important events and the deeds of kings. In about 2700BCE, Gilgamesh became king of Uruk and fought several wars. He was so famous that many stories were told and written about him.

SACRED CITIES

At the centre of each city was a *ziggurat*, a massive artificial hill topped by a temple. Built of layers of mud brick and straw, the ziggurats were up to 100m across and 100m tall. Mud brick was not strong

254

THE LAW CODES

Rulers set out law codes, often carved on a stone pillar and set up for public display. The oldest known was made by Ur-Nammu, who ruled Ur in about 2100BCE. The code dealt with slaves, personal injury and witchcraft. Ur was also famous for its ziggurat, an enormous stepped temple to the Moon god Nanna, also built by Ur-Nammu.

enough to support such huge structures for long and most ziggurats had to be repaired every 100 years or so. The ziggurat was dedicated to the god or goddess of the city. The prestige of the gods and goddesses depended on the power of their particular city. Gods could gain or lose worshippers if their city won or lost a battle. Many of the rulers were both kings and priests, or the posts in neighbouring cities were held by members of the same family.

WARRIOR EMPIRES

Around 2370BCE, King Sargon of Akkad (Agade), the area around Nippur, conquered Mesopotamia. He and his successors then conquered lands as far away as Syria. Soon after 2000BCE, invaders from the north and west destroyed the empire and overran several cities. The invaders settled in Mesopotamia and adopted local customs. By about 1792BCE, King Hammurabi of Babylon claimed to rule all Mesopotamia. Gradually the northern cities grew more wealthy and powerful. In 1250BCE the Assyrians, based at Nineveh, conquered a new empire, covering Mesopotamia, Syria, Palestine and Egypt.

END OF AN ERA

Mesopotamia enjoyed a final period of power from 626BCE to 539BCE, under the Chaldean rulers. It was then conquered by Persia, and became a part of larger empires. Mesopotamia is now divided between Iraq, Syria and Turkey.

◄ Cuneiform writing and a carving of a king. Cuneiform symbols represent an object and the sound of its name. They were used to write a variety of languages from 3200BCE to 100CE.

▲ One of two statues of goats made of gold, silver and lapis lazuli found in one of the royal tombs at Ur.

SEE ALSO

Babylon, Egypt (Ancient), Empire, Seven wonders of the world, Warfare

METAL

A metal is a shiny material such as iron, gold or copper. Most are solid at room temperature, easy to shape when hot and good at conducting heat and electricity.

▲ Metals can be joined by welding – the application of heat, pressure or both. Here an electrical current is being used to heat steel in a process called arc-welding.

▼ Aluminium alloys are used in aircraft construction because they are light but strong.

The Earth has a huge supply of some metals such as tin and iron – used to make tools, machines and large structures. Other metals, such as gold and platinum, are rare. They are usually used in small quantities.

WORKING WITH METAL

People have known how to extract and use metals since c. 8000BCE. If a metal is heated until it becomes molten (liquid), it can be poured into a mould. As soon as it cools, it hardens and keeps its shape until melted again. Metals can also be hammered into any shape or pulled into long strands. Most solid metals are very strong and hard, which is why they are used to make things like building frames and engine parts that have to keep their shape when put under pressure.

METALS THAT RUST

If something made of iron is left outside, it will go rusty. This is because the surface of the iron reacts with oxygen in the air to form a new compound – iron oxide. Many other metals react with oxygen or other elements, so are not found in their pure state in the ground. Instead, they are found as ores – compounds of metal and oxygen. A common way of extracting metal from oxide ores is to heat them with charcoal to remove the oxygen, leaving the pure metal.

ALLOYS

People have discovered many ways to mix metals with each other, and with non-metals, to make useful materials. These mixtures are called alloys. Steel is an alloy made from iron and small amounts of carbon and other metals. It is harder and stronger than pure iron. Bronze is a hard alloy made from copper and tin.

METAL FATIGUE

You need a large force to break a lump of metal apart in one go. But some metal objects break when bent many times by a small force. This way of breaking a metal, called metal fatigue, can be a real hazard. Machines like aeroplanes that must not fail are checked for signs of metal fatigue.

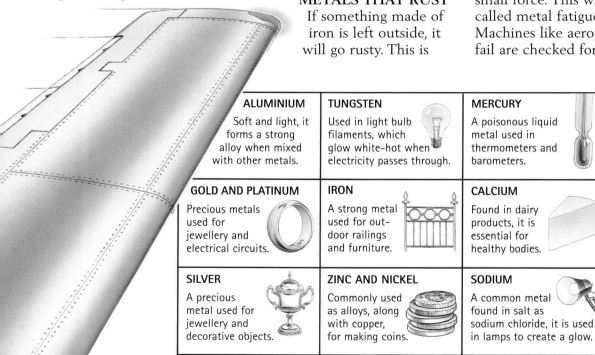

ALUMINIUM Soft and light, it forms a strong alloy when mixed with other metals.	**TUNGSTEN** Used in light bulb filaments, which glow white-hot when electricity passes through.	**MERCURY** A poisonous liquid metal used in thermometers and barometers.	**STEEL** An extremely strong alloy made of iron, carbon and other metals.
GOLD AND PLATINUM Precious metals used for jewellery and electrical circuits.	**IRON** A strong metal used for out-door railings and furniture.	**CALCIUM** Found in dairy products, it is essential for healthy bodies.	**BRASS AND BRONZE** Copper alloys used for sculpture and decorative objects.
SILVER A precious metal used for jewellery and decorative objects.	**ZINC AND NICKEL** Commonly used as alloys, along with copper, for making coins.	**SODIUM** A common metal found in salt as sodium chloride, it is used in lamps to create a glow.	**PEWTER** An alloy of tin and lead, once widely used to make tableware.
COPPER A good conductor of electricity, commonly used for electrical wiring.	**TIN** Commonly used to cover steel cans to stop them rusting.	**MAGNESIUM, STRONTIUM AND BARIUM** Used to create the bright colours in fireworks.	

SEE ALSO

Construction, Gold, Iron and steel, Mineral and gem, Mining, Silver

MEXICO

Mexico, North America's third largest country, lies between the United States to the north and Central America to the south.

Area: 1,958,201 sq km
Population: 112,338,000
Capital: Mexico City
Language: Spanish
Currency: Mexican peso

In north and central Mexico, mountain ranges called *sierras* enclose a high plateau. This plateau, the country's most thickly populated region, contains active volcanoes. Mexico's highest peak, Mount Orizaba (5,700m), also called Citlaltépetl, is a dormant volcano.

▲ At Christmas, children try to burst a hollow papier-mâché *piñata*, full of sweets.

DESERTS AND FORESTS
Seven tenths of Mexico has little rainfall. The north is largely desert, but rainforests grow in the south. Temperatures vary according to the height of the land. Acapulco on the coast is much warmer than Mexico City, which is 2,300m above sea level. Mexico City was built on the site of the ancient Aztec capital founded around 1325.

▲ Tourists visit Mexico to see ancient ruins such as the Great Pyramid and *Chac-mool* figure in the Yucatán Peninsula.

MESTIZOS
Many Mexicans are *mestizos*, of mixed European and Native American origin. Most white people are descendants of Spaniards who arrived in Mexico in 1519. Spanish is the official language but some Mexicans speak Native American languages. Most Mexicans are Roman Catholics and more than three quarters of the people live in cities and towns.

TRADE AND FOOD
Mexico is rich in minerals, including silver, while oil, gas and oil products are the main exports. Factories also produce chemicals, clothing, iron and steel, processed food and vehicles. Food crops include maize (used to make flour for traditional pancakes called *tortillas*), beans, rice and wheat. Coffee, cotton, vegetables and fruits are also important.

MODERN TIMES
Mexico became independent from Spain in 1821. It lost land to the United States in the Mexican War (1846–48) and this war ruined Mexico's economy. There were revolutions between 1910 and 1921, but since then Mexico has been mainly at peace. Poverty has led many people to enter, illegally, Mexico's rich neighbour, the United States, in search of jobs.

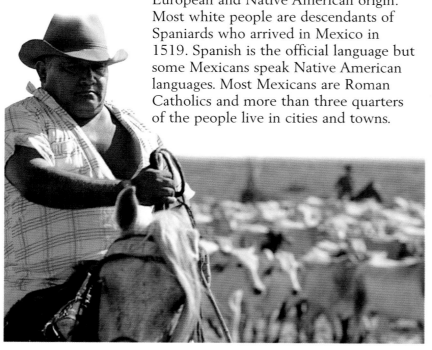

◄ Cattle are reared in the northern part of Mexico's plateau, where there is little rainfall.

SEE ALSO

Aztecs, Central America, Maya, Native Americans, North America

MICRO-ORGANISM

Micro-organisms are tiny living creatures that cannot be seen without a microscope. They can be bacteria, viruses, protists (protozoans), or tiny algae or fungi.

The Ebola virus is long and worm-like in shape. It is often deadly.

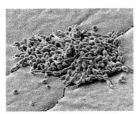

Yeast cells are fungi and can be used to ferment alcohol and make bread.

A colony of rod-like, food-poisoning bacteria growing on cooked roast beef.

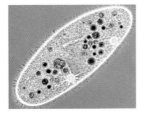

Paramecium protists are abundant in water and soil and feed on bacteria.

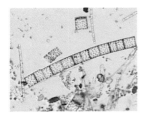

Many varieties of single-celled algae form colonies in or on top of water.

Bacteria are single-celled specks of living matter, mostly well under one hundreth of a millimetre long. There are three main shapes: rods, spheres and spirals. Bacterial cells differ from other cells because their DNA, which controls all living things, floats free through the cells instead of being contained in a nucleus. They get food and energy by breaking down all kinds of living or dead substances and, unlike most other living things, many of them can survive without oxygen.

GOOD AND BAD
Bacteria reproduce by simply splitting into two. This can happen every 15 minutes in good conditions, so bacteria exist in huge numbers. Many bacteria cause illnesses, including tuberculosis, cholera and food-poisoning. These are often called germs or microbes. But not all bacteria are harmful. Some help to keep the soil in good condition, while others can be used to manufacture yoghurt and other foodstuffs.

PROTISTS

Protists are single-celled organisms in which the DNA is wrapped up in a nucleus near the cell's centre. They live everywhere, especially in watery surroundings. The best known members of the group are amoeba, which continually change shape as they move. Some live harmlessly in water and swallow bacteria by simply flowing over them. Others live inside animals and cause illness. Many protists cause illnesses such as malaria and sleeping sickness.

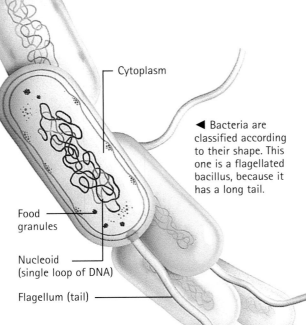

Cytoplasm

◄ Bacteria are classified according to their shape. This one is a flagellated bacillus, because it has a long tail.

Food granules

Nucleoid (single loop of DNA)

Flagellum (tail)

VIRUSES
Viruses are even smaller than bacteria. On the border between living and non-living things, most consist of a piece of DNA inside an envelope of protein. Viruses can form crystals like salt and other chemicals, and can survive in this state for a long time. But they can reproduce only when they get inside other living things. In such cases, the DNA of a virus invades the cells, forcing them to make more viruses. All viruses therefore cause disease in other living things. Human illnesses caused by viruses include measles, AIDS and the common cold. Prions are even smaller than viruses and have only recently been discovered. BSE, or mad-cow disease, is thought to be caused by prions.

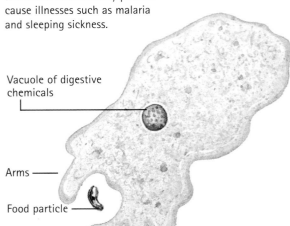

Vacuole of digestive chemicals

Arms

Food particle

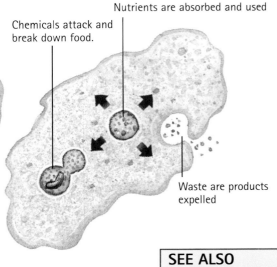

Chemicals attack and break down food.

Nutrients are absorbed and used

Waste are products expelled

SEE ALSO

Cell, Disease, Fungi, Genetics, Microscope

MICROSCOPE

Microscopes are instruments that magnify tiny objects or reveal fine details on larger objects. They have opened up a whole world that is invisible to our eyes.

An electron scan (x20) of velcro, used as a clothes' fastener, showing the nylon hooks and loops.

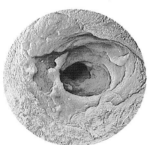

A false-colour electron scan (x200) of a sweat pore from a blister on the palm of a man's hand.

An electron scan (x 500) of individual fibres that make up a single thread of cotton.

An electron scan (x1,300) of human hairs protruding from the surface of the scalp (coloured pink).

The first microscope was made by the Dutch spectacle-maker Zacharias Janssen in 1609. The first scientist to see bacteria was the Dutchman Anton van Leeuwenhoek, who made his own microscopes in the 1670s. The first microscopes were optical, which means that the object, or specimen, being studied was viewed through an eyepiece. For this to work, the specimen needed to be thin enough to let light through.

ELECTRON MICROSCOPES

Electron microscopes were first used in the 1930s. Instead of light, they use a beam of electrons controlled by magnetic fields. Electron microscopes are very powerful and can show details 1,000 times larger than optical microscopes can. However, the specimen must be dried out

OPTICAL MICROSCOPES

In an optical microscope, light shining through an object is bent as it passes through a lens. This makes the object appear much bigger. Adding a second lens makes the magnification even greater. Optical microscopes with several lenses are called compound microscopes and can magnify things by up to about 2,000 times their real size.

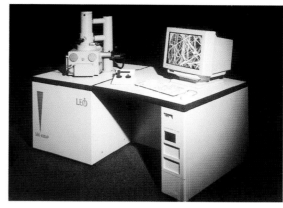

▲ In an electron microscope, the electrons are invisible, so a fluorescent screen is used instead of an eyepiece.

and sliced very thinly (about a thousandth – the thickness of this page). In addition, the air must be removed from inside an electron microscope and from around the specimen, as electrons are easily scattered.

OTHER MICROSCOPES

Scanning electron microscopes move a beam of electrons over the surface of the specimen. The electrons that bounce off are collected to make an image. Scanning probe microscopes and atomic force microscopes were invented in the late 1980s. They can magnify a million times, showing up individual atoms. An extremely sharp probe moves over the surface of the specimen, 'feeling' its shape in tiny detail. A computer turns signals from the probe into a 3-D image, which is displayed on a television screen.

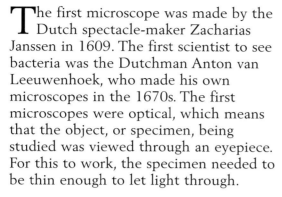

Binocular lenses

Specimen mounted on a rectangular slide

Magnification and focusing are electronically adjustable

Dyes are used to make the specimen visible

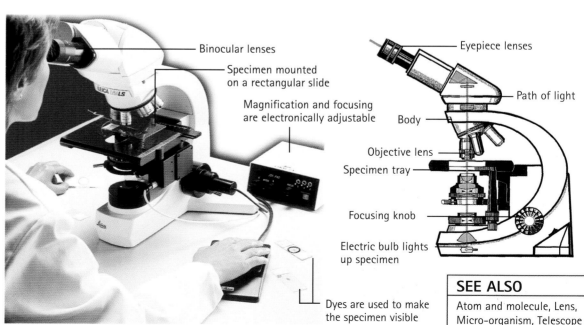

Eyepiece lenses

Path of light

Body

Objective lens

Specimen tray

Focusing knob

Electric bulb lights up specimen

SEE ALSO

Atom and molecule, Lens, Micro-organism, Telescope

MIDDLE AGES

The Middle Ages was the period in European history which began in about 750CE and ended in the 1400s with the dawn of the period known as the Renaissance.

▶ During the 1400s in France, Christine de Pisan wrote for a living — this was unusual in an age when few people, particularly women, knew how to read and write.

Society was divided into three estates: the clergy and the nobility ...

... and the third estate, made up of farm workers, traders and craftsmen.

Following the collapse of the Roman Empire in the 5th century CE, western Europe was overrun by pagans (non-Christians). By 1400, Europe shared a common Christian culture and was about to begin centuries of expansion through exploration, trade and conquest.

EMPEROR AND POPE
In 800, Charlemagne, king of the Franks, was crowned emperor by the pope. This was an attempt to reunite Europe under a Christian ruler. The power of pope and emperor dominated the Middle Ages.

FEUDAL SOCIETY
In this period, Europe was divided into many kingdoms, dukedoms, bishoprics and other states. The source of most wealth was farmland. The feudal system of controlling land and people was developed in France in the 10th century. Kings gave land to lords and knights in return for military services. Each lord had to swear fealty (loyalty) to his overlord. The lord's land was farmed by peasants, who paid him in labour and surplus crops. The Church also held a lot of land and many monasteries used their wealth to encourage learning and the arts.

A VIOLENT PERIOD
After the defeat of invading Vikings, Muslims and Avars, the rulers of Europe fought each other for power and wealth. The Hundred Years' War (1337–1453) was fought between the kings of England and France over who should rule France. The Habsburg family of Austria and the Hohenzollerns of Germany fought long wars to conquer new lands.

TRADE AND INDUSTRY
After about 1100, Europe became increasingly wealthy. Merchants and craftsmen formed guilds – organizations that imposed regulations and controlled prices. They helped spread skills and encourage trade between regions. By 1400, a growing number of people were working in manufacturing and trade.

MEDIEVAL BANQUETS
The wealthy lords and ladies of the Middle Ages held banquets for special occasions. These formal meals began early in the day — around 10 or 11am — and continued for several hours. Guests ate with their fingers or with knives and spoons (forks had not yet been invented). The food included a great many meat dishes and was often heavily spiced.

SEE ALSO

Castle, Crusades, Renaissance, Roman Empire

MIDDLE EAST

The Middle East is a group of countries in southwest Asia lying between Africa and Europe. It has great economic importance and is an area of unrest.

AFGHANISTAN
Area: 645,807 sq km
Population: 23,994,000
Capital: Kabul
Languages: Pashto and Dari
Currency: Afghani

BAHRAIN
Area: 716 sq km
Population: 1,235,000
Capital: Manama
Languages: Arabic and Indian languages
Currency: Bahraini dinar

CYPRUS (part of Europe)
Area: 9,251 sq km
Population: 1,041,000
Capital: Nicosia
Languages: Greek, Turkish
Currency: Euro and Turkish pound

IRAN
Area: 1,641,918 sq km
Population: 74,733,000
Capital: Tehran
Languages: Farsi and Azeri
Currency: Rial

IRAQ
Area: 434,128 sq km
Population: 32,105,000
Capital: Baghdad
Languages: Arabic, Kurdish
Currency: Iraqi dinar

Much of the Middle East is desert, with rugged mountain ranges in eastern Turkey, Iran and northern Afghanistan. Afghanistan contains the region's highest peak, Nowshak (7,485m), in a range called the Hindu Kush. Most people live along the coasts, in inland valleys or around oases.

ANCIENT RIVERS
The main rivers, the Tigris and Euphrates, rise in Turkey and flow through Syria and Iraq. They join to form a river called the Shatt al Arab, which empties into the Persian Gulf. The world's first city-states were founded along these rivers in Mesopotamia, by a people called the Sumerians, in around 3500BCE. The Middle East's most famous inland body of water is the Dead Sea, which lies in a deep valley between Israel and Jordan. Its shoreline is the world's lowest point on land, 432m below sea level.

▲ The Elburz mountains run along Iran's northern border close to the Caspian Sea, and make up one of the Middle East's many mountain ranges.

RAIN, SNOW AND DESERT
The areas with the highest rainfall are in the northeast: the Turkish city of Istanbul has an average rainfall of 690mm a year, while Saudi Arabia's capital Riyadh has only 106mm. Snow falls on the mountains and temperatures drop below freezing in winter. The desert plains are hot. Few plants grow in the deserts, though date palms flourish around oases. ▶

▼ The Middle East has been transformed by the discovery of oil.

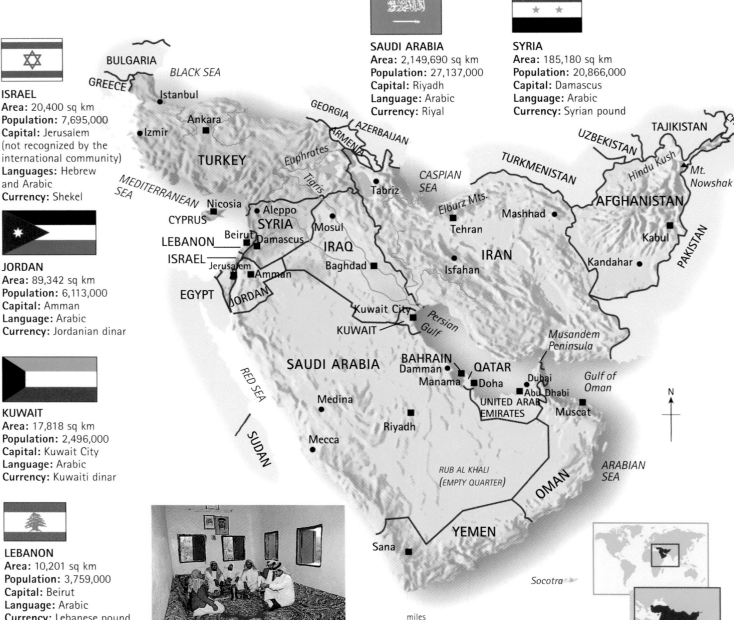

ISRAEL
Area: 20,400 sq km
Population: 7,695,000
Capital: Jerusalem
(not recognized by the
international community)
Languages: Hebrew
and Arabic
Currency: Shekel

JORDAN
Area: 89,342 sq km
Population: 6,113,000
Capital: Amman
Language: Arabic
Currency: Jordanian dinar

KUWAIT
Area: 17,818 sq km
Population: 2,496,000
Capital: Kuwait City
Language: Arabic
Currency: Kuwaiti dinar

LEBANON
Area: 10,201 sq km
Population: 3,759,000
Capital: Beirut
Language: Arabic
Currency: Lebanese pound

OMAN
Area: 309,500 sq km
Population: 2,773,000
Capital: Muscat
Language: Arabic
Currency: Omani rial

QATAR
Area: 11,427 sq km
Population: 1,699,000
Capital: Doha
Languages: Arabic and
Indian languages
Currency: Qatari riyal

SAUDI ARABIA
Area: 2,149,690 sq km
Population: 27,137,000
Capital: Riyadh
Language: Arabic
Currency: Riyal

SYRIA
Area: 185,180 sq km
Population: 20,866,000
Capital: Damascus
Language: Arabic
Currency: Syrian pound

▲ In Saudi Arabia, men often relax and
drink tea together. Tradition means that
women do not attend such gatherings.

DESERT ANIMALS

In some areas, nomadic tribes herding
camels, goats and sheep move around in
search of pasture. The best-known animal
of the Middle East is the camel, which can
go for long periods without water. Another
desert animal, the Arabian oryx, once lived
throughout the Arabian peninsula and in
Lebanon, Iran and Iraq. By 1972, it was
extinct in the wild because people had
overhunted it in their cars. Arabian oryxes
bred in captivity have now been released
in Oman and are increasing in number.

PEOPLE AND RELIGION

Many of the people of the Middle East are
Arabs and Arabic is their chief language.
There are also Turks, Iranians, Kurds,
Pashtuns, Azeris, Uzbeks, Armenians and
Jews. The Middle East was the birthplace
of Judaism, Christianity and Islam, and all
three religions regard Jerusalem in Israel as
a holy city. Muslims also make pilgrimages
to Mecca and Medina in Saudi Arabia.
Islam is now the main religion, although
Christians live in Cyprus and Lebanon,
and Judaism is the chief religion in Israel.

◀ In cities such as Damascus in Syria, hand-crafted goods are sold at markets called *souks*.

MIDDLE EASTERN WARS

The boundaries of many countries in the Middle East were fixed after World War I (1914-18). Israel was created in 1948, leading to a number of Arab-Israeli wars. The Palestinians are still fighting to have their own land. Cyprus has been divided since 1974 into a Turkish-speaking Muslim area and a Greek-speaking Christian area. In 1991 and 2003, US-led coalitions fought Saddam Hussein's regime in Iraq. The Kurds, who live in Armenia, Iran, Iraq, Syria and Turkey, are fighting to have their own country, Kurdistan. In the Arab Spring of 2011, there were uprisings and protests across the Middle East, notably in Bahrain, Syria, Yemen and Iraq.

HOW PEOPLE LIVE

Until about 50 years ago, most people lived on farms or in farming villages. Today, over 70 per cent of the people live in cities and towns. The largest cities are Tehran, capital of Iran, Istanbul in Turkey and Baghdad, capital of Iraq. Many cities have tall modern buildings as well as older areas.

OIL POWER

The region's chief resource is oil, and Saudi Arabia has about a fifth of the world's known oil reserves. Other leading oil producers are Iran, Kuwait, United Arab Emirates, Qatar and Oman. Qatar's riches also derive from huge reserves of natural gas. Money from oil sales has been used to build new cities and roads, and to develop new industries to make oil products such as chemicals and plastics.

INDUSTRY AND FARMING

Iran and Turkey have many other industries, while Israel, the most developed country in the Middle East, is known for its aircraft, electrical goods, electronics, precision instruments and textiles. Agriculture employs over three quarters of people in Afghanistan and Yemen, but in desert nations such as Bahrain and Qatar less than two per cent of the population are farmers.

▶ Kuwait's water towers are part of a desalination plant, where fresh water is produced by removing salt from sea water.

SADDAM HUSSEIN
Saddam Hussein (1937–2006) became Iraq's president in 1979. He led Iraq into a war with Iran which lasted from 1980 to 1988. In 1990, Iraq invaded Kuwait, but an international force drove the Iraqis out during the Gulf War in 1991. In 2003, a US-led coalition invaded Iraq and overthrew Saddam and his government. He was executed in 2006 for crimes against humanity.

TURKEY
Area: 779,452 sq km
Population: 73,723,000
Capital: Ankara
Languages: Turkish and Kurdish
Currency: Turkish lira

UNITED ARAB EMIRATES
Area: 83,600 sq km
Population: 4,765,000
Capital: Abu Dhabi
Languages: Arabic and Indian languages
Currency: Dirham

YEMEN
Area: 527,970 sq km
Population: 22,492,000
Capital: Sana
Language: Arabic
Currencies: Rial

SEE ALSO

Asia, Christianity, Europe, Islam, Israel, Judaism, Mesopotamia, Oil

MIGRATION

Migration is the regular, instinctive movement of animals between one place and another. Their journeys are usually made to tie in with the seasons.

► Reindeer (known as caribou in North America) migrate from the Arctic tundra in vast herds to winter in the great coniferous forests farther south.

▼ When the insects on which swallows feed die out in the autumn, the birds fly south to find a fresh supply.

▲ Humpback whales migrate thousands of kilometres to reach warm waters, but they do not cross the Equator.

► Monarch butterflies fly more than 3,000km, over mountains and cities, to reach their winter home.

FINDING THE WAY

The map shows the routes taken by various migratory animals. Migrants are believed to use a range of methods to find their way. Some follow geographical features such as mountains and coastlines, others use their sense of smell. Birds, in particular, may be guided by the Sun or the stars, or by sensing the Earth's magnetic field.

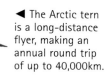

◄ The Arctic tern is a long-distance flyer, making an annual round trip of up to 40,000km.

◄———►	Swallow
◄———►	Reindeer/caribou
◄———►	Monarch butterfly
◄———►	Arctic tern
◄———►	Humpback whale

▲ Salmon battle their way upstream to reach their breeding grounds.

Every year, many animals journey hundreds, sometimes thousands, of kilometres to avoid cold winters – when food is hard to find – or to reach their summer breeding grounds. The animals usually travel in one direction before the onset of winter, then make the return journey the following spring.

BIRD MIGRANTS

Birds are among the most common migrants. Cuckoos, swallows, and many other insect-eating birds live in Europe and North America during the summer, when insects are plentiful, then fly south to spend the winter in warmer lands. Certain geese and ducks breed during the summer in the far north but, when the lakes begin to freeze over, they fly south in search of food. The Arctic tern makes the longest journey of all. Each year, it flies from the Arctic to the Antarctic and back again, so that it can enjoy the summer months in both places.

BREEDING TIME

Whales commonly feed in cold waters in the far north and south, but they migrate to warmer subtropical waters to breed. Seals travel long distances across the sea to rocky islands where they bear their young, and turtles head for warm sandy beaches in which to lay their eggs. Some fish also migrate, though not annually. Salmon live in the sea, but return to the same river in which they hatched in order to spawn (breed). European eels, on the other hand, live in fresh water but travel to the Sargasso Sea, east of Florida, to breed.

INSECT MIGRANTS

Certain insects migrate. Millions of monarch butterflies, for example, fly south from Canada and the northern US to winter in warmer areas. They breed in the spring and die soon afterwards. Then their young make the journey north again.

SEE ALSO

Bird, Butterfly and moth, Reptile, Whale and dolphin

MILLIPEDE AND CENTIPEDE

Millipedes and centipedes are long-bodied animals with many pairs of legs. Millipedes feed mainly on rotting vegetation, but centipedes are active hunters.

The word millipede means 'thousand legs', whereas centipede means 'hundred legs'. Neither animal tends to have as many legs as its name suggests, but both have an impressive number, which makes them easy to identify.

SEGMENTED BODIES
Millipedes and centipedes belong to a group of animals called arthropods. Like other arthropods, they have a tough outer case, or exoskeleton, and their bodies are divided into segments. In most millipedes, the segments are circular in cross-section, and each one carries two pairs of tiny legs. In centipedes, the segments are flatter and, instead of carrying four legs, each segment carries just two.

DANGERS OF DRYING OUT
Millipedes and centipedes do not have fully waterproof bodies, which means that they have to be careful not to dry out. To

► When threatened, millipedes usually coil up tightly with their tough coat on the outside.

avoid this danger they tend to live in damp places, such as scattered leaves and soil, and are active mainly at night.

DIFFERENT LIFE STYLES
In other ways, these animals live quite differently. Millipedes have small jaws and they feed on the remains of decaying plants. They move quite slowly and, if they are threatened, they rarely run away. Instead, they often protect themselves by coiling up into a spiral. Some millipedes have special glands that produce a poisonous fluid. If another animal tries to eat them, the fluid soon puts the attacker off its meal. Centipedes, on the other hand, are aggressive hunters with large claws surrounding their head. Many can move quite fast, either to scurry after their prey or to escape danger.

Two of the 10,000 species of millipede. Most have 120 to 160 legs, but the record is 750.

Two of nearly 3,000 types of centipede. Most have 30 to 50 legs, though one species has 177 pairs.

FEROCIOUS HUNTERS
A centipede's flattened body allows it to slip easily in and out of crevices while it is hunting. Centipedes are armed with special claws on either side of the head that inject poison into their prey. Most centipedes feed on small creatures such as worms, snails and beetles, but large tropical species – which can reach over 25cm long — sometimes attack frogs, mice and even birds. Their claws are strong enough to pierce human skin, with very painful results.

Leg muscles anchored to the rigid body wall enable the limbs to move freely

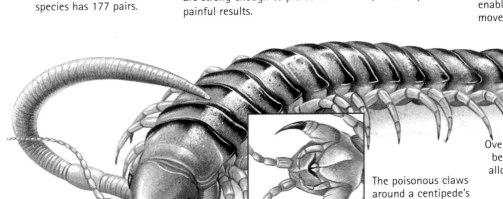

The poisonous claws around a centipede's head are actually modified front legs

Overlapping membranes between the segments allow greater flexibility of movement

A centipede has long antennae which it uses to search for food

SEE ALSO
Animal, Insect

MINERAL AND GEM

Minerals are the natural elements or compounds that make up rocks in the Earth's crust. Gems, metal ores, sand, salts and even talc are all forms of minerals.

Jade is a hard, often green, semi-precious gemstone that can be carved to form fine ornaments.

Turquoise ranges in colour from blue to grey-green. Sky blue specimens are popular as gems.

The gem opal shows a characteristic play of colours, known as opalescence.

There are over 3,000 different minerals, but only 30 of them make up the majority of rocks, soils and sand on Earth. Some minerals form glassy crystals, others are like brightly coloured rocks. They vary in colour, density and hardness, and also in their ability to reflect light, and conduct heat or electricity.

MINERAL COMPOUNDS

Some minerals, such as gold, consist of one pure element. Many others are made up of two or more elements, combined to form a compound. The most common mineral – quartz – is a combination of silicon and oxygen. Most grains of sand are quartz, which is used for making glass.

MINERAL ORES

Many mineral compounds contain metals. The mineral hematite, for example, is iron oxide, and galena is lead sulphide. Minerals such as these, from which the metals can easily be removed, or extracted, are called ores, and are widely mined.

FORMING CRYSTALS

Many minerals form distinct three-dimensional shapes called crystals. The shapes are the result of the neat arrangement of atoms and molecules inside the mineral. Minerals that produce fine, hardwearing crystals that can be cut and polished to a beautiful finish are called gemstones.

PRECIOUS GEMS

Gems are most commonly worn as jewellery. They include diamonds, rubies, sapphires and emeralds. Diamonds, which are incredibly hard, are also used in industry and mining for drilling, cutting and grinding. Industrial-grade diamonds can now be made artificially.

SCALE OF HARDNESS

An Austrian scientist, Friedrich Mohs (1773–1839), devised a scale to grade the hardness of minerals. His scale ranges from grade 1 for talc, the softest, to grade 10 for diamond, the hardest.

On Mohs' scale, a fingernail rates as 2.5, a copper coin as 3.5 and a steel penknife as 5.5.

A SELECTION OF MINERALS

Galena has a metallic grey colour and forms cubic crystals. It is the main ore of lead, and is commonly found with quartz.

Gold is a soft, malleable (easily worked) metal which has been used since ancient times to make jewellery.

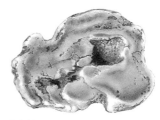

Malachite is a copper ore, well known for its bright green colour. It is often granular, and rarely forms crystals.

The iron ore hematite often forms kidney-shaped lumps, which earns it the name kidney ore.

Talc (magnesium silicate) is the softest mineral on Mohs' scale. It is widely used as talcum powder.

Quartz forms fine crystals and comes in many colours. The colourless variety is called rock crystal.

SEE ALSO

Earth, Gold, Metal, Mining, Oil, Rock, Silver, Soil

MINING

Mining is the process of taking from the Earth useful or valuable substances such as coal, gas, salt, mineral ores, gemstones or building stone.

The earliest mines were built to find useful metals like lead, copper, iron and tin, and precious metals such as silver or gold. But, because there were no effective methods for removing excess water or supplying workers with air, the mines always had to be near the surface.

▲ Gold is found as small grains, or nuggets, of pure metal. Here, gold nuggets are being washed out of the soil using water.

MINING AND MACHINES

Over the last two centuries, problems with drainage and ventilation have been solved by using machines, and mines can now be sunk deep into the ground. As well as pumping out water and circulating air, machines are used for drilling and cutting, and carry materials, men and equipment to and from the surface. Deep mining has always involved dangers from cave-ins,

▶ A vast bucket-wheel excavator is used to dig up rocks and minerals in an open-cast mine.

flooding and poisonous gases. In the future, work in dangerous conditions is likely to be done by robots controlled from the surface.

REACHING THE DEPOSITS

There are many different methods of mining – the type and depth of deposit usually determine the method used. Materials such as stone, gravel and sand are mined in quarries. Mineral deposits near the surface can be removed by open-cast mining, using mechanical diggers or high-pressure water jets. Deep deposits are reached by sinking vertical shafts into the ground, or driving a tunnel into the side of a hill or mountain – called drift mining. Explosives are often used to blast rocks apart so the minerals can be broken up.

MINING METHODS

A shaft mine is used to reach deep deposits. Where deposits are closer to the surface, minerals can be hauled up a slope in wagons. Drift mines are used where the seam reaches the surface, as on a hillside. Deposits close to the surface are removed in an open-cast mine, and oil beneath the sea is tapped by an oil rig.

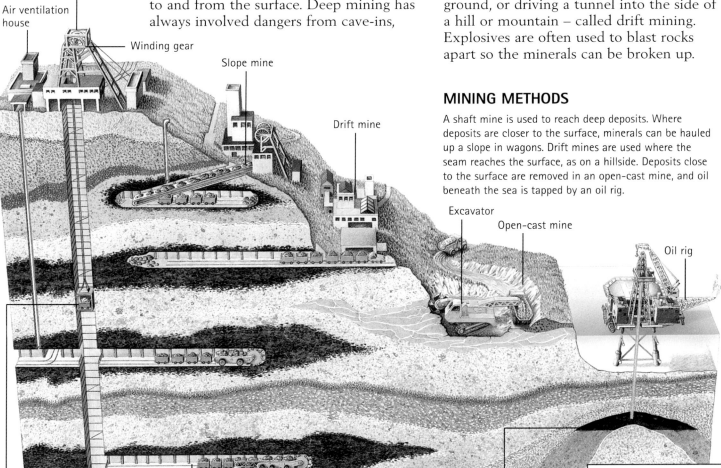

Shaft mine

Air ventilation house

Winding gear

Slope mine

Drift mine

Excavator

Open-cast mine

Oil rig

Cage (lift)   Main shaft   Tunnel   Ore vein (or coal seam)   Oil reservoir

SEE ALSO

Coal, Gas, Gold, Industry, Iron and steel, Metal, Mineral and gem, Oil, Rock, Silver

MONEY

Money is used to buy things or to save wealth for future needs. Money may take the form of notes, coins, or anything accepted as payment.

Native Americans used beads and shells made into decorative patterns.

The Ancient Chinese used bronze cast into spade, knife and other shapes.

Coins are popular as they are easy to produce and last a long time.

Paper money began as promises by banks to pay a certain amount of coins.

Credit cards and cheques are convenient substitutes for cash.

Before there was money, trade took place through barter, the exchange of one commodity or service for another. Barter only works if the person with one item wants what the other has to offer. Money allows people to sell things for money, then swap the money for what they want. It also makes borrowing possible, so that exchanges can be spread over time.

BEADS TO COINS

Many things have served as money. Useful products, such as salt or knives, have been used, as have decorative beads or even natural items such as shells or cattle. Coins made of precious metal and stamped with a design to show how much metal they contain were probably invented in Lydia (part of modern Turkey) around 700BCE.

PROMISES TO PAY

Paper money is not valuable itself, but is a promise to pay real money. It was invented in China in around 1000CE. Until the 20th century, notes could be exchanged for gold. Most modern notes represent promises made by a bank or government, as do cheques or credit cards.

► In 1923, German money lost value rapidly. Money became so worthless that bundles of notes were used as toys.

MAKING COINS

Coins are made from metals such as bronze or copper, which are stamped with a design showing how much they are worth and which country produced them. An artist draws the design on paper.

The design is engraved, in reverse, onto metal dies.

The metal for the coins is melted into thin sheets

Round 'blanks' are cut from the metal sheet.

The dies stamp the coin design onto the blanks.

THE MEASURE OF WEALTH

Money can be used to store and measure wealth, but the value of money is not stable. Wars may cause governments to collapse, so that their money becomes worthless. If a government prints too many notes, or allows excessive borrowing, the money loses value and inflation occurs.

HIGH FINANCE

Large sums are lent and borrowed by governments and large companies in the money markets. Brokers and banks arrange loans or sell shares allowing businesses to grow and trade.

> **SEE ALSO**
> Gold, Great Depression, Silver, Trade

MONGOLS

The Mongols, a people of eastern Asia, conquered vast areas of Asia and Europe in the 13th century to create a huge, united and very powerful empire.

Genghis Khan (c. 1162–1227) united the Mongols and founded the empire.

Kublai Khan (c. 1217–94) organized the conquests in China into a stable state.

Tamerlane (1336–1405) conquered an empire in central and western Asia.

The speed and brutality of the Mongol conquests stunned and terrified their enemies. But the Mongols failed to organize their new empire and it collapsed as quickly as it had been created.

THE TIDE OF CONQUEST
In 1206, Temujin, leader of the Mongols, united the nomadic Asian tribes, taking the title Genghis Khan, or supreme ruler. By 1215, he had conquered northern China, killing about 35 million Chinese. Genghis Khan then turned west, taking western Asia, the Caucasus and southern Russia before his death in 1227. Genghis's son Ogedai then became khan, smashing Russia, Hungary and Poland by 1241. That year Ogedai died and the new khan, Mongke, turned on China and Persia.

MONGOL WARFARE
Mongols were mounted on hardy ponies, able to travel long distances in a short time. The light cavalry was armed with bows and trained to shoot while galloping. Heavier cavalry had lances and armour. This combination of speed and shock smashed every army they met.

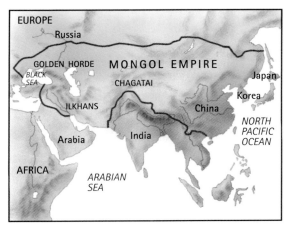

▲ The Mongol Empire at its largest in 1280 under Kublai Khan. The Golden Horde, Chagatai and Ilkhans later became smaller independent empires.

THE NEW EMPIRE
By 1279, all China had been conquered and the Mongol Empire stretched from Korea in the east to the Black Sea in the west. Kublai Khan moved his capital to China, from where he was able to enjoy the wealth and luxuries of the conquests.

COLLAPSE OF THE KHANS
After 1300, the khan in China lost control of Mongol rulers elsewhere. The Mongols abandoned the tough life of warriors and, in 1368, were driven out by the Chinese. In the west, Mongol power was broken by the early 1400s. Today, Mongolia is a vast but poor country north of China.

SEE ALSO
Asia, China, Empire

MONKEY AND OTHER PRIMATES

Monkeys and apes belong to a group of mammals known as the primates, which also includes lorises, lemurs and bushbabies, as well as human beings.

Monkeys differ from apes in having a tail, although this is sometimes very short. Both have their eyes at the front of the head, giving them human-looking faces. They are intelligent creatures with good brains, and they learn quickly. They live in family groups or larger colonies and spend a lot of time grooming each other and looking after their babies. Apes are the nearest living relatives of human beings.

The woolly monkey is a New World monkey.

The South American spider monkey uses its tail as an extra hand.

The Old World colobus monkey rarely comes down from the trees.

The mandrill is one of the largest Old World monkeys.

LIFE IN THE TREES

Monkeys and apes are very active and nimble animals, with excellent eyesight. Except for the South American night monkey, or douroucouli, they feed in the daytime and sleep at night. Most of them live in the trees, where they can run along branches and swing from branch to branch with amazing ease. They grasp branches with hands and feet, and some South American monkeys can even hold on to the branches with their tail. Baboons, the largest of the monkeys, live mainly on the ground, although they usually sleep in the trees at night. With their pointed muzzle and large teeth, they look more like domestic dogs than monkeys.

TWO MONKEY GROUPS

There are about 200 kinds, or species, of monkey, nearly all of which live in the tropical and subtropical parts of the world. They fall into two main groups – the New World monkeys of South and Central America and the Old World monkeys of Africa and Asia. New World monkeys, which include the little tamarins and marmosets, have a

▲ Ring-tailed lemurs walk on the ground holding their long tail up in the air. The word lemur means 'ghost', a name derived from the weird cry of some species.

broad nose with the nostrils facing to the sides. Old World monkeys have a narrower nose with the nostrils pointing downwards.

THE BIGGEST APE

About 16 different kinds of ape live in the forests of the Old World; no apes are found in the Americas. The gorilla, the chimpanzee and the bonobo, or pygmy, chimpanzee live in Africa. Weighing up to 200kg, the gorilla is the largest and strongest of all the primates. It usually walks on all fours, with its knuckles on the ground. Gorillas are not the fierce creatures that people once thought them to be. In fact, they live peacefully in the forest in small family groups.

▲ An adult chimpanzee, closely observed by its young, uses a stick as a tool to probe for termites. Chimpanzees are among the most intelligent apes, able to imitate humans and solve simple problems.

◄ Baboons live in close family groups called troops. Like other monkeys and apes, the female carries her babies until they are old enough to look after themselves.

▲ The loris is a slow-moving primate that lives in Southeast Asia. It has huge, forward-pointing eyes and broad grasping hands and feet.

INTELLIGENT CREATURES

Chimpanzees look like small gorillas, but usually have a paler face. They live in large communities, often with over 100 individuals. They are probably the most intelligent of the apes, often using simple tools to help them find food.

ORIENTAL APES

The orang-utan and the dozen or so species of gibbon live in Southeast Asia. Orang-utans reach up to 1.3m when standing upright, and their bodies are covered in rather sparse, reddish-brown hair. Gibbons are small apes, rarely weighing more than 6 or 7kg, and they are wonderful acrobats. They use their very long arms to swing and leap through the branches at high speed. Unlike chimps, gibbons and orang-utans rarely come down to the ground.

FAMILY LIVING

Gorillas live in family groups, or troops. Each group is made up of one or more males and several females with their young. The group is ruled by a large mature male, known as a silverback because of the silver-grey hairs on his back. Gorillas are vegetarian, eating a diet consisting mainly of leaves and shoots but also of bark, stems, roots and fruit. They may live for up to 37 years.

VEGETARIAN DIETS

Monkeys and apes are basically vegetarian, although they often eat insects and other small animals. Chimpanzees even catch monkeys and small antelopes. Fruit is plentiful at all times of the year in the tropical areas and is the main food of most monkeys and apes. The gorilla and a few monkeys feed mainly on leaves and shoots.

OTHER PRIMATES

Bushbabies, lorises and lemurs have smaller brains than monkeys and apes, and are often called 'lower' primates. Their snouts are more pointed than those of most other primates. They live mainly in the trees and feed mostly on fruit, leaves or insects. Bushbabies live in tropical Africa and lorises in southern Asia. Both are active at night and have very large eyes. Lemurs are found only on the island of Madagascar, off the east coast of Africa.

▲ The orang-utan is an endangered species. Special rehabilitation centres in Sumatra and Borneo care for young animals and introduce them back into the wild.

SEE ALSO

Animal, Conservation, Mammal

MOON

The Moon is the Earth's only natural satellite. Its diameter is 3,476km and it lies at an average distance of 384,400km from the Earth.

Crescent Moon (waxing)

Half Moon (first quarter)

Full Moon (appears round)

Half Moon (Last Quarter)

Crescent Moon (waning)

The Moon shines because it reflects light from the Sun. The phase of the Moon (how much of its surface we can see) depends on the position of the Moon in its orbit.

SOLAR ECLIPSE
Sometimes the Moon passes exactly between the Earth and the Sun. When this happens, there is a total solar eclipse and, for a few minutes, the Sun's bright disc is blotted out. Since the Moon takes exactly the same time (27.3 days) to complete one orbit of the Earth as it does to spin around once on its axis, it always keeps the same side facing towards us.

BLEAK AND LIFELESS
The Moon is a bleak place with no atmosphere which means there is no weather – no clouds, rain, nor wind. There is no life, although ice has now been found on the dark side. The Moon consists mostly of solid rock with a small central core of molten rock or iron. A thin layer of dust covers its surface. During the day, the surface temperature may climb to 127°C (more than the boiling point of water), but at night it can plunge to as low as –173°C.

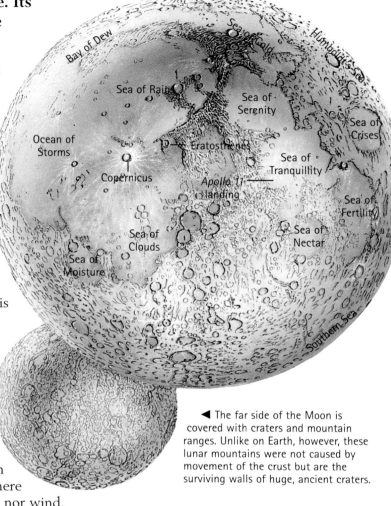
◄ The far side of the Moon is covered with craters and mountain ranges. Unlike on Earth, however, these lunar mountains were not caused by movement of the crust but are the surviving walls of huge, ancient craters.

ORIGIN OF THE MOON
The Moon was formed just over four and a half billion years ago. It may have been gouged out of our own world when a large object struck the Earth. Another possibility is that the Moon has always been a separate body and was captured by the Earth when it strayed too close.

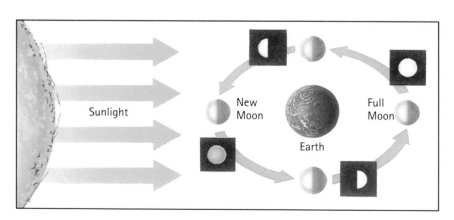

◄ At New Moon, the unlit side of the Moon, which is invisible, faces the Earth. It grows (Crescent Moon) until half, then all, the unlit side becomes visible (Full Moon). The phases then continue in reverse until the Moon is new again.

PLAINS AND CRATERS

The dark regions of the Moon's surface, known as maria (seas), are low-lying plains of solidified lava surrounded by brighter, mountainous areas. Craters, formed by the impact of meteorites and asteroids, occur everywhere on the Moon, but are especially common in the highlands. They range in size from a few metres to 1,100km across (Imbrium Basin in the Sea of Rains).

PULL OF THE MOON

Just as the Moon is held in orbit around the Earth by gravity, so the Earth itself is affected by the Moon's gravity. This is noticeable in the movement of the oceans and seas, which are pulled up when the Moon is directly above them. As the Earth rotates, these tidal bulges shift from east to west twice daily, causing high tides.

MYTHS AND LEGENDS

For centuries, the Moon has given rise to various myths and legends. Early peoples saw it as a god or goddess, while some philosophers thought that it was linked with birth and death, because it waxed and waned. It was also feared that eclipses signalled famine or war. In astrology, the Moon is believed to have an important influence over our lives and destiny.

▼ The Collision Theory suggests that a large body struck the Earth.

◀ This body added its own material to the debris thrown off into space (1). The debris formed an orbiting cloud (2), which finally solidified into a solid mass – the Moon (3).

1

2

3

▶ The Capture Theory suggests that the Moon was a passing body caught by the Earth's gravity. This explains its different composition, although calculations show that a collision with another body was more likely.

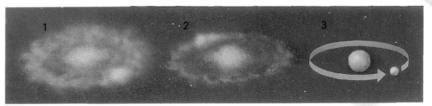

Moon's new orbit
Original path of Moon
Moon   Earth

▲ The Earth and Moon may have formed together as a double planet from the cloud of debris left over after the formation of the Sun. However, this argument does not explain why their surface rocks are so different and why the Moon has such a small iron core compared with the Earth.

▼ Moon rock brought back from the *Apollo* missions ranges in age from about 4.5 billion years, just after the Moon was formed, to 3.1 billion years, when the lava plains were created.

Anorthosite

Vasicular basalt

Typical basalt

SEE ALSO

Astronaut, Earth, Gravity, Planet, Solar system, Space exploration

MOUNTAIN AND VALLEY

A mountain is a mass of land that is much higher than its surroundings, pushed upwards by movement of the Earth's crust. Valleys are formed on mountain slopes.

As glaciers melt, they leave behind deep, U-shaped valleys gouged by the ice.

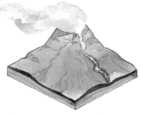

Erupting volcanoes build up mountains made of lava and ash.

Block mountains form along breaks, or faults, in the Earth's crust.

A mountain is higher than a hill, but there is no strict distinction between the two. Mountains are natural barriers to communications, while valleys offer trade routes, places for settlement, and pastures for farming. Some mountains are found under the sea. One of them, Mauna Kea in the Pacific Ocean, is higher than Everest.

HIGHEST PEAKS

Mountains are formed over millions of years through plate tectonics – movement of the Earth's crust. The crust is made up of rigid plates which are continuously moving. The highest mountains are the youngest. The longest mountain range on Earth, the Andes (7,200km long), is being formed as the Pacific plate plunges beneath the South American plate. The highest, the Himalayas, is being formed as the Indian plate crushes up against the Asian plate.

FOREVER WEARING AWAY

All the time a mountain is being pushed up, forces of erosion (such as wind and water) are wearing it down. Water flowing down the slopes gathers in streams and rivers, which carve out deep V-shaped valleys. Flat-bottomed, U-shaped valleys are formed by glaciers. Some straight valleys, like the Great Rift Valley, in East Africa, are formed along a crack or fault in the Earth.

MOVING THE EARTH

The highest mountains are fold mountains. These are found in chains, or ranges, and are formed like folds in a blanket when the ends are pushed together. They are pushed up when rocky plates of the Earth's crust collide. When one plate plunges beneath another, the rocks of the uppermost plate crumple up, making the mountain range.

THE WORLD'S HIGHEST PEAKS	
Top five (all in Asia)	Other continents
Everest, Himalayas, 8,848m	Aconcagua, South America, 6,960m
K2, Karakoram, 8,611m	McKinley, North America, 6,194m
Kanchenjunga, Himalayas, 8,597m	Kilimanjaro, Africa, 5,895m
Lhotse, Himalayas, 8,510m	Elbrus, Europe, 5,633m
Makalu, Himalayas, 8,460m	Vinson Massif, Antarctica, 5,140m

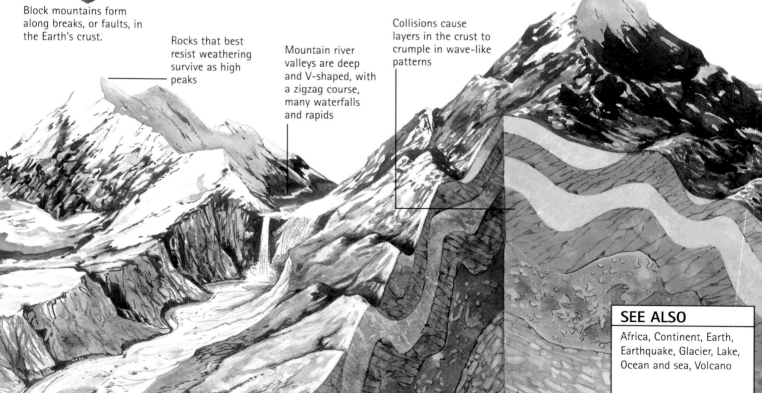

Rocks that best resist weathering survive as high peaks

Mountain river valleys are deep and V-shaped, with a zigzag course, many waterfalls and rapids

Collisions cause layers in the crust to crumple in wave-like patterns

SEE ALSO

Africa, Continent, Earth, Earthquake, Glacier, Lake, Ocean and sea, Volcano

MUSCLE

The body has 640 muscles, each specialized to contract (become shorter) to make the body move. All body actions, from blinking to sprinting, are muscle-powered.

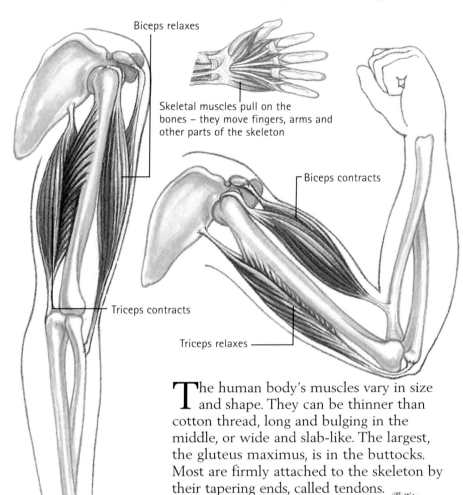

Biceps relaxes

Skeletal muscles pull on the bones – they move fingers, arms and other parts of the skeleton

Biceps contracts

Triceps contracts

Triceps relaxes

▲ When you bend your arm, the biceps muscle in the upper arm pulls the forearm, and so bends the elbow. Its opposing partner, the triceps, pulls the forearm the other way and straightens the elbow.

The human body's muscles vary in size and shape. They can be thinner than cotton thread, long and bulging in the middle, or wide and slab-like. The largest, the gluteus maximus, is in the buttocks. Most are firmly attached to the skeleton by their tapering ends, called tendons.

WORKING IN PAIRS
Muscles can only pull, not push. So they are arranged in opposing pairs. One of the pair pulls the body part one way. To move the part back again, its opposing partner pulls it the other way. Animal muscles have the same structure, and work in the same way, as human muscles.

INSIDE A MUSCLE
Muscles are made up of bundles of long fibres called muscle fibres or myofibres. Each one of these contains bundles of even thinner microscopic parts – muscle filaments or myofilaments. In turn, muscle

▼ Inside a muscle are bundles of long muscle fibres (myofibres), thinner than human hair, joined by connective tissue.

Skeletal muscle

Smooth muscle

Cardiac muscle

filaments are made of bundles of thread-like structures, called actin and myosin.

MUSCLE POWER
For a muscle to pull, each myosin 'grabs' its neighbouring actin and makes it slide past, like pulling in a rope with a hand-over-hand movement. Millions of myosins and actins doing this make the whole muscle shorten. The amount and strength of contraction are controlled by nerve signals to each muscle from the brain.

THREE MUSCLE TYPES
Skeletal muscles have a striped appearance under the microscope, so they are known as striped, or striated, muscles. As we can make them contract when we want to (by thinking), they are called voluntary muscles. Cardiac muscle (called the myocardium) forms the thick walls of the heart. It contracts regularly to pump blood. Visceral muscle forms layers and sheets in the walls of the body's inner parts – viscera – such as the stomach, intestines and bladder. Both of these work automatically, so they are known as involuntary muscles.

The eye has six muscles which help rotate the eyeball in its socket

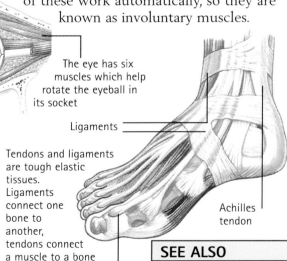

Ligaments

Tendons and ligaments are tough elastic tissues. Ligaments connect one bone to another, tendons connect a muscle to a bone

Achilles tendon

Tendons

SEE ALSO
Heart, Human body, Lens, Lungs, Sight, Stomach, Touch

MUSIC

The word 'music' comes from the Greek muses, who were said to inspire song and dance. In more scientific terms, music is the art of organized sounds.

As painters or sculptors use lines, colours and shapes, so musicians use the properties of sound. They use notes of different pitch (highness or lowness) and combine them with the beat of a rhythm, to make a melody, or tune. They can add harmony – the sounding together of two or more notes of different pitch. Tone, or timbre – the special quality of sound produced by different instruments or voices – is another aspect of music.

African tribal music is one of the oldest surviving musical forms and is always accompanied by the rhythm of drums.

MUSIC WITH A PURPOSE

The earliest music was probably functional. People danced and sang or chanted because the strange power of music gave them courage to hunt wild animals. They also sang and danced to honour their gods, or to accompany themselves as they worked. All these ancient types of music are with us still.

John Lee Hooker (1917–2001) was a leading blues player. Blues have greatly influenced US pop music.

MUSIC AS AN ART

With the growth of civilizations, people turned music into an art. The ancient *ragas* (rhythmic or melodic patterns) of India are a fine example of this. In the Western world, music as an art grew and changed rapidly. In medieval Europe, music still had a functional purpose, since it was sung in church and so served religion. But there was also the singing and the playing of minstrels, whose music was intended for pleasure and entertainment.

Elvis Presley (1935–1977) revolutionized pop music in the 1950s. He was one of the first rock'n'roll stars.

▲ Jazz music originated in New Orleans, USA, during the early 1900s and has remained a major form of music ever since. Unlike written music, it requires musicians to improvise, or make up music on the spur of the moment.

THE RENAISSANCE

From about 1400 to the present day, Western music has beens divided into periods. The Renaissance, about 1400–1600, was a period when the rich had time to enjoy themselves. There was a big increase in secular (non-religious) music, and much more music for instruments, including the harpsichord and lute, by such composers as William Byrd and John Dowland.

▶ British musician Evelyn Glennie (born 1965) is one of the top percussionists in the world. She is deaf, but feels the vibrations of the music through her sense of touch.

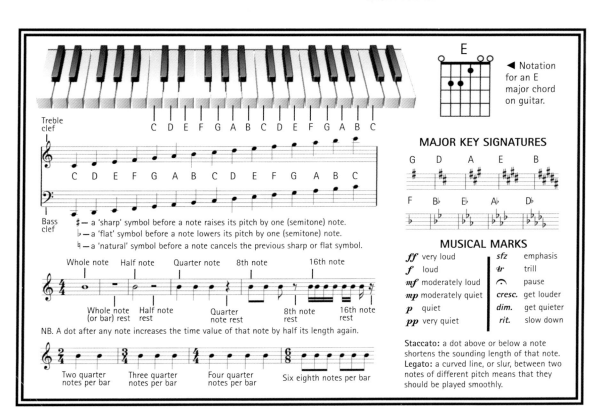

◄ Notation for an E major chord on guitar.

Treble clef

C D E F G A B C D E F G A B C

C D E F G A B C D E F G A B C

Bass clef

♯ — a 'sharp' symbol before a note raises its pitch by one (semitone) note.
♭ — a 'flat' symbol before a note lowers its pitch by one (semitone) note.
♮ — a 'natural' symbol before a note cancels the previous sharp or flat symbol.

Whole note Half note Quarter note 8th note 16th note

Whole note (or bar) rest Half note rest Quarter note rest 8th note rest 16th note rest

NB. A dot after any note increases the time value of that note by half its length again.

Two quarter notes per bar | Three quarter notes per bar | Four quarter notes per bar | Six eighth notes per bar

MAJOR KEY SIGNATURES

G D A E B

F B♭ E♭ A♭ D♭

MUSICAL MARKS

ff	very loud	**sfz**	emphasis
f	loud	**tr**	trill
mf	moderately loud	⌢	pause
mp	moderately quiet	**cresc.**	get louder
p	quiet	**dim.**	get quieter
pp	very quiet	**rit.**	slow down

Staccato: a dot above or below a note shortens the sounding length of that note.
Legato: a curved line, or slur, between two notes of different pitch means that they should be played smoothly.

THE BAROQUE PERIOD

During the baroque period, about 1600–1750, much music was composed on a grand and opulent scale. There were operas (musical dramas in which the characters sing most of their lines) by Monteverdi and Handel, great choral works by Handel and J. S. Bach, and clear-sounding music for string orchestras by Vivaldi and others.

CLASSICAL ERA

The classical period, about 1750–1820, focused on new music forms for orchestras and instrumental groups: string quartets, sonatas, concertos and symphonies. Haydn, Mozart and Beethoven were masters of these new forms, with their emphasis on 'classical' order and proportion.

THE ROMANTICS

Beethoven's dramatic and expressive music also opened the way for the romantic period, about 1820–1900. Composers now wanted to express their own thoughts and feelings through poetic songs, descriptive pieces or operas full of passion and drama. Schubert, Mendelssohn, Schumann, Chopin, Berlioz, Wagner, Verdi, Brahms and Tchaikovsky all lived during this period.

GROWTH OF WORLD MUSIC

The 20th century saw an explosion of musical styles. Blues and jazz developed and later gave rise to rock and pop. Composers have been influenced by jazz and music from the Far East and elsewhere. Every kind of music has been touched by electronics and computers. TV, radio, satellites, CDs, mp3s and the Internet make music instantly available to people all around the world.

▶ Traditional instruments, as well as synthesizers, can be connected to a computer using MIDI (Musical Instrument Digital Interface). Once stored in the computer's memory, the notes can be made to trigger any sound or effect.

Johann S. Bach (1685–1750) influenced almost every composer after him.

Wolfgang Mozart (1756–91) was a child prodigy. He began to compose at five.

Ludwig van Beethoven (1770–1827) composed music despite being deaf.

Franz Liszt (1811–86) was a brilliant pianist who wrote difficult piano music.

Richard Wagner (1813–83) wrote dramatic operas of a romantic nature.

George Gershwin (1898–1937) was famous for his popular songs and musicals.

SEE ALSO

Dance, Film, Musical instrument, Radio, Sound

MUSICAL INSTRUMENT

Musical instruments create vibrations that are turned into sound. Most have their own range of pitched (high or low) notes. All have their own tone, timbre or 'voice'.

Musical instruments may be classified scientifically as: aerophones, in which the air itself vibrates; chordophones, in which one or more strings vibrate; membranophones, in which a stretched skin, or membrane, vibrates; and idiophones, in which the whole body of the instrument vibrates as one. The better-known way of classifying them is: strings, woodwind, brass, percussion, as well as keyboard instruments, electronic instruments and the voice.

Irish harps were carried from town to town by wandering minstrels.

The 1.8m-long serpent was very popular during the 1600s and 1700s.

From the 1100s, the hurdy-gurdy accompanied singers at feasts and dances.

The Jew's harp is placed inside the mouth, while a finger plucks its tongue.

STRINGED INSTRUMENTS

Stringed instruments produce their sounds from vibrating strings. With violins, violas, cellos and double-basses, the strings are usually scraped with a bow to make them vibrate. In other stringed instruments, notably the guitar, the strings are plucked. The player presses down on the strings with his or her fingers to change their 'playing length', which is the section that vibrates. This is called 'stopping'. The wooden body vibrates in sympathy with the strings, giving them volume and tone.

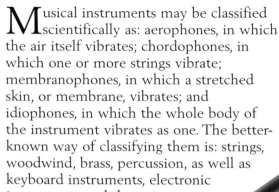

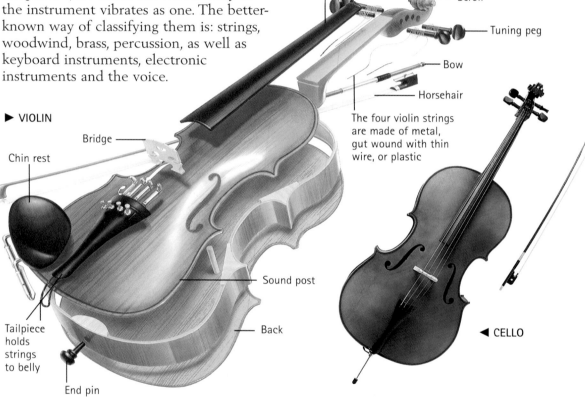

▶ VIOLIN

Fingerboard

Scroll

Tuning peg

Bow

Horsehair

The four violin strings are made of metal, gut wound with thin wire, or plastic

Bridge

Chin rest

Sound post

Back

Tailpiece holds strings to belly

End pin

◀ CELLO

SYMPHONY ORCHESTRA

A typical orchestra includes a string section of violins, violas, cellos and double-basses; a brass section of French horns, trumpets, trombones and tuba; a wind section of clarinets, oboes, bassoons, flutes and piccolos; and a percussion section of timpani, gong, glockenspiel, bass drum, and various other percussive instruments.

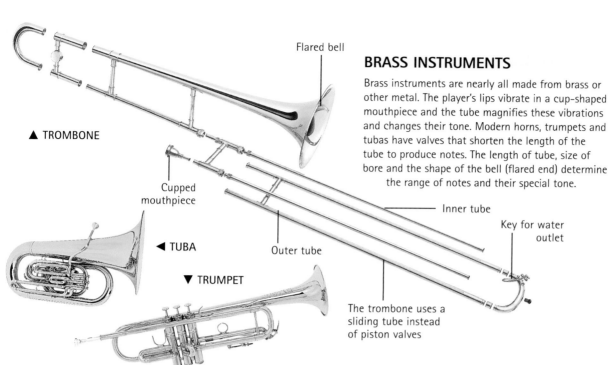

▲ TROMBONE

Cupped mouthpiece

◄ TUBA

▼ TRUMPET

Flared bell

Outer tube

Inner tube

Key for water outlet

The trombone uses a sliding tube instead of piston valves

BRASS INSTRUMENTS

Brass instruments are nearly all made from brass or other metal. The player's lips vibrate in a cup-shaped mouthpiece and the tube magnifies these vibrations and changes their tone. Modern horns, trumpets and tubas have valves that shorten the length of the tube to produce notes. The length of tube, size of bore and the shape of the bell (flared end) determine the range of notes and their special tone.

The electric guitar has a flat, solid body and electric pick-ups under each string.

The saxophone has a flared bell, single-reed mouthpiece and is very popular in jazz.

The rock drumkit includes a bass drum, floor toms, cymbals and snare drum.

WOODWIND INSTRUMENTS

Woodwind instruments make air vibrate in a tube. Many are made from wood, but this is not what classifies them as woodwind, it is the way they are played. Some, like the flute and recorder, have a mouth-piece that turns the player's breath directly into vibrations. The oboe, clarinet and bassoon have small vibrating reeds. The player sounds different notes by opening or closing holes in the tube's side, so changing the length of the tube in which the air vibrates.

▼ FLUTE

Foot joint

Finger hole covered by key

Finger key

Cork pads make airtight seal

Head joint

Body joint

Lip plate

Blow hole

▼ CLARINET

▼ OBOE

Single (clarinet) reed
Double (oboe) reed

▼ TIMPANI (KETTLEDRUM)

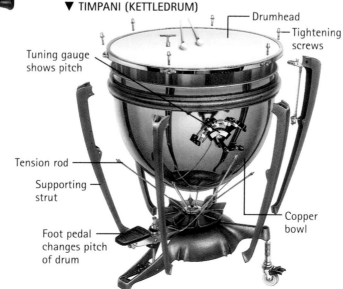

Tuning gauge shows pitch

Drumhead

Tightening screws

Tension rod

Supporting strut

Foot pedal changes pitch of drum

Copper bowl

PERCUSSION INSTRUMENTS

Percussion instruments are struck. Drums have a tight membrane across a frame, which the player strikes with hands, fingers or sticks. The air inside the frame, or the frame itself, makes the vibrating membrane sound louder. Bells, cymbals and gongs are all made from a single piece of material and vibrate as a whole when struck. Some percussion instruments, such as drums and bells, sound notes of definite pitch. But with gongs and cymbals it is difficult to place the pitch.

The powerful church organ has one or more keyboards and several banks of pipes.

SEE ALSO

Dance, Music, Sound

MYTH AND LEGEND

Myths and legends are the names given to the stories which early peoples told about their heroes and religious beliefs, and to explain the world about them.

In earlier times, when people knew little about science or nature, they explained things like how the Sun rose and set or how the world began through stories called myths. Before writing was developed, myths were passed down from generation to generation by word of mouth. By studying myths, we can learn much about a people's way of life, customs and values.

▲ In Greek legend, the magical winged stallion Pegasus was ridden by the hero Bellerophon. Pegasus later became a carrier of thunderbolts for Zeus.

HEROIC EXPLOITS

Unlike myths, which early peoples regarded as sacred and true, legends are folktales about the imaginary exploits of a hero. The hero often existed. But over many tellings the story became exaggerated. The earliest recorded literature in the world is the Sumerian legend *The Epic of Gilgamesh*. It was based on a real person, King Gilgamesh, who lived around 2700BCE. However, in the legend, the hero Gilgamesh is described as being half-god.

▲ Baba Yaga is a witch in Slavic mythology who guards the gate to the Other World. She has power over animals and birds, and day and night.

THE UNKNOWN EXPLAINED

All early peoples had their own myths to explain how natural events happened. The Ancient Greeks believed that the Sun was their god Apollo driving a flaming chariot across the sky each day. The Ancient Egyptians believed that the Sun god Ra sailed across the sky in a boat.

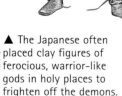

▲ The Japanese often placed clay figures of ferocious, warrior-like gods in holy places to frighten off the demons.

▲ The Zuni tribe of the American Southwest believed the first people came from underground and were black and scaly. They were guided by the medicine man, Yanauluha.

CREATION MYTHS

Most early peoples had their own myths to explain how the world began. Many myths start with nothingness, darkness or water. Out of this comes a god, who then starts the process of creation. According to an Indian myth, the world began when a creature shaped like a man divided into man and woman. From their marriage came the human race and, later, animals.

FAVOURITE GODS

At the centre of most myths were a people's gods. The functions of particular gods depended on what was important to the people. For instance, farming was very important to the Aztecs of Mexico and so they worshipped, among others, a group of maize gods. The gods of the seafaring Vikings were mostly concerned with war.

HOMES OF THE GODS

A people's gods usually belonged to one 'family'. Often they looked and behaved like people. They had mythical homes, usually in the sky or on a mountain top as gods needed to be all-seeing. Some gods inhabited sacred groves or the sea. However, the chief god in African mythologies lived on the Earth.

EPIC TALES

The Greeks and Romans also told long stories to entertain. Among them are the Greek poet Homer's epic poems about Troy – the *Iliad* and *Odyssey*. He wrote these during the 700s BCE and they are great works of literature. Such myths have inspired artists and writers ever since.

▲ According to Greek legend, Perseus, son of Zeus, killed the Gorgon Medusa by cutting off her head. The sight of her head, which had snakes for hair, turned people to stone. Here, Perseus holds it up to King Polydectes and his courtiers in anger.

◀ In Hindu mythology, the half-man, half-eagle creature Garuda was said to be the Sun in the form of a bird. Here, he carries the god Vishnu and his wife Lakshmi.

▶ The Norse (Scandinavians) believed that giants were a constant threat to both gods and human beings. Here, Surt leads the fire giants of Muspell against the gods at Ragnarok in what would be the last battle — and the end of the world.

SEE ALSO

Greece (Ancient), Literature, Religion

NAPOLEONIC WARS

The Napoleonic Wars were fought between Napoleon, ruler of France from 1799 to 1814, and his allies, and other European states, such as Britain and Russia.

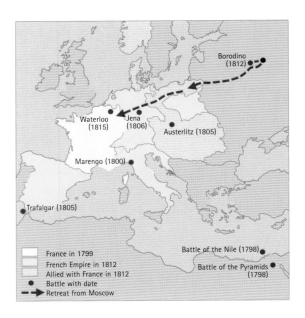

Napoleon was helped on campaigns by marshals like Michael Ney (1769–1815).

Cavalry Marshal Joachim Murat (1767–1815) became King of Naples.

Marshal Louis-Alexander Berthier (1753–1815) was Chief of Staff from 1805.

In 1799, General Napoleon Bonaparte (1769–1821) seized power in France. He introduced liberal freedoms and went to war with countries who opposed his rule. In 1804, he crowned himself emperor of France and crowned his wife empress.

THE CONQUEST OF EUROPE
In 1805, Napoleon defeated Austria at Ulm and Austerlitz. Prussia was defeated at Jena in 1806, and in 1807 the Russian army lost at Friedland. From 1808 to 1814, a British army fought in Portugal and Spain against a French invasion. In 1812, Napoleon invaded Russia, but was cut off by winter weather. Of his 500,000 men, only 75,000 returned. In 1814, Napoleon was forced to go into exile.

STRATEGY AND TACTICS
Napoleon tried to cut the enemy off from supplies and force them to fight where and when he chose. On the battlefield, he relied on artillery to pound the enemy before columns of infantry broke through the enemy lines, followed by cavalry to hunt fugitives. Bright uniforms helped soldiers to recognize each other through the dense battlefield smoke.

DEFEAT AT WATERLOO
In 1815, Napoleon returned to France. His new army marched quickly, but was defeated by the British and Prussians at Waterloo. He was banished to the Atlantic island of St Helena, where he died in 1821.

BATTLE OF MARENGO
Napoleon made his reputation at the Battle of Marengo in Italy on June 14, 1800. Attacked by 31,000 Austrians, Napoleon led a fierce defence by his 18,000 men until 10,000 reinforcements arrived under General Louis Desaix. Napoleon's brilliant counter-attack crushed the Austrians.

SEE ALSO
France, Revolution, Warfare

NATIVE AMERICANS

Native Americans were the first peoples to settle in North America, before the discovery and settlement of those lands by Europeans.

The Tlingit lived along the northwest coast.

Navajo farmed the south west of North America.

The Creek lived in the eastern woodlands area.

Native Americans developed into many different tribes and cultures, but were overwhelmed by European invaders after the 15th century. Today they make up a minority of the North American population.

EARLY ARRIVALS
Before 20,000BCE, humans crossed into the Americas along a land bridge that stretched from eastern Asia across the Bering Strait. By about 10,000BCE, they had spread south to the tip of South America. The Inuit of Canada and Alaska came from Asia only 3,000 to 5,500 years ago.

NATIVE CULTURES
The earliest Native Americans hunted wild animals and gathered wild plants. In about 1500BCE, some peoples began farming. Maize, beans and squashes were grown in most areas. Few animals were domesticated and Native Americans relied on wild game for meat. The great plains were dominated by tribes hunting bison, buffalo and other animals. Southwestern tribes were farmers and sheep herders. In the eastern woodlands, tribes lived off the game that was plentiful there. Along the northwest coast, cultures based on fishing developed.

DISEASE AND MASSACRE
In 1492, Christopher Columbus sailed to the Americas from Europe. Over the next 400 years, the European settlers spread over most of the Americas. European diseases killed many Native Americans, who had no immunity. About 80 per cent of the Mandan tribe in the northern plains died of smallpox.

▲ This thriving smoked fish business in Wisconsin shows how traditional skills have been adapted to modern times.

CULTURES
- Arctic
- Subarctic
- Northwest coast
- California
- Plains
- Eastern woodlands
- Southwest

Many other surviving tribes were driven from their lands or killed in warfare. The last battle of the Indian Wars was fought at Wounded Knee, South Dakota in 1890.

TRIBAL LANDS
In the late 1970s, some tribes started legal battles against the US federal government to try to reclaim land that had been taken from them. Today, North America is home to about two million Native Americans. Many live on reservations and keep alive traditional cultures. Some are poor, while others run thriving businesses.

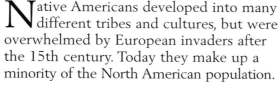

◄ The Cheyenne were one of the plains tribes. During war, the warriors were organized into seven societies, with the 'dog soldiers' acting as scouts and forward troops.

SEE ALSO
Aztecs, Canada, Central America, Incas, Maya, North America

NAVIGATION

Navigation is the science of finding the way. It is used mainly to guide ships, aircraft and spacecraft, but can also be used for vehicles on land.

The magnetic compass was invented in China around 1000CE.

The backstaff helped find latitude by measuring the height of Sun and stars.

The astrolabe was used by navigators before the invention of the sextant.

The sextant, which also determines latitude, is still in use today.

For thousands of years, ever since people began to travel by sea, navigation has been necessary. Early navigators relied on skill and guesswork, but today are helped by satellite technology and computers.

ANCIENT ARTS
Many early peoples travelled for trade or war, but the first to navigate seriously were the Phoenicians and Greeks, who sailed throughout the Mediterranean from about 750BCE. By 300BCE, some Greeks could find latitude by studying the stars, but after the fall of the Roman Empire, most navigational skills were lost.

HENRY THE NAVIGATOR
In 1418, Prince Henry of Portugal set up a school of navigation, which made many advances in exploration and navigation.

MODERN NAVIGATIONAL SYSTEMS
The idea of bearings from beacons is used with satellite technology. The US military Geostat system has satellites in orbit around the Earth positioned so that at least two are within radio range from any place on Earth. It is claimed a soldier with a computerized hand-held receiver can find his position to within 2m.

Lines of longitude

◄ The lines of latitude and longitude marked on globes and atlases can be used to pinpoint specific places. Lines of latitude show how far north or south of the Equator a place is. Lines of longitude run from the North to the South Pole.

Lines of latitude

The tools developed depended on compass readings and sightings of the stars and Sun. Although this early equipment underwent many changes, it remained the basis of navigation until well into the 20th century.

PINPOINTING A TARGET
World War II brought a major boost to navigation. Bomber aircraft needed to find their way to a target accurately. One way was to direct two radio beams into enemy territory so they crossed over the target. Aircraft followed one beam until they found the second. Another system was based on radio beacons. By taking a bearing on two beacons, the navigator could find his position to within a few hundred metres. The system was adapted to cover shipping lanes as well as air routes, and remains in use today as a major navigational aid for boats and ships.

Signals from satellites help aircraft pinpoint their position to within 100m

Navigation satellites beam radio signals to Earth

A receiver on board uses signals from land-based radio beacons to calculate the boat's position

Radar reflectors on floating buoys warn of hidden dangers

A computer on board uses satellite radio signals to guide the boat with great accuracy

An echo sounder measures the water depth by beaming high-pitched sound waves towards the sea bed

SEE ALSO
Explorer, Magnetism, Map, Warfare

NETHERLANDS, BELGIUM AND LUXEMBOURG

The Netherlands, Belgium and Luxembourg make up a group of countries in northwest Europe called the Low Countries. The Netherlands is also known as Holland.

BELGIUM
Area: 30,528 sq km
Population: 10,667,000
Capital: Brussels
Languages: Dutch, French
Currency: Euro

LUXEMBOURG
Area: 2,586 sq km
Population: 512,000
Capital: Luxembourg
Languages: French, German, Letzeburgish
Currency: Euro

NETHERLANDS
Area: 41,526 sq km
Population: 16,575,000
Capitals: The Hague, Amsterdam
Language: Dutch
Currency: Euro

The name Netherlands means 'lowlands' – two fifths of the country lies below sea level and the countryside is criss-crossed with canals. Half the country's freight is carried on the inland waterways. The landscape is dotted with windmills, originally built for controlling the water level. Belgium is also low lying and mostly flat, rising to hills called the Ardennes in the south, which extend across the border into the small country of Luxembourg.

TRADE AND NEW LAND

From the 1500s, the Dutch became seafarers, growing rich from fishing and trade, and built up an empire in Southeast Asia. Rotterdam remains Europe's largest port. The Dutch became experts at flood control, draining the land and reclaiming it from the sea, by building dykes and using pumps. This has created rich farmlands – cheese and butter are major exports.

INDUSTRIES AND CITIES

Belgium's textile industry dates back to the Middle Ages. Today, the country is a heavily industrialized nation. Luxembourg is a leading steel producer, but Belgium's steel industry is in decline. The city of Luxembourg is a major centre of banking, and Luxembourg is one of the wealthiest nations in Europe.

The Netherlands is densely populated – in Europe, only the tiny states of Monaco, Vatican City and San Marino have more people per sq km. Amsterdam, its largest city, is the national capital, but the government sits at The Hague.

HISTORY AND HERITAGE

The Netherlands fought for freedom from Spanish rule in the 16th century. Belgium and Luxembourg were part of the Netherlands until the 19th century. These three countries remain closely linked as members of the European Union, which has its headquarters in Brussels.

◄ Cut flowers and bulbs are important crops in the Netherlands, as well as fruit and vegetables.

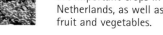

SEE ALSO
Europe

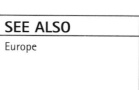

NEWSPAPERS AND MAGAZINES

Newspapers and magazines are publications that print international or local news, alongside comments on important events and interviews with celebrities.

©DC Thomson, Dundee

Children's comics have been around since the late 1800s. The *Dandy* started in 1937.

Superheroes, popularized by DC Comics, US, include *Wonder Woman* from 1941.

©DC Comics

©Hachette Filipacchi Presse

Magazines concentrate on particular subjects or age groups.

Tabloids are small-sized newspapers with a more sensationalist style.

Broadsheets are larger and the news reports have a more serious tone.

People all over the world find out about events by reading newspapers and magazines. National daily and weekly newspapers carry news from around the world. Some magazines specialize in one subject, such as football or medicine.

TABLOIDS AND BROADSHEETS

The first newspapers were printed in Europe in about 1650, after the introduction of the printing press. They may be printed every day or once a week, and may concentrate on local events or cover worldwide news. Most newspapers are either tabloid, with a page size of about 30x40cm, or broadsheet, about twice as large. Tabloids tend to print short stories, often about film stars and popular events. Broadsheets usually print longer stories, looking at serious events in more detail. Although newspapers are all different, most have similar features. Sports news is usually printed towards the end of a paper, while national, political and international news is printed at the front.

GATHERING NEWS

News is gathered by reporters who may visit events, such as political conventions and sports matches, or interview people taking part. Politicians, sports personalities and commercial companies often write a press release and send it to reporters to let them know about events or new products.

MAGAZINES

Magazines may be published weekly or monthly. They often feature full-colour, glossy pages with in-depth interviews and features. Some magazines cover a wide range of subjects, but some can be very specialized. Magazines may deal with fashion, sport or celebrities. Those which concentrate on a particular business are called 'trade press'. They often have a long lead-time (written several weeks or months in advance).

▲ Using computers, newspaper designers decide on the look of a page, choosing the style of type and the size and number of pictures.

► An editor and designer discuss the content of the lead, or front, page.

◄ A photographer shows the shots she took of an event to the art editor, using an onscreen digital light box. Later, the art editor will select the best images for publication with the article.

▼ Reporters write their stories straight on to the computer network. They are cut to length by an editor, who also checks facts and spellings.

CREATING A NEWSPAPER

Newspapers, magazines and books are put together on computers (desk-top publishing), before they are sent to be printed. A newspaper staff includes writers, photographers, designers and sub-editors, working under an overall editor.

SEE ALSO

Cartoon and animation, Design, Language, Media, Printing

NEW ZEALAND

New Zealand lies in the South Pacific, 1,900km southeast of its nearest neighbour Australia. It has two main islands, both of which are long and narrow.

Area: 270,534 sq km
Population: 4,368,000
Capital: Wellington
Language: English
Currency: New Zealand dollar

▲ In the greeting *hongi*, Maoris rub noses. Other traditions include carving, weaving and tattooing.

Eighty-six per cent of New Zealanders live in towns or cities. Three quarters of the population live on North Island, where it is warmest, but South Island is the largest of the two main islands.

NATURAL HAVEN
The coasts are ideal for sailing, surfing and fishing, and the mountains attract many skiers. There are active volcanoes, geysers and pools of bubbling mud. Because New Zealand has been isolated from other land masses for millions of years, it has developed distinct native wildlife such as the kiwi, a flightless bird, and many different kinds of fern. Cattle and sheep outnumber people by ten to one.

◄ Most of New Zealand's landscape is hilly, but there are fertile valleys and plains, such as South Island's Canterbury Plains.

EARNING A LIVING
Farming is in decline in New Zealand and employs just one in 14 people. Major exports include wood and wood products, crude oil, dairy products, meat and manufactured goods. Industry is concentrated around Auckland, the largest city. Tourism is a fast-growing business. More than two thirds of the country's wealth comes from the service industries.

TWO TRADITIONS
New Zealand was first settled by Maoris from Polynesia around 900CE. Today less than a fifth of the population are Maori or of mixed Maori-European heritage. British settlement began in 1840. Settlers transformed the country by founding cities and introducing cereal crops, sheep and cattle. Independence came in 1907, but ties between New Zealand and Britain remain close through trade and sport.

◄ The All Blacks is New Zealand's national rugby football team. It is one of the best in the world.

SEE ALSO
Custom, Pacific Islands

287

NIGERIA

Nigeria is a republic on the west coast of Africa. It has a greater population than any other African country and a rich blend of cultures.

Area: 923,103 sq km
Population: 140,003,000
Capital: Abuja
Language: English
Currency: Naira

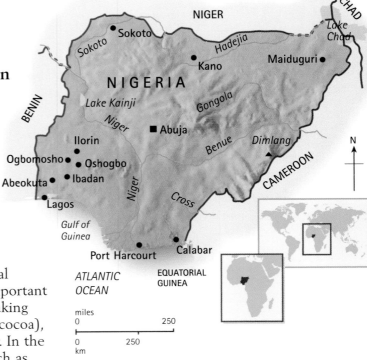

Nigeria's coastline consists of mangrove swamps. To the north of these lies a belt of dense tropical rainforest. Farther north, open woodland and savanna grassland merge into areas of semi-desert.

RICH IN RESOURCES

The country's most valuable natural resources are oil and gas. Other important products are palm oil (used for making soap), tin, cacao (used for making cocoa), peanuts, rubber, cotton and timber. In the dry north, livestock and cereals such as millet and sorghum are important. In the wetter south, fish, rice, yams and cassava are the main foods. The biggest city is the former capital Lagos, a major port and home to more than 12 million people.

ARTS AND CRAFTS

Nigeria has a rich tradition in arts, music and literature. The craftworkers of the kingdom of Benin were famous for casting fine sculptures in bronze 500 years ago. Wood carving and weaving are other traditional crafts. Nigerian authors writing in English, such as Chinua Achebe, have won fame, and in 1986, Wole Soyinka was the first African to be awarded the Nobel Prize for Literature.

NEW NATION OF OLD PEOPLES

Nigeria's boundaries were established by its British colonizers in the early 1900s. The new nation brings together over 200 ancient tribes and kingdoms, as well as many different languages and religions. Half the people live in villages and the rest in towns and cities. Half the people are Muslims who make up most of the population in the north. The other main religion is Christianity. There are more than 250 ethnic groups: the main ones are the Hausa and Fulani, living in the north, and the Yoruba and Igbo in the south. Nigeria became independent of British rule in 1960.

▲ Although elections were held in Nigeria in 1979 and 1993, the army ruled for most of the time between 1960 and the end of the 1990s. Democratic elections ended military rule in 1999, but regional disputes have led to instability in the country.

◄ Zuma Rock dominates the landscape at Abuja. The city, which was built in 1979 to replace Lagos as the capital, is centrally located.

SEE ALSO

Africa

NORTH AMERICA

North America is the third largest of the world's seven continents and the fourth largest in population. It stretches from the Arctic Ocean to Central America.

▼ The world's first skyscraper was built in Chicago, USA, in 1884. It no longer stands, but two other early skyscrapers, the Wrigley Building (left) and the Tribune Tower (right), are still Chicago landmarks.

The largest part of North America is made up of Canada and the United States. The rest consists of Mexico, the seven countries in Central America and the islands in the Caribbean Sea, which include 13 independent countries and 18 overseas territories still linked with a colonial partner. The UK territory of Bermuda lies in the North Atlantic Ocean and is also part of North America.

LARGEST ISLAND

Greenland, in the north, is a self-governing territory linked with Denmark and is the world's largest island.

▲ In the province of Quebec in Canada, average January temperatures range from –12°C to –29°C.

MOUNTAINS AND PLAINS

In the western half of the continent are the Rocky Mountains, the world's second longest mountain chain. The continent's highest peak, Mount McKinley (6,194m), is in Alaska. There are smaller mountain ranges in the east, including the Appalachians. The Canadian Shield is a huge area of ancient rock with poor soils but rich in minerals. Across the centre of the continent is a vast grassland region, known as the prairies.

GREAT LAKES AND RIVERS

The five Great Lakes – Superior, Huron, Erie, Ontario and Michigan – form the world's largest grouping of this kind. The thundering waters of Niagara Falls, on a strait between Lakes Erie and Ontario, are an impressive spectacle. The Mississippi, Missouri and Ohio rivers together form the continent's longest river system, more than 7,500km long.

COLD AND HOT

North America has every kind of climate. The north has bitterly cold winters – in the Arctic regions of Canada and Alaska it is too cold for trees to grow. In the south, huge forests of evergreen and deciduous trees cover the land. Still farther south, there are hot deserts and tropical forests.

GIANT TREES

Some of the world's tallest trees, the giant redwood and the sequoia, grow on the west coast of North America. In the eastern forests, the leaves of maple, hickory and other deciduous trees provide a brilliant colour show in the autumn. Mesquite, prickly pear and saguaro cactus grow in desert regions. ▶

ARCTIC OCEAN

GREENLAND
(Denmark)

ALASKA
(USA)

Mt. McKinley

NORTH PACIFIC
OCEAN

YUKON
TERRITORY

Mackenzie

Yukon

ROCKY MOUNTAINS

Hudson
Bay

CANADA

CANADIAN   SHIELD

GREAT
PLAINS

Vancouver

Lake
Superior

Lake
Huron

Quebec

Ottawa

Lake Ontario

Lake
Michigan

Lake Erie

New York

NORTH
ATLANTIC
OCEAN

UNITED STATES
OF AMERICA

GREAT
BASIN

Chicago

Washington D.C.

Missouri   Ohio

APPALACHIANS

CALIFORNIA

Los Angeles

BERMUDA (UK)

Mississippi

Dallas

Rio Grande

Gulf of California

MEXICO

Gulf of
Mexico

BAHAMAS

CUBA

DOMINICAN
REPUBLIC

PUERTO
RICO (US

ISLANDS

CARIBBEAN

HAITI

PACIFIC
OCEAN

Mexico City

BELIZE

HONDURAS

JAMAICA

CARIBBEAN
SEA

VENEZUELA

GUATEMALA

CENTRAL AMERICA

EL SALVADOR

NICARAGUA

COSTA RICA

COLOMBIA

PANAMA

miles
0   500

0   500
km

KEY TO MAP
1 ST KITTS & NEVIS
2 ANTIGUA &
  BARBUDA
3 DOMINICA
4 BARBADOS
5 ST LUCIA
6 ST VINCENT &
  THE GRENADINES
7 GRENADA
8 TRINIDAD &
  TOBAGO

ANIMAL LIFE

Wildlife has been reduced by hunting and settlement, so buffalo, wolves and bears are no longer widespread. There are caribou, moose, mountain lions, wild goats, porcupines, beavers, rattlesnakes and alligators. Birds include the turkey, macaw, roadrunner and bald eagle – the national symbol of the United States.

FARMING

North America is rich in farm land and the continent is the world's biggest grain exporter. The vast prairies have been ploughed for cereals or are used as grazing land for cattle and sheep. Important crops are maize, soya, cotton, wheat and flax. There are also plantations growing bananas, coffee, cotton and sugar cane, and huge orchards of apples, oranges, cherries and other fruits.

▼ North American bison, also known as buffalo, graze in Yellowstone National Park. These animals live mostly in reserves. Their numbers have been greatly reduced by overhunting and strict laws now exist to protect them.

GOODS AND RESOURCES

Both Asia and Europe make more factory goods than North America, but it is still a major producer of vehicles, aircraft, electronics and chemicals. It is rich in minerals, including silver, natural gas, oil, copper and coal. Some of the world's leading companies are based here.

CITIES AND TRANSPORT

Most North Americans live in towns and cities. The continent has some of the world's largest cities, including Mexico City, New York and Los Angeles, where skyscrapers make dramatic skylines and

▲ At carnival time in Mexico, people dress in traditional costume. Many Mexicans are of Spanish ancestry, but there are also descendents of the Ancient Aztec and Mayan people living in Mexico and Central America.

where cars and trucks move along multi-lane highways. In this huge continent, trains and aeroplanes carry passengers and freight long distances. Many North Americans enjoy a high standard of living, but in the inner cities of the United States and in Mexico and parts of the Caribbean, people are relatively poor.

VARIED ROOTS

North America has been a melting pot for peoples from many parts of the world. English is the main language but French is used in parts of Canada, while Spanish is spoken in Mexico and by many people in Central America and the United States. Many North Americans have European or Asian roots. African Americans are the descendants of black people who were brought from Africa as slaves.

THE FIRST AMERICANS

People came to North America from Asia around 16,000 years ago and settled across the continent. They were hunters, some of whom, over the ages, became farmers and town-builders. Another group was the ancestors of the Inuit people, who settled in the far north. The Maya and Aztecs of Mexico created civilizations of which impressive ruins still remain.

EUROPEANS ARRIVE

Vikings came to North America more than 1,000 years ago but did not settle for long. In 1492, the explorer Christopher Columbus discovered the American continent, which soon became known as the New World. He was followed by other explorers from Spain, who came seeking gold. From the 1600s, the British and French settled in Canada and along the east coast. Spain ruled Mexico, Florida and Central America. Canada and Mexico became independent in the 19th century.

THE UNITED STATES

The United States was created in 1776 when 13 colonies broke away from Britain. It grew rapidly into an industrial giant. Native Americans were driven from their lands as settlers moved west across the Great Plains and reached the Pacific coast. Immigrants from Africa, Europe, Asia and Central America have helped to shape the modern United States.

▲ Sequoias, growing on the west coast of the continent, are some of the world's tallest trees.

◄ Grenada is one of 13 independent island nations in the Caribbean. Its capital, St George's, lies on the southwest coast among forested hills.

SEE ALSO

Arctic, Aztecs, Canada, Caribbean, Central America, Explorer, Maya, Mexico, Native Americans, Slavery, USA, Vikings

NUCLEAR POWER

Nuclear power is the generation of electricity using heat released by changes in the nuclei of atoms. The process is known as a controlled nuclear reaction.

▲ The mushroom cloud from a nuclear explosion is made up of particles of rock, soil, water and other materials that eventually fall back to Earth as radioactive 'fall-out'.

Lise Meitner (1878–1968) proved that heavy atoms can be split into lighter ones – a process she called 'nuclear fission'.

Otto Hahn (1879–1968) worked with Meitner to split the atom, for which he was awarded the 1944 Nobel Prize for Chemistry.

Enrico Fermi (1901–54) built the first nuclear reactor in a squash court in 1942 and later worked on the atomic bomb project.

The centre of an atom is called the nucleus. Radioactive elements such as uranium have nuclei which sometimes split, releasing energy including heat. When these nuclei split, they throw out two or three tiny particles called neutrons. These can hit other nuclei, making them split, shooting out more neutrons.

AN IDEAL FUEL
Compared to coal, oil or gas, very small amounts of uranium can make a lot of electricity, and it does not pollute the air with chemicals or solids. Nuclear power is ideal for spacecraft and submarines: a nuclear-powered spacecraft can keep its instruments working for years, while a nuclear-powered submarine can travel around the world without refuelling and does not pollute the air with waste gases.

HOPEFUL SOLUTION
In the 1950s, nuclear power was seen as the solution to the world's energy needs. The world's first commercial nuclear power station, Calder Hall, in the UK, started generating electricity in 1956. Some countries, such as France, rely heavily on nuclear power. But few nuclear power stations are now being built because of the dangers.

NUCLEAR HAZARDS
Nuclear waste is hard to dispose of, remaining dangerously radioactive for thousands of years. Making old nuclear reactors safe is expensive. There is also the chance of an accident, such as the one in 1986 at Chernobyl in the Soviet Union, when an explosion contaminated thousands of square kilometres. Nuclear fusion, which releases energy by joining nuclei together rather than splitting them apart, may provide safe and clean energy in the future.

THE NUCLEAR REACTOR
In a reactor, a moderator such as graphite or water is used to slow down the neutrons released from fuel rods containing uranium. Slowed neutrons are much better at splitting other uranium atoms, causing a sustained chain reaction that releases huge amounts of heat. Control rods stop the reaction going too fast by absorbing neutrons. The heat boils water into steam, which turns turbines to make electricity.

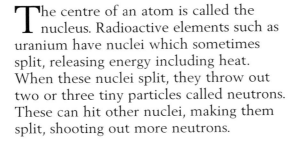

Reactor vessel

Water and steam separator

Control rod

Core (nuclear fuel assembly)

Steam outlet

Pump

Water inlet

Control rod drive

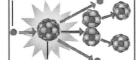

Concrete shield

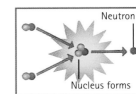

Neutron

Nucleus splits

Neutron

Nucleus forms

▲ In nuclear fission, neutrons are used to split heavy atoms, such as those in uranium, which in turn release more free neutrons and energy.

▲ In nuclear fusion, two nuclei of a lightweight substance such as hydrogen combine to form heavier ones, releasing a further neutron and energy.

SEE ALSO
Atom and molecule, Electricity, Energy, Submarine, World War II

NUTRITION

Nutrition is the process by which we take in and use food. Chemical substances found in food, called nutrients, provide energy and help the body function.

Fruit and vegetables are rich in vitamins. We should eat five portions each day.

Carbohydrate foods contain natural sugars and starches for energy.

Fats can be animal (butter, milk, cheese) or vegetable – from plants and nuts.

Meat, fish, cheese, pulses and nuts are all sources of protein.

There are five important nutrients – carbohydrates, proteins, fats (in small quantities), vitamins and minerals. We also cannot live without water.

ENERGY AND GROWTH

Carbohydrates and fats provide the body with energy. Proteins are necessary for growth and repair of cells. Vitamins and minerals like calcium, potassium and iron are essential for the health of nerves, skin, bones, muscle and brain. Research has shown that eating food rich in vitamins A, C, E and beta-carotene can help protect against the cell damage that causes cancer.

FIBRE AND WATER

Fibre, the indigestible part of fruits and vegetables, is essential in the diet. It adds bulk to food and helps it move through the large intestine during digestion. Water

A BALANCED MEAL

A healthy meal can take many forms. Most national diets are based on locally grown produce, animals or fish and a traditional staple food that is usually starchy and relatively cheap, such as rice, bread or pasta.

▲ A Sudanese mother in a refugee camp shows all the food she has to feed her family. Lack of food can result in malnutrition and lowered resistance to disease.

is vital. The human body is made up of about 65 per cent water. Its cells need water to keep chemical reactions going. We need about two litres of water a day.

A BALANCED DIET

The energy value of food is measured in calories. The more work your body does, the more calories you need. A man needs, on average, 2,555 calories a day and a woman 1,925; a 16-year-old boy needs 2,755 calories a day and a girl 2,110.

FOOD SHORTAGES

Many people do not get enough to eat. Malnutrition (not getting sufficient nutrients) causes weakness and disease. Around 20 million people die each year from hunger-related causes, more than six million of whom are under five years old.

▼ Pasta is a good energy source; adding cheese increases protein. Tomato sauce provides Vitamin C.

▼ The traditional Thanksgiving dinner in America is a typical well-balanced meal.

◀ Research shows the Japanese diet is especially beneficial to long-term health. Tofu (beancurd) contains protein, calcium and other minerals. Raw fish is used to make sushi.

◀ A healthy meal in one bowl. In parts of West Africa, meat, beans and nuts are mixed in a stew (gumbo) along with yam, a root vegetable.

▶ Many of our most popular foods originally come from South America.

▲ Fresh, raw vegetables are simply prepared in hot countries like Australia. Grilling meat reduces fat.

SEE ALSO
Farming, Food, Fruit, Vegetable

OCEAN AND SEA

Seventy-one per cent of the Earth's surface is covered by water. Nearly all of this vast area is made up of salt water oceans and seas.

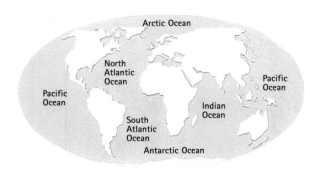

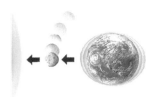

High spring tides are caused by the combined gravitational pull of the Sun and Moon when they are in line with the Earth. This occurs at the full Moon and new Moon.

Weak neap tides occur during the Moon's first and third quarters, when the gravitational forces of the Sun and Moon are at right angles and their combined force is less.

The Earth's crust is of two types: dense oceanic crust and lighter continental crust. The continental crust forms the great land masses of the Earth and these, being relatively light, stand high above the general level of the Earth's surface. The water-filled hollows that lie between the continents are called oceans.

OCEAN FOUNDATIONS
The ocean floor is made of denser crustal material, which is constantly being created and destroyed through the process of plate tectonics. Along each ocean lies a volcanic ridge, forming a vast underwater network that encircles the Earth. This is where new crustal material is generated. The old material is destroyed along the edges of some of the oceans as one crustal plate is drawn down and swallowed up beneath the edge of another.

OCEAN FEATURES
All this movement gives the basic features of any ocean – the oceanic ridge, which can rise to about 1,000m beneath the surface; the abyssal plains, which comprise the greatest area of ocean floor and average 5,000–6,000m deep; and the oceanic trenches, many of which are over 9,000m deep with the deepest – the Marianas Trench – plunging to nearly 11,000m.

THE SOFT COVERING
The sediments of the ocean floor consist of oozes, which are made up of tiny skeletons and shells, volcanic dust and mud that has washed off the land. Sediments are very thin close to the oceanic ridges, but thicker farther away. This is because the new ocean crust close to the ridges has not had enough time to collect much debris.

SHALLOW SEAS
Seas differ from oceans in that they are much shallower. They are the areas of the continents that happen to be below sea level – the continents' flooded edges. Sea floors tend to be thickly covered in sediment, such as sand and mud, brought

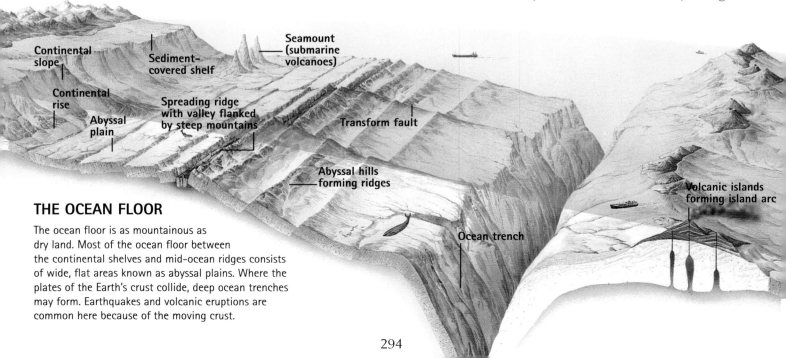

Continental slope

Continental rise

Abyssal plain

Sediment-covered shelf

Seamount (submarine volcanoes)

Spreading ridge with valley flanked by steep mountains

Transform fault

Abyssal hills forming ridges

Ocean trench

Volcanic islands forming island arc

THE OCEAN FLOOR
The ocean floor is as mountainous as dry land. Most of the ocean floor between the continental shelves and mid-ocean ridges consists of wide, flat areas known as abyssal plains. Where the plates of the Earth's crust collide, deep ocean trenches may form. Earthquakes and volcanic eruptions are common here because of the moving crust.

down by the rivers. Some seas do not lie on the continental shelf but are inland. The Caspian Sea is completely landlocked, and the Black Sea is only narrowly connected with the Mediterranean Sea. The Red Sea is an oddity – although it is small and almost landlocked, its floor is true oceanic crust and it has a central ridge.

LIVING THINGS

Most ocean life is found within a layer of water about 100m deep, where sunlight penetrates. Plankton is the mass of tiny plants and animals that drifts in the sea and is the basis of the entire ocean food chain. All sea creatures depend directly on plankton for food or on animals that feed on plankton. Planktonic plants (*phytoplankton*) grow here, and also planktonic animals (*zooplankton*), which include one-celled animals, baby crabs and fish. Larger creatures feed upon these animals, and even larger predators feed upon them in turn. The final link in the food chain is humans – the sea provides a source of food for much of the world's population.

MYSTERIOUS DEPTHS

Scuba divers and submersibles are still exploring the sea, studying its creatures and geological features and discovering submerged cities and ship-wrecks. Although the oceans have been travelled by many generations, the sea has always retained its mystery. It has been the source of many legends, such as that of the mermaid and the sea serpent, and has inspired artists throughout the centuries.

MARINE LIFE

Life forms in the ocean are more varied than those on land. New creatures are often discovered in the deep sea.
1 Herring **2** Sperm whale **3** Prawn **4** Kat-tail **5** Angler fish **6** Grenadier **7** Cod **8** Gulper eel **9** Sea spider, tube worms, clam, white ghost crab **10** Tripod fish **11** Viper fish **12** Swallower **13** Lantern fish **14** Swordfish **15** Yellowfin tuna **16** Giant squid **17** Hammerhead **18** Barracuda **19** Portuguese man-of-war **20** Plankton **21** Green turtle **22** Sea lion **23** Common dolphin

ATOLLS

An atoll begins as a coral reef surrounding a volcanic island. As the island sinks, the reef grows upwards to keep pace. Eventually, the island disappears completely and all that remains is a ring-shaped reef, or atoll, surrounding a lagoon.

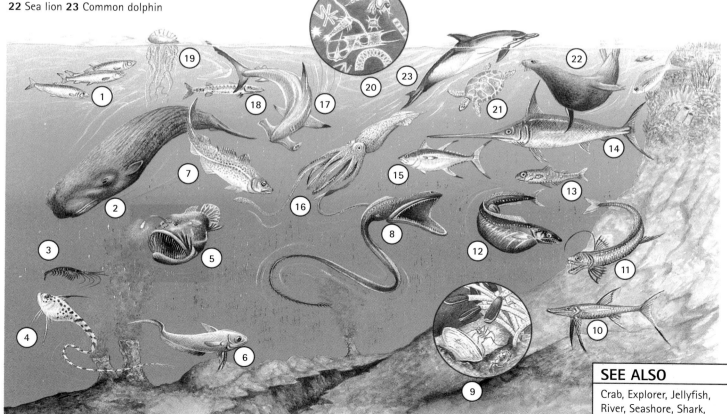

SEE ALSO

Crab, Explorer, Jellyfish, River, Seashore, Shark, Snail, Starfish, Swamp and marsh, Water

OIL

Oil, or petroleum, is a thick, black liquid, sometimes called crude oil. It is a valuable raw material for fuels such as petrol, and in the chemical industry.

► In a refinery, parts, or fractions, of the crude oil are separated out in a process called fractional distillation. Fuels such as paraffin and petrol are made by mixing these fractions. Other fractions are sent to chemical plants to be made into drugs, paints, plastics and other products.

OTHER OIL SOURCES
Many oil products are derived from animal and vegetable sources.

Animal fats, such as pig lard, are used for cooking.

Vitamin-rich cod liver oil is used in medicine.

Most of the world's olive crop is grown for its oil.

Oil from sunflower seeds is used to make margarine.

Oil is a complex mixture of chemical compounds consisting of the elements hydrogen and carbon. These hydrocarbons release heat when they burn. This is what makes them useful as fuels.

THE ORIGINS OF OIL
The story of oil began millions of years ago, with plants and animals that lived in the ancient seas. After they died, the bodies of these plants and animals decayed and gradually turned into oil. The oil has remained trapped in rocks ever since. Like coal and gas, oil is a fossil fuel.

FINDING OIL
The search for oil is called oil exploration. Crude oil is always found in certain patterns of rock, so geologists look for these patterns in areas where oil is likely to be found. They use magnetic and seismic surveys (which send sounds from explosions at ground level to bounce off rocks underground) to find rock formations that may contain oil.

DRILLING FOR OIL
To get the oil out, a hole is drilled down through the rocks. This is an oil well. The most expensive method is using oil rigs at sea (offshore), although onshore drilling is also common. The oil is sent by pipeline or by ship to an oil refinery for processing.

THE FUTURE OF OIL
Like other fossil fuels, oil pollutes the environment when it is burned. It also contributes to acid rain and to global warming. The modern world uses increasing amounts of oil for vehicles, power generation, heating and industry. New oil finds are being made but known reserves may have run out by 2060. In future, alternative fuels will be needed so that the world's oil reserves do not completely run out.

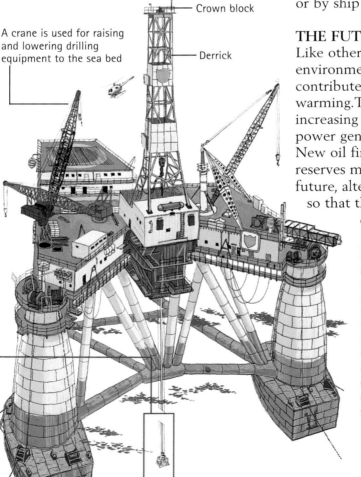

A crane is used for raising and lowering drilling equipment to the sea bed

Crown block

Derrick

◄ A large-toothed bit is used to drill through soft rock.

► The drill shaft rotates within an outer casing. Mud is pumped down to clean the bit and bring up the rocks.

OFFSHORE DRILLING
An offshore oil rig is more dangerous to work on than a land rig as storms can damage the structure. It also costs about ten times more to build. The rig itself has to be floated out to sea in sections and then assembled, while the equipment and crew are carried out to the site by helicopter. Because of the huge expense involved, several test drillings are carried out to make sure that there are enough oil reserves to justify the cost of setting up a permanent rig.

SEE ALSO
Coal, Gas, Medicine, Mining, Plastic, Pollution

OLYMPIC GAMES

The Olympic Games are a world athletic and sports competition that takes place every four years. About 200 nations enter competitors in about 300 events.

The first modern Olympic Games were opened by King George I of Greece in Athens on April 5, 1896. They were a huge success, but it took several attempts to get it established as a successful global event. The modern Olympics were inspired by the ancient Olympic Games, which were first held in Olympia, Greece in 776BCE.

▲ The ancient Olympians, such as this discus thrower, competed naked.

OLYMPIC SPIRIT

The aim of the Olympic Games is to promote peace, equality and friendship, and to inspire athletes around the world. Competition between individuals rather than countries is encouraged and on the scoreboard at every Olympic Games is the message: "The most important thing in the Olympic Games is not to win but to take part…"

▲ The Olympic symbol of five linked rings represents the five continents of Africa, Asia, Australia, Europe and North America. It was designed so that at least one of the six colours in the symbol (including the white background) would appear in all the flags of the competing nations.

OPENING CEREMONY

At every Olympic opening ceremony, the parade of nations is led by Greece, the founder nation, with the host country coming last and the nations in between appearing in alphabetical order. During the celebrations, the athletes and officials take the Olympic oath, the Olympic torch is lit and the Olympic flag raised. As a sign of peace, doves are released into the stadium. ▶

FAST FACTS

• Since 1896, only five countries have been at all the Games – Australia, France, Greece, Great Britain and Switzerland

• The marathon used to be 25 miles, but in the 1908 London Games it was extended to over 26 miles so that Princess Mary could see it start from the nursery window at Windsor Castle

• The Beijing Games opening ceremony began at 8pm on 8 August, 2008. The number 8 means prosperity in Chinese culture.

• Newer Olympic sports include tae kwondo and the triathlon (introduced for Sydney 2000) and women's boxing (introduced for London 2012)

THE 2008 BEIJING GAMES

The 2008 Games were held at Beijing in China. The opening ceremony was spectacular, and featured over 15,000 performers. There were new events for the Games, including BMX biking and an open–water swimming marathon. A total of 10,500 athletes took part in the Games and over 950 medals were won. China topped the medal table with 51 golds.

▲ US athlete Jesse Owens became the star of the 1936 Games at Berlin, Germany, when he walked away with four gold medals. In the face of Nazi propaganda for white superiority, Owens's victory was a huge embarrassment for Nazi officials.

▲ Not all Olympic events go smoothly, as was the case when Britain's Zola Budd (right) collided with America's Mary Decker in the women's 3,000m event in 1984 at Los Angeles. Mary Decker fell and was robbed of the chance of victory. This caused a great uproar.

RECORD BREAKERS

- The first men's gold medallist was James Connolly, from the USA, in 1896 in the triple jump

- The first women's gold medallist was British tennis player Charlotte Cooper in 1900

- Johnny Weissmuller of the USA won five gold medals altogether for swimming, in 1924 and 1928, and went on to play Tarzan in 18 films

- British rower Steve Redgrave won gold medals in five successive Games between 1984 and 2000

- Swimmer Michael Phelps of the USA has won more medals in one Olympics than any other competitor. In 2008, he won eight swimming gold medals

- Swimmer Kristin Otto of East Germany was the first woman to win six medals at one Olympic Games, in 1988

THE OLYMPIC TORCH

Four weeks before the start of the Games, the Olympic flame is lit in Greece by magnifying the Sun's rays with mirrors. It is then carried across the world in a torch by a series of runners. On the opening day of the Games, the last runner enters the stadium and the arena flame is lit. It stays burning until the close of the Games.

THE ANCIENT GAMES

The ancient Olympic Games were first organized as a religious, sporting and cultural festival held in honour of Zeus, the most powerful of the Greek gods. Every four years, Greek athletes travelled from all over the country to Olympia, a village near Mount Olympus (home of the gods) in Greece. Only Greek citizens could compete, although no women were allowed to take part in or even watch the Games on pain of death. The Games were taken so seriously that a truce between any warring states within Greece was called so that competitors could travel safely to Olympia.

BANNING OF THE GAMES

At the first ancient Olympic Games in 776BCE, there was only one event, a 200m stadium race. Gradually, more events were added, including chariot racing in 680BCE. The Games were finally banned in 394CE by the Roman Emperor Theodosius. The Romans had conquered Greece and Theodosius banned all pagan festivals, including the Olympic Games.

THE WINTER OLYMPICS

The modern Olympics falls into two parts: the Winter and the Summer Olympics. The first Winter Olympics were held in Chamonix, France in 1924. Until 1994, they were always held the same year as the Summer Olympics but is now held two years earlier. Winter Olympic sports include ice hockey, luge (small toboggan), skating, skiing and bobsleigh.

Thomas Burke (USA) wins the 100m event in the 1896 Olympics in Athens, Greece.

The Canadian ice hockey team triumphs in the first-ever Winter Olympics in Chamonix, France in 1924.

Attilio Pavesi (Italy) wins the cycling road race in the 1932 Games in Los Angeles, USA.

Dawn Fraser (Australia) wins 100m freestyle swimming event in Melbourne, 1956.

Joe Frazier (USA) is heavyweight boxing champion at the 1964 Games in Tokyo, Japan.

THE SUMMER OLYMPICS

The Summer Olympics include 26 sports: combat sports include judo and boxing; ball games include volleyball and handball; court games include tennis and badminton; and water sports include rowing and swimming. Athletics is classified as one sport in the Olympics, but includes nearly 50 events, including 24 track events. As well as running events, athletics includes the high jump and long jump, the discus and javelin, and the decathlon (ten athletic events spread over two days).

POLITICAL PROBLEMS

Because the Olympic Games are the world's greatest sporting event, they have sometimes been used as a political tool. In 1972, Israeli competitors were attacked and killed by Arab terrorists at the Olympics in Munich, Germany. Eight years later, the Games in Moscow were boycotted by the USA and its allies because of the Soviet invasion of Afghanistan. In 1984, the Soviet Union and its allies refused to compete in the Olympics in Los Angeles because of fears over security arrangements.

TODAY'S GAMES

The Olympic Games are considered to be the ultimate sporting event and attract athletes from all over the world. Over 4.5 billion viewers tuned in to watch the 2008 Games, which saw the Marshall Islands, Montenegro and Tuvalu competing for the first time, proving that the Games are becoming even bigger and more competitive.

▲ The Paralympics is a competition for disabled competitors. It is separate from, and held after, the main Olympics, although it takes place in the Olympic stadium and is no less competitive.

14-year-old Nadia Comaneci (Romania) is gold medallist in the combined athletics event in the 1976 Games in Montreal, Canada.

Steffi Graf (Germany) wins the women's tennis singles event in the 1988 Games held in Seoul, South Korea.

Jan Zelezny (Czech Republic) wins the javelin event in the 1996 Games in Atlanta, USA.

Sprinter Usain Bolt (Jamaica) broke three world records at the 2008 Games in Beijing, China: the 100m and 200m races and the 4x100m relay.

SEE ALSO
Greece (Ancient), Sport

PACIFIC ISLANDS

Before the 1960s, most of the thousands of islands in the Pacific Ocean were ruled by the UK, US or France, but there are now 13 independent countries.

The Pacific Islands are part of a vast region called Oceania (which also includes Australia). Some of the islands are the mountainous tips of volcanoes and others are coral islands which rest on the tops of sunken volcanoes.

ISLAND GROUPS

The Pacific Islands are divided into three areas. Melanesia, meaning 'black islands' after the dark skin of the people, includes Fiji, Papua New Guinea and the Solomon Islands. Micronesia, meaning 'tiny islands', includes part of Kiribati, the Federated States of Micronesia and several island groups associated with the United States. Polynesia, meaning 'many islands', includes the islands in a triangle formed by New Zealand, Hawaii and Easter Island.

 FIJI
Area: 18,272 sq km
Population: 837,000
Capital: Suva
Languages: English, Fijian
Currency: Fiji dollar

KIRIBATI
Area: 717 sq km
Population: 93,000
Capital: Bairiki
Languages: English and I-Kiribati
Currency: Australian dollar

 MARSHALL ISLANDS
Area: 181 sq km
Population: 56,000
Capital: Majuro
Languages: Marshallese and English
Currency: US dollar

 FEDERATED STATES OF MICRONESIA
Area: 701 sq km
Population: 103,000
Capital: Palikir
Language: English
Currency: US dollar

 NAURU
Area: 21 sq km
Population: 9,300
Capital: Yaren
Language: Nauruan
Currency: Australian dollar

 NEW ZEALAND
Area: 270,534 sq km
Population: 4,368,000
Capital: Wellington
Language: English
Currency: NZ dollar

 PALAU
Area: 458 sq km
Population: 19,900
Capital: Ngerulmud-Melekeok
Languages: Palauan and English
Currency: US dollar

 PAPUA NEW GUINEA
Area: 462,840 sq km
Population: 5,370,000
Capital: Port Moresby
Language: English
Currency: Kina

 SAMOA
Area: 2,831 sq km
Population: 179,000
Capital: Apia
Languages: Samoan and English
Currency: Tala

SOLOMON ISLANDS
Area: 28,370 sq km
Population: 495,000
Capital: Honiara
Language: English
Currency: Solomon Islands dollar

TONGA
Area: 748 sq km
Population: 102,000
Capital: Nukualofa
Languages: English, Tongan
Currency: Pa'anga

TUVALU
Area: 24 sq km
Population: 11,000
Capital: Fongafale
Languages: Tuvaluan and English
Currency: Australian dollar

 VANUATU
Area: 12,190 sq km
Population: 243,000
Capital: Port-Vila
Languages: Bislama, English and French
Currency: Vatu

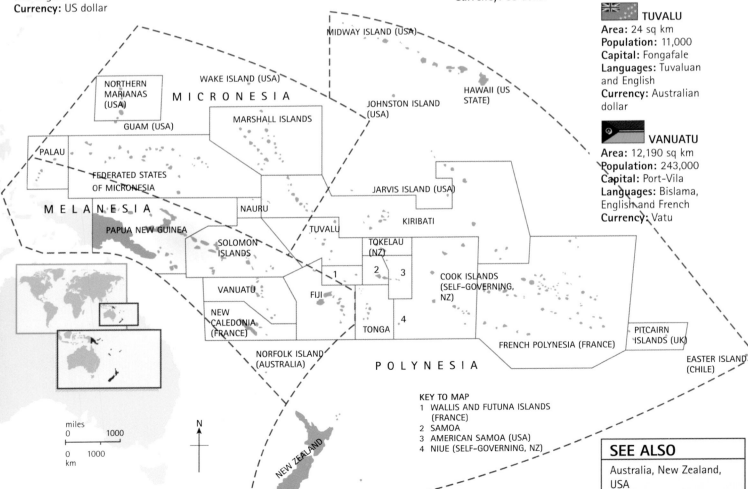

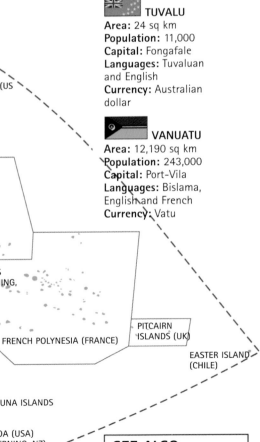

MIDWAY ISLAND (USA)

WAKE ISLAND (USA)

NORTHERN MARIANAS (USA)

MICRONESIA

GUAM (USA)

JOHNSTON ISLAND (USA)

HAWAII (US STATE)

PALAU

MARSHALL ISLANDS

FEDERATED STATES OF MICRONESIA

MELANESIA

NAURU

JARVIS ISLAND (USA)

PAPUA NEW GUINEA

SOLOMON ISLANDS

TUVALU

KIRIBATI

TOKELAU (NZ)

VANUATU

FIJI

1   2   3

COOK ISLANDS (SELF-GOVERNING, NZ)

NEW CALEDONIA (FRANCE)

TONGA   4

FRENCH POLYNESIA (FRANCE)

PITCAIRN ISLANDS (UK)

NORFOLK ISLAND (AUSTRALIA)

POLYNESIA

EASTER ISLAND (CHILE)

NEW ZEALAND

miles
0   1000
0   1000
km

N

KEY TO MAP
1 WALLIS AND FUTUNA ISLANDS (FRANCE)
2 SAMOA
3 AMERICAN SAMOA (USA)
4 NIUE (SELF-GOVERNING, NZ)

SEE ALSO
Australia, New Zealand, USA

PAINT AND DYE

Paint is a colouring which is used to cover a surface, usually to protect or decorate it. A dye is a substance that sinks into the material, colouring it inside and out.

▲ In textile dyeing, the cloth is immersed in the dyeing solution and the temperature is raised until enough dye has moved out of the solution and onto the cloth fibres.

Paints and dyes were traditionally produced in small batches from natural substances such as earth, fruits or flowers. Today, most are mass-produced in factories.

INSIDE PAINT
Paint is usually applied as a liquid and dries by evaporation to form a thin layer. It consists of a liquid – called a binder or medium – which may be water, an oil or a resin, and a solid – the pigment which gives paint its colour. Chemicals are often added to improve the paint. They may prevent the paint from becoming solid in the can, or make the paint resistant to damage from exposure to the Sun or frost once applied. Buildings or furniture may be treated with paints that, in the event of fire, break down chemically to slow up the spread of the flames.

MAKING PAINT
In the first stage of making paint, oils, resins and solvents (thinners) are blended together. Coloured pigment is then added and the mixture is ground in a ball mill until the paint is thoroughly mixed.

▶ Pigment gives paint its colour. Today's pigments are usually made from chemicals although artists often grind their own paints by hand.

◀ In 1856, English chemist William Perkin accidentally invented the world's first artificial chemical dye, a mauve derived from coal tar waste.

ORIGINAL MAUVENE PREPARED BY SIR WILLIAM PERKIN IN 1856

USING DYES
Dyes are used to colour plastics and paper as well as textiles. They usually need a fixative, or mordant, to help them penetrate fibres and stay in them. Most mordants are chemical solutions of metal salts. Until the 1850s, dyes were derived from natural substances such as leaves and berries. Indigo, a plant, was used to dye cloth blue, the cheapest colour, usually worn by servants in 18th-century Europe. By 1880, chemists had learned how to make an artificial indigo. Nowadays, almost all dyes are industrially produced. To ensure an even colour, the material being dyed must not resist the dye and it must be moved continually during dyeing.

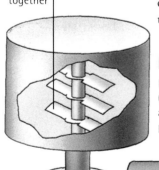

Oil and resin are blended together

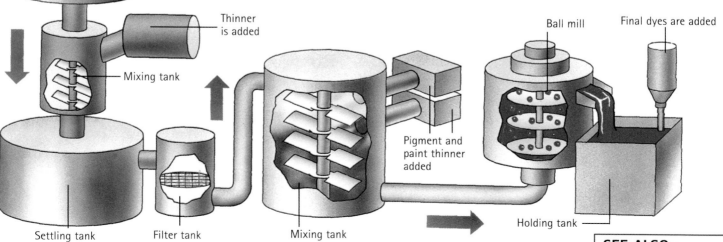

Thinner is added

Mixing tank

Settling tank

Filter tank

Mixing tank

Pigment and paint thinner added

Ball mill

Final dyes are added

Holding tank

SEE ALSO
Colour, Textile

PAPER

Paper is a material made from plant fibres that are webbed together to form sheets. It is used for many different purposes, including writing and packaging.

Waxed paper can be used to make cartons for holding liquids.

Filter paper is used inside cars to stop grit from entering the engine.

Furnishings such as lampshades and wallpaper can be made from paper.

Paper is used for communication – it can be printed or written on.

Paper is used to mop up liquids, both in industry and in the home.

People have known how to make paper for over 2,000 years. The earliest paper-makers lived in Ancient China. They made thick, coarse sheets of paper by flattening and drying out a pulp (mush) of water, chopped bark, plants and fishing nets. Some 500 years before them, the Egyptians had discovered they could make something like paper by pressing papyrus strips together. Our term 'paper' comes from the word papyrus.

STRONG FIBRES

Like Ancient Chinese paper, modern paper is made from a pulp, but most of it contains shredded, softened wood from conifer trees such as pine, spruce or fir. The fibres in wood, or any other plant, are made of a strong material called cellulose. This makes the paper very strong, so that it does not fall apart easily when pressed, folded or stretched.

MAKING PAPER TODAY

In a modern paper-making machine, wood chips are boiled with caustic soda or another chemical to soften them and strip them of everything but their long, stringy fibres. This pulp is spread over a conveyor belt, blasted with air, then squeezed between rollers to turn it into dry paper.

DIFFERENT SOURCES

Over the years, people have experimented with cellulose from sources other than wood. Bank notes and expensive writing paper often contain fibres from cotton rags, which are made from cotton plants. The fibres make the paper very smooth and tough.

WASTE PAPER

On average, every person in the United States uses about 340kg of paper a year. Over a third of the paper we use is recycled to make newspapers, toilet rolls and other low-quality papers. The rest is dumped in landfill sites.

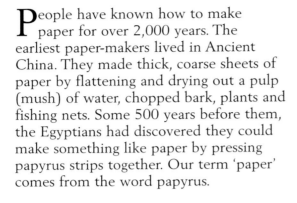

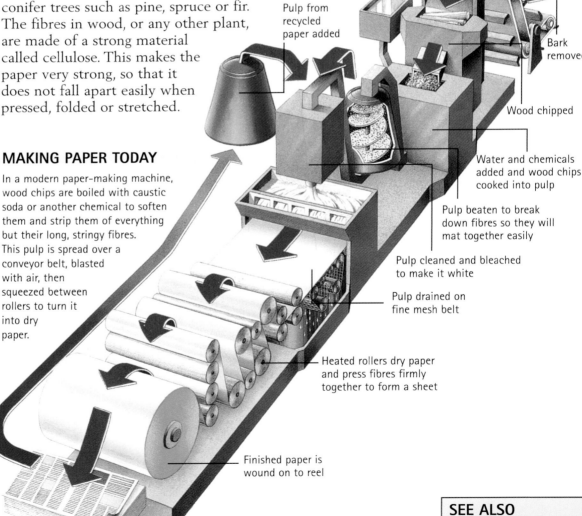

Pulp from recycled paper added

Bark removed

Wood chipped

Water and chemicals added and wood chips cooked into pulp

Pulp beaten to break down fibres so they will mat together easily

Pulp cleaned and bleached to make it white

Pulp drained on fine mesh belt

Heated rollers dry paper and press fibres firmly together to form a sheet

Finished paper is wound on to reel

SEE ALSO

Egypt (Ancient), Conservation

PHILIPPINES

The Republic of the Philippines is a country in the southwest Pacific Ocean, off the coast of mainland Asia. It is made up of more than 7,000 islands.

Area: 300,076 sq km
Population: 88,575,000
Capital: Manila
Language: Filipino and English
Currency: Peso

The Philippines is in one of the Earth's most violent geological zones, the 'ring of fire', where there are many volcanoes. The dormant volcano Mount Apo (2,954m) is the country's highest peak. The two largest islands are Luzon and Mindanao. Off the northeast coast of Mindanao is one of the deepest points in the Pacific Ocean, the Philippine Trench, reaching 10,439m below the surface. The climate is tropical, with monsoon rains in July and August.

FORESTS AND FARMING

Forests cover a quarter of the land. The fibre from kapok trees is used to make cushions, and bamboo provides a useful building material. With many trees being felled for timber, deforestation is a problem. In the fertile soil, farmers grow rice, corn, cassava, sweet potatoes, sugar cane, and abaca (Manila hemp). The seas provide fish, clams and shrimp.

▲ Just over a third of the people live in rural areas and many are farmers. The carabao, a type of water buffalo, is used to pull ploughs and haul loads.

▲ Gold is one of the Philippines' valuable resources. The country also has large reserves of copper, chromium, nickel, oil and natural gas.

BOOMING CITY

Manila, founded in 1571, grew from a collection of shore villages into a teeming metropolis. It symbolizes the country's growth as an industrial nation. More than 11.5 million people live in and around it, and it is the busiest port. Factories make clothing and electronic goods for export.

THE FILIPINOS

The people of the Philippines, Filipinos, are related to Malays. Chinese, Europeans, Indians, Japanese and mountain peoples called Negritos also live there. Catholicism has been the main religion since the Spanish arrived in 1565. The islands are named after Philip II of Spain. They were ruled by the USA after 1898, invaded by Japan during World War II (1939–45) and became independent in 1946.

◀ Around 45 per cent of the population is under 20 years old. Basketball is the country's national sport.

SEE ALSO

Asia, Volcano, World War II

PHOTOGRAPHY

Photography is the process of capturing images by focusing light onto a light-sensitive surface using a camera. It is used in the arts, media and sciences.

As early as 1515, Leonardo da Vinci described how an image could be made on the wall of a darkened room by letting light through a tiny hole in the opposite wall. This was called a *camera obscura*, meaning dark chamber. Apart from sketching it by hand, there was no way of recording the image until the 18th century, when the British scientists Sir Humphry Davy (1778–1829) and Thomas Wedgwood (1771–1805) caught outlines of leaves and faces on paper or leather coated with light-sensitive silver chloride.

THE FIRST PHOTOGRAPHS

The first photographs, called heliograms, were made in the 1820s by the French doctor Joseph Niépce (1765–1833) on

bitumen-coated pewter plates using a camera obscura. In the 1830s, the French painter Louis Daguerre (1787–1851) made photographs on plates coated with light-sensitive silver iodide. The British inventor William Fox Talbot (1800–77) found a way to 'fix' the silver iodide permanently so that it would not react to light and darken after a picture was taken. He also invented a process that made it possible to make many copies of one photograph.

PHOTOGRAPHY FOR EVERYONE

Photography was a complex procedure until 1888, when the American George Eastman (1854–1932) invented roll film and the small box camera. It soon became a hobby that any keen amateur could take up. More technical advances, such as the invention of flash bulbs and colour film in the 1930s, led to the growing popularity of photography as it is enjoyed today.

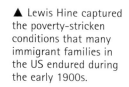

PHOTO-JOURNALISM

Journalists quickly learned that a good photograph could often tell a story with more impact than written words. The first British war correspondent, Roger Fenton (1819–69), began taking battlefield photographs of the Crimean War in the 1850s, while in the 1860s, the American Matthew Brady (1823–96) captured the grim reality of the US Civil War.

SOCIAL REALISM

American sociologist Lewis Hine (1874–1940) was one of the first to use photography to show the terrible living conditions of poor people. His striking portraits of children at work in factories and mills helped to change child labour laws. Modern photo-journalists often risk their lives to take pictures of war-torn countries or to reveal injustices in society.

ART PHOTOGRAPHY

Some early photographers used the principles of painting in their photographs. In the 1860s, the British photographer Julia Margaret Cameron (1815–79) created stunning portraits using blur and soft focus. The French photographer Nadar (1820–1910) captured many Paris intellectuals and artists, encouraging them to pose naturally.

In the 1920s, the American photographer Man Ray (1890–1976) experimented with artistic effects. His original style combined fantasy with reality, inspiring many generations of budding photographers.

FUTURE PHOTOGRAPHY

Today, cameras are becoming smaller and easier to use. Images from digital cameras can be viewed on a television or loaded onto a computer for editing, printing or sending across the Internet. An image can be processed in many ways to change its colour, shape, size and composition. Holography is a method of photography that uses lasers to show all sides of a subject in 3-D.

▲ Lewis Hine captured the poverty-stricken conditions that many immigrant families in the US endured during the early 1900s.

▲ Fast shutter speeds freeze a moving image, but blur still occurs with a racing fairground ride.

HOW A DIGITAL CAMERA WORKS

When you take a picture, the camera's shutter flicks open and shut to let light enter the camera and hit the charge coupled device (CCD) for the correct length of time. The lens does the focusing and the aperture controls how much light gets through. The CCD converts the light into binary digital code. The data is stored on the camera's memory chip, and can then be displayed on the camera's screen or transferred to a printer or computer.

Electronic flash

This button is pressed to take a photo

Viewfinder

Camera mode selector dial

A large, precisely-shaped lens captures plenty of light and brings the image to a sharp focus

A charge coupled device (CCD) captures the image

▲ Images are transferred from a digital camera to a computer using a special cable. On screen, the images can be viewed, changed, uploaded to the Internet or emailed.

SEE ALSO

Art, Computer, Film, Internet, Lens, Newspaper and magazine, Printing

PILGRIM

Pilgrims are people who travel to take part in religious or spiritual events. Often they travel along a specific route or path known as a pilgrim way.

Holy relics of Christian saints are often stored in jewelled boxes.

Buddhists climb Mount Fuji to view the dawn during summer months.

Followers of Shinto in Japan return to their family shrine once a year.

Ancient Egyptians held festivals at Bubastis for the cat goddess Bastet.

PILGRIM WAYS

During the Middle Ages, a network of roads, called pilgrim ways, ran across Europe, linking major sites of pilgrimage. Pilgrims made donations and bought badges and relics, creating wealth for the churches and cities they visited. Monasteries were built along most routes to provide shelter for travellers.

Many religions have places which are considered sacred or where holy rituals are held. The most popular ritual of ancient times was the Greek festival of Demeter, the farming goddess. Each year people travelled to the town of Eleusis, where secret ceremonies, called the Mysteries, took place.

CULT OF THE SAINTS

Many Christians believe that visiting the grave of a saint brings them closer to God. During the Middle Ages, Canterbury drew pilgrims from Britain and northern Europe to the tomb of St Thomas à Becket, while Compostela in Spain held the tomb of St James. But the greatest pilgrimage was to Jerusalem, where Christ was crucified. Today, Christians visit holy places such as Fatima in Portugal or Lourdes in France.

THE HAJJ

Muslims have a duty to visit Mecca, in Saudi Arabia, at least once. This

▲ Muslims who have completed the hajj pilgrimage decorate their homes with paintings of the journey.

pilgrimage, the *hajj*, centres on a sacred black stone – which Muslims believe was given by God to Adam to absorb the sins of mankind – and sacred pillars and hills.

MOUNTAINS AND RIVERS

Japanese Buddhists believe Mount Fuji to be a gateway to another world. During the summer, pilgrims climb the mountain to watch the Sun rise. Hindus believe the River Ganges in India to be sacred and many place the ashes of their relatives in the river after cremation.

SEE ALSO

Buddhism, Christianity, Crusades, Hinduism, Islam, Middle Ages, Religion

PLANET

Planets are the largest objects that circle around stars. They may be rocky, like the Earth, or made mostly of gas and liquid, like Jupiter.

Sir William Herschel (1738–1822) discovered Uranus in 1781.

In 1846, Urbain Le Verrier (1811–77) found the position of Neptune.

John Couch Adams (1819–92) predicted in 1845 that an eighth planet existed.

Percival Lowell (1855–1916) began the search for a ninth planet in 1905.

Clyde Tombaugh (1906–97) found Pluto. It was classed as a planet from 1930 to 2006.

The Sun is orbited by eight planets, most of which have moons. They range in size from Mercury, less than half as wide as Earth, to Jupiter, which is 11 times wider than Earth.

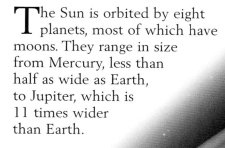

THE WANDERERS

The word planet is Greek for 'wanderer'. The name comes from the way planets appear to move against the stars over time. It is thought that the planets formed at about the same time as the Sun. As the original cloud of gas and dust collapsed to form the Sun, some matter was spun out into a flattened disc. Over several million years, the dust and gas gathered together to form the planets and moons. Denser rocks gathered near the Sun and lighter gases farther out.

MERCURY

Mercury is the planet closest to the Sun,

PLANET SYSTEMS

Planets in the solar system and around other stars share several features. The solid centre is often surrounded by layers of gas forming an atmosphere. Circling the planet may be smaller planet-like objects called moons. Around the equator may be found bright rings consisting of tiny particles of rock and ice.

at an average distance of 58 million km. With a diameter of just 4,878km, Mercury is the smallest of the eight planets. During the day, its temperature soars to 430°C, hot enough to melt lead, but at night it cools down to –170°C. Mercury's day, the time it takes to spin around once on its axis, is equal to 59 Earth days. Its year, the time it takes to go once around the Sun, is equal to 88 Earth days.

VENUS

With a diameter of 12,142km, Venus is nearly the same size as Earth. However, most of Venus's atmosphere consists of carbon dioxide, a gas that traps the Sun's heat. This 'greenhouse effect' makes Venus hotter than Mercury, although it is about twice as far from the Sun. Most of its surface is covered in lava that flowed out of giant volcanoes millions of years ago. Venus is the only planet to spin the opposite way to the direction of its orbit. It spins so slowly that one of its days lasts for as long as 243 days on Earth. ▶

PLANETARY NAMES

Mercury The Roman god of merchants and travellers

Venus The Roman goddess of love

Mars The Roman god of war

Jupiter The king of the Roman gods

Saturn The Roman god of seeds and sowing

Uranus The Greek and Roman god of the sky

Neptune The Roman god of the sea

MARS

The fourth planet from the Sun, Mars is only about half the size of the Earth and is much cooler. Its strong red colour is due to rust in the rocks on its surface. Its atmosphere consists mostly of carbon dioxide and is about 100 times thinner than the Earth's. The largest volcano and the largest canyon ever discovered are to be found on the Martian surface. There are also features on Mars that look like dried-up river beds. This suggests that Mars was once warmer and wetter than it is now. Under these conditions, life may have developed and there is even a chance that primitive life may exist there today. Mars has two tiny moons: Phobos and Deimos. The larger of these, Phobos, is only about 24km across.

JUPITER

The biggest of the planets, Jupiter, could swallow up over 1,000 Earths. It has a

MERCURY
The surface of Mercury is rocky, often covered in sand and marked by large meteorite craters. There is no atmosphere and the planet is roasted by the nearness of the Sun.

VENUS
Venus has broken slabs of rock and some dust on its surface. Most sunlight is blocked by the clouds of sulphuric acid in the atmosphere of carbon dioxide and nitrogen.

EARTH
Only Earth is known to support life. The rocky surface is covered by water and soils. The atmosphere of nitrogen and oxygen contains clouds of water vapour.

MARS
The reddish surface of Mars is made up of rock and sand. The atmosphere is thin and consists mostly of carbon dioxide. Both poles are covered with caps of ice.

▲ The space probe *Voyager 2* was launched in 1977 and by 1989 had passed close to Jupiter, Saturn, Uranus and Neptune, sending data back to Earth.

JUPITER
As a gas giant, Jupiter has no surface. Instead, dense layers of gas surround a core. Io, one of 63 known moons, has a rocky surface dyed red by sulphur from its many volcanoes.

SATURN
Like Jupiter, Saturn is a gas giant. The 91 per cent hydrogen atmosphere has dense clouds of ammonia, water and methane coloured by phosphorous and other elements.

URANUS
Hydrogen and helium make up most of the gas giant Uranus. The planet is surrounded by rings of blackish particles 'shepherded' in place by two small moons.

NEPTUNE
The blueness of the gas giant Neptune is due to methane gas. The surface of the moon Triton is frozen methane and nitrogen. Geysers of nitrogen gas erupt to 8km.

diameter of 142,800km, but most of this is made of gases and liquids rather than solid rock. Like the Sun, Jupiter contains a great deal of hydrogen. Jupiter spins so fast that its day lasts less than ten hours. But a year on Jupiter is nearly 12 times longer than one of ours. Jupiter has a single ring and 63 known satellites. One of these, Ganymede, is the largest moon in the solar system – bigger than Mercury.

SATURN

Measuring 120,000km across, Saturn is second only to Jupiter in size. Like Jupiter, Uranus and Neptune, it is a gas giant. It is famous for its bright rings, made of billions of particles of rock and ice. The rings are more than 272,000km across, but they are very thin. Saturn has at least 60 moons. The largest of these, Titan, is the only moon known to have an atmosphere.

URANUS

Orbiting the Sun 19 times farther out than the Earth, Uranus receives little heat. The temperature at the top of its clouds is –220°C. With a diameter of 52,000km, Uranus is less than half the size of Saturn but still four times bigger than the Earth. It was the first planet to be discovered through a telescope. Uranus has a set of thin, dark rings and 27 known moons.

NEPTUNE

Similar in size and appearance to Uranus, the blue-green planet Neptune orbits the Sun at an average distance of 2.8 billion km. It is bitterly cold and 85 percent of its atmosphere is hydrogen, while violent winds blow at over 1,000km/h. Neptune has several thin rings and 13 known moons.

DWARF PLANETS

Smaller round objects, known as dwarf planets, also orbit the Sun. The best known is Pluto, which was classed as a planet from its discovery in 1930 until 2006. This cold, icy world is just 2,300km across, and its orbit around the Sun takes 248 Earth years to complete. The other known dwarf planets are Ceres, discovered in 1801 and originally classed as an asteroid, Haumea, Makemake and Eris.

PLANETS OF OTHER STARS

Planets that are orbiting stars other than our Sun are called extrasolar planets. The first ones were discovered in the 1990s, and since then more than 500 have been found. There are also another 1,200 or so that are waiting to be confirmed as planets. The first found to be rocky like Earth was CoRot-7b. As more and more are found, the chances grow that billions of planets may exist, and that there may be life on some of them.

▲ Life from other planets has featured in the movies. The alien in the movie *E.T.* was friendly, but other movie aliens are warlike.

▲ Saturn's rings are made up of dust, ice crystals and rocks up to 10m across. The rings are 66,000km wide, but only 1km deep. As Saturn orbits the Sun, the rings are seen from different angles from Earth.

GREAT RED SPOT

The Great Red Spot on Jupiter has existed since at least 1665. It is a circular storm with winds blowing at about 80m per second. The red colour may be due to sulphur in the clouds.

SEE ALSO

Astronomy, Moon, Solar system, Spacecraft, Space exploration, Sun

PLANT

Plants are living organisms that harness the energy of the Sun to feed themselves. Without plants for animals to feed on, there would be no animal life on Earth.

Ferns are among the oldest plants, appearing about 350 million years ago.

The dodder is a parasitic plant. It inserts suckers into other plants to get food.

The carnivorous Venus flytrap feeds on insects that it traps in its leaves.

We make textiles from the fibres of the ripe fruit of the cotton plant.

Some plants are dangerous to eat – hemlock can be used to make poison.

Plants provide timber. Wood from the oak tree is heavy, hard and strong.

Most plants are able to absorb sunlight by means of a green substance inside them called chlorophyll. They use the energy from the Sun's light to make food by a chemical process called photosynthesis. This results in the production of oxygen, which all plants and animals, including humans, need to live.

PLANTS OF ALL KINDS

There are about 400,000 different kinds of plant, ranging in size from tiny mosses only a few millimetres long to giant redwood trees, which grow to over 100m tall. Each has adapted to absorb light, find water and minerals and withstand the temperature range in its own habitat. Desert plants such as cacti have long, widely spreading roots to collect water, which they store in their expandable stems. Succulent plants store water in swollen fleshy leaves. Plants in cold places grow in thick, low clumps which protects them from the cold and wind.

DESIGNED TO CATCH LIGHT

Plants need to catch as much light as possible. Each one has leaves which are shaped and arranged on the stem so they over-shadow the leaves below as little as possible. Tall trees have strong, woody trunks to hold their leaves high above the ground and other plants. Plants like vines climb up through the trees with clinging tendrils. Plants called epiphytes grow entirely suspended in tree branches, never touching the ground.

OTHER SOURCES OF FOOD

Some parasitic plants, such as mistletoe, obtain extra nourishment by growing into the tissues of larger plants. Other plants, such as the dodder, cannot make any of their own food. The dodder attaches itself to another plant for nourishment. There are also carnivorous (meat-eating) plants, such as the pitcher plant and the Venus flytrap, which can catch and digest insects.

PLANTS AND PEOPLE

People learned to grow plants as crops about 10,000 years ago. Today, over four fifths of the world's food comes from

GERMINATION

Inside the seed are all the parts needed to form a new plant. The stage when a seed starts to sprout is called germination. In order to begin the germination process, a seed must have warmth, moisture and oxygen.

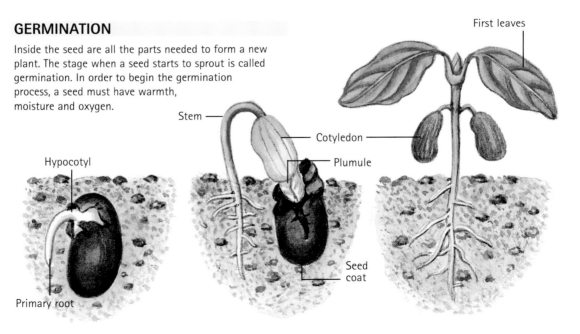

First leaves

Stem

Cotyledon

Plumule

Seed coat

Hypocotyl

Primary root

Stage 1

When a seed starts to germinate, it splits and the primary root is formed from the hypocotyl.

Stage 2

The stem pushes up through the soil and the cotyledon starts to break out of the seed coat.

Stage 3

The plumule breaks free of the cotyledon, the stem grows upwards and the first leaves are formed.

CLASSIFYING PLANTS

Plants are classified according to certain similarities they share. One way is to divide them into ten groups, or divisions. The division Bryophyta is made up of non-vascular plants. These plants do not have the tissues that carry food and water from one part of the plant to another. The other nine divisions are all vascular. The division Anthophyta contains all flowering plants (also called angiosperms), which contain their reproductive cells in flowers. Angiosperms used to be divided into two classes, monocots and dicots. Monocots have one seed leaf (or cotyledon) and dicots have two. Today, scientists recognize four main clades, or groups, of flowering plant: monocots and eudicots, and two clades of primitive flowering plants – the basal angiosperms and the magnoliids. Together, they include a huge variety of plants, from water lilies to broad-leaved trees.

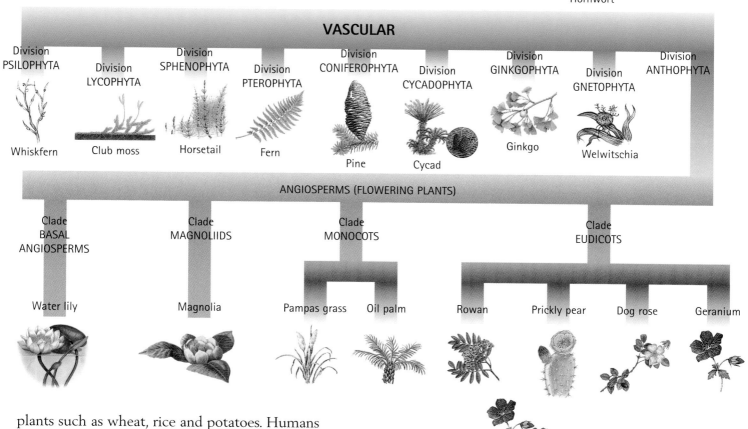

NON-VASCULAR

Division BRYOPHYTA

Class HEPATICAE — Liverwort

Class ANTHOCEROTAE — Hornwort

Class MUSCI — Moss

VASCULAR

Division PSILOPHYTA — Whiskfern

Division LYCOPHYTA — Club moss

Division SPHENOPHYTA — Horsetail

Division PTEROPHYTA — Fern

Division CONIFEROPHYTA — Pine

Division CYCADOPHYTA — Cycad

Division GINKGOPHYTA — Ginkgo

Division GNETOPHYTA — Welwitschia

Division ANTHOPHYTA

ANGIOSPERMS (FLOWERING PLANTS)

Clade BASAL ANGIOSPERMS — Water lily

Clade MAGNOLIIDS — Magnolia

Clade MONOCOTS — Pampas grass, Oil palm

Clade EUDICOTS — Rowan, Prickly pear, Dog rose, Geranium

plants such as wheat, rice and potatoes. Humans eat a variety of fruits, nuts and vegetables and make drinks from tea, coffee and grains. Plants also provide products such as vegetable oils, cotton, rubber and – perhaps the most useful of all – wood. Many of the drugs we use to treat disease come from plants. Even fuels such as coal are the fossilized remains of prehistoric plants.

PLANT BREEDING

Most plants we use today are quite different from their ancestors. Using methods such as genetic engineering, plant breeders have made improvements to cereals such as wheat to make them more productive or more resistant to pests.

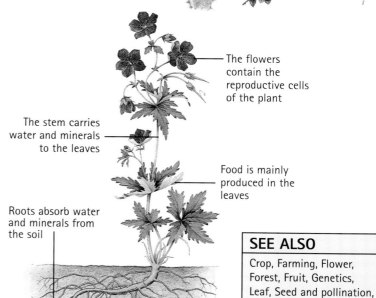

The flowers contain the reproductive cells of the plant

The stem carries water and minerals to the leaves

Food is mainly produced in the leaves

Roots absorb water and minerals from the soil

SEE ALSO

Crop, Farming, Flower, Forest, Fruit, Genetics, Leaf, Seed and pollination, Soil, Tree, Vegetable

PLASTIC

Plastics are materials that can easily be stretched or moulded into shape. Most are made from the chemicals obtained from petroleum oil.

Plastic replaces many metal and ceramic items because it is light but durable.

Many items are wrapped and sealed in plastic rather than paper bags.

Strong and lightweight plastics can replace the metal bodywork in cars.

Polyester is a plastic that is widely used in clothing manufacture.

Instead of wood, boats today are often made of strong, lightweight plastic.

Plastic is used for replacement body parts, such as false teeth.

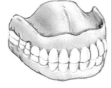

Plastics are man-made and consist of long chains of molecules called polymers. The arrangement of these chains gives plastics their different qualities. Hard plastics can be used to replace metals, in cars for example. Soft plastics can be used to create fabrics, leather and even fur.

NATURAL INGREDIENTS
In 1862, the British chemist Alexander Parkes showed the first plastic, known as cellulose nitrate, at the London Exhibition. It was later named celluloid and developed by American inventor John Wesley Hyatt. Although celluloid became brittle and changed colour in strong light, it was used to make many objects, from billiard balls to false teeth and photographic film.

CHEMICALLY BASED PLASTIC
The first plastic to be chemically based was a material called Bakelite, invented in 1909. More modern plastics, however, such as polyester and PVC, are lighter and easier to colour. They can also be made flexible and can withstand moisture and strong sunlight.

HARD OR SOFT
Plastics do not all behave the same way when reheated. Some, called 'thermoplastics', melt and can be reshaped

PLASTIC MOULDING
Two common methods for moulding plastic are that of injection moulding, in which plastic pellets are heated and then injected into a mould, and hot extrusion, in which hot plastic is forced through openings to make rods or sheets.

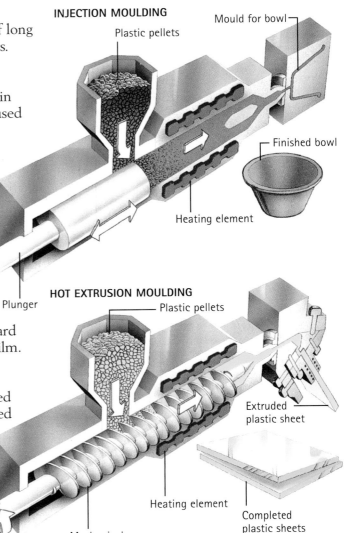

INJECTION MOULDING
Plastic pellets

Mould for bowl

Finished bowl

Heating element

Plunger

HOT EXTRUSION MOULDING
Plastic pellets

Extruded plastic sheet

Heating element

Completed plastic sheets

Mechanical screw

after reheating. Polythene, a material used to make plastic bowls, is like this, which is why it often loses its shape if something hot is placed on it. Other plastics are 'thermosetting'. Once they have cooled and set during manufacture, they cannot be reshaped. In fact, if a thermosetting plastic is heated up, it gets harder. Electric plugs are made of thermosetting plastics, which is why they do not melt if the wires inside them overheat.

◄ Perspex is an ideal plastic for a squash court as it is transparent like glass but much stronger.

SEE ALSO
Clothing, Materials, Oil, Textile

PLATYPUS

The platypus is an unusual mammal with a beak like a duck and a tail like a beaver. It lays eggs, but it has fur and it feeds its young with milk like other mammals.

▲ Echidnas are found in Australia and New Guinea. The female lays one egg a year, which hatches in a pouch on her belly. The young echidna stays in the pouch for several weeks, feeding on its mother's milk.

The platypus is often called the duck-billed platypus because of the shape of its jaws, which resemble a duck's bill. It is one of just five mammals that lay eggs (monotremes). The others are four species of echidna, or spiny anteater. The platypus is found in Australia and Tasmania. It lives by rivers and lakes, where it digs a burrow in the bank with its strong claws. It sleeps in its burrow for most of the day and comes out to feed mainly at night, when it uses its flat bill to catch large numbers of insects and worms.

▲ Platypuses are very good swimmers, pushing themselves through the water with their broad, paddle-like front feet and steering with their hind feet and tail.

A FAKE?

The platypus is up to 75cm long, including its tail, and it weighs up to 2.5kg. When European scientists first saw the skin of a platypus, they thought it was a fake – as if someone had sewn a duck's beak and a beaver's tail onto the body of another animal. The platypus's bill is not hard like that of a duck. It is soft and leathery and very sensitive, and it has no teeth. The platypus stores energy-giving fat in its broad tail.

POISONOUS SPINES

The male platypus has a poisonous spine on each back leg. The animals use their spines when they fight each other during the breeding season. Wounded platypuses are not seriously hurt by the poison, although there is enough in each spine to kill a dog.

HATCHING FROM EGGS

When the female is ready to lay her eggs, she makes a tunnel in the river bank up to 30m long. At the end of it she makes a nest of leaves to lay her eggs in. Three or four months after hatching, the young are ready to leave the burrow, but they stay there a few more weeks while they learn to swim and find food.

▶ The female platypus has no teats (nipples) – instead, the babies lap up the milk as it oozes from pores on her body.

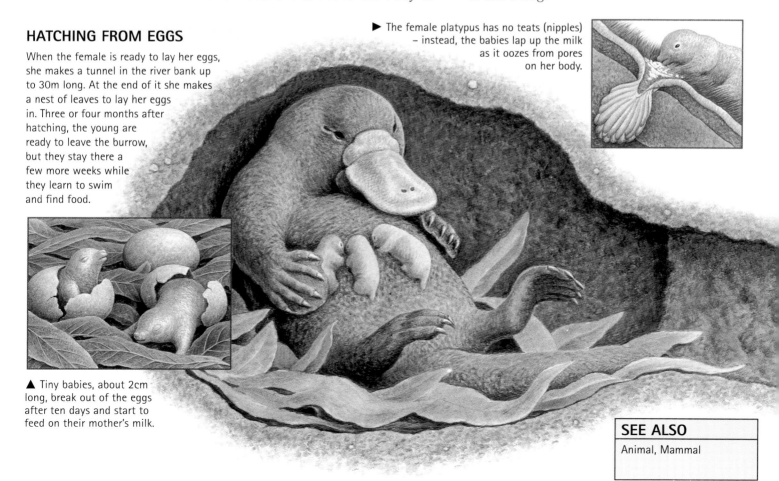

▲ Tiny babies, about 2cm long, break out of the eggs after ten days and start to feed on their mother's milk.

SEE ALSO
Animal, Mammal

POLITICS

Politics is the art and science of seeking public office through elections or appointment, controlling government policies and influencing those in power.

▲ Then-Senator Barack Obama speaks at a rally during the 2008 presidential election in the United States. Campaign rallies gain television coverage, encourage party workers and allow politicians to get their message across.

▼ A meeting of Chartists in London in 1848. The Chartists staged mass meetings and organized petitions demanding political reform, in particular universal suffrage and vote by secret ballot.

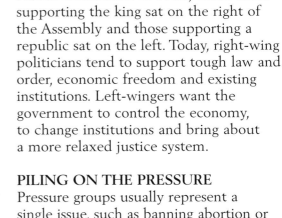

Politics is about power in government. People who seek to form governments or affect policy are politicians.

ELECTION POLITICS
During elections, parties put forward candidates and publish their ideas and programmes. Politicians make speeches, appear on radio and television, and knock on doors to meet the people. There are two main election systems: the 'first past the post' system (the candidate with the most votes wins) and proportional representation (where voters may vote for more than one candidate, and for more than one party). Politics today has much to do with media management – the skilful use of the Internet, TV and advertising. Politicians are now more likely to debate on TV than in public.

LEFT AND RIGHT
Politics is often divided into Left and Right. These terms come from the French Revolution of 1789, when those supporting the king sat on the right of the Assembly and those supporting a republic sat on the left. Today, right-wing politicians tend to support tough law and order, economic freedom and existing institutions. Left-wingers want the government to control the economy, to change institutions and bring about a more relaxed justice system.

PILING ON THE PRESSURE
Pressure groups usually represent a single issue, such as banning abortion or preventing the construction of a new road. They try to mobilize opinion through the press or by organizing public demonstrations.

SEE ALSO
Communism, Democracy, Government, Revolution

POLLUTION

Pollution happens when a harmful substance is released into the environment in such large quantities that it causes damage to people, wildlife or habitats.

The control of pollution is a major problem facing the world. Large areas may soon become uninhabitable and many plants and animals may become extinct. Public opinion is now forcing governments and industry to combat pollution.

SMOKES AND SMELLS

Car exhausts and factories pump fumes into the air. Some of these gases mix with clouds to form acid rain which kills plants. Carbon dioxide traps the Sun's heat, and may lead to global warming. Other gases, called CFCs, are thought to destroy ozone – the gas barrier that blocks harmful radiation from the Sun. Noise can also be a form of pollution, with traffic or aircraft noise ruining the quality of life.

OIL SPILL

Oil tankers carry up to two million barrels of oil, so accidents can be devastating. The oil floats, forming a slick that blocks the sunlight needed by seaweed and other algae. Birds and fish may be trapped or poisoned by the oil, but the wildlife usually recovers in a few years.

▲ Smoke and other pollutants can travel thousands of kilometres before falling as deposits or as acid rain.

▲ Liquid waste dumped into rivers may poison wildlife and threaten supplies of drinking water for humans.

A LOAD OF RUBBISH

Rubbish is created in large quantities, and the world is running out of places to put it all. Recycling glass, paper and other waste reduces the need for dumping. Radioactive waste created by nuclear power stations remains dangerous for thousands of years.

DEAD RIVERS

Industrial waste dumped into rivers can kill all life. Fertilizers can produce growths of algae, which absorb the oxygen in the water, killing fish and plants. International agreements have been drawn up to stop countries dumping waste at sea and to reduce the pollution of lakes and rivers.

SEE ALSO

Conservation, Ecology, Habitat

PREHISTORIC ANIMAL

Prehistoric animals are animals that lived before people began to record things in writing. Animal life began around one billion years ago in the oceans.

Mammoths lived
around 5 million
years ago (mya)

Hyracotherium –
first horse (size of
a terrier)

Paramys – early
rodent of 55 mya

Archaeopteryx –
first bird with
feathers

Sailback reptile –
from Permian
period

Oldest land
vertebrate from
Devonian period

Trilobites,
570 mya

We know that prehistoric animals existed because some of their remains have been preserved in the rocks as fossils. The fossils tell us a lot about the shape and size of the animals. From this, scientists can work out how they lived and what they ate.

ARMOURED CREATURES
The first living things appeared about 3,500 million years ago. We don't know much about them because they were microscopic, and did not leave many traces in the rocks. About 600 million years ago, animals began to develop shells or other hard coverings, and these hard parts were often preserved as fossils. Trilobites were among the earliest of the armoured creatures. They looked rather like woodlice and lived mainly on the sea bed. Corals and many kinds of shellfish lived with trilobites. Huge sea scorpions, up to about 2m long, fed on the smaller animals.

OUT OF THE WATER
The first animals with backbones were fish, which appeared about 500 million years ago. Many of them had bony armour to protect them from sea scorpions. The earliest prehistoric animals all lived in the sea, but they gradually spread into fresh water and then onto the land. The amphibians were the first backboned animals to move on to the land. These early

▶ *Meganeura* was like a giant dragonfly, with a wingspan reaching to about 75cm. It probably grew large because of the warm Carboniferous

▼ *Diplocaulus*, an amphibian from the Permian period, was a pond dweller. His head shape would have made him hard to swallow.

amphibians were rather like fish with stumpy legs that could only just lift their bodies off the ground. Some of them looked like big newts or salamanders. The early amphibians all lived in damp places and, just like today's frogs and toads, they had to go back to the water to breed. One group of amphibians started to change: their skins got thicker and they laid eggs with tough shells. These animals became the first reptiles. They could live in drier places and they spread all over the land.

TAKING TO THE SKIES
Some reptiles, called pterosaurs, learned to fly. Others went back to the sea, where they lived like today's dolphins. The best known prehistoric reptiles were the dinosaurs, which ruled the Earth for over 100 million years during the Triassic, Jurassic and Cretaceous periods. Many small, rat-like mammals wandered over the land at the same time as the dinosaurs. Some probably fed on dinosaur eggs, but only when the dinosaurs died out, about 65 million years ago, could mammals really have a chance of survival.

Dzungaripterus' pincer-like beak crushed shellfish.

Dimorphodon had strong jaws and sharp teeth.

Tropeognathus fed on fish caught by the mouthful.

▲ Scientists get clues to these pterosaurs' diets by studying their jaws. Strong jaws and sharp teeth were used for meat, while *Tropeognathus*'s odd beak steadied it in the water.

FLYING GIANT

Quetzalcoatlus was the largest pterosaur. It lived in North America about 68 million years ago and had a wingspan of at least 12m (almost five times bigger than our largest bird). Its loose throat pouch may have held fish.

▲ Evidence of prehistoric animals comes from fossils and ancient cave paintings like those at Lascaux, France showing deer, horses, elephants, and bison, which lived in Europe over the last 50,000 years.

EXPERIMENTAL MAMMALS

As nature experimented with different shapes and sizes, many very strange prehistoric mammals appeared. *Baluchitherium* was a giant, giraffe-shaped rhinoceros that lived in Asia between 20 million and 30 million years ago. With its huge head carried about 8m above the ground, it was probably the largest mammal ever to live on land. Most of these 'experimental' mammals died out completely, but some of them survived and gradually evolved into the mammals that we see around us. Like the reptiles

before them, some invaded the sea and became whales and seals and some, such as the bats, developed wings and learned how to fly.

MAMMALS IN THE ICE AGES

During the last two million years, there have been several very cold periods called ice ages. Many northern parts of the world were covered with ice. Most animals moved south to avoid the cold, but some managed to survive close to the ice because they were able to grow thick coats, like the woolly rhinoceros and the woolly mammoth. These cold-climate mammals died out when the climate began to warm up about 10,000 years ago, and new species evolved to replace them.

▼ *Smilodon* was one of the sabre-toothed cats of the Pleistocene period. It had massive fangs, about 15cm long, and huge neck muscles to power its jaws.

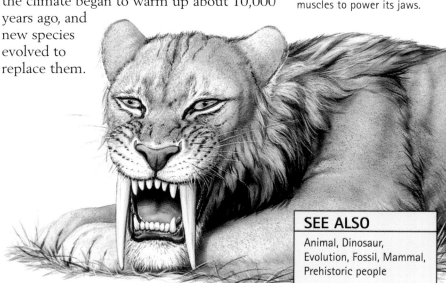

SEE ALSO

Animal, Dinosaur, Evolution, Fossil, Mammal, Prehistoric people

PREHISTORIC PEOPLE

Prehistoric people lived in 'pre-history', that is, before about 3500BCE when people first began to write and so record their lives. They include our earliest ancestors.

Neanderthals shaped sophisticated hand tools.

Cro-Magnons made arrowheads from flint.

A bone needle used in the Palaeolithic era.

The first human beings lived in Africa more than two million years ago. But small, human-like creatures who walked upright on their back legs were living on the Earth more than four million years ago. Today, scientists have named them australopithecines, and we know about them because their bones and footprints have been discovered. One of the most famous finds was the skeleton of a female, nicknamed 'Lucy', who lived about 3.75 million years ago in Ethiopia.

APE MEN AND WOMEN
Australopithecus probably looked and lived very like apes. This species was overtaken by a more advanced species,

ARRIVAL IN EUROPE

The Cro-Magnons (named after the site in France where their bones were first discovered) were the oldest known modern humans (*Homo sapiens*) in Europe, appearing around 40,000 years ago. They were taller (1.7m tall) and more slender than the Neanderthals, and had bony chins and domed heads.

▼ The various species of australopithecines, around 3.5 million years ago, were probably proficient hunters, using sticks and stones to kill prey and dig up edible roots.

known as *Homo habilis* (skilful man), who was certainly a tool-maker, with the ability to shape stones to make cutting and scraping tools. Animal bones have been found with scratches on them, suggesting that *Homo habilis* cut off the skins and meat from dead animals with stone tools.

STONE AGE PEOPLE
The Old Stone Age, or Palaeolithic period, began with *Homo habilis*. Some 1.8 million years ago, a new human species appeared. This was *Homo erectus* (upright man), who spread from Africa as far as Europe and Asia. *Homo erectus*

▲ An encampment of hunters in Eastern Europe, about 25,000 years ago. Hunting together they could kill large animals.

had a bigger brain, made better tools, and was probably the first human being to use fire. Some time after 230,000 years ago, yet another human species came on the scene. This was *Homo neanderthalensis*. The Neanderthal people (named after a valley in Germany), lived in Europe and the Middle East until about 28,000 years ago. The Neanderthals used simple tools and had probably developed a language to speak to one another. The Neanderthals successfully survived the cold of the Pleistocene Ice Age by living in caves.

PREHISTORIC CULTURES
Modern humans, *Homo sapiens*, appeared about 195,000 years ago and lived alongside the Neanderthals. The two species shared a common ancestor around

500,000 years ago and also interbred around 45,000 years ago. When the Neanderthals died out, ours was the only human species left on Earth. Prehistoric peoples, such as the Cro-Magnons, lived all over Europe during the Stone Age period. They built simple wooden huts, fished, and hunted deer and wild cattle, moving on in search of food. They began to express themselves through art, drawing pictures on cave walls and carving stones into human shapes. There are famous examples of detailed cave paintings in Lascaux in France and Altamira in Spain.

SETTLING DOWN
In the Neolithic, or New Stone Age, people moved from a nomadic life based on food-gathering and hunting to a more settled existence, growing crops and domesticating animals. This happened by about 11,000 years ago. People began to make metal tools about 5,500 years ago. The timing of events differs from area to area. The Ancient Greeks were living in the Bronze Age at the height of their success 3,000 years ago, historical times for them, but in Britain, prehistory lasted until the Romans invaded 2,000 years ago in the Romans' Iron Age.

Mesolithic people learnt to attach blades to handles.

Mesolithic antler spear thrower, still used by Inuits.

FAST FACTS
- The Palaeolithic period, (Old Stone Age) stretches back two million years to the time of *Homo habilis*
- Mesolithic times (the Middle Stone Age) were when Europe was recovering from the Ice Age, around 18,000BCE
- The Neolithic period (New Stone Age) was marked by the beginning of agriculture

◀ This mummy, found in 1991 in the Similaun glacier, Austria, is estimated to be 5,300 years old. Such finds tell us about our ancestors' lifestyles.

SEE ALSO
Evolution, Fossil, Prehistoric animal

PRINTING

Printing is the mass production of identical images of writing or pictures on books, posters, packaging and fabrics. It is used in education, business, art and fashion.

The first attempts at printing were made in China in the eighth century AD. Wooden blocks were carved with characters and pictures, which were then inked and pressed onto paper.

▲ With the Gutenberg press, books could be printed and circulated on a large scale. As printing became quicker and less expensive, books became cheaper, spreading information to a greater number of people. Printing inventions in the 19th century aided revolutions in science and mechanics.

EARLY PRESSES

The German Johann Gutenberg (c. 1398–1468) invented the first printing press around 1455. Gutenberg used moveable type, with raised pieces of metal for each letter so that words could be rearranged easily. The type was laid on a forme and then covered with ink. A sheet of paper was placed over it, held down by screws to give a clear, even image. Later inventors added mechanisms for automating the printing press. By 1830, a steam press could produce 1,000 sheets per hour.

MODERN PRINTING

In 1904, the American printer Ira Rubel invented offset lithography printing. He discovered that the inked image from a printing plate could be offset, or stamped, onto a rubber roller, which could then be printed onto paper. In 1930, this system was combined with a method of making pictures up from small dots. When used with four basic colour inks, this made mass-production colour printing possible. Today, many publications are printed from computer-generated pages. Laser printers work by spraying ink onto the page; dot matrix printers form images from tiny dots.

PICTURE PRINTS

Artists use intaglio to make engravings: they cut a design into the printing plate. Gravure printing uses a copper plate, which is engraved with a picture using a photographic process. Different tones and strengths of colour are produced by engraving deeper or shallower holes.

OFFSET LITHOGRAPHY PRINTING

Rubber rollers are offset with a printing image, one for each of four basic colours: yellow, magenta, cyan (blue) and black. Paper is then printed with the coloured inks in turn until the complete picture is built up.

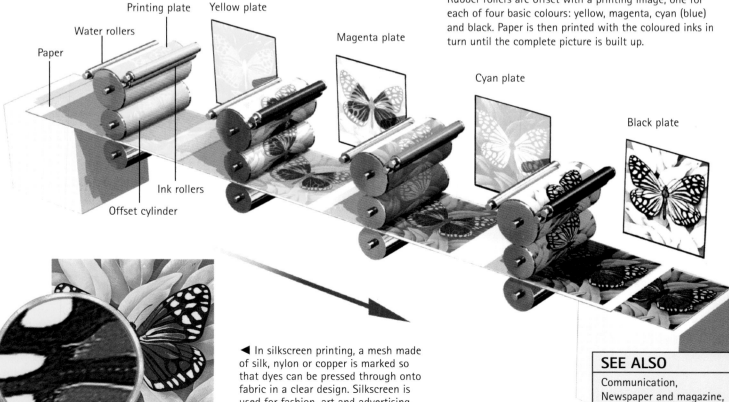

Paper

Water rollers

Printing plate

Yellow plate

Magenta plate

Cyan plate

Black plate

Ink rollers

Offset cylinder

◀ In silkscreen printing, a mesh made of silk, nylon or copper is marked so that dyes can be pressed through onto fabric in a clear design. Silkscreen is used for fashion, art and advertising.

SEE ALSO

Communication, Newspaper and magazine, Paint and dye, Paper, Textile

RADAR AND SONAR

**Radar and sonar are systems that locate objects.
They work by sending out waves, detecting echoes
from objects and measuring the distance in between.**

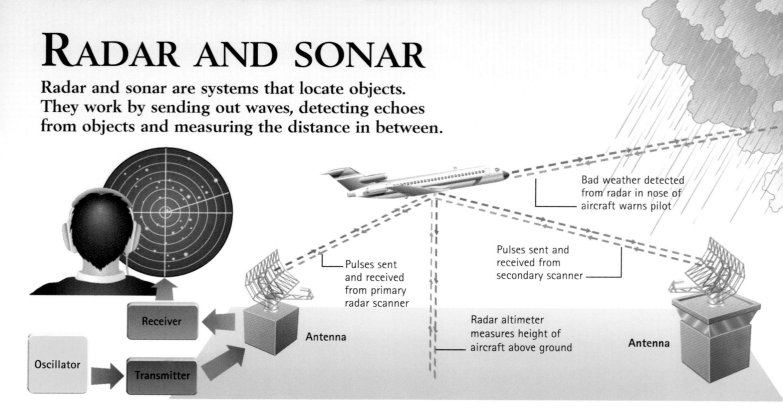

Bad weather detected from radar in nose of aircraft warns pilot

Pulses sent and received from secondary scanner

Pulses sent and received from primary radar scanner

Radar altimeter measures height of aircraft above ground

Antenna

Antenna

Receiver

Oscillator

Transmitter

Radar and sonar are used to find the location of objects that are difficult to see. They also help people to judge how fast objects are moving. Radar is used at airports to track aircraft in the surrounding airspace. Boats use sonar to measure the depth of the sea floor or river bed and to spot any obstacles under water.

HOW RADAR WORKS
Radar, which is short for RAdio Detection And Ranging, works by sending out a narrow pulse of radio waves. Any car, aircraft or other large metal object in the way of this pulse will reflect it, in the same way that a mirror reflects light. A receiver on the radar system picks up

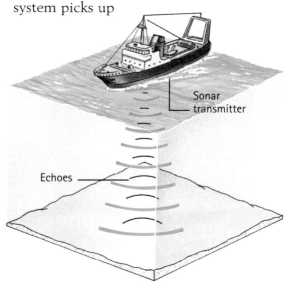

Sonar transmitter

Echoes

AIRCRAFT RADAR
Air traffic controllers need to know the height and position of aircraft around busy airports to prevent collisions between planes. They have small display screens that relay information they have found. The displays show a realistic map of the area, marked with objects. Large aircraft have on-board radar to detect other planes and bad weather.

the reflected waves and measures how long the radio wave took to bounce back. This information can be used to calculate the object's distance. Radar is used by scientists to find out the distance to other planets and by police to catch speeding motorists. It is also used to track storm fronts and forecast the weather.

HOW SONAR WORKS
Sonar, meaning SOund Navigation And Ranging, works in a similar way to radar. Instead of radio waves, it sends out a pulse of high-pitched sound. Known as ultrasound, the sound from a sonar system is so high that humans cannot hear it. The ultrasound bounces off any dense objects in its path, such as rocks, shipwrecks and shoals of fish, back towards the ship. Hydrophones (underwater microphones) pick up the reflected sound and use it to calculate the distance of the objects.

◄ Survey ships use sonar to chart the contours of the seabed. The time it takes sound waves to reflect back to the ship indicates the depth of the seabed.

▲ Radar was first used to detect enemy aircraft during World War II. Information was sent to a central control room, where it was used to track enemy action and plot battle strategies on a map.

SEE ALSO
Aircraft, Medicine, Navigation, Radio, Ship, Sound, Submarine, Weather, World War II

RADIO

Radio is an invention we can use to send and receive information through the air and even deep into space without connecting wires.

GUGLIELMO MARCONI
In 1895, this Italian inventor (1874–1937) was the first to send telegraph signals through the air without the use of wires.

Radio waves are a form of energy that travels through the air. There are radio waves around all the time, but you are unaware of them until you turn on your radio (strictly called your radio receiver) and tune in to one of them.

DIFFERENT FREQUENCIES

All waves vibrate to and fro. The rate at which they do this is their 'frequency'. Radio waves vibrate at amazingly high frequencies – anything from a few thousand to a few billion times a second. Different radio stations broadcast on different frequencies so that their transmissions do not get jumbled.

1 A microphone turns sound waves from the DJ's voice into a vibrating electric current.

2 This current combines with another current that vibrates very rapidly.

MAKING A RADIO BROADCAST

When a DJ makes a radio broadcast, a microphone picks up his voice and turns it into an electric current. This current, which vibrates exactly as his voice does, is sent to a transmitter for broadcasting. In the transmitter, the vibrating current is mixed with another one that vibrates millions of times a second. This very rapid current is called a 'carrier wave'. Once they are mixed together, the two currents are turned into a radio wave which can be beamed out through the air.

SENDING OUT SOUNDS

There are two analogue ways of sending out radio waves: AM (amplitude modulation) and FM (frequency modulation). An AM broadcast sends out a radio show by varying the amplitude (extent of vibration) of a radio wave. An FM broadcast sends it out by varying the radio wave's frequency. An analogue radio picks up these changes and turns them back into sounds. In digital broadcasts, the analogue radio signal is turned into digital 1s and 0s and compressed to take up less bandwidth. A digital radio picks up the digital signal and turns it back into audio.

A VARIETY OF USES

Radio is regularly used by the police and by the crews on board ships and aeroplanes to keep in touch with staff back at base or in ground control. Entertainers often use radio microphones on stage to relay their voices to amplifiers. Radio waves are also used to send signals to remote-controlled model cars, boats and planes.

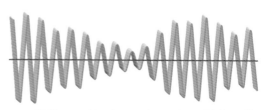

3 The combined currents are turned into radio waves, which are beamed through the air. A tuned-in radio picks up these waves.

4 The radio waves are amplified.

5 Circuits inside the radio pick out the current originally made by the DJ's microphone.

6 A loudspeaker turns this current into sound waves again.

SEE ALSO
Electronics, Sound, Telecommunication, Wavelength

RAINFOREST

These dense, damp forests are mainly found near the Equator. They contain more types of plants and animals than all the other habitats put together.

The world's biggest rainforests are the tropical rainforests of South America, Africa and Southeast Asia, where the climate is always warm and wet. There is no winter at the Equator, so there is nothing to stop the plants growing. The result is a huge variety of trees, ferns, vines and epiphytes (plants that grow on other plants).

TROPICAL RAINFORESTS

Although they cover only six per cent of the Earth's surface, tropical rainforests contain about three fifths of all known species of animals and plants. Wherever you look, there are always some plants in flower or producing fruit, so there is a constant supply of food for birds, bats, insects, snakes, tree frogs, antelopes, monkeys and a host of other animals. Most of the animals live in the trees.

◀ Tropical forest animals have adapted to life in the trees. The sloth uses its hooked claws to move from branch to branch.

RAINFOREST LIFE CYCLE

Tropical rainforests are made up of several layers. The main canopy (tree-top layer) is usually 30-50m above ground, where the slender trunks break out into a cluster of branches, but the tallest trees reach 60m. The under-storey, dark beneath the canopy, consists of tree trunks covered with lianas (climbing plants) and laced together by creepers. The forest floor is surprisingly free of clutter. Leaves, fruit, animal droppings and bodies decompose quickly when they fall to the ground, and their chemical building blocks are immediately taken up again by plant roots and used to make new growth. It is nature's most efficient recycling system.

TEMPERATE RAINFORESTS

Farther from the Equator are temperate rainforests, formed in coastal regions where onshore winds bring constant rain. These lie chiefly in northwestern North America, southern Chile, Tasmania, southeastern Australia and New Zealand. The dominant trees are redwoods and sitka spruce in the Northern Hemisphere and eucalyptus and Antarctic beech in the Southern Hemisphere. Some temperate rainforest trees are even taller than those in the tropical forests, but the animal and plant life is not as rich.

THREATS TO THE FOREST

Large areas of the Amazon, Congo and Malaysian rainforests have been destroyed by logging for timber. Vast areas have also been cut down to make way for plantations of rubber, coffee, bananas and sugar cane, or to provide pasture for cattle. Rainforests play an important part in keeping the Earth's climate healthy, and they contain many medicinal plants. International organizations are trying to protect the remaining forests before it is too late.

Emergent tree

Canopy

Understorey

Lianas wind around the tree trunks and rafflesias grow on the forest floor

SEE ALSO
Brazil, Conservation, Forest, Habitat, Plant

RAT AND OTHER RODENTS

Rodents are mammals that have sharp, chisel-like front teeth. They use these for gnawing through food, as well as through anything that gets in their way.

Black (and brown) rats carry the germs of several diseases, including typhus.

The European red squirrel is one of several species of tree squirrel.

House mice live among people – 'mouse' comes from a word meaning thief.

Most hamsters have large cheek pouches. They use these to carry food in.

Porcupines defend themselves with their sharp, spiny quills.

Found in cold, northern regions, lemmings migrate to prevent overpopulation.

Rats belong to a large group of mammals called rodents. There are about 2,050 kinds of rodent, and they include rats, mice, voles, hamsters, squirrels, beavers and porcupines. The smallest rodent is the swamp mouse from marshes and forests in Africa, which weighs just 5g. The biggest is the capybara from South America, which can weigh over 75kg. Together, rodents make up almost half of the world's mammal species.

SHARP TEETH
All rodents share one important feature – a set of four sharp front teeth, called incisors, which work like chisels. They use these to gnaw their way through their food, to chop up nesting material and to get through anything that blocks their path. Beavers use their incisors to gnaw through solid tree trunks, while rats and mice use them to gnaw through household timber,

▲ Like all rodents, rats have four sharp front teeth. These are self-sharpening, and grow throughout the animal's life.

WIRE CUTTERS
Both the black rat and the much more common brown rat (shown right) eat almost any kind of plant or animal. With their strong teeth, they are able to cut through materials as strong as wire to get to food. When eating, they often use their front feet to hold their food while their teeth set to work.

▲ In order to supply wood for its lodge (nest) and its winter food store, the beaver uses its teeth to trim branches and even to fell small trees.

food packaging and even electric cables, which can trigger off fires.

FAST BREEDERS
Compared with many other mammals, rodents can breed very rapidly if they have enough food. A female brown rat can start to breed when just two months old, and may produce as many as five litters a year, with up to 12 babies in each litter. Poisons or traps are often used to keep rats under control, but their fast breeding rate makes this difficult.

SEE ALSO
Animal, Black Death, Mammal

REFORMATION

The Reformation was a period in Europe's history when the Christian Church in the West was split by disagreements and Protestantism became established.

LUTHER'S 95 THESES

In 1517, the German priest Martin Luther (1483–1546) was so upset at the scandal of the sale of indulgences (pardons for sins) by corrupt Church officials that he listed 95 theses, or arguments, against the practice and nailed them to the door of the church in Wittenberg.

John Calvin (1509–64) was influenced by Luther and set up a Protestant Church in Geneva, Switzerland.

King Henry VIII of England (r. 1509–47) broke away from the Catholic Church in order to get a divorce.

John Knox (1514–72) established the Protestant faith in Scotland with help from Elizabeth I.

► During the 1200s, the Catholic Church set up the Inquisition (meaning 'inquiry') to deal with heresy. In 1478, Spain set up its own. In 1542, the Pope created a Roman Inquisition to cope with Protestantism. Like the civil courts, the Inquisition used torture as a form of questioning.

The Reformation grew out of the ideas of the Renaissance. People no longer shared the same beliefs about religion and wanted greater freedom of worship. Religious arguments became mixed with political struggles, leading to bitter wars. The Reformation led to great changes within the Roman Catholic Church.

BEGINNINGS

The Pope in Rome was the head of the Catholic Church. However, by 1500, many people saw the Church as corrupt. Early protesters, such as Jan Huss (c.1370-1415) in Bohemia and John Wycliffe (c.1330-84) in England, spoke out against the Church. But the Reformation really began in 1517 when Martin Luther attacked Church corruption with his 95 theses. The Pope expelled Luther from the Church. But Luther continued to lead the Protestant revolt until his death in 1546.

PROTESTANTISM SPREADS

Religious leaders, including Huldrych Zwingli and John Calvin in Switzerland, took up Luther's cause. In England, King Henry VIII broke with the Pope over his divorce (which the Church refused), and made himself head of the Church of England. In the Netherlands, many Dutch people adopted Protestantism in order to break free from Spanish (Catholic) rule.

MARTYRS AND WARS

Europe was split into two religious camps, often at war, with cruelties on both sides. Under Queen Mary I in England, Catholics persecuted Protestants. Under Mary's sister, Queen Elizabeth I, Protestants did the same to Catholics. France was torn by civil wars between Catholics and Protestants, and religious conflict reached its height during the Thirty Years' War (1618–48), which killed about half the people of Germany.

SEE ALSO
Christianity, Crusades, Religion, Renaissance

REFUGEE

Refugees are people who are driven from their homes through wars, revolution, natural disasters like floods, or because of political, racial or religious persecution.

▲ Some refugees are forced to flee for religious reasons. The Huguenots in France suffered for 250 years. Many were murdered in the Massacre of St Bartholemew's Day, 1572.

▲ Frequent famines in Ethiopia, like this one in the mid-1980s, force many villagers to congregate in camps, reliant on food aid.

When refugees flee from war or famine they can carry little with them. They travel in large, sudden movements, often bringing problems with them. Some refugees are welcomed in their new homelands, others are treated badly.

MASS MOVEMENTS

In the past, refugees were often met with hostility and forced to act brutally themselves. In 370 when the Huns invaded Europe from Asia, the Goths and Germans were defeated and fled west into the Roman Empire. A lack of land and food led to fighting and the Roman Empire was destroyed. Other refugees have been made more welcome. In the 1700s, the Protestants in Catholic France were persecuted and moved to nearby countries, like the Netherlands and Britain, bringing with them weaving and banking skills.

INTERNATIONAL HELP

In the 1920s, recognizing that refugees could disrupt stable nations, the League of

Nations set up an agency for refugees. The United Nations formed a new commission after World War II to help resettle the millions of displaced people. The aim was to provide food and shelter until refugees could return home or find a new one.

HUMAN DISASTERS

In Iraq, millions have fled their homeland in the last 30 years or so, forced out by wars including the Iran–Iraq War (1980–88) and Second Gulf War (2003). The worst refugee disasters of all, however, have been in Africa. The Second Sudanese Civil War (1983–2005) displaced four million people in what is now South Sudan, while the Darfur conflict (2003–10) uprooted another three million Sudanese, many into Chad. In the Democratic Republic of Congo, civil war (1998–2003) caused widespread famine and disease. In 2004 alone almost half a million Congolese crossed into neighbouring states as refugees.

FAST FACTS

- About 5 million Hindus and Sikhs moved from West Pakistan into India in 1947, while Muslims left India for Pakistan

- After the Vietnam War ended in 1975, hundreds of thousands of Vietnamese fled by boat

- Almost 4 million Afghans left their homeland following Soviet invasion in 1979

UNWANTED VICTIMS

Some of these Rwandan refugees had been walking for a month before reaching the border at Zaire (now the Democratic Republic of Congo). Most had taken refuge in Zaire in 1995, to escape conflict between Rwanda and Burundi, only to be forced back on the road in November 1996, when civil war broke out in Zaire.

SEE ALSO

Israel, Gaza and West Bank, Judaism, United Nations, Warfare

326

RELIGION

A religion usually involves a belief in a god or gods. It may have rituals, recognize certain places as holy and recommend a certain way of life.

Zoroaster (c. 600BCE) believed Earth was fought over by good and evil gods.

Siddhartha Gautama (c. 500BCE), the Enlightened One, founded Buddhism.

Confucius (551-479BCE) established the way of life now called Confucianism.

Jesus Christ (c. 4BCE–c. 30CE) preached the teachings of Christianity in Palestine.

Abu Bakr (c. 573–634CE) led Islam after the death of the prophet Muhammad.

There have been, and still are, many religions around the world. Most religions teach that people should lead good lives and behave in certain ways.

GODS
Gods are thought to be greatly superior to humans, endowed with wonderful powers. The Ancient Greeks had hundreds of gods, each for a different thing – such as the sea, wind or love. This collection of gods is known as a pantheon. Many peoples, such as the Vikings and ancient Egyptians, had a pantheon of gods. Other religions, including Judaism, Christianity and Islam, have only one god.

REVELATIONS
Some religions are based on a revelation – the passing on of sacred knowledge – from a god or gods to a human. Islam is based on the teachings of God as given to the prophet Muhammad in Arabia nearly 1,400 years ago. The Mormon Church of Latter Day Saints is based on visions and a holy book revealed to Joseph Smith in Palmyra, New York, USA in the 1820s.

▼ In New Guinea, dancers in colourful costume take the roles of spirits during ceremonies.

TALKING TO THE GODS
The Ancient Greeks believed that the Oracle at Delphi, dedicated to the Sun god Apollo, could foretell the future. The chief priestess gave answers to questions in a trance. These answers were often ambiguous, but even the government of the day sometimes consulted the Oracle.

PRIESTS AND TEMPLES
Many religions have priests, who study the holy teachings and make sure that rituals are carried out properly and that holy places are respected. Other religions, such as Islam, have no priests. The Ancient Egyptians built vast temples that were considered to be the home of a god. In many societies, great wealth is lavished on the temple or church. However, Australian Aboriginals believe that certain places are sacred to the spirits and should not be built on.

HOLY COMMUNITIES
The followers of some religions may form a special community and treat non-believers as outsiders. In some religions, people form communities where they follow the teachings of the religion very strictly. Such dedicated communities include the monasteries and convents of Christianity and Buddhism.

SEE ALSO
Buddhism, Christianity, Hinduism, Islam, Myth and legend, Pilgrim

RENAISSANCE

The Renaissance was a revival in arts and sciences which began in Italy around 1350 and spread across Europe. It marked the end of the Middle Ages.

Astronomers developed more accurate telescopes to observe the stars.

The invention of printing in 1440 made the spread of learning possible.

In the late 14th century, Italy was the richest and most populated of all the European countries. However, Italy was not a unified country at this time – the region was divided up into about 250 states, and each state was based around a city and governed by the wealthiest families in that particular area of the country.

THE REBIRTH
The word "Renaissance" means "rebirth". Italy had preserved much of the Ancient Roman civilization, but this had been largely ignored until the 1300s. Then, around 1350, Italian scholars began to copy the old manuscripts and circulate them. These manuscripts contained the history of the ancient (classical) world and passed on its knowledge of architecture, science and art. There was also an influx of Ancient Greek learning from the city of Constantinople after it fell to the Turks in 1453. Renaissance thinkers became increasingly influenced by the way ancient

KEY DATES
1300s Florentine artist Giotto di Bondone is the first painter to show realistic (not symbolic) settings
1430s The Medici family dominates Florence's ruling class, paying architects to design impressive buildings
1518 Baldassare Castiglione writes *The Book of the Courtier*, describing proper conduct for noblemen
1519 Pope Leo X appoints the painter Raphael superintendent of Rome's antiquities
1526 The Bible is first translated into English

scholars studied subjects such as philosophy, literature and science, and wanted to recreate the spirit of the classical age. During the Middle Ages which had immediately preceded the Renaissance, people had been much more concerned with theology (religion).

POWERFUL BACKERS
The rich noblemen who ruled the Italian cities paid for the classical manuscripts to be copied. In Florence, the powerful Medici family of bankers spent lavishly as patrons of the arts. Lorenzo Medici, who ruled Florence from 1469 to 1492, was called 'The Magnificent' because he attracted the finest scientists and artists to the area. Francesco Sforza, a mercenary who became Duke of Milan in 1450, was another great Italian patron.

GREAT ARTISTS
Renaissance artists began to paint and sculpt in a completely new style. Instead of stiff, formal poses, they drew people more naturally and put them in real landscapes and rooms. By 1424, Tomasso Masaccio was decorating churches in Florence with beautiful frescos. At the same time, Filippo Brunelleschi was building startling new structures. His masterpiece is the dome on the cathedral in Florence, which he began in 1420. It blends excellent engineering with graceful design and was the largest dome in the world at the time.

◀ Hans Holbein's *The Ambassadors* (1533) typifies the spirit of the Renaissance: the richly robed ambassadors are surrounded by objects from science and the arts.

FUTURISTIC IDEAS OF FLYING MACHINES

The great minds of the Renaissance, like Leonardo Da Vinci, did not take all their inspiration from the past. His sketch books show a fascination with flight and the possibility of flying machines long before the invention of the first successful aircraft.

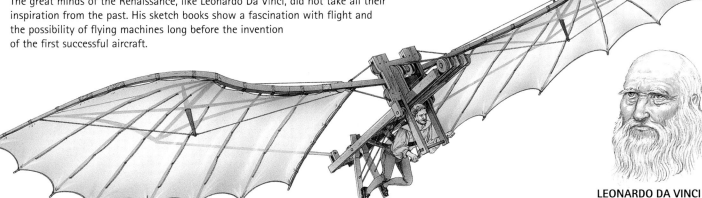

▲ A modern artist's impression of Leonardo's flying machine — turning paddles moved the wings.

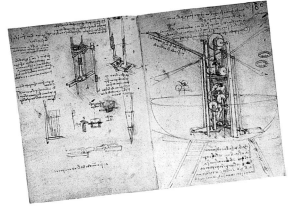

▲ Da Vinci's original sketches

COMBINING SKILLS

The ability to mix very different skills was typical of the artists and scientist of the Renaissance. Michelangelo Buonarroti is best known for his marble sculptures, such as the famous *Pietá*, but he was also a painter and poet. He even worked as an architect on St Peter's Basilica in Rome in 1547. Most versatile of all was Leonardo da Vinci, who created several great paintings, studied science and designed irrigation systems for farms. Other famous figures of the era include the artists Giotto, Botticelli and Raphael, sculptors Donatello and Ghiberti and the architect Bramante.

Scientists began to make their own detailed observations instead of simply accepting the teachings of the Church. The Polish astronomer Nicolaus Copernicus (1473–1543) realized that the Earth moved round the Sun. However, he was too afraid to publish his findings until he was very close to death, as his thinking opposed the Church view that the Earth was the centre of the universe.

THE SPREAD OF LEARNING

As the new art and learning developed in Italy, other countries began to take note. The universities of Oxford, Cambridge and Paris became centres of a Renaissance in England and France. Scholars such as Erasmus of Rotterdam in Holland and Thomas More of England developed and spread the ideas. In both Holland and Germany, artists such as the van Eycks, Dürer and Holbein took Renaissance ideals and developed a distinct northern European style. In England, the writers Shakespeare and Spenser began a revolution in poetry and drama. Then, in 1600, Marie de Medici married King Henri IV of France, and took Italian craftsmen, artists and cooks to France, which further spread the new thinking through Europe.

◀ Bramante's Tempietto in Rome reflects classical styles of building.

LEONARDO DA VINCI
As well as being a painter (masterpieces include the *Mona Lisa*) and inventor, da Vinci (1452–1519) studied biology, anatomy and mechanics.

DESIDERIUS ERASMUS
(1466–1536) was a Dutch priest and leading Christian humanist whose writings attacked the morals of church leaders.

▲ Michelangelo's statue of Moses, carved in about 1513, is typical of the realistic style of sculpture of the Renaissance.

SEE ALSO

Architecture, Art, Astronomy, Dance, Design, Explorer, Invention, Italy, Printing, Sculpture

REPRODUCTION

Reproduction is the process of producing new organisms so that life continues from one generation to the next. All living things make more of their own kind.

▲ Single-celled organisms, such as the amoeba, reproduce asexually by dividing in two – a process called 'binary fission'.

Reproduction is one of the most important functions of all living organisms – from the tiniest microbes to the biggest trees, elephants and whales. It means making more of your own kind, or species. There are two main types of reproduction: asexual and sexual.

ONE BECOMES TWO

The simplest form of asexual reproduction is that of organisms consisting of a single cell, such as amoebas or bacteria. These reproduce by simply dividing in two. Each offspring cell grows larger and then also divides, and so on. In conditions that suit them, some bacteria can double their numbers like this every 15 to 20 minutes.

ONE-PARENT REPRODUCTION

Many plants reproduce asexually by vegetative propagation. A part of the plant grows roots into the soil and sprouts a stem, which then becomes a separate individual. Gardeners make use of this process by slicing off a part of a plant and growing it into a new individual. Some simple animals reproduce in a similar way, by budding. The parent sprouts a 'bud' that grows into a new individual. Hydras, tiny anemone-like water creatures, multiply by budding.

AVERAGE PREGNANCY TIME FOR MAMMALS:	
Species	Days
Common shrew	15
House mouse	17
Horseshoe bat	45
Cat	63
Dog	63
Tiger	103
Goat	150
Moose	245
Gorilla	260
Human	266
Horse	333
Blue whale	350
Asian elephant	660

FERTILIZATION

Reproduction is very similar in all mammals, including humans. The female or mother has reproductive organs called ovaries that make hundreds of tiny eggs. The male or father has reproductive organs called testes (testicles) that make millions of even tinier sperm. During mating, the male passes his sperm cells into the reproductive tubes, or tract, of the female. Here, one of the sperm joins with, or fertilizes, an egg. The genes in the egg and sperm come together to create a new individual.

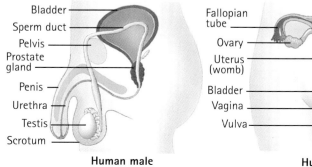

Human male   Human female

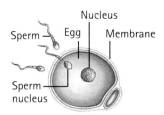
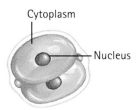

1 Day 1: a sperm cell penetrates and fertilizes an egg inside the Fallopian tube, forming a zygote.

2 The zygote divides into two and continues to travel along the Fallopian tube toward the uterus.

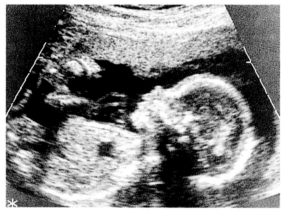

▲ Ultrasound scans, as of this 20-week-old foetus, are used to keep check on a baby's development in the womb.

DIFFERENT GENES – VARIATION

Most plants and animals breed by sexual reproduction. This requires two parents – female and male. Each parent contributes a unique selection of genes, so the offspring vary in the genes they inherit and grow up to be slightly different from each other. This variation means that at least some offspring will be suited to the world's ever-changing conditions, and so will survive in the struggle for life.

HAVING BABIES

Some young mammals, such as mice, are born fur-less, with eyes closed, and depend totally on their parents. A human baby is similarly helpless, although it has certain built-in reflexes, such as crying when it is hungry or cold. Other mammal babies, such as whales, giraffes and antelopes, are alert and able to move about within minutes of birth. The number of young born at one time varies. Mother seals, dolphins, bats and humans usually have one baby. Mother dogs, cats and rats have several babies. A mother opossum may give birth to more than 30 babies.

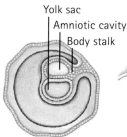

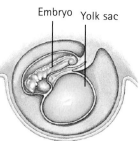

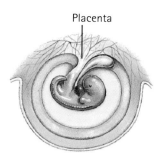

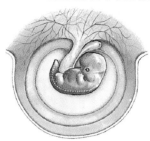

Yolk sac
Amniotic cavity
Body stalk

Embryo   Yolk sac

Placenta

3 The cells continue to divide until, after 4 to 5 days, a tiny ball of 16 cells has formed.

4 Day 13: the ball settles into the lining of the uterus, which forms supportive structures.

5 Day 21: the embryo feeds off the yolk sac and its spine and brain begin to form.

6 Day 28: the stomach, arm and leg buds have all begun to form and the heart starts pumping blood.

7 Day 35: bones and muscles start to form, while the arms and legs continue to grow.

HOW THE HUMAN BABY DEVELOPS

During development, the cells multiply rapidly, move around and change into specialized shapes, gradually forming the basic body organs. This rapid growth is called the embryo stage. As the tiny, tadpole-like body develops, it takes on a recognizable shape. It develops muscles, bones, skin and other features. Eight weeks after fertilization, it is called a foetus. It is nourished by the mother through a specialized organ, the placenta. Finally, it leaves the womb through the birth canal to begin life in the outside world.

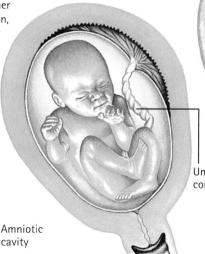

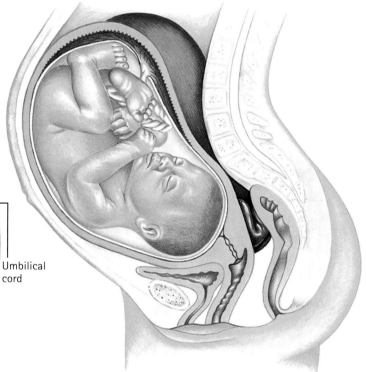

Amniotic cavity

Umbilical cord

8 Day 56: the 2cm-long foetus has developed its main body parts, including fingers and toes, and some of its muscles and nerves function.

9 After four months, the baby has doubled in size and has well-developed features such as fingers and toes.

10 After five months, the lungs and most of the other body organs are working properly. The foetus usually repositions itself, so that at the end of nine months (above) it is ready to be born head first.

LAYING EGGS

Mammals, some snakes and fish, and a few insects give birth to their young. But the vast majority of animal mothers reproduce by laying eggs, out of which the offspring hatch. On land, the eggs are usually encased in a tough shell for protection and to prevent drying out. Examples are bird and reptile eggs. These contain a yolk, which is the food store for nourishing the baby as it develops. Insects, spiders and similar smaller creatures also lay tough-cased eggs, but without large food stores inside. The offspring must hatch out and feed straight away.

REPRODUCING IN WATER

Eggs laid in water do not need a waterproof casing. Amphibians' eggs are jelly-like, and the eggs of most fish, crabs and similar creatures have thin walls. On land, the male usually transfers his sperm into the female's body during mating, otherwise the sperm would dry out and die. In water, females can release their eggs, and males their sperm, without the risk of them drying out. Male and female cast their sperm and eggs into the water and fertilization is left to chance. In many fish and crabs, males and females come together and release their eggs and sperm into one place.

> **SEE ALSO**
> Amphibian, Animal, Butterfly and moth, Evolution, Fish, Flower, Human body, Insect, Mammal, Micro-organism, Seed and pollination

REPTILE

Reptiles are air-breathing animals with backbones and a covering of tough scales. Most of them live on land, but some live in the sea or in fresh water.

▲ The Australian frilled lizard raises its collar in a display of aggression that frightens its attacker away.

When frightened, the poisonous cobra rises and spreads its hood.

Reptiles are usually described as cold-blooded creatures, and this means that their body temperature goes up and down as the air or water temperature changes. Most reptiles live in warm places, but they are found everywhere except in the far north or south. Those living in cooler places have to warm themselves up in the mornings by sitting in the sun. Reptiles are vertebrates (they have backbones), and there over 8,700 different species divided into five main groups: turtles or tortoises; lizards and snakes; crocodiles and alligators; worm lizards; and the tuatara, a species in its own group. The tuatara is described as a living fossil – it has hardly changed in 200 million years.

The crocodile is a large flesh-eater that seizes its prey with powerful jaws.

TORTOISES – AN ANCIENT GROUP
Reptiles first appeared on the Earth over 300 million years ago, and many different kinds have come and gone since then. The oldest group of reptiles still living are the tortoises and turtles, which have not changed much in 200 million years. They are easily recognized by their shells, which are made of bone and usually have a horny covering. There are 300 different species. Those living in the sea are usually called turtles and those living on land tortoises. Freshwater species are called terrapins. In the United States, however, the name turtle is often used for all the shelled reptiles. Land-living tortoises feed mainly on plants, but the other species are mainly flesh-eaters. Tortoises have no

SEA-GOING CREATURES

Most reptiles lay eggs. **1** The sea-going marine turtle comes ashore to find a safe place in the sand for her brood. **2** She lays her eggs in a sheltered spot. **3** Weeks later, the hatchlings break out of their shells. **4** They scramble out and race for the safety of the water. **5** Aquatic turtles all have limbs that act as paddles or flippers, which makes them excellent swimmers.

teeth, and they bite their food with sharp, horny beaks.

DINOSAUR RELATIVES

The huge dinosaurs that roamed the Earth millions of year ago were reptiles. Their nearest living reptile relatives are the crocodiles and alligators. These dangerous flesh-eaters live in and around tropical rivers. There are 23 species, and some of them reach lengths of about 9m.

LIZARDS AND SNAKES

These animals form the largest group of reptiles alive today. There are about 4,450 species of lizard and 2,900 species of snake. Scientists believe that snakes descended from a group of burrowing lizards that gradually lost their legs about 100 million years ago. Some snakes are poisonous and bite with grooved fangs that inject venom from sac-like glands. Lizards nearly all live on land and are mostly very active animals. They include both vegetarians and flesh-eaters. The world's biggest lizard is the Komodo dragon, which lives in Indonesia. Up to 3m long, it eats animals as large as pigs. It is one of the monitor lizards, which have long necks and powerful teeth. Some monitors steal crocodile eggs and even eat young crocodiles. Small lizards feed mainly on insects, slugs and other species of invertebrate animals.

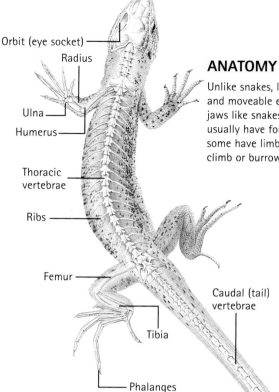

Orbit (eye socket)
Radius
Ulna
Humerus
Thoracic vertebrae
Ribs
Femur
Caudal (tail) vertebrae
Tibia
Phalanges

ANATOMY OF A TYPICAL LIZARD

Unlike snakes, lizards have an outer ear opening and moveable eyelids. They cannot unhinge their jaws like snakes to swallow large prey. Lizards usually have four well-developed limbs, but some have limbs modified to help them run, climb or burrow. A typical lizard has a long tail.

The slow-worm looks like a snake but is really a lizard without legs.

The tortoise can pull its head, legs and tail into its hard, protective shell.

The gecko can climb walls using sucker-like pads on its feet.

CHAMELEONS

These are slow-moving lizards, some of which are famous for their ability to change colour. A chameleon surrounded by green leaves is usually some shade of green, but if it is then put among brown leaves or bare twigs it will gradually turn brown. Chameleons feed on insects, which they catch by firing out their long, sticky tongue at great speed. Their bulging eyes are also very unusual because each one can be moved separately: one eye can look forward while the other one looks behind. This is very useful for finding insects and also for spotting enemies.

A STRANGE SURVIVAL TRICK

Many birds and mammals like to eat lizards, but most lizards run away quickly when they are frightened. Their enemies often manage to grab no more than the tail – and then a surprising thing happens. The lizard snaps off its tail and races away, leaving the predator with just a wriggling tail. The lizard grows a new tail.

▲ A chameleon lashes out its tongue to catch a hapless insect. Its tongue is almost the same length as its body.

FAST FACTS

- The lifespan for a giant tortoise can be longer than 175 years

- The Gila monster and the beaded lizard can kill people with their poisonous saliva

- The only seagoing lizard is the marine iguana, which lives in the Galapagos Islands

SEE ALSO

Alligator and crocodile, Desert, Ocean and sea, Snake

REVOLUTION

A revolution is an overwhelming uprising by the people which aims to destroy the social or political system of a country and replace it with a new system.

Wat Tyler (*d.* 1381) led the Peasants' Revolt of southern England in 1381.

George Washington (1732–99) led colonial troops in the American Revolution.

Simon Bolívar (1783–1830) led many revolts in South America.

Georges Danton (1759–94) led the republican faction in the French Revolution.

Giuseppe Garibaldi (1807–82) led revolutions in Italy to create a united nation.

Revolutions are unpredictable. They may achieve all their aims or lose sight of the ideals that were fought for. Their leaders may go down in history as heroes or traitors.

MASS MOVEMENTS
Revolutions occur when most of the people in a country are suffering hardship, or when they want changes to be made. If they cannot gain what they want, anger and the demand for more radical change builds up. However, revolutions need an incident to start them. The uprising of Sicilians against French rulers in 1282 began when a Sicilian stabbed a Frenchman who had insulted his wife.

REASONS FOR FAILURE
Most revolutions fail. The government has many advantages over ordinary people, including wealth, control of the army and better organization. Revolutions are often disorganized, starting as separate protests

▲ Medieval peasant revolts were generally aimed at abolishing harsh taxes. Rebels often burned the books in which taxes were recorded.

which can be put down by force. Even if rebel forces unite, they often argue later. The revolutions that succeed are those with a clear aim and strong leadership. But even these may fail. In 133BCE, the Roman army officer Tiberius Gracchus led the poorer citizens in demands for reform of land and property laws. The revolution failed when noblemen killed Gracchus, his brother and over 300 supporters.

MEDIEVAL PEASANTS
During the Middle Ages, the peasants of Europe had to pay taxes and work long hours for their masters. Some nobles treated their peasants harshly. In 1381,

FARMERS AGAINST MERCENARIES
During the American Revolution of 1775 the British hired 30,000 German mercenaries, mostly Hessians. The American farmers and frontiersmen were expert marksmen and won many skirmishes, but, compared with the mercenaries, they were poorly trained. It was only after George Washington began proper training and discipline that the Americans won major battles and, eventually, the war.

the peasants of England demanded an end to such conditions. Although the uprising collapsed, reforms were slowly introduced. In 1524, German peasants launched a violent uprising. They murdered nobles and organized an army. The nobles hired foreign troops and defeated the peasants at Frankenhausen in 1525. Most of the rebels were killed.

THE AMERICAN REVOLUTION
The American Revolution began in 1775 when British colonists protested against being taxed by Britain with no representation in Parliament. At first, the uprising aimed at changing the status of the colonies, but in 1776 the colonies declared independence. After full-scale war with Britain, the new United States established a democratic republic.

THE FRENCH REVOLUTION
In France, in 1789, the king ruled without a parliament or constitution, spending vast sums on luxuries. Involvement in wars, including the American Revolution, had drained the treasury. At the same time, food prices doubled after the harvest failed,

TO THE BARRICADES
The *sans-culottes*, the working class of Paris, formed the shock troops of the French Revolution. On July 14, 1789 they attacked the royal prison of the Bastille, marking the start of violence. July 14 is now the most important public holiday in France. During fighting, the *sans-culottes* built barricades across the narrow streets of Paris, from which to defy troops and police.

and many people were close to starvation. The middle classes demanded an end to the injustices. In May 1789, Louis XVI called a meeting of the States General (parliament) for the first time in about 175 years. This body demanded tax reforms. Food riots broke out and mob violence spread. The new government introduced radical measures to please the mob. In 1793, Louis XVI was arrested while trying to flee the country, and beheaded. In the Reign of Terror that followed, almost 20,000 people were executed as enemies of the Revolution. Ten months later, moderates established a new government based on the ideals of the Revolution. ▶

◀ In 1848, people supporting democracy and social reforms rose against the monarchies of Europe. King Louis Philippe was overthrown in France, and major reforms were introduced in Belgium, Denmark and the Netherlands. Elsewhere, the armies and peasants remained loyal to their monarchs. Revolts were crushed in Prussia and Italy, though some reforms were made. Only in Austria, Poland and the smaller German states did the revolutions fail totally.

▲ Demonstrations in Tunis and across Tunisia led to the overthrow of President Zine El Abidine Ben Ali's regime in 2011.

▲ Government symbols may be destroyed by revolutionaries, as was this portrait of Stalin by Hungarians in 1956.

► Civilians may take over military weapons in a revolution. The Hungarian Rising of 1956 failed when better-trained Soviet troops invaded.

REVOLUTION IN RUSSIA

In spring 1917, Russia's tsar, or emperor, was overthrown by middle class democrats, but many social problems remained. Vladimir Lenin, leader of the Communist Party, began an uprising. It ended in 1921 with Communist victory.

REVOLUTION FROM ABOVE

In 1959, a force of Communist guerrillas overthrew the Cuban government. The guerrilla leader, Fidel Castro, then began a revolution from above by introducing communism to Cuba.

VELVET REVOLUTIONS

In 1956, the Hungarians tried but failed to peacefully to overthrow their Communist government. By 1989, however, Russia was too weak to interfere in Eastern Europe. Peaceful protests began in Poland, East Germany, Czechoslovakia, Bulgaria and Hungary. These 'velvet revolutions'

replaced communism with democracy within a few months.

THE ARAB SPRING

In December 2010 a Tunisian market seller set himself on fire after his cart was confiscated by a police officer. He later died. The event triggered protests and, eventually, revolution in Tunisia. It also inspired other uprisings across the Arab world. During this wave of protest, known as the Arab Spring, the presidents of both Egypt and Libya were forced from office.

STORMING THE PALACE

Taking key buildings and communication centres is vital to any successful revolution. On October 25, 1917, Russian Communists and supporting troops seized government buildings, including the famous Winter Palace in St Petersburg. Within days, the government of Russia was communist.

SEE ALSO

Civil war, Communism, Fascism, France, Russia and the Baltic States, USA

RHINOCEROS

A rhinoceros is a large, thick-skinned mammal that is distantly related to the horse. It has one or two horns on the nose and three hoofed toes on each foot.

▲ Rhinos may fight each other with their horns, which can sometimes be torn from the nose in the struggle.

The two-horned black rhino has a hooked upper lip and lives on the African plains.

The two-horned African white rhino has square lips and lives on scrubland.

The one-horned Indian rhino has large folds of skin and lives in marshy jungles.

The two-horned Sumatran rhino has hairy skin and lives in rainforests.

The one-horned Javan rhino lives in the rainforests but is now nearly extinct.

There are five species of rhinoceros, also called rhino. Two live in Africa and three in southern Asia. They are all plant-eaters. The African white rhino, which is actually grey like all the others, lives mainly on scrubland, where it feeds off grass. Nearly 2m high, up to 4m long and weighing over 2 tonnes, it is the biggest of the five. The Sumatran rhino is the smallest species, weighing only 1 tonne, and unlike the others it is quite hairy.

HORN OR HAIR?

A rhino's horn is not made of bone or horn. It is actually made of very coarse hairs which are firmly stuck together. African black rhinos and white rhinos have two horns and the one furthest forward can be nearly 1.5m long. The Sumatran rhino also has two horns, but the Indian

A rhino's horns are used for self-defence and for digging up bushes and shrubs.

A black rhino uses its hooked upper lip for grasping leaves.

and the Javan rhinos have only one horn. A young rhino begins to grow horns when it is four to five weeks old.

ENDANGERED SPECIES

All rhinos are rare animals. There are probably only about 60 Javan rhinos left in the world and about 300 Sumatran rhinos. The animals have been hunted for their horns, which are often ground up and used to make traditional medicines in Asia. The white rhino lives in various National Parks in Africa and is the most numerous, but the other rhinos are in serious danger of becoming extinct.

A rhino's foot has three toes, each of which ends in a hoof. The middle toe takes most of the rhino's weight.

THE BLACK RHINOCEROS

Like all rhinos, the African black has excellent hearing and a good sense of smell. Its eyesight is not good, however, and the animal often charges almost blindly when it is disturbed by an unfamiliar smell or sound. A charging black rhino is a terrifying sight, since it can run more than 45km/h, faster than a human.

SEE ALSO
Africa, Conservation, Indian subcontinent, Mammal

RIVER

When water falls as rain and snow over the land, it eventually flows back to the seas and oceans. Usually, it flows back in the form of a river.

WORLD'S LONGEST RIVERS		
Name	Outflow	Length
Nile	Mediterranean Sea (Egypt)	6,690km
Amazon	Atlantic Ocean (Brazil)	6,570km
Missouri	Mississippi River (USA)	4,090km
Chang Jiang	East China Sea (China)	5,980km
Yenisey	Kara Sea (Russia)	5,870km
Amur	Tartar Strait (Russia)	5,780km
Ob-Irtysh	Gulf of Ob (Russia)	5,410km

A river that flows quickly down a steep slope, over hard rocks, cuts a deep gorge in the land.

When a river flows more slowly over softer rocks, the valley is worn back into an open V-shape.

▲ Waterfalls occur when a river tumbles over the edge of a steep cliff or ledge, as in the powerful Dettifoss Falls in Iceland.

A river goes through many stages in its development. First, water falls as rain on hills and mountainsides and seeps into the ground until the soil and rock are completely saturated with it – so full that they cannot hold any more. The top level of this saturated zone is called the water table. When the water table reaches the surface of the soil, as on a steep slope, water pours out, and forms into a spring. Water from the spring runs downhill as a stream, and in time, many streams flow into one another to form a river.

YOUNG RIVER

When a river is young, it runs swiftly down the hill or mountainsides. High up, close to the springs, the falling water is full of energy and may even carry rocks and boulders with it. This rocky debris scrapes and crashes along the bed of the river, carving out a deep V-shaped valley or a gorge. This constant erosion is typical of a river in its early stage, and waterfalls and rapids (fast currents) are common here.

MATURE RIVER

In the second stage of the river's development, some of the rocky debris begins to settle out in a process called deposition. However, erosion continues to take place. The river valley becomes broad and flat, and the river winds, or meanders, around in it. When the course of the river swings towards the valley's edge, the sides are worn back, and the valley becomes even wider. At the same time, rocks and sand are deposited on the valley floor, forming what is known as a flood plain. This whole area can be under water during flooding. As it flows, the river constantly changes direction, and eats into the sediment (solid matter) which has already been dropped, lifting it and depositing it elsewhere.

▼ Rivers are used all over the world to move goods and people. This river market in Zaire is part of a river trade route, where people travel by boat to buy and sell goods.

LOOPING CURRENTS

When a river flows round in a loop, its current is faster on the outside. The faster current can erode more quickly than the slower current on the inside, so the outside bank of the loop is worn back. In the meantime, sand and pebbles are deposited by the slower current, and build up the inside bank. The loop gradually becomes more pronounced, and the course of the river changes.

OLD MAN RIVER

In its final stage of development, the river becomes so slow that there is no erosion anywhere, only deposition. The river is now a long way from its source high up in the mountains, and is meandering slowly across a flat plain. The river overflows its banks during times of flood, depositing fertile sediment on the plains as the water slows down away from the main current. The banks are often built up so that the river may actually flow at a higher level than the plain around it. Such a river alters its course continually during flooding, spreading valuable fertile soil on the plain, but making the water difficult to manage.

MEETING THE SEA

Eventually, the river reaches the sea at its mouth. If there are no sea currents at this point, the rest of the river's sediment is deposited as sand banks. These sand banks may even form islands, and the river water splits up into individual streams between them, forming a delta. More often, the sediment is carried away, and the river has a broad tidal mouth called an estuary.

When the channel of a river flows in a snake-like pattern across its valley, it is said to meander.

1 Some meanders swell to broader loops than others.

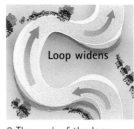

2 The neck of the loop then becomes very narrow.

3 The old channel is cut off to form an oxbow lake.

Glacier · Meltwater · Waterfall · Rapids · Stream · Tributary stream · River · Oxbow lake · Estuary · Meander

Flood plain

River mouth

THE IMPORTANCE OF RIVERS

Although rivers make up only a tiny percentage of the Earth's surface water, they are very important. Rivers form the landscape and provide natural barriers. They also provide vital links from seas to inland areas, and are used for trading goods. Most inland villages, towns and cities began as settlements around rivers; when bridges were built, the settlements grew. Rivers supply food, and water for drinking, washing and crop irrigation.

SEE ALSO

Lake, Mountain and valley, Transport, Water

ROAD

People build and use roads for travel and for moving freight. Cars and trucks on the roads now carry most of the world's passengers and goods.

Interchanges are systems of slip roads that allow traffic to switch smoothly and safely between motorways.

Unpaved roads have stony or earthen surfaces and can be muddy after rain.

Track surfaces are made of gravel. They lie in remote areas with little traffic.

Main roads have all-weather surfaces and can support heavy trucks.

The earliest roads were rough tracks, made by people's feet as they travelled between villages. Sometimes, trackways of timber were laid over boggy ground. Few early roads were suitable for wheeled carts, especially in wet weather.

ROMAN ROADS
The Romans were one of the first peoples to build good roads. Surveyors planned the route, following old tracks or setting out a new, straight line. The roads were suitable for wagons or an army on the march. Towns grew at points where roads crossed.

DECLINE AND REVIVAL
After the Romans, road-building declined in Europe. Both the Inca of South America and the Chinese had advanced road systems, but in Europe, most roads were no better than rough tracks. Improvements were not made until the 18th century,

Natural soil
Compacted soil
Sub-base
Base course
Pavement
Shoulder

ROAD CONSTRUCTION
The lowest layer in modern highways is the sub-base of stone which evens the ground. The base course is made up of stones 4cm in size. The top pavement may be made of concrete or of bitumen and small stones. Lane markings, lights and signs make roads safer for driving.

when armies built better roads to move supplies. In 1816, British engineer John MacAdam (1756–1836) published new designs for roads. He used well-drained layers of stones and gravel bound together with sand. The design was used around the world for major routes.

MOTOR CARS
In the 1890s, early motorists demanded better roads, as cars could not cope with cart tracks. By the 1930s, the first motorway networks had been built in Italy and Germany. Today, many towns are dominated by roads and traffic, causing pollution and safety problems. Road building has opened up regions such as the Amazon, causing environmental damage. Roads are needed for business and pleasure, but town planners need to solve the problems that roads create.

◀ Roman roads were built of flat stones laid over concrete. They were built and used by the army.

SEE ALSO
Car, Transport, Truck and bus

ROBOT

A robot is a machine designed to imitate human actions. It can perform a range of tasks that are often too dangerous or monotonous for a human to do.

Robots are widely used in factories. Here, robotic hands solder parts onto electronic circuit boards.

The name 'robot' comes from *robota*, the Czech word for the work peasants had to do for their landlords. Robots free humans from heavy and boring work; they perform routine tasks in industry such as painting or welding. They can be used in dangerous conditions, such as where there are poisonous fumes or around volcanoes. Robots equipped with electronic 'eyes' can also be used to inspect or sort goods.

Radio-controlled bomb disposal robots check out suspect packages and make controlled explosions.

ROBOTS IN INDUSTRY

The first robot was introduced in 1961 by General Motors in New Jersey, USA. Although they were invented in America, Japan soon became the world's leading maker and user of industrial robots. The first robot in Japan was brought from the USA in 1967. By 1978 Japan was making 10,000 robots a year, by 1980 twice as many. By the 21st century, however, the European Union boasted more industrial robots than Japan.

ROBOTS VERSUS HUMANS

Uses are being developed for robots outside industry. In 1990, the US Army

Robots have taken on cult status in films. Robby the robot starred in *Forbidden Planet* (1956).

▲ Early robots and sci-fi film robots (left) looked like humans. Later, useful robots were tiny and bug-like or resembled industrial machines. By the 1990s, robotic research seemed to have gone full circle. Honda's (right) can walk, climb and make simple decisions.

introduced the 'Robo-spy', a remote-controlled, all-terrain vehicle equipped with a video camera. This was designed to roam enemy territory, sending back information about forces and equipment. In 1991, a robotic sheep-shearer was introduced in Australia; it could work almost twice as fast as a human shearer. In 2011, *Robonaut 2* became the first humanoid robot in space, when it arrived at the International Space Station.

▶ Tiny robots are used in micro-surgery. Here a 'bug-bot' is sweeping away fatty cholesterol deposits clogging up human arteries.

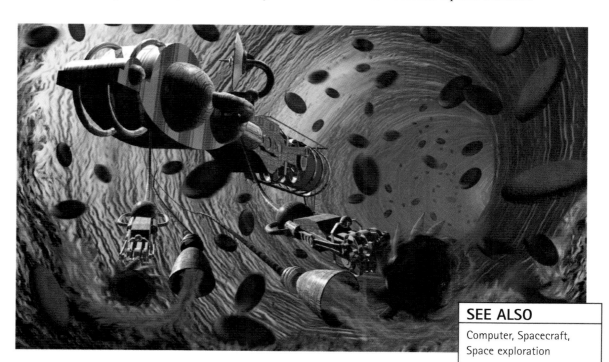

SEE ALSO

Computer, Spacecraft, Space exploration

ROCK

Rocks are the solid substances that make up the surface of the Earth. There are three types of rock, each of which forms in a different way.

▲ Basalt is an igneous rock formed from volcanic lava. It cools very fast, often producing these pencil-like columns.

Granite is a coarse-grained igneous rock that has formed slowly underground.

Pumice is a light igneous rock that often forms in a volcanic eruption.

Marble is a medium-grained rock that forms in metamorphic terrains.

Slate is a dense, fine-grained metamorphic rock that splits into thin slabs.

Limestone is a sedimentary rock that often contains tiny fossilized remains.

Sandstone is a sedimentary rock made of fine or coarse grains cemented into beds.

Igneous rocks are formed from heat. Sedimentary rocks are formed underwater from layers of soil and organic remains. Metamorphic rocks are the result of changes made to existing rocks.

ROCKS FROM HEAT
Hot molten magma from inside the Earth can break out at the surface through a volcano as lava. It then cools and solidifies quickly, forming very fine rock such as basalt. Or, it may cool slowly underground, forming big, coarse, mineral crystals. Granite is a rock formed in this way. In both cases, the rock is igneous – formed from fire.

ROCKS FROM WATER
Loose material, such as sand or mud, can build up in layers at the bottom of the sea. These layers, or beds, may eventually be buried, compressed and cemented into a

solid mass. The resulting rock is called a sedimentary rock – built from layers. The layers may consist of small fragments such as sand, creating sandstone. Or they may be built from minerals dissolved in the sea water, such as limestone, or built up from things that were once alive, such as coal. We find fossils in sedimentary rocks.

NEW ROCKS FROM OLD
The third kind of rock forms when a rock that already exists is heated or squeezed. This may occur in the heart of a mountain chain when it is being pushed up, as the heat and pressure change the minerals that it contains. This produces a metamorphic rock – a rock of change. Great heat gives a rock with an even, crystalline structure, such as marble. Great pressure produces a rock in which the crystals are all twisted and deformed, such as schist.

ROCK CYCLE
New rock is constantly being pushed up towards the Earth's surface, where it is broken down by the elements and deposited at the bottom of lakes, rivers and seas. These sedimentary layers are compressed into new rock, which may later be uplifted or sink to depths where it melts to form igneous rocks again. It can also become so roasted and compressed that it forms metamorphic rock.

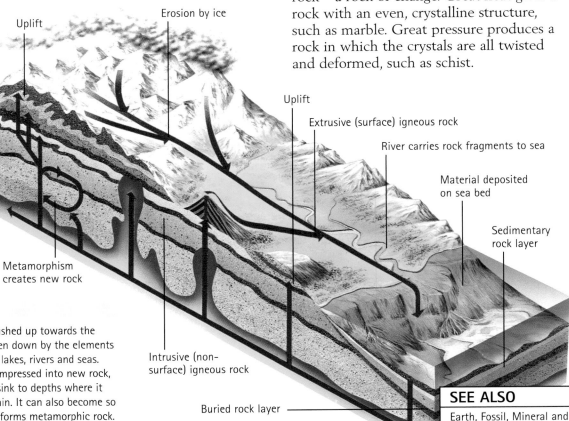

Uplift

Erosion by ice

Metamorphism creates new rock

Intrusive (non-surface) igneous rock

Buried rock layer

Uplift

Extrusive (surface) igneous rock

River carries rock fragments to sea

Material deposited on sea bed

Sedimentary rock layer

SEE ALSO
Earth, Fossil, Mineral and gem, Mining, Oil, Soil

ROCKET

Rockets provide the thrust needed to lift spacecraft above the Earth's atmosphere. They do this by burning fuel and shooting out the exhaust gases behind them.

Rockets make use of a law of physics: a force in one direction gives rise to an equal force in the opposite direction. The backward force of the escaping gases leads to an equal and opposite thrust that pushes the rocket forward. Because rockets have a supply of liquid oxygen, they can work in the emptiness of space.

MULTI-STAGE ROCKETS

Most space rockets consist of three separate sections, or 'stages'. After the powerful first stage has run out of fuel, it falls away and the second-stage engines ignite. After this fuel has been used up, the spacecraft completes its journey away from Earth with the help of the third-stage engines.

MILESTONES IN ROCKETRY

c.1000 Chinese fireworks propelled by gunpowder

1805 Englishman William Congreve develops a rocket for use in battle

1903 Russian Konstantin Tsiolkovsky designs a spacecraft powered by liquid fuel

1926 First liquid-fuelled rocket

1944 Germany launches its destructive V2 rockets

1957 First rocket to lift a spacecraft into Earth's orbit

1981–2011 The Space Shuttle is the first reusable rocket system

SPACE SHUTTLE

The US Space Shuttle had the first reusable rockets. It consisted of an orbiter; an external fuel tank that supplied the orbiter's main engine; and two solid-fuel rocket boosters. When the boosters ran out of fuel they parachuted into the ocean, to be recovered. The empty fuel tank was jettisoned next, burning up on reentry into the Earth's atmosphere. The orbiter continued into space to carry out its mission, returning to land on a runway like an aeroplane. During its 30 years of service, the five-strong Shuttle fleet flew 135 missions.

FUTURE ROCKETS

Almost all rocket engines today use chemical fuels, but their use in long distance space travel is limited. Nuclear rockets may be the answer, if scientists can eliminate the risk of accidents at take-off. Another idea for deep-space missions is the use of a matter-annihilation device, which emits a beam of photons.

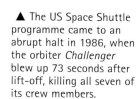

▲ The US Space Shuttle programme came to an abrupt halt in 1986, when the orbiter *Challenger* blew up 73 seconds after lift-off, killing all seven of its crew members.

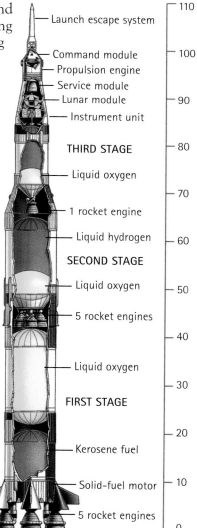

Height in metres

- Launch escape system
- Command module
- Propulsion engine
- Service module
- Lunar module
- Instrument unit

THIRD STAGE
- Liquid oxygen
- 1 rocket engine
- Liquid hydrogen

SECOND STAGE
- Liquid oxygen
- 5 rocket engines
- Liquid oxygen

FIRST STAGE
- Kerosene fuel
- Solid-fuel motor
- 5 rocket engines

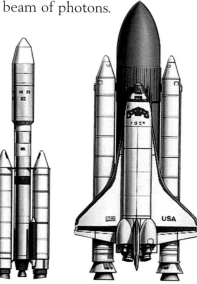

German V2 first tested in 1942.

US *Atlas* developed in 1960s.

Soviet *Soyuz II* launched in 1968.

European *Ariane IV* makes first flight in 1986.

US *Titan* launched *Viking* spacecraft to Mars in 1974.

Reusable US Space Shuttle makes first flight in 1981.

Saturn V takes US *Apollo II* crew to Moon in 1969.

SEE ALSO

Engine, Spacecraft, Space exploration, Warfare

ROMAN EMPIRE

The Romans ruled the Mediterranean and much of Europe for nearly 400 years. Many modern law codes and government systems are based on those of Rome.

Julius Caesar (c.100–44BCE) was a dictator, taking power from the Senate.

Caligula (12CE–41CE) ordered many executions and may have been insane.

Hadrian (76–138) ordered the building of defences along the Empire's borders.

Septimus Severus (146–211) reformed the Empire into a military state.

The cruelty of Commodus (161–192) plunged the Empire into civil war.

Constantine the Great (c.280–337) was the first Christian emperor.

The Roman Empire was built up by the people of Rome from about 250BCE and lasted until 476CE. The Romans were good at organization and were feared for their powerful army and navy. The Empire had one language, one economy and one government.

THE REPUBLIC

According to legend, Rome was founded in 753BCE, and in 509BCE became a republic. Rome's main rival was the city of Carthage in North Africa, and in 218BCE the two went to war. The Carthaginian leader, Hannibal, wiped out the main Roman army at Cannae in 216BCE, but he could not capture Rome, and Carthage was later defeated. By 44BCE, Rome had conquered Greece and large areas of the Near East, North Africa, Spain and France.

AGE OF AUGUSTUS

As the Roman Empire grew, patricians, or noblemen, gained vast wealth and the ordinary citizens, or plebeians, lost political power. The army was more loyal to successful commanders than to the government. These tensions led to a series

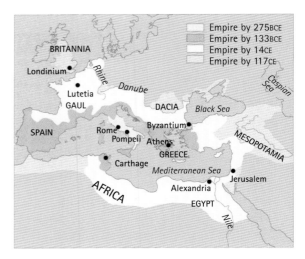

▲ The territory of the Roman Empire expanded rapidly during wars with Egypt, Carthage and Greece. After 117CE, remote areas, such as Mesopotamia, were abandoned.

of civil wars from 49BCE to 30BCE. The wars were won by Octavian, nephew of the dictator Julius Caesar. He took the title Augustus, meaning 'the sacred one', and established a new type of government, giving power to the emperor.

CITIZENS OF ROME

Being a citizen of Rome had many advantages. Citizens could vote, stand in elections or work in the government. At first only people from Rome were citizens, but gradually men from other cities or who had served in the army for 30 years became citizens. Finally, in 212CE, every free man in the Empire became a citizen of Rome.

THE ROMAN ARMY

The Roman army was organized into legions of about 6,000 armoured infantry, with a few archers and cavalry. In battle, the legion was trained to fight in tight formations, such as the *testudo*, or tortoise (below). The army built roads and forts to guard the frontiers. Each legionary had to carry all his equipment, including weapons, cooking pot, blanket and tools (right).

ROMAN HOUSING

Most Romans lived in the countryside, or in blocks of flats called *insulae*, but wealthy families would have a town house, or *domus*. The front rooms were rented out to shopkeepers, while the family lived in rooms around the atrium (courtyard) or the peristyle (garden). The triclinium (dining-room) and reception rooms were close to the kitchen.

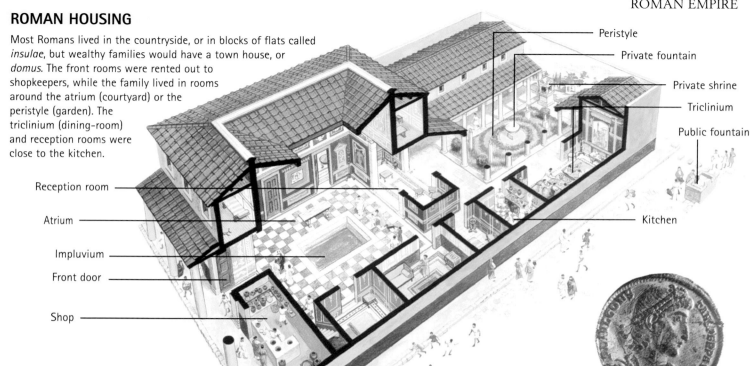

Peristyle
Private fountain
Private shrine
Triclinium
Public fountain

Reception room
Atrium
Impluvium
Front door
Shop

Kitchen

BREAD AND CIRCUSES

Most people in the Roman Empire lived in country areas and worked on farms. The cities were centres for business and government. To keep the people entertained, games were held in which gladiators fought each other or wild beasts in the arena. Criminals might be thrown to the lions as a form of execution. Also popular were chariot races held at the arena called the *Circus*. Free bread was distributed in Rome to the poorer citizens.

BARBARIAN ONSLAUGHT

After about 300CE, plagues and famines reduced the population, while heavy taxation and bad government reduced trade and wealth. In 395CE, the Empire was divided in two, with capitals at Rome and Constantinople. The Eastern Empire became the Byzantine Empire, which had strong Greek influences. After 370CE, waves of Germanic Goths, Saxons and Franks invaded and raided the Empire. The Roman army kept the invaders under control for a while, but in 410CE the Goths captured Rome. In 447CE, the Huns, under Attila, invaded the Empire.

Although the Huns were defeated in 453CE, the power of Rome had been broken. The last Roman emperor, Romulus Augustulus, abdicated in 476CE and the Empire split into small Germanic kingdoms. The Byzantine Empire survived until conquered by the Turks in 1453.

THE LEGACY OF ROME

The laws of Rome influenced legal codes in many countries, while Latin, the Roman language, developed into French, Italian and Spanish. It was the discovery of Roman art and architecture which laid the foundations for the Renaissance, and for the modern world.

▲ A gold coin of the later Empire. Coins of known value were essential for trade and prosperity.

▲ The ruins of a temple in Ephesus, now in Turkey, one of the richest cities in the Roman Empire.

▶ The Romans worshipped many gods. Among these were (clockwise from left) Mars, god of war; Jupiter, king of the gods; Roma, patron goddess of Rome; Neptune, god of the sea; Diana (far right), goddess of hunting; Apollo, god of the Sun and music; and Venus, goddess of love.

SEE ALSO

Architecture, Celts, Civil war, Empire, Government, Greece (Ancient), Italy, Revolution, Slavery, Warfare

RUSSIA AND THE BALTIC STATES

The Russian Federation is the largest country in the world. Its western neighbours – Estonia, Latvia and Lithuania – are known as the Baltic states.

ESTONIA
Area: 45,227 sq km
Population: 1,340,000
Capital: Tallinn
Language: Estonian
Currency: Euro

LATVIA
Area: 64,610 sq km
Population: 2,230,000
Capital: Riga
Language: Latvian
Currency: Lats

LITHUANIA
Area: 64,210 sq km
Population: 3,245,000
Capital: Vilnius
Language: Lithuanian
Currency: Litas

RUSSIA
Area: 17,075,400 sq km
Population: 142,905,000
Capital: Moscow
Language: Russian
Currency: Rouble

Western Russia is mostly flat and low-lying, and is separated from the east by the Ural mountains. In the east, Siberia consists of tablelands and ridges while to the south, the landscape is mountainous. Much of the north is tundra – treeless land where the soil is frozen below the surface. The north is bounded by the world's longest Arctic coastline. Estonia is flat and two fifths of it is farmland, while Latvia has low, forested hills. Lithuania's coast of white sand dunes is popular with tourists.

WINTER AND SUMMER
Most of Russia has long, cold winters, with half the country covered by snow for six months. Summers are mild or warm, but short. In winter, most northern ports, such as St Petersburg, are closed by ice. Rivers such as the Volga, Don and Dnieper are an important part of the transport system and are joined at many points by major canals.

▲ Russian ballet became internationally famous in the 1800s. The Moscow State Academy of Choreography is one of the training grounds for children.

RICH IN RESOURCES
Russia's rich resources include coal, oil, gas, iron, copper, gold and platinum. Many of these reserves, however, are in remote areas and their use is hampered by the harsh climate and by transport problems. The railway system radiates out from Moscow and St Petersburg, around which industry is concentrated. More than three quarters of the population lives in towns and cities. Agricultural produce includes

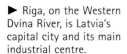

▶ Riga, on the Western Dvina River, is Latvia's capital city and its main industrial centre.

miles
0 — 500

0 — 500
km

N

ARCTIC OCEAN

Franz Josef Land
Severnaya Zemlya
New Siberian Islands
Novaya Zemlya
BERING SEA
Kolyma
Indigirka

NORWAY
FINLAND
ESTONIA
LATVIA
LITHUANIA
RUSSIA
POLAND
BELARUS

Murmansk
Tallinn
Arkhangel'sk
Riga
Vilnius
St. Petersburg
W. Dvina
Dnieper

Lena
CENTRAL SIBERIAN PLATEAU
SEA OF OKHOTSK

Moscow
Nizhniy Novgorod
Kazan
Perm
Samara
Yekaterinburg
Chelyabinsk
Omsk
Novosibirsk

R U S S I A

Ural Mts.
Ob
Yenisey

Sakhalin
Kuril Islands

UKRAINE
Don
Volga

Rostov-na-Donu
KAZAKHSTAN

GEORGIA
CASPIAN SEA
AZERBAIJAN

Lake Baikal
CHINA
Amur
JAPAN

CHINA
MONGOLIA

Vladivostok

cattle, cotton, barley, maize, sunflower seeds, tobacco, wine and reindeer. The main exports of the Baltic States are foods, chemicals and manufactured goods.

PEOPLE AND RELIGION

Russians account for around 80 per cent of the population of Russia. Important minorities include Tatars and Ukrainians. There are 170 different nationalities in all. Russia, Estonia and Latvia are largely non-religious. In Lithuania, nearly 80 per cent of people are Roman Catholic. Average levels of education are high, although researchers, especially in technology and medicine, have been held back by shortages of funds.

RUSSIA'S EXPANSION

The Russian state emerged from the Rus civilization in the 9th century. Its rulers took the title of tsar. Peter the Great, tsar from 1682 to 1725, introduced Western European culture and technology and founded a new capital, St Petersburg. By conquering Estonia and Latvia, he

began a programme of expansion which his successors extended to Lithuania, Belarus, Ukraine and the Crimea. Russian settlement of Siberia began in the 18th century and in the 19th century Finland, the Caucasus and Central Asia were added to the Russian Empire. ▶

▼ Lake Baikal in Siberia is the world's deepest lake.

▲ Like Latvia and Lithuania, Estonia became independent in 1991. It had been taken into the Soviet Union in 1940.

▲ Boris Yeltsin (above) served as Russia's first president from 1991 until 1999. His successor, Vladimir Putin, was in office until 2008, and then again from 2012.

▲ Long, harsh winters are an accepted part of life in Siberia. Local people use sledges to carry shopping.

EARLY 20TH CENTURY RUSSIA
Russia was held back by its very size and a lack of resources. Poverty increased as the population grew within overcrowded settlements. Russian achievements, nevertheless, included the development of modern ballet, the music of Tchaikovsky and the writings of Tolstoy and Chekhov.

RUSSIAN REVOLUTION
Revolution finally came in 1917, in two stages. Alexander Kerensky – a moderate – was brought to power, then overthrown by the Bolsheviks, led by Vladimir Ilyich Ulyanov (Lenin). Lenin ruthlessly led the Bolsheviks to victory and, in 1922, established the communist-run Union of Soviet Socialist Republics (USSR), or Soviet Union. This covered almost all of the former Russian Empire, except Finland and the Baltic States.

SOVIET CONTROL
After Lenin's death in 1924, Joseph Stalin ruled as a brutal dictator. He took the peasants' land to create government-run farms and built up heavy industry, dams, railways and an electric power system. After World War II, the USSR gained control over much of

Eastern Europe, either by forcing countries to become Soviet republics or by controlling their governments. After Stalin's death in 1953, Soviet life was dominated by the Cold War between the Soviet-led communist countries and the US-led Western democracies.

TOWARDS DEMOCRACY
Mikhail Gorbachev became Soviet leader in 1985 and introduced political reforms. He encouraged other Eastern European countries to do the same and many abandoned communism. The Soviet Union broke up in 1991 and countries including the Baltic States became independent. Since the 1990s, oil and natural gas have brought greater prosperity to Russia, but state control has also increased.

► The Kremlin, in Moscow's Red Square, was originally a fortress. Under communist rule, it became the government headquarters.

SEE ALSO
Asia, Astronaut, Civil War, Cold War, Communism, Europe, Revolution

SATELLITE

Satellites are objects that move in orbit around other objects of greater mass. A satellite may be natural, like the Moon, or artificial, like an orbiting spacecraft.

Spacecraft orbiting high above the Earth can be used to relay messages over very long distances. Some satellites are used to send television signals around the world or to track the movement of hurricanes and large weather fronts. Communication satellites are used to pass on telephone conversations and computer data. These satellites receive signals from a transmitting station on Earth, amplify them, and beam the signals down to another Earth station, which may be thousands of kilometres away.

▲ *Sputnik 1*, the world's first artificial satellite, was launched by Russia on October 4, 1957. It was used to broadcast scientific data and orbited the Earth for six months.

▼ Satellites can sometimes give us a clearer picture of activity on the Earth's surface than we can get from the ground. The Earth is surrounded by craft designed specifically for different purposes.

GEOSYNCHRONOUS ORBIT
Most communication satellites move in a special orbit known as a geosynchronous orbit, which is about 35,900km above the Equator. This orbit allows the satellite to remain over the same point on the Earth's surface at all times.

ASTRONOMICAL SATELLITES
By carrying telescopes and other instruments above the Earth's atmosphere, astronomical satellites can see distant objects, such as stars, nebulae and galaxies, much more clearly than we can from the ground. They can also pick up types of waves, such as infrared, ultraviolet, X-rays and gamma rays, which are partly or totally blocked by the atmosphere. For example, X-ray satellites have helped scientists to study black holes and dense, remote binary (double) stars.

SURVEYING THE EARTH
Remote-sensing satellites, equipped with powerful cameras and other equipment, provide valuable information about our planet's natural resources. They can reveal changes to the polar ice caps or the rate at which human beings are destroying the rainforests. Weather satellites can track the movement of hurricanes and supply data that allows accurate weather forecasts several days in advance.

Landsat 5 can spot areas where the Brazilian rainforest has been cleared

The European Remote Sensing satellite (ERS) carried instruments to monitor Earth's land, oceans and atmosphere. It was replaced by Envisat in 2011

Spy satellites use powerful telescopes to detect potential trouble spots

Aqua (EOS PM-1) is a research satellite that studies the Earth's water cycle

The Meteosat Second Generation (MSG) satellite stays in geostationary orbit above the Atlantic to track weather fronts such as hurricanes and cyclones

SEE ALSO
Communication, Radar, Telecommunication, Telephone, Television, Weather

SCANDINAVIA

Scandinavia consists of the neighbouring north European countries of Denmark, Norway, Sweden, Finland, Iceland and the Faeroe Islands.

DENMARK
Area: 43,094 sq km
Population: 5,535,000
Capital: Copenhagen
Language: Danish
Currency: Krone

FINLAND
Area: 338,145 sq km
Population: 5,375,000
Capital: Helsinki
Languages: Finnish and Swedish
Currency: Euro

ICELAND
Area: 102,819 sq km
Population: 319,000
Capital: Reykjavik
Language: Icelandic
Currency: Krona

NORWAY
Area: 323,878 sq km
Population: 4,920,000
Capital: Oslo
Language: Norwegian
Currency: Krone

SWEDEN
Area: 449,964 sq km
Population: 9,416,000
Capital: Stockholm
Language: Swedish
Currency: Krona

▶ Stockholm, capital of Sweden, is built on 14 small islands connected by about 50 bridges.

The name Scandinavia refers to the large peninsula made up of Sweden and Norway. Often included in this term are the neighbouring countries of Denmark and Finland, as well as Iceland and the Faeroe Islands, which have cultural and language links with the region. Danish, Swedish, Norwegian and Icelandic all come from a common ancestor language, but Finnish is quite different.

THE FAEROE ISLANDS

These 18 islands in the North Atlantic Ocean have a population of about 49,000. They were ruled by Norway until 1380, and many of the inhabitants are of Norse origin. For the last 600 years, they have been under Danish control, and in 1948, Denmark allowed them to become self-governing. The representatives of their parliament, or *Lagting*, hold seats in the Danish parliament in Copenhagen.

LONG SUMMER DAYS

Due to their northerly location, the countries of Scandinavia have long, cold, snowy winters. In Iceland and in the northernmost parts of Finland, Norway

▲ Norway's coast is famous for its many fjords – long, narrow inlets of the sea that make fine natural harbours.

and Sweden around the Arctic Circle, it is light for 24 hours a day around midsummer and dark for most of the day towards the end of December.

RICH IN RESOURCES

Flat Denmark is famous for its agriculture, Finland for its lakes, Sweden for its forests, Norway for its spectacular coastal fjords (inlets) and Iceland for its dramatic geysers (hot springs) and volcanoes. The region is rich in natural resources, including oil, gas, iron and timber. Since oil was discovered in the North Sea in the 1960s, Norway has become self-sufficient in natural gas and oil, and expert at oil rig construction. Sweden is the most industrial of the Scandinavian nations and

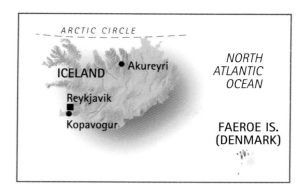

is one of the wealthiest countries in Europe. Fishing has been an important industry for the whole region. Modern Scandinavian styles of architecture and design, especially of furniture, metalwork and glassware, are influential worldwide.

NORTHERN PEOPLES

Most Scandinavians are descendants of Germanic peoples who moved into the area around 2,000 years ago, while most Finns migrated around the same time from western Russia. North of the Arctic Circle are the Sami – descendants of the earliest inhabitants of Sweden and Finland. Some Sami live a traditional way of life herding reindeer, which they keep for their meat, milk and hides. But most earn a living from farming, fishing or mining. In Norway, Finland and Sweden, the Sami have their own parliaments, or *Sameting*s.

▼ In Denmark, surrounded as it is by sea, both fishing and ship-building are important. Danish fishing fleets bring in mackerel, herring, cod, shrimp and flatfish.

SCANDINAVIAN POLICIES

Norway, Denmark and Sweden are all constitutional monarchies, but Finland and Iceland are republics. The Scandinavian countries have traditionally been strong supporters of international organizations, human rights, health and welfare programmes and conservation. Many of these efforts are co-ordinated by the Nordic Council, founded in 1953.

NORSE MYTHOLOGY

In pre-Christian times, early Scandinavian and Germanic peoples shared a common mythology, known as Norse mythology. The myths, originally passed on by word of mouth, were first written down in the 1200s. Four of the early Norse gods – Tiw, Odin, Thor and Freya – are remembered in the days of the week, Tuesday, Wednesday, Thursday and Friday. Today, Lutheran Protestant Christianity is the main religion in all Scandinavian countries.

▲ Found in Arctic regions, reindeer migrate several hundred kilometres a year in search of food.

SEE ALSO

Arctic, Europe, Myth and legend, Vikings

SCULPTURE

Sculpture is a piece of three-dimensional art that gives you different views as you walk around it. It can be carved, moulded or shaped out of a range of materials.

▲ Rachel Whiteread's award-winning *House* (1995) used a house in East London as a mould.

The two traditional ways of making a sculpture are carving and moulding. Carving means cutting into wood or stone; moulding involves making a model in clay and using it to cast a replica in concrete or a metal. Sculpture can also be carved in 'relief', by cutting a raised picture into flat stone or wood. Modern sculptures have been made from plastic, glass and everyday objects – the British artist, David Mach, uses papers and magazines.

▲ Michelangelo's bold and lifelike marble statue of *David* (1504) followed the classical Greek style.

GODS AND IDOLS
Since people began using tools, they have made figures of people and animals, or religious idols to please their gods and scare away evil spirits. Tiny figures possibly made by shamans (magician-priests) about 30,000 years ago are among the earliest-known sculptures. The Ancient Egyptians cut huge figures out of solid rock, and there are other massive ancient sculptures in the Americas and Asia. Tribal totem poles are a form of sculpture, while Ancient Greeks created impressive lifelike figures.

CHANGING IMAGES
In the Middle Ages, European sculpture was mostly religious – the decoration in and on church buildings. During the Renaissance, artists returned to the realism of the classical Greeks. Their works were for religious and private patrons who paid for marble and bronze sculptures.

BREAK WITH TRADITION
In the 20th century, sculptors began to explore new styles, using solid shapes to represent abstract ideas and feelings. This included using ordinary objects in unusual ways, assembling moving pieces or mobiles – known as installation art. The US artist Christo wrapped buildings in plastic, which linked art and architecture in a new way.

▲ American sculptor Andy Goldsworthy's *Slits Cut Into Frozen Snow* (1988), a form of land art, shows that art is not confined to galleries.

▶ Hundreds of years ago, Easter Islanders carved more than 600 huge stone statues, known as *moai*, using handpicks.

SEE ALSO

Art, Renaissance

SEASHORE

There are many types of seashore, from rocky cliffs to sandy beaches. Each habitat has its own creatures and plant life, specially adapted to live there.

Tidal pools contain plants and small marine animals.

Rocky cliffs are a favourite nesting place for kittiwakes.

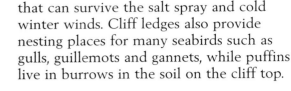

Many salt-resistant grasses thrive on sand dunes.

The narrow zone where land and sea meet, the seashore, is one of the most varied and fascinating habitats on Earth. It contains creatures that have evolved to live half their lives on land and half at sea.

BEACHES

The most common type of shore is the sandy beach, made of tiny particles of rock (sand) worn down by being constantly rolled together by waves. Plants can't grow in the loose sand between high- and low-water marks, but just below the surface, sand-worms and burrowing shellfish feed on tiny food particles washed in with the tide. Sandy and muddy shores are favourite feeding places for shorebirds.

CLIFFS

Where waves hammer against hard rocks, a steep cliff may form. Here, the tiny ledges and cracks are home to specialized plants that can survive the salt spray and cold winter winds. Cliff ledges also provide nesting places for many seabirds such as gulls, guillemots and gannets, while puffins live in burrows in the soil on the cliff top.

ROCKY SHORES

Rocky coasts are home to a huge variety of red, brown and green seaweeds, some like long leather belts, some like mosses. The seaweed fronds provide a cool, damp hiding place for sand-hoppers, crabs, barnacles, winkles and limpets. Rock pools provide another place in which sea creatures can survive while the tide is out. Some molluscs, such as mussels and limpets, attach themselves to rocks.

SANDY SEASHORES

A vast array of birds, plants, molluscs and crustaceans live around the world's seashores. Crashing waves constantly change the shape of sandy beaches, so all forms of life must be adaptable – most shore plants and animals are able to live in and out of water. Shorebirds feed on worms, fish and other small creatures.

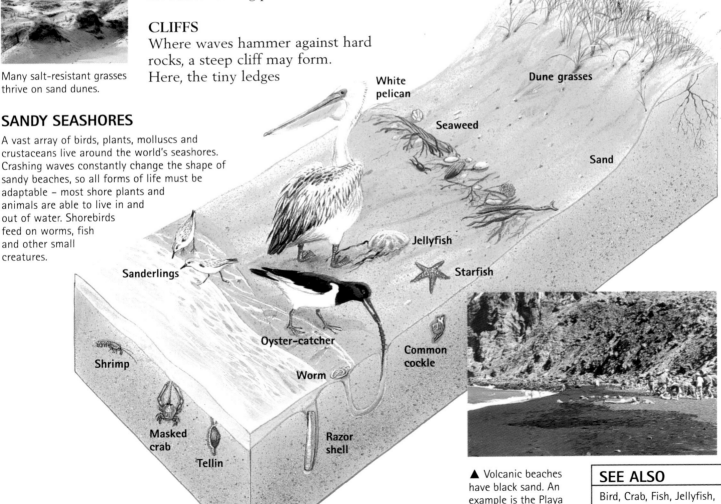

White pelican

Seaweed

Dune grasses

Sand

Jellyfish

Starfish

Sanderlings

Oyster-catcher

Common cockle

Worm

Shrimp

Masked crab

Tellin

Razor shell

▲ Volcanic beaches have black sand. An example is the Playa Anglais, Canary Islands.

SEE ALSO

Bird, Crab, Fish, Jellyfish, Snail, Starfish, Ocean and sea, Volcano, Worm

SEASON

As the Earth orbits the Sun, the tilt of its axis causes changes in the length of day and the temperature. This creates what we call the seasons.

MARCH 21
Spring begins in the Northern Hemisphere, autumn in the Southern Hemisphere. The days and nights are of equal length.

DECEMBER 21
Winter begins in Northern the Hemisphere, summer begins in the Southern Hemisphere.

JUNE 21
Summer begins in the Northern Hemisphere, winter begins in the Southern Hemisphere.

SEPTEMBER 23
Autumn begins in the Northern Hemisphere, spring begins in the Southern Hemisphere. Days and nights are of equal length again.

▲ December in Alberta, Canada brings the typically snowy and cold weather of a Northern Hemisphere winter.

▲ Southern Hemisphere areas like Green Island Beach, Australia enjoy the beginning of their summer season in December.

The seasons affect everything we do. They determine when we plant our crops and harvest them, what kind of clothes we wear, what we eat, how much energy we use for heating and lighting, and even how we feel. The seasons are caused by the tilt of the Earth's axis during its yearly journey around the Sun.

THE EARTH'S TILT
The Earth is always spinning, tilted at an angle of 23.5°, so that the North Pole tilts towards the Sun for part of the year. In the Northern Hemisphere, the Sun is high in the sky and the days are long and warm, resulting in summer. At the same time, the South Pole is tilted away from the Sun, and the Southern Hemisphere has its winter.

THE SOLSTICES
As the Earth orbits the Sun, its axis points towards the same spot in space, so that six months later, the North Pole tilts away from the Sun. It is now winter in the Northern Hemisphere and summer in the Southern Hemisphere. In the Northern Hemisphere, the longest day (the summer solstice) is June 21, and the shortest day (the winter solstice) is December 21. For the Southern Hemisphere, the longest day of the year is December 21 and the shortest day is June 21.

THE EQUINOXES
Halfway between the solstices are the autumn and spring equinoxes. On March 21 and September 23, the tilted Earth is sideways-on to the Sun, and day and night are of equal length. Spring in the Northern Hemisphere begins on March 21, when the Southern Hemisphere has autumn. On September 23, the Northern Hemisphere autumn begins, and it is spring south of the Equator.

SEE ALSO
Climate, Earth, Hibernation, Sun, Weather, Wind

SEED AND POLLINATION

Seeds are the means by which flowering plants reproduce to make other plants of the same species. But pollination must take place before a seed is formed.

Stone fruits (drupes) such as the peach have a large stone that contains a seed.

The coconut is a very large seed, with edible flesh and milk inside its tough husk.

The acorn is the fruit of the oak tree. Its woody cup holds a hard, smooth nut.

Ash seeds have papery wings that help them scatter on the wind.

An apple has several seeds in its core, to increase its chances of reproduction.

A seed consists of a tiny new plant, called an embryo, and a store of food, all contained within a tough protective coat. Some seeds can remain dormant (in a resting state) for over 100 years before they grow into new plants. To make a seed, pollen (male cells) from one plant must fertilize, or pollinate, the eggs (female cells) of another plant.

POLLINATION

Some plants, such as grasses and trees, rely on the wind to blow their pollen from one plant to the next. Other plants have large flowers, with bright colours, scents and nectar, to attract insects, bats, birds or small animals. These visitors feed on the nectar, and as they do so, the pollen sticks to them and is carried to the next flower they visit. When a pollen grain sticks to

another flower's sticky end (stigma), it send out a tube that grows down inside a stalk leading to the ovary (style), so that male cells can reach the egg and fertilize it. Once the egg has been fertilized, it develops into a seed.

GERMINATION

A seed must have moisture, warmth and oxygen to grow into a new plant. This process, called germination, begins with the seed absorbing water. The embryo begins to grow, and its root pushes its way through the seed coat. The seed leaves, or cotyledons, and the shoot soon follow.

SEEDS AS FOOD

When a seed falls to the ground, its starchy food store feeds the young plant, and it is this starch that people use as food. The seeds of wheat, barley, maize, rice and other members of the grass family are cooked to make basic foods, or ground into flour to make bread and pasta.

▶ A wheat grain is a seed made up of starch (used to make flour), covered with a shell (bran).

Bran
Starch
Husk
Embryo

▲ When a windborne seed falls to the ground, its food store gives it the nutrients it needs to take root.

▲ The soil provides additional nutrients so that the plant can push above ground level and grow to full size.

SEED DISPERSAL

Plants scatter, or disperse, seeds using many methods. Mice and other small animals eat grass seeds (grain) and berries, and spiky burrs from plants such as thistles stick to their fur. Later, mouse droppings move seeds to a different area, and burrs drop off along the way. Dandelion seeds have soft, feathery tufts and poppies have tiny, light seeds, which make it easy for them to become windborne.

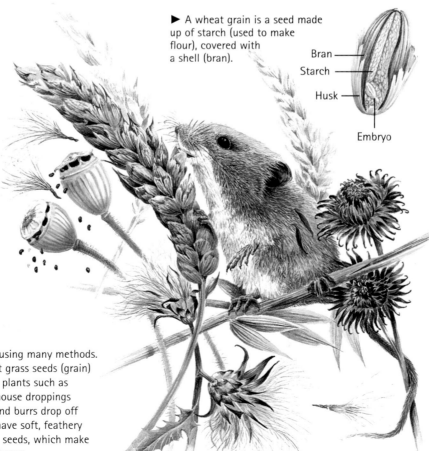

SEE ALSO

Crop, Flower, Fruit, Plant, Tree, Vegetable

SEVEN WONDERS OF THE WORLD

The Seven Wonders of the World were the most impressive and famous buildings and monuments known to the Ancient Greeks.

In about 146BCE, the Greek architect Philo of Byzantium produced a list of the finest engineering feats of the known world. Of these, only the Pyramids of Giza, the ruins of the Temple of Artemis, the Mausoleum and the Pharos remain.

IN MEMORY

The greatest of the Egyptian Pyramids were built at Giza as tombs for the pharaohs Cheops (Khufu), Chephren (Khafre) and Mycerinus (Menkure) between 2600BCE and 2500BCE. The Mausoleum was built as the tomb of King Mausolus of Caria in 353BCE by his widow, Artemisia, in the city of Halicarnassus in Egypt. The finest craftsmen were employed to create a tomb so beautiful that even today, elaborate tombs are called mausoleums. The Hanging Gardens of Babylon were built in about 580BCE by King Nebuchadnezzar II of Babylon to remind his wife, a princess from the mountain kingdom of Media, of home.

BUILT FOR THE GODS

The great Temple at Ephesus, Turkey was built in 350BCE by the Greek architects, Scopas and Apelles. It had over 100 columns, each 20m tall and decorated with sculptures. It was dedicated to Artemis, goddess of nature. The statue of Zeus at Olympia, home of the Olympic Games, was made in 433BCE by Phidias of Athens. The wooden statue stood 12m tall and was covered in ivory and gold. The Colossus of Rhodes was a 40-m tall bronze statue of the Sun god Helios, erected by the city of Rhodes after invaders were defeated in 305BCE. It fell in an earthquake in 224BCE and was sold for scrap in 653CE.

THE FIRST LIGHTHOUSE

The approach to the harbour of Alexandria in Egypt was extremely dangerous. To help ships arrive safely, the great Pharos was built in about 280BCE. The tower stood over 140m tall and was topped by a statue of a god – perhaps Poseidon, Greek god of the sea. The tower could be seen from far out to sea and guided ships to harbour. At night, it is said, a fire was lit to guide ships. The tower gradually crumbled into ruins after 1,500 years.

The Great Pyramids of Giza in Egypt.

The Colossus on the island of Rhodes.

The Mausoleum of Halicarnassus.

The statue of Zeus at Olympia.

The Hanging Gardens of Babylon.

The Temple of Artemis at Ephesus.

SEE ALSO

Babylon, Egypt (Ancient), Greece (Ancient)

SHARK

Sharks are fish whose skeletons are made of gristly cartilage instead of bone. Almost all of them live in the sea and they feed mainly on other fish.

The aggressive tiger shark can grow to over 7m long and is known as a dangerous man-eater.

The hammerhead shark can grow up to 6m long and has a flattened head like the head of a hammer.

The basking shark can grow to 15m long and swims close to the surface of the water to feed on plankton.

The fast and powerful mako shark grows up to 3.5m long and is a popular catch for sea anglers.

The thresher shark grows to about 6m long and uses its long tail to stun the fish it feeds on.

The harmless whale shark grows up to 15m long but feeds only on plankton and small fish.

There are about 400 kinds of shark, from little dogfish, less than half a metre long, to the huge whale shark, which is 15m long and weighs 14 tonnes. Most sharks are fast swimmers, with streamlined bodies. Their fins are thick and leathery, and cannot be folded like those of other fish.

GILL SLITS FOR BREATHING

A shark has five to seven gill slits just behind the head on each side. Water taken in through the mouth flows out through these slits after passing over the gills, where life-giving oxygen is taken from it. Most sharks must keep swimming to keep this oxygen flow going.

SKIN LIKE SANDPAPER

The skin of a shark is covered with denticles – tooth-like scales that make it very rough. In fact, sailors once used shark skins as sandpaper to scrub the decks of their wooden ships. A shark's teeth have

serrated, razor-sharp edges and can easily slice through flesh. Its digestive juices are strong enough to corrode steel.

THE BIGGEST FISH

Although most sharks are ferocious hunters, the biggest ones are actually quite harmless. The whale shark is the biggest fish in the world. It has a huge mouth, but it feeds by straining tiny animals and plants from the water, just as many whales do.

SKATES AND RAYS

Skates and rays are closely related to sharks, but their bodies are very flat. Their head and body and massive front fins are all fused together to form a circular or diamond-shaped disc. They live mainly on the sea bed and feed on shellfish and other bottom-living animals, which they crush with rows of flat teeth. Some of them are armed with poisonous spines.

Sense pores on the nose can detect the electrical signals given off by the twitching muscles of the shark's prey

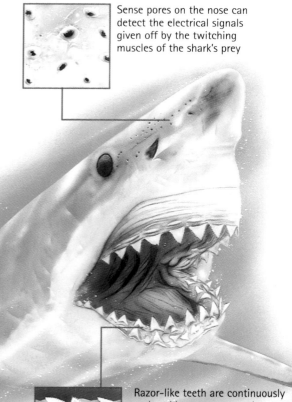

THE GREAT WHITE

Up to 8m long, the great white is the most dangerous of all sharks. It preys on large animals such as dolphins, sea lions and other sharks. It will also attack human beings and even fishing boats.

The skin consists of tiny, tooth-like scales and is used to make rough shark leather

Gill slits open and close to take in oxygen from the water

Razor-like teeth are continuously replaced by new ones as they are lost. During its lifetime, a shark will get through thousands of teeth

SEE ALSO
Fish, Ocean and sea, Whale and dolphin

357

SHIP

Ships are craft that weigh more than 1,000 tonnes. They are used to carry passengers and freight or to catch fish. They may also be used in warfare.

▲ Tankers transport liquids, usually oil, in bulk. The liquid is stored in tanks, while empty chambers give added buoyancy. The engines and crew quarters are usually placed at the rear.

Viking longships of 900ce had open decks and were powered by sails and oars.

Galleons of the 16th century had high sides on which to mount guns.

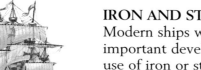

Clippers of the 19th century had streamlined hulls for extra speed.

Large wooden ships were first built for transport in the countries around the Mediterranean Sea and in the Far East about 300BCE. These ships were powered by sails or oars and were up to 50m in length. Later wooden ships, which had tall masts and several sails, reached as much as 115m in length.

IRON AND STEAM

Modern ships were made possible by two important developments. The first was the use of iron or steel construction, which is strong enough for very large ships. The second was the steam engine, which made ships independent of the direction in which the wind was blowing. The only practical limit to the size of a steel ship is the depth of coastal waters and the size of docks. The largest ships afloat today are the 'supertankers', which sail between oil fields and refineries in Europe, America and Japan. Supertankers are far bigger than any liner or warship, weighing up to one million tonnes when fully loaded and measuring over 400m long.

The *Great Eastern* of 1855 combined steam and sail power and was the first liner.

CARGO CARRIERS

Modern cargo ships include bulk carriers and container ships. The bulk carrier transports large, solid cargoes such as coal or iron ore, using special equipment to load and unload. The container ship carries packed containers, each small enough to be loaded onto a lorry. A very large ship may carry several thousand containers. These big merchant ships have an 'island' at the back (the stern) containing the bridge, the crew quarters and the engine room. They also have a long centre deck above the cargo holds, and a further small island close to the front (the bow).

PASSENGER SHIPS

Luxurious passenger ships called liners were used to carry passengers between continents, but today, large passenger-carrying ships are used for cruising. They take people on holiday, allowing them to visit different ports while enjoying a luxurious life on board. Another passenger ship is the ferry, used for carrying people and vehicles on short sea crossings. Ferries are designed to load and unload their passengers quickly, usually through huge doors at the bow and stern. A modern cruise liner may weigh 80,000 tonnes, and some ferries weigh over 20,000 tonnes.

WARSHIPS

As trade by sea became more important and nations competed for dominance, they began to develop navies of fighting ships. Warships now include destroyers, cruisers, and submarines, armed with guns, missiles and torpedoes. The largest warships are aircraft carriers, which can weigh 80,000 tonnes or more. They act as offshore air bases from which air strikes on enemy targets can be made.

ENGINES AND STEERING

Most modern ships are driven by one or two propellers, powered by large diesel engines or by gas turbines, although some warships use nuclear power. The diesel engine is cheaper and more reliable, while the gas turbine is small and light. A rudder is used for steering, but small propellers, or thrusters, are used to control the ship when it is manoeuvring.

SKIMMING THE SURFACE

A ship uses most of its energy pushing the water aside, so some modern craft skim above the water. Hydrofoils are supported by 'wings' under the water, while hovercraft float on a cushion of air. Both are fast, but cannot be built too large.

FACTORY FISHING

Factory ships catch large numbers of fish, and waste almost nothing. The net is hauled in, spilling the catch into the fish bin where it is sorted before passing to the cleaning room where heads and guts are removed. The waste is processed into fish meal, while the clean fillets are packed and frozen. The frozen fish is stored in the refrigerated hold until the ship reaches port. The entire operation is controlled from the bridge, where sonar and other electronic aids help the skipper to find giant shoals of fish.

▲ A multi-purpose cargo ship carrying containers, tanks and crates. Lifting gear along the centre of the ship is used to load and unload the cargo.

Air strikes against enemy fleets are launched from aircraft carriers.

Cruise ships are luxurious floating hotels carrying thousands of passengers.

Missiles and torpedoes are launched from submarines beneath the sea surface.

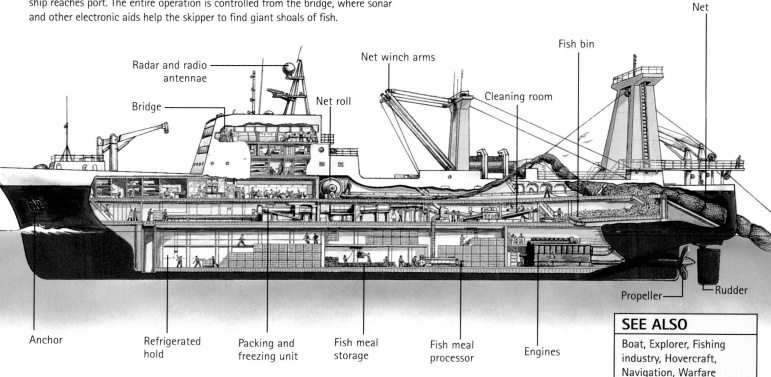

Radar and radio antennae

Bridge

Net roll

Net winch arms

Cleaning room

Fish bin

Net

Anchor

Refrigerated hold

Packing and freezing unit

Fish meal storage

Fish meal processor

Engines

Propeller

Rudder

SEE ALSO

Boat, Explorer, Fishing industry, Hovercraft, Navigation, Warfare

SIGHT

Sight is the ability to detect light and form it into an accurate view of the shapes, colours and distances of surrounding objects.

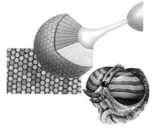

Insect compound eyes have a mosaic of cells which build up an image.

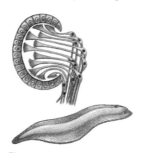

Flatworms have cupped organs able to detect the direction of a light source.

Sight is the most important sense for most animals, providing over half of all the information that enters the brain. Animals use their eyes to look for food and mates and to watch for danger. Most invertebrates (creatures without backbones) have simple eyes, able to give only a rough picture of their surroundings.

ADVANCED VISION

Animals with backbones (vertebrates) have eyes that are able to see clearly. At the front of the eye is a transparent area, known as the cornea, through which light enters. Behind the cornea is a coloured ring of muscle, the iris, with a central hole, the pupil. The iris changes shape to make the pupil wider in dim light, so that more light enters the eye, for clearer vision. Behind the pupil is the lens, which focuses light rays. A ring of ciliary muscles changes the shape of the lens to adjust the focus.

THE HUMAN EYE

The human eyeball, about 25mm across, is set into a bowl-shaped socket in the skull. Six small muscles move the eye up, down and sideways. The eye's whitish outer layer, the sclera, is strong and tough. Inside is the choroid layer, soft and blood-rich, which nourishes the inner parts of the eye. The main bulk of the eyeball is filled with clear jelly, or vitreous humour, which keeps it firm.

▲ Cats' eyes stand out in poor light (left) as they have an extra layer, the guanine, which reflects light back past the retina. The guanine allows cats to see clearly in poor light (right), although they cannot distinguish colours.

LIGHT TO NERVE SIGNALS

Light rays focused by the lens shine onto the retina. This contains millions of light-sensitive cells, called rods and cones, which send nerve signals to the brain where they are translated into a picture. The rods are sensitive in dim light and detect movement and the contrast between black and white. The cones, which are clustered in one small area, see colour. Only humans and a few other types of animal can see in full colour.

TWO EYES

Most animals have two eyes, which help to judge distance in two ways. Each eye sees an object from a slightly different position. The brain compares the view it receives from each eye and, the more different they are, the nearer the object. The brain also measures how much the eyes swivel inwards to look at an object that is very near.

▲ Nerve cells on the retina react to light. They send signals along the optic nerve to the brain.

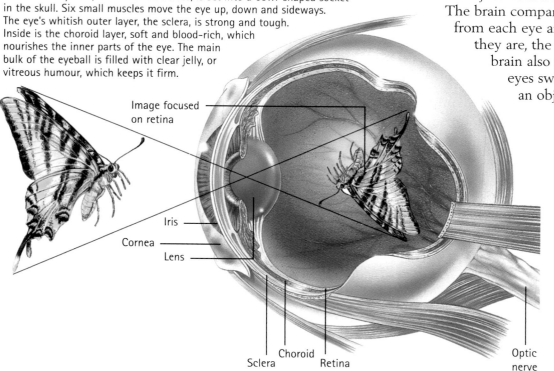

Image focused on retina

Iris

Cornea

Lens

Sclera

Choroid

Retina

Optic nerve

SEE ALSO

Brain, Cat, Eagle, Human body, Insect, Lens, Light, Wavelength

SILVER

Silver is a white-coloured precious metal. It is best known for its use in jewellery, coins and silverware, but it is also used in electronics and photography.

Silver on calcite

Silver ore

Silver wiry form

In addition to its beauty, silver has important properties that make it unique. One of the most important is its conductivity: it allows heat and electric current to pass through it (conduct) more easily than any other metal.

MINING SILVER
The amount of silver in the Earth is tiny, but it occurs in many types of rock. Some rocks contain pure silver metal. Others combine silver with other chemical elements in silver ores. Silver is separated from these ores (smelted) using heat and electricity. Like gold, silver is an important by-product of copper and lead mines. Mexico leads in the world's production of silver, followed by Peru and China.

SILVER JEWELLERY AND COINS
Silver jewellery has been made for at least 6,000 years, even before the smelting of metals began. Most modern silver jewellery is made of an alloy (mixture) of 80 per cent silver and 20 per cent copper.

◀ Silver is often used with turquoise in Native American jewellery such as necklaces.

This 17th-century ▼ ewer is an example of Spanish silver tableware.

▼ Pegasus features on this ancient silver coin from Corinth, c. 350BCE.

Like gold, silver is used as a form of money. Coins have been made out of silver for at least 2,800 years. For much of that time, large quantities of silver have been held in reserve by governments as a sign of their wealth. Today, however, silver has other more important uses.

OTHER USES OF SILVER
At one time, nearly two fifths of all silver went into making photographic film. The rise of digital cameras means that now less than 10 per cent is put to that use. Silver is used in modern electronic circuit boards and in some surgical equipment. Most household mirrors are made by coating glass with a thin layer of silver.

SILVER ELECTROPLATING
In electroplating, a metal object is coated with a plate (thin layer) of another metal, such as silver or gold, using an electric current. The jug is immersed in a water and silver solution. One wire is connected to a strip of silver, and another is connected to the jug. The wires are both connected to a power source. When the current is switched on, electrolysis occurs: silver moves from the solution to coat the jug with a smooth layer.

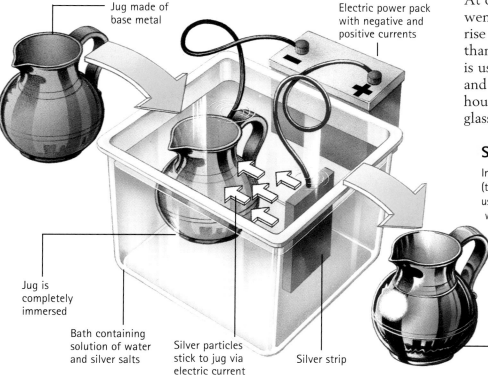
Jug made of base metal

Electric power pack with negative and positive currents

Jug is completely immersed

Bath containing solution of water and silver salts

Silver particles stick to jug via electric current

Silver strip

Finished silver-plated jug

SEE ALSO

Electronics, Metal, Mineral and gem, Mining, Money

SINGAPORE

Singapore is a small island nation in Southeast Asia. It lies at the southern tip of the Malay Peninsula, to which it is connected by a causeway.

SINGAPORE
Area: 704 sq km
Population: 5,077,000
Capital: Singapore City
Languages: Chinese, English, Malay, Tamil
Currency: Singapore dollar

The Republic of Singapore is made up of just under 50 islands, of which the largest is linked to Malaysia by road across the Johor Strait. It is a flat country with a warm, wet, tropical climate. Nearly a quarter of Singapore is made up of rainforest and nature reserves.

PROSPERITY

Singaporeans enjoy one of the highest living standards in Asia. Lacking raw materials of its own, Singapore has prospered from the skills of its well-educated, hardworking people. Although 77 per cent of the population is Chinese, 14 per cent Malay and most of the rest from India, English is the main language

▲ Traditional life mixes with modern – Chinese rickshaws ferry passengers along Singapore's main highways.

of government, business and education. Singapore is one of Asia's leading international financial centres. Other main industries include electronics, building and repairing ships, refining oil, fishing and tourism.

NEW COUNTRY, NEW NATION

Singapore supported small farmers and fishermen until Sir Stamford Raffles, a British trader, saw the advantages of its natural harbour and location on major trade routes, and made it a British possession in 1819. Under British rule, the population grew, gaining many Chinese and Indians, who came as traders and labourers. The port handled products like rubber, tin and timber from Malaya. British rule ended in 1959, and Singapore became part of the Federation of Malaysia (1963–65). Since then, it has been an independent republic.

▼ The city of Singapore developed around its harbour. It is the third largest port in the world, after Shanghai and Ningbo (both in China).

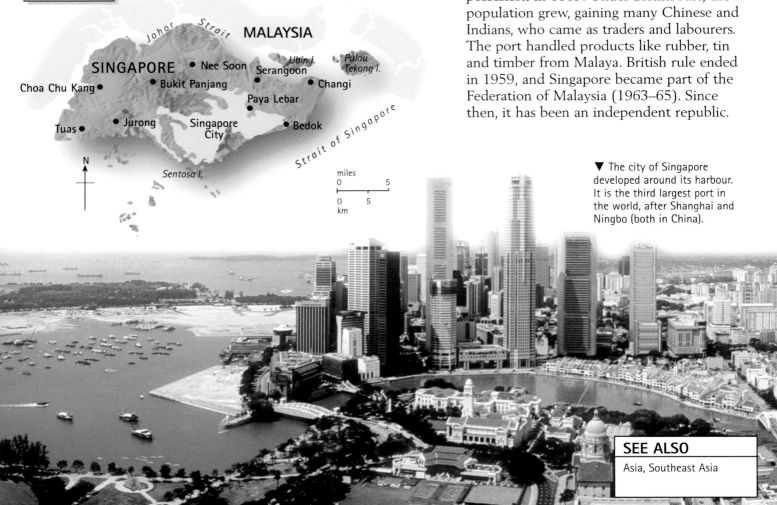

MALAYSIA

Johor Strait

SINGAPORE

Choa Chu Kang ●   ● Nee Soon   Serangoon   *Ubin I.*   *Pulau Tekong I.*

● Bukit Panjang   ● Changi

Paya Lebar

Tuas ●   ● Jurong   Singapore City   ● Bedok

Strait of Singapore

N

Sentosa I.

miles
0   5

0   5
km

SEE ALSO

Asia, Southeast Asia

SKELETON

The strong framework of more than 200 bones called the skeleton gives the body shape, support and protection, and allows it to move.

A bird's skeleton is very light in weight, making flight easier.

Large mammals such as cows need strong bones to carry their body weight.

Fish have spiny bones to support fins and flexible backbones for swimming.

The body's firmness, shape and strength are due to its skeleton. The skeleton has two main parts. The skull, backbone, and ribs form the central, or axial, skeleton, and the arms and legs make up the appendicular skeleton. This system of 206 tough, rigid parts, called bones, forms the body's internal framework and protects delicate organs such as the brain, heart and lungs. Bones are linked to each other at joints and are anchored to muscles, which pull on them to move the body.

BONE STRENGTH

Each bone's size, shape and strength depend on how it supports its part of the body and its muscle attachments. Bones are stiff because they contain crystals of minerals such as calcium and phosphate. But they are also slightly flexible, because they contain fibres of the body protein collagen, so that they bend slightly under stress, rather than crack.

INSIDE A BONE

Bones are pale yellow and have their own blood vessels and nerves. They are a combination of living cells and minerals. Bone cells, called osteocytes, produce tiny rod-like structures of bone minerals, called osteons (Haversian systems). Most bones have a strong outer layer of compact bone, with the osteons packed together. Inside this is a layer of spongy, or cancellous, bone.

BONE MARROW

In the middle of some bones is jelly-like marrow. This makes new cells for the blood, producing millions every second. All of a baby's bones contain marrow, but by adulthood, marrow is found mainly in the breast bone, backbone, ribs and skull.

THE HUMAN SKELETON

The skull is made up of eight bones joined together; the face has 14 bones. Inside each ear are three of the body's tiniest bones called ossicles. The backbone has 26 bones called vertebrae; 12 pairs of ribs join the breast bone at the front of the chest. Each shoulder and arm has 32 bones, including eight carpals in the wrist. Each hip and leg has 31 bones, including seven tarsals in the ankle.

◄ About one third of bone is living tissue. The rest consists of minerals like calcium and phosphorus, which produce a hard, yet slightly elastic, material.

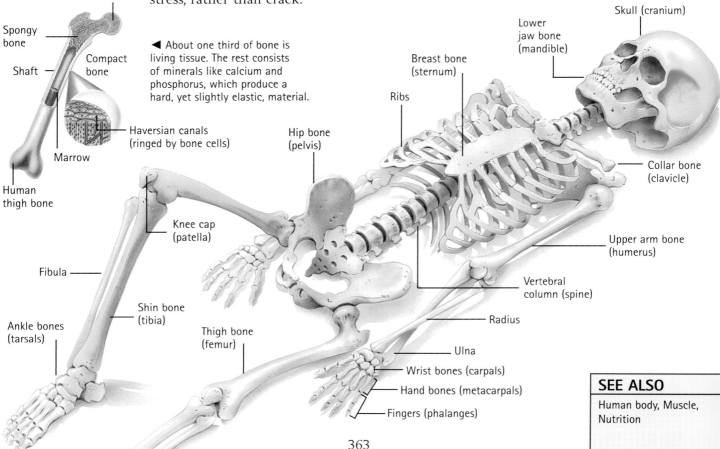

Head

Spongy bone

Shaft

Compact bone

Haversian canals (ringed by bone cells)

Marrow

Human thigh bone

Knee cap (patella)

Fibula

Shin bone (tibia)

Ankle bones (tarsals)

Thigh bone (femur)

Hip bone (pelvis)

Breast bone (sternum)

Ribs

Lower jaw bone (mandible)

Skull (cranium)

Collar bone (clavicle)

Upper arm bone (humerus)

Vertebral column (spine)

Radius

Ulna

Wrist bones (carpals)

Hand bones (metacarpals)

Fingers (phalanges)

SEE ALSO
Human body, Muscle, Nutrition

SKIN AND HAIR

Skin protects our delicate insides from wear, knocks, dirt, germs and rain. It also helps to cool or warm the body, and gives us our sense of touch.

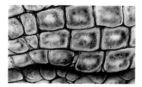

Reptiles such as lizards have dry, scaly skin.

Pigskin: only mammals' skin is covered with hair.

Slug skin: glands secrete slime on the skin.

Skin is our all-over, hard-wearing, living overcoat, covering an area of about 2m square. It weighs around 4kg and varies in thickness from 0.5mm on the eyelids to 5mm on the soles of the feet; the average thickness is 1–2mm. Skin is continually growing and renewing, and with pressure and wear, it becomes thicker and tougher.

THE OUTER LAYER

The skin's surface, the epidermis, is dead, but just underneath it is one of the body's busiest parts, the dermis. Microscopic cells at the base of the epidermis continually multiply, which pushes old cells upwards. Over about four weeks, these cells fill with the tough body protein, keratin (which also makes up hair and nails), flatten and die. The dead cells then reach the surface, and rub and flake off with daily wear and tear.

GETTING UNDER YOUR SKIN

There is an outer and inner layer of skin. The outer layer is the epidermis, underneath is the thicker dermis. This contains fibres of stiff collagen and stretchy elastin, making it strong yet flexible. In the dermis are sweat glands, hair roots, tiny blood vessels, and microscopic nerve endings for our sense of touch. Each hair is anchored in a follicle. It has a sebaceous gland that makes a natural wax or oil called sebum.

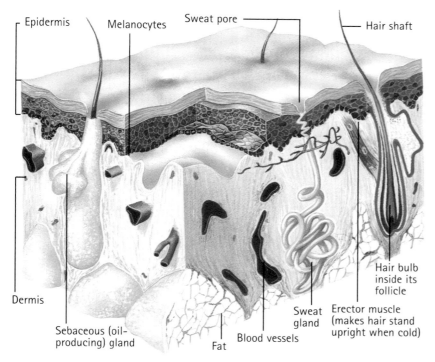

Epidermis — Melanocytes — Sweat pore — Hair shaft

Dermis

Sebaceous (oil-producing) gland — Fat — Blood vessels — Sweat gland — Erector muscle (makes hair stand upright when cold) — Hair bulb inside its follicle

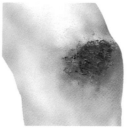

When skin is damaged, a scab forms to protect the body from germs while new skin develops under it.

1 Broken blood vessels become narrow to stop blood loss. White blood cells destroy bacteria.

2 Substances in the blood called platelets cause it to clot. This clot hardens into the scab.

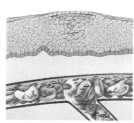

3 In the dermis, cells called fibroblasts produce new tissue. When healed, the scab falls off.

SKIN COLOUR

Our melanocyte cells produce tiny flecks of dark brown melanin (pigment). More active melanocytes make more melanin and thus produce darker skin. We inherit our normal level of melanocyte activity, and therefore our skin colour, from our parents. However, strong sunlight makes melanocytes more active to protect the body from the sun's ultraviolet rays – and this produces a sun tan.

COOLING SWEAT

Skin helps to control our temperature. If the body is too hot, tiny blood vessels in the dermis widen, allowing more blood to lose heat to the air. The microscopic sweat glands also ooze sweat through the pores (tiny holes) onto the skin. As this dries, it draws more warmth from the body.

HAIR AND GOOSEBUMPS

If the body is too cold, the blood vessels narrow, to reduce heat loss. The erector muscle, attached to a hair, pulls it upright. This traps air near the skin's surface which keeps warmth in, and causes goosebumps. Hairs are long rods of dead, keratin-filled cells. The only living part is the hair bulb inside the follicle.

SEE ALSO

Amphibian, Blood, Cell, Gland, Human body, Snail, Touch

SKYSCRAPER

Skyscrapers are very tall buildings found in cities where land is expensive. Usually built of concrete on a metal frame, they are used for offices and apartments.

▲ High-rise building is a risky operation. A builder climbs a spire during construction of the Bank of China in 1990.

When US mechanic Elisha Graves Otis created an elevator with a safety device in 1852, he made skyscrapers possible – tall buildings could now be used comfortably. In 1884, William Le Baron Jenney built the world's first skyscraper in Chicago (now demolished). Its ten storeys would not qualify as a skyscraper today, but its metal frame structure set a new trend.

HIGH-RISE LIVING
From 1895, the lead in skyscraper-building passed to New York. Famous examples include the Woolworth Building (1914), the Chrysler Building (1930) and the Empire State Building (1931), which was the world's tallest building until the 1960s.

SWAYING WEIGHT
A skyscraper has to support a heavy weight (the Empire State Building weighs around 400,000 tonnes) and resist strong winds. Its frame can be made of pre-stressed or reinforced concrete, although steel girders form the skeleton of most skyscrapers. The Sears Tower (1974) is made of nine huge steel tubes welded together.

UNDERGROUND SUPPORT
The foundations (section below ground) of tall buildings stop them toppling over. Piles (supporting poles of concrete and metal) are driven deep into the ground. London's Tower 42 (1980) has 18m-deep foundations, with piles driven down a further 24m.

GOING UP
Some skyscrapers (like the John Hancock Center) have their steel skeleton on the outside, others show a wall of glass. During construction, factory-made sections of glass, concrete and steel are brought onto the site and put into place by cranes. The cabling and service pipes go between the floors.

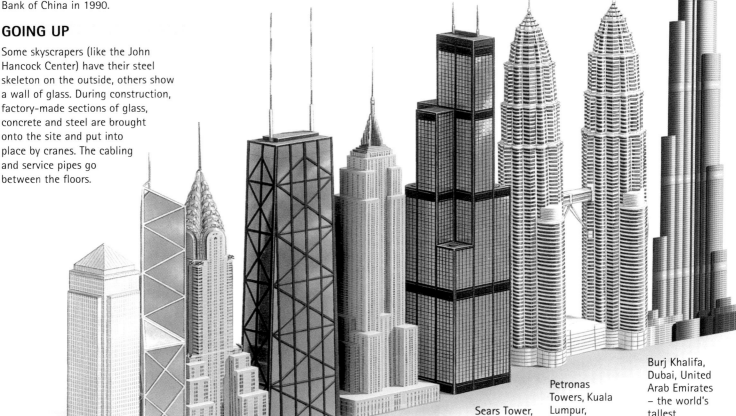

Canary Wharf, London, 244m, 50 floors

Bank of China, Hong Kong, 315m, 72 floors

Chrysler Building, New York, 319m, 77 floors

John Hancock Center, Chicago, 344m, 100 floors

Empire State Building, New York, 381m, 102 floors

Sears Tower, Chicago, 443m, 110 floors

Petronas Towers, Kuala Lumpur, 452m, 88 floors

Burj Khalifa, Dubai, United Arab Emirates – the world's tallest building at 828m tall, 162 floors

SEE ALSO
Architecture, Construction, North America

SLAVERY

Slavery is when one person becomes the property, or slave, of another. The slave must do as the owner wishes and has few, if any, rights under the law.

William Wilberforce (1759–1833) led Britain to abolish slavery in 1833.

Ex-slave Harriet Tubman (c.1820–1913) helped 300 slaves escape in the USA.

Nat Turner (1800–31) led a failed uprising of slaves in America in 1831.

Today, the idea of slavery is horrifying, but it was once an accepted part of society. Slaves were kept as servants or as workers on farms or in factories.

BONDAGE OF WAR
In early times, prisoners captured in battle belonged to the victors. In 146BCE, the Greek city of Corinth rebelled against the Romans. When the city was recaptured, all its 80,000 inhabitants were sold into slavery. In some areas of the Roman Empire, over half the people were slaves.

THE SLAVE TRADE
By the 18th century, the slave trade was a major industry. Thousands of slaves were transported from Africa to the Americas to work on plantations. Some were treated well, but many suffered harsh conditions. In the United States, the North campaigned to abolish slavery. In 1861, several southern states left the Union, partly because they wanted to keep slavery, and this began the American Civil War (1861–65). Slavery was abolished in 1865 after the victory of the northern states.

▲ An Arabian slave market in the 13th century. The Arabs traded slaves from Africa, Europe and Asia through the great markets of Zanzibar, Samarkand and Mombasa.

SLAVERY CONDEMNED
From about 1780, public opinion in many countries began to turn against slavery. Slavery was abolished in the British Empire from 1833, and by the 1890s most other countries had followed. In 1948, the United Nations declared that freedom from slavery was a universal human right.

SLAVERY TODAY
Slavery is illegal in all countries, but it still goes on. Some slaves are working to pay off a family debt. Others, including children, are being forced to work against their will, in sweatshops or labour camps, for example. According to some estimates, as many as 27 million men, women and children are being kept as slaves worldwide.

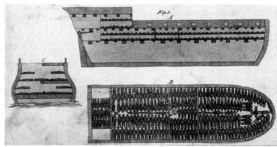

THE TRIANGULAR TRADE
The largest slave trade was between West Africa and the Americas, in the Triangular Trade. Ships left Bristol or Liverpool in England with weapons and tools to be traded in Africa for slaves. The slaves were so tightly packed onto ships (above) that many died during the voyage to the Americas, where they were sold for sugar or tobacco destined for England. From 1680 to 1800, about seven million slaves were traded.

SEE ALSO

Civil rights, Civil War (American)

SLEEP

Sleep is a state of decreased consciousness, during which the body rests from its normal activities. It is essential for a healthy body and mind.

SLEEP CYCLES

Laboratory studies show the electrical patterns the brain produces during sleep. Electrodes from an EEG, or electroencephalograph, are attached to the sleeper's head – these record changes in brain activity, shown as a wavy line on the graph. In an 8-hour sleep period, sleepers go through REM and NREM cycles every 90 minutes, starting with NREM in stage 1. Sleep gets deeper until stage 4, the deepest sleep. After 60–90 minutes, dreaming (REM) occurs during stage 2, when the brain becomes more active again. Longer REM periods occur as sleep continues.

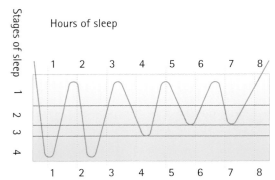

When we sleep, the electrical activity of the brain slows down in stages, along with the heart rate, temperature and breathing. However, when we dream, the brain's activity increases again, and the eyes move rapidly under the eyelids in REM (rapid eye movement) sleep. We go through several cycles of non-dreaming (NREM, or non-rapid eye movement) and dreaming sleep every night.

SLEEP AND GROWTH

Although we spend a third of our lives asleep, no one really knows why it is so important. Sleep rests the body, but we use almost as much energy asleep as when we are awake. Sleep is important for growth, which is why children need more than adults. It may also help with learning and memory. As people age, they need less sleep. A baby sleeps most of the time, and a four-year-old needs 10–14 hours of sleep a night. A young adult may sleep for eight hours, but people over 60 sleep only about 5–6 hours, and wake often during the night.

SLEEP DISTURBANCES

Sleep is essential. When a person has insomnia (the inability to sleep) for even one night, he or she feels irritable and clumsy. If insomnia continues, lack of concentration and hallucinations (seeing things that are not real) can occur. Some people have nightmares; others get out of bed and walk around while they are asleep (sleepwalking). Jet lag is the disruption of sleep caused by air travel across time zones.

DREAMS

Many people believe that dreams are the working through of thoughts and feelings that happen during the day. Some people remember dreams and some do not. Dreams are often fantastic and colourful, and provide people with inspiration for art, music, stories and films.

SLEEP FACTS

- Human beings are mostly diurnal – they are awake during the day and sleep at night
- Some animals, such as badgers, are nocturnal – they sleep by day and are active at night
- Reptiles, fish and insects have periods of inactivity that resemble a sleeping state
- Donkeys need three hours' sleep per day
- Bats need 20 hours' sleep per day

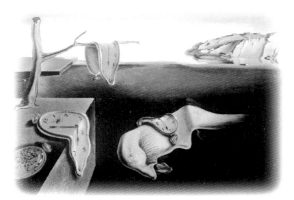

◀ The Spanish painter Salvador Dali (1904–89) was inspired by his dreams and called his art 'hand-painted dream photographs'. In *The Persistence of Memory* (1931), he illustrates his idea of time.

SEE ALSO

Animal, Hibernation, Human body, Season, Time

SNAIL AND OTHER MOLLUSCS

Molluscs are soft-bodied invertebrate animals that have no bones and no legs. They include snails, slugs, clams, cockles, limpets, oysters, octopuses and cuttlefish.

The great black slug (which can be orange) has a tough skin flap on top.

The common mussel, a bivalve, has a shell in two parts, hinged at the front.

The spiny murex, a type of sea snail, is a univalve – it has a single, coiled shell.

Cuttlefish, octopuses and squid are among the most active and mobile molluscs.

Most molluscs are protected by hard shells. Snails have a one-piece shell that is usually coiled; bivalves, such as cockles and mussels, have a two-piece shell hinged along one side. Cuttlefish and squid have a shell that grows inside their body and some slugs have a small, flat shell under the skin. A few kinds of mollusc, like octopuses and some kind of slugs, have no shell at all, just a tough skin cover protecting the organs.

SLIMY TRAILS
A snail moves from place to place by gliding along on a muscular part of its body called the foot. It lubricates its path with slime poured out from glands near the front. The head is at the front and carries one or two pairs of feelers or tentacles. Land snails have eyes at the tips of their tentacles, sea snails' eyes are at the base.

▲ A baby leopard slug emerges from a pearl-like cluster of eggs. It takes about 30 days for the eggs to hatch.

THOUSANDS OF TEETH
Land snails are usually active at night or in damp weather. They feed mainly on plants. A snail's tongue, called a radula, carries thousands of tiny teeth and it works like a strip of sandpaper to shred up the stems and leaves of the plants. The tongues of some sea snails are so strong that they can drill through the shells of other animals.

MOLLUSCS WITH HINGED SHELLS
Bivalves all live in water, most of them in the sea. Some are fixed to rocks and never move, but others can burrow in sand and mud. They feed by drawing a current of water into the open shell and filtering small particles of food from it, taking oxygen from the water at the same time.

LIFE SUPPORT BACKPACK
Molluscs have a skin-like mantle that makes the shell. Most of the snail's internal organs are in its coiled hump, which stays inside the shell. When it is alarmed, the snail can pull its head and foot right inside its shell as well.

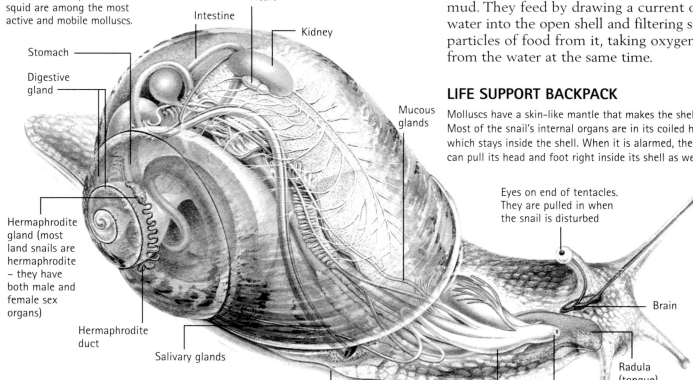

Heart
Intestine
Kidney
Stomach
Digestive gland
Mucous glands
Hermaphrodite gland (most land snails are hermaphrodite – they have both male and female sex organs)
Hermaphrodite duct
Salivary glands
Foot
Penis
Genital pore
Eyes on end of tentacles. They are pulled in when the snail is disturbed
Brain
Radula (tongue)

SEE ALSO
Animal, Evolution, Ocean and sea, Soil

SNAKE

Snakes are slender reptiles with no legs and, like all reptiles, they are covered with scales. There are about 2,800 species and all of them prey on other animals.

▲ Snakes regularly shed their skins (epidermis), including the scale covering their eyes (the brille), in order to grow.

Although they have no legs, snakes can slither surprisingly quickly over the ground. Most of them move by throwing their bodies into curves and pushing backwards against the ground. Some also push themselves along by digging their belly scales into the ground. Many snakes can even climb trees in this way. Snakes are generally inactive and are seldom seen except when they are hunting or disturbed.

Most snakes live alone, but rattlesnakes and corn snakes hibernate in groups.

HUG OF DEATH

A snake finds its food largely by smell. It picks up scent particles from the air by flicking out its forked tongue, and it homes in on the scent of its prey. Some snakes merely grab their prey in their jaws and swallow it live. Others poison or suffocate their prey first. Snakes that suffocate their prey are called constrictors. They include boas, pythons, and the anaconda – the largest snake, which can grow to 9m long. They coil their powerful bodies around their victims and squeeze.

The bright yellow eyelash viper is well camouflaged in the golden palm fruit.

DEADLY INJECTION

Poisonous snakes, which include vipers and cobras, inject venom into their prey through large teeth called fangs. The venom of around 270 snakes is harmful or fatal to humans. The saw-scaled viper of Africa, Indian cobra and Australian taipan are among the world's most dangerous snakes.

SWALLOW IT WHOLE

All snakes swallow prey whole since they have no broad back teeth for crushing and cannot chew. A snake can swallow animals larger than itself because it can open its mouth extremely wide. And, as its ribs are not joined together, they open out to let the food pass along the body.

A huge meal, like a baby zebra, could last a python more than six months.

Snakes don't have eyelids so they never close their eyes or blink

Fangs
Venom canal
Venom gland
Hinged jaw

Elastic ligaments stretch between the bones

ONE BIG GULP

Wagler's pit viper (Southeast Asia) feeds mainly on birds, lizards and rodents, which it swallows whole. The bones of the lower jaw are not fixed to the skull, and they can be separated from each other at the front. Using its backward-pointing teeth, the snake gradually works its mouth over the prey and swallows it. Enzymes break down the food so that it can be digested, except for hair or feathers. One meal may keep a snake going for weeks.

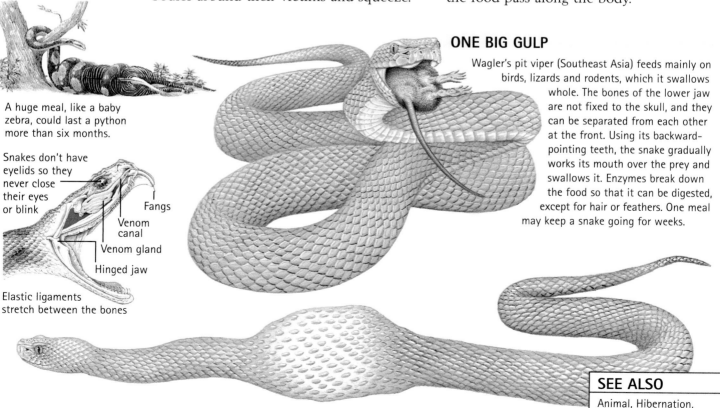

SEE ALSO
Animal, Hibernation, Reptile, Skin and hair

SOIL

Soil is the loose material that lies on the Earth's surface and in which plants grow. It consists mainly of small particles of broken-down rock and plant material.

Deciduous forests form deep, humus-rich soils.

Dry, lime-rich soils form on grasslands.

Mountains have only a thin covering of poor soil.

Desert soils are rich in salts, but lack humus.

Tropical rainforests form fertile, but thin, soils.

Swamps have wet and often acidic soils.

▶ Farmers add manure and other organic matter to soil to boost the fertility of their land.

Soil covers the rocks of the Earth and is sometimes quite deep. It is made up of small pieces of rock, along with plant material, fungi, bacteria and a host of tiny animals.

HOW SOILS FORM

Rocks are broken down by rain and wind to produce a layer of grit. Leaves and stems falling on the grit rot away to provide food for fungi, worms and microscopic organisms. Some plant fibres remain in the soil as humus, which binds the grit together and helps it hold water. The rest of the plants, and the remains of animals, are broken down by fungi and bacteria into simple chemicals that provide nutrients for new plants.

A MATTER OF LAYERS

Soil is made up of layers. The dark topsoil is rich in humus and nutrients. Below that is the subsoil, a layer of fine material containing a lot of clay. The thickness of the layers and their chemical composition vary according to the climate, the type of rock the soil is made from, and the kind of vegetation growing in it.

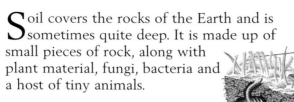

Water table   Topsoil   Subsoil

Broken rock   Bedrock

A HIDDEN WORLD

Living within the soil are creatures that break down plant and animal matter into nutrients that can be taken up by plant roots. Earthworms pull plant waste into the soil and are eaten by moles whose tunnels help circulate air. Microscopic beetles, centipedes and other creatures feed on rotting plant and animal matter, and on each other.

VALUABLE RESOURCE

The plants that take root in soil form the basis of the food chain for all land animals. People plant food crops in the soil as well as fodder crops to feed farm animals. Most farmers care for their soil, but in some areas, cutting down trees or intensive farming leads to soil erosion and crop failure.

SEE ALSO

Climate, Conservation, Crop, Farming, Habitat, Seed and pollination

SOLAR POWER

Solar power harnesses the energy in the Sun's rays. It is a non-polluting source of energy that will not run out until the Sun dies, billions of years in the future.

The Sun is our chief source of energy. Coal, oil and gas come from the fossilized remains of ancient plants which used sunlight to grow. The Sun's energy is stored in oceans and rivers, and in the winds. All living things need the Sun. Yet we use only a fraction of the energy reaching us from the Sun.

SOLAR POWER STATIONS

By using mirrors, the Sun's rays can be used to heat a water-filled boiler. Steam from the boiler turns a turbine which makes electricity. A station called Solar 1 in California, USA, uses 1,818 computer-controlled mirrors to concentrate the sunlight onto a boiler tower 91m high. However, solar power stations need to be in sunny places, and much of the electricity they make is lost during distribution.

▼ Solar cells mounted in wing-like panels are used to power satellites because they require almost no maintenance.

SOLAR HEATING

Sunlight can provide heat for the home, saving other energy resources. Modern buildings with large windows and heat-absorbing collectors on the roof can take in enough energy from sunlight to provide room and water heating, even on cloudy days. Even a simple, insulated glass panel with a black-coated bottom will collect enough solar energy to warm the water inside, as black absorbs the most sunlight.

▲ A solar furnace uses a huge curved mirror to focus the Sun's rays. It uses the Sun's energy to provide a clean, non-polluting source of heat.

▼ Energy from the Sun can be used directly to heat water for a home's hot water system through the use of solar panels.

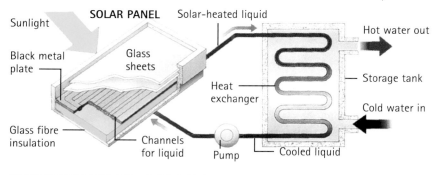

SOLAR PANEL — Sunlight — Solar-heated liquid — Hot water out — Black metal plate — Glass sheets — Heat exchanger — Storage tank — Glass fibre insulation — Channels for liquid — Pump — Cooled liquid — Cold water in

ELECTRICITY FROM SUNLIGHT

Solar cells, first developed in the 1950s, make electricity when light shines on them. They are made of wafers of silicon, as are computer chips. The cells change some of the energy in sunlight into electrical energy. They are ideal for places where there is plenty of sunlight but no electricity supply, such as orbiting space satellites like the Hubble Space Telescope (below) and space stations. In the future, there may be a huge orbiting solar power station which beams microwave energy down to an antenna on Earth.

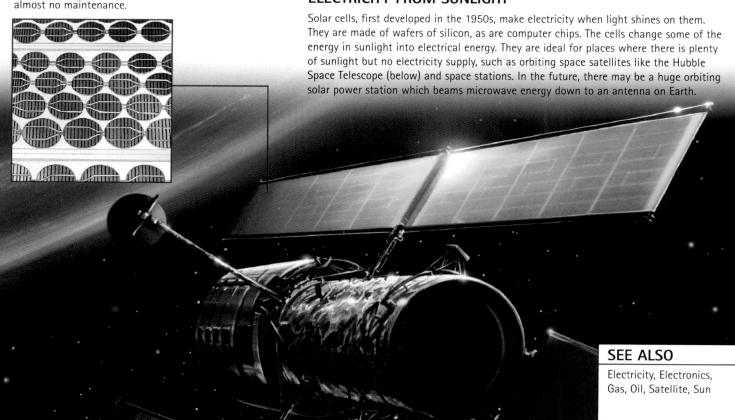

SOLAR SYSTEM

Our solar system is made up of the Sun and the objects that orbit it, including eight main planets and their moons, as well as dwarf planets, asteroids, comets and meteors.

THE PLANETS	
Distance from Sun (million km)	Average time to orbit Sun
Mercury	
58	88 days
Venus	
108	225 days
Earth	
150	1 year
Mars	
228	1.9 years
Jupiter	
778	11.9 years
Saturn	
1,427	29.5 years
Uranus	
2,870	84 years
Neptune	
4,498	164.8 years

The Sun is at the centre of the solar system. Its mass, which makes up 99.86 per cent of all the mass in the solar system, holds the planets and other objects in their orbits through gravity.

ROCKY WORLDS AND GAS GIANTS

Most of the matter from which the planets formed consisted of hydrogen and helium. The planets nearest the Sun – Mercury, Venus, Earth and Mars – were too warm to hold on to these plentiful light gases and instead became small worlds of rock and metal. Farther from the Sun, where temperatures were very low, the planets attracted huge amounts of hydrogen and helium. They became the gas giants – Jupiter, Saturn, Uranus and Neptune.

ASTEROIDS AND COMETS

Between the orbits of Mars and Jupiter is a band of space where asteroids – rocks as big as mountains – are common. This is the asteroid belt. Occasionally asteroids collide. When this happens, bits break off that may eventually arrive on Earth as meteorites. A vast cloud of frozen comets is thought to lie much farther from the Sun than Pluto. This cloud, which may be 100 times farther from the Sun than the Earth is, marks the outer edge of the solar system.

HOW THE SOLAR SYSTEM FORMED

The Sun was born about five billion years ago out of a great cloud of gas and dust in space. Scientists believe that the planets, as well as the asteroids and comets, gradually formed out of this spinning cloud.

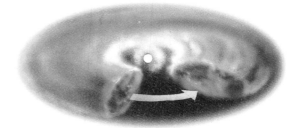

1 Material that was left over from the cloud of dust and gas formed a disc that circled the Sun.

2 As particles within the disc collided, they began to stick together, forming larger objects.

3 The objects grew into planets, moons, asteroids and comets, which often collided.

4 Eventually, the remaining objects circled the Sun in orbits that rarely crossed.

◄ The planets of our solar system drawn to scale: 1 Mercury; 2 Venus; 3 Earth; 4 Mars; 5 Jupiter; 6 Saturn; 7 Uranus and 8 Neptune.

SEE ALSO

Astronomy, Big Bang theory, Comet, meteor and asteroid, Constellation, Earth, Galaxy, Gravity, Planet, Star, Sun, Universe

SOLID, LIQUID AND GAS

Solids, liquids and gases are the three states in which substances, or matter, can exist. Each state depends on how strongly the molecules are bound together.

BOILING POINTS (at sea level)	
Substance	°Celsius
Iron	2,800°
Mercury	357
Water	100
Ethanol	78
Oxygen	–183
Nitrogen	–195

MELTING POINTS (at sea level)	
Substance	°Celsius
Iron	1,539
Mercury	–39
Water	0
Ethanol	–117
Oxygen	–218
Nitrogen	–210

As you read this book, you may well be sitting at a table. The table is probably made of wood, plastic, or steel. At room temperature, these materials are all solids. They are made of molecules that are strongly bound together. That is why the table keeps its shape. Scientists call a solid a 'state' of matter.

LIQUIDS
If you have a drink nearby, you can see another state of matter: liquid. Water, milk and ethanol (ordinary alcohol) are all liquid at room temperature. Like all other liquids, they are made of molecules that are only loosely bound together. When you pour a liquid into a glass, its molecules are able to flow around the bottom of it. That is why the liquid fills the container evenly, forming a level surface.

GASES
All around you is air. Air is in another state, called a 'gas'. Gases are made of molecules that are hardly bound to each other at all. When you release a gas into any space, its molecules are free to move around the space randomly, spreading around and filling the whole space evenly. That is why a beach ball forms a spherical shape even though you only puff air into one end of it.

CHANGING STATE
If we change a substance's temperature enough, its state will usually change. When iron is heated to over 1,539°C, for instance, it melts into a liquid. Similarly, if we cool water to below 0°C, it freezes to form ice, a solid. Oxygen, one of the gases that makes up air, will condense to form a liquid if we cool it to a chilly –183°C.

HOW TEMPERATURE CHANGES MATTER
At room temperature, water is in a liquid state. However, water can be turned into a gas by heating it until it boils and turns into water vapour. Alternatively, if the water's temperature is lowered to below freezing point, it will turn into ice, which is its solid state. These changes take place because temperature affects the way in which the individual atoms and molecules of a substance are bound together.

Gas molecules move randomly and independently of one another

The molecules in liquids are free to move around

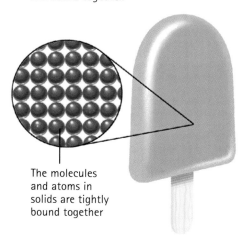

The molecules and atoms in solids are tightly bound together

SOLID
Solids, such as ice, have a fixed shape and size.

GAS
Gases, such as water vapour from boiling water, have no fixed shape or size.

LIQUID
Liquids, such as water, have a fixed size, or volume, but no fixed shape.

SEE ALSO
Atom and molecule, Heat, Iron and steel

SOUND

Sound is a form of energy that can be heard. It is caused by vibrations and travels in waves through solids, liquids and gases.

▼ When you tap a tuning fork against a hard surface, it starts to vibrate rapidly, giving out a constant pitch. When the prongs vibrate outwards, they compress the air near them, creating high pressure. When they vibrate inwards, the air expands, leaving an area of low pressure.

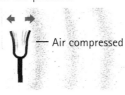
Air compressed

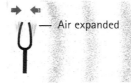
Air expanded

We normally think of sound travelling only through air, but it can also move through other substances. If you put your head under the bath water, for example, you can still hear sounds in the room around you. That is because sound can travel through water – or any other liquid. Noisy neighbours are a problem because the sounds they make can travel through walls and floors – solid materials.

MAKING SOUND

You can make a sound in air if you hit together two objects, such as a pair of saucepan lids. The objects create sound because you give them some energy, making them vibrate (shake). As the objects vibrate, they squash, then release the air each side of them, over and over again. This makes the air pressure around them rise and fall repeatedly.

THE HUMAN VOICE

The human voice produces sound when air from the lungs is forced past the vocal cords. How high or low the voice is depends on how quickly or slowly these cords vibrate. The diaphragm controls the flow of air in and out of the lungs. The muscles around the mouth turn the noise produced by the vocal cords into recognizable sounds. The cavities in the nose, throat and chest help the sounds to resonate.

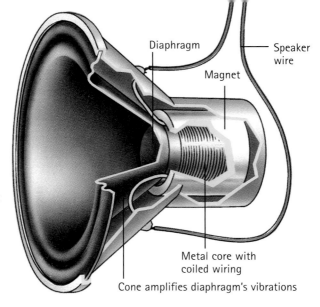
Diaphragm
Speaker wire
Magnet
Metal core with coiled wiring
Cone amplifies diaphragm's vibrations

▲ Loudspeakers turn electrical signals back into sounds. The signals cause a diaphragm inside the speaker to vibrate, and this motion reproduces the original sound.

AIR VIBRATIONS

Sound is caused by only tiny changes of air pressure. When someone nearby talks to you, they make the air pressure rise and fall by about 1/10,000 of normal air pressure. That is roughly the pressure change you feel when you put a single sheet of paper in your palm. As air vibrates, it shakes a thin membrane in our ear called our 'ear drum'. That is why we can hear the vibrations as sound. Our ears can not pick up all kinds of vibration. The vibrations have to be loud enough for us to hear. They also have to happen at a rate that our ears can detect – in other words, they have to be the right frequency.

SPREAD OF SOUND

When an object vibrates, sound waves spread out from it. The farther you are from the object, the more the energy from it has spread, so the quieter it is. Sound waves bounce off hard objects such as brick walls or windows. When you listen to someone speaking in a room, for example, you hear both the sound that has come directly from their voice and the sound that has bounced off the walls, ceiling and floor. This effect is called 'reverberation'.

LOUDNESS

The harder you hit something, the louder the sound you make with it. That is because it vibrates more, creating a greater pressure change in the air around it. Our

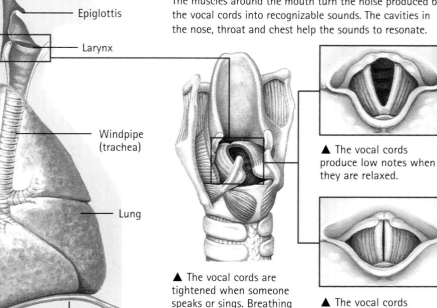

Nasal cavity
Mouth
Epiglottis
Larynx
Windpipe (trachea)
Lung
Diaphragm

▲ The vocal cords produce low notes when they are relaxed.

▲ The vocal cords produce high notes when they are taut.

▲ The vocal cords are tightened when someone speaks or sings. Breathing out makes the cords vibrate and produce sound.

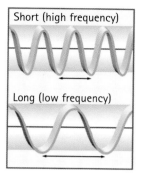

Short (high frequency)

Long (low frequency)

▲ The pitch of a sound – whether it is high or low – depends on its frequency or wavelength. Long waves have a lower frequency and pitch than short waves.

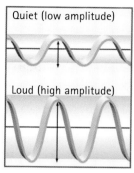

Quiet (low amplitude)

Loud (high amplitude)

▲ A sound's loudness depends on the height of its waves, called its amplitude. Quiet sounds have a smaller amplitude than loud sounds.

▲ A visual display of three different sounds: a symphony orchestra in full swing (top); the spoken word 'hello' (above left); and two hand claps (above right). Rich, complex sounds involve thousands of waveforms, of differing amplitudes and frequencies, all intermingling at the same time to make up the waveform shapes above.

ears can pick up a wide range of pressure changes. At best, they can detect sounds made by pressure changes that are a mere 5 billionths of normal air pressure. A pin drop is this quiet. At the other extreme, our ears can detect pressure changes about one fifth of normal air pressure. A road drill is this loud.

FREQUENCY AND PITCH

Whistles and women's voices make sounds that are much higher in pitch than bass guitars and men's voices. That is because

they make sounds that have a higher frequency, or shorter wavelength. Frequency is measured in hertz (Hz). Our ears can only pick up sounds that are between 20 Hz and 20,000 Hz. A car horn makes a sound with a frequency of about 200 Hz, women can sing notes as high as 1,200 Hz and men can sing notes as low as 60 Hz.

SPEED OF SOUND

On a warm day, sound travels through air at about 330m per second. On colder days, it travels more slowly. Sound travels at different speeds through other materials. It travels four times faster through water than air. Sound travels through solid concrete (such as the concrete partition between two offices) over ten times faster than it travels through air.

BREAKING THE SOUND BARRIER

When a vehicle, such as the British jet car Thrust SSC (below), travels at the speed of sound, pressure waves build up in front of the vehicle and form a shock wave. As the car accelerates through the sound barrier and travels faster than sound, the shock wave breaks away and can be heard, after the car has passed, as a sonic boom. You cannot hear a vehicle approaching at supersonic speeds.

LOUDNESS SCALE

Loudness is measured in decibels (dB). As the sound energy increases ten times, the decibels go up by the number ten. The following table shows the loudness of some sounds.

• Rocket lift-off	150–190 dB
• Jet take-off	120–140 dB
• Thunder	95–115 dB
• Motorbike	70–90 dB
• Vacuum cleaner	60–80 dB
• Orchestra	50–70 dB
• Talking	30–60 dB
• Whispering	20–30 dB
• Falling leaves	20 dB

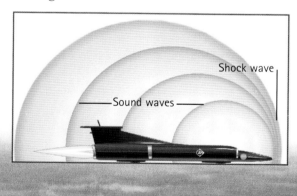

Shock wave

Sound waves

SEE ALSO

Hearing, Musical instrument, Radar and sonar, Radio, Wavelength

SOUTH AFRICA

Occupying the southernmost tip of the African continent, the country of South Africa consists mostly of a vast plateau, 1,200m above sea level.

Area: 1,224,691 sq km
Population: 48,502,000
Capitals: Pretoria – executive; Cape Town – legislative
Languages: Afrikaans and English
Currency: Rand

South Africa's high, flat-topped hills are surrounded by fertile, low-lying coastlands varying from 55km to 240km across. The spectacular Drakensberg Mountains rise to 3,482m and, in the north, the Limpopo River marks much of the country's northern boundary. The separate, mountainous kingdom of Lesotho is entirely surrounded by South African territory. The climate is mostly dry and sunny, averaging 17°C.

DESERT, GRASSLAND AND SCRUB

In the north, the Kalahari Desert stretches into neighbouring Botswana. Most of the vast central plateau is occupied by an area of coarse grassland called the Highveld. The Middleveld, in the northwest, is more suited to livestock than crops because of its poor soil, owing to erosion and little rain. The northeast of the plateau is the Transvaal basin, where farmers grow citrus fruits, maize and tobacco. Elephants, lions, leopards and great herds of antelope and zebras live on Transvaal's thorny scrub and are protected in the Kruger National Park.

▲ Apartheid forced many blacks to live in sprawling slums, or townships, such as Soweto – South Africa's largest black residential area.

PRECIOUS RESOURCES

South Africa has a vast wealth of natural resources, in particular minerals. It exports more diamonds than any other country, and also produces gold, platinum, chrome and manganese. It has large reserves of gas, coal, copper, iron, asbestos, silver, nickel and uranium. It is Africa's most industrial country and could be one of the world's richest nations. It can provide enough of its own grain and meat to feed its population, and nearly a third of its wealth comes from industries such as chemicals, textiles and machinery.

▲ The Drakensberg mountains form a long line of sharp cliffs where South Africa's high central plateau drops down towards coastal lowlands.

▶ For many visitors, the first sight of South Africa is Cape Town, set against the dramatic backdrop of Table Mountain, at the southern tip of the country.

POLICY OF APARTHEID

The wealth of South Africa's natural resources has benefited only a minority of the population. This is because a policy of apartheid (separateness) was introduced in 1950 by the white government, which separated blacks from whites and refused blacks equal rights. With black people making up almost three quarters of the population, millions of people were left in abject poverty. Many other countries protested against the cruelty of apartheid, and imposed sanctions which limited South Africa's overseas trade.

THE AFTERMATH OF APARTHEID

The process of apartheid began to collapse in 1990, under the presidency of F.W. de Klerk. In 1994, the first multi-racial elections were held in South Africa, bringing to power a majority black government. Although this struck a blow for equality, the young democracy still faces enormous problems: supplying education, social services, electricity and clean water, for example, as well as tackling unemployment, crime and diseases such as HIV-AIDS, which is lowering life expectancies. South Africa has made great advances since 1994, but there is still much work to be done.

▲ The elections of 1994 brought to power the African National Congress (ANC), headed by Nelson Mandela. Between 1964 and 1990, Mandela had been imprisoned for his opposition to the apartheid regime.

FIGHTING FOR TERRITORY

The first South Africans were the San and the Khoi peoples. From about 300CE, Bantu-speaking peoples such as the Zulus, Xhosa and Sesotho moved into the region. From 1652, Dutch settlers came by sea, soon followed by other Europeans. In 1806, the British took over the coastal areas, where the Dutch farmers (called Boers or Afrikaners) had settled. In order to keep their independence and claim new land for themselves, the Afrikaners made a 'Great Trek' inland in 1834–38, during which time they founded Transvaal and the Orange Free State. The discovery of gold and diamonds on Afrikaner territory led to two wars between the Boers and the British. Final Afrikaner defeat in 1902 led to a united South Africa in 1910.

PLANS FOR THE FUTURE

South Africa's population is 79 per cent black, 9.6 per cent white, 8.9 per cent of mixed descent and 2.5 per cent Asian. The government intends to build a 'rainbow society' where all peoples can live in harmony. South Africa's public holidays celebrate Human Rights, the Family, Freedom, Workers, Youth, Women, Heritage, Reconciliation and Goodwill.

▲ One of the main peoples of South Africa is the Zulus. Over 11 million of them live here, mostly in the province of Natal.

SEE ALSO

Africa, Civil rights

SOUTH AMERICA

Covering 12 per cent of the planet's land area, South America is the fourth largest continent. Its people make up 17.6 per cent of the world's population.

▲ Ecuador's Cotopaxi (5,897m) is the continent's highest active volcano. Here it is seen from the volcano Illiniza.

KEY FACTS

- **Area:** 17,819,000 sq km
- **Population:** 396,700,000
- **Number of countries:** 12
- **Largest country:** Brazil
- **Smallest country:** Suriname (163,270 sq km)
- **Highest point:** Aconcagua (6,960m)
- **Largest lake:** Lake Maracaibo (13,512 sq km)
- **Longest river:** Amazon (6,448km)

South America's varied landscape includes the rocky islands of Tierra del Fuego (belonging to Argentina and Chile) and the immense grasslands of Argentina and Venezuela. There are also snow-capped mountains and active volcanoes. The Andes, running along the Pacific coast for 8,000km, form the longest mountain range in the world. Aconcagua in Argentina is the continent's highest peak.

WET AND DRY

The Amazon River basin holds a fifth of the world's fresh water. It occupies two fifths of the continent and is the world's largest tropical rainforest. The Amazon River is second only to the Nile in length. Quibdo in Colombia is South America's rainiest place, receiving over 10,700mm of rain a year. The Atacama desert in Chile is one of the world's driest places – the port of Arica in northern Chile averages less than 1mm of rain a year – but the hottest temperatures are recorded in the Gran Chaco region of northern Argentina.

CLIMATIC DIFFERENCES

The great range of climates is due to the fact that there is a wide variation in the distance of the different countries from the Equator, and in the height of different areas above sea level. Lake Titicaca, between Bolivia and Peru, is the highest lake in the world, 3,811m above sea level.

COASTAL CITIES

High mountains, dense forests and vast distances make overland transport difficult and costly. Most major cities lie along the coast or on large rivers, where they can be served by shipping. Away from cities, most

▲ Venezuela's Angel Falls has a longer drop (979m) than any other waterfall in the world.

▶ In Bolivia, llamas graze high up in the Andes and are kept for their wool and meat. They are also able to carry heavy loads.

GALAPAGOS IS.
(Ecuador)

▲ The giant tortoise is one of the many unusual forms of wildlife on the Galapagos Islands, which lie 960km off the coast of Ecuador.

roads are unpaved and in rural areas, donkeys and carts drawn by oxen, or horses are used to carry goods. Aviation has developed rapidly since about 1950, especially in Brazil, which has more than 725 airports and 3,300 landing strips.

UNIQUE WILDLIFE

South America's isolation from the rest of the world has led to the evolution of many unique forms of wildlife. These include the rhea (a large flightless bird), the capybara (the world's largest rodent) and the llama. Other South American creatures include the tapir, armadillo, jaguar, condor, iguana, giant anteater, tree sloth, vicuña, piranha fish, manatee and many varieties of parrot and monkey.

PLANTS AND PRODUCTS

The Amazon region contains more kinds of plants than anywhere else in the world, including at least 11,200 types of tree and hundreds of species of orchid. South American plants yield products such as rubber, quinine, sisal and chocolate and woods such as mahogany and balsa.

▼ The Pan-American highway, which runs through the Atacama Desert, links most South American countries to each other and to North America.

VARIED DESCENT

The native peoples of South America came from Asia by way of North America. From 1500 onwards, Europeans came to settle, mostly from Spain and Portugal. Many intermarried with local peoples, producing children of mixed race known as *mestizos*. In Andean countries such as Bolivia and Peru, native peoples still make up a large proportion of the population. Argentina's population is largely white, with many people of Italian, German or British descent, while Brazil's population includes many descendants of African slaves brought to work on sugar plantations. Since 1940, South America's population has more than tripled.

▲ Sugar cane is Guyana's most important crop. It is grown near the coast.

379

TODAY'S PEOPLES

One person in three in South America is under 15. About three quarters of the population lives in cities, the three largest cities being Brazil's São Paolo and Rio de Janeiro, and Argentina's Buenos Aires. Ninety per cent of adults can read and write. Most of the people are Roman Catholics. In most South American countries, there is a small governing class of officials, businessmen, landowners and military leaders, a growing professional middle class and a poor majority. Many of the poor are unemployed and live in overcrowded conditions. Living standards are lower in rural areas, many of which still lack electricity, telephones, schools and medical care. Official development programmes are trying to improve rural conditions to reverse the movement of people to the cities.

SPORT AND LEISURE

Soccer has passionate fans throughout the continent – Brazil's Pelé has been called the world's greatest footballer of all time. Bullfighting is still popular in Colombia, Venezuela and Peru. South America has

▲ Indians make up much of the population in Bolivia. Many wear traditional clothes, especially for festivals. Panpipes are a popular local instrument.

▲ Brazil produces a third of the world's coffee. The beans must be washed in order to remove the outer skin.

produced many popular forms of music and dance such as the tango and samba. Colourful fiestas (festivals) are held on national and religious holidays. South American writers who have won the Nobel Prize for Literature include Chilean poets Gabriela Mistral and Pablo Neruda, and Colombian novelist Gabriel Garcia Marquez.

MINERAL RESOURCES

Since European settlement began, South America has developed as a supplier of raw materials. At first this meant gold and silver, then timber, sugar, coffee and

▼ Bolivia is rich in tin. Local people sift through the mountains of slag for tin ore.

rubber and, after the coming of railways and steamships, beef, wheat and wool. Venezuela is rich in oil, Brazil in iron, manganese and bauxite. Colombia has nickel and emeralds and Chile has copper as well as guano (bird droppings) and nitrates – used as fertilizer and to make explosives. Mineral exports pay for imports of manufactured goods, but modern mining creates few jobs.

INDUSTRIALIZATION
Brazil is the most industrialized South American country, producing vehicles, light planes, televisions and machinery for the rest of the continent. Shortages of money and skills hold back industry in other countries, but most now produce basic items such as clothes, shoes, furniture and drinks for local use, reducing the need for imports.

NEW VERSUS OLD
Brazil and Argentina both have vast plantations and ranches. Large-scale forest clearance has created environmental problems, as well as disturbing the traditional way of life of tribal peoples, who live by hunting and gathering. Offshore fishing is a major industry for both Chile and Peru.

EUROPEAN SETTLEMENT
During the 1400s, the Inca built up a great empire in the Andes. In the early 1500s, European settlers from Spain and Portugal – greedy for gold and silver – enslaved or killed many Indians, and brought with them diseases

unknown to the continent, which wiped out millions of others. Missionaries introduced Christianity to replace traditional beliefs. The Napoleonic Wars in the early 1800s, however, weakened the hold of Spain and Portugal on their South American colonies.

TO INDEPENDENCE
Revolutions in the early 1800s brought independence. The leading revolutionary figures were Simón Bolívar and José de San Martín. The former Spanish colonies became republics, but Brazil was ruled by emperors until 1889. South American trade remained tied to Europe and, from the late 1800s onwards, increasingly to the United States. Centuries of European influence are clearly shown in the Spanish-style architecture of many older cities.

▲ Paraguay's capital city Asunción was built by the Spanish, who arrived in the 1500s and ruled the country for 300 years.

▲ *Ariane IV* is one of a number of rockets launched from the Kourou Space Centre in French Guiana.

STONE STATUES
Some 300 stone statues have been found in the hills near San Agustín in Colombia. They are at least 1,000 years old and appear to mark burial sites. Colombia was originally home to many groups of indigenous people, some living in rainforest settlements, others wandering the open plains.

MILITARY RULE
Many South American countries have been ruled by dictators, usually backed by the military, and revolutions were once common. Since the 1980s, civilian rule has been restored across South America. However, only seven of its 12 nations are full democracies.

SEE ALSO
Argentina, Aztecs, Brazil, Continent, Incas, Maya

SOUTHEAST ASIA

The region of Southeast Asia consists of seven mainland countries and four island nations that lie east of India and south of China.

BRUNEI
Area: 5,765 sq km
Population: 409,000
Capital: Bandar Seri Begawan
Language: Malay
Currency: Brunei dollar

Southeast Asia covers an area of over four million sq km. Its population of over 580 million is growing swiftly. The landscape of the region is mainly composed of mountainous uplands and tropical forests, with swampy coastland. Countries north of the Equator, such as Thailand, get heavy rain from May to October, while Indonesia, south of the Equator, has rain from November to April. Temperatures are usually above 25°C all year round.

VOLCANIC LAND
A chain of volcanoes runs through the Indonesian islands of Sumatra, Java and the Lesser Sunda Islands. Seventy-six have erupted in the last 200 years. The eruption on the island of Krakatoa which took place in 1883 was the loudest explosion in modern history.

OLD CULTURES
Early centres of civilization emerged in the valleys of rivers such as the Irrawaddy, Chao Praya and Mekong, where annual flooding fertilized the soil. Rich harvests of rice supported ruling classes of warriors and

BURMA (MYANMAR)
Area: 676,577 sq km
Population: 52,171,000
Capital: Naypyidaw
Language: Burmese
Currency: Burmese kyat

CAMBODIA
Area: 181,035 sq km
Population: 13,396,000
Capital: Phnom Penh
Language: Khmer
Currency: Riel

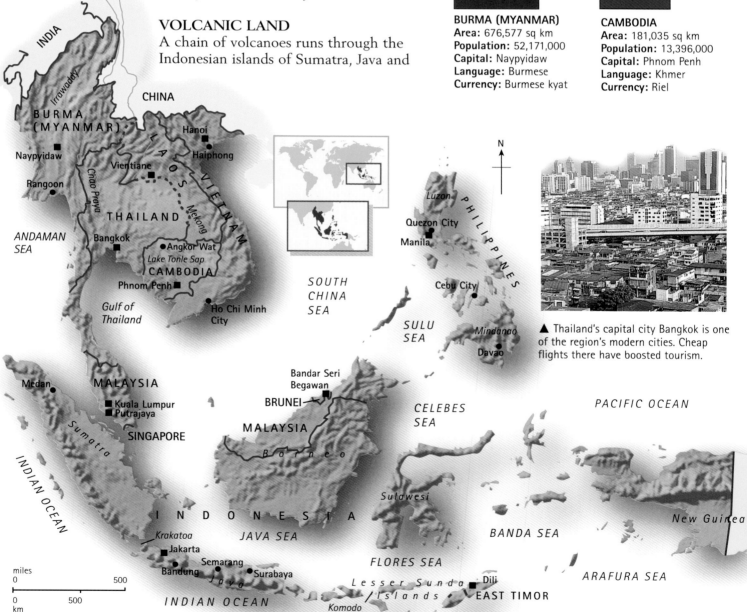

▲ Thailand's capital city Bangkok is one of the region's modern cities. Cheap flights there have boosted tourism.

▲ Most Cambodians live in farming villages and work in paddy fields. On Cambodia's Lake Tonle Sap, there are floating villages.

priests. The harvests also fed the craftsmen and labourers who made luxurious goods and built palaces, forts and temples for the same ruling classes. Thailand and Burma (Myanmar) are famed for their historic pagodas. In Cambodia are the ruins of the temple-city of Angkor Wat, the capital of the great Khmer Empire (900CE to 1500).

MATERIALS FOR TRADE
Southeast Asia is rich in raw materials such as oil, tin and timber. Burma and Thailand are the two leading ruby producers. Burma also has sapphires (only Madagascar produces more). Five hundred years ago, European merchants came trading for spices such as cloves, nutmeg and cinnamon. Apart from Thailand, the whole region gradually came under European rule and plantation crops such as rubber and coffee were introduced.

Many Chinese and Indians moved there as traders and labourers.

MODERN TIMES
Since regaining their independence after 1945, Southeast Asian countries have dramatically raised their standards of living, health and education, despite the damage caused by the Vietnam War (1955 –73). Malaysia, Singapore and Thailand have developed modern industries, making cars and electronic goods. Farming is the main occupation in East Timor, Laos and Burma, the chief crops being rice, maize, palm oil, sugar, tea and coffee.

FUTURE CONCERNS
The rapid use of the region's resources is raising concern about pollution problems, the destruction of forests and threats to wildlife. Almost all the nations of the region belong to the Association of South East Asian Nations (ASEAN), which was founded in 1967 to help co-operation in trade, education and development.

▲ The Komodo dragon, the largest living lizard, is named after one of the Indonesian islands on which it is found.

PHILIPPINES
Area: 300,076 sq km
Population: 88,575,000
Capital: Manila
Language: Filipino and English
Currency: Peso

SINGAPORE
Area: 704 sq km
Population: 5,077,000
Capital: Singapore City
Languages: English, Malay, Mandarin Chinese, Tamil
Currency: Singapore dollar

THAILAND
Area: 513,115 sq km
Population: 65,479,000
Capital: Bangkok
Language: Thai
Currency: Baht

VIETNAM
Area: 329,315 sq km
Population: 85,847,000
Capital: Hanoi
Language: Vietnamese
Currency: Dong

EAST TIMOR
Area: 14,874 sq km
Population: 1,067,000
Capital: Dili
Language: Tetum, Portuguese
Currency: US dollar

INDONESIA
Area: 1,904,413 sq km
Population: 237,641,000
Capital: Jakarta
Languages: Bahasa Indonesia, Javanese
Currency: Rupiah

LAOS
Area: 236,800 sq km
Population: 6,128,000
Capital: Vientiane
Language: Lao
Currency: Kip

MALAYSIA
Area: 329,758 sq km
Population: 28,334,000
Capitals: Kuala Lumpur and Putrajaya
Language: Bahasa Melayu
Currency: Ringgit (Malaysian dollar)

SEE ALSO
Asia, Indonesia, Malaysia, Philippines, Singapore

SPACECRAFT

There are three main types of spacecraft: artificial satellites, unmanned probes and manned spacecraft. All require powerful rockets to lift them into space.

Unmanned spacecraft that orbit the Earth are satellites. They are used for surveying our planet, communication, forecasting the weather or, as in the case of the Hubble Space Telescope, investigating the universe. They carry a variety of equipment, including radio receivers and transmitters, measuring instruments, cameras and computers. The energy needed to run the onboard equipment comes from solar panels that convert sunlight into electricity.

GETTING THERE

The Space Shuttle took off like a rocket, landed like a plane and could reach speeds of 28,000km/h. The launch in 1981 of the first Space Shuttle, *Columbia*, by NASA meant that a reusable vehicle could launch craft into space instead of a new rocket having to be built for each mission.

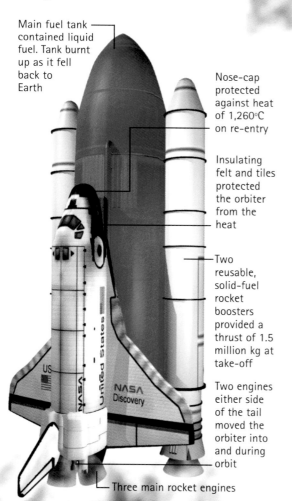

Main fuel tank contained liquid fuel. Tank burnt up as it fell back to Earth

Nose-cap protected against heat of 1,260°C on re-entry

Insulating felt and tiles protected the orbiter from the heat

Two reusable, solid-fuel rocket boosters provided a thrust of 1.5 million kg at take-off

Two engines either side of the tail moved the orbiter into and during orbit

Three main rocket engines

▼ Two minutes after launch, the booster rockets fell away; six minutes later, the main liquid-fuelled tank dropped away. The boosters splashed down in the Atlantic Ocean and were retrieved by ships.

▲ Shuttles were used to launch satellites and other cargo into orbit. The Shuttle's speed at the time of launch was crucial: if it was too fast, the satellite would fly off into space; too slow and it would drop to Earth.

Sputnik (USSR), the first satellite, launched in 1957, orbited for six months.

Mir space station (USSR, 1986) was almost continuously occupied.

Luna 9 was the first craft to land on the Moon and send back pictures, in 1966.

The European Space Agency's *Ariane* rocket was first launched in 1981.

ROBOTS IN SPACE

Robotic spacecraft called probes have been sent to fly past, orbit or land on other planets. They carry cameras and instruments to gather scientific data which is sent back to Earth as a stream of radio signals. Space probes have small rocket engines which are fired to alter course or slow down before they enter orbit. Some probes send a lander down to a planet's surface, where it soft-lands using rocket-braking and parachutes.

MANNED SPACECRAFT

Early spacecraft able to carry people include the USSR's 1961 *Vostok I*, which carried the first man into space, and the US 1969 *Apollo* craft, which carried the first astronauts to the Moon. Later came orbital space stations and the Space Shuttle. Manned spacecraft must carry enough air, food, and water to keep their crew of astronauts alive and working for what may be months in space. Fresh supplies can be brought from Earth by unmanned vehicles that dock with the manned spacecraft.

ROCKETS

To gather enough speed to go into orbit around the Earth, or to escape from Earth's gravity, spacecraft need rocket launch vehicles. These usually come in three parts, or stages. As one stage runs out of fuel, it falls away, and the next stage fires.

SEE ALSO

Astronaut, Planet, Rocket, Satellite, Solar system, Space exploration

SPACE EXPLORATION

Space exploration began in 1957 with the launch of the first artificial satellite. By 1961, people were orbiting the Earth. Most major planets have now been investigated.

Unmanned *Luna 2* (USSR) was the first spacecraft to reach the Moon, in 1959.

Five unmanned *Surveyor* craft (USA) landed on the Moon in the 1960s.

Radio-controlled *Lunokhod* (USSR) travelled on Moon's surface in 1970 and 1973.

The Moon, being nearest to Earth, was the first target for space probes. In 1959, Russia's *Luna 1* flew past the Moon at a distance of 5,955km. Later that year, *Luna 2* crash-landed on the Moon and *Luna 3* went around it, to send back the first pictures of the 'far side' – not visible from Earth. In the 1960s, several US and Russian probes landed on the Moon and sent back pictures of its surface. These, and a series of manned orbital flights to practise docking the spacecraft, prepared the way for manned landings, beginning with *Apollo 11* in 1969. Altogether, the six successful Apollo missions brought back 381kg of lunar rock and dust.

▲ A dog named Laika was the first astronaut, sent into orbit in *Sputnik 2* in 1957. It stayed up for two weeks.

HOT VENUS

Although Venus is the planet closest to the Earth (about 41.4 million km away), its surface is always hidden by thick clouds, so it's hard to get a clear picture of it by telescope or spacecraft. In 1967, the Russian probe *Venera 4* parachuted down through the gaseous clouds and sent back information about their make-up.

SEARCHING PROBES

During the 1970s, several Russian probes landed on Venus and took measurements of their surroundings. But in scorching temperatures of over 450°C, none of the spacecraft survived for more than about an hour. In 2005, the European spacecraft *Venus Express* was launched into orbit around Venus, to study the planet's atmosphere. In 2006 it began sending back detailed images. ▶

APOLLO COMMAND MODULE

APOLLO LUNAR MODULE

A GIANT LEAP FOR MANKIND

In 1969, US astronaut Neil Armstrong made history when he stepped from *Apollo 11*'s lunar module onto the Moon. Later missions, like this fourth US landing in 1971, used lunar rovers to explore and collect soil samples. The lunar module took them back to the orbiting command module.

The Sun
Ulysses, 1994–5 examined the polar regions

Comets
Giotto met Halley's Comet, 1986, and Grigg-Skjellerup, 1992

Earth

Saturn
Pioneer 11, 1979
Voyager 1, 1980
Voyager 2, 1981
Cassini, launched 1997

Neptune
Voyager 2, 1989 (stunning photographs)

Uranus
New Horizons flies by, 2011

Mercury
Mariner 10 is the only spacecraft to have visited Mercury. It flew by three times in 1974 and 1975, taking photographs

Venus
Soviet *Venera* craft 1–13, first landed in 1970
Mariner 10, 1974
Magellan orbited three times – 1990/91/94
Venus Express, 2006
Solar-sailed *IKAROS* launched, 2011

Mars
Mariner 4, 1965 first photos
Mariner 9, 1971-72 (discovered Mariner Valley)
Viking 1, 1976, landed on Mars
Pathfinder/Sojourner, 1997
Mars Polar Lander, 1999
Mars Reconnaissance Orbiter, 2006
Phoenix lands, 2008

Jupiter
Pioneer 10 and *Pioneer 11*, 1973/74
Voyager 1, March 1979
Voyager 2 July 1979, took photos and discovered sulphur volcanoes on Io
Galileo, 1995, parachute probe
Galileo Europa Mission studying Jupiter's moons Io and Europa, 1999
Juno, launched 2011

The *Mars 96 Penetrator* (USSR) has a 6-m long spike full of instruments to monitor soil composition.

Artist's impression of the *Magellan* radar-mapping spacecraft orbiting Venus in 1994.

Earth-controlled exploring robot designed to roam Mars or the Moon and send back images.

▲ Unmanned probes have now visited all the major planets – and *New Horizons*, launched in 2006, should reach faraway dwarf planet Pluto in 2015. Recent ventures include further deep-space missions and the 2011 launch of *Juno*, on its way to Jupiter.

MAPS AND PHOTOS

The most accurate maps of Venus came from the *Magellan* probe, which went into orbit around Venus in August 1990. It discovered the longest canyon in the solar system and a landslide that happened while the craft was taking measurements. The probe *Mariner 10*, which skimmed past Venus in 1974, also flew by Mercury, sending back the first clear photos of this small world's heavily cratered surface.

LIFE ON MARS?

One of the most exciting moments in space exploration came in 1971 when the American probe *Mariner 9* photographed what looked like dried-up riverbeds on Mars. This suggested that millions of years ago, Mars had water and a thicker, warmer atmosphere, and therefore may have supported life. In 1976, the American spacecraft *Viking 1* and *Viking 2* went into orbit around Mars, named the 'Red Planet', after the colour of its soil. Probes descended to the surface by parachute. Each lander collected samples of the Martian soil and ran tests to see if they contained any life. Results were uncertain.

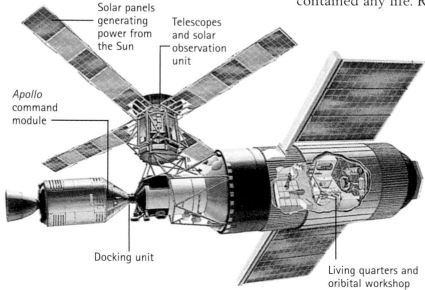

Solar panels generating power from the Sun

Telescopes and solar observation unit

Apollo command module

Docking unit

Living quarters and orbital workshop

◀ *Skylab*, launched in 1973, was built by NASA as a laboratory in space. It lasted until 1979, when it broke up and fell back to Earth. Astronauts now live and work in orbit in the International Space Station, which received its first resident crew in the year 2000.

IS ANYONE OUT THERE?

Planet	Probability
Mars	Top runner among scientists who suspect life could exist underground
Titan, Saturn's moon	Orange, nitrogen-rich atmosphere
Europa, Jupiter's moon	Pictures have hinted at a possible ocean beneath its crust and tests suggest oxygen may be present
Jupiter	Scientists say a chemical pre-life form could exist in its clouds
Comets	Some scientists suggest dust fragments in a comet's tail contain pre-life forms and viruses

◀ The Mars *Global Surveyor*, launched in 1996, orbited Mars (the Red Planet) taking photographs, assessing the planet's geology and finding a landing site for the next mission due to land there.

RETURN TO THE RED PLANET

In 1997, *Mars Pathfinder* made the most unusual landing of any spacecraft so far. Parachutes and small rocket engines helped to slow it down. It bounced along the Martian surface using big balloons until it finally came to rest. The probe released a roving vehicle, *Sojourner*, which analyzed rocks and returned 550 images.

DEEP SPACE

Beyond Mars lie the giant planets Jupiter, Saturn, Uranus and Neptune. These are much more remote worlds and it was only in 1973 that the first probe to Jupiter, *Pioneer 10*, flew past its target. Its sister craft, *Pioneer 11*, used the gravity pull of Jupiter to swing it on to an encounter with Saturn. This 'sling-shot effect' was also used by the later probes, *Voyager 1* and *Voyager 2*. In 1979, *Voyager 2* swung past Jupiter on its way to Saturn in 1981, Uranus in 1986 and Neptune in 1989.

TO SATURN AND BEYOND

Launched in 1997, NASA's *Cassini* spacecraft took seven years to reach Saturn. In 2004, it arrived at the planet and released a robot probe, *Huygens*, which successfully landed on the surface of Titan, Saturn's largest moon. The probe sent back images of the surface of Titan showing ice blocks scattered all around. It also sampled and sent back information on the chemical composition of the atmosphere. Since then, *Cassini* has flown by other, smaller moons of Saturn, sending back views of their surfaces.

Like the three earlier deep space probes, *Voyager 2* is now heading out of the solar system. In 1995, the *Galileo* spacecraft went into orbit around Jupiter. It released a probe that dropped by parachute through Jupiter's clouds and sent back details on the weather conditions and make-up of the atmosphere before burning up.

MANNED EXPLORATION

More than 520 astronauts have flown in space, and 12 have set foot on the Moon. The next target for manned exploration is Mars. A craft to make this journey could be built in space by astronauts aboard the International Space Station orbiting the Earth.

▼ *Huygens* took two-and-a-half hours to parachute to Titan's surface, sending back information about the moon's atmosphere to *Cassini*, which relayed it back to Earth.

SEE ALSO

Astronaut, Planet, Satellite, Solar system, Spacecraft, Star, Sun

SPAIN AND PORTUGAL

Spain and Portugal lie in the most southwesterly part of Europe, in an area known as the Iberian Peninsula. The countries have a linked history.

SPAIN
Area: 504,782 sq km
Population: 46,158,000
Capital: Madrid
Languages: Spanish, Catalan, Galician, Basque
Currency: Euro

PORTUGAL
Area: 92,391 sq km
Population: 10,627,000
Capital: Lisbon
Language: Portuguese
Currency: Euro

▲ Forests of cork oak trees in central and southern Portugal are stripped of their bark to provide large quantities of cork, a major product.

▶ Spain has about 1,400 castles and palaces. The fortified Alhambra Palace in Granada was built in the 1200s and 1300s.

Much of the Spanish mainland is a huge plateau called the Meseta. The country's high mountains include the Sierra Nevada and the Cantabrian ranges. The Pyrenees separate Spain from France. The Mediterranean coastline consists of fertile plains and, together with Spain's Balearic Islands, it attracts many tourists. The Canary Islands in the Atlantic are also popular with tourists and Spain's highest peak, Pico de Teide (3,718m), lies on the island of Tenerife. Central Spain has hot summers, reaching 42°C, and cold winters, but the coasts have a more moderate climate. Portugal is also mountainous, with high cliffs along its sandy Atlantic coastline. It has a milder climate than Spain. Its territory includes the islands of the Azores and Madeira in the Atlantic.

KEY CITIES
Spain's capital city, Madrid, is in the centre of the country. Other major cities include the industrial ports of Barcelona, Valencia, Malaga and Bilbao, as well as the historic fortress-cities of Granada, Cordova, Seville and Murcia. Portugal's capital city, Lisbon, stands on the River Tagus, which divides the country. Lisbon

▲ Traditional costume, like that of these women and children from Seville, is still worn by many Spanish people for festivals and other celebrations.

was rebuilt after being destroyed by an earthquake in 1755. Portugal's other major city, Porto, is the centre of the port wine trade. Over a third of the Portuguese people live in rural villages.

TOURISM AND TRADE
In Spain, tourism and industry have grown rapidly since the 1950s, alongside traditional crafts, winemaking, fishing, and growing fruits and vegetables. Portugal's main products are textiles and clothing, wine, fish, cork and marble. Portugal also depends heavily on tourism. Many Portuguese work abroad, sending money back home. Nearly seven per cent of the country's adults cannot read or write.

THE SPANISH LANGUAGE
Southern Spain was ruled by Moors – Muslims from North Africa – from 711CE to 1492. Moorish civilization left its mark on language, architecture, food and music.

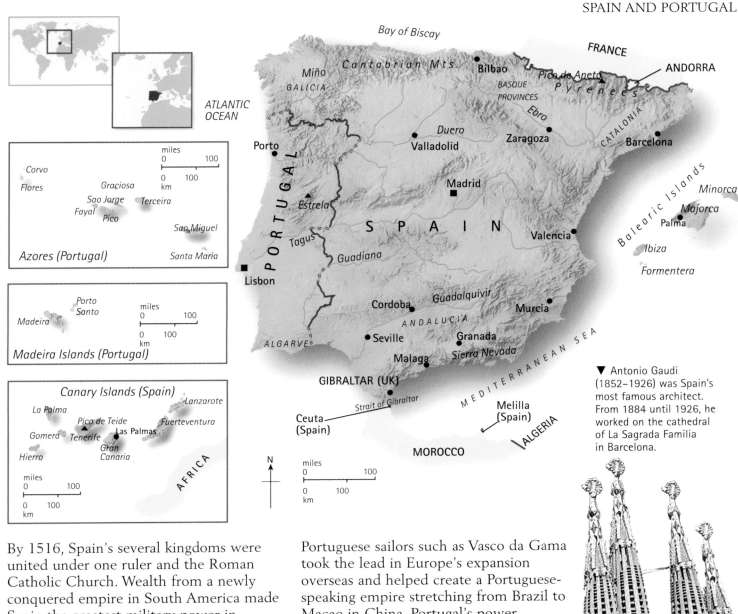

ATLANTIC OCEAN

Bay of Biscay

FRANCE

ANDORRA

Cantabrian Mts.

Bilbao

Pico de Aneto

Pyrenees

BASQUE PROVINCES

Miño

GALICIA

Ebro

CATALONIA

Porto

Duero

Valladolid

Zaragoza

Barcelona

Balearic Islands

Minorca

Madrid

Majorca

Estrela

PORTUGAL

S P A I N

Palma

Tagus

Valencia

Ibiza

Guadiana

Formentera

Lisbon

Cordoba

Guadalquivir

Murcia

ANDALUCIA

ALGARVE

Seville

Granada

GIBRALTAR (UK)

Malaga

Sierra Nevada

MEDITERRANEAN SEA

Strait of Gibraltar

Melilla (Spain)

Ceuta (Spain)

ALGERIA

MOROCCO

N

miles
0   100

0   100
km

Azores (Portugal)

miles
0   100

0   100
km

Corvo

Flores

Graciosa

Sao Jorge

Terceira

Fayal

Pico

Sao Miguel

Santa Maria

Madeira Islands (Portugal)

miles
0   100

0   100
km

Madeira

Porto Santo

Canary Islands (Spain)

miles
0   100

0   100
km

La Palma

Lanzarote

Pico de Teide

Fuerteventura

Gomera

Tenerife

Las Palmas

Hierro

Gran Canaria

AFRICA

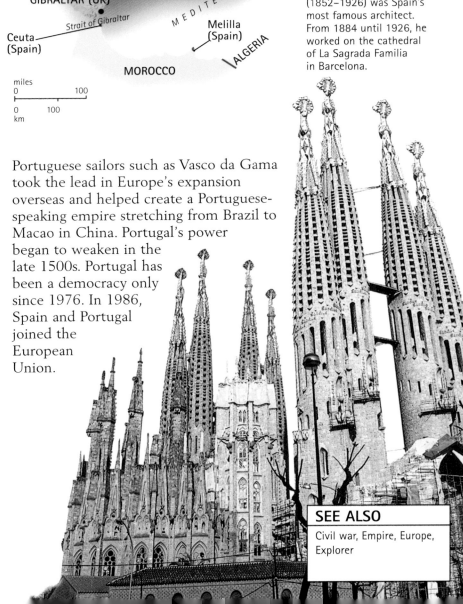

▼ Antonio Gaudi (1852–1926) was Spain's most famous architect. From 1884 until 1926, he worked on the cathedral of La Sagrada Familia in Barcelona.

By 1516, Spain's several kingdoms were united under one ruler and the Roman Catholic Church. Wealth from a newly conquered empire in South America made Spain the greatest military power in Europe, and colonization, especially in the Americas, made Spanish a world language.

SETBACKS TO PROGRESS

From 1800, Spain was weakened by wars, revolutions and poverty. After the Spanish Civil War of 1936–39, General Francisco Franco ruled as a dictator until his death in 1975. The monarchy was then restored with King Juan Carlos I and a democratic form of government was established.

PORTUGAL'S HISTORY

Although overshadowed by Spain, Portugal has managed to keep its language, identity and independence. Like Spain, Portugal has a Moorish heritage, is strongly Roman Catholic and has suffered from wars, dictatorship and poverty. From 1400,

Portuguese sailors such as Vasco da Gama took the lead in Europe's expansion overseas and helped create a Portuguese-speaking empire stretching from Brazil to Macao in China. Portugal's power began to weaken in the late 1500s. Portugal has been a democracy only since 1976. In 1986, Spain and Portugal joined the European Union.

SEE ALSO

Civil war, Empire, Europe, Explorer

SPIDER AND SCORPION

Spiders and scorpions are invertebrates (animals with no backbone) belonging to a group called arachnids. They have four pairs of legs – insects have only three.

The wind scorpion (or Sun spider) uses the wind to run and has huge jaws.

Mites, like this giant desert mite, are members of the arachnid family.

Unlike spiders, harvestmen have just one body section and eight slender legs.

A scorpion has large claws at the front to crush prey, and a sting in its tail.

All spiders and scorpions are predatory animals, feeding mainly on insects. Some of the big tropical spiders eat both lizards and mice and even take baby birds from their nests.

WEB OF DEATH
Spiders are famous for the silk webs they spin to trap their prey. There are lots of different web designs, the best-known being the circular orb webs. These have sticky spiral threads fixed to a set of radial threads that look like the spokes of a bicycle wheel. They are designed to catch flying insects. Other webs are designed to trap insects that scuttle over the ground.

HUNTING OR TRAPPING
The Australian dinopis spider spins a net, and holding this in its front legs, waits for an insect to pass by. Then it throws the net over the insect. But not all spiders make webs. Wolf spiders run after their prey, and crab spiders usually sit on plants, seizing insects that come within range.

POISONOUS FANGS
A spider kills its prey with poison, which is injected with a pair of needle-like fangs close to its mouth. The poison also starts to digest the prey, making it liquid, so the spider can suck the juices into its tiny mouth. It

◄ Crab spiders use their colours to hide in the centre of flowers, ready to pounce on pollen-hunting bugs.

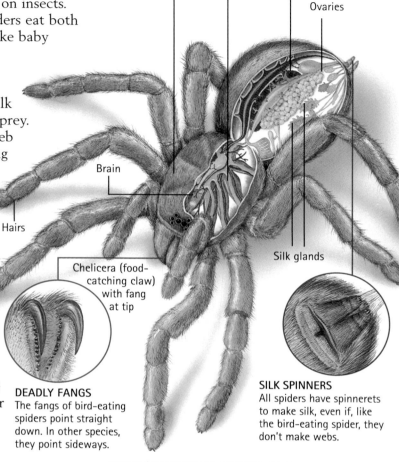

Spiders have two body parts – an abdomen (back end) and a cephalothorax (head and chest). The legs are joined to the cephalothorax

Sucking stomach

Heart

Ovaries

Brain

Hairs

Claws

Chelicera (food-catching claw) with fang at tip

Silk glands

DEADLY FANGS
The fangs of bird-eating spiders point straight down. In other species, they point sideways.

SILK SPINNERS
All spiders have spinnerets to make silk, even if, like the bird-eating spider, they don't make webs.

BIG, HAIRY BIRD-EATER

Bird-eating spiders are among the largest spiders in the world, with a leg-span of up to 25cm and 6cm-wide bodies. Despite their eight eyes, they have poor eyesight and use their sense of touch and body hairs to detect vibrations. They leave trails of silk to help would-be mates find them, to help them climb and to wrap their eggs.

cannot eat solid food. Some spider poisons are powerful enough to kill people, but only about 30 of the 38,000 or so species of spider are really dangerous. They include the black widow and the funnel-web spiders. The most venomous spider known to humans is the wandering spider from Brazil, and there is still no antidote for the bite of the recluse spider, also found in South America. The fangs of most spiders are too small or weak to pierce human skin.

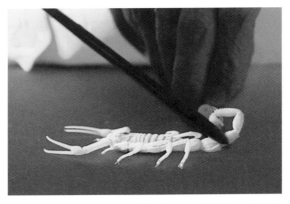

▲ Scorpions are fluorescent. Their outer shell glows bright green when an ultraviolet light is shone at it. This helps scientists to spot them at night when they are most active.

SENSITIVE HAIRS

Each leg of a spider has seven segments. Most species have three claws at the tip of the leg and a pad of hairs that helps them stick to surfaces. The legs are covered with three kinds of sensory hairs. On most spiders, the hairs are irritants that can be rubbed off onto attackers. They are also used to taste (by detecting chemicals in the surroundings), to feel and to 'hear', picking up vibrations either on the ground or in the web. A male spider often drums on a female's web as a mating signal.

A DANGEROUS COURTSHIP

Mating can be dangerous for many arachnids. The male spiders are mostly smaller than the females and often risk being mistaken for prey and eaten when they approach a would-be mate. In fact, the female often eats the male after, or even during, mating. The male nursery web spider gives his partner a gift of an insect wrapped in silk. As she eats the insect, he can mate safely.

EGGS IN SILK BAGS

A female spider wraps her eggs in silk bags, or sacs. Wolf spiders carry these around with them, and even carry their babies on their backs for a while. Some spiders, such as the pink-haired bird-eating spider, lay 3,000 eggs in one batch – the hatched spiderlings are bigger than many fully-grown species.

▶ A scorpion's sting is at the end of a long flexible tail which it can quickly flick over to inject venom into its prey. The poison comes from two glands at the base.

STICKY TRAPS

Spiders have a variety of ways to trap prey. The orb-web spider (like many common garden spiders) creates a circular web in which unsuspecting flies get stuck. Bolas spiders 'fish' for prey using a sticky line of silk which they throw at nearby insects. Trap door spiders lurk in tunnels with little trap doors. They dart out to catch passing insects and drag them below.

SCORPIONS

There are about 1,500 species of scorpion and all live in hot countries. Many of them live in deserts, where they can survive the high temperatures without ever needing a drink. Scorpions range from 2–20cm in length, the largest being the imperial scorpion of West Africa. All scorpions and spiders moult or shed their skin around five to ten times as they grow.

A STING IN THE TAIL

Scorpions have large pincers – pedipalps – at the front and use them to catch lizards, insects and other small animals. A scorpion also has a sting at the end of its slender tail. The sting is used mainly for defence and some species are dangerous to people. The fat-tailed scorpion, found in parts of north Africa and the Middle East, is one of the most venomous scorpions. Its sting can kill a human in six to seven hours.

Common garden spiders spin sticky, circular orb webs between branches.

Water spiders make a tent of silk underwater, using air bubbles to breathe.

Trap door spiders make a silk-lined tunnel in the ground with a lid on top.

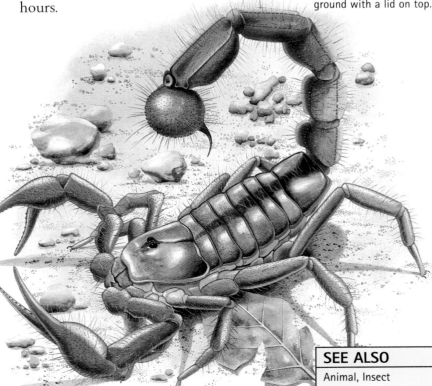

SEE ALSO
Animal, Insect

SPORT

Sport is a game or activity involving physical skills, usually in competition. It is enjoyable as a form of exercise and also provides big-business entertainment.

Sports can be played either in teams or individually, on a professional or an amateur basis. Most sports are competitive and winning may be decided in a number of ways: by timing speeds (running or swimming events), measuring distances (jumping or throwing events), scoring points (most ball games) or judging performances (diving, boxing and gymnastics).

In ice hockey, players reach speeds of 48km/h and drive a hard, disc-shaped puck over the ice at 160km/h.

In scrambling, strong, light bikes with chunky tyres race across rough and hilly cross-country terrain.

A discus thrower spins around one-and-a-half times before releasing the discus from the hand.

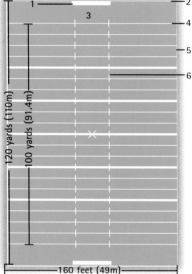

Goal post

KEY

1 Goal post	4 Goal line
2 End line	5 Sideline
3 End zone	6 Hash marks

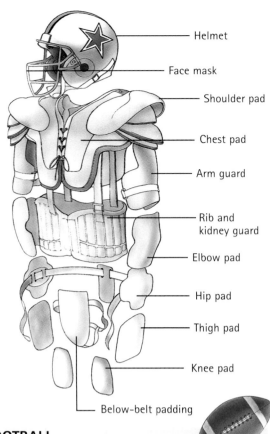

AMERICAN FOOTBALL

American football evolved from English soccer and rugby. Professional sides have squads of up to 45 players divided into three teams: one for offence, another for defence and the third for taking kicks. The team in possession (offence) has four plays, or 'downs', to advance the ball 10 yards (9.1m) by running with it or passing it. If successful, the team has another series of plays. If it fails, the opposition takes possession of the ball. All plays start on or between the hash marks. Six points are awarded for a touchdown, plus an extra point for converting the ball over the crossbar. Place kicking the ball over the crossbar from anywhere in the field gains three points. The defence also scores two points from a 'safety' either by tackling the ball carrier in his own end zone or if the carrier steps out of the back or side of his zone.

TENNIS

The modern game of lawn tennis was developed in Britain in the 1860s. The object of the game is to score points by hitting the ball with a racket over the net into the opponent's court so that it cannot be returned. The ball may be struck either before it has hit the ground or after one bounce. Tennis is played in sets, usually the best of three or five. A set is won when one side wins six games, with a lead of at least two games. A game's scoring goes from 'love' (0) to 15, 30, 40 and 'game'. If the score reaches 40–40 ('deuce'), it continues until one side leads by two clear points.

◄ Success in men's tennis depends greatly on having a powerful serve, as Pete Sampras of the USA demonstrates.

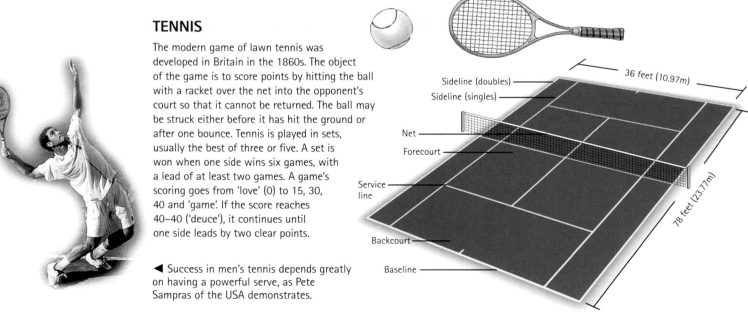

SOCCER

Professional soccer is played 11-a-side, with three substitutes allowed, and consists of two 45-minute halves. The object of the game is to kick or head the ball into the opponents' net to score a goal. The team with the most goals at the end of play wins. Players can move the ball with their feet, head or body, but not their hands or arms. Only the goalkeeper may handle the ball, and then only inside his penalty area. A free-kick is given if a player commits a foul or is off-side. A player is off-side when fewer than two defending players are positioned between him and the goal-line as the ball is being passed forward to him.

▼ Holland's Mark Van Bommel attempts to tackle Carles Puyol of Spain in the FIFA 2010 World Cup Final. Spain won after extra time.

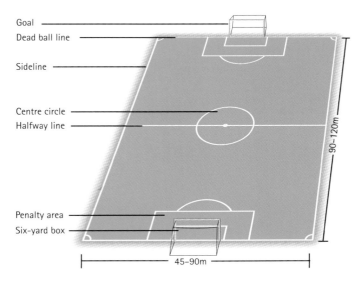

Goal
Dead ball line
Sideline
Centre circle
Halfway line
Penalty area
Six-yard box
90–120m
45–90m

TRACK AND FIELD EVENTS

Outdoor running events, except for the marathon, take place on the 400m track. They include the 100m, 200m and 400m sprint. The longest middle-distance track race is 10,000m (25 laps), and other running events include the steeplechase and relay. Field events include: high, long and triple jump; hammer, discus and javelin throwing; pole vaulting; and shot putting. Combined track and field events include the ten-event decathlon and seven-event heptathlon.

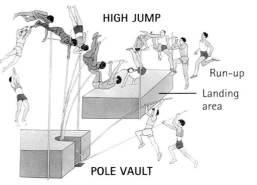

HIGH JUMP
Run-up
Landing area
POLE VAULT

◄ Leading high jumpers use a technique called the 'Fosbury flop'. This involves clearing the bar head first, followed by the back, and, last of all, the legs. In pole vaulting, the pole may be of any length or width.

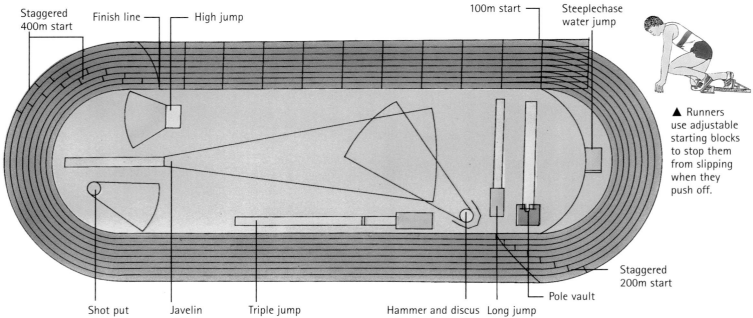

Staggered 400m start
Finish line
High jump
100m start
Steeplechase water jump

▲ Runners use adjustable starting blocks to stop them from slipping when they push off.

Shot put
Javelin
Triple jump
Hammer and discus
Long jump
Pole vault
Staggered 200m start

An old Scottish game, golf is now one of the most popular sports worldwide.

Horse-racing can either be flat racing or racing over jumps, and is a major betting sport.

Skiing is a snow sport that includes downhill, slalom (obstacle course), ski-jumping and cross-country.

BASKETBALL

Basketball was invented in Massachusetts, USA, in 1891, and is now one of the most popular team sports worldwide. It is played by two teams of ten, although only five players may be on court at any one time. The object of the game is to score points by throwing the ball into the opposition's basket. Players move the ball around with their hands by passing, dribbling and shooting. Running with the ball is not allowed. Baskets may be scored from any part of the court and are worth three points from outside the three-point arc, two from inside it and one from a free throw.

▲ Michael Jordan 'slam dunks' for the Chicago Bulls.

Backboard
Basket
Free-throw line
Sideline
End line
Centre circle

FENCING

As a combat practice, fencing dates from the Middle Ages. Three weapons are now used – the épée, sabre and foil. The object of fencing is to touch your opponent on the target area with your sword to score a hit. The fencers are wired up so that any hit can be registered electronically. Only the point of the weapon may be used in épée and foil, but with the sabre the edge of the blade also counts.

Face mask
Target areas
SABRE
Handle
Guard
EPEE
Blade
FOIL
On-guard line
Centre line
Electronic scorer
Rear limit

CRICKET

Organized cricket began in late 17th-century England, although its origins probably go as far back as 1300. The modern game is played 11-a-side. At each end of the pitch is a wicket, which is defended by a batsman. The object of the game is to get the opponents' side out with the least number of runs. A side's innings end when ten batsmen have been dismissed, caught or run out. Any member of the fielding side may bowl an 'over', consisting of six balls. After each over, another bowler starts from the other end of the pitch. A run is scored when a batsman hits the ball with the bat and both batsmen run to the opposite end of the pitch without being dismissed. A hit over the boundary scores four runs, or six runs if it does not touch the ground first.

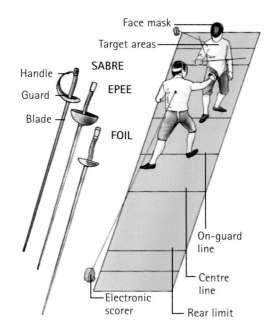

▲ The possible fielding positions for a right-handed batsman (only 11 fielders allowed):
1 Bowler; 2 Wicket-keeper; 3 First slip; 4 Second slip; 5 Gully; 6 Point; 7 Cover point; 8 Extra cover; 9 Silly point; 10 Silly mid-off; 11 Mid-off; 12 Deep mid-off; 13 Long-off; 14 Long-on; 15 Deep mid-on; 16 Mid-on; 17 Mid-wicket; 18 Silly mid-on; 19 Deep square-leg; 20 Square-leg; 21 Forward short-leg; 22 Backward short-leg; 23 Leg slip; 24 Short extra cover; »25 Backward point; 26 Short third man; 27 Third man; 28 Deep mid-wicket; 29 Deep extra cover.

Batting glove
Bails
Leg pad
Stumps

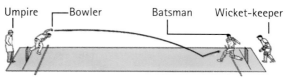

Umpire — Bowler   Batsman   Wicket-keeper

BASEBALL

Baseball probably developed from games such as cricket and rounders. It was first played in 1846 in New Jersey, USA. It is played nine-a-side on a square field called the diamond, within a larger outfield. At one point of the diamond is home plate, where the batter stands, and at the other points are first, second and third bases, each of which is defended by a baseman. The pitcher throws the ball from a mound in the centre of the diamond. To score a run, the batter moves around the bases to reach home plate. He may do this with one hit or on hits of succeeding batters. Each side has nine turns at batting. The fielding side must get three batters out to close an inning and take its next turn at batting.

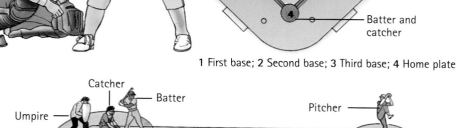

Outfield
Centre field
Left field
Right field
Shortstop
Foul line
Pitcher
Infield
Batter and catcher

1 First base; 2 Second base; 3 Third base; 4 Home plate

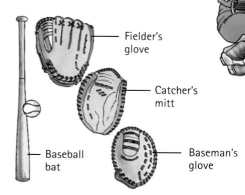

Fielder's glove
Catcher's mitt
Baseball bat
Baseman's glove

Umpire
Catcher
Batter
Pitcher

GYMNASTICS

After its birth in Ancient Greece, gymnastics was revived in the late 18th century and was held at the first modern Olympic Games in 1896. In competition, gymnasts are marked out of ten by a panel of judges. The classic events involve floor exercises, high bar, parallel bars, pommel horse, rings and vault. Rhythmic gymnastics is performed to music and involves ballet steps and hand apparatus. Its individual exercises include twirling, throwing, catching, rolling, bouncing or swinging the apparatus. Sports acrobatics, for individuals or teams, includes somersaults and springs.

WOMEN'S VAULT

Handspring
Landing
Springboard
Horse

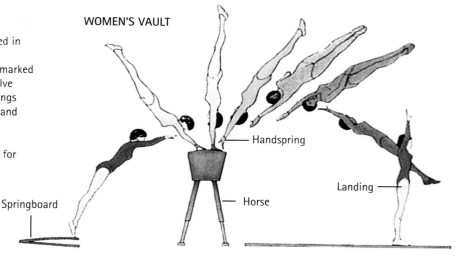

SWIMMING AND DIVING

The earliest swimming races took place 2,000 years ago in Japan. Today, they involve four main strokes – front crawl, backstroke, breaststroke and butterfly – as well as freestyle. There are also separate diving events, either from a highboard or springboard, which involve specific somersaults, twists and turns while in the air.

Dive
Recovery
Turn

SEE ALSO

Olympic Games

STAR

Stars are large balls of hot gas that produce light and heat through nuclear reactions. Our Sun is an average yellow star, but it seems bright because it is so close.

THE BIRTH OF A STAR

A star begins its life by condensing out of material from a cloud of dust and gas. When the star's temperature is hot enough, nuclear reactions begin, and hydrogen converts to helium, creating a steady glow. Yellow stars, such as the Sun, may shine steadily for billions of years before expanding and cooling into red giants. Finally, they collapse into small, dense, white dwarfs, and then die.

1 A nebula (cloud of dust and gas), the birth-place of a star.

2 The gas and dust condense, and the star begins to form.

3 Nuclear reaction takes place: hydrogen is converted to helium.

4 The new star generates light and heat.

5 The yellow star remains stable for billions of years.

▲ The constellation of Orion is a place where new stars are being born, in areas such as the Orion Nebula (M42).

BRIGHTEST STARS

Name	Constellation
Sun	–
Sirius	Canis Major
Canopus	Carina
Rigil Kent	Centaurus
Arcturus	Bootes
Vega	Lyra
Capella	Auriga
Rigel	Orion
Procyon	Canis Minor
Achernar	Eridanus

Stars form from large clouds of gas and dust in space, called nebulae. These clouds shrink due to the inward pull of their own gravity. At the centre of a shrinking cloud, the gas becomes hotter and denser. Eventually, nuclear reactions start, in which hydrogen is turned into helium by a process known as nuclear fusion, and a new star is born.

STAR TEMPERATURES
At the centre of a star, where nuclear fusion takes place, the temperature is over 10 million°C. Stars may be classified according to their temperature. The temperature at the surface varies from star to star. A red dwarf may be as little as 3,000°C, while a blue supergiant star may be over 20,000°C. Stars also have different luminosities, or brightnesses, so that a bright, distant star may look closer than a nearby star that is very dim.

STARS IN OLD AGE
When all the hydrogen at the centre of a star is used up, the star begins to change. Its outer layers swell until the star is many times larger than before, and it becomes a red giant. After this, the fate of the star is decided by its mass. Stars such as the Sun end up as small, hot stars called white dwarfs. More massive stars, however, are shorter-lived and blow up in huge explosions called supernovae. One of two final stages may follow: in the first, the remaining part of the star collapses until it becomes a neutron star, the densest type of star. A handful of its material weighs billions of tonnes. The second possibility is that a star of very great mass may collapse and become a black hole, a funnel-like shape that sucks all nearby material into it – even light cannot escape.

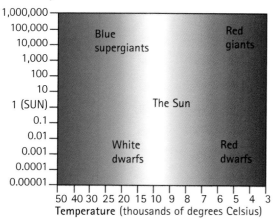

Luminosity

Blue supergiants	Red giants
The Sun	
White dwarfs	Red dwarfs

Temperature (thousands of degrees Celsius)
50 40 30 25 20 15 10 9 8 7 6 5 4 3

▲ The diagram plots the temperature and luminosity of stars. The more material a star has, the hotter it is. Blue giants are the hottest, and red dwarfs the coolest.

SEE ALSO
Astronomy, Black hole, Colour, Constellation Galaxy, Sun, Universe

STARFISH AND OTHER ECHINODERMS

Starfish are star-shaped, marine invertebrates with between five and 40 arms. Other echinoderms include brittle stars, sea urchins and sea cucumbers.

A sea cucumber can grow up to 50cm. It uses its suckered feet for climbing.

Echinoderm means 'spiny-skinned' and all members of the group have a rough or spiny skin to protect them. All live in the sea, although brittle stars often live at great depths, while most starfish and sea urchins live in fairly shallow water. There are about 1,600 different kinds of starfish, ranging in size from about 1cm to 60cm.

POWERFUL SUCKERS
Using its suckers, a starfish can move in any direction it chooses. It feeds on other small animals, including fish and worms, and can even open the shells of cockles and other bivalves with its powerful suckers. The starfish wraps its arms around a shell and grips with its suckers, which gradually pull the two halves of the shell apart. The starfish then pushes its stomach through the crack and digests the soft body inside.

DRIFTING YOUNGSTERS
Starfish do not mate. The males and females release clouds of sperms and eggs into the water and fertilization takes place there. The young starfish (or larvae) are

▲ A starfish digests a mussel. It turns its stomach inside out and pushes it into the shell to eat the soft body.

blob-like with no arms and, instead of living on the sea bed, they float near the surface of the sea so they spread to new areas. They alter shape as they grow, and metamorphose (change) into adults.

SLENDER RELATIVES
Brittle stars look like starfish, but their arms are more slender and are clearly separated from the central disc. Some brittle stars catch small animals with their arms, but most species shovel mud into their mouth and digest any tiny creatures living there. Sea cucumbers have feeding tentacles around their mouth to filter food from the water. Some sea urchins also feed like this.

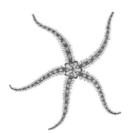

A brittle star has no suckers. It uses its long arms to pull itself along.

A rock urchin grows up to 6cm and has sharp spines. It scrapes up algae to eat.

A violet heart urchin has furry spines on top. It burrows in sand and mud.

SYMMETRICAL STAR
Like all echinoderms, the starfish is built on a circular plan, with no head or brain, although it has a simple network of nerves in its body. The mouth is on the underside. Common starfish have five arms, which can regrow if they are cut off.

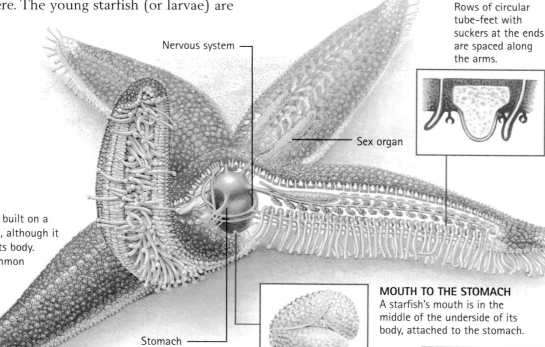

Nervous system

Sex organ

Stomach

SOFT SUCKERS
Rows of circular tube-feet with suckers at the ends are spaced along the arms.

MOUTH TO THE STOMACH
A starfish's mouth is in the middle of the underside of its body, attached to the stomach.

SEE ALSO
Animal, Ocean and sea, Seashore

STOMACH AND DIGESTIVE SYSTEM

The food we eat is broken down into nutrients by the stomach and intestines, and then taken into the body for energy, growth, maintenance and repair.

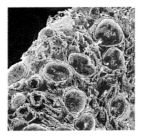

▲ A magnified view of human taste buds, which detect sweet, sour, bitter, salt and umami flavours.

The stomach is the widest part of the digestive system, a long passageway or tube within the body. This begins at the mouth and continues through the throat, gullet, stomach, small intestine and large intestine, ending at the anus. The whole tube is about 9m long.

CHEWED TO PULP
Chewing mashes food into a pulp so that digestive juices can reach it more easily.

DIGESTIVE JOURNEY
Food takes 24 to 36 hours to pass through the human digestive system. It is digested, or broken down, by physical squeezing and mashing, and by strong chemical juices called digestive enzymes.

1 In the mouth, food is chewed into a pulp and mixed with watery saliva (spit). This makes food slippery and easy to swallow. Each mass of swallowed food is called a bolus.

2 As food passes down the throat and the oesophagus (gullet), it is squeezed and massaged along by wave-like contractions of the muscles in the gullet wall.

3 Strong muscles in the stomach wall churn and squash the food. After 3 to 6 hours, the soupy, semi-digested food, called chyme, trickles into the small intestine.

4 In the small intestine, the chyme is broken down into chemicals. The nutrients are taken into the bloodstream.

5 Undigested food and wastes pass into the large intestine. Water and body salts are taken into the bloodstream before the faeces are expelled through the anus.

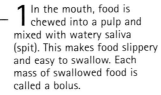

▲ Sugar and fat contain important nutrients, but are converted to fat if not enough exercise is taken.

Three pairs of glands pour saliva into the mouth. The saliva contains enzymes to break down starches and sugars.

DIGESTING AND ABSORBING
In the stomach, the food is mixed with powerful acid and digestive enzymes. From there food passes to the small intestine, which is 4cm wide and 6m long. Its lining is covered with thousands of villi (tiny projections), each about 1mm long. This provides a huge area for absorbing nutrients. The small intestine lining and nearby pancreas gland make more strong enzymes to digest chyme (semi-digested food). Another digestive fluid, bile, is made in the liver and stored in the gall bladder. Bile is especially good at digesting fatty substances in food.

LARGE INTESTINE
Undigested food passes into the large intestine, which is about 6cm wide and 1.5m long. The semi-solid faeces are stored near the end of the tract, in the rectum, until it is convenient to expel them through the anus.

LIVER
Blood from the intestines flows to the liver, which stores some nutrients from digestion, and converts sugars into starch for storage. It also breaks down possibly harmful substances, such as alcohol.

SEE ALSO

Food, Gland, Human body, Nutrition, Taste and smell

SUBMARINE

A submarine is a craft that can travel under the sea. It can be a deadly naval weapon, but can also explore the sea bed and carry out repairs on underwater pipelines.

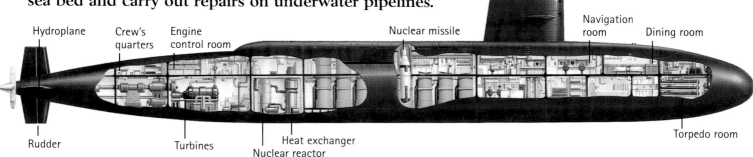

Periscope, radio and radar antennae

Hydroplane

Crew's quarters

Engine control room

Nuclear missile

Navigation room

Dining room

Rudder

Turbines

Nuclear reactor

Heat exchanger

Torpedo room

▲ David Bushnell's *Turtle* was the first submarine to be used in warfare, in the American Revolution, 1776. The craft was driven by hand- and foot-propellers and steered by a rudder.

KEY DATES

c.1620 First submarine is built by Dutchman Cornelius Drebbel

1864 USS *Hunley* becomes first submarine to sink an enemy ship, in American Civil War

1954 USS *Nautilus* is the first nuclear submarine

1960 *Trieste* submersible dives to a record depth of 10.9km in the Pacific

The earliest submarines were barrel-like vessels powered by hand-cranked propellers or oars during the 17th and 18th centuries. The US engineer Robert Fulton (1765–1815) tried in vain to interest the French navy in his submarine in 1800. Submarine warfare was tried during the American Civil War (1861–65) and it was the US Navy that used the first practical submarine, built in 1898 by Irish-born inventor John P. Holland (1840–1914).

SUBMARINES IN WAR

Submarines armed with torpedoes sank ships in both world wars. They had electric motors for use under water, but moved faster on the surface, using diesel engines to recharge the electric motors' batteries. The United States launched the first nuclear-powered submarine in 1955. Modern naval submarines have nuclear reactors driving turbine engines and can travel around the world under water without refuelling. They can fire guided missiles and, with the aid of computerized navigation systems, can go almost anywhere in the world's oceans.

▲ Much of the space in a nuclear submarine is taken up by the turbines that drive it and the reactor. The crew's quarters and operating area take up a very small space.

HOW A SUBMARINE WORKS

A submarine's depth in the sea is controlled by ballast tanks. When the tanks are filled with water, the submarine sinks. When water in the tanks is forced out by compressed air, the submarine rises. Under water, the submarine is steered by rudders, while its depth is controlled by wing-like hydroplanes at the front and back. The submarine's whale-like shape helps it slip through the water with the least resistance. The largest nuclear submarines are huge, weighing more than 20,000 tonnes, and have room for about 150 crew members and 16 nuclear missiles.

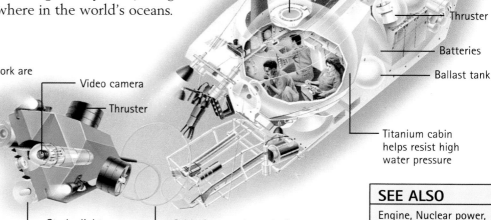

Hatch

Thruster

Thruster

Batteries

Ballast tank

Titanium cabin helps resist high water pressure

Video camera

Thruster

Strobe light

Cable for remote control

SUBMERSIBLES

Submarines used for scientific and industrial work are called submersibles. Some are unmanned and are guided by remote control as they explore the oceans. Others, such as US *Alvin* (right), can seat up to three crew members. The *Alvin* can dive to depths of 4,000m and has been used to locate ocean mineral deposits and marine life. A remotely operated vehicle, *Jason Junior* (near right), can be operated from within the submersible to explore places too small or dangerous for the *Alvin*.

SEE ALSO

Engine, Nuclear power, Ship, World War I

SUDAN AND SOUTH SUDAN

Until 2011, Sudan and what is now South Sudan were all one country, Sudan, and Africa's biggest. Now Sudan is the second largest country in Africa, after Algeria.

Area: 1,886,070 sq km
Population: 30,894,000
Capital: Khartoum
Language: Arabic
Currency: Sudanese pound

Area: 619,745 sq km
Population: 8,260,000
Capital: Juba (new capital will be built at Ramciel)
Languages: English, Dinka, Nuer
Currency: South Sudan pound

▲ Khartoum is divided into three areas: Khartoum itself, Omdurman (above) and Khartoum North. Omdurman has the largest population.

Most of the people of Sudan and South Sudan live along the banks of the White Nile and the Blue Nile. These rivers join at Sudan's capital, Khartoum, flowing north into Egypt. Much of Sudan is desert, which gives way to grassy plains. In South Sudan, where there is more rainfall, there are forests and a swamp called the Sudd which is the size of England. South Sudan is rich in wildlife, including giraffes, lions, leopards and elephants, with hippos and crocodiles along the Nile. The climate is hot, reaching 46°C in the north in summer.

A DIVIDED LAND
For centuries, the north of this region has been home to Arabs, who were Muslims. The south was home to dozens of different black African peoples. From the late 19th century, some of these peoples became Christians, but most remained followers of traditional African religions. Today, more than 100 different African languages are spoken in South Sudan.

FARMING AND INDUSTRY
Cotton is Sudan's major export, while wheat and millet are the main food crops. Mining produces chromium, gypsum and gold. Sudan is also the world's largest supplier of gum arabic, used in ink and medicines. South Sudan is much poorer.

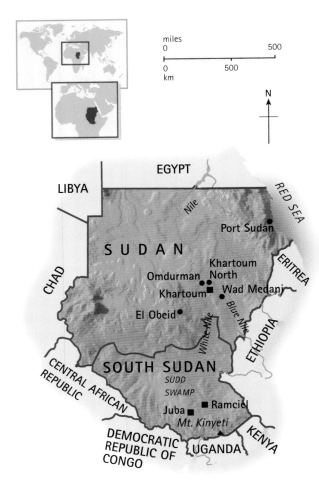

More than 75 per cent of its people are farmers. However, it has oil reserves that it exports through Sudan to Port Sudan.

ANCIENT LAND
People first settled in the Sudan region around 9,000 years ago and farming began 6,000 years ago. Missionaries brought Christianity from 500CE but Muslims later conquered the area. Britain and Egypt controlled Sudan from 1899, until Sudan became an independent country in 1956. Civil war between the north (now Sudan) and south (now South Sudan) broke out in the 1950s and 1960s and fighting recurred from 1983. War and drought created a major refugee problem and stopped the development of oil fields in the south. A peace agreement signed in 2005 led to a vote in the south in favour of independence. In 2011 South Sudan became a separate republic and Africa's newest country.

◀ The Dinka people make up South Sudan's largest black African group. They live by herding and farming.

SEE ALSO
Africa

400

SUN

The Sun is the closest star to Earth. It is a globe of hot gas, mostly hydrogen, and lies at the centre of our solar system. It contains no solid material.

The Sun is so big that more than a million Earths would fit inside it. It looks different from other stars because it is so much nearer to Earth. At the Sun's core, high temperatures and pressures cause nuclear reactions to take place in which hydrogen is turned into helium. This process releases huge amounts of energy, which eventually finds its way to the Sun's surface, called the photosphere. From there, it escapes into space as light, heat and other radiations.

EVER-CHANGING

Cooler areas of the Sun form dark patches on the Sun's surface known as sunspots. From these, releases of energy, called solar flares, send bursts of radiation into space. Other eruptions, known as prominences, reach into the Sun's inner atmosphere, the chromosphere, and into its outer atmosphere, the corona. From the corona, there is a constant stream of particles into space, called the solar wind.

GOOD AND BAD RAYS

Without the warmth and light of the Sun, life on Earth would be impossible. But the Sun also gives off other kinds of radiation, including ultraviolet rays and X-rays, which can be harmful. We are shielded from most of this damaging radiation by the ozone layer of the Earth's atmosphere, but enough ultraviolet radiation penetrates to the surface to be able to cause sunburn.

LIFE STORY OF THE SUN

The Sun was formed about five billion years ago from a cloud of gas and dust. In another four or five billion years, its supply of hydrogen will run out and the core will collapse. The outer layers will swell as it becomes a red giant, then it will end its life as a slowly cooling white dwarf star.

THE SUN'S ENERGY

The Sun's energy is produced in the core. It flows out as radiations, through the radiative zone to the convective zone. The energy reaches the visible surface of the Sun (the photosphere) by a churning motion called convection. Hot gas rises to the surface, gives off its energy and cools, then sinks back. The surface gives off the energy as light and heat.

▼ Solar flares occur over sunspots. They can disturb Earth's magnetic field and interfere with radio transmissions on Earth.

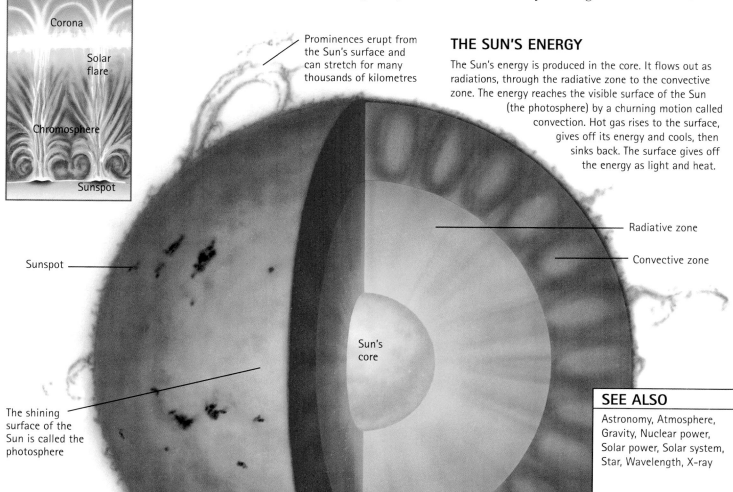

Corona

Solar flare

Chromosphere

Sunspot

Prominences erupt from the Sun's surface and can stretch for many thousands of kilometres

Radiative zone

Convective zone

Sun's core

Sunspot

The shining surface of the Sun is called the photosphere

SEE ALSO

Astronomy, Atmosphere, Gravity, Nuclear power, Solar power, Solar system, Star, Wavelength, X-ray

SURGERY

Surgery is a branch of medicine that involves cutting into the body to remove or repair a body part that is damaged or diseased.

Artificial limbs were made over 2,000 years ago. In the 1500s, they were made of metal or wood.

18th-century military surgeons carried their surgical instruments with them in a wooden case.

The surgeon Joseph Lister (1827–1912) used carbolic acid to disinfect the air during operations.

An early surgical knife is the forerunner of the modern-day scalpel, used to cut into the body.

Anaesthetics can be given as gases inhaled through a mask, but they are now more likely to be injected.

A surgical procedure is called an operation and is usually done in hospital. Operations are performed in an operating theatre – a room designed to protect the patient from infection.

THE SURGICAL TEAM
Operations are carried out by a specially qualified doctor called a surgeon. He or she works with an assistant, a theatre nurse and an anaesthetist (a doctor who gives the patient an anaesthetic). The surgical team all wear sterile gowns, gloves and masks to make sure that they neither receive nor transmit germs.

SURGICAL INSTRUMENTS
The surgeon uses various instruments during an operation. A scalpel is a knife which cuts into the body. Retractors hold the incision (cut) open. Forceps are used to handle tissue, which may be cut with surgical scissors. After the operation, the surgeon sews up the incision or seals it with special tape.

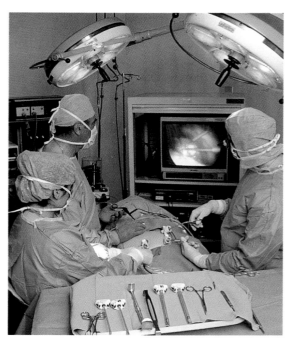

▲ Cameras are often used in the operating theatre so that the surgical team can see the area they are operating on in greater detail on a video screen.

▲ Until the 1600s, the Church did not allow people to cut open human bodies for scientific purposes. The study of anatomy, shown here in Rembrandt's painting of 1632, enabled surgeons to perform more complex operations.

TYPES OF SURGERY
There are several types of surgery. In transplant operations, diseased organs such as the liver or heart are removed and replaced by healthy organs from human donors. Plastic surgery involves repairing skin that has been damaged by burns or injury. It is also done to improve a person's appearance. Today, many operations are done using keyhole surgery, which helps the patient recover more quickly. Here, the surgeon makes a tiny incision and uses miniature instruments to do the surgery.

DULLING THE PAIN
Without anaesthetics, most of the surgery done today would be impossible. An American dentist, William Clarke, was the first to use an anaesthetic in 1847. He used ether to make a patient unconscious while he pulled out a tooth. Nitrous oxide, which is still used today, was another early anaesthetic.

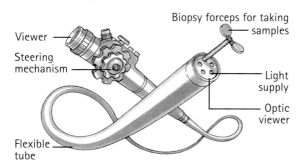

Viewer

Steering mechanism

Flexible tube

Biopsy forceps for taking samples

Light supply

Optic viewer

▲ The endoscope is a long, flexible tube with its own fibre-optic light source. This allows doctors to see inside the body before making an incision.

SEE ALSO
Drug, Medicine

SWAMP AND MARSH

Swamps, marshes, bogs and fens are all varieties of wetlands, in which the soil is permanently waterlogged or even completely covered with water.

A swamp is a wetland area dominated by trees and shrubs – a kind of permanently flooded forest. Waterlogged areas without trees are called marshes.

UNDERWATER ROOTS

The species found growing in swamps are those that can withstand having their roots permanently under water. Some of the world's largest swamps are found in southern Asia. Here, mangrove swamps form a tangle of tall, stilt-like roots along thousands of kilometres of coast. Strange fish called mudskippers scurry about on exposed areas of mud and archer fish spit water to knock insects off overhanging branches. Other creatures include crab-eating frogs and monkeys, and some of the world's most poisonous water snakes.

MARSHLAND

Marsh vegetation consists mainly of grasses and sedges. Dense patches of reeds and rushes surround patches of open water, which may contain water-lilies, rooted to the bottom but with their leaves floating on the surface, or true 'floaters' such as the water hyacinth and duckweed. Many of Europe's big rivers

have marshlands alongside them, providing homes for a huge variety of birdlife – from herons, egrets and avocets to tiny reed warblers and bearded tits. Salt marshes are common around the coasts in temperate regions. They contain a variety of grasses depending on how saline (salty) they are and whether they are permanently flooded. Like freshwater marshes, they contain huge numbers of insects, snails and frogs and are vital breeding and feeding areas for waterbirds.

BOGS AND FENS

The term 'bog' is usually used for a waterlogged area consisting of thick layers of peat. There is usually no water on the surface, but the ground is soggy, and the surface usually covered with spongy sphagnum moss. The peat is so acidic and contains so little oxygen that 2,000-year-old bodies have been found in it, perfectly preserved. Less acidic wetland areas are often called fens.

THE EVERGLADES

The Florida Everglades in the USA are the best known Northern Hemisphere swamps, extending nearly 8,000 sq m. The region is essentially a river filled with coarse grasses and rushes and scattered with dense stands of cypress, red maple and gum trees, draped with Spanish moss.

Rough green snake

Pileated woodpecker

Zebra butterfly

Raccoon

Roseate spoonbill

Green tree frog

Mississippi alligator

Mangrove roots

Terrapin

Oxeye tarpon

SEE ALSO

Alligator and crocodile, Bird, Fish, Habitat, Insect, Snake, USA

SWITZERLAND AND AUSTRIA

Switzerland and Austria lie north of Italy, in Europe, with Liechtenstein sandwiched between them. The Alps cover a large area of the two countries.

AUSTRIA
Area: 83,858 sq km
Population: 8,404,000
Capital: Vienna
Language: German
Currency: Euro

SWITZERLAND
Area: 41,285 sq km
Population: 7,786,000
Capital: Bern
Languages: German, French, Italian and Romansch
Currency: Swiss franc

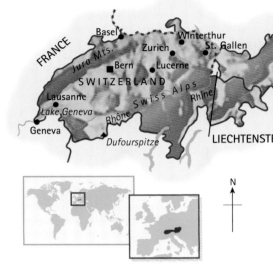

▲ Switzerland is famous for its beautiful lakes, including Lake Geneva.

▲ Swiss banks are probably the most secure banks in the world. Gold bars are stored in their vaults.

Two of Europe's greatest rivers, the Rhine and the Rhône, both start in the Swiss Alps within 25km of each other, while the mighty Danube flows through Austria. The mountainous landscape of both countries attracts many tourists.

ALPINE INDUSTRY
Switzerland is one of the richest countries in Europe, despite its lack of natural resources and flat farmland. Its wealth has come from banking, tourism and industry – it produces cheese, chocolate, medicines, machinery and watches. Nearly half of Austria is forested, supplying timber and paper. Austria's mountain waters feed hydroelectric plants that provide more than two thirds of the nation's power.

SWISS GOVERNMENT
Switzerland is divided into 26 self-governing regions called cantons, although central government controls the army, railways and post, and links with foreign countries. Twenty-five major international organizations have their headquarters in Switzerland, including the Red Cross, founded there in 1864. Through all the wars of modern history, Switzerland has remained neutral, but all Swiss men must train as soldiers. About a fifth of the population was born outside Switzerland.

AUSTRIA'S PEOPLE
Until 1918, Austria ruled Europe's sprawling Austro-Hungarian Empire from Vienna. Vienna is Austria's capital city today and almost a quarter of the people live there. The majority of Austrians are Roman Catholic and keep up old customs and festivals. Many country people wear traditional dress, such as leather breeches.

POPULAR PASTIMES
Austria has a rich musical history as the home of the waltz and of the composers Mozart, Schubert and Strauss. Favourite Swiss and Austrian pastimes include folk dancing, yodelling, shooting and cycling.

▲ Skiing is a popular pastime in both countries and attracts many tourists. In Austria, there are around 60 resorts.

SEE ALSO
Europe

404

TASTE AND SMELL

Taste and smell are two of our five main senses. They warn us of harmful fumes or rotten food – and also allow us to enjoy a delicious meal.

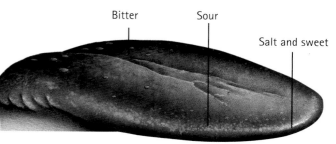

Bitter   Sour   Salt and sweet

▲ There are five tastes: sweet, salty, sour, bitter and umami. The first four are detected by a certain part of the tongue, but umami tastes are sensed throughout.

Smell and taste are called chemosenses as they both work by detecting tiny particles of chemicals. In the case of smell, these particles, called odorants, float in the air that we breathe. In the case of taste, they are flavour particles in food and drinks.

DETECTING SMELLS
When odorant particles land on the sticky liquid, or mucus, at the top of the nose, they touch the hairs of the smell cells. Different smells have differently-shaped particles and the hairs have differently-shaped pits or holes, called receptors. If an odorant particle fits exactly into a receptor, this triggers the smell cell to generate a nerve signal. This passes along the olfactory nerve to the brain, where it is analyzed and identified. Unlike other senses, smell has direct nerve connections with the parts of the brain that deal with memory and emotion. This is why certain aromas, such as seaside air, can arouse strong memories and feelings.

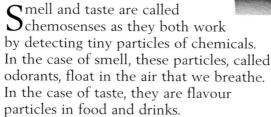

▲ A snake uses its tongue to pick up scents in the air, so it can tell whether a mate, a meal or an enemy is near.

DOWN IN THE MOUTH
The tongue's upper surface has pimple-like protrusions called papillae, which help to grip and move food during chewing. It also has 10,000 microscopic taste buds, scattered mainly between and on the sides of the papillae. A taste bud is a tiny pit containing a ball-shaped cluster of 20 to 30 gustatory (taste) cells, which are arranged like segments of an orange. Flavour particles dissolve in saliva (watery fluid) and, as in the nose, probably fit into receptors on the hairs of the gustatory cells. This triggers nerve signals that travel along two main nerves to the taste centre of the brain for analysis and identification.

TASTING SMELLS
When we eat, the mouth mainly tastes the food, but we also smell it. This is because some odorant particles in the mouth float around the back of the roof of the mouth up into the nasal cavity. There, they are smelled in the same way as odorant particles breathed in through the nose.

NOSE AND MOUTH CELLS
Inside the nose is a two-part chamber called the nasal cavity. The roof of each part has a thumbnail-sized patch of lining which contains about 12 million microscopic olfactory (smell) cells. The tip of each of these cells is covered with 10 to 20 tiny hairs, called cilia. These stick into the thin mucus (sticky liquid) that coats the nasal cavity lining. The gustatory (taste) cells of the tongue's taste buds also have tiny hairs, projecting into the saliva (watery fluid) that coats the tongue.

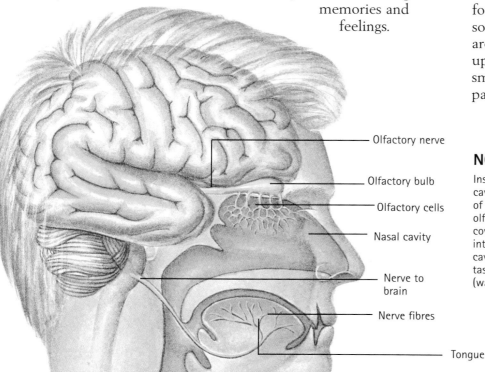

Olfactory nerve

Olfactory bulb

Olfactory cells

Nasal cavity

Nerve to brain

Nerve fibres

Tongue

SEE ALSO
Brain, Cell, Food, Human body

TECHNOLOGY

Technology is the practical use of knowledge to construct things, to make work easier and to make our lives more comfortable. It is also used to cure diseases.

The invention of the wheel meant easier travel, as chariots and carts could carry goods and people.

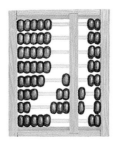

The abacus – a type of early calculator – was widely used in China from around 5000BCE.

No one knows when technology began. The earliest examples – hand-axe flints – are about 250,000 years old. Technology is now advancing very quickly, dramatically changing the way we live.

MATERIALS
Before 6000BCE, wood, bone, hide, stone and shell were used to make things. By controlling fire, ancient peoples could heat ores, such as iron and bronze, to make tools, weapons and jewellery. In India and Egypt, people became skilled at making pottery and glass. Eventually, processed natural materials such as leather, rubber and bricks were developed. Synthetic materials, such as plastics, have been made only since the mid-1800s.

POWER AND PRODUCTION
The invention of the wheel (c. 2000BCE) eventually led to the watermill and the windmill, which provided power for

► The Romans developed expert engineering skills to construct viaducts and aqueducts across valleys.

manufacturing. The steam engine paved the way for the Industrial Revolution. The internal combustion engine of 1876 led to the use of road vehicles. Machines using wheels, gears, cranks and cams were built to carry out repetitive processes such as weaving.

MODERN TECHNOLOGY
Nano technology, using tiny, computerized robots, is allowing us to make ever-smaller and more complex machines. Medical technology, used to help people live longer and healthier lives, includes biotechnology (manipulating cells) and genetic engineering (manipulating genes). Today's technologists must find ways to enrich our lives in ways that respect the Earth's environment and do not cause pollution.

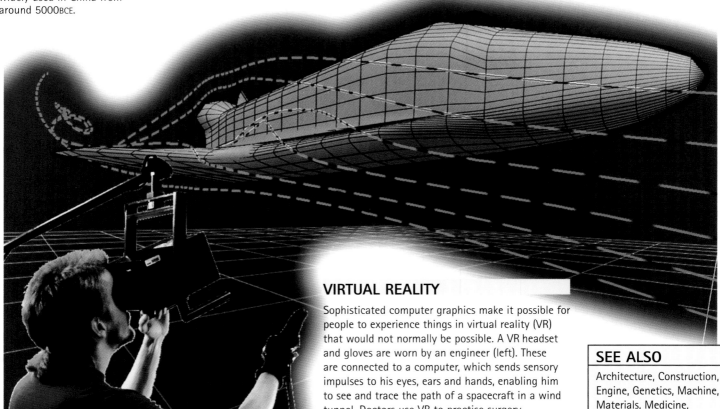

VIRTUAL REALITY
Sophisticated computer graphics make it possible for people to experience things in virtual reality (VR) that would not normally be possible. A VR headset and gloves are worn by an engineer (left). These are connected to a computer, which sends sensory impulses to his eyes, ears and hands, enabling him to see and trace the path of a spacecraft in a wind tunnel. Doctors use VR to practise surgery.

SEE ALSO
Architecture, Construction, Engine, Genetics, Machine, Materials, Medicine, Telecommunication

TEETH

Teeth are hard, bone-like, enamel-coated structures embedded in the jawbones of animals, including humans. They are used mainly for biting and chewing.

Meat-eaters such as the hyena have sharp teeth for tearing and crushing.

The male African savanna elephant's tusk is the largest incisor tooth of any animal.

Snakes have teeth that curve backwards to help pull prey into the throat.

A spider's fangs are hollow and filled with poison for paralyzing its victims.

Teeth are extremely strong and hard-wearing, and are covered with the body's hardest substance – enamel. But to prevent toothache, tooth decay and gum disease, they need regular cleaning.

TYPES OF TEETH

Our four main kinds of teeth do different jobs. Incisors at the front are thin and square-tipped, like a chisel or spade, to slice and bite off food. Next are canines, or eye teeth, which are taller and more pointed in order to tear and rip. Premolars and molars, or cheek teeth, at the back of the mouth, are broad and wide-topped for powerful grinding and chewing.

FIRST SET OF TEETH

Humans grow two sets of teeth. The first set – baby, milk or deciduous teeth – numbers 20. It begins to appear about six months after birth, and is complete by the age of three. Baby teeth consist of two incisors, one canine and two premolars in both the left and right halves of the upper jaw, and the same in the lower jaw.

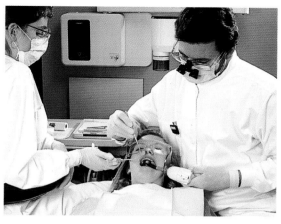

▲ A dentist looks after his patient by diagnosing and treating diseases of the teeth and gums. Regular visits to the dentist help detect problems early.

SECOND SET OF TEETH

From the age of about seven, a child's first teeth loosen and fall out naturally, to be replaced by 32 permanent, or adult, teeth. In each half of each jaw there are two incisors, one canine, two premolars and three molars. The rear molars, or wisdom teeth, are usually the last to erupt, or grow, above the gum, which happens at around the age of 20. In some people they never erupt, staying small and hidden in the jawbone.

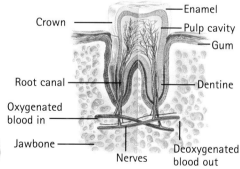

INSIDE THE TOOTH

All teeth have the same basic structure. The upper part, or crown, of the tooth shows above the gum, and the root is in the jawbone. At the base of the crown, soft gum tissue (gingiva) joins to the neck of the tooth. In between the crown and root is the pulp cavity. This contains tiny blood vessels to nourish the tooth, and nerves to detect pressure, temperature and pain. The vessels and nerves pass into the jawbone through a tiny hole, the root canal, at the root's base.

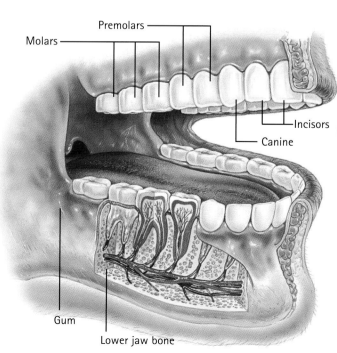

A shark's teeth are serrated and are regularly replaced as they fall out.

SEE ALSO

Elephant, Horse, Human body, Shark, Snake, Spider and scorpion

TELECOMMUNICATION

Telecommunication is the transmission of words, sounds, images or other data over long distances as electronic or electromagnetic signals.

Simple communication systems were already in use in the early 19th century. A code, known as semaphore, that used two moveable arms for each letter and a mirror called a heliograph to flash sunlight, allowed people within sight of each other to send messages.

▲ Semaphore telegraphy became the fastest way to send messages across long distances in the early 19th century.

▲ The first submarine cables were laid between Dover in southern England and Cap Gris-Nez in northern France in 1850.

▲ ATMs, or cashpoints, use telephone lines for fast communication with a cardholder's bank. Once the bank has sent its approval of the cash withdrawal, the ATM dispenses the money.

ELECTRIC PULSES
The electric telegraph allowed coded messages to be sent much farther than ever before, as pulses of electric current along copper wires. It was invented in Britain in 1837 by William Cooke and Charles Wheatstone and was soon used by railway companies. Developed at the same time, Samuel Morse's American telegraph system used coded pulses to transmit messages from place to place. The dots and dashes of the Morse code were internationally recognized right up until 1997.

MESSAGES WITHOUT WIRES
In 1876, Alexander Graham Bell discovered how to send the human voice along wires. In doing so, he invented the telephone. Later, by using the discoveries about electromagnetic waves made by German physicist Heinrich Hertz in 1894, the Italian inventor Guglielmo Marconi made a 'wireless' telegraph. Sending messages as radio waves, Marconi linked telegraph operators on opposite sides of the Atlantic Ocean in 1901. As the use of radio developed, speech, and later pictures as well, could be transmitted. Today, high-frequency microwave radio signals can carry tens of thousands of telephone conversations, text messages, emails, Internet chats and tweets all at the same time, as well as television and data signals.

AROUND THE WORLD IN SECONDS
Microwave radio signals travel in straight lines, so they need to be passed along by relay stations in order for them to carried smoothly around the curve of the Earth's surface. The British science fiction writer

▲ The invention of radio in 1901 helped police and armed forces keep in contact with staff working outside.

Arthur C. Clarke came up with an ingenious solution to the problem in 1945. He suggested putting the relay equipment onto satellites which could orbit the Earth every 24 hours, staying fixed in one point in the sky 36,000km above the ground. His dream become a reality in 1964, when the first geostationary satellite *Syncom 3* was successfully launched and put into orbit. Complete networks of satellites and ground stations can now link any two places on the Earth almost instantly.

TOO MUCH INFORMATION?
The kinds and amount of information being carried by telecommunication systems is increasing all the time. The conversion of voice, sound and pictures into digital code allows increasingly more

▲ Fax (facsimile) machines sent words and images down telephone lines. They were first demonstrated in 1902 and in use by the 1920s. Today, however, they have largely been replaced by paperless email communication.

THROUGH THE CABLES
Multimode fibres have glass cores which can carry several light messages at once over short distances.

Outer sheath
Filter
Fibre
Cushion

Satellite

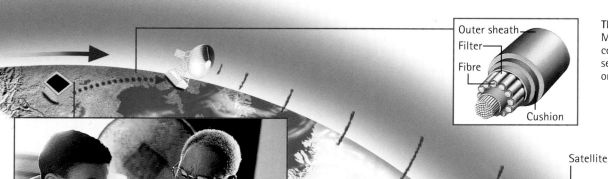

▲ Improvements in technology mean that email can now zip between continents in a matter of seconds.

CHATTING ELECTRONICALLY

The rapid growth of the Internet has revolutionized the telecommunication industry. An electronic mail (email) message sent from one country to another can travel by a variety of routes. Here, it travels from the computer by fibre-optic cable, then by microwaves relayed by a satellite. It finishes its journey by cable.

Ground station transmits and receives signals

information to be carried across continents and seas, and this information travels almost instantaneously. Today, fibre-optic cables made of bundles of fine glass fibres are used to transmit telephone calls. A caller's voice is changed into digital signals and carried as rapidly flashing pulses of laser light. Fibre-optic cables channel light round corners and can carry far more digital information than the copper wires that carry analogue signals.

INFORMATION SQUEEZE

It has become possible to squeeze more information through existing networks by compression. The capacity, or bandwidth, of the networks is increased, and this helps to ease the flow of data while new networks are designed and built. A purely digital system called ISDN (Integrated-Services Digital Network) began operating in Japan in 1988 and has since been adopted by many countries.

FAST FACTS

- Worldwide, there are about 1.3 billion fixed landlines and more than 4.6 billion mobile phone subscriptions

- Cable carries 90% of all Internet traffic

- More than three quarters of people in the USA are Internet users

- About 2.8 million emails are sent every second

▲ By checking her electronic mailbox, this user can receive any mail and reply immediately. There is no rushing out to catch the post.

SEE ALSO

Communication, Computer, Internet, Laser, Satellite, Telephone

TELEPHONE

Telephones are instruments for communicating over long distances. They send speech to another location as electric currents, laser light or radio waves.

Alexander Graham Bell's prototype telephone (1876) had an exposed coil, electromagnet and wires.

The telephone of 1919 had a body with a mouthpiece, a rotary number dial and a separate earpiece.

Mobile phones are small and portable. They allow people to communicate while on the move.

The telephone was invented in 1876 by the Scottish engineer Alexander Graham Bell (1847–1922). He had been working in the United States on improvements to the telegraph, which could only send Morse code dots and dashes. By 1880, the first public telephone systems were in use, although at first they had very few subscribers.

GETTING CONNECTED

Early telephones were connected by wires to a telephone exchange, where operators connected one line to another by hand. The invention of automatic switches in the 1890s allowed exchanges to connect calls without going through an operator. Modern telephone systems change the varying electrical signal of older telephones into a digital signal made up of pulses that are handled by computerized exchanges, removing the need for mechanical switches.

HOW DOES A TELEPHONE WORK?

A telephone handset has a mouthpiece and an earpiece. When a caller speaks, sound waves made by their voice hit a diaphragm (thin metal disc) in the mouthpiece, making it vibrate. This pushes against carbon grains, making their resistance to an electric current flowing through them vary in a pattern that copies the sound wave pattern. At the receiver's end, this current causes an electromagnet to make the diaphragm in their earpiece vibrate. This makes sound waves that reproduce the sound of the caller talking.

▲ Until the early 1900s, telephone operators connected phone calls manually through a switchboard. A caller gave the operator the number; the operator then connected the caller's line to the line of the person being called.

SENDING THE SIGNAL

Calls can be sent around the world as radio signals relayed by satellites, or digital signals can be sent as pulses of laser light along fibre-optic cables under the oceans. The fibre-optic cables can carry thousands of calls at once. Mobile, or cellular, phones use microwave radio frequencies to connect to nearby transceivers, which transmit and receive calls in a network.

NEW TECHNOLOGY

Phones are becoming even more useful as the technologies of telephones and computers mix. Internet access, email and video telephones, which display images of the caller, are all possible from a small, mobile handset using digital technology.

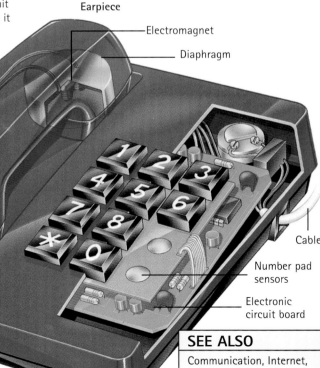

Earpiece

Electromagnet

Diaphragm

Mouthpiece

Cable

Number pad sensors

Electronic circuit board

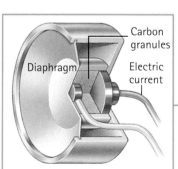

Diaphragm

Carbon granules

Electric current

◄ Sound waves vibrate the diaphragm, compressing carbon granules to alter the flow of electricity and send the caller's voice.

SEE ALSO
Communication, Internet, Laser, Light, Sound, Telecommunication

TELESCOPE

Telescopes are instruments for studying objects that are far away. Astronomers use various kinds of telescope to find out more about stars and planets.

Sir Isaac Newton (1642–1727) invented a reflecting telescope that used curved mirrors to reflect light.

Galileo (1564–1642) used this telescope to view the phases of Venus and the moons of Jupiter.

William Herschel (1738–1822) built a reflector with an aperture of 120cm to study faint objects.

Edwin Hubble (1889–1953) used this 2.4-m reflector to discover the expansion of the universe.

The Hubble Space Telescope orbits Earth and sends back pictures from the farthest parts of the universe.

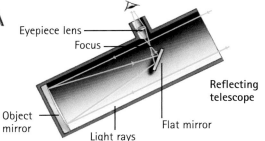

Object lens

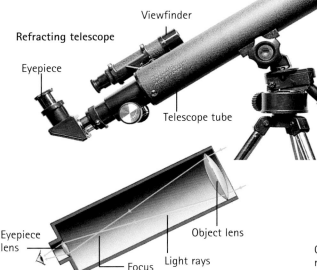

Refracting telescope

Viewfinder

Eyepiece

Telescope tube

Eyepiece lens

Object lens

Focus

Light rays

OPTICAL TELESCOPES

The two main types of optical telescope are refractors and reflectors. Refractors, such as the Simmons 100X magnification telescope, use a lens to form an upside-down image. Reflectors have a large, curved mirror instead of a lens. The mirror gathers light, which is reflected off a second mirror into the eyepiece. The image seen is right side up.

Eyepiece lens

Focus

Reflecting telescope

Object mirror

Flat mirror

Light rays

The first telescope was built by a Dutch scientist called Hans Lippershey (c. 1570–1619) in 1608. It was an optical telescope, with glass lenses that made distant objects appear larger.

REFRACTING TELESCOPES

Refractors have two lenses. A large lens at the front of the telescope, called the objective, collects light. A small eyepiece lens focuses the light into the observer's eye. Galileo used this kind of telescope in 1609 to look at the Moon, which he could see 30 times more clearly than before.

REFLECTING TELESCOPES

Modern astronomers mainly use reflectors, which have a big, curved mirror to collect light, and a small, flat mirror to shine the light through an eyepiece lens. The first reflector, built by Isaac Newton in 1668, used a primary mirror only 7.5cm wide. Modern reflectors use bigger mirrors. The Keck telescope in Hawaii has 36 six-sided mirrors joined together to make a mirror 10m across. Its images are viewed on a computer screen or camera film.

SEEING THE UNSEEN

Light reaching us from distant parts of the universe is very faint, and the Earth's

atmosphere blurs what we can see through optical telescopes. To record faint images, astronomers use electronic detectors called charged-coupled devices (CCDs) instead of their eyes. The Hubble Space Telescope (HST) orbits high above the Earth's atmosphere, so the light it collects is not distorted. Radio, X-ray, infrared, gamma-ray and microwave telescopes collect other kinds of energy radiating from stars and galaxies that we cannot see with our eyes.

▲ The Hanbury Brown radio telescope in New South Wales, Australia picks up long-wavelength radio waves from space.

SEE ALSO
Astronomy, Lens, Radio, Satellite, Wavelength, X-ray

TELEVISION

Television (TV) is the transmission of pictures and sound from one place to another. It is one of the most important means of mass communication in the world.

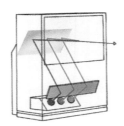

John Logie Baird's 1926 television system used lenses set in revolving discs to scan an object.

The first regular high-quality television broadcasts began in 1936, from Alexandra Palace in London. Several scientists had worked on developing television, including the Scot John Logie Baird and Americans Vladimir Zworykin and Philo Farnsworth.

Some large-screen televisions use a back projection system with mirrors to enlarge the image.

IN THE PICTURE
Television pictures are made up of electronic signals produced by a camera and recreated by a television set. A TV camera has lenses which focus the picture onto a surface that converts light to electronic signals. These can be recorded for later transmission. The signals can be turned into radio waves, to be broadcast from radio transmitters, beamed via a satellite or sent along cable networks directly to the TV sets in homes.

▲ A Serb army officer stops a TV news crew from filming during the Bosnian crisis of 1995. Television is a powerful media tool which many governments try to control.

MAKING A TV PROGRAMME
Producing a TV show is a team effort. Camera operators take the pictures, while mike boom operators keep microphones in position. The director in a control room cuts from one camera to another. There are also script writers, make-up artists, costume designers, caterers, lighting crews, post-production teams and technical staff.

TV TODAY
Most of today's televisions use either liquid crystal displays (LCDs) or plasma screens. These screens can be very large, but are also light and thin enough to mount on a wall. They give very sharp images – especially when showing programmes on High Definition TV (HDTV) channels.

HOW TELEVISION WORKS
Light detectors in a TV camera convert light into electronic signals, which are processed before being transmitted as radio waves to a television receiver. The TV camera will also convey sound information to the receiver. The television set displays the transmitted information, displaying moving pictures on its screen and producing sound from its speakers. An LCD television contains tiny crystals with light behind them. The crystals twist when electricity is applied and this allows light to shine through them onto the screen.

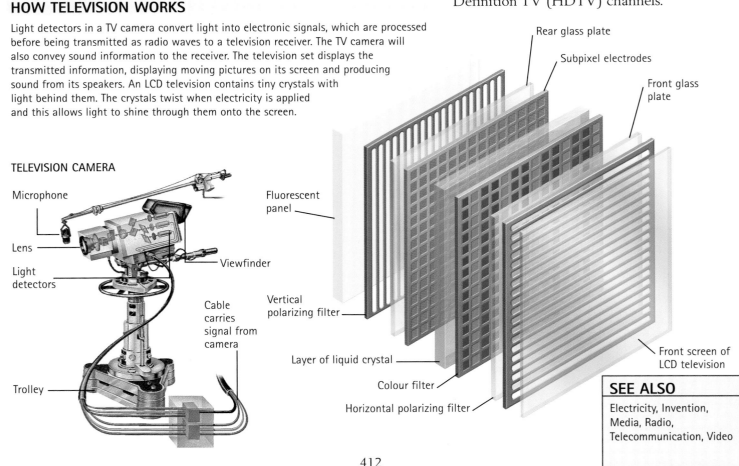

TELEVISION CAMERA

Microphone
Lens
Light detectors
Viewfinder
Cable carries signal from camera
Trolley

Rear glass plate
Subpixel electrodes
Front glass plate
Fluorescent panel
Vertical polarizing filter
Layer of liquid crystal
Colour filter
Horizontal polarizing filter
Front screen of LCD television

SEE ALSO
Electricity, Invention, Media, Radio, Telecommunication, Video

TEXTILE

The word textile means 'to weave' and the first textiles were all woven. Now they can be created from natural fibres or manufactured using chemical processes.

▲ A Chinese woman weaves silk on a hand loom. Woven fabrics use two sets of yarns: one lengthwise (the warp) and one crosswise (the weft).

▲ Cotton machines in a Ugandan factory. The raw cotton has been arranged into long fibres and coiled. The fibres are twisted into yarn and woven.

Originally, textiles were fabrics made by spinning natural fibres into threads and then weaving them together on a loom. Modern textiles are also produced by other methods such as knitting (using a single yarn or set of loops) or felting (matting fibres together by heat and pressure) and include such materials as lace, braid and net.

GROWING MATERIALS

The five most important natural fibres are wool, cotton, silk, linen and jute. Wool comes from sheep, goats or llamas; cotton has been grown in Egypt and India since ancient times, and silk was first made in Ancient China. Linen, made from the flax plant, is used for shirts, sheets and table napkins, and jute, which grows best in India and Bangladesh, is used to make sacks, matting, ropes and twine.

WEARING CHEMICALS

The chemical industry produces synthetic (artificial) fibres such as nylon and acrylic, which can be made stronger, cheaper, more elastic and easier to wash than natural fibres. These include neoprene, a synthetic rubber used in wet suits, Gore-Tex, a waterproof fabric used in climbing and outdoor clothing and stretchy nylon Lycra, used in everyday casual wear.

▲ Tapestries are textile art. They are woven in different colour threads to create a picture. Some tell a story. The Bayeux Tapestry recounts the Battle of Hastings in 1066.

FROM HOME TO FACTORY

Textile-making has often made great use of women's labour. Weaving was traditionally practised at home and still is in many parts of the world. Textile-making was the first industry to be completely mechanized, starting with cotton in Britain in the 18th century. Modern textile machinery is often computer-controlled to produce intricate designs.

A WAY OF LIFE

Many areas of the world have depended on textiles for employment. Special types of cloth, such as denim, duffel, muslin and chantilly, take their names from the towns which specialized in making them. Making rugs and carpets is still a major industry in countries such as Turkey, Iran, Afghanistan and Pakistan. Indonesia is famous for a resist-dyeing process called batik.

TEXTILE USE

The largest demand for textiles comes from the clothing industry, but they are also used for upholstery, sports and car accessories.

◀ In a factory, textile patterns are printed using rollers on a rotary printer – each prints a single colour. Some textiles are still hand-printed by batik or screen printing.

▶ A young child makes a traditional Jaipur carpet in India. He pulls threads through using a hand tool.

SEE ALSO
Clothing, Design, Paint and dye, Printing, Technology

THEATRE

Theatre is the production of a drama, comedy, music or other artistic performance in front of an audience. It usually takes place in a specially designed building.

Sophocles (c. 496–406BCE) wrote 123 tragedies in Ancient Greece.

William Shakespeare (1564–1616) was England's finest playwright.

Okuni (c.1620) established the Japanese style of theatre called *Kabuki*.

Molière (1622–73) created a new kind of comedy in the French theatre.

Irishman Samuel Beckett (1906–89) wrote abstract, philosophical plays.

Tennessee Williams (1911–83) wrote tense plays about the southern USA.

THE GLOBE THEATRE

The Globe opened in London in May 1599. The circular structure was built of wood and up to 3,000 people sat in galleries or stood around the protruding stage in an area known as the pit. William Shakespeare wrote exclusively for his own theatre company, and many of his plays had their first showing at the Globe. He not only wrote the plays, but also acted in some of them. Entry to a performance cost one penny to stand in the pit, two to sit in the gallery.

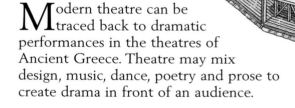

Modern theatre can be traced back to dramatic performances in the theatres of Ancient Greece. Theatre may mix design, music, dance, poetry and prose to create drama in front of an audience.

ANCIENT PLAYS

The Ancient Greeks established both tragedy and comedy. In Greek theatre, the chorus (a group of singers) chanted the story, while the actors mimed their roles. At first, the audience sat on hillsides and the action took place on a level space known as the orchestra. By 450BCE, theatres with banks of stone benches for the audience, like the one at Epidaurus, had been constructed. The Romans added an elaborate 'scene house', which provided backdrop scenery for the action. In front of this there was a stage that was raised above the orchestra, as in modern theatres.

REVIVAL IN EUROPE

During the Middle Ages, theatre in Europe almost ceased to exist. In the 16th century, William Shakespeare and others led a revival. All the roles were played by men and boys, not women. Actresses first appeared in Europe with the Italian travelling players performing *commedia dell'arte* – plays with themes of love and intrigue using familiar characters. In Japan, actors developed the formal *No* and popular *Kabuki* plays.

ARCHES AND STAGES

In the 1590s, English theatres were circular wooden buildings with an open stage. In the 17th century, the proscenium arch – a frame around the front of the stage – was introduced. This masked the areas where actors or scene shifters waited. The most important figure of 18th-century European theatre was David Garrick (1717–79), an actor-manager who put on new plays, as well as works by Shakespeare.

MUSIC HALL AND DRAMA

Increasingly popular in the 19th century was music hall, known as vaudeville in North America. These shows had actors, singers and comedians performing to enthusiastic and noisy audiences. Opera (drama in which the actors sing) and ballet (dance-drama) also flourished in the 19th century. At the same time, electric lighting, larger sets, revolving stages and exciting special effects with water, smoke and illusions developed. Productions became so elaborate that, by 1910, some directors preferred a simple approach with little scenery. New ideas included the open-thrust stage, which projected forwards, theatre in the round (with the audience all around the stage) and open-air theatre.

THEATRE TODAY

Modern theatre productions involve a team of backstage people – designers, set-builders, technicians, wardrobe and make-up artists, as well as the actors and director. Professional theatres offer the latest electronic gadgetry, lighting and sound systems, although plays are still performed very successfully by amateurs in small halls and schools. The Ancient Greek theatre of Epidaurus continues to stage classic Greek dramas, while in London, the reconstructed Globe Theatre offers modern audiences the opportunity to experience Shakespeare's plays as they were originally performed.

THE 'MET'

There has been a Metropolitan Opera House, known as the 'Met', in New York City since 1833. The New House at Lincoln Center opened in 1966 and presents both opera and ballet. Each time a performance is put on, the theatre employs a team of about 1,000 people.

▲These Indian puppets are three metres high. They are used in dramatic performances to tell tales of love and bravery.

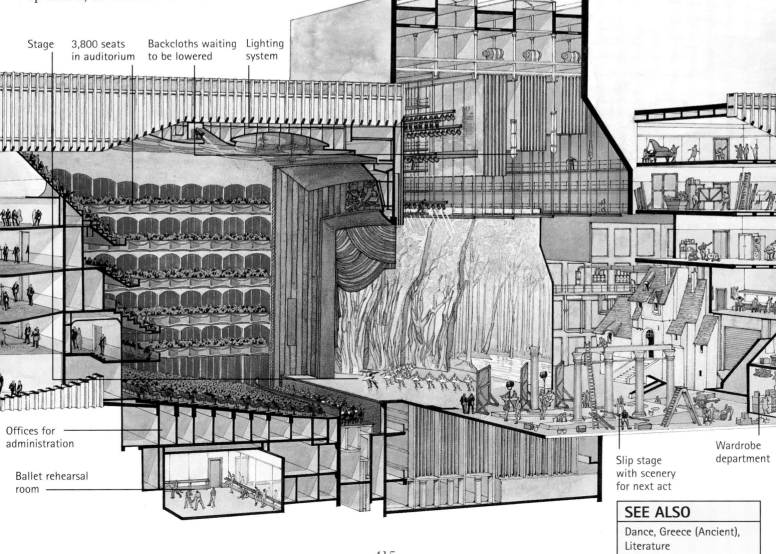

Stage   3,800 seats in auditorium   Backcloths waiting to be lowered   Lighting system

Offices for administration

Ballet rehearsal room

Slip stage with scenery for next act

Wardrobe department

SEE ALSO

Dance, Greece (Ancient), Literature

TIGER AND OTHER BIG CATS

Tigers, lions and leopards belong to a group of the cat family known as 'big cats'. The cat family also includes many smaller wild cats, as well as the domesticated cat.

▲ Although not classed as a 'big cat', the puma is as big as a leopard. Also known as the cougar, mountain lion and panther, it ranges through the Americas and eats a varied menu, from deer to rabbits and birds.

The cheetah is the only cat to outrun its prey rather than stalk it.

A panther is a natural, black-furred variation of a leopard or jaguar.

The lynx is a wild cat that lives in the forests of Asia, Europe and North America.

Tigers belong to the cat family (*Felidae*). So do four other kinds of big cat – lions, jaguars, leopards and snow leopards. The cat family also includes about 35 kinds of smaller wild cat, from the cheetah, puma, bobcat and lynx down to the smaller margay, kodkod and sandcat. The black-footed cat of southern Africa is even smaller than a domesticated cat.

CAT FEATURES

All cats are meat-eaters, members of the carnivore group. They live by hunting, although a few scavenge dead meat. They have keen senses, with excellent sight even at night-time, and amazing balance for climbing. Long whiskers feel the way in darkness. The cat's body is lithe and agile, with stealthy movements. The fur is striped, spotted or patterned for camouflage, so the cat can creep silently and unseen. Long claws grip, scratch and slash, and can be pulled or retracted into the toe-tips, keeping them sharp. Long, sharp teeth bite and tear flesh.

NIGHT HUNTER

Like other cats, the tiger hunts mainly at twilight or night. It prefers dense, swampy forest and ambushes deer, wild pigs, wild cattle, and the occasional baby elephant or rhino. Very rarely, a tiger preys on people. The record-holding 'man-eater' killed over 400 people.

BIGGEST OF THE BIG CATS

Tigers live across India, on some islands of Indonesia and in parts of China. Siberian tigers of Manchuria are huge and powerful predators, up to 4m long from nose to tail and weighing more than 300kg. Like most cats, tigers live alone. They are only together when mating, or when a mother is with her cubs.

▲ Lions are the only cats that live and hunt in groups (or prides). The lionesses do the hunting, usually at night. One lioness stalks the prey, driving it towards the other lionesses who lie in wait. The adult male does not join in, but claims a share of the kill. Lions sleep during the day.

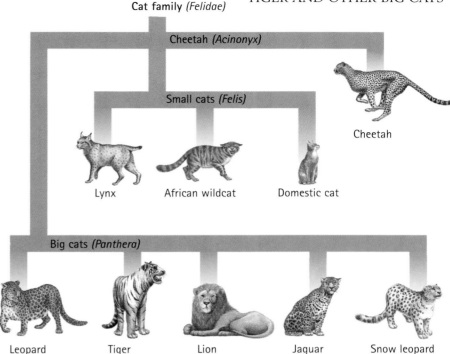

Cat family (Felidae)

Cheetah (Acinonyx)

Small cats (Felis)

Cheetah

Lynx

African wildcat

Domestic cat

Big cats (Panthera)

Leopard

Tiger

Lion

Jaguar

Snow leopard

THE LEOPARD

The leopard is the most widespread big cat, ranging across Africa and Southern Asia, into China and Indonesia. It is adaptable, too, living in high hills, deserts, scrub, rainforests, and even near towns and villages. Leopards eat a wide variety of prey and will drag a carcass into a tree to store it away from scavengers. The rare snow leopard, or ounce, lives in the Himalayas and nearby mountains. It has long, thick, pale fur for warmth and camouflage.

THE CHEETAH

This lean, long-legged cat is the fastest land animal. It sprints at almost 100km/h after swift prey such as antelope, hares and even young ostriches. It has spotted fur and a long tail to help it balance and turn at speed. The cheetah is the only cat that cannot retract its claws. For this reason, it is classed on its own in the cat family.

THE LION

Prides of lions can be found only in protected areas south of the Sahara Desert in Africa and in the Gir forest, a wildlife sanctuary in India. They live in open, grassy plains where water is available and are territorial, fiercely protecting their hunting ground, where they stalk zebras, wildebeest and antelope.

THE CAT FAMILY

The cat family is divided into three groups. The *Panthera* group is made up of the five big cats: the leopard, tiger, lion, jaguar and snow leopard. The *Felis* group includes the domestic cat, as well as about another 34 types of small cat. The cheetah forms a group of its own.

THE JAGUAR

The only American big cat, the muscular jaguar is found in the southern USA and in Central and South America. With its spotted coat, it resembles a leopard, but is larger and more powerful, weighing about 100kg. Jaguars like thick forests with swamps, lakes and rivers. They are excellent swimmers.

▼ The leopard has a full body length of about 150cm. As with most cats, the males are larger than the females, at 60–70kg. The leopard's larger spots are not single black patches, but circular groups, or rosettes.

SEE ALSO
Animal, Cat, Mammal

TIME

We use time to track the passing of days, in hours, minutes and seconds. In addition to natural units of time, people have invented other ways to measure it.

One day

One day is exactly the time it takes for the Earth to revolve on its axis once.

One year

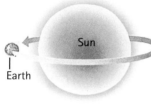

One year is approximately the time it takes for the Earth to orbit the Sun.

One lunar month

A month is based roughly on the time it takes the Moon to orbit the Earth.

When you need to know the time, you look at a watch or clock. This tells you how many hours and minutes it is since noon (midday) or midnight. For example, if your watch says the time is exactly 3:30 ('half past three') in the afternoon, you know that three hours and thirty minutes have passed since noon. If your watch is very precise, it may also tell you how many seconds have passed.

DAYS

The measurement of time is based on the position of the Sun in the sky. Every day, the Sun seems to rise at dawn, move across the sky, then set at dusk. This happens because the Earth is continually spinning around. Each place on Earth can only see the Sun for part of the day; when the Sun is out of view, it is night-time in that part of the world. The Sun appears to rise as it comes into view and set as it disappears again. At one moment in the day, each place faces the Sun directly. When this happens, the Sun is highest in the sky and the daylight is brightest (on a sunny day).

▲ The Greenwich Observatory, England, is the place where astronomers first devised the Greenwich meridian in 1866. This is the line at zero longitude that divides east from west; time zones are still calculated from it.

HOURS

As early as 2400BCE, the Babylonians divided the day into 24 equal parts, called hours. The modern day starts at midnight, a time when the sky is dark in most areas. A few hours later, the Sun rises. Twelve hours after midnight it is noon, the time when the Sun is highest. In another 12 hours, it is midnight again.

CALENDARS

Every civilization has used some kind of calendar to keep track of years, months, weeks and days. Calendars are used to plan planting and harvesting, but also to mark special holidays and festivals. The Julian calendar was instituted by Julius Caesar in 46BCE. Pope Gregory XIII (1502–85) adjusted it in 1582, and his Gregorian calendar is still used in Western countries today. The Chinese calendar is lunar, with a 60-year cycle, but the Chinese use the Western calendar, too. The Jewish calendar is a combines solar and lunar cycles, and has 12 or 13 months.

CALENDARS OF THE AMERICAS

The Aztecs of Central America made a calendar in the ground from a huge stone shaped liked the Sun. The face of the Sun god, Tezcatlipoca, was carved in the middle, and signs for the days were carved around the edges. The Maya – also of Central America – used a calendar with two interlocking cog-wheels to represent circular time. Native American tribes in North America kept track of time by watching the seasons and phases of the Moon.

THE AZTEC CALENDAR

TIME ZONES

Because the Earth is spinning, different places on Earth face the Sun at different times of day. When it is midday in London, UK, it is dawn in New York, USA, and in Adelaide, Australia, it is still night. If people read the time directly from the Sun's position, watches worldwide would be set to thousands of different times. Chaos would result; for example, it would be impossible to write accurate train timetables.

GREENWICH MEAN TIME

To get around this timing problem, governments approximate time by dividing the world into 24 time zones. These zones follow the Earth's longitude lines, and are based on Greenwich Mean Time (GMT), the time at Greenwich, UK. Tokyo, Japan is nine hours ahead of GMT, so when it is 2:00 am in Greenwich, it is 11:00 am in Tokyo.

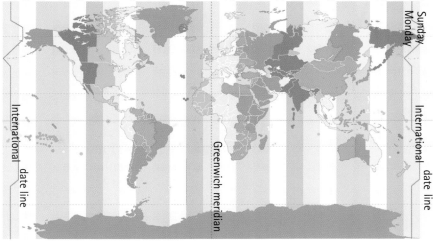

Hours -12-11-10 -9 -8 -7 -6 -5 -4 -3 -2 -1 0 +1 +2 +3 +4 +5 +6 +7 +8 +9 +10 +11 +12

International date line

Greenwich meridian

Sunday Monday

International date line

▲ The world is divided into 24 time zones, centred on the prime meridian at Greenwich, UK. Each zone west of the meridian is an hour earlier than the last; each zone to the east is one hour ahead.

THE FOURTH DIMENSION

All objects have three dimensions: width, height and breadth (the dimensions of space). Scientists believe that objects also have a fourth dimension: time. Every day, we move through the four dimensions (called space time). We can move in all directions through space (up and down, or from side to side); however, it is believed that we can only move forward through time. Many science fiction writers have played with the idea that time travel into the future (or into the past) is possible.

▼ Stonehenge in England (begun c. 2700BCE) is a stone circle thought to have been used as an astronomical observatory and calendar. Its axis was aligned with midsummer sunrise (June 21), which suggests it was used to track the movements of the Sun, Moon and planets.

▲ H. G. Wells' (1866–1946) remarkable science fiction novel, *The Time Machine* (1895), tells the story of a man who builds a machine that carries him into the future. In the 1960 film above, the machine vanishes forward in time without its maker.

▲ The giant Sun clock in New Delhi, India tells the time as the Sun casts shadows on graduated markings.

SEE ALSO

Astronomy, Clock, Earth, Moon, Navigation, Season, Star, Sun

TOUCH

Touch is one of the body's five main senses. It allows us to detect not only physical contact, but also temperature, pressure, heat, cold and pain.

▲ Touch sensors are packed closer together in places such as the lips and fingertips, with hundreds in a pin-head-sized area. These body parts are most sensitive to touch.

Touch can distinguish between light and heavy pressure and between things that are soft and hard, cold and hot, dry and wet, rough and smooth, still and moving. From this variety of information, we build up an impression of what our skin comes into contact with – from a cold, slippery ice cube to a warm, furry kitten.

TOUCH SENSORS

There are millions of microscopic sensors in the skin. Each is the specialized ending of a nerve fibre. When stimulated, the sensor sends bursts of nerve signals along its fibre to the brain. Touch sensors are all over the body in the skin. Hairs are mostly dead, so they cannot feel. But touch sensors are

▲ Braille is a special raised-dot type system that enables blind people to read with their fingertips. The system was invented by Louis Braille (1809–52).

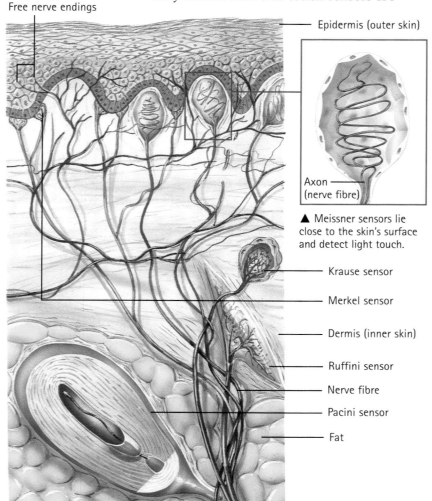

Free nerve endings

Epidermis (outer skin)

Axon (nerve fibre)

▲ Meissner sensors lie close to the skin's surface and detect light touch.

Krause sensor

Merkel sensor

Dermis (inner skin)

Ruffini sensor

Nerve fibre

Pacini sensor

Fat

wrapped around each hair root. When the hair is rocked or tilted, the sensors send out nerve signals. Similarly, nails are dead but have touch sensors in the skin underneath.

TYPES OF SENSOR

There are different types of touch sensor. Merkel sensors are tiny discs in the base of the skin's upper layer, or epidermis. Meissner sensors are slightly larger and egg-shaped, in the upper part of the skin's lower layer, or dermis. Krause sensors, also egg-shaped, and Ruffini sensors, larger and sausage-like, are in the middle of the dermis. Pacini sensors are multi-layered, like onions. At up to 1mm long, they are the largest sensors and are just visible to the naked eye. The most numerous sensors are free nerve endings, each one resembling a tiny, many-branched tree.

WHAT DO THEY DETECT?

Some types of sensor respond better to certain kinds of touch. Meissner and Merkel sensors detect light touch, while Pacini sensors respond better to heavier pressure. Ruffini sensors pick up vibrations well. But in daily life, most types of sensor respond to most kinds of touch. Free nerve endings, which are the most widespread, respond to almost any kind of touch, including heat and cold, as well as the great pressure and damage that cause pain.

SEE ALSO
Brain, Skin and hair

420

TRADE

Trade is the buying and selling of goods. It takes place between individuals or companies, but the largest exchanges take place between different countries.

International trade allows countries to exchange what they have for what they need. A country with plenty of farmland, but no coal mines can export (sell abroad) food and import (buy in) coal. Some countries specialize in one product, others produce a variety of goods and services.

During the Renaissance (1400–1600), trade in Europe increased greatly until it overtook farming as a source of wealth.

VISIBLES AND INVISIBLES
International trade is divided into visible and invisible trade. Most goods, such as food, computers and washing machines, which are moved from one country to another are visibles. Invisibles include banking charges, insurance policies and people spending money on holiday. Some countries, such as Switzerland and Britain, rely heavily on invisible trade.

PROTECTION
Some countries limit import trade to try to protect jobs and industries at home.

▲ A customs officer uses a dog to sniff out smuggled goods. People sometimes try to smuggle in goods that are illegal or will be heavily taxed.

A special tax, called a tariff, may be placed on imported goods, or a limit set on imports. This is known as protection.

LAISSEZ FAIRE
Free trade, also known as laissez faire, means that people are free to import or export without restrictions or tariffs. A laissez faire policy encourages trade and is believed to increase employment and wealth. International trading organizations, such as the European Union (EU) and the North American Free Trade Agreement (NAFTA), establish free trade between member states. The World Trade Organization works to reduce trade barriers between all countries.

BALANCE OF PAYMENTS
The difference between the money coming into and going out of a country (both for visible and invisible items) is called the balance of payments. Large amounts of money or goods continually flowing in one direction may damage the economy of the country. If the value of the nation's currency is allowed to fall or rise, it affects the price of imports and exports and helps to bring the balance of payments back to zero.

◄ Most visible trade is carried out by sea. Ships transport goods relatively cheaply, using large, packed containers. Goods that need to be moved quickly are carried by aircraft.

SEE ALSO
Explorer, Great Depression, Industry, Money, Slavery, Transport

TRAIN

Trains are lines of coaches or wagons pulled along a steel track by an engine. They are used for transporting goods or people above or below ground at speed.

The fastest steam train was the *Mallard* at 201km/h.

The first diesel train was built in Germany in 1912.

Diesel locomotives haul heavy goods trains.

Subway trains carry people beneath crowded cities.

Rack and pinion railways climb steep slopes up hills.

Trains were developed during the Industrial Revolution in the 18th century. At first, horses were used to pull trucks carrying heavy loads along simple metal tracks at mines and factories. Later, steam engines mounted on wheels were developed, and these were used to link cities with one another and achieved much higher speeds.

GETTING GOING
In 1802, the British engineer Richard Trevithick patented a high-pressure steam engine mounted on wheels. Later, in 1825, the British engineer George Stephenson overcame problems with engine power and track-laying to build the Stockton and Darlington Railway. He went on to build the Liverpool to Manchester line in 1829.

STEAM TRAINS
After the success of George Stephenson's Liverpool to Manchester Railway, trains quickly became extremely successful and popular for moving both freight and passengers.. At the time, there were few proper roads and no powered vehicles to run on them. By 1900, most of the developed countries of the world had built extensive networks of railway lines that were able to carry millions of passengers and a great deal of freight.

STEEL ON STEEL
Most modern trains have steel wheels which run on twin steel rails. This arrangement means that resistance

▲ On February 21, 1804, Cornish engineer Richard Trevithick won a bet when he built the first steam locomotive able to haul 10 tons of freight over 10 miles (16km).

to the motion is small, so that a heavy train can be propelled using relatively little power. It also means there is no need to worry about steering the train, since it will always follow the rails. A railway line therefore needs to be only centimetres wider than the widest train that is intended to pass along it.

UNDERGROUND RAILWAYS
Many cities have railways running in tunnels under their streets. These ease congestion and move people at speed. The first underground railway was the Metropolitan, which opened in London, England, in 1863. The smoke from the steam engines underground caused problems, so later lines used electric trains. Other cities began building underground railways – Boston in 1895, Budapest in 1896, Paris in 1898 and the subway system in New York in 1904.

▼ In 1981, the French national railways introduced the TGV, or *Train à Grande Vitesse* – a high-speed train service between major cities. Today it is the fastest train in the world, reaching 320km/h on its eastern line. On test lines it has travelled even faster - its record was more than 570km/h.

RAIL SYSTEMS

Trains run on a number of tracks, switching from one track to another at points. The points and signals are controlled from a signal box with the aid of computers. The signal controllers keep the lines free for high-speed passenger trains, or express trains, by moving local and freight trains on to side tracks called sidings. Modern trains are either electric or diesel, although steam trains are still used in some countries.

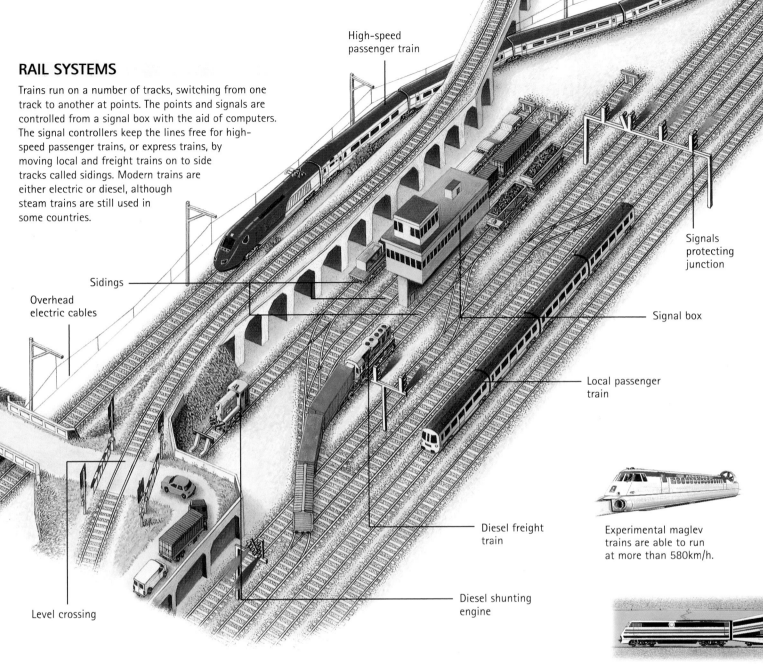

High-speed passenger train

Sidings

Overhead electric cables

Signals protecting junction

Signal box

Local passenger train

Diesel freight train

Diesel shunting engine

Level crossing

Experimental maglev trains are able to run at more than 580km/h.

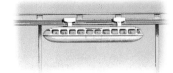

Car drivers can relax while they travel on car trains from country to country.

Monorails have been built in many cities high above the crowded streets.

RAILWAYS DECLINE

In the second half of the 20th century, railways began to lose both passenger and freight traffic to the roads and to the airlines. Railways were not 'flexible' – they could not deliver to everyone's front door as the roads could – and they were very expensive to maintain to the high standard that safety demanded. Trains need long distances for acceleration and braking. This meant that they had to be a long way apart, limiting the number that could use a line. Railways began to lose money. During the 1960s and 1970s, several lines were closed or services cut.

FUTURISTIC DESIGNS

Railway engineers have worked hard to attract passengers and freight back onto the rails. After many years when train speeds remained almost the same, most systems now operate some kind of high-speed train running at 200km/h or more, for example the French TGV. More adventurous designers have eliminated the steel rails altogether. They have used magnets, for example, to lift the train above a track. This 'maglev' system, which has been pioneered in Germany and Japan, allows even higher speeds while at the same time reducing noise.

SEE ALSO

City, Engine, Industrial Revolution, Transport

TRANSPORT

Transport is a means of carrying people, animals or goods from one place to another. This can be by land, water or air, or through space.

Britain's *Flying Scotsman* made the world's longest non-stop run in 1928, from London to Edinburgh.

▲ The Japanese inter-city bullet train can travel up to 300km/h and provides smooth and noiseless transport for thousands of commuters daily.

Humans have always needed transport, to move from place to place and to carry their goods. This is why the earliest civilizations were built alongside rivers. Eventually, people began to ride on horseback to cover long distances more quickly. They also used pack animals and carts to carry goods.

TRADE BY WATER

As civilizations developed, the need for transport continued to grow. Any trading centre close to water built a harbour and began to send heavy goods to other centres by boat. At the same time, vehicles with wheels also became important. But few roads were strong enough to support heavily laden carts. For this reason, right up to the 19th century, water transport, in the form of ships and barges, developed more quickly than land transport, and most of the world's trade went by sea.

STEAM ENGINES

At the end of the 18th century, the first practical steam engine was invented. This gave birth to the steamship and, in the 1820s, railway transport. Railways became so successful that they soon put inland

ON THE ROAD

The first travellers had to carry or drag their belongings. Then they trained animals to carry loads and drag sleds. Around 3500BCE, the Sumerians began to use wheeled carts. From that time and for hundreds of years, people travelled in various types of carriages pulled by animals. However, for many years there were no roads. Since the invention of the motor car, a vast network of roads and motorways has run across countries.

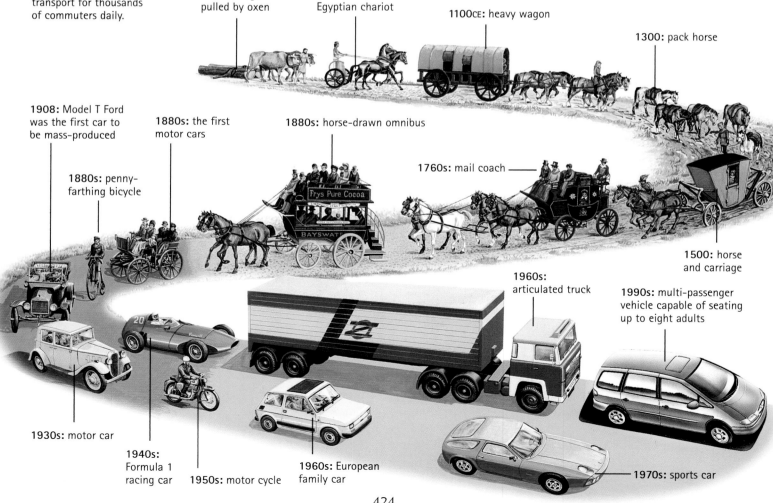

300BCE: logs pulled by oxen

1500BCE: Ancient Egyptian chariot

1100CE: heavy wagon

1300: pack horse

1908: Model T Ford was the first car to be mass-produced

1880s: the first motor cars

1880s: horse-drawn omnibus

1760s: mail coach

1880s: penny-farthing bicycle

1500: horse and carriage

1960s: articulated truck

1990s: multi-passenger vehicle capable of seating up to eight adults

1930s: motor car

1940s: Formula 1 racing car

1950s: motor cycle

1960s: European family car

1970s: sports car

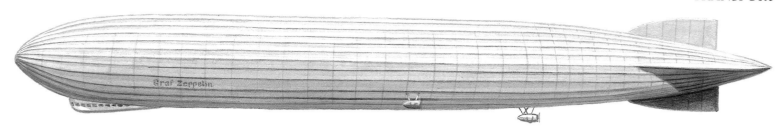

canals out of business. At the same time, larger, faster steamships were carrying more and more passengers and goods across the oceans.

▲ Rigid airships, such as the German Zeppelin, were a successful form of transport in the early 1900s. With a length of 120–240m, they could reach speeds of up to 130km/h.

TRADE BOOM
This progress had the effect of further boosting trade. By the end of the 19th century, the world's major ports were huge places employing thousands of people, and the railways in most countries had been fully extended. Also, networks of metalled (hard-topped) roads were being built. This meant that goods could be delivered from the ports and railway yards directly to the front doors of shops and houses, and people could travel to work. The development of the roads was aided by two inventions: the pneumatic (air-filled) tyre and the internal combustion engine, which, between them, led to the invention of the modern motor vehicle.

▲The largest jet airliners, known as jumbo jets, can carry as many as 850 passengers.

MOTOR TRANSPORT
Roads quickly became the most useful form of transportation. Anyone with a motor vehicle could travel almost anywhere, for business or pleasure. At first, few people could afford a car of their own. During the 1920s, however, cheap motor cars began to be mass-produced, and heavy lorries became much more efficient. By about 1950, road transport had taken a great deal of business away from the railways. In addition, by this time, air transport, with the development of bigger planes and jet engines, was attracting passengers away from ocean-going liners, which had become too expensive to run.

Great ocean liners had six or more decks with luxury extras for passengers such as lifts, suites, ballrooms and swimming pools.

MERCHANT SHIPPING
Today, most short-distance transport – of people or goods – is by road, while almost all long-distance transport is by air and sea. Heavy cargo is usually transported by merchant shipping, which consists of specially built cargo carriers, such as oil tankers, bulk carriers and container ships.

DEATH OF THE RAILWAYS
An increase in air traffic has meant that the role of the railways in many countries has been reduced to carrying people to and from work in city centres. However, the growth of electric underground train systems in many large cities has helped take the strain off street buses and trams, as well as cut down on city pollution.

▲ The daily congested road traffic in cities such as Los Angeles, USA, has become a real global problem because of the pollution it creates and the damage this does to the ozone layer.

The bicycle still remains one of the most efficient means of short-distance transport and in addition causes no pollution.

SEE ALSO
Aircraft, Balloon and airship, Bicycle and motorbike, Boat, Car, Horse, Hovercraft, Road, Ship, Train, Truck and bus

TREE

A tree is a large, upright plant with a single, woody main stem. The biggest trees are among the largest, heaviest and longest-living organisms on Earth.

Trees come in all shapes and sizes, but most are over 6m tall. Some, such as oaks, have a short main trunk that divides into huge, spreading branches. Others, such as redwoods, are tall and conical, with trunks 100m high and 9m thick at the base.

CLASSIFYING TREES

The two main tree families are the conifers, or softwood trees, and the deciduous trees, or hardwoods. Scientists refer to conifers as gymnosperms (meaning 'naked seeds'), because their seeds form on the woody scales that make up their cones. Deciduous trees are called angiosperms ('enclosed seeds'), because their seeds are enclosed inside fruits. Pines, firs, spruces, larches and hemlocks are all conifers – also called evergreens because most keep their thin, needle-shaped leaves throughout the year. Deciduous trees, such as oak, ash, maple, beech, elm and horse chestnut, shed their leaves in the autumn.

TREE PARTS

The three main parts of a tree are its roots, trunk and leaves. The roots take in water and nutrients from the soil. The trunk supports the tree and carries water and nutrients to the leaves through tubes, and food from the leaves back down to the rest of the tree.

The silver birch has pure white bark, often pocked with black marks. It has a tall and elegant shape.

Like the sugar maple, the silver maple is tapped for its syrup. Its five-lobed leaves are deeply toothed.

▲ The horse chestnut has spreading branches, and pink or whitish blossom clusters in spring. Its seed, the conker, is covered in a spiky shell, and its leaves have 5–7 leaflets.

Blossom

Conker

▲ After deciduous trees drop their leaves in the autumn, their bare branches are exposed during the winter.

Bud

Cork layer

Dead leaf

▲ Losing leaves in autumn helps deciduous trees to conserve water in winter. The leaf is sealed off from the stem's food supply near the bud; it dies and falls.

Deciduous trees are ▶ broad-leaved and have spreading crowns and roots, with spring flowers that develop into fruits.

Roots

▶ Acorns are the fruits of the oak tree. On the English oak, they are attached to stalks.

Oak leaf

Acorn

The bark of the oak tree is fissured (ridged) and brownish-grey in colour.

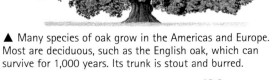

▲ Many species of oak grow in the Americas and Europe. Most are deciduous, such as the English oak, which can survive for 1,000 years. Its trunk is stout and burred.

▲ The banyan tree, native to India, has branches that hang down to the ground and root themselves. On one banyan in Sri Lanka, over 3,300 trunks were counted.

Monkey puzzle female pine cone

Monkey puzzle bark

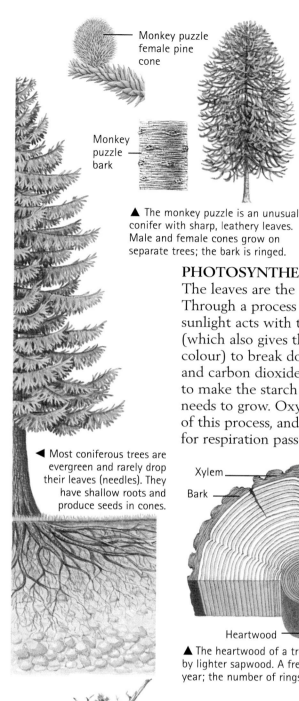

Chinese windmill palm leaf

Stem

▲ The monkey puzzle is an unusual conifer with sharp, leathery leaves. Male and female cones grow on separate trees; the bark is ringed.

▲ The spiky, fanned fronds of the Chinese windmill palm leaf can spread to a width of 1m.

◄ Most coniferous trees are evergreen and rarely drop their leaves (needles). They have shallow roots and produce seeds in cones.

▲ Deciduous trees produce vivid and beautiful autumn colours in North American woodlands. Leaves may change from green to all shades of red, orange and gold.

PHOTOSYNTHESIS

The leaves are the tree's chemical factory. Through a process called photosynthesis, sunlight acts with the chemical chlorophyll (which also gives the leaves their green colour) to break down molecules of water and carbon dioxide, rearranging their atoms to make the starch and sugars the tree needs to grow. Oxygen is the waste product of this process, and whatever is not needed for respiration passes back into the air.

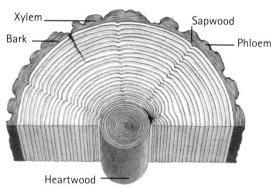

Xylem

Bark

Sapwood

Phloem

Heartwood

▲ The heartwood of a tree trunk section is surrounded by lighter sapwood. A fresh growth ring is added every year; the number of rings shows the tree's age.

USES OF TREES

Trees were among the first natural resources used by people. They provided fuel for fires; wood for shelters, tools and weapons; and fruits and nuts for food. Today, three billion people in developing countries still rely on wood for fuel. The industrial world also uses huge amounts of lumber, plywood and hardboard. Wood pulp is used to make paper and fibres.

TREES AND THE ENVIRONMENT

Trees help to keep the atmosphere healthy, because they remove carbon dioxide from the air and give off oxygen not used during photosynthesis. Trees also protect the land from erosion. Their large canopies of leaves and branches absorb heavy rainfall; their roots bind the soil and prevent it from being washed away. This is why it is important to preserve rainforests in Brazil and Indonesia. In parts of Africa, where natural forests have been cut down, fast-growing trees are being planted to help prevent the desert taking over.

◄ Bristlecone pines of North America are the world's oldest trees. Some are over 6,000 years old.

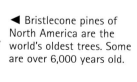

Fan-shaped leaf

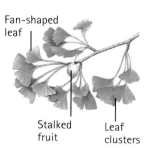

Stalked fruit

Leaf clusters

► The baobab tree is native to Africa and Australia. It has a wide, bulbous trunk with thick, short branches.

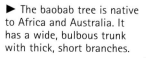

▲ Bonsai is the art of growing miniature trees. Almost any tree seedling can be grown as a bonsai by pruning its roots and branches, but evergreens are the most popular.

▲ The ginkgo biloba, or maidenhair tree, has remained unchanged for 160 million years. The tree was cultivated for centuries in Chinese temple gardens.

SEE ALSO

Conservation, Ecology, Forest, Fruit, Habitat, Leaf, Plant, Rainforest, Seed and pollination

TRUCK AND BUS

Trucks and buses are commercial road vehicles. Trucks are used to carry goods and products, while buses provide public transport for people.

Commercial trucks and buses have many features in common and are often built by the same companies.

A Foden C-type steam lorry of 1922. Steam trucks were popular until the 1930s.

A 1914 Hallford 3-ton truck used by the British army in World War I.

A London double-decker bus. The second deck boosts passenger capacity.

Modern trucks carry pre-packed containers of goods for easy loading.

RANGE OF SIZES

Unlike cars, most trucks and buses have a separate chassis, or wheeled frame, on which is mounted a body designed for a particular purpose. A truck may be a light local delivery vehicle, a middle-range goods transporter or a heavy-load carrier weighing up to 44 tonnes, while the largest public service buses – bendy buses – carry as many as 200 passengers.

ROAD TRAINS

There are two main types of truck: rigid and articulated. Rigid trucks are built as a single unit, with all the wheels attached to one chassis. The articulated truck, or 'artic', consists of a 'tractor' unit, which contains the engine and cab, and a trailer which carries the goods. Artics are easier to handle and more flexible in operation. Truck chassis may be adapted for special purposes, as with tankers (which carry liquids such as milk, fuel or chemicals), cement mixers and fire engines. In some countries, such as Australia, heavy trucks may tow trailers as a 'road train'.

▲ Long-distance bus routes were established in the USA in 1925 by the Greyhound Corporation, and are now found in most countries with a good road system.

CARRYING PASSENGERS

Buses may be single-decked or double-decked. A double-decker can carry more passengers in the same road space. Very long single-deck buses are hinged near the centre so they can turn tightly. Most buses operate in cities, but others run long-distance routes, usually offering much lower fares than the railway. The tram, a bus-like vehicle on rails, follows a fixed route through a city. Many cities are planning tram lines to solve traffic jams.

▲ Road trains (articulated trucks pulling several trailers) are used for long-haul transport in remote areas.

ARTICULATED TRUCKS

An articulated truck is made up of a tractor and a semi-trailer. The tractor contains the engine, cab, fuel tanks, brakes and other equipment. The semi-trailer carries the main load. It has wheels at the rear, and rests on the tractor at the front via a device called the fifth wheel.

> **SEE ALSO**
> Car, Engine, Road, Transport

TUNNEL

Tunnels are natural or artificial passageways built underground. They can be built through hills or mountains, or under land or water.

Tunnels are constructed to carry roads, railways, water, sewage or cables. They are also built to reach mineral deposits, or to create underground shelters or storage areas. Tunnels that carry traffic or people need ventilation systems to remove fumes and circulate fresh air.

ANCIENT TUNNELS

Tunnelling began in prehistoric times when cave-dwellers began to extend natural caves and dig for useful flints to make into tools. Ancient empires had tunnels built to house royal tombs and temples and to carry water to irrigate fields. The Romans built tunnels to connect the aqueducts that carried their water supply.

EXPLOSIVES AND SHIELDS

The first major traffic-carrying tunnel was built in the 1670s, when a 158-m tunnel was blasted through a rocky hill near Béziers in France. Tunnel builders today still use explosives to blast through solid rock. Building tunnels through less dense

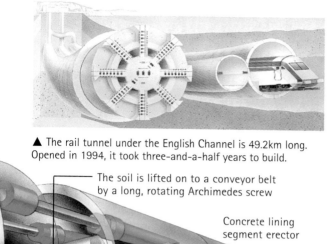

▲ The rail tunnel under the English Channel is 49.2km long. Opened in 1994, it took three-and-a-half years to build.

The soil is lifted on to a conveyor belt by a long, rotating Archimedes screw

Concrete lining segment erector

An operator sits in a control cab behind the cutting head

Spoil (muck) conveyor

Powerful rams force the cutting head forward

The cutter head has tough cutting rollers and teeth

TUNNEL–BORING MACHINE (TBM)

Modern tunnelling machines use very tough, tungsten carbide cutting teeth. These can bore through soft rock, such as chalk, at a rate of up to 1,000m a month. The cutting machine is immediately followed by a segment erector, which places the lining sections in position.

materials requires a tunnelling shield. Invented in Britain in 1825 by the French-born engineer Marc Isambard Brunel (1769–1849), the shield protects labourers as they dig. As the shield is gradually moved forward in sections, the walls of the tunnel are shored up with brickwork or concrete to stabilize them. Brunel used this method to build the first tunnel under the River Thames, London, completed in 1843.

UNDERWATER TUNNELS

A cheaper method of building tunnels under water is to dig a trench, drop in pre-formed sections of metal or concrete and then, after divers have fitted them together, pump out the water and fill in the trench. The Hong Kong Cross Harbour Tunnel was built this way.

▲ A mole can dig five times faster than a TBM using just its two front paws, although its tunnels are, of course, smaller.

◄ The Thames Tunnel, built by Marc Brunel in the early 1840s, was the first underwater tunnel. It is still in use today as part of the London Underground train system.

FAST FACTS

• The world's widest tunnel, which is 63m wide, is the eight-lane Fort McHenry Tunnel, Baltimore, USA

• The world's longest road tunnel is the Laerdal Tunnel in Norway. It was completed in 2000 and is 24.5km long

• The longest railway tunnel is the Seikan, joining the Japanese islands of Honshu and Hokkaido. Completed in 1988, it is 53.9km long

SEE ALSO

Hibernation, Mining, Oil

UNITED KINGDOM

England, Scotland and Wales lie on the island of Great Britain in northwest Europe. Together with Northern Ireland, they are governed as a United Kingdom.

UNITED KINGDOM
Area: 244,088 sq km
Population: 62,262,000
Capital: London
Languages: English and Welsh
Currency: Pound sterling

Much of England is lowland, with the flattest areas in the east. Upland regions include the Lake District and the Pennines. Scotland, Wales and Northern Ireland are more mountainous than England. Scotland's Ben Nevis (1,343m) is the United Kingdom's (UK's) highest peak. Loch Neagh, in Northern Ireland, is the UK's largest lake, and the Severn (354km), which runs through Wales and the west of England, is the UK's longest river. In most parts, summers are generally cool and winters mild, with rainfall all year round.

TOWN AND COUNTRY
The UK is a crowded nation. Four out of every five British people live in cities and towns. England – especially the southeast around London – is the most densely populated country. London is one of the world's greatest cultural centres. The UK has an extensive road system with many motorways, and London's Heathrow is the world's busiest airport for international traffic. Since 1994, the Channel Tunnel, under the English Channel, has physically linked Great Britain with France.

▲ Many commuters use London Bridge, over the river Thames, to reach the City of London, the heart of the capital's business community.

INDUSTRY AND FARMING
Natural resources include oil and natural gas deposits in the North Sea. The UK's many rivers provide drinking water, as well as water for crops. Much of the countryside is farmed and the crops include wheat, sugar beet, potatoes and oil-seed rape. Dairy cattle and sheep are raised as well as pigs and poultry. Manufacturing industries include aerospace, chemicals, telecommunication and electronics. Scotland also produces fine woollens and Northern Ireland is famous for its pure white linen. Service industries such as banking, publishing and tourism are also important.

▲ Northern Ireland has been the scene of violent conflict between Catholics and Protestants. Here the Protestant Orange Order celebrate the anniversary of the victory of William of Orange over Catholic King James II in the Battle of the Boyne in 1690.

► Wales is a land of green valleys, grassy plains, hill farms and mountains. Its castles include Carreg Cennen in the southwest, shown here.

◄ The word *loch* means 'lake' in Gaelic. Loch Tulla is one of many lakes lying between Scotland's peaks.

Shetland Is.

Orkney Is.

Outer Hebrides

Isle of Skye

Inverness

Loch Ness

SCOTLAND

Aberdeen

Ben Nevis ▲

L. Tulla

Dundee

ATLANTIC OCEAN

Edinburgh

Glasgow

NORTH SEA

NORTHERN IRELAND

Londonderry

Lough Neagh

Belfast

Newcastle-upon-Tyne

LAKE DISTRICT

PENNINES

ISLE OF MAN

Bradford

Leeds

Blackpool

Manchester

REPUBLIC OF IRELAND

IRISH SEA

Liverpool

Sheffield

Nottingham

Mt. Snowdon ▲

WALES

Severn

Leicester

Norwich

Birmingham

Coventry

Cambridge

ENGLAND

Swansea

Newport

Oxford

London

Cardiff

Bristol

Thames

ATLANTIC OCEAN

Southampton

Brighton

Plymouth

Dartmouth

ENGLISH CHANNEL

CHANNEL ISLANDS

miles
0   100

0   100
km

N

FROM CONQUEST TO KINGDOM

The Romans conquered lowland Britain from 43CE. After the Romans came Anglo-Saxons, Vikings and Normans. The United Kingdom of Great Britain and Ireland was formed in 1801. It became the United Kingdom of Great Britain and Northern Ireland in 1922, after the southern part of the island of Ireland became independent.

WORLD POWER

During the 18th century, Britain colonized large parts of North America, Africa and Asia. Wealth from the colonies supplied money for the Industrial Revolution to begin at home, and factories and machinery were built. By 1900, the British Empire had become the biggest empire in the world, defended by the biggest navy.

DECLINE OF EMPIRE

In the first half of the 20th century, two world wars caused loss of life and economic strain. From the 1950s, the UK's wealth and power declined as many of the colonies became independent and Britain's traditional manufacturing

industries such as coal, iron, steel and ship-building declined.

THE UK TODAY

The UK remains a major player in finance and the service industries, and takes a lead in world affairs through the United Nations, the European Union and the Commonwealth. The UK is a constitutional monarchy, which means the king or queen is head of state but political power is controlled by parliament. In 1997, some power was devolved to a regional parliament in Scotland and an assembly in Wales. Northern Ireland has had its assembly since 2007. The Isle of Man and the Channel Islands (Jersey and Guernsey) are largely self-governing.

▲ England's south coast, including Dartmouth Quay in Devon, is popular with tourists for its scenery and climate.

▲ Tower Bridge, across the River Thames in London, is a moveable bridge. The two halves of its roadway are raised for passing tall ships.

SEE ALSO

Civil war, Empire, Europe, Government, Industrial Revolution, Middle Ages, United Nations, World War I, World War II

UNITED NATIONS

The United Nations is an international organization based in New York City. Its member nations meet there to discuss problems and try to find solutions.

The United Nations flag features the world surrounded by the olive branch, a symbol of peace.

UN AGENCIES
World Health Organization (WHO)
Food and Agricultural Organization (FAO)
International Monetary Fund (IMF)
UN Educational, Scientific and Cultural Organization (UNESCO)
International Civil Aviation Organization (ICAO)
World Bank
UN Children's Fund (UNICEF)

Founded in 1945 by the allies after World War II, the United Nations (UN) has grown to include 193 of the nearly 200 independent states on Earth. The UN sponsors negotiations between disputing members, and its many agencies carry out humanitarian work.

GENERAL ASSEMBLY

Each UN member country has one vote in the General Assembly, which meets in New York City, USA. The General Assembly approves UN work, debates important issues and decides how to spend its money. The 15-member Security Council is responsible for peace and security. It can send a peace-keeping force to any country, and may condemn aggressive action. Five countries are permanent members: China, France, Russia, the UK and the USA.

HUMANITARIAN WORK

The UN works to promote trade, health education and cultural understanding. This work is carried out by the bodies of the Economic and Social Council (ESC), which pays for aid projects in poor countries, encourages health care and promotes the rights of minorities. UNICEF (UN Children's Fund) promotes the welfare of children in poor countries. In 1991, the UN held an Earth Summit in Rio de Janeiro, so that world leaders could discuss environmental problems.

PROBLEMS IN THE UN

The UN cannot always find solutions that suit all its member states. The USA has accused the UN of bias against developed countries and has refused to pay its share until reforms are made. In 2003, there was disagreement about whether to take military action against Iraq. A US-led coalition attacked Iraq without UN backing.

▲ United Nations forces are stationed in many parts of the world, such as Cambodia, to help keep the peace. Here, a UN soldier talks to a Cambodian woman and her child.

◀ The United Nations General Assembly meets for three months every autumn to decide important issues. It can hold a Special Session during an emergency, such as the Soviet invasion of Hungary in 1956.

SEE ALSO
Civil war, Government, World War II

UNITED STATES OF AMERICA

The United States is a republic in the continent of North America and is made up of 50 states. It is rich in natural resources and advanced in technology.

Area: 9,629,091 sq km
Population: 307,007,000
Capital: Washington, D.C. (District of Columbia)
Language: English
Currency: US dollar

▼ The Statue of Liberty stands at the entrance to New York Harbor. It was a gift from France in 1884 and represents freedom for the American people.

The United States (US) is the third largest country in the world both in terms of population and area. Two states sit apart from the others. Alaska, lying west of Canada, includes Mount McKinley (6,194m), the highest peak in the US. The state of Hawaii is made up of a group of islands in the Pacific Ocean.

THE EASTERN STATES
In the eastern US, rocky, forested New England centres on Boston, famed for universities such as Harvard. Also in the east are the federal capital of Washington, D.C., the historic cities of Philadelphia and New York City and the industrial cities of Detroit and Cleveland. Spectacular Niagara Falls and the country's largest lake, Michigan, are in the north. The southeast includes booming cities such as Atlanta, sunny Florida with its rich wildlife in the Everglades swamps, and historic settlements such as Charleston.

ACROSS THE COUNTRY
The north-central part of the US is known as the Midwest. It is a rich farming region and has mighty rivers, including the longest river in the US, the Mississippi-Missouri river system, which is 6,020km long. There are

▲ New York City is the largest city in the US. One of its key symbols is the yellow taxi, a common sight on the streets of Manhattan and the other four boroughs – the Bronx, Queens, Staten Island and Brooklyn.

also huge grasslands known as prairies. Farther west are the Rocky Mountains, the geysers of Yellowstone National Park, ski resorts and bustling cities such as Denver. The south has scorching deserts in Arizona and business centres such as Houston and Dallas in Texas. The far west is dominated by the most populous and richest state, California. Los Angeles, in California, is the second largest city in the US and home of the Hollywood film industry. ▶

▲ The Grand Canyon lies in the state of Arizona, in the warm, dry southwest. It is one of the most spectacular gorges in the world, carved from the desert rock by the Colorado River.

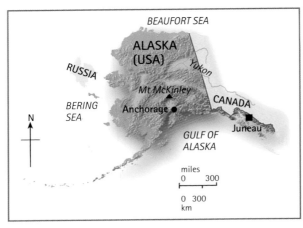

▲ The Trans-Alaska pipeline carries oil from the north of Alaska to its south coast. The state of Alaska has a cold climate and is thinly populated.

THE PEOPLE

Since 1940, the population of the United States has more than doubled. Native Americans, who lived in North America for thousands of years before Europeans began arriving, now make up just one per cent of the population. About half of all Americans are Protestants and nearly a quarter are Roman Catholics. About two per cent of the population are Jewish, and less than one per cent is Muslim.

SETTLEMENT AND REVOLUTION

Permanent European settlement of what was to become the US began with a British colony founded in 1607 at Jamestown, Virginia. British colonists spread along America's east coast. In the south, they grew tobacco, cotton and indigo on plantations worked by slaves shipped from Africa. In the north, timber and furs were key products and fishing was a major industry. French and Spanish explorers and colonists began to settle other territories to the west. Disputes between Britain and its 13 colonies

over trade, taxes and defence led to the American Revolution (1775–83) and on July 4, 1776, a group of colonial leaders signed the Declaration of Independence. The war ended in victory for the colonists, led by General George Washington.

THE NEW REPUBLIC

The colonies united to form a republic. In 1787, the US Constitution was written, dividing power between a central, federal government and the ex-colonies, which became separate states and were given powers of self-government. National laws were to be made by the president together with Congress, which is made up of the House of Representatives and the Senate.

▲ The casinos and nightclubs of Las Vegas, in the state of Nevada, attract thousands of visitors. Neon signs light up the city.

▶ About 80 per cent of Americans are white or Hispanic. African Americans form 13 per cent of the population, Asians four per cent, people of mixed race two per cent and Native Americans one per cent. This classroom reflects the multicultural make-up of the United States.

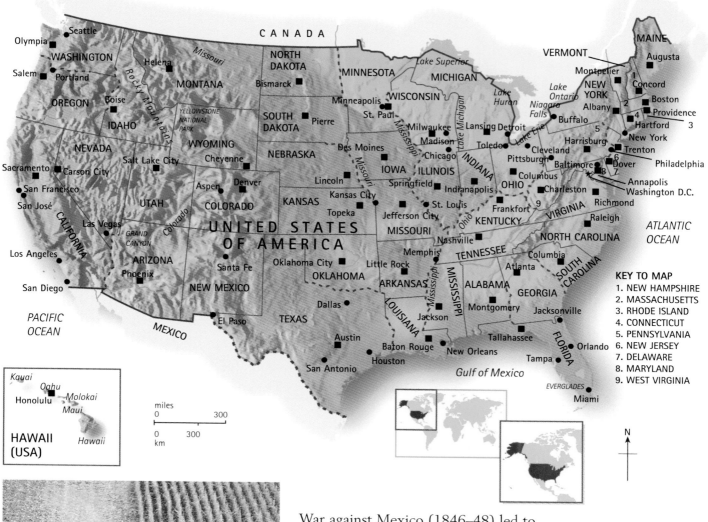

HAWAII (USA)

KEY TO MAP
1. NEW HAMPSHIRE
2. MASSACHUSETTS
3. RHODE ISLAND
4. CONNECTICUT
5. PENNSYLVANIA
6. NEW JERSEY
7. DELAWARE
8. MARYLAND
9. WEST VIRGINIA

▲ Wheat is harvested on the prairies – the vast grasslands of the Midwest.

GROWTH OF A NATION

George Washington was the first president and a new national capital was founded and named in his honour. In 1791, a Bill of Rights was added to the Constitution, guaranteeing the rights of all US citizens. In 1802, President Thomas Jefferson bought vast western territories claimed by France, doubling the size of the new nation. In 1804, he sent an expedition to explore the continent from east to west.

War against Mexico (1846–48) led to the conquest of the southwest and Pacific coast. Lured by the discovery of gold in California in 1848 and by the prospect of free land on the prairies, Americans headed west. Washington Irving and other writers helped create a new national identity and Noah Webster compiled the first dictionary of American English.

WAR AND PEACE

From 1861 to 1865, America was torn by civil war which made the south poor but boosted industry in the north. Peace brought a boom in railway building. By 1869, the railway joined the east and west coasts. San Francisco, Chicago and St Louis grew from frontier posts into great cities. ▶

▼ Surfing and other water sports are popular on all the Hawaiian islands, including Oahu, where 76 per cent of Hawaii's population lives.

▲ Like baseball and basketball, American football is a popular national sport.

▲ The White House, in Washington D.C. has been the home of US presidents since it was built in 1800. It was rebuilt after a fire in the War of 1812.

INDUSTRY AND IMMIGRATION

Millions of Europeans moved to the US and Native Americans were driven from their traditional lands. America grew rich from its farms and factories. By 1900, the average American was better off than the average European. Half of all Americans still lived on farms, but cities were booming. Inventions made in America, such as the light bulb, elevator, skyscraper and aeroplane, were to change the world.

A WORLD POWER

In 1867, the United States bought Alaska from Russia. In 1898, it took over the Pacific islands of Hawaii and also went to war with Spain. This led to independence for Cuba and American rule over the Philippines. The US developed a great navy. In 1917, the country joined in World War I to help Britain and France to defeat Germany and its allies.

BOOM, BUST AND WAR

In the 1920s, the US was the first country in which millions of people drove cars, listened to radio and enjoyed the movies, but the 'roaring twenties' ended in a business collapse in 1929, with millions out of work. President Franklin D. Roosevelt used government money from taxes to create new jobs. Following Japan's attack on the US naval base at Pearl Harbor (Hawaii) in 1940, Roosevelt led the country into World War II, but died just before the German surrender in 1945.

SUPERPOWER

War boosted industry in the US and left the country as a superpower, armed with atomic bombs and with a new role as leader of the democratic world. American wealth helped Europe recover from war damage. Today, the US is the world's most powerful nation and US culture has spread across the world.

▲ In 1620, English Puritans who called themselves Pilgrims sailed to America and founded a colony in Plymouth, Massachusetts. A recreation of their settlement now stands on the site of the original colony.

◄ In the early 1900s, jazz emerged in New Orleans and developed as a new and distinctly American style of music. Today, the New Orleans jazz festival is world famous.

SEE ALSO

Bridge, Civil rights, Civil War (American), Cold War, Habitat, Native Americans, North America, Slavery, World War I, World War II

UNIVERSE

The universe is made up of stars, planets and other matter scattered throughout space. It may contain up to 100 billion galaxies with 100 billion stars in each.

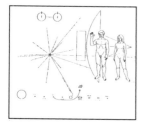

▲ NASA sent a diagram of humans into space, so that it could be found by intelligent life elsewhere in the universe. The dumb-bell represents a hydrogen atom; the symbols below it represent the solar system.

Most scientists believe that the universe began with an enormous explosion called the Big Bang, which happened about 13.7 billion years ago. During this event, all the matter and energy that would ever exist was created in a fraction of a second, in an area smaller than the size of a grape. Ever since the Big Bang, the universe has been expanding outward into space.

SEEING INTO THE PAST

A galaxy that is five billion light years away is seen by astronomers as it was five billion years ago. Therefore, looking at very remote objects gives us a way of seeing the universe when it was much younger than it is today. The most distant objects ever seen are newborn galaxies or galaxies that are still being formed. At even greater distances and earlier times, astronomers can detect only faint radio waves, which come from all parts of space. These are the cooled-down remains of the fireball that erupted out of the Big Bang.

HISTORY OF THE UNIVERSE	
Time after Big Bang	Event
0 minutes	Time, space and energy created
3 minutes	Universe 90 per cent hydrogen and 10 per cent helium
300,000 years	Atoms were formed
1 billion years	First galaxies appeared
13.7 billion years	The present day

MYSTERIES OF THE UNIVERSE

Scientists ask: will the universe go on expanding forever, or will it eventually begin to shrink and end in a Big Crunch? At present, the answer is unknown, but it seems that the universe may be delicately balanced between the two options. Another question is: does life exists elsewhere in the universe? Again, the answer is not yet known, but the evidence suggests that life may be common throughout space. Space probes sent to other planets search for water, the main ingredient that supports life as we know it. Over 90 per cent of the universe consists of dark matter, which cannot be seen. The composition of this remains another great mystery.

SEE ALSO

Astronomy, Big Bang theory, Galaxy, Planet, Solar system, Star, Time

VEGETABLE

Vegetables are plants grown to provide food. Most are grown from seeds, bulbs or tubers, then harvested within a year. A few grow on long-lived plants.

EDIBLE VEGETABLE PARTS

Eight different parts of vegetable plants are eaten: the bulbs of onion and garlic; the flowers of broccoli and cauliflower; the leaves of lettuce and kale; the roots of carrots and turnips; the seeds and pods of peas and beans; the stems of celery and rhubarb; and the tubers of potatoes and yams. Tomatoes, peppers, aubergines and squashes such as pumpkins and marrows, are really fruits since they contain seeds, but are grown as vegetables.

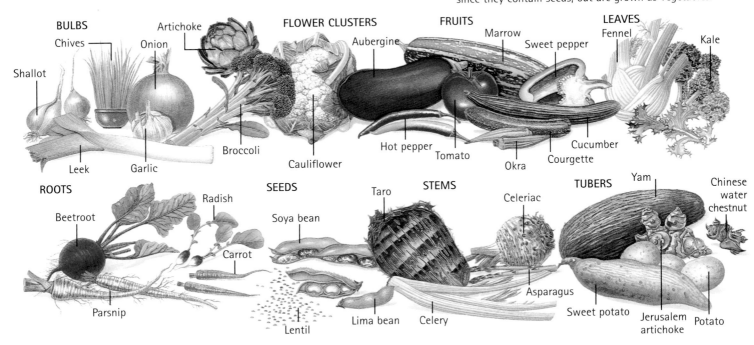

BULBS — Chives, Shallot, Onion, Artichoke, Leek, Garlic

FLOWER CLUSTERS — Broccoli, Cauliflower, Aubergine

FRUITS — Marrow, Sweet pepper, Hot pepper, Tomato, Okra, Courgette, Cucumber

LEAVES — Fennel, Kale

ROOTS — Beetroot, Radish, Carrot, Parsnip

SEEDS — Soya bean, Lentil, Lima bean

Taro, Celery

STEMS — Celeriac, Asparagus, Celery

TUBERS — Yam, Chinese water chestnut, Sweet potato, Jerusalem artichoke, Potato

VEGETABLE FACTS

- Potatoes, tomatoes, pepper and sweet corn are native to the Americas and were unknown in Europe before 1500CE
- Some types of bean are poisonous if eaten raw
- Organic vegetables are grown without pesticides

Vegetables are very important to a healthy diet: they are low in fat, and different types provide protein, carbohydrates in the form of starches and sugars, vitamins, minerals and fibre. Some vegetables, such as potatoes, must be cooked before being eaten; others are best eaten raw, while many vegetables may be eaten either way. Cooking vegetables for too long destroys some of their vitamins.

SEASONAL VEGETABLES

Vegetables are harvested at different times of the year. Some, such as lettuce, are usually eaten fresh, but others, such as peas and beans, can be dried or frozen and cooked later. Root vegetables last for a long time when stored in cool, dry conditions – they can even be left in the soil. Freezing and canning make it possible to eat from a wide selection the whole year, although fresh vegetables have the highest nutritional value.

CROPS AND BREEDING

All vegetables contain stored food. Cultivated crops have much larger food stores than their wild ancestors. Many people, particularly in developing countries, have to rely on their own crops for food. If crops fail, they face starvation, so over thousands of years, farmers have selected and bred edible plants that give the best yield for the climate in their area. Through plant-breeding techniques, scientists have developed new varieties of vegetables that are resistant to attack by pests and diseases.

◄ Giant vegetables, such as green beans, are grown in competitions, but they are too tough to eat.

SEE ALSO

Crop, Farming, Nutrition, Plant, Seed and pollination

VIDEO

Video technology turns moving pictures and sounds into electronic form, stores them, then plays them back on a screen.

▲ Modern DV (Digital Video) camcorders store images in digital form. These give high-quality recordings, which can be edited on a PC.

▲ Closed-circuit television (CCTV), with small video cameras, is used for security surveillance in buildings and public places.

Signals from TV aerials, satellite dishes, cables or video cameras can be recorded in many ways: on magnetic tape, optical discs, computer hard disc drives or an electronic system called 'flash memory'.

GET THE PICTURE
Before video, silent home movies were made using cartridges containing reels of photographic film. These had to be sent off for developing before they could be played back with a projector. Early video systems used a big TV camera connected to a separate, heavy recording system. All this changed in the mid-1980s with the invention of the camcorder – a portable video camera with built-in recorder.

VIDEO CAMERAS
In a camcorder, a lens bends the incoming light to form a sharp image on a flat light sensor called a charge coupled device (CCD). This turns the image into an electronic signal, which is recorded together with a sound track. The user looks at a viewfinder, which has a small liquid-crystal display (LCD). Camcorders

▲ Computer-controlled video-editing suites are used to assemble images and add special effects.

are built into many mobile phones and digital cameras, and their quality is improving all the time.

VIDEO-CONFERENCING
The use of video has become increasingly widespread. For instance, video-equipped police cars and traffic cameras help to monitor roads and enforce speed limits. Early video telephones never caught on, but the arrival of web-cams (small cameras mounted on computer monitors) made video calls over the Internet possible. Using this technology, people can 'meet' and talk even when they are on different continents. In the same way, the latest smartphones enable users to make face-to-face calls while on the move.

HOW A DIGITAL VIDEO RECORDER WORKS

Until recently, people recorded TV programmes onto video tapes, but now they are stored either on the hard disc of computers or onto DVDs (Digital Versatile Discs) in the form of digital files. The quality of these recordings is higher than that of video tapes, the discs are less bulky and any part of the recording can be reached quickly, without the need to wind through a long tape.

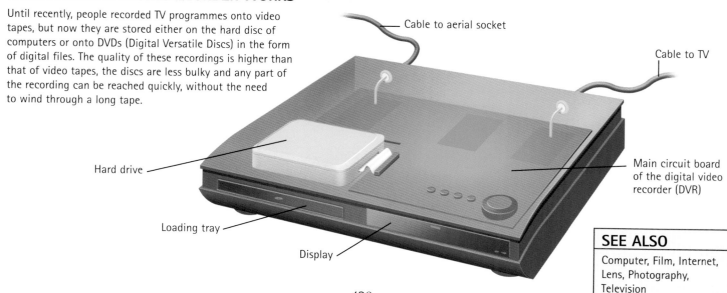

Cable to aerial socket

Cable to TV

Hard drive

Main circuit board of the digital video recorder (DVR)

Loading tray

Display

SEE ALSO

Computer, Film, Internet, Lens, Photography, Television

VIKINGS

The Vikings were a warrior people from Norway, Sweden and Denmark, who invaded much of northern Europe during the ninth and tenth centuries.

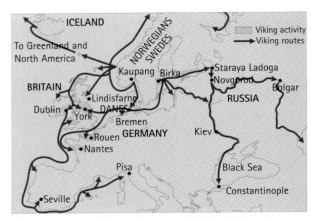

▲ Viking trade and expansion routes in the ninth and tenth centuries ran east through Russia, as far south as Seville and Pisa, and, by 1000CE, west to North America.

Thor was the Viking god of thunder and war. Thursday is named after him.

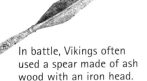

In battle, Vikings often used a spear made of ash wood with an iron head.

A Viking silver amulet in the shape of Thor's hammer and decorated with a face.

During the eighth century, the population of Scandinavia rose dramatically, but there was not enough land there for farming. At about the same time, the Vikings developed the longship, which gave them the means to reach other lands.

EARLY RAIDS

The first Viking raids were carried out by one or two longships. They would land on the coast, raid a village or two and escape with their loot. In 793CE, a Viking force destroyed the monastery on Lindisfarne, in northern England. Within a few years, raids were made on the coasts of Scotland, Wales, Ireland and northern France.

FIERCE RELIGION

Viking gods were fierce and warlike. The Vikings told stories of the gods and heroes in long poems called sagas. They believed the world would end in a mighty war between the gods and giants at Ragnarok, meaning the 'twilight of the gods'. Odin was their chief god. Men who died bravely in battle were thought to be collected by the Valkyries, 12 handmaidens from Odin's court, and taken to Valhalla, a great hall, to spend eternity feasting and fighting.

INVASION OF ENGLAND

In 851CE, Vikings arrived in England with a great army and 350 ships. They invaded Kent, destroying Canterbury. In 866CE, an even larger Viking army, led by Halfdane and Basecg, invaded Kent. Within five years nearly all of England had been defeated and conquered. The victory of King Alfred the Great (849CE–899CE) over Guthrum's Viking army at Edington in 878CE saved southern and western England.

VIKING SETTLEMENTS

Large numbers of Vikings sailed to England and settled in the conquered lands as farmers and traders. York, Lincoln and Derby became Viking towns. In Ireland, the Vikings founded Dublin and Waterford as trading cities. A large section of northern France – later known as Normandy (from Norsemen) – was captured by Earl Rollo and settled by Vikings. Some Vikings sailed east to travel up the rivers of eastern Europe. At Kiev, they founded a kingdom called the Russ, or Russia.

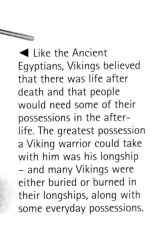

◄ Like the Ancient Egyptians, Vikings believed that there was life after death and that people would need some of their possessions in the after-life. The greatest possession a Viking warrior could take with him was his longship – and many Vikings were either buried or burned in their longships, along with some everyday possessions.

FEARLESS RAIDERS FROM THE SEA

From the 8th to the 11th centuries, fearless Viking warriors from the Scandinavian countries of Norway, Sweden and Denmark made several raids on the coasts of Christian countries, inflicting great terror on the local inhabitants. They plundered monasteries and churches, killing, burning houses and driving away the cattle.

OCEAN VOYAGES

The Vikings were skilled navigators. By studying the stars and the Sun they could travel accurately across vast distances of open sea. In about 825CE, they reached and settled the Faeroe Islands. Fifty years later, they reached Iceland. There, they founded an assembly – the Althing – to discuss and decide communal matters. It still meets and is the oldest parliament in the world. In 982CE, the first Viking settlements on Greenland were founded. About the year 1000, a Viking named Leif Ericsson travelled to Newfoundland in search of timber, which was scarce in Greenland. Although they visited North America over many years, the Vikings never settled there.

VIKING TWILIGHT

By 900CE, the great Viking raids were over. Wars between Viking settlements and surrounding kingdoms remained common, but most Vikings settled down to a more peaceful existence. The Viking kingdoms in England and Ireland were taken over by the native kingdoms by 970CE.

CHRISTIAN CONVERTS

Vikings and English lived side by side and, for a time, England became part of the Scandinavian empire, under Cnut (1016–35). A last attempt at conquest was made by the Norwegian Viking Harald Hardrada when he invaded England in 1066, but he was defeated and killed. From then on, most of the Vikings adopted Christianity and turned to farming and trading, abandoning raiding and conquest.

▲ Swords were highly valued by the Vikings and were often richly decorated with gold and silver.

▲ A Viking man and woman dressed in everyday clothes.

SEE ALSO

Myth and legend, Religion, Ship, Warfare

VOLCANO

When lava bursts through an opening in the Earth's crust, a volcano forms. The word 'volcano' comes from Vulcan, the Roman god of fire and metalworking.

The Earth's surface is continually moving through the action of plate tectonics, as sections of the Earth's crust are moved along by currents in the molten rock below. There are two types of volcano: basaltic volcanoes, found where new plate material is being created, and andesitic volcanoes in areas where plates are being destroyed.

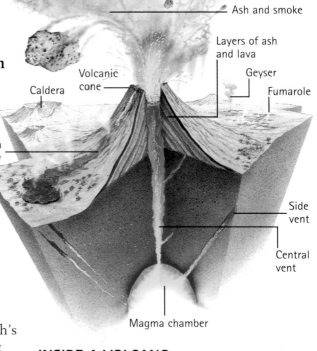

Ash and smoke

Layers of ash and lava

Geyser

Fumarole

Volcanic cone

Caldera

Lava flow

Side vent

Central vent

Magma chamber

BASALTIC VOLCANOES
Where new crust forms along oceanic ridges, the molten material from the Earth's mantle wells up and spreads out, pushing the plates apart. This usually happens at the bottom of the ocean, but in Iceland it has risen above the ocean and produced a whole island. The molten material, or lava, that erupts from these basaltic volcanoes is very runny and flows a long distance before becoming solid. Basaltic volcanoes are also found a long way from the edges of the plates. The Hawaiian islands were formed as basaltic material pushed its way up through the plate from the Earth's mantle. These so-called 'hot-spot' volcanoes have produced many other islands of the Pacific, such as the Galapagos Islands and Fiji.

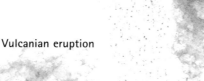

Volcanic activity has formed the whole landscape of Iceland. The terrain is littered with hot jets of boiling water, called geysers.

FAMOUS ERUPTIONS

• In 79CE, Vesuvius erupted, destroying the Roman city of Pompeii

• About 90 eruptions have been recorded at Mount Etna, in Sicily, since 1800BCE

• Krakatoa, a volcanic island in Indonesia, erupted in 1883 and killed 36,000 people

• In 1980, the eruption of Mount St Helens, USA, was predicted – the area was evacuated and only a few people died

INSIDE A VOLCANO

A typical volcano has a crater and a cone of solidified lava and ash. Eruptions take place through a chimney-like vent. Far below the surface is a chamber of magma (molten rock), containing bubbling gases that make some volcanic rock frothy. A caldera forms when a violent eruption empties the magma chamber that feeds it. The roof then collapses, leaving a hole. Fumaroles are openings that let out only gas and steam, and geysers sometimes shoot fountains of boiling water high into the air.

VIOLENT ERUPTIONS

Andesitic volcanoes are found where plates are being drawn beneath one another and destroyed. Molten plate material rises through the overriding plate and bursts through at the surface. These andesitic volcanoes occur in the great mountain chains, and in island arcs around the edges of oceans, close to deep ocean trenches. The lava of an andesitic volcano is stiff and sticky, and when it erupts, it does so explosively. Mount St Helens, in Washington, USA, and the island of Montserrat are recent examples of such violent and destructive eruptions. Because of accurate forecasting, few people were killed, but the hot ash from Mount St Helens destroyed trees up to 30km away.

Vulcanian eruption

Plinian eruption

Hawaiian eruption

Volcano cones created by Hawaiian eruptions slope gently, because the lava flow is quite runny

A vulcanian eruption, after Vulcano in Italy, throws out almost solid magma during its rare explosions

Plinian eruptions, such as the one that destroyed Pompeii in 79CE, explode with great clouds of ash and pumice

SEE ALSO

Earth, Earthquake, Mountain and valley, Ocean and sea, Rock

WARFARE

Warfare is armed conflict between the military forces of two nations or states, or between organized groups within a state.

Much of recorded history tells of war and conflict. This is often because one group seeks to impose its will on another for some form of gain, such as territory, food or natural resources.

TURNING TO ARMS

Wars start for different reasons. In Scotland in 1692, the Clan Campbell attacked the MacDonald Clan of Glencoe in revenge for cattle raids. Other wars are begun for gain. In the 8th century, Vikings attacked European countries to steal gold and other treasures, while the Romans went to war to expand their Empire. The Crusades started for religious reasons. The Franco-Prussian War of 1870 began when France blocked plans for a united Germany.

OUTBREAK OF WAR

Countries going to war want to appear to be in the right. This encourages citizens to support the war, and deters other countries from helping the enemy. Often a relatively minor incident will trigger a war. In 1914,

▲ Samurai warriors used their discipline and skill with weapons to control Japan from 1200 to 1871.

the Habsburg Empire declared war on Serbia after a Serb killed the Austrian Archduke. The Habsburgs really wanted to stop Serbia encouraging unrest within the empire. Their act triggered World War I.

INTELLIGENCE

Once at war, commanders need to know about the strengths and plans of the enemy. The lack of such knowledge left France vulnerable to the German attack of 1940. Information may be gathered by watching the enemy from satellites and aircraft, by capturing or decoding messages, or by using spies. The information is given to commanders to help them make battlefield decisions. ▶

The earliest Ancient Egyptians used stone for maceheads, knives and arrow- and spear heads.

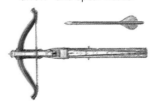

Medieval crossbows shot bolts accurately, but were slow to load and use.

OARS AND RAMS

The Battle of Salamis in 480BCE was fought between the oared galleys of Greece and the Persian Empire. The Greeks defeated the larger Persian fleet as their *triremes* (ships with three banks of oars) were faster and easier to handle than the Persian ships.

▲ Hand weapons of the Middle Ages included:
1 Daggers for stabbing **2** Maces to crack metal armour **3** War hammers, used as maces **4** Spiked staffs **5** Pikes with handles up to 2m long to keep horsemen at a distance.

▲ In 15th-century Europe, armour covered the body with carefully shaped metal plates, each curved and ribbed to deflect blows.

▲ Helmets fringed with chain mail gave protection while allowing movement.

TOTAL WAR

In a total war, an entire country is organized for fighting. In the 19th-century Zulu Empire, every young man had to serve in the army, while boys, older men and women provided supplies. Both world wars of the 20th century were total wars. Men were conscripted into the armed forces and many industries switched to producing weapons. It was considered fair to bomb cities in which factories were located, even though this meant killing civilians.

THE FATE OF PRISONERS

Some prisoners are taken in all wars, but the treatment they receive has varied. The soldiers of Ancient Rome sold prisoners as slaves. The Aztecs sacrificed prisoners to their gods. In the 19th century, in wars with the British, the Afghans tortured all prisoners to death – the British often shot their men if they could not rescue them. World War II prisoner of war camps in

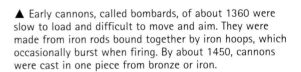

▲ Early cannons, called bombards, of about 1360 were slow to load and difficult to move and aim. They were made from iron rods bound together by iron hoops, which occasionally burst when firing. By about 1450, cannons were cast in one piece from bronze or iron.

Japan were notorious for bad conditions. The Geneva Convention of 1864, which has been signed by most nations, lays down strict rules about the treatment of prisoners of war. They must be given the same food and shelter as the troops who capture them, and cannot be forced to do any work to help the war effort. Prisoners are usually released at the end of a war.

LIMITED BLOODSHED

War by its nature is violent. Soldiers may kill civilians, steal goods and burn houses, so attempts have been made to reduce the violence. During the 12th century, the idea of chivalry encouraged knights to avoid hurting women or children and to take prisoners rather than killing captives. In 1631, the German city of Magdeburg was captured by an army of Croats and Walloons. The soldiers looted the city and slaughtered thousands. European monarchs were appalled and developed

---

KEY DATES

c. 5000BCE Cities in Mesopotamia form first armies

c. 90BCE Marius reforms the Roman armies into professional and full-time forces

c. 800CE Feudal armies made up of semi-professional knights form in Europe

c. 1350 Gunpowder is invented

1916 Tanks are used for the first time

1945 Nuclear weapons are used for the first time

1991 The first major use of cruise missiles in the Gulf War by the USA

THE BATTLE OF WATERLOO

The Battle of Waterloo was fought in 1815 between the French, led by Napoleon Bonaparte, and a joint British, Dutch and German army. The muskets and cannons of the time had only a limited range. The colourful uniforms helped soldiers tell friend from foe in the smoke of the battlefield.

the idea of limited war, which meant that civilians were to be unharmed and armies could surrender peacefully.

OBEYING THE RULES

Many wars have been fought according to a set of rules. In Ancient Greece, most cities depended on olive oil for food, so olive trees were not usually destroyed when an enemy city was captured. The people of each city knew that they might be defeated at some time, and wanted to have enough food to survive. During the Middle Ages, prisoners were given a chance to buy their freedom immediately by paying a ransom.

WAR CRIMES

Before 1945, any enemy soldier or leader who broke the rules of war was hanged or put in prison. At the end of World War II, the Allies set up special courts to try

▲ In 1906, HMS *Dreadnought* was a new type of battleship, armed with 12-inch guns and able to steam at over 20 knots. Battleships remained the most powerful ships afloat until aircraft carriers took over in the 1940s.

certain people as war criminals for breaking the Geneva Convention or for the mass murder of Jews and others in the Holocaust. In the 1990s, new war crimes courts were set up to try people who had killed civilians during the Bosnian civil war.

GUERRILLAS

Some wars are fought by irregular troops called guerrillas. Such wars are usually fought when the enemy is too strong to be faced in battle. Using any weapons to hand and operating in small groups, ▶

A hand gun of 1400.

A 16th-century wheel-lock.

A 17th-century flintlock.

The Colt revolver of 1851.

A matchlock musket.

A 19th-century breech-loading rifle.

The German Mauser pistol of 1896.

The Gatling gun of 1862 was an early machine gun.

▲ The British Mark IV tank of World War I was designed to crush barbed wire and cross trenches while protecting its crew from machine gun fire.

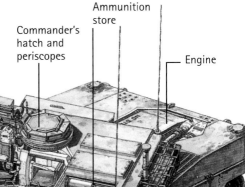

A German 50-tonne siege cannon of 1867.

Commander's hatch and periscopes · Ammunition store · Engine · Machine gun · 105-mm cannon · Sloped armour · Driver's seat · Tracks

THE MAIN BATTLE TANK

The Abrams M1 is the main battle tank (MBT) of the USA. MBTs are the most important weapons in any army. They have guns up to 120mm calibre that are able to destroy enemy strongpoints and tanks; armour protects the crew from all but the heaviest guns; and their mobility allows them to move through enemy territory to reach targets.

Modern warships have guns, missiles and complex electronics.

The Mustang was the fastest American fighter of World War II.

During World War II, the V-1 was the first guided missile used in combat.

The American 'Honest John' missile could reach a range of 20km.

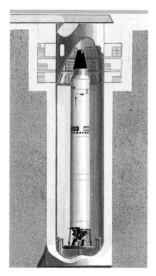

Modern Intercontinental Ballistic Missiles (ICBMs) carry nuclear warheads.

FIGHTING TOMCAT

The Grumman F14-A Tomcat is a twin-engined, two-seater fighter. It served as part of the US Navy fleet from 1974 until 2006, and is still in use by the Iranian Air Force.

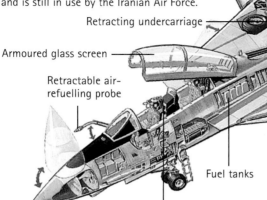

Wing pivot mounting

Retracting undercarriage

Armoured glass screen

Retractable air-refuelling probe

Fuel tanks

Ejector seat

guerrillas cut enemy supply lines and ambush patrols. The aim is to wear down the enemy forces, so that they give in.

PSYCHOLOGICAL WEAPONS

Many commanders try to persuade the enemy to surrender or to retreat by tricking them. In the 1740s, King Frederick the Great of Prussia had a special regiment of men over 2.2m tall. Because he only used his 'Giants' when he thought he would win, enemies seeing them advancing would think they were beaten. During World War II, British aircraft dropped leaflets on Germany urging troops to surrender. They failed as the leaflets contained obvious lies.

RADIO TRICKS

During World War II, a British radio station aimed at German troops claimed to be broadcast by a German army officer. Because the 'officer' used army slang, many Germans believed the stories of German defeats. Tokyo Rose, a Japanese radio show, mixed stories of American defeats with popular music during this time.

▶ Soldiers of the US 82nd Airborne Division wear gas masks during the Gulf War of 1991. Chemical and biological weapons can cause massive casualties.

PEACEFUL SOLUTIONS

At the end of every war is a period of peace. This is often agreed between the two sides in a document called a treaty. Treaties set out conditions, such as the handing over of territory and the return of prisoners, which are signed by all parties. The Treaty of Amiens ended a war between Britain and France in 1802, but it left so many issues unresolved that the two were at war again just one year later. Other treaties have been more successful. The Treaty of Vienna in 1815 was signed by every nation in Europe and meant that peace lasted for nearly a century. After World War II, the United Nations was set up to solve international disputes with the aim of preventing war from breaking out.

SEE ALSO

Castle, Celts, Civil war, Crusades, Greece (Ancient), Mongols, Napoleonic Wars, Rocket, Roman Empire, United Nations, World War I, World War II

WATER

Water is the most common substance on Earth. It is the main ingredient in all living organisms – without water, life on the planet could not exist.

WATER FACTS

- The average person drinks 44,000 litres of water in a lifetime

- Human beings will die if they lose more than 20% of the body's normal water content

- Each flush of the toilet uses between six and 17 litres of water; it takes 140 litres to fill a bath; nearly 40 litres to wash the dishes; and up to 120 litres to run a washing machine

- The wettest place on Earth is Mawsynram in India, where about 26,000mm of rain fell in 1985

▲ Climate change is reducing the amount of fresh water frozen in glaciers and polar ice caps.

Water vapour condenses and forms clouds

Rain and snow

Transpiration from plants

Water vapour in atmosphere

River flows back to oceans

Evaporation from seas and lakes

Water vapour cools and forms rain

Groundwater runs off

THE WATER CYCLE

Water is constantly being recycled. When the Sun heats the Earth's surface, water evaporates into the atmosphere. Over 80 per cent of this comes from oceans, but some comes from plants giving off water vapour (transpiration). As water in the atmosphere cools, it condenses to form clouds. Some of this water falls again as rain.

Water vapour	0.05%
Moisture in soil	0.2%
Rivers and lakes	0.35%
Salt water lakes and inland seas	0.4%

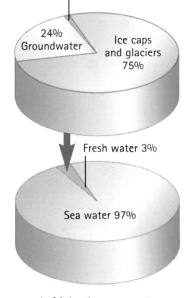

▲ Of the three per cent of the world's water that is not in the sea, 75 per cent is in ice and glaciers.

Water exists naturally in three different forms: solid (frozen as ice), liquid (water) and gas (water vapour in the air). It can dissolve more substances than any other liquid. The force of natural water power has shaped the world's mountains, valleys, coastlines and plains.

UNIVERSAL SUBSTANCE

Water covers 70 per cent of the Earth's surface – over 1.4 billion cubic kilometres. But only a tiny fraction is of any use to humans. Almost 97 per cent of the world's water is sea water, containing up to 35kg of dissolved mineral salts in every 1,000kg. That is eight times too salty to drink or to use for watering crops. Only about three per cent of the world's water is fresh – and three quarters of that is locked up in polar ice caps and mountain glaciers. Every living thing on Earth depends on the small amount of fresh water (less than one per cent of the total) that falls as rain and fills our rivers and lakes.

WATER FOR LIVING

Life began in the sea 3.5 billion years ago, and water is still essential for all life forms. The human body is made up of about two thirds water. People need 2.5 litres of water a day to stay alive, but many of us use far more – the average American uses 570 litres, the average Norwegian 300 litres and the average Briton 150 litres. We also use vast amounts of water in industry and agriculture. It takes 1,000 litres of water to grow 1kg of wheat, and 240 litres of water to produce 1kg of steel.

SHAPING THE LAND

Water is the most important force in shaping the land. Rivers and glaciers carve valleys, wear down mountain ranges, and carry gravel, sand, silt and clay onto lowland plains and eventually out into the sea. Even spectacular desert scenery is carved mainly by water from flash floods.

SEE ALSO

Lake, Mountain and valley, Ocean and sea, River, Water power, Weather

WATER POWER

Water power uses the movement of water to turn machinery or to generate electricity. It is a renewable, non-polluting source of energy.

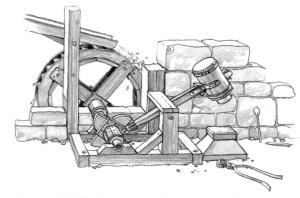

▲ In the Middle Ages, waterwheels were used to power hammers for ironworking. They saved time and labour.

Waterwheels have been used to grind grain into flour since Ancient Greek times. In 19th-century Britain, they provided the power for big textile mills during the Industrial Revolution. Electric generators that could convert the turning motion of a waterwheel into electricity led to the rapid development of hydroelectric power in the early 20th century.

HYDROELECTRIC POWER
Water is first stored in a reservoir, often made by damming a river and flooding its valley. The water flows down pipes through turbines, propeller-like blades that are spun around by the flow of the water. In turn, these spin the electricity generators. Pumped storage plants can push the water back up into the reservoir using cheap, off-peak electricity, then generate electricity again when demand is high, rather like charging up a giant battery. Just over six per cent of the world's electricity is from hydroelectric power, but it is available mainly in mountainous areas, far away from large cities, where most of the power is needed.

▲ A huge wave crashing against the shore shows the awesome force of natural water power. The sea can be harnessed to generate electricity in tidal power stations and wave-power generators.

TIDAL POWER
Dams built across river estuaries trap the rise and fall of ocean tides. The trapped water turns turbines as it flows through holes in the dam. These use the 'head' of water made by the rise and fall of ocean tides to spin turbines. The largest tidal power plant, on the River Rance in Brittany, France, has been generating 240 megawatts of electricity since 1966.

WAVE POWER
The up-and-down movement of sea waves can be used to make electricity, but this is more difficult than using flowing water to turn a turbine. Since the 1980s, more than a dozen different types of device have been developed to harness wave power. There are wave farms off the coasts of Scotland, Australia and Portugal.

TURBOGENERATOR
Water flows past turbogenerators inside the dam wall of a hydroelectric power plant. A turbogenerator converts the energy of flowing water into electrical energy. The turbine shaft is turned by the pressure of water against its curved blades, and this moves the generator rotor, which generates (produces) an electric current.

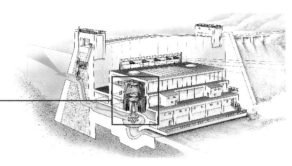

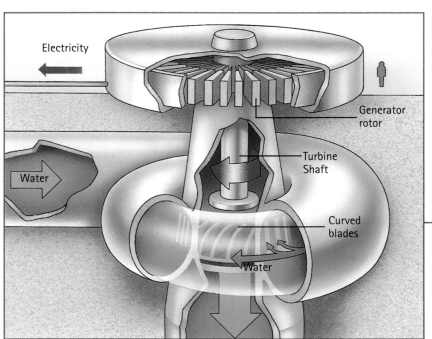

Electricity

Water

Generator rotor

Turbine Shaft

Curved blades

Water

SEE ALSO
Dam, Electricity, Energy, Engine, Water

WAVELENGTH

Wavelength is the distance between two identical points on a wave. This is usually measured from one peak of the wave to the next.

Most of us have seen waves on the sea. Before they reach the coast, these waves make the seawater ripple. The highest points of these ripples are called peaks, the lowest points are called troughs. The distance between one peak and the next is called the wavelength of the waves.

SOUND WAVES

All forms of moving energy, including sound, light and heat, travel in waves. All of them have a wavelength just like waves on the sea. When sound waves travel through air, for example, they create tiny changes in the air pressure. The peaks of a sound wave are where the air pressure is greatest. Our ears pick up the changes in air pressure and send signals to the brain.

DIFFERENT WAVELENGTHS

Just like frequency (the speed at which a wave moves up and down), wavelength affects a wave's properties. That is because wavelength and frequency are closely related. For instance, low-frequency sound waves have a longer wavelength than high-frequency ones. Similarly, red light waves have a longer wavelength than blue ones. Light itself is one of a range of energy waves, including radio waves, microwaves, infrared rays, ultraviolet rays, X-

rays and gamma rays, all of which travel at 300,000km/second. Together, these form the electromagnetic spectrum.

▲ Police often use radar to catch speeding motorists. Radar waves from a gun bounce off a moving vehicle. The frequency at which they return gives its speed.

WAVELENGTH AND FREQUENCY

If you divide the speed of a wave (measured in metres per second) by its frequency (measured in Hertz), you can work out its wavelength (in metres). For example, a sound wave that travels at 344m/second and has a frequency of 688Hz has a wavelength of 0.5m (because 344 ÷ 688 = 0.5).

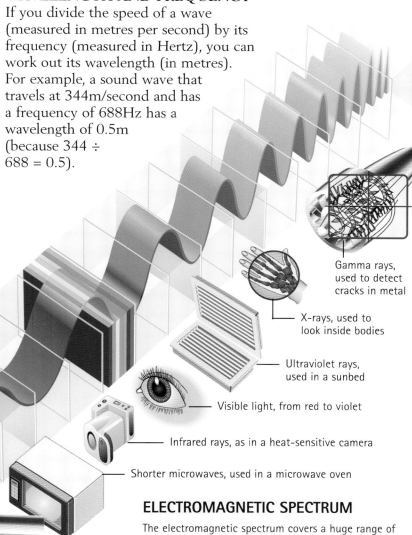

Gamma rays, used to detect cracks in metal

X-rays, used to look inside bodies

Ultraviolet rays, used in a sunbed

Visible light, from red to violet

Infrared rays, as in a heat-sensitive camera

Shorter microwaves, used in a microwave oven

Wavelength

Peak

Trough

Longer microwaves, used in radar

Ultra High Frequency (UHF) radio waves for TV transmissions

Radio waves used in radio broadcasts

ELECTROMAGNETIC SPECTRUM

The electromagnetic spectrum covers a huge range of energy waves, all of which travel in the same way. As different parts of the spectrum have different wavelengths, they have different properties. A light wave, for example, is one that we can see. An X-ray is a part of the spectrum that can pass through some solid objects, such as skin.

SEE ALSO

Energy, Light, Musical instrument, Radar and sonar, Radio, Sound, X-ray

WEATHER

Atmospheric conditions, such as rain, wind and sunshine, make up the weather at a particular place and time. Weather may change slowly or rapidly.

An anemometer is used to measure the speed of the wind. Its sensitive shells move in the wind's path.

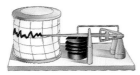

A barograph records changes in air pressure on a rotating drum, using an inked pen to draw a graph.

The psychrometer uses a dry bulb and a wet bulb to measure the humidity in the air.

Thermometers measure air temperature. They are used either inside or outside buildings.

The weather depends on the way air masses move around the globe. The climate of a place is the average of these weather conditions over a long period of time. Though weather may change within hours, climates change over years.

CAUSES OF WEATHER

The way that air masses are driven depends on factors such as distance from the Equator and the presence of mountains or seas. When an air mass moves from the sea over high ground, it cools, and the water it contains falls as rain. If an air mass moves from the centre of a continent, it contains no water and brings dry weather. If a mass of air rests over tropical waters for a long time, it becomes extremely moist and warm, leading to severe storms.

REGULAR CYCLES

The weather follows regular cycles. In many areas, the summer has warmer weather than the winter because more solar (Sun) energy is received during long, hot days. In Southeast Asia, the monsoon period is dominated by warm, wet winds from the Indian Ocean, causing heavy rains. Every ten years or so, a phenomenon called El Niño occurs: the temperature of the southeast Pacific Ocean rises slightly, which alters the movements of air masses. This can lead to drought, severe rainstorms and economic disaster.

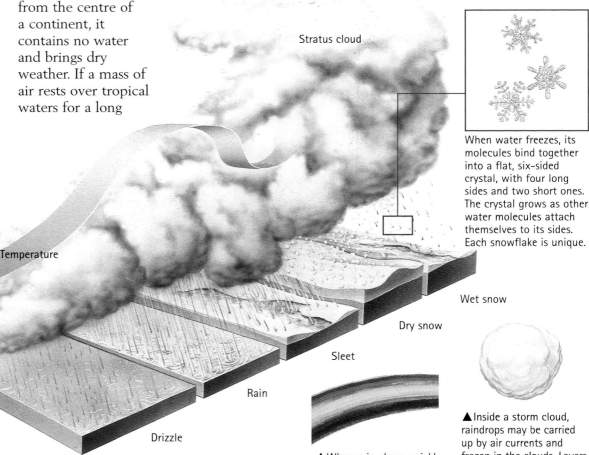

Stratus cloud

Temperature

Drizzle

Rain

Sleet

Dry snow

Wet snow

When water freezes, its molecules bind together into a flat, six-sided crystal, with four long sides and two short ones. The crystal grows as other water molecules attach themselves to its sides. Each snowflake is unique.

▲When rain clears quickly after a shower, a colourful rainbow may stretch across the sky. Sunlight shines on water droplets, and light is bent, or refracted, until it is split into spectrum colours.

▲ Inside a storm cloud, raindrops may be carried up by air currents and frozen in the clouds. Layers of ice build up as water vapour freezes onto these icy crystals. The growing hailstones fall to warmer levels, then rise again until they are heavy enough to fall from the clouds.

RAIN AND SNOW

Two main types of rain occur. In the tropics, rain forms when tiny droplets bump into each other in a cloud, join together and fall. Rain outside the tropics is caused by melting snowflakes. If the base of a stratus cloud is low enough, rain falls as drizzle. Dry snow falls when the ground temperature is cold, but if snow falls into air that is above freezing, sleet (a mixture of rain and snow) occurs.

1 The Sun heats one area of ground, such as bare soil, more than others. On warm days, bubbles of hot air form over these areas, and rise up through the cooler air around them.

2 Warm air rises into low-pressure air, then expands and cools. The air cools so much that water vapour condenses into droplets, and a small cumulus cloud is formed.

3 As it is fed by a series of air bubbles, the cloud grows, and the wind detaches it. Fair-weather cumulus clouds look like cotton balls. They do not carry enough water to cause rain.

▲ Radiosondes are balloons that carry instruments to measure temperature, air pressure, and humidity in the upper atmosphere.

HIGH AND LOW PRESSURE

In most parts of the world, weather is determined by areas of low air pressure (cyclones) or areas of high pressure (anticyclones). Some last for months, for example, the Bermuda High is an anticyclone that appears in the North Atlantic during summer. Others last only a few days or weeks. In tropical areas, belts of low pressure can be massive and move slowly westward. As they suck in warm air, heavy rains and storms are created.

FRONTS

When a mass of cold air meets a mass of warm air, a front develops. If cold air cuts sharply under warm air, a cold front forms. The warm air rises rapidly, cools and produces heavy rains. If warm air rises slowly, it produces a warm front marked by long periods of gentle rain and drizzle.

DESTRUCTIVE WEATHER

Although most thunderstorms are harmless, a large storm can produce strong winds, heavy rain, lightning and hail. In 1986, a storm in Gopalganj, India, created a downpour of hailstones weighing 1kg each and killing 100 people in a few seconds. Lightning is thought to kill 200 people a year and to start over 20,000 fires. Tornadoes form when thunderstorms create strong updraughts. The spinning air can reach 500km/h and wreak destruction along a path 1km wide and 100km long.

FORECASTING

Traditionally, people have forecast weather either by watching the sky or by noticing the behaviour of animals, which is affected by basic weather changes. Modern weather forecasting follows the global movement of areas of low and high pressure and fronts. Satellite photographs of cloud patterns help produce accurate forecasts.

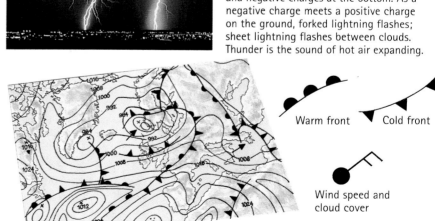

▲ As water droplets collide in a large cloud, water becomes electrically charged. Positive charges collect at the cloud's top, and negative charges at the bottom. As a negative charge meets a positive charge on the ground, forked lightning flashes; sheet lightning flashes between clouds. Thunder is the sound of hot air expanding.

Warm front   Cold front

Wind speed and cloud cover

Isobar

▲ Weather maps, such as this synoptic chart, use standard symbols. Isobars are lines that connect places where air pressure is the same. Winds flow parallel to isobars; the closer together they are, the stronger the wind. Air pressure (in millibars) is shown at centres of low and high pressure. Wind speed, and warm and cold front symbols, are also shown.

SEE ALSO

Climate, Ecology, Electricity, Light, Satellite, Season, Water

WEIGHTS AND MEASURES

Weights and measures are the standard units that we use to work out how much we have of things. Each form of measurement needs its own kind of 'ruler'.

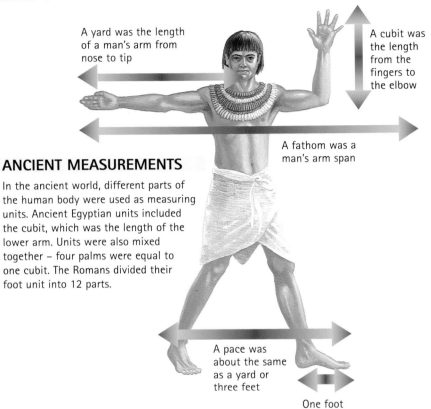

A yard was the length of a man's arm from nose to tip

A cubit was the length from the fingers to the elbow

A fathom was a man's arm span

A pace was about the same as a yard or three feet

One foot

ANCIENT MEASUREMENTS

In the ancient world, different parts of the human body were used as measuring units. Ancient Egyptian units included the cubit, which was the length of the lower arm. Units were also mixed together – four palms were equal to one cubit. The Romans divided their foot unit into 12 parts.

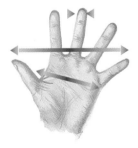

▲ Units based on the hand included the digit, which was the width of a finger. This later became the inch. A span was the length from thumb to little finger and there was also the palm unit.

Ever since people started making things, trading goods or carrying out experiments, they have needed to measure amounts. Ancient civilizations based their measurements on parts of the body. These would have been standard (the same) only within each civilization. An Egyptian cubit, for example, was different from a Greek or Roman cubit. This caused many problems, especially when people needed to trade with one another. That is why, over centuries, standard measurement systems have come into use.

IMPERIAL SYSTEM

Until about 30 years ago, most people used the imperial system of measurement. This measured length in inches, feet, yards and miles; and weight in ounces, pounds, stones and tons. The use of the foot as a unit of measurement dates back to Anglo-Saxon times. The inch (three grains of barley laid lengthwise) dates to the 1300s, and the

mile has its origins in measuring thousands of paces. Ounces and pounds are units of the avoirdupois ('goods sold by weight') system, in use since the 1400s. The imperial system was not always easy to use, however, and people who took complex measurements realized they needed a simpler set of units. In the 1790s, the metric system was created in France.

METRIC SYSTEM

Many countries now use the metric system, or SI (Système International). The units are the metre (length) and the kilogram, (weight). There are many other units with their own special names such as the joule, the newton and the volt. However, scientists can relate most of them to this basic set – one newton (1N), for example, the unit of force, can also be written as one kilogram metre per second per second ($1kg\ m/sec^2$).

SETTING STANDARDS

A laboratory near Paris holds examples of the SI units – the Standard Metre is the length of a certain number of wavelengths of a specially made laser beam. The Standard Kilogram is the weight of a special ingot of platinum-iridium metal, stored at a controlled temperature.

▲ Scales have been used to weigh objects for sale for thousands of years. In this case, they are being used to weigh dried flower and plant remedies for sale at a herbalist dispensary.

452

WEIGHT

SI units

1,000 milligrams (mg)	=	1 gram (g)
1,000g	=	1 kilogram (kg)
100kg	=	1 quintal (q)
1,000kg	=	1 metric ton or tonne (t)

Imperial units

16 ounces (oz)	=	1 pound (lb)
14lb	=	1 stone
112lb	=	1 hundredweight (cwt)
20cwt	=	1 (long) ton (= 2,240lb)
2,000lb	=	1 short ton (US)

Conversions

1 gram	=	0.035oz
1kg	=	2.205lb
1 metric ton or tonne (t)	=	2,200lb
1t	=	0.984 (long) tons
1oz	=	28.35g
1lb	=	454g
1 (long) ton	=	1.02t

AREA

SI units

100 square mm (mm^2)	=	1 square cm (cm^2)
10,000cm^2	=	1 square metre (m^2)
100m^2	=	1 are (a)
100a	=	1 hectare (ha)
100ha	=	1 square kilometre (km^2)

Imperial units

144 square inches (in^2)	=	1 square foot (ft^2)
9ft^2	=	1 square yard (yd^2)
4,840yd^2	=	1 acre
640 acres	=	1 square mile (mile^2)

Conversions

1cm^2	=	0.155in^2
1m^2	=	10.76ft^2
1 hectare	=	2.47 acres
1km^2	=	0.386 square miles
1in^2	=	6.45cm^2
1ft^2	=	0.093m^2
1 acre	=	0.405 hectares
1 square mile	=	2.59km^2

LENGTH

SI units

10 millimetres (mm)	=	1 centimetre (cm)
100cm	=	1 metre (m)
1,000m	=	1 kilometre (km)

Imperial units

12 inches (in)	=	1 foot (ft)
3ft	=	1 yard (yd)
1,760 yd	=	1 mile

Conversions

1mm	=	0.0394in
1cm	=	0.394in
1m	=	1.094yd
1km	=	0.621 miles
1in	=	2.54cm
1ft	=	30.48cm
1yd	=	0.914m
1 mile	=	1.609km

VOLUME

SI units

1,000mm^3	=	1 cubic centimetre (cm^3)
1,000cm^3	=	1 cubic decimetre (dm^3)
1,000dm^3	=	1 cubic metre (m^3)

Imperial units

1,728 cubic inches (in^3)	=	1 cubic foot (ft^3)
27ft^3	=	1 cubic yard (yd^3)

Conversions

1cm^3 = 0.061in^3	1m^3 = 35.3ft^3
1in^3 = 16.4cm^3	1ft^3 = 0.028m^3

CAPACITY

SI units

1,000 millilitres (ml)	=	1 litre (l)
100 litres	=	1 hectolitre (hl)

Imperial units

4 gills	=	1 pint (= 20 fluid ounces)
2 pints	=	1 quart
4 quarts	=	1 UK gallon

Conversions

1 litre = 0.22 UK gallons	1 pint = 0.568 litres
1 UK gallon = 1.2 US gallons	

The Egyptians used delicate balancing scales to weigh gold and precious stones. Later, the Babylonians (who lived in what is now Iraq) made standard weights from metal to use at markets.

The builders of the pyramids in Egypt had to measure length so that they knew how many stones they needed, as well as how to drive shafts accurately through the huge structures.

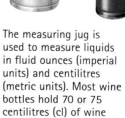

The measuring jug is used to measure liquids in fluid ounces (imperial units) and centilitres (metric units). Most wine bottles hold 70 or 75 centilitres (cl) of wine when they are full.

SEE ALSO

Babylon, Clock, Gravity, Time

WHALE AND DOLPHIN

Whales, dolphins and porpoises are collectively known as cetaceans, which means 'large sea animal'. They are divided into two groups: toothed and baleen whales.

A white-sided dolphin eats fish and has 92–128 teeth. It is found in big schools of up to 1,000 dolphins.

A rough-toothed dolphin is a small (up to 2.5m), tropical species known to follow ships.

Porpoises are the smallest cetaceans (up to 2m). The most common species is the harbour porpoise.

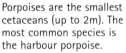

The adult beluga, or white whale, is pure white, but the young are grey. Belugas have no dorsal fin.

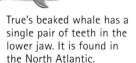

True's beaked whale has a single pair of teeth in the lower jaw. It is found in the North Atlantic.

A male bottle-nosed whale grows up to 9m (females are smaller). It eats squid, cuttlefish and herring.

There are 14 species of baleen whale and about 74 toothed whale species, including 38 types of marine dolphin, four river dolphin species and six types of porpoise. Cetaceans may look like fish, but whales and dolphins are warm-blooded, air-breathing mammals.

FROM EARTH TO SEA
Whales first appeared on the Earth over 50 million years ago. Their ancestors once lived on land, but then moved into the water and gradually lost their back legs; their front legs became flippers. The flippers are used for steering and balance, but the power comes from the big tail with its horizontal fins or flukes. The tail is waved up and down to drive the whale forward. (Fish have vertical tail fins, waved from side to side.)

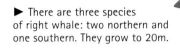

▶ There are three species of right whale: two northern and one southern. They grow to 20m.

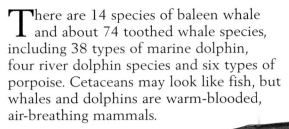

◀ Fin whales belong to the rorqual and humpback family that have grooved throats. They grow to 20m.

▶ Bowhead whales grow up to 18m and their baleen plates can be 3m long. They belong to the right whale family.

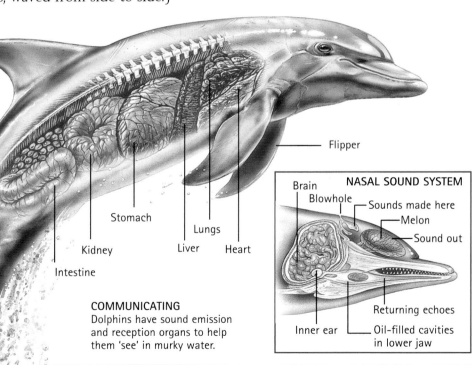

Flipper

Stomach

Kidney

Lungs

Liver   Heart

Intestine

NASAL SOUND SYSTEM
Brain
Blowhole — Sounds made here
— Melon
— Sound out
Inner ear — Oil-filled cavities in lower jaw
Returning echoes

COMMUNICATING
Dolphins have sound emission and reception organs to help them 'see' in murky water.

SEEING WITH SOUND
Dolphins communicate, find food and navigate using a kind of radar sound system under water. They make high-frequency clicking noises by blowing air through their nasal passages. Then the melon (a waxy cavity in the dolphin's head) focuses the sound into a beam. Sound vibrations travel through the water and bounce off objects. A dolphin receives the sound echoes through an area in its jaw where the bones are thinner. The echoes then travel to the inner ear.

SIEVE OR BITE

There are two types of whale: baleen whales and toothed whales. Baleen whales are filter feeders that sieve tiny creatures from the water through fringed curtains of a horny material called baleen or whalebone.

◀ Blue whale.

▲ The number and size of teeth varies with species. Dolphins (above) have conical, interlocking teeth, porpoises have spade-shaped teeth and most beaked whales only have two visible pairs.

THERE SHE BLOWS

Whales come to the surface to breathe. As they breathe out, warm moist air rushes out through nostrils on the top of the head – the blowhole. This 'blow' may reach 10m into the air. They then take a few breaths through the blowhole and dive down for several minutes. Toothed whales have just one blowhole, baleen whales have two.

FRIENDLY GIANT

The blue whale is the largest animal that has ever lived on Earth. It can reach a length of 30m and a weight of 150 tonnes – as heavy as 20 fully grown elephants. Like most of the other large whales, the blue whale has no teeth. It is a baleen whale that feeds on tiny plankton and krill living near the surface of the sea. Other whales and dolphins have lots of teeth and feed on fish, squid, seals, and penguins.

SMILING DOLPHINS

Dolphins are small whales with a pointed snout and appear to have a permanent smile. They are playful and intelligent animals. They live in groups called schools and communicate with clicks and whistles. They use sound location to navigate and find fish to eat. An injured dolphin will usually be helped by other members of the school. There are even reports of dolphins helping drowning people. Like all whales, dolphins never come ashore. They mate and give birth to their young in the sea. A mother dolphin feeds her baby on her milk for a year and they often stay together for several years.

▲ Narwhals grow up to 5.5m with no dorsal fin and two teeth. In males, one tooth develops into a 3-m long spiral tusk.

◀ Sperm whales are a family of three species. They are the largest toothed whales (growing up to 20m) and the deepest divers. They eat mostly squid – even giant ones.

◀ Orcas, or killer whales, are dolphins with a tall (2m) shark-like fin. They have long, sharp teeth and eat young whales, seals, squid or fish.

SEE ALSO

Animal, Conservation, Mammal, Migration

WIND

Wind is the movement of air over the Earth's surface. It can range from a gentle summer breeze to the destructive power of a hurricane or tornado.

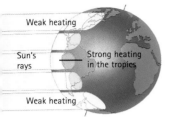

▲ The Sun is strongest in the tropics, where it is almost overhead. Closer to the poles, the Sun's rays are more spread out and are therefore weaker.

North Pole (high pressure)

South Pole (high pressure)

▲ Wind is the flow of air from high- (H) to low-pressure areas (L). This creates six main bands of air across the globe.

Wind is the movement of air from an area of high pressure to an area of low pressure. A wind is named after the direction from which it is blowing. So a north wind is one blowing from the north.

BLOWING HOT AND COLD

Big global wind systems such as the Trade winds and Easterlies are caused by the heating effect of the Sun. Near the Equator, the Sun is almost overhead, and so the land, sea and air receive the maximum amount of heat. Warm air tends to rise (just as a hot air balloon rises) and because it is rising, it does not press down so much on the Earth's surface. This creates a low-pressure area. Colder, heavier air sinks down towards the Earth's surface in cooler regions, farther from the Equator, and this creates high-pressure areas. The cooler, heavier air flows over the Earth's surface from high-pressure areas to low-pressure areas, creating winds.

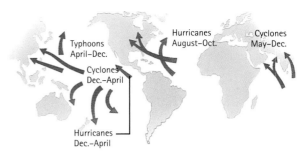

▲ Hurricanes form in late summer and autumn over warm areas in the Atlantic, Pacific and Indian oceans. They then move westwards, along the coasts.

LOCAL WINDS

Local winds arise from a combination of weather patterns and the shape of the land. Land heats up and cools down quicker than water and this produces the gentle breezes you often feel at the coast. During the day, the land heats up, the air above it warms up and rises, and moist air flows in from the sea to replace it, creating a cool sea breeze. At night, the land cools quickly, the air above it descends and spreads out, and this produces a light offshore breeze. Other local winds form round mountains, especially where there are glaciers. At night, cold, heavy air pours down the hillsides and valleys, and out over the surrounding lowlands.

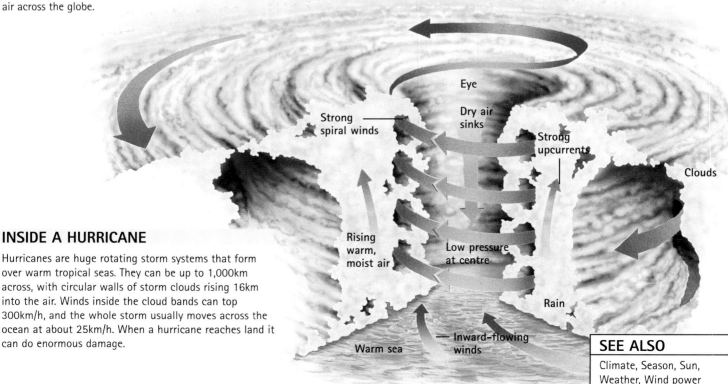

INSIDE A HURRICANE

Hurricanes are huge rotating storm systems that form over warm tropical seas. They can be up to 1,000km across, with circular walls of storm clouds rising 16km into the air. Winds inside the cloud bands can top 300km/h, and the whole storm usually moves across the ocean at about 25km/h. When a hurricane reaches land it can do enormous damage.

SEE ALSO

Climate, Season, Sun, Weather, Wind power

WIND POWER

Wind power uses the power of the wind to turn machinery or generate electricity. It is a renewable, non-polluting source of energy.

Fantail

Windmills have been used to grind corn or pump water from the ground for hundreds of years. Simple windmills may have been used in Ancient Persia (now Iran) in the 7th century CE. Modern windmills, called wind turbines, use the turning motion of the blades to spin a turbine, which generates electricity.

▲ The addition of a fantail, invented in 1745, automatically turned the top of the mill so that the sails caught the wind.

SPINNING SAILS
In a windmill, four to eight wind sails, each 3–9m long, catch the wind. As the sails spin, a shaft turns. Gears transfer the power to turn a heavy grinding stone at the bottom of the building. Spring sails made of wood shutters were invented in 1772 and could be adjusted to turn at a steady speed in varying winds.

WIND TURBINES
Windmills were largely replaced in the 20th century by engine power. But wind turbines are a growing source of energy. Pioneered in Denmark in the 1890s, these use airfoils like an aeroplane's propellers to

▲ Although often only 500m across, tornadoes unleash a devastating force. They form over land, like dark funnels of cloud hanging from the base of storm clouds, and can contain winds of over 400km/h – strong enough to demolish buildings and throw cars around like toys.

turn a turbine and make electricity. Used to supply electricity in remote areas, wind farms may consist of hundreds of wind turbines, with blades 15–30m in diameter. The largest wind farms can generate more than 750 megawatts – nearly as much electricity as a nuclear power plant produces. Although they do not cause pollution, they take up a lot of land.

WIND FARMS
Wind turbines need to be made so that they turn even in gentle wind, but still cope with gales. They also need to be built where there is plenty of wind, such as along the coast or on flat plains. These places are usually a long way from where the electricity is needed, and so much energy is lost sending it along power lines.

FAST FACTS
• The sailing boat is one of the most common users of wind power

• The largest wind farms are in California and Texas, USA, but Shepherds Flat, which will be largest when built, is in Oregon

• By 2050, 12 per cent of the world's electricity may be generated using wind power

SEE ALSO
Boat, Electricity, Wind

WOLF AND OTHER WILD DOGS

Wolves, coyotes, jackals and foxes are all kinds of wild dog. They are strong, quick, alert carnivores, many of which hunt in packs.

A skilful hunter, the red fox lives in Asia, Europe and North America.

In winter, the long fur of the Arctic fox turns from brown or grey to white.

Known for its eerie howl, the coyote is found in Canada, the USA and Mexico.

Wolves belong to the group known as *Canidae*, or the dog family. This group also includes the grey, red and maned wolf, coyote and dingo, African and Asian (dhole) wild dogs, raccoon and bush dogs, four kinds of jackal, about 20 kinds of fox – as well as the hundreds of breeds and varieties of domestic dog. These were probably tamed and bred from wolf ancestors at least 10,000 years ago.

FEATURES OF THE HUNTER
All members of the dog family are meat-eaters, or carnivores. They live by hunting or scavenging. But they eat almost anything if they are hungry, even fruits and berries. They have keen senses, including sharp eyesight and hearing, and an excellent sense of smell. Their long, strong legs, which they use for fast running and relentless pursuit, have clawed toes for good grip and scratching. Their long, sharp teeth bite and tear flesh.

WOLF HABITATS
The grey, or timber, wolf, usually just known as the wolf, is widespread across North America, parts of Europe, the Middle East and northern Asia. It prefers forests, but can live in mountains, grasslands and even deserts. The red wolf is extremely rare, limited to a small area of southeast North America.

◄ When gathering to begin a hunt, wolves greet each other with loud howls. This warns wolves from other packs to stay out of their territory.

▲ In each pack, some wolves are more dominant than others. Here, a dominant wolf stands with its tail and ears held up, while a subordinate wolf approaches it in a crouched position, tail between legs and ears flattened.

The maned wolf, which is really more like a long-legged fox, dwells in grassy scrubland in central South America.

WILD DOGS AROUND THE WORLD
The coyote, with its mournful howl, is a wolf-like wild dog that has extended its territory from the southwestern United States and Mexico across the whole North American continent. In Australia, the dingo is probably descended from the part-tamed dogs of Aboriginal people, brought to the continent more than 7,000 years ago. Jackals live across Africa, the Middle East and southern Asia. Different kinds of bushy-tailed fox dwell in almost every habitat, from the Arctic fox of the snowy far north, to the Cape fox of southern Africa's deserts, and the well-known, widespread and adaptable red fox, which scavenges bins in towns and cities.

KEY FACTS
- Various members of the dog family can breed with each other. For example, a domestic dog and a coyote produce 'coydog' puppies. This interbreeding makes it difficult to know exactly how many true species are in the dog family

- The main difference between wolves and dogs that look like them is that wolves carry their tail hanging down while dogs carry it curled up

- The crab-eating fox of South America really does eat crabs, and tortoises too, but it prefers easier meat, such as mice, birds, lizards, insects and eggs

HUNTING IN PACKS

Many kinds of wild dog, especially wolves and African and Asian wild dogs, hunt with others of their kind. The group is called a pack. It can catch much larger prey than one dog hunting alone. A pack of wolves can bring down a full-grown moose over 2m high. Each pack has dominant males, or leaders, who get the best food, and mate with females at breeding time.

A VARIETY OF PREY

Other kinds of wild dog, especially foxes, live and hunt alone, or with a mate. Jackals have a mistaken reputation as scavengers. In fact, they usually hunt live prey – from frogs, lizards and mice to small gazelles and young zebras. Smaller wild dogs usually eat smaller meals. Most foxes have a diet of mice, voles, fish, frogs, birds, eggs and insects. The smallest kind, the fennec fox, with huge ears, survives in the Sahara and Middle Eastern deserts by consuming small beetles, spiders, locusts and worms.

▲ The dingo, which can be bred with the domestic dog, howls, but rarely barks. Dingoes come together to run down and kill large prey, such as kangaroos.

THE HUNTER IS HUNTED

Wolves have long been feared in legend and have therefore been persecuted. In fact, wolves attack people only when threatened or if they are extremely hungry. Many other wild dogs are also hunted, and some are endangered. People shoot, poison or trap them in case they raid farm animals. Also some kinds, especially foxes, are still killed for their handsome fur pelts.

The jackal is up to 75cm in length. Like the fox, it has a strong body smell.

The raccoon dog lives throughout eastern Asia and is mainly nocturnal.

The African wild dog lives in large parts of Africa, and hunts its prey in packs.

PACK HUNTERS

Wolves hunt in packs, feeding on almost any animal that they can catch. In order to kill prey such as reindeer and elk, which are faster and stronger than they are, wolves must be quick and skilful. Wolves hunt by day and by night, roaming through territory until they find prey. They stalk it by moving towards it against the wind to prevent it from picking up their scent. Once close enough, the wolves break into a run and the chase begins. If they succeed in catching their victim, they weaken it through injury, then grab it by the throat.

459

SEE ALSO

Animal, Desert, Dog, Mammal

WOMEN'S RIGHTS

Women's rights are those civil rights that have traditionally been denied to women in many societies. Women have had to struggle to gain these rights.

MARY WOLLSTONECRAFT (1759–97), English-born writer of one of the first feminist books, *Vindication of the Rights of Women*, 1792. A later pamphlet, *Thoughts on the Education of Daughters* (1797) criticized girls' schooling.

ELIZABETH CADY STANTON (1815–1902), organized the first women's rights assembly in the USA in 1848. She fought for fair property and divorce laws for married women, co-education and the right to vote (suffrage).

EMMELINE PANKHURST (1828–1928), a women's rights leader in the UK, who founded the Women's Social and Political Fund (1902), campaigning for the right to vote. She and her daughter, Christabel, were imprisoned many times.

In different societies the status of men and women has varied greatly. Today it is generally thought that men and women should have equal rights and some countries have laws to make forms of discrimination (unfair treatment) illegal.

ANCIENT RIGHTS
The role of women within society has varied greatly. In Ancient Greece, women had few rights. They were expected to stay at home and to take no part in social life. Some Greek teachers believed it was wrong to teach women to read in case they learned too much and disagreed with the men. In Egypt, however, women played a full part in society. They could take jobs, own property and divorce their husbands. Some became rulers, but usually after the death of a husband or son.

DIVISION OF LABOUR
In traditional farming communities the work of a family was divided. Men mainly carried out heavy physical work. Women took on household tasks and childcare. Other jobs in society were also

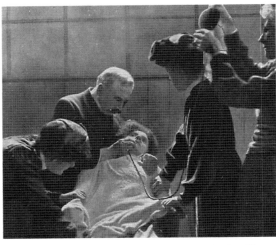

▲ Imprisoned women's rights campaigners in the UK often went on hunger strike and were brutally force-fed.

divided. Traditionally, men fought in the army, while women often cared for the sick.

CHANGING RIGHTS
Industrial Revolution in the 1800s brought changes. The work in many new industries did not need strength, but skill. Women were able to do many factory jobs just as well as men. A family could be supported by a woman instead of a man. By the late 19th century, most industrialized nations

► The US Army 24th Infantry in Saudi Arabia. The Gulf War, in 1990–91, was the first conflict that saw women soldiers of the US Army fighting alongside men.

KEY DATES

1893 Women in New Zealand get the right to vote

1958 Moroccan women have right to choose husbands

1960 Sirimavo Bandaranaike in Ceylon (now Sri Lanka) becomes the world's first woman prime minister

1963 Equal Pay Act of 1963 in the USA rules that men and women should receive equal pay for the same job

1971 Women in Switzerland get the right to vote

1975 Sex Discrimination Act (UK) makes it illegal to choose men over women for jobs, on grounds of sex

1984 Women in Liechtenstein get the right to vote

2011 Saudi Arabia announces that women will be allowed to vote in the next election

had civil rights for women. Women were allowed to keep their own property when they married, instead of giving control to their husbands. They could enter into contracts and sign legal papers, teach and become nurses and doctors, although education for girls was still less formal than for males, and ended at an earlier age.

THE VOTE

Some people argued that only those who owned property or fought in wars had a right to vote. But during the 19th century these ideas were challenged. The right to vote was extended to poor men, but not to women. In the late 19th century, in many parts of the world a movement began to win suffrage (the right to vote) for women. Its followers, known as suffragettes, used publicity and persuasion to gain the vote. Others led demonstrations and turned to violence. One British campaigner, Emily Davison, was killed when she threw herself under the King's horse at a race.

SLOW PROGRESS

Women in New Zealand were the first to get the vote, in 1893. By the 1920s, most democracies had given women the vote, although Swiss women won it only in the 1970s. Many Arab countries only gave women the right to vote in the early years of the 21st century.

SHIFTING HORIZONS

During the 1960s, a new movement, called Women's Lib (Liberation), aimed to make women equal to men in social and economic terms. Gradually women's choices have widened. Today there are women doctors, judges and company directors. It is not unusual to see women as fire-fighters or builders, and women have taken front-line roles in some Western armies. Even so, the balance between a career and motherhood is still a dilemma for many women.

▲ During the two world wars, many Western women took jobs making weapons in factories. It was their war efforts that led to greater recognition of women's value.

▲ Israel's Golda Meir was deputy foreign minister in 1948, and later foreign minister. She became the Israeli prime minister in 1969.

◄ In 1996, the Taliban (fundamentalist Muslims) took over the government of Afghanistan. They banned girls from schools, women from working and made women cover themselves. This government was overthrown in 2001.

SEE ALSO

Democracy, Education, Industrial Revolution, Israel, Middle Ages, Textile, World War I, World War II

WORLD WAR I

World War I was a terrible war fought between 1914 and 1918 in which millions of people died. It began in Europe, but spread to many parts of the globe.

Kaiser Wilhelm II (1859–1941) of Germany led an aggressive foreign policy against other nations.

Lloyd George (1863–1945), British prime minister from 1916, reorganized the war effort for victory.

Russia's Tsar Nicholas II (1868–1918) backed Serbia against Austria, bringing Russia into the war.

People living at the time called World War I 'the Great War' because no other war had been so widespread nor so destructive. Millions of soldiers were killed and the world economy changed for ever.

OUTBREAK OF WAR
In 1914, Europe was divided into two major alliances. The Habsburg Empire was allied to Germany to block Russian moves in the Balkans, while France sided with Russia against the growing might of Germany. On June 28, 1914, the Habsburg archduke Franz Ferdinand was shot dead by a Serb terrorist, prompting the Habsburgs to declare war on Serbia. Serbia, in turn, asked for help from the Russians, who then declared war on the Habsburgs. This brought Germany and France into the war. Britain joined the war when Germany invaded Belgium.

EARLY BATTLES
In the East, Russian armies were smashed by the Germans at Tannenberg, while Habsburg armies were defeated by the Russians in several encounters during the month of September. In the West, the Germans intended to capture Paris and defeat France, but were stopped on the River Marne on September 8, 1914, while the British army blocked outflanking moves to the North. By October, the armies had settled into trenches for the winter.

NEW WEAPONS
Barbed wire barriers, machine guns and artillery made defence so strong that attacks were almost useless. Troops experimented with poison gas to help attackers, but it rarely had much effect. Tanks, first used by the British in 1916,

Russian Cossacks and other cavalry were used for scouting, but were useless in the trenches.

▲ World War I began after Serb terrorist Gavrilo Princip killed the Habsburg archduke Franz Ferdinand. Princip was sentenced to 20 years in prison, but fell ill and died in 1918.

could defeat barbed wire or machine guns, but they often broke down. Aircraft were more successful, and were used to spy out enemy troops, target artillery shells and drop bombs. The German pilot Manfred von Richthofen, nicknamed the 'Red Baron', successfully shot 80 enemy aircraft down in flames.

WORLD WAR
In Africa, British and French troops attacked German colonies. In 1915, Australian and New Zealand troops attacked Turkey at Gallipoli, but were badly defeated and sustained heavy losses. At sea, German ships and submarines sank Allied ships, and in 1917 began attacking any ships heading for Allied ports. The United States first protested about these attacks on its ships, and then joined the Allies, declaring war on Germany.

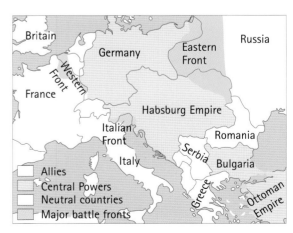

▲ Trench warfare led to small battle fronts. Only on the Eastern Front were sweeping movements made.

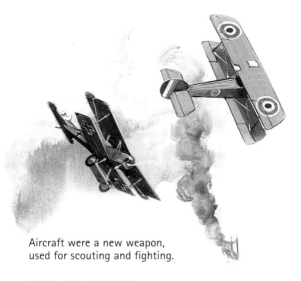

Aircraft were a new weapon, used for scouting and fighting.

The small Serb army was driven out of Serbia into Greece in December 1915.

Britain had the smallest army in 1914, but it was made up of professionals.

In 1914, the German army was the largest and best trained in the world.

KEY DATES

August 1914 War breaks out between the Allies (France, Britain, Russia, Belgium, Serbia and Montenegro) and the Central Powers (Germany and Habsburg Empire)

November 1914 Turkey joins the Central Powers

May 1915 Italy joins the Allies

October 1915 Bulgaria joins the Central Powers

August 1916 Romania joins the Allies

April 1917 The USA joins the Allies

December 1917 Russia makes peace with Germany

November 1918 Fighting ceases

1919 Peace Treaties signed at Versailles in France

FINAL MOVES

In 1917, the Communists took over Russia, and made peace. The German troops, freed from Russia, launched a massive attack in March 1918 in France. American troops helped to stop the attack. But Bulgaria, Turkey and the Habsburgs were close to collapse and Germany asked for peace. A ceasefire was finally agreed on November 11, 1918.

TRENCH WARFARE

The war in the West was fought from trenches guarded by barbed wire and machine guns. Conditions were appalling, with knee-deep mud, constant shelling, sniping and raids. The battles of the Somme and Verdun in France in 1916 cost over two million casualties, although neither side managed to advance more than a few hundred metres.

THE WAR ENDS

The cost of World War I was immense. Germany lost 1.9 million men, Russia 1.7 million, France 1.5 million and Britain and the Habsburgs 1 million each, as well as vast amounts of money. The Habsburg Empire was split into Austria, Hungary, Czechoslovakia and Yugoslavia. Poland, Estonia, Latvia and Lithuania became independent. European countries lost economic power as others built up their industries. The world was changed for ever.

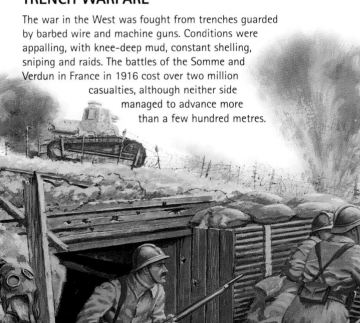

Machine gun post in the French trenches

German troops

SEE ALSO
Communism, Empire, Warfare, World War II

WORLD WAR II

World War II was fought between 1939 and 1945. It involved more countries, cost more lives and caused more destruction than any other war.

Erwin Rommel (1891–1944) was a daring leader of German armoured units.

Yamamoto Isoroku (1884–1943) planned Japan's attack on Pearl Harbor.

Bernard Montgomery (1887–1976) led the British in North Africa and Europe.

Georgy Zhukov (1896–1974) commanded the Soviet Red Army.

Dwight D. Eisenhower (1890–1969) led the D-Day invasion of 1944.

The dictators Adolf Hitler in Germany, Benito Mussolini in Italy and General Tojo Hideki in Japan wanted to extend the power and territories of their countries. They formed a pact, called the Axis, to gain what they wanted.

BLITZKRIEG

In September 1939, Germany invaded Poland to regain land it had lost in World War I. Britain and France supported Poland. The Germans used a tactic called *Blitzkrieg* – 'lightning war'. Bomber aircraft began the attack, then tanks, or panzers, plunged deep behind enemy lines, followed by infantry and artillery. Poland was defeated in just five weeks. In April 1940, Hitler invaded Denmark, Belgium, Holland, Norway and France. By July, only Britain had not surrendered. In the Battle of Britain which followed, the Royal Air Force beat off German air attacks.

INTO RUSSIA

Hitler wanted to expand Germany and create new 'living space' for the German nation. In June 1941, 3.5 million German, Italian, Romanian and Hungarian troops stormed into Russia, capturing vast territories and over a million prisoners. In December, a reinforced Red Army finally stopped the invaders just outside Moscow.

The American B17 Flying Fortress

The Japanese Mitsubishi Ki-67, codenamed 'Peggy'

The German Dornier Do217

The British Lancaster

▲ Small bombers, such as the Dornier and Mitsubishi, were used to destroy battlefield targets, such as tanks and artillery. The Lancaster, Flying Fortress and other heavy bombers pounded cities and factories.

PEARL HARBOR

Japan wanted to capture large areas of Southeast Asia to secure industrial raw materials. The Japanese hoped that a quick defeat of the USA would persuade the Americans to allow Japanese expansion, so they launched a surprise attack on Pearl Harbor, Hawaii. The USA did not give way, but declared war. The same day, Japan invaded Southeast Asia. By May 1942, Japan had conquered Burma, Malaya, the Philippines and the East Indies.

THE TIDE TURNS

After three years of war, the Allies had built up their armed forces. In North Africa, German and Italian troops were defeated at El Alamein in October 1942, and in December 1942, the German 6th Army was

◄ On December 7, 1941, 360 Japanese aircraft attacked Pearl Harbor, Hawaii, the base of the US Pacific Fleet. The attack opened the way for Japanese conquests and brought the USA into the war.

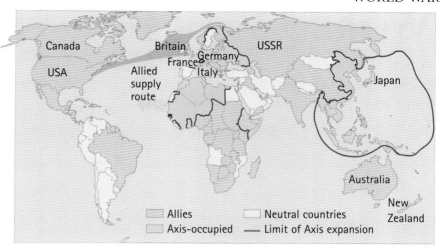

► The Axis powers – Germany, Japan and their allies – made large conquests in 1939–42. But the greater resources of the Allies were brought into action after 1942, leading to eventual victory.

wiped out by the Russians at Stalingrad. The Japanese were halted by British, Australian and American troops in February 1943. The Allies then organized strike forces to reconquer Burma, and to use 'island-hopping' tactics in the Pacific.

GERMANY COLLAPSES

In June 1944, Germany was caught between the D-Day landings in Normandy, France and the Russian advance in the East. In April 1945, the Russians reached Berlin. On April 30, Hitler killed himself, and two days later Germany surrendered. Allied troops discovered that the Nazis had killed millions, six million of them Jews, in what became known as the Holocaust.

THE ATOM BOMBS

In April 1945, the Americans attacked the island of Okinawa, from which Japan could be invaded. American casualties were high as the Japanese fought back. US President Harry S. Truman decided to use the atom bomb. The cities of Hiroshima and Nagasaki were destroyed in August with the loss of about 200,000 lives. Japan surrendered on September 2, 1945.

PEACE AND COLD WAR

The war had cost the lives of some 15 million troops and 35 million civilians. After the war, the world divided into two powerful blocs: the Communist countries, led by the Soviet Union and China and the democratic world, led by the USA. The Cold War had begun.

▲ The Allied leaders, Winston Churchill (left), Franklin D. Roosevelt (centre) and Joseph Stalin (right), met at Yalta in 1945 to decide the post-war arrangements for Europe.

D–DAY

At dawn on June 6, 1944, the largest invasion fleet in history landed Allied forces on the coast of Normandy. In all, 1,200 warships and 4,100 landing craft put 132,500 men ashore, while 10,000 aircraft attacked German positions inland. The success of the D-Day invasion allowed American, British and French troops to drive the Germans out of France.

SEE ALSO

Cold War, Fascism, Great Depression, Warfare, World War I

WORM

Worms are legless invertebrates (animals with no backbone). There are four major groups: ribbon worms, flatworms, roundworms and segmented worms.

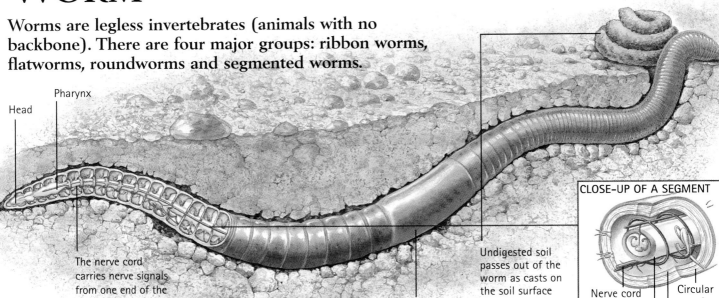

Head

Pharynx

The nerve cord carries nerve signals from one end of the worm to the other

Clitellum – produces cases for worm eggs

Undigested soil passes out of the worm as casts on the soil surface

CLOSE-UP OF A SEGMENT

Nerve cord
Intestine
Longitudinal muscle
Circular muscle

A lugworm (segmented) has feathery gills.

A horse leech (segmented) can grow up to 30cm.

Flatworms can cause serious illnesses in humans.

Roundworms make up the largest group of worms.

Most ribbon worms live in the sea and grow up to 2m.

A ragworm (segmented) has strong jaws to eat prey.

There are thousands of kinds of worm. The simplest kinds, such as flatworms, are found mostly in the sea or are parasites that live inside animals and humans. Ribbon worms are like long flatworms – the bootlace worm grows up to 25m.

EARTHWORMS
The earthworms that tunnel in gardens belong to a group called annelids, or segmented worms. Their bodies are made of many ring-like sections. There are hundreds of species of earthworm and all feed by swallowing soil and digesting any decaying matter in it. They also pull dead leaves into their tunnels and eat them. Earthworms are important for farmers and gardeners because their tunnels drain and bring air into the soil and allow plant roots to grow properly. There are no separate males and females: each worm has both male and female parts. After mating, which usually takes place above ground at night, each worm lays its own eggs.

BLOOD-SUCKING LEECHES
Leeches are related to earthworms, but instead of having bristles for moving they have a large sucker at each end. Most of them live in water or damp soil and feed on other animals. Some of the bigger ones are bloodsuckers and may attack people.

SLITHERING SEGMENTS
Each segment of an earthworm's body has several little bristles on the underside and these enable the worms to move through their tunnels. The bristles of one group of segments dig into the walls like anchors, while powerful muscles push or pull the others forward. There are no lungs; respiration takes place through the body surface.

PARASITIC WORMS
Many flatworms and roundworms (also called nematodes) live inside other animals as parasites. Hooks or suckers on their head cling to the lining of the host's intestines and the worms soak up digested food there. Tapeworms, which can reach 30m, produce huge numbers of eggs, which pass out with the host's droppings. Some eggs find their way into new host animals.

▲ Peacock worms live in the sea. They catch food with bristles and live in a tube made from secretions.

SEE ALSO
Animal, Earth, Sight, Zoology

466

X-RAY

X-rays are a form of energy that can pass straight through many solid materials. We use X-rays to look inside bodies and machines and to kill some cancers.

▲ X-ray radiation was discovered by the German physicist Wilhelm Roentgen (1845–1923), who was awarded the first Nobel Prize for Physics in 1901.

▼ High doses of X-rays can damage body cells. The harmful effects of X-rays are often used to help cure cancers. Powerful beams of X-rays are directed at cells in a tumour, killing them off.

If you break a bone, you will probably go to the hospital for an X-ray. An X-ray image lets the doctor see where your bone is fractured or damaged. A special machine directs a narrow beam of X-rays at the part of your body that needs examining. Unlike light waves, these X-rays can pass right through the soft parts of your body, such as the skin and muscles.

X-RAY IMAGE

When X-rays come out the other side of your body, they hit a photographic plate, where they form an image. As your bones and teeth are heavy and dense, they block the path of the X-rays. This is why they leave blank patches on the X-ray image. Trained people can look at these blank areas and work out the exact shape of your skeleton.

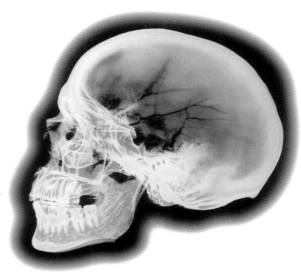

▲ An X-ray image of a human skull found at a Roman burial site, revealing a missing top molar tooth.

SOFT TISSUE

Sometimes, doctors use X-rays to look at softer, lighter parts of your body, such as the liver or bladder. To do this, they inject you with a special chemical called barium sulphate, which makes these tissues block the path of X-rays. The body gets rid of this chemical naturally after a few hours.

MACHINES AND CRYSTALS

X-rays are not only used to look inside people. They are also used to examine the insides of certain machines. Aircraft makers, for example, take X-ray images of various machine parts to make sure they have no inner cracks. Chemists take X-ray images of crystals. They use these to study how the X-rays bounce off a crystal's inner structure. This can help them work out how the atoms in crystals are arranged.

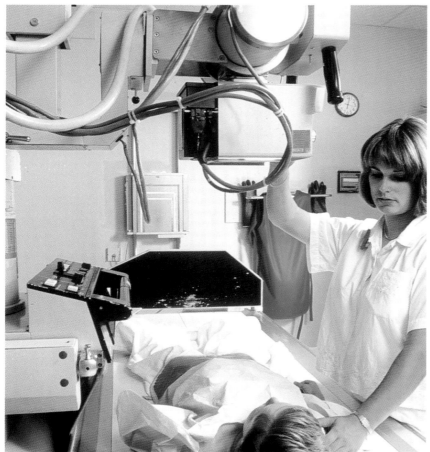

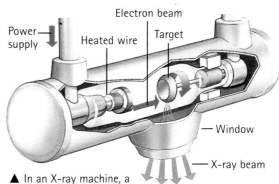

▲ In an X-ray machine, a hot wire produces a stream of electrons. These are fired at a tungsten metal target, giving out X-rays. Some pass through the patient's body, making an image on film or a fluorescent screen.

SEE ALSO

Astronomy, Atom and molecule, Light, Medicine, Wavelength

ZOOLOGY

Zoology is the scientific study of all animals – their body structure, how they live, feed, breed, move and behave – in nature or captivity.

◄ The roe deer is one of the few animals that is naturally confined to the Palaearctic Realm. It has relatives in other areas.

Nearctic Realm

Palaearctic Realm

Oriental Realm

Neotropical Realm

Ethiopian Realm

Australasian Realm

▲ The bald eagle is a species of eagle found in the Nearctic Realm. It is the USA's national bird.

▲ The giant panda weighs up to 160kg, lives in China and eats mainly bamboo. Most attempts to breed it in zoos have failed.

► Sloths are a family of South American animals that move slowly and hang upside down in trees.

◄ A pygmy hippopotamus can be 1.5–1.8m tall. It faces extinction through being hunted in Africa.

▲ Australia has many marsupials, such as the kangaroo rat, found only in the Australasian area.

GROUPING ANIMALS

Zoologists divide the Earth into six distinct regions, or realms, following the work of British wildlife expert, Alfred Russel Wallace, in the 1800s. He first noticed that whole orders or families of animals, birds and freshwater fish may be confined to one region. This map shows the six realms and an example of the animals found only in each area.

The animal kingdom is vast, varied and complicated. Zoology has many specialist branches. These often overlap. Some branches deal with particular groups of animals. For example, entomology is the detailed study of insects. Ichthyology specializes in fish. Herpetology is the study of amphibians and reptiles.

LEARNING ABOUT ANIMALS

Other branches of zoology deal with the features that animals share. Anatomists study the structure of an animal's body and the parts inside, such as the heart, nerves, guts and kidneys. Physiologists look at how these parts work, such as how worms take food from soil or how fish take in oxygen through gills. Embryologists deal with how animals develop before they are born.

THE LIVING AND THE DEAD

Some areas of zoology are very wide-ranging. Ethologists watch animal behaviour – their actions and instincts. Ecologists study how a creature fits into its surroundings or habitat. They observe its needs, such as food and shelter, and its predators. Palaeontologists study fossil remains that tell us about prehistoric life, such as dinosaurs. They deal with 'dead' remains, but still need a good knowledge of living animals to reconstruct finds and compare them with other creatures.

WHAT ZOOLOGISTS DO

Some zoologists are desk-based, writing reports or books. Others work in laboratories, carrying out tests and experiments. Some are based in museums, zoos or wildlife parks and others are in the field – watching, taking notes on and photographing animals in the wild. Many deal with the media: for example, campaigning to save endangered creatures or giving pet advice.

▼ A keeper at Marwell Zoo (UK) bottle-feeds a baby okapi, a very rare African animal. Breeding threatened species such as these is one invaluable role of a zoo. Many breed animals in captivity to help boost their dwindling numbers in the wild.

SEE ALSO

Animal, Conservation, Evolution, Mammal, Prehistoric animal

Propelled by rocket engines, the supersonic X-15 holds the world air speed record at 7,274km/h, set in 1967.

The funeral mask of Tutankhamun, boy-king of Egypt (1361–52BCE), was discovered in1922.

The first washing machine (invented by Hamilton Smith, USA, 1858) still relied on muscle power.

On April 12, 1961, Yuri Gagarin of the USSR became the first man in space on board *Vostok 1*.

The steam gun carriage of 1769, invented by French engineer Cugnot, was the first motorized vehicle.

FACTFINDER

This section provides facts, figures and other essential information – from a world map to kings, queens and presidents, and on to biographies of famous figures, finishing with the highlights of the last 100 years. Timelines present key historical events internationally (top) and locally (bottom).

The *chanoyu*, a Japanese tea ceremony that can last for four hours, originated in China.

The Arctic tern is a long-distance flyer, making an annual round trip of up to 40,000km.

In 1834, Charles Babbage (1792–1871) designed the first mechanical computer, but he never saw it built.

Camptosaurus was an ornithopod ('bird-footed') dinosaur that lived about 150 million years ago.

The Venus flytrap is a carnivorous plant that feeds on insects that it traps in its leaves.

US astronauts use a Manned Manoeuvring Unit (MMU) to guide themselves when floating free in space. This contains several small rocket thrusters pointing in different directions. When one is fired, the astronaut moves in the opposite direction.

The American Edgar Allan Poe (1809–49) was a poet and writer of mystery and horror stories.

COUNTRIES OF THE WORLD

Abbreviations
B&H	– BOSNIA & HERZEGOVINA
CRO	– CROATIA
KOS	– KOSOVO
LIE	– LIECHTENSTEIN
LUX	– LUXEMBOURG
MAC	– MACEDONIA
MONT	– MONTENEGRO
RUSS FED	– RUSSIAN FEDERATION
SAN	– SAN MARINO
SWITZ	– SWITZERLAND

A R C T I C

Greenland
(Denmark)

Jan Mayen
(Norway)

Arctic Circle

UNITED STATES
OF AMERICA
(ALASKA)

ICELAND

C A N A D A

ATLANTIC

OCEAN

Faeroe Islands
(Denmark)

UNITED
KINGDOM   DENM

REPUBLIC OF
IRELAND   of Man
(UK)   NETHERLAN

BELGIUM

St Pierre &
Miquelon
(France)

Channel Islands
(UK)

FRANC
MON

UNITED STATES
OF AMERICA

Bermuda
(UK)

ANDORRA

PORTUGAL   SPAIN

Azores
(Portugal)

Gibraltar
(UK)

Tropic of Cancer

Madeira
(Portugal)

MORROCO

ALGER

Hawaiian Islands
(US)

MEXICO

BAHAMAS

Turks &
Caicos Is (UK)

CUBA

Cayman Is
(UK)

Canary Islands
(Spain)

WESTERN
SAHARA
(occupied by Morocco)

British
Virgin Is (UK)

Virgin Is
(US)

Johnston Atoll
(US)

Navassa
Island

GUATEMALA

DOMINICAN
REPUBLIC

HAITI

Puerto
Rico
(US)

Anguilla (UK)
St Martin (France and Neth)
St Barthélemy (France)
ANTIGUA & BARBUDA
Montserrat (UK)
Guadeloupe (France)
DOMINICA
Martinique (France)
ST LUCIA

MAURITANIA

MALI

JAMAICA

St Eustatius (Neth)
ST KITTS & NEVIS

CAPE VERDE

BELIZE

HONDURAS

Aruba
(Neth)

Bonaire (Neth)

Curaçao (Neth)

BARBADOS

ST VINCENT & THE GRENADINES

SENEGAL

GAMBIA

EL SALVADOR

NICARAGUA

GRENADA

TRINIDAD & TOBAGO

GUINEA-BISSAU   GUINEA

BURKINA
FASO

BEN

Kingman Reef (US)

COSTA
RICA   PANAMA

VENEZUELA

French
Guiana
(France)

SIERRA LEONE

IVORY
COAST

GHANA

TOG

Palmyra Atoll (US)

Clipperton Island
(France)

COLOMBIA

GUYANA

LIBERIA

EQUATORIAL GU

P A C I F I C

SURINAME

Equator

Jarvis Island
(US)

ECUADOR

Galapagos Islands
(Ecuador)

SÃO T
& PRIN

KIRIBATI

O C E A N

PERU

BRAZIL

Ascension
Island
(St Helena)

American
Samoa
(US)

Cook
Islands
(NZ)

BOLIVIA

St Helena
(UK)

Niue
(NZ)

French Polynesia
(France)

PARAGUAY

Tropic of Capricorn

Easter Island
(Chile)

Pitcairn Islands
(UK)

Juan
Fernández Islands
(Chile)

URUGUAY

ATLANTIC

OCEAN

C
H
I
L
E

A
R
G
E
N
T
I
N
A

Tristan da Cunha
(St Helena)

Gough Island
(Tristan da Cunha)

Falkland Islands
(UK)

Bouvet Island
(Norway)

South Georgia
(UK)

South Sandwich Islands
(UK)

S O U T H

Antarctic Circle

A N T A R C T I C A

INTERNATIONAL ORGANIZATIONS

Logo for the League of Arab States. This organization has its head-quarters in Cairo, Egypt.

APEC
Asia-Pacific Economic Co-operation group, founded in 1989 to promote trade between members and the rest of the world. Members are Australia, Brunei, Canada, Chile, China, Hong Kong, Indonesia, Japan, Malaysia, Mexico, New Zealand, Papua New Guinea, Peru, Philippines, Russia, Singapore, South Korea, Taiwan, Thailand, Vietnam and USA.

ASEAN
Association of Southeast Asian Nations, founded in 1967 to promote economic, social and cultural co-operation and development. Members are Brunei, Burma (Myanmar), Cambodia, Indonesia, Laos, Malaysia, Philippines, Singapore, Thailand and Vietnam.

AU
African Union, formerly the Organization of African Unity, which was founded in 1963 to promote African unity and co-operation. It has 54 member states.

Logo for the European Union. This was known until 1994 as the EC (European Community).

CARICOM
Caribbean Community and Common Market, founded in 1973. Its full members are Antigua and Barbuda, Bahamas, Barbados, Belize, Dominica, Grenada, Guyana, Haiti, Jamaica, Montserrat, St Kitts & Nevis, St Lucia, St Vincent and the Grenadines, Suriname and Trinidad and Tobago.

Commonwealth
A grouping of mainly former British-ruled states, founded in 1949. It has over 50 members.

ECOWAS
Economic Community of West African States, founded in 1975.

EFTA
European Free Trade Association, founded in 1960 to promote the expansion of trade within Europe. Most of its original members have joined the EU; those remaining are Iceland, Liechtenstein, Norway and Switzerland.

The AU flag features an outline of Africa and a circle of stars that stand for its member states.

European Union (EU)
Originally a free trade and customs union, founded in 1952. Now a closer political and economic union of 27 members: Austria, Belgium, Bulgaria, Cyprus, Czech Republic, Denmark, Estonia, Finland, France, Germany, Greece, Hungary, Ireland, Italy, Latvia, Lithuania, Luxembourg, Malta, Netherlands, Poland, Portugal, Romania, Slovakia, Slovenia, Spain, Sweden, UK.

Group of Eight (G8)
An informal group of eight leading developed nations, established in 1975, which meet to discuss economic issues. Members are Canada, France, Germany, Italy, Japan, Russia, UK and USA.

Group of Twenty (G20)
A group of 19 countries, plus the EU, founded in 1999 to promote international financial stability. Its members contribute more than 80 per cent of the world's trade. Members are Argentina, Australia, Brazil, Canada, China, the EU, France, Germany, India, Indonesia, Italy, Japan, Mexico, Russia, Saudi Arabia, South Africa, South Korea, Turkey, UK and USA.

Interpol
International Criminal Police Organization, founded in 1956, to promote co-operation between police authorities. It has over 180 members.

League of Arab States
Also known as the Arab League. Founded in 1945 to promote cultural, political and economic links among Arab states. It has 21 members, including Palestine, which is considered to be an independent state by the League.

NATO
North Atlantic Treaty Organization, founded in 1949. A military alliance of Western nations set up to defend Europe and the North Atlantic from military aggression. Its 28 members are Albania, Belgium, Bulgaria, Canada, Croatia, Czech Republic, Denmark, Estonia, France, Germany, Greece, Hungary, Iceland, Italy, Latvia, Lithuania, Luxembourg, Netherlands, Norway, Poland, Portugal, Romania, Slovakia, Slovenia, Spain, Turkey, UK and USA.

OAS
Organization of American States, founded in 1948. It has 35 members, including Cuba, which was suspended from activities from 1962 to 2009.

OECD
Organization for Economic Co-operation and Development, founded in 1961 to promote social and economic welfare in its 34 member countries and to co-ordinate efforts on behalf of developing nations.

OPEC
Organization of Petroleum Exporting Countries, founded in 1960 by oil-producing states to co-ordinate oil production and prices. Members are Algeria, Angola, Ecuador, Iran, Iraq, Kuwait, Libya, Nigeria, Qatar, Saudi Arabia, United Arab Emirates and Venezuela.

United Nations (UN)
Formed in 1945 to maintain international peace and security and to develop friendly relations between nations. By 2011, it had 193 member nations; its headquarters are in New York City, USA. Its main parts include: General Assembly with representatives of all member nations; Security Council of 15 members, five of which (China, France, Russia, UK and USA) have permanent seats and ten of which are elected for two years; and the International Court of Justice, which sits in The Hague, Netherlands.

21ST-CENTURY WARS AND CONFLICTS

Afghanistan
In 1992, the Taliban, an extreme Islamic group, seized power. In 2001, al-Qaeda suicide bombers led attacks on the USA, which then invaded Afghanistan to wipe out al-Qaeda training camps. By the end of 2001, the Taliban had been removed from power. Elections in 2004 left the Afghan government controlling about 30 per cent of the country. Taliban insurgents occupy areas in the south and east. Attempts by US and NATO troops to contain the Taliban and an associated group, the Haqqanis, have had limited success and the country faces an uncertain future when most Western forces withdraw in 2014.

Burma (Myanmar)
Ruled by a military junta since 1962, Burma has faced guerrilla attacks by border ethnic minorities, such as the Karen and Mon, for half a century.

Since the end of the Cold War in the 1990s, NATO has had to reassess its military role.

First settlement in Britain — 250,000BCE

First Aboriginals reach Australia — 50,000BCE

Britain separated from mainland Europe — 5000BCE

Bronze Age in Britain and Europe — 2000BCE

Stonehenge built — 2000BCE

Earliest Hindu writings — 1500BCE

c. 1792–50 BCE — King Hammurabi rules Babylonia

800s–600s BCE — Assyrian Empire

551BCE — Birth of Confucius

500–323BCE — Golden Age of Greece

563BCE — Birth of Buddha

331BCE — Alexander the Great conquers Persian Empire

Most guerrilla groups signed a ceasefire in 2004, but violence has continued, particularly against the Karen people who seek autonomy.

Burundi
In 2005, after 12 years of conflict between Hutu and Tutsi tribes, a new, elected president and constitution were put in place. Sporadic violence continued until 2008, however.

Chad
In 2002, a peace treaty ended three years of civil war, but in 2005, new rebel groups attacked in the east. Adding to the instability, hundreds of thousands of refugees entered Chad from Sudan's Darfur region in 2003.

Chechnya
This republic in southwest Russia has a tradition of Chechen nationalism. Fighting began in 1994, when Russian troops invaded to put down an uprising. Violence continued between Russian troops and Chechen guerillas for over ten years and is still a threat.

Colombia
Guerilla wars funded by the drug trade escalated in the 1990s and despite two ceasefires, in 2002 and 2005, violence continues. By 2011, the authorities had pushed back Farc (Revolutionary Armed Forces of Colombia) rebels into rural areas of the south and east. Farc has become less concerned with politics and more with drug dealing, producing half of the world's cocaine.

Congo, Democratic Republic
The scene of "Africa's world war" (1998–2003). Government forces, supported by forces from Angola, Namibia and Zimbabwe, faced rebels in the east backed by Rwanda and Uganda. Up to three million died in the conflict itself or as a result of disease or starvation caused by the war. Much of the east remains in the hands of rebel groups and militias.

Georgia
After Georgia became independent in 1991, the regions of Abkhazia and South Ossetia broke away. In 2008, conflict over the separatist regions led to war between Georgia and Russia. Russia recognizes the two breakaway regions' independence.

India
In early 2002, Pakistan and India appeared close to war, mainly over Kashmir (a predominantly Muslim territory, disputed since 1947). In June, India pulled back its military from Pakistani borders and in 2004, a ceasefire was agreed in Kashmir.

Iraq
In 2003, a US-led coalition invaded Iraq and overthrew Saddam Hussein's military regime, which was suspected of making chemical weapons. In 2007–08 US coalition forces pushed back Shia militias, but Iraq remains volatile after the withdrawal of coalition forces in 2009–11.

Israel
Israel has been at odds with the neighbouring Palestinians since the foundation of a Jewish state in 1948. Israeli-Palestinian violence escalated between 2000–2005, despite peace talks. An agreement reached in 2005 saw a reduction in violence, but the political situation is still unstable.

Ivory Coast
In 2002, an armed rebellion in the Muslim north led to civil war. French troops and forces from neighbouring countries established a buffer zone between north and south. Elections were held in 2010 but the defeated (southern) president refused to step down. A second, month-long civil war was ended when northern forces, supporting the presidential victor, eventually took control.

Lebanon
After civil war in 1975-90, Lebanon enjoyed relative peace but remained politically divided between various religious and ethnic groups. The Shia Muslim armed group Hezbollah controls part of the country and, in 2006, Israel launched a military campaign against the group, damaging Lebanon's infrastructure.

Liberia
Civil war began in 1990 after rebels overthrew President Samuel Doe. In 2003 a peace agreement brought an end to the war and in 2005, a democratically elected president took power, although the political situation remains unstable.

Libya
In early 2011, a rebellion against the dictatorship of Muammar Gaddafi broke out in the city of Benghazi. A six-month civil war resulted, in which the rebels were supported by NATO air strikes to protect civilians. In August, the rebels took the capital, Tripoli, and were recognized as the legitimate government. In October, Gaddafi was killed in his last stronghold, Sirte.

Pakistan
In 2001 Pakistan ended its support for the Taliban in Afghanistan but elements of the Taliban remain along its Afghan border. Pakistani forces have struggled to control tribal areas, such as Waziristan, and a military campaign against militants has increased since 2009. See also India.

Sri Lanka
In 2002, the Tamil Tigers, a guerrilla force, and the Sri Lankan government signed a ceasefire, but fighting broke out again in 2004 and 2005. The civil war intensified in 2009; in May, the last areas in Tamil hands were taken by government troops. A UN report accused both sides of war crimes.

Somalia
Since 1991 Somalia has had no effective government: the country is divided between competing warlords while the north, the former British Somaliland, has seceded and operates as a separate stable but unrecognized state. The Somali government, supported by AU forces, controls little more than the capital, Mogadishu, where it is besieged by the militant Islamist al-Shabab movement which occupies most of southern Somalia. The northeast, Puntland, is also beyond the government control.

Syria
In 2011 the Arab Spring, a wave of pro-democracy protest in several Arab nations, was initially suppressed by the dictatorship of Bashir al-Assad in Syria. However, a brutal crackdown on protesters led to uprisings in several cities and brought Syria to the brink of civil war.

Yemen
Since 2009 Shia rebels have been active in the north, despite a ceasefire signed in 2010. Islamic militants allied to al-Qaeda have established in other areas, and separatists in the south have taken up arms, too. The Yemeni government has also violently resisted popular protests for democracy and a change of government.

During the Six-Day War in 1967, Israel gained land in Jerusalem, Sinai, the Golan Heights and West Bank.

From the 1969 to 1998, the IRA (Irish Republican Army) waged a terrorist bombing campaign in the UK.

In Rwanda, approximately 100,000 people died in two weeks in May 1994. Many fled as refugees.

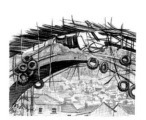

Civil wars in the former Yugoslavia (1991–95) resulted in its break up into seven new states.

Iron Age Celts in Britain — 700BCE

Nok civilization in Nigeria / Bantu peoples in East Africa — 500BCE

Mauru dynasty in India — 321BCE

Julius Caesar visits Britain — 55-54BCE

Romans invade Britain — 43CE

Boudicca's rebellion in Britain — 61CE

KINGS AND QUEENS OF GREAT BRITAIN

Brought up by monks, Edward the Confessor preferred prayer to politics.

Mary I's attempts to restore Roman Catholicism led to the execution of many Protestants.

Cromwell came to power after the civil war of the 1640s, but he did not crown himself king.

George Washington was commander of the troops that won independence from the English in 1781.

SCOTLAND

Malcolm III Canmore	1057–1093
Donald Bane	1093–1094
Duncan II	1094
Donald Bane (restored)	1094–1097
Edgar	1097–1107
Alexander I	1107–1124
David I	1124–1153
Malcolm IV	1153–1165
William The Lion	1165–1214
Alexander II	1214–1249
Alexander III	1249–1286
Margaret of Norway	1286–1290
INTERREGNUM	1290–1292
John Balliol	1292–1296
INTERREGNUM	1296–1306
Robert I The Bruce	1306–1329
David II	1329–1371

HOUSE OF STUART

Robert II	1371–1390
Robert III	1390–1406
James I	1406–1437
James II	1437–1460
James III	1460–1488
James IV	1488–1513
James V	1513–1542
Mary Queen of Scots	1542–1567
James VI (I of England)	1567–1625

ENGLAND

SAXONS

Egbert	827–839
Ethelwulf	839–858
Ethelbald	858–860
Ethelbert	860–865
Ethelred I	865–871
Alfred The Great	871–899
Edward The Elder	899–924
Athelstan	924–939
Edmund	939–946
Edred	946–955
Edwy	955–959
Edgar	959–975
Edward The Martyr	975–978
Ethelred II The Unready	978–1016
Edmund II Ironside	1016

DANES

Canute	1016–1035
Harold I Harefoot	1035–1040
Hardecanute	1040–1042

SAXONS

Edward The Confessor	1042–1066
Harold II	1066

HOUSE OF NORMANDY

William I The Conqueror	1066–1087
William II	1087–1100
Henry I	1100–1135
Stephen	1135–1154

HOUSE OF PLANTAGENET

Henry II	1154–1189
Richard I The Lionheart	1189–1199
John	1199–1216
Henry III	1216–1272
Edward I	1272–1307
Edward II	1307–1327
Edward III	1327–1377
Richard II	1377–1399

HOUSE OF LANCASTER

Henry IV	1399–1413
Henry V	1413–1422
Henry VI	1422–1461

HOUSE OF YORK

Edward IV	1461–1483
Edward V	1483
Richard III	1483–1485

HOUSE OF TUDOR

Henry VII	1485–1509
Henry VIII	1509–1547
Edward VI	1547–1553
Mary I	1553–1558
Elizabeth I	1558–1603

BRITAIN

HOUSE OF STUART

James I (VI of Scotland)	1603–1625
Charles I	1625–1649

COMMONWEALTH

Oliver Cromwell (Lord Protector)	1649–1658
Richard Cromwell (Lord Protector)	1658–1659

HOUSE OF STUART (restored)

Charles II	1660–1685
James II	1685–1688
William III (and)	1688–1702
Mary II (jointly)	1688–1694
Anne	1702–1714

HOUSE OF HANOVER

George I	1714–1727
George II	1727–1760
George III	1760–1820
George IV	1820–1830
William IV	1830–1837
Victoria	1837–1901

HOUSE OF SAXE–COBURG

Edward VII	1901–1910

HOUSE OF WINDSOR

George V	1910–1936
Edward VIII	1936
George VI	1936–1952
Elizabeth II	1952–

PRESIDENTS OF THE UNITED STATES OF AMERICA

(D) Democrat *(DR)* Democratic Republican *(F)* Federalist *(NU)* National Unionist *(R)* Republican *(W)* Whig

George Washington *(None)*	1789–1797	Abraham Lincoln *(R)*	1861–1865	Herbert Hoover *(R)*	1929–1933
John Adams *(F)*	1797–1801	Andrew Johnson *(NU)*	1865–1869	Franklin D. Roosevelt *(D)*	1933–1945
Thomas Jefferson *(DR)*	1801–1809	Ulysses S. Grant *(R)*	1869–1877	Harry Truman *(D)*	1945–1953
James Madison *(DR)*	1809–1817	Rutherford Hayes *(R)*	1877–1881	Dwight Eisenhower *(R)*	1953–1961
James Monroe *(DR)*	1817–1825	James Garfield *(R)*	1881	John F. Kennedy *(D)*	1961–1963
John Quincy Adams *(DR)*	1825–1829	Chester Arthur *(R)*	1881–1885	Lyndon Johnson *(D)*	1963–1969
Andrew Jackson *(D)*	1829–1837	Grover Cleveland *(D)*	1885–1889	Richard Nixon *(R)*	1969–1974
Martin Van Buren *(D)*	1837–1841	Benjamin Harrison *(R)*	1889–1893	Gerald Ford *(R)*	1974–1977
William H. Harrison *(W)*	1841	Grover Cleveland *(D)*	1893–1897	Jimmy Carter *(D)*	1977–1981
John Tyler *(W)*	1841–1845	William McKinley *(R)*	1897–1901	Ronald Reagan *(R)*	1981–1989
James K. Polk *(D)*	1845–1849	Theodore Roosevelt *(R)*	1901–1909	George Bush *(R)*	1989–1993
Zachary Taylor *(W)*	1849–1850	William Taft *(R)*	1909–1913	Bill Clinton *(D)*	1993–2001
Millard Fillmore *(W)*	1850–1853	Woodrow Wilson *(D)*	1913–1921	George W. Bush *(R)*	2001–2009
Franklin Pierce *(D)*	1853–1857	Warren Harding *(R)*	1921–1923	Barack Obama *(D)*	2009–
James Buchanan *(D)*	1857–1861	Calvin Coolidge *(R)*	1923–1929		

PRIME MINISTERS OF GREAT BRITAIN

(C) Conservative *(Coa)* Coalition *(Lab)* Labour *(L)* Liberal *(P)* Peelite *(T)* Tory *(W)* Whig

Sir Robert Walpole *(W)*	1721–1742	Sir Robert Peel *(T)*	1834–1835	Andrew Bonar Law *(C)*	1922–1923
Earl of Wilmington *(W)*	1742–1743	Viscount Melbourne *(W)*	1835–1841	Stanley Baldwin *(C)*	1923–1924
Henry Pelham *(W)*	1743–1754	Sir Robert Peel (T)	1841–1846	James Ramsay MacDonald *(Lab)*	1924
Duke of Newcastle *(W)*	1754–1756	Lord John Russell *(W)*	1846–1852	Stanley Baldwin *(C)*	1924–1929
Duke of Devonshire *(W)*	1756–1757	Earl of Derby *(T)*	1852	James Ramsay MacDonald *(Lab)*	1929–1931
Duke of Newcastle *(W)*	1757–1762	Earl of Aberdeen *(P)*	1852–1855	James Ramsay MacDonald *(Coa)*	1931–1935
Earl of Bute *(T)*	1762–1763	Viscount Palmerston *(L)*	1855–1858	Stanley Baldwin *(Coa)*	1935–1937
George Grenville *(W)*	1763–1765	Earl of Derby *(C)*	1858–1859	Neville Chamberlain *(Coa)*	1937–1940
Marquess of Rockingham *(W)*	1765–1766	Viscount Palmerston *(L)*	1859–1865	Winston Churchill *(Coa)*	1940–1945
William Pitt (The Elder) *(W)*	1766–1768	Earl Russell *(L)*	1865–1866	Winston Churchill *(C)*	1945
Duke of Grafton *(W)*	1767–1770	Earl of Derby *(C)*	1866–1868	Clement Atlee *(Lab)*	1945–1951
Lord North *(T)*	1770–1782	Benjamin Disraeli *(C)*	1868	Winston Churchill *(C)*	1951–1955
Marquess of Rockingham *(W)*	1782	William Gladstone *(L)*	1868–1874	Anthony Eden *(C)*	1955–1957
Earl of Shelburne *(W)*	1782–1783	Benjamin Disraeli *(C)*	1874–1880	Harold Macmillan *(C)*	1957–1963
Duke of Portland *(Coa)*	1783	William Gladstone *(L)*	1880–1885	Alec Douglas–Home *(C)*	1963–1964
William Pitt (The Younger) *(T)*	1783–1801	Marquess of Salisbury *(C)*	1885–1886	Harold Wilson *(Lab)*	1964–1970
Henry Addington *(T)*	1801–1804	William Gladstone *(L)*	1886	Edward Heath *(C)*	1970–1974
William Pitt (The Younger) *(T)*	1804–1806	Marquess of Salisbury *(C)*	1886–1892	Harold Wilson *(Lab)*	1974–1976
William Wyndham Grenville *(W)*	1806–1807	William Gladstone *(L)*	1892–1894	James Callaghan *(Lab)*	1976–1979
Duke of Portland *(T)*	1807–1809	Earl of Rosebery *(L)*	1894–1895	Margaret Thatcher *(C)*	1979–1990
Spencer Perceval *(T)*	1809–1812	Marquess of Salisbury *(C)*	1895–1902	John Major *(C)*	1990–1997
Earl of Liverpool *(T)*	1812–1827	Arthur Balfour *(C)*	1902–1905	Tony Blair *(Lab)*	1997–2007
George Canning *(T)*	1827	Sir H. Campbell–Bannerman *(L)*	1905–1908	Gordon Brown *(Lab)*	2007–2010
Viscount Goderich *(T)*	1827–1828	Herbert Asquith *(L)*	1908–1915	David Cameron *(Coa)*	2010–
Duke of Wellington *(T)*	1828–1830	Herbert Asquith *(Coa)*	1915–1916		
Earl Grey *(W)*	1830–1834	David Lloyd–George *(Coa)*	1916–1922		
Viscount Melbourne *(W)*	1834				

Pitt the Elder was a great war leader in the Seven Years' War against France and Austria (1756–63).

In Britain, Thatcher was the first woman prime minister. She held office for ten years.

PRIME MINISTERS OF NEW ZEALAND

Joseph Ward	1906–1912
Thomas MacKenzie	1912–1915
William Massey	1915–1925
Francis Bell	1925
Joseph Coates	1925–1928
Joseph Ward	1928–1930
Georges Forbes	1930–1935
Michael Savage	1935–1940
Peter Fraser	1940–1949
Sidney Holland	1949–1957
Keith Holyoake	1957
Walter Nash	1957–1960
Keith Holyoake	1960–1972
John Marshall	1972
Norman Kirk	1972–1974
Hugh Watt	1974
Wallace (Bill) Rowling	1974–1975
Robert Muldoon	1975–1984
David Lange	1984–1989
Geoffrey Palmer	1989–1990
Michael Moore	1990
Jim Bolger	1990–1997
Jenny Shipley	1997–1999
Helen Clark	1999–2008
John Key	2008–

PRIME MINISTERS OF AUSTRALIA

Edmund Barton	1901–1903			
Alfred Deakin	1903–1904			
John Watson	1904			
George Reid	1904–1905			
Alfred Deakin	1905–1908			
Andrew Fisher	1908–1909			
Alfred Deakin	1909–1910			
Andrew Fisher	1910–1913			
Joseph Cook	1913–1914			
Andrew Fisher	1914–1915	Harold Holt	1966–1967
William Hughes	1915–1923	John McEwen	1967–1968
Stanley Bruce	1923–1929	John Gorton	1968–1971
James Scullin	1929–1932	William McMahon	1971–1972
Joseph Lyons	1932–1939	E. Gough Whitlam	1972–1975
Earle Page	1939	Malcolm Fraser	1975–1983
Robert Menzies	1939–1941	Robert Hawke	1983–1991
Arthur Fadden	1941	Paul Keating	1991–1996
John Curtin	1941–1945	John Howard	1996–2007
Francis Forde	1945	Kevin Rudd	2007–2010
Joseph Chifley	1945–1949	Julia Gillard	2010–
Robert Menzies	1949–1966		

Bob Hawke sought to increase trade with countries such as the USA, Japan and China.

Nehru played a key role in negotiating independence for India before he became prime minister.

PRIME MINISTERS OF INDIA

Jawaharlal Nehru	1947–1964
Gulzarilal Nanda	1964
Lal Shastri	1964–1966
Gulzarilal Nanda	1966
Indira Gandhi	1966–1977
Morarji Desai	1977–1979
Charan Singh	1979–1980
Indira Gandhi	1980–1984
Rajiv Gandhi	1984–1989
V. P. Singh	1989–1990
Chadra Shekhar	1990–1991
P. V. Narasimha Rao	1991–1996
H. D. Deve Gowda	1996–1997
Inder Kumar Gujral	1997–1998
Atal Behari Vajpayee	1996; 1998–2004
Dr. Manmohan Singh	2004–

BIOGRAPHIES

ARTISTS

Leonardo excelled not only in art, but also as an inventor, mathematician, engineer and anatomist.

Picasso was the most famous artist of the 20th century. His work changed the course of modern art.

Chaucer's *Canterbury Tales* was a collection of stories told by imaginary people while on a pilgrimage.

Brought up in poverty himself, Dickens wrote knowledgeably about the lives of the poor.

Adams, Ansel (1902–84)
American photographer. Noted for his landscapes of the western USA, particularly Yosemite National Park.

Botticelli, Sandro (c. 1444–1510)
Italian painter. His paintings reflect the humanist and classical interests of his time. *Primavera* (Spring), *Birth of Venus*.

Cézanne, Paul (1839–1906)
French painter. At first an Impressionist, painting the effects of light on objects rather than the objects themselves. Later he moved towards more solid forms.

Degas, Edgar (1834–1917)
French painter and sculptor. He was influenced by Impressionism and Japanese woodcuts and interested in the human form. *Rehearsal of the Ballet, Dancer Lacing her Shoe*.

Eyck, Jan van (c. 1389–1441)
Dutch painter. Greatest Flemish artist of 15th century, his work is characterized by realistic light effects. *The Adoration of the Holy Lamb, Arnolfini*.

Giotto di Bondone (c. 1266–1337)
Italian painter. His realistic style became a strong influence on the Renaissance painters of the 1400s. *Life of Christ* and the *Last Judgement*.

Goya y Lucientes, Francisco (1746–1828)
Spanish painter. He painted portraits and scenes from real life. *The Family of Charles IV, The Disasters of War*.

Hepworth, Barbara (1903–75)
British sculptor and painter. One of the most important non-figurative sculptors of her time.

Leonardo da Vinci (1452–1519)
Italian painter and scientist. Considered to be supreme example of Renaissance genius. *Last Supper* (fresco), *Mona Lisa* (painting).

Michelangelo (1475–1564)
Italian painter, sculptor and architect. Most famous for the frescoes on the ceiling of the Sistine Chapel and his sculpture, *David*.

Monet, Claude (1840–1926)
French painter. One of the creators of the Impressionist movement. *Rouen Cathedral, Waterlilies*.

Moore, Henry (1898–1986)
British sculptor. One of the most original and powerful modern sculptors, he produced mainly semi-abstract figures and groups. *Madonna and Child*.

Picasso, Pablo (1881–1973)
Spanish painter. First painted in a mainly blue palette, then with Georges Braque developed Cubism (in which forms are broken down into geometric shapes). *Guernica*.

Pollock, Jackson (1912–56)
American artist. His work developed from Surrealism to abstract art on huge canvases. *Autumn Rhythm (Number 30), 1950*.

Rembrandt (Harmenszoon van Rijn) (1606–69)
Dutch painter. *The Night Watch, The Anatomy Lesson of Dr Tulp* and self-portraits.

Rubens, Peter Paul (1577–1640)
Flemish painter, master of baroque style. Painted portraits, landscapes, religious and historical subjects.

Turner, Joseph M. W. (1775–1851)
British landscape painter. Painted in both watercolours and oils. *The Fighting Temeraire, Old Chain Pier at Brighton*.

Van Gogh, Vincent (1853–90)
Dutch painter. Post-impressionist famous for his use of colour. *Sunflowers, The Chair and the Pipe*.

Warhol, Andy (1926–87)
American pop artist and film-maker. A pioneer of 'pop art' with colourful reproductions of familiar objects, such as the Campbell's soup-tin label.

Wren, Sir Christopher (1632–1723)
English architect. An astronomer and mathematician, he designed many churches and buildings in London after the Great Fire (1666). St Paul's Cathedral.

WRITERS

Andersen, Hans Christian (1805–75)
Danish writer. One of the world's greatest story-tellers, best known for his fairy tales. 'The Emperor's New Clothes', 'The Snow Queen', 'The Ugly Duckling'.

Austen, Jane (1775–1817)
British novelist. Wrote six novels of English country life with detailed characters. *Emma, Pride and Prejudice*.

Brontë sisters
Three British novelists. Anne (1820–49), Charlotte (1816–55), Emily (1818–48) wrote respectively, *The Tenant of Wildfell Hall, Jane Eyre, Wuthering Heights*.

Cervantes, Miguel (1547–1616)
Spanish novelist and dramatist. His greatest work, *Don Quixote*, tells the life of a poor gentleman who wants to be a knight and do knightly deeds.

Chaucer, Geoffrey (c.1345–1400)
English poet. Wrote in the southern English dialect, which he established as the literary language of England. *Troilus and Criseyde, Canterbury Tales*.

Dante Alighieri (1265–1321)
Italian poet. Wrote in Italian rather than the literary Latin of the period. *Divina Commedia (Divine Comedy)*.

Dickens, Charles (1812–70)
English novelist. His 16 novels provoked reform, drawing attention to the plight of the poor. *Oliver Twist, David Copperfield*.

Goethe, Johann Wolfgang von (1749–1832)
German lyric poet and dramatist. Of unequalled importance in German literature. *Faust* and *Werther*.

Hugo, Victor (1802–85)
French poet and novelist. He led the French Romantic movement and was a great defender of political liberty. *Notre Dame de Paris, Les Miserables*.

Johnson, Dr Samuel (1709–84)
English writer. Compiled *The English Dictionary* (1747–55), the model for all English-language dictionaries.

Joyce, James (1882–1941)
Irish novelist and poet. His skilful use of the English language can be seen in *Dubliners*, *Ulysses* and *Finnegan's Wake*.

Keats, John (1795–1821)
English poet. *The Eve of St Agnes*, many great odes, such as 'To a Nightingale', 'To Autumn'.

Lewis, C. S. (1898–1963)
British writer of children's fiction, science fiction and religious works. *The Screwtape Letters*, *The Chronicles of Narnia*.

Melville, Herman (1819–91)
American writer. He used his early experiences as a sailor for his most popular books. *Moby Dick*, *Typee*.

Shakespeare, William (1564–1616)
English dramatist and poet. Wrote tragedies (*Hamlet*), histories (*Richard III*) and comedies (*Twelfth Night*).

Shaw, George Bernard (1856–1950)
Irish playwright. His plays dealt with a wide range of subjects reflecting his socialist views. *Man and Superman*, *Pygmalion*.

Stevenson, Robert Louis (1850–94)
British author. Wrote travel sketches as well as romantic novels. *Kidnapped*, *The Strange Case of Dr Jekyll and Mr Hyde*.

Swift, Jonathan (1667–1745)
Anglo-Irish poet and satirist. He directed his wit at politics and religion. *Gulliver's Travels*.

Tolkein, J. R. R. (1892–1973)
South African-born author. Became a professor of English language and literature. *The Lord of the Rings*.

Tolstoy, Count Leo (1828–1910)
Russian writer. After fighting in the Crimean War he settled down to write. *War and Peace*, *Anna Karenina*.

Twain, Mark (1835–1910)
Pen name of American novelist and journalist, Samuel Langhorne Clemens. *The Adventures of Tom Sawyer*, *The Adventures of Huckleberry Finn*.

Wordsworth, William (1770–1850)
British poet. His poetry explores the lives of humble folk in contact with nature. 'Tintern Abbey', 'Ode to Duty'.

COMPOSERS AND MUSICIANS

Bach, Johann Sebastian (1685–1750)
German composer. Wrote concertos, sacred cantatas, clavier works, *St Matthew Passion* and *B Minor Mass*.

Beethoven, Ludwig van (1770–1827)
German composer. Wrote sonatas, symphonies, chamber music, concertos and opera *Fidelio*.

Bizet, Georges (1838–75)
French composer. Most famous for his opera *Carmen*, on which his reputation is based.

Brahms, Johannes (1833–97)
German composer. A gifted pianist, his music was solidly classical. Wrote piano sonatas, symphonies and a choral requiem.

Britten, Benjamin (1913–76)
British composer. Large-scale instrumental works were followed by vocal and choral pieces. *The Young Person's Guide to the Orchestra*.

Copland, Aaron (1900–90)
American composer. His works employed jazz rhythms and American traditional and folk music. *Appalachian Spring*.

Gershwin, George (1898–1937)
American composer. He produced, sometimes with his brother Ira, concert works and Broadway musicals. *Porgy and Bess*, *Rhapsody in Blue*.

Handel, Georg Friedrich (1685–1759)
German-English composer. After beginning as an organist and orchestral player, Handel produced incidental and choral music, as well as operas. *Messiah*.

Haydn, Franz Joseph (1732–1809)
Austrian composer. The most famous composer of his day, his vast output included 104 symphonies, about 50 concertos, 84 string quartets.

Lennon, John (1940–80) and McCartney, Paul (1942–)
British pop singers and composers. As part of The Beatles, Lennon and McCartney produced numerous hit songs. *Yesterday*.

Monteverdi, Claudio (1567–1643)
Italian composer. A proficient violinist, he also wrote some of the earliest operas. *Orfeo*.

Mozart, Wolfgang Amadeus (1756–91)
Austrian composer. Works include 41 symphonies, nearly 30 piano concertos, and several operas (*Don Giovanni*, *The Marriage of Figaro*, *The Magic Flute*).

Sibelius, Jean (1865–1957)
Finnish composer. His series of symphonic poems were based on well-known Finnish legends. He is famous for his symphonies and violin concerto. *Finlandia*.

Strauss, Johann (1825–99)
Austrian composer and violinist. Like his father and brothers, he composed waltzes which gained great acclaim and popularity. *The Blue Danube*.

Stravinsky, Igor Fedorovich (1882–1971)
Russian composer. He produced symphonies and opera as well as the ballet music for which he is famous. *The Firebird*, *The Rite of Spring*.

Tchaikovsky, Piotr Ilyich (1840–93)
Russian composer. He was a master of orchestration with a gift for writing melody, some of which was melancholy. Wrote ballet music, symphonies, piano concertos and operas. *Swan Lake*.

Tippett, Sir Michael (1905–98)
British composer whose pacifist ideas are reflected in his operas and symphonies. *A Child of Our Time*, *The Midsummer Marriage*.

Verdi, Giuseppe (1813–1901)
Italian composer. The leading Italian operatic composer of his day and a master of theatrical effect. *Rigoletto*, *La Traviata*, *Aida*.

Vivaldi, Antonio (1678–1741)
Venetian violinist and composer. He wrote operas, some sacred music and concertos. *The Four Seasons*.

Wagner, Richard (1813–83)
German composer. Known mainly for his major opera cycle, *The Ring*, which consists of four operas based on old Germanic tales. He built a theatre at Bayreuth, Germany in which to perform his works.

Tolstoy introduced a new form of Christianity into Russia, writing religious works as well as novels.

Tom Sawyer's adventures on the Mississippi River were based on Twain's own boyhood experiences.

Beethoven was deaf for the last eight years of his life. Before this, he used ear trumpets to help him hear.

Mozart began writing music at the age of five. Two years later, he was playing in concerts.

1904–5	1912	1914–18	1917	1929	1933	1936–39
Russia defeated in Russo–Japanese War	Chinese overthrow Manchu dynasty; establish republic	World War I	Communists seize power in Russia	Wall Street Crash starts worldwide depression	Hitler comes to power in Germany	Civil war in Spain

Marie and Pierre Curie devoted their lives to research, spending their own money on equipment.

One of Edison's most famous inventions was the phonograph – a recording device invented in 1877.

Aristotle studied under Plato for 20 years before becoming tutor to Alexander the Great.

Gandhi is often called the 'father of modern India' for his work in freeing India from British rule.

SCIENTISTS AND INVENTORS

Becquerel, Antoine-Henri (1852–1908)
French scientist who discovered that uranium gives off radiation; shared the 1903 Nobel Prize with the Curies.

Bell, Alexander Graham (1847–1922)
Scottish-born American inventor of the telephone.

Copernicus, Nicolaus (1473–1543)
Polish astronomer who explained that the Earth revolves around the Sun.

Curie, Marie (1867–1934)
Polish physicist who discovered radium, a radioactive substance. She worked with her husband, Pierre.

Darwin, Charles (1809–82)
British naturalist whose studies of animals and plants helped formulate his theory of evolution by natural selection.

Edison, Thomas Alva (1847–1931)
American inventor of, among other things, the electric light bulb and sound recording.

Einstein, Albert (1879–1955)
German-born physicist who changed our view of the universe with his General Theory of Relativity (1915). Nobel Prize for Physics (1921).

Faraday, Michael (1791–1867)
British physicist and chemist, pioneer of electricity, whose work made both the dynamo and the electric motor possible.

Fermi, Enrico (1901–54)
Italian nuclear physicist who helped design the first nuclear reactor.

Fleming, Alexander (1881–1955)
British bacteriologist who developed penicillin, the first antibiotic, from the mould penicillium.

Franklin, Benjamin (1706–90)
American scientist, publisher and statesman. He proved lightning is electrical and invented the lightning conductor.

Freud, Sigmund (1856–1939)
Austrian physician who introduced the science of psychoanalysis (investigation of the unconscious human mind), thereby advancing the treatment of the mentally ill.

Galilei, Galileo (1564–1642)
Italian astronomer and physicist whose discoveries include the motion of pendulums and falling bodies, and observations of the Moon and planets.

Halley, Edmond (1656–1742)
English astronomer noted for his work on comets. He correctly predicted that a comet first observed in 1682 would return in 1758 and he produced the first accurate map of the stars.

Jenner, Edward (1749–1823)
British physician who discovered vaccination as a means of preventing smallpox.

Lavoisier, Antoine (1743–94)
French chemist, regarded as the founder of modern chemistry. Published his findings in *Elementary Treatise on Chemistry*.

Linnaeus, Carolus (1707–78)
Swedish botanist who introduced a standard method of naming and classifying living things.

Marconi, Guglielmo (1874–1937)
Italian electrical engineer, the first person to transmit long-distance radio signals.

Mendel, Gregor (1822–84)
Austrian monk who researched the mechanisms of heredity using pea plants.

Newton, Sir Isaac (1642–1727)
English mathematician who devised laws of motion, theorized about gravity and showed the nature of light and colour.

Niepce, Joseph Nicéphore (1765–1833)
French inventor credited with taking the first photograph in 1826.

Pasteur, Louis (1822–95)
French scientist who proved that bacteria cause decay and disease.

Rutherford, Sir Ernest (1871–1937)
New Zealand-born physicist who worked on radioactivity and the structure of the atom.

Watt, James (1736–1819)
British engineer who improved the steam engine to make it a suitable power plant for all kinds of machinery.

PHILOSOPHERS AND REFORMERS

Aristotle (384–322BCE)
Greek philosopher who studied under Plato. Opened school of philosophy in Athens. His work gave rise to the science of logic or reasoning.

Calvin, John (1509–64)
French religious reformer and leader of the Protestant Reformation. Believed that all people, not just bishops and kings, should share in religious and political policy-making.

Confucius (c. 551–c. 480BCE)
Chinese philosopher whose teachings on moral responsibility have been a strong influence on Chinese thought for over 2,000 years.

Gandhi, Mohandas Karamchand (1869–1948)
Indian spiritual and political leader who helped free India from British control through non-violent resistance. Known as Mahatma, or 'Great Soul'.

Gautama, Siddhartha (Buddha) (c. 563–483BCE)
Indian religious teacher and founder of Buddhism, one of the world's great religions. He gave up his life as a prince to become a wandering monk in search of enlightenment.

Jesus Christ (c. 4BCE–c. 33CE)
Religious leader on whose teachings the Christian religion was founded.

Joan of Arc, Saint (c. 1412–31)
French national leader and heroine. She believed God had chosen her to free France from English rule and led French armies to many victories.

King, Martin Luther (1929–68)
Black American minister and leader of US civil rights movement. Won the 1964 Nobel Peace Prize.

Luther, Martin (1483–1546)
German religious reformer and leader of the Reformation – the religious movement that led to the birth of Protestantism.

Marx, Karl (1818–83)
German political philosopher and main founder of the socialist and communist movements. Wrote *The Communist Manifesto* and *Das Kapital* with Friedrich Engels.

1939–45; 1945	1949	1957	1957–75	1979	1989–90	1994	2001
World War II; United Nations founded	Communists take over China	EEC founded	Vietnam War	Islamic Revolution in Iran	Democracy sweeps Eastern Europe	Black rule in S. Africa	Terrorist attacks on the USA

Montessori, Maria (1870–1952)
Italian educator and doctor. She designed an educational system to help children develop their intelligence and independence, now used throughout the world.

Mother Teresa of Calcutta (1910–97)
Roman Catholic nun born in Yugoslavia. She founded a religious order in Calcutta in 1950 called Missionaries of Charity, which now works in more than 130 countries.

Muhammad (570–632CE)
Arabian prophet and founder of Islam. He felt himself called as God's prophet and preached that there is only one God (Allah).

Nightingale, Florence (1820–1910)
English nursing pioneer who reformed the nursing profession.

Pankhurst, Emmeline (1858–1928)
English political reformer. She led the fight for women's right to vote in England.

Plato (c. 427–c.347BCE)
Greek philosopher who founded what is probably the first ever university, known as the Academy. Wrote *The Republic*, in which he outlined the ideal state or society.

Sanger, Margaret (1883–1966)
American leader of the birth control movement.

Socrates (c. 469–399BCE)
Greek philosopher and teacher. He devoted himself to seeking truth and goodness.

Stanton, Elizabeth Cady (1815–1902)
American leader of the women's rights movement. She also worked for the abolition of slavery.

Wesley, John (1703–91)
English clergyman and founder of Methodism, who travelled over 8,000km a year preaching sermons.

Wilberforce, William (1759–1833)
English politician and reformer. He led the fight to abolish slavery in the British Empire.

Wollstonecraft, Mary (1759–97)
English author who argued that women should have equal rights to men in her book, *A Vindication of the Rights of Women*.

EXPLORERS

Amundsen, Roald (1872–1928)
Norwegian explorer. The first man to navigate the Northwest Passage and reach the South Pole (1911).

Balboa, Vasco Nuñez de (1475–1519)
Spanish explorer. The first European to sight the Pacific Ocean.

Battuta, Ibn (c. 1304–68)
Moroccan explorer. Journeyed throughout East Africa, Arabia, Russia, India and China and left a description of his travels.

Bering, Vitus (1680–1741)
Danish navigator who proved that Asia and North America are separated by water, now known as the Bering Strait.

Cabot, John (1461–98)
Italian-born explorer and navigator. Sailed across the North Atlantic to Canada in search of the Northeast Passage (round America to Asia).

Champlain, Samuel de (c. 1570–1635)
French explorer. Navigated the St Lawrence River in Canada; founded Quebec.

Columbus, Christopher (1451–1506)
Italian explorer. 'Discovered' the American continent (actually the Caribbean islands) by accident while seeking a route to Asia.

Cook, James (1728–79)
British explorer and navigator. Explored coasts of Australia and New Zealand.

Días, Bartholomeu (1450–1500)
Portuguese navigator. Took a two-ship expedition around the Cape of Good Hope, so opening the route to India.

Ericsson, Leif (10th–11th century)
Viking sailor. Crossed the Atlantic and settled in Vinland, said to be North America (c. 1003CE).

Gama, Vasco da (c. 1469–1524)
Portuguese navigator and explorer. Led the first European expedition to reach India.

Hillary, Sir Edmund (1919–2008)
New Zealand mountaineer and explorer. In 1953, he was the first to climb Mount Everest with Tenzing Norgay. Also travelled overland to the South Pole, the first to do so since Scott and Amundsen.

Kingsley, Mary (1862–1900)
British traveller and writer. Journeyed to West Africa twice, living among peoples such as the Fang and the Hausa.

Lewis, Meriwether (1774–1809) and Clark, William (1770–1838)
In 1804, these American explorers led an expedition to explore the interior of the USA. They covered over 12,400km in more than two years.

Livingstone, David (1813–73)
Scottish missionary and traveller. Travelling in Africa, he became the first European to navigate the Zambezi and view the Victoria Falls.

Magellan, Ferdinand (c. 1480–1521)
Portuguese navigator. Commanded the first expedition to sail round the world (1519–22). Was killed in Philippines on return journey.

Polo, Marco (c. 1254–c. 1324)
Venetian traveller. Lived at court of Kublai Khan in China. Account of his travels (1271–95) encouraged Europeans to seek a sea route to Asia.

Scott, Robert Falcon (1868–1912)
British Antarctic explorer. Reached South Pole in early 1912, but discovered Amundsen had been there a month earlier. The whole party died on the return journey.

Tasman, Abel (1603–c. 59)
Dutch navigator. In 1642, he discovered Tasmania and New Zealand. He also visited Tonga, Fiji and the northwest coast of Australia.

Tenzing Norgay (1914–86)
Nepalese mountaineer. Nearly 20 years after his first climb, he reached summit of Mount Everest with Sir Edmund Hillary in 1953.

Vespucci, Amerigo (1451–1512)
Italian explorer. Sailed to Caribbean and South America. Gave his name to the Americas.

Zheng He (15th century)
Chinese admiral. Between 1405 and 1433, he led seven naval expeditions to Southeast Asia, the coasts of India and Arabia and Africa.

Emmeline Pankhurst and her followers engaged in violence such as window-breaking to gain attention.

Ibn Battuta recorded his travels in the book *Rihla (Journey)*. He travelled for over 24 years.

Vasco da Gama reached India in 1498 by sailing around the Cape of Good Hope in southern Africa.

Henry Morton Stanley, a reporter, found Livingstone (feared dead in Africa) at Lake Tanganyika in 1871.

History highlights since 1900

Hitler's aggressive policies in Germany led to the outbreak of World War II.

DNA determines which traits children inherit from their parents.

Home computers became widely available in the early 1980s.

US spacecraft *Viking I* and *2* landed probes on Mars by parachute.

Over a million industrial robots work in factories around the world.

In 1953, Hillary and Tenzing scaled the highest mountain in the world.

POLITICAL EVENTS

1914–18: World War I

1917: Russian Revolution

1920: Women win the vote in USA (and in the UK,1928)

1929 (October): Great Depression: sparked by Wall Street Crash

1939–45: World War II

1941–45: Holocaust: six million Jews are killed in German-occupied Europe

1945: United Nations established

1957–75: War in Vietnam

1948: Cold War rivalry between USA and Soviet Union begins

1948: Foundation of state of Israel

1957: Founding of European Common Market (now European Union)

1989: Collapse of communism in Europe; reopening of Berlin Wall

1990: Apartheid ends in South Africa

1991: Gulf War. Break-up of Soviet Union

2001: Terrorist attacks on USA

2003: US-led coalition invaded Iraq

2005: Terrorist attacks on London's transport system

2009: Barack Obama is the USA's first black president

2010–11: Arab Spring

MEDICINE AND SCIENCE

1905: Einstein's Theory of Relativity

1919: Ernest Rutherford (New Zealand) splits atom for the first time

1928: Alexander Fleming (UK) discovers penicillin, though it was 1940 before the substance was isolated for use as an antibiotic

1944: First kidney machine

1945: First atomic bomb

1953: Work by Francis Crick, James Watson and Rosalind Franklin (UK) leads to the discovery of the double-helix structure of DNA

1954: First kidney transplant

1955: First anti-polio vaccine

1956: First nuclear power station

1967: First heart transplant (by Dr Christiaan Barnard, South Africa)

1978: First test-tube baby: Louise Brown is born in the UK

1983: HIV retrovirus (from which AIDS can result) first identified

1990: First use of gene therapy

1990–2003: Human Genome Project sequences the human genome

1997: Dolly the sheep is the first mammal to be cloned

2010: A da Vinci robot surgeon and *McSleepy* robot anaesthetist carry out the first all-robot surgery

TELECOMMUNICATIONS

1936: First public TV broadcast in UK

1946: First electronic computer (ENIAC)

1953: First colour TV broadcast in USA

1960s: Internet begins as a military security network

1962: First live TV signals between USA and UK, using *Telstar* satellite

1971: Microprocessor invented

1981: IBM introduces its first personal computer

1992: IBM's Simon, the world's first smartphone,goes on sale

1993: Mosaic web browser helps to popularize public use of the Internet

1997: FLAG (fibre-optic link around the globe) is completed

2001: Broadband technology enters mainstream usage

2006: Social networking site Facebook is launched for everyone

SPACE EXPLORATION

1957 (October): First artificial satellite *Sputnik 1* launched from USSR

1961 (April): Yuri Gagarin (USSR) the first man in space in *Vostok 1*

1963 (June): Valentina Tereshkova (USSR) the first woman in space

1965 (March): Alexei Leonov (USSR) makes the first walk in space

1969 (July 20): First Moon landing made by Neil Armstrong and Edwin Aldrin (USA) from *Apollo 11*

1976: First successful soft landing on Mars made by US *Viking* probes

1981 (April): First flight of reusable Space Shuttle (USA)

1986: First close-up pictures of Uranus (and Neptune, 1989) from *Voyager 2* probe, launched in 1977

1986: First close encounter with comet Halley, by *Giotto* probe

1997: *Sojourner* (USA) the first robot vehicle to explore Mars

2005: Space Shuttle *Discovery* docks to the International Space Station

2006: Spacecraft *Venus Express* orbits Venus, taking detailed images

2011: Final Space Shuttle mission

THE ARTS AND SOCIETY

1932: First self-service supermarket

1937: Disney's first full-length cartoon, *Snow White*

1938: First ballpoint pen

1949: National Health Service started in UK

1950s: Environmental campaigns spurred by books such as *Silent Spring* by Rachel Carson

1965: Mini-skirt launched in UK

1970: Feminist movement publicized by books such as *The Female Eunuch* by Germaine Greer

1994: Launch of the PlayStation, the first games console to use CDs

1995: Pixar releases first full-length CG animation, *Toy Story*

2009: Birth of 'twitterature', classics shortened to 140-character tweets

FAMOUS ACHIEVEMENTS

1903: First powered flight: Wilbur and Orville Wright fly a biplane in Kitty Hawk, North Carolina, USA

1909 (April): Robert Peary and Matthew Hensen (USA) the first to reach the North Pole

1909: First cross channel flight made by Louis Blériot (France)

1911 (December): Roald Amundson (Norway) the first person to reach the South Pole

1912: First parachute descent from an aircraft

1953 (May): Sir Edmund Hillary (New Zealand) and Tenzing Norgay (Nepal) the first people to reach the summit of Mount Everest

1981: Completion of the longest bridge (Humber suspension bridge, UK: 1,410km)

1988: Completion of the longest railway tunnel (Seikan, Japan: 53.9km)

1996: Ashok Gadgill introduces new water-purification technique, using ultraviolet light

2010: Official opening of the Burj Khalifa in Dubai, United Arab Emirates, the world's tallest building at 828m

INDEX

Page numbers shown in **bold** indicate where the main reference to the subject can be found. Numbers in *italic* refer to pages where illustrations can be found.

ACKNOWLEDGEMENTS

The publishers wish to thank the following for supplying photographs for this book:

ABBREVIATIONS (*t* = top; *b* = bottom; *c* = centre; *l* = left; *r* = right)
PICTURE LIBRARY ABBREVIATIONS: **AAA:** The Ancient Art & Architecture Collection; **AKG:** AKG London; **BAL:** The Bridgeman Art Library; **B&C Alexander:** Bryan & Cherry Alexander; **BC:** Bruce Coleman Collection; **EB/JD:** Eye Ubiquitous/James Davis Travel Photography; **ET:** E.T. Archive; **FLPA:** Frank Lane Picture Agency; **FS:** Frank Spooner Pictures; **GI:** Getty Images; **HL:** The Hutchison Library; **NHPA:** Natural History Photographic Agency; **OSF:** Oxford Scientific Films; **Panos:** Panos Pictures; **PE:** Planet Earth Pictures; **Popper:** Popperfoto; **RGA:** The Ronald Grant Archive; **RHPL:** Robert Harding Picture Library; **SP:** Still Pictures; **SPL:** Science Photo Library

Front Cover: *top* Shutterstock/Gusev Mikhail Evgenievich; *cl* Shutterstock/Mike Truchon; *c* Shutterstock/holbox; *r* Getty/RHPL; *bl* Shutterstock/Matej Pavlansky; *bc* Shutterstock/erlire74; spine Getty/RHPL; inside front flap Shutterstock/Ammit; inside back flap Shutterstock/Ky Cho; back cover: Shutterstock/Yokobchuk Vasyl; Shutterstock/Joseph Calev; Shutterstock/Mircea Bezergheanu; Shutterstock/Ekkachai; Shutterstock/Alfred Bondarenko; Kingfisher artbank. Pages: viii: Colorific 1: NHPA *(tl, br)*, GI *(tr)*, Panos *(b)* 2: RHPL *(tr)*, NHPA *(b)* 3: SP *(b)* 4: BAL *(tr)*, SP *(tl)*, RHPL *(bl)* 5: RHPL *(tl)*, Empics *(cr)*, Panos *(b)* 8: Telegraph Colour Library *(tr)* 9: OSF *(tr)* 10: PE *(tr)* 12: NHPA *(tl)*, PE *(tr)* 16: Popper *(tl)*, BC *(cr)*, NHPA *(bl)* 17: The British Museum, EA24957 *(bl)*, AAA *(br)* 18: RHPL *(tr)* 20: NHPA *(cr)*, B&C Alexander *(bc)* 21: RHPL *(cl)*, GI *(cr)*, HL *(bl)* 22: AKG *(clt)*, AKG/©ADAGP, Paris and DACS, London 1998 *(tr)*, BAL *(tl, clb, cr, bl, br)* 23: AKG/©Estate of Roy Lichtenstein/DACS, 1998 *(tl)*, AKG/©Man Ray Trust/ADAGP, Paris and DACS, London 1998 *(tr)*, ET/©Succession Picasso/DACS, 1998 *(cr)*, BAL *(br)*, ©Duane Hanson/Saatchi Collection, London 1998 *(bl)* *(br)* 24: SP *(tr)*, NHPA *(bl)*, RHPL *(b)* 25: Panos *(b)* 26: HL *(tl, b)*, FS *(tr)* 27: Panos *(cr, tl)*, BAL *(tr)* 28: Popper *(tr)*, SPL *(tr)*, Portfolio Pictures *(br, clb, clt)*, Genesis Space Photo Library *(bc)* 30: SPL *(trt, trb)* 32: SPL *(tl)*, National Oceanic and Atmospheric Administration, United States Department of Commerce *(tr)* 34: PE *(tr)*, OSF *(bc)* 35: PE *(bc)*, NHPA *(br)* 36: Colorific *(tl)*, SP *(bc)* 37: RHPL *(tr)*, Colorific *(bl)*, NHPA *(cl)* 40: Virgin *(cl)*, Images Colour Library *(tr)* 43: GI *(tr)* 44: SPL *(tr)* 46: NHPA *(br)* 49: SPL *(br)* 50: Corbis *(tl)*, SPL *(tr)* 51: Zefa *(br)* 54: EB/JD *(tr)*, RHPL *(cl)*, GI *(b)* 55: GI *(cl)*, EB/JD *(br)* 57: Graham Harrison *(tr, cl)*, GI *(tr)* 58: BC *(c, bc)* 60: Zefa *(tr)*, RHPL *(b)*, Robert Estall Photo Library *(cr)*, FS 61: Robert Estall Photo Library *(cr)*, RHPL *(br)* 62: Allsport *(tl)*, ©Aerospace Publishing *(t)*, Ford Motor Company *(b)* 64: Panos *(tr)*, HL *(b)* 65: SuperStock *(br)*, HL *(tl)* 66: Portfolio Pictures *(tl)*, ©Uli Meyer Studios *(br)* 70: SPL *(tl, clt, cl, clb, bl)* 71: The National Museum of Ireland *(tl)*, AAA *(cl)*, BAL *(b)* 72: RHPL *(tr)*, Panos *(b)* 73: GI *(tr, b)*, Panos *(cl)* 75: SP *(cl)*, Image Bank *(b)* 76: BC *(tl)* 77: GI *(tc, tr, bl)*, RHPL *(br)* 78: Panos *(tr, bl)* Shutterstock/haak78 *(br)* 79: GI *(c, bcl)*, Zefa *(bl)*, FS *(bcr)*, Rex Features *(br)* 80: ©Amnesty International *(tl)*, Popper *(tr)*, Corbis *(b)* 81: Corbis *(tl)*, Popper *(bl)*, Camera Press *(br)* 82: Peter Newark's Military Pictures *(tl)* 86: RHPL *(tr)*, Camera Press *(cl)* 87: Zefa *(tc)*, FS *(tr)*, GI *(c)*, RHPL *(br)* 88: RHPL *(cr)* 89: Gamma-Rapho via Getty Images *(b)* 90: AKG *(tr)* 91: SPL *(tl, clt, clb, bl)* 92: SPL *(tl)* 93: Camera Press *(bl, clb)*, AKG *(br)* 94: GI *(tr)* 95: Corbis *(tr)* 96: SPL *(tl)*, AKG *(tr)* 98: Travel Ink *(cr)*, RHPL *(br)* 104: RHPL *(br)* 106: Allsport *(bl)*, Performing Arts Library *(br, tr)* 107: EB/JD *(tl)*, Rex Features *(cr)*, Performing Arts Library *(b)* 108: Popper *(b)* 109: GI *(t)* 110: ©Salvador Dali - Fundacion Gala-Salvador Dali, DACS, London 1998 *(tl)*, Shutterstock/Slaven *(bl)*, Steve Shott *(bl)* 112: The Natural History Museum, London *(cl)* 114: FS *(tl)*, SPL *(bl)* 115: Farmers Weekly Picture Library *(br)* 120: Corbis *(tl)* 121: Panos *(tl)*, GI *(b)* 122: Panos *(b)* 123: Panos *(tl)*, GI *(tr)*, Rex Features *(b)* 124: Panos *(br)* 125: Panos *(tl)*, EB/JD *(cl)*, GI *(cr, b)* 126: GI *(tl, bl, bc)* 127: Simon Farrell *(tr)* 133: GI *(cr)* 134: RHPL *(bc)* 136: Popper *(tl, cl)*, Colorsport *(tr)* 138: FLPA *(tr)*, GI *(b)* 139: FLPA *(br)* 140: Zefa *(tl)*, GI *(tr)*, Rex Features *(b)* 141: RHPL *(cl)*, Rex Features *(b)* 145: W.J. Hatt Ltd, The Institute of Explosives *(tl, clt, clb, bl, br)* 146: Topham *(cl)* 147: Popper *(tl, bl)*, Camera Press *(clb)*, Corbis *(br)* 149: Photofest *(tr, cr)*, Kobal Collection/Walt Disney Pictures *(cl)*, Kobal Collection/Dreamworks Animation *(bl)* 150: NHPA *(tr)* 152: FLPA *(tr)* 156: NHPA *(bc)* 158: GI *(c)* 159: RHPL *(cl)*, GI *(c)* 160: Telegraph Colour Library 161: Robin Keeley/The Forensic Science Service, London *(tl)*, Topham *(cl)* 162: GI *(tl)* 164: GI *(tr, br, cl)* 165: FS *(tl)*, Popper *(bl)*, RHPL *(br)* 168: SPL *(tl)* 169: SPL *(tl, clt, clb, bl)* 170: SP *(bl)*, Telegraph Colour Library *(bcl, br)*, GI *(bcr)* 171: Popper *(tr)* 172: Zefa *(tr)*, FS *(cl)*, RHPL *(b)* 173: Popper *(cl)*, GI *(b)* 176: Sonia Halliday Photographs *(cl)* 177: SPL *(tr, bc)*, The Wallace Collection, London *(tl)* 178: RHPL *(cr)*, Topham *(br)* 179: NHPA *(b)* 180: Corbis *(tl)*, GI *(b)* 181: Corbis *(tr, br)* 182: GI *(tr)*, RHPL *(cl)*, Panos *(br)* 183: Popper *(cl)*, RHPL *(cl)*, Panos *(b)* 185: RHPL *(tr)*, NHPA *(tr)*, RHPL *(b)*, GI *(cr)* 189: RHPL *(tr)* 192: FS *(tr)*, GI *(b)* 193: BC *(tr)*, GI *(tr)* 194: Image Bank *(tr)*, GI *(tr)* 196: Neff (UK) Ltd *(tr)* 197: GI *(tr)*, Panos *(bl)*, Zefa *(tr)* 198: OSF *(tr)* 199: FS *(tr)*, GI *(br)*, Panos *(bl, clt)*, EB/JD *(clb, cr, tl)* 201: Image Bank *(tc)* 204: Panos *(tr)*, GI *(b)* 205: Panos *(cr)*, Image Bank *(bl)* 206: Colorific *(tl)*, GI *(tr)*, FS *(b)* 207: OSF *(tl)*, Panos *(bl)* 208: GI *(cl, bl)*, Panos *(cr)* 210: GI *(tl)*, Panos *(b)* 212: RHPL *(tr)*, Panos *(b)* 213: OSF *(cr, br)* 214: OSF *(tl, clt, clb, bl)*, BC *(br)* 215: FS *(tr)*, BAL *(cl, bl)*, Houghton's Horses Picture Library *(br)* 219: GI *(tr)* 220: RHPL *(cl)*, GI *(b)* 221: FLPA *(tr)*, GI *(cl)*, Network/Mike Abrahams *(bl)* 222: GI *(tr, b, cl)* 223: FS *(cr)*, John Ferro Sims *(br)* 224: GI *(tr)*, Panos *(cl)* 225: Panos *(cr)*, Zefa *(b)* 226: Zefa *(tr)* 227: GI *(tr, cl)*, Image Bank *(bl)*, Colorific *(bc)* 229: Panos *(cl)*, PE *(bl)*, GI *(br)* 230: SPL *(tl)* 232: EB/JD *(tl)*, BAL *(b)* 233: RHPL *(tl)*, Zefa *(tr, bl)*, TRH Pictures *(cr)* 234: Image Bank *(tr)* 237: Zefa *(tr, cr)*, Corbis *(tr)*, Image Bank *(cl)*, OSF *(bc, bc)* 238: Image Bank *(tl)* 244: SPL *(tr)* 245: HL *(cl)*, Panos *(bl)*, RHPL *(br)* 249: Image Bank *(tr)* 250: Panos *(tr)* 251: Alpha *(tr, bc)*, A.C. Edwards *(bl)* 252: Glaxo Group Research *(bc)* 253: SPL *(tr, bc)* 255: AAA *(cr, b)* 256: Telegraph Colour Library *(tl)* 257: South American Pictures *(tr)*, Spectrum Colour Library *(cl)*, Panos *(b)* 258: SPL *(tl, cl, cl, clb, bl)* 259: LEO Electron Microscopy Ltd *(tr)*, Leica Microsystems (UK) Ltd *(bc)*, SPL *(tl, clt, clb, bl)* 261: RHPL *(tr)*, Panos *(b)* 262: HL *(c)* 263: Spectrum Colour Library *(tr)*, FS *(tr)*, HL *(bc)* 264: PE *(b)* 265: OSF *(tr)* 267: SP *(tl)* 271: OSF *(tr)* 276: Zefa *(tl)*, Redferns *(cl, bl, br)* 277: RHPL *(b)* 278: Edinburgh University *(cr)*, Keith Saunders/LSO with Michael Tilson Thomas *(b)* 283: Corbis *(tr)* 285: FS *(bl)* 287: Spectrum Colour Library *(tc, cl)*, FS *(bl)* 288: Panos *(cl, b)* 289: Panos *(tl)*, HL *(bl)* 290: NHPA *(tr)* 291: Panos *(tr)*, HL *(tr)*, Zefa *(b)* 292: Popper *(tr)* 293: Getty Images *(tr)* 296: SPL *(tr)* 297: Allsport *(cr)*, Bob Thomas Sports Photography/Getty Images *(b)* 298: Topham *(tl)* 299: Allsport *(tr)* 301: SPL *(tl)* 303: HL *(cl)*, Panos *(bl, bc)* 304: Polaroid *(clb)*, Canon *(bl)*, BAL *(b)* 305: Science & Society Picture Library *(tr)*, Alamy/Sandra Seckinger *(br)* 306: HL *(tr)* 309: Universal/courtesy Kobal Collection *(tr)* 312: ICI *(b)* 313: NHPA *(tl, tr)* 314: Shutterstock/Alan Hainkel *(t)* 315: HL *(tr)* 317: AAA *(tr)* 319: Popper *(tr)* 323: NHPA *(tr)* 324: PE *(tr)* 326: SP *(tl)*, Jean-Loup Charmet *(tr)*, Popper *(tr)* 327: HL *(b)* 328: BAL *(bl)* 329: BAL *(cl)* 330: GI *(cr)* 336: Getty Images/AFP *(tl)*, Popper *(tr)*, GI *(cl)* 337: PE *(tr)* 338: NHPA *(bl)*, HL *(bc)* 340: GI *(tl)*, HL *(bc)* 341: SPL *(tl, cl)*, UFA/courtesy Kobal Collection *(tc)*, Honda Motor Company *(tr)* 342: NHPA *(tr)* 343: Sophie Mortimer/NASA *(tr)* 345: Zefa *(crt)*, GI *(crb)* 346: SCR Photo Library/Novosti *(tr)*, RHPL *(b)* 347: HL *(br)* 348: Rex Features *(tl)*, Novosti, London *(cl)*, HL *(bl, br)* 350: GI *(tr, b)* 351: RHPL *(bl)*, FLPA *(b)* 352: AKG *(tl)*, Rex Features *(tr)*, ©Andy Goldsworthy *(cl)*, GI *(br)* 353: GI *(tl, cl)*, HL *(br)* 354: HL *(tr)*, Spectrum Colour Library *(tr)* 359: Zefa *(tc)* 61: RHPL *(tr)*, AAA *(cl)*, Christie's Images *(cr)* 362: GI *(tr, b)* 365: Travel Ink *(tl)* 366: BAL *(tr)*, Mary Evans Picture Library/Explorer *(br)* 367: SPL *(tr)*, AKG/©Salvador Dali - Fundacion Gala-Salvador Dali, DACS, London 1998 *(tr)* 368: OSF *(tr)* 369: NHPA *(tr)* 370: Zefa *(b)* 371: Topham *(tr)* 375: Popper *(b)* 376: RHPL *(cl, tr)*, GI *(tr)* 377: FS *(bl)*, RHPL *(cr)* 378: South American Pictures *(tr, cl, b)* 379: HL *(tl)*, South American Pictures *(bl)*, Panos *(br)* 380: Panos *(tl, b)*, South American Pictures *(tr)* 381: South American Pictures *(tr)* 382: Panos *(cr)* 383: Panos *(tl, c)*, HL *(tr)* 385: SPL *(tr)*, Portfolio Pictures/NASA *(bl)* 386: SPL *(cl, clb, bl)* 388: GI *(tr)*, HL *(cl)*, RHPL *(b)* 389: HL *(t)* 391: NHPA *(tr)* 392: Allsport *(tr)* 393: Corbis/Eva-Lotta Jansson *(tr)* 394: Sporting Pictures *(cr)* 396: SPL *(cl)* 397: NHPA *(tr)* 398: SPL *(tl)*, GI *(tr)* 400: HL *(cl)*, Panos *(bl)* 402: AKG *(tr)*, RHPL *(b)* 404: RHPL *(cl, bl, br)* 406: SPL *(tr)* 407: Zefa *(tr)* 408: Mary Evans Picture Library *(tl)*, British Telecommunications plc *(cl)*, Corbis *(bl)*, Philips UK *(b)* 409: Corbis *(br)*, GI *(tr)* 410: Panasonic UK Ltd *(clb)* 411: Simmons Ltd *(tc)*, SPL *(br)* 412: Popper *(tr)* 413: AKG *(tr)*, SPL *(bl)*, RHPL *(br)* 418: Topham *(tr)* 419: Panos *(cl)*, RGA *(cr)*, RHPL *(b)* 420: GI *(tr)* 421: Panos *(b)*, Corbis *(cl)* 424: SPL *(cl)* 425: FS *(bl)* 427: Telegraph Colour Library *(tr)* 428: Greyhound Ltd *(tr)* 429: GI *(bl)* 430: Popper *(cl)*, RHPL *(tr)*, BTA/Britain On View *(b)* 431: BTA/Britain On View *(tl)*, HL *(bl)*, RHPL *(br)* 432: FS *(cr)*, Popper *(b)* 433: Panos *(tr)*, RHPL *(bl, br)* 434: RHPL *(tl, cl)*, Zefa *(bl)* 435: RHPL *(b)* 436: RHPL *(tl, cl)*, Corbis *(cr)*, Redferns *(b)* 437: SPL *(tl)* 438: Popper *(b)* 439: Sanyo UK *(tl)*, SPL *(tr, cl)*, Sony *(bl)* 442: HL *(tl)* 446: Topham *(br)* 447: HL *(tc)* 448: Corbis *(tl)* 449: SPL *(c)* 451: SPL *(b)* 452: SPL *(tr)*, SPL *(b)* 457: RHPL *(tr)*, SPL *(b)* 459: NHPA *(tc)* 460: Corbis *(b)* 461: Corbis *(cr)*, Popper *(bl)* 466: PE *(br)* 467: SPL *(tr, bl)* 468: Gaynor Worman/Marwell Zoo *(br)*

The publishers would also like to thank the following for their help in supplying information used as visual reference: 6-7: Boeing Aircraft Corporation (Boeing 747); 11: Zoological Society of London (fire salamander cutaway); 17: Geoscan Research (scanner); 19: Ove Arup & Partners (Sydney Opera House); 30-31: W.M. Keck Observatory (Keck observatory); 62-63: John Willoughby, The Mustang Owners Club of Great Britain, Selby (Mustang); 146: Fullwood Ltd (milking shed); 190: Bell Helicopter Textron (helicopter cutaway); 196: Dyson Appliances Ltd (Dyson vacuum cleaner cutaway); 198: The Hovercraft Museum Trust; 242-243: Otis plc, Ove Arup & Partners (lift); 252-253: Picker International Ltd, Siemens Medical Engineering (CAT scanner); 292: Nuclear Electric (nuclear reactor); 296: British Petroleum (platform); 297-299: Olympic Museum; 361: Balco Ltd (electroplating system); 410: British Telecom (telephone); 425: Ford Motor Company (people carrier).
Every effort has been made to trace the copyright holders of the photographs. The publishers apologize for any unavoidable omissions.

INTERNET LINKS

There are countless websites that can help you research your area of interest. Below are some of the better ones.

General
www.enchantedlearning.com
www.gridclub.com/info/
www.infoplease.com/encyclopedia.html

Earth
kids.earth.nasa.gov/site.htm

Continents and countries
www.cia.gov/cia/publications/factbook

Plant life
www.sciencekids.co.nz/sciencefacts/plants.html

Animal life
www.wwf.org.uk
www.kidsplanet.org/factsheets/map.html

Human body
kidshealth.org/kid

Science and technology
www.bbc.co.uk/science

Transport
www.ltmuseum.co.uk

Construction and buildings
www.greatbuildings.com

History
www.historyforkids.org

Politics
http://www.direct.gov.uk/en/YoungPeople/DG_10016203

Sport
library.thinkquest.org/10480

Religion
www.bbc.co.uk/religion

The arts and media
www.louvre.fr/en/

Space
starchild.gsfc.nasa.gov